T0270923

ESSENTIAL MICROECONOMICS

Essential Microeconomics is designed to help students deepen their understanding of the core theory of microeconomics. Unlike other texts, this book focuses on the most important ideas and does not attempt to be encyclopedic. Two-thirds of the textbook focuses on price theory. As well as taking a new look at standard equilibrium theory, there is extensive examination of equilibrium under uncertainty, the capital asset pricing model, and arbitrage pricing theory. Choice over time is given extensive coverage and includes a basic introduction to control theory. The final third of the book, on game theory, provides a comprehensive introduction to models with asymmetric information. Topics such as auctions, signaling, and mechanism design are made accessible to students who have a basic rather than a deep understanding of mathematics. There is ample use of examples and diagrams to illustrate issues, as well as formal derivations.

John G. Riley is Distinguished Professor of Economics at the University of California, Los Angeles. A Fellow of the Econometric Society, his research has appeared in eminent journals such as the *American Economic Review, Econometrica, Journal of Political Economy, Quarterly Journal of Economics, Review of Economic Studies, Journal of Economic Theory*, and the *RAND Journal of Economics*. With the late Jack Hirshleifer, Professor Riley coauthored *The Analytics of Uncertainty and Information* (Cambridge University Press, 1992), a new edition of which is forthcoming with Sushil Bikhchandani of UCLA.

ESSENTIAL MICROECONOMICS

JOHN G. RILEY

University of California, Los Angeles

CAMBRIDGE
UNIVERSITY PRESS

University Printing House, Cambridge CB2 8BS, United Kingdom

One Liberty Plaza, 20th Floor, New York, NY 10006, USA

477 Williamstown Road, Port Melbourne, VIC 3207, Australia

314-321, 3rd Floor, Plot 3, Splendor Forum, Jasola District Centre, New Delhi - 110025, India

79 Anson Road, #06-04/06, Singapore 079906

Cambridge University Press is part of the University of Cambridge.

It furthers the University's mission by disseminating knowledge in the pursuit of education, learning and research at the highest international levels of excellence.

www.cambridge.org
Information on this title: www.cambridge.org/9780521827478

First published 2012

A catalogue record for this publication is available from the British Library

Library of Congress Cataloging in Publication data
Riley, John G.
Essential microeconomics / John G. Riley, University of California, Los Angeles.
pages cm
Includes index.
ISBN 978-0-521-82747-8 (hardback)
1. Microeconomics.   I. Title.
HB172.R55   2012
338.5–dc23   2011052561

ISBN 978-0-521-82747-8 Hardback

Additional resources for this publication are available at www.essentialmicroeconomics.com.

Brief Contents

1 **Prices and Optimization** *page* 1

2 **Consumers** 43

3 **Equilibrium and Efficiency in an Exchange Economy** 85

4 **Firms** 106

5 **General Equilibrium** 139

6 **Dynamic Optimization** 182

7 **Uncertainty** 218

8 **Equilibrium in Financial Markets** 259

9 **Strategy: Games in Which Preferences and History Are Common Knowledge** 303

10 **Games with Asymmetric Information** 347

11 **Incentive Compatibility and Mechanism Design** 382

12 **Auctions and Public Goods** 436

Appendix A: Mathematical Foundations 491

Appendix B: Mappings of Vectors 521

Appendix C: Optimization 567

Answers to Odd-Numbered Exercises 593

Index 691

Contents

Preface   *page* xi

Synopsis of the Text   xiii

Approach of the Text and Summary of Chapters and Appendixes   xv

Web Site   xxi

1 Prices and Optimization   1
    1.1 Supporting Prices   1
    1.2 Shadow Prices   14
    1.3 The Envelope Theorem   23
    1.4 Foundations of Constrained Optimization   30
    1.5 Application – Monopoly Pricing with Joint Costs   37

2 Consumers   43
    2.1 Theory of Choice   43
    2.2 Budget-Constrained Choice with Two Commodities   51
    2.3 Consumer Choice with n Commodities   65
    2.4 Consumer Surplus and Willingness to Pay   73
    2.5 Choice over Time   78

3 Equilibrium and Efficiency in an Exchange Economy   85
    3.1 The 2×2 Exchange Economy   85
    3.2 The Fundamental Welfare Theorems   101

4 Firms   106
    4.1 What Is a Firm?   106
    4.2 Decision Making by Price-Taking Firms   108
    4.3 Returns to Scale   117
    4.4 Firm and Industry Analysis   123
    4.5 Monopoly Pricing   130

5 General Equilibrium   139
  5.1 The Robinson Crusoe Economy   139
  5.2 Equilibrium and Efficiency with Production   145
  5.3 Existence of Equilibrium   153
  5.4 Public Goods   163
  5.5 Equilibrium Futures Prices   167
  5.6 Equilibrium with Constant Returns to Scale   173

6 Dynamic Optimization   182
  6.1 Life-Cycle Consumption and Wealth   182
  6.2 A Family of Dynamic Optimization Problems   191
  6.3 The Ramsey Problem   196
  6.4 Dynamic Programming Reformulation   201
  6.5 Optimal Control   206

7 Uncertainty   218
  7.1 Risky Choices   218
  7.2 Attitudes toward Risk   229
  7.3 Comparing Risky Alternatives   240
  7.4 Principal-Agent Problem   250

8 Equilibrium in Financial Markets   259
  8.1 Arrow-Debreu Equilibrium   259
  8.2 Security Market Equilibrium   269
  8.3 Capital Asset Pricing Model   284
  8.4 Arbitrage Pricing Theory   292

**9 Strategy: Games in Which Preferences and History Are
Common Knowledge**   303
  9.1 Strategic Equilibrium   303
  9.2 Games with a History   319
  9.3 Duopoly Games   328
  9.4 Infinitely Repeated Games   338

10 Games with Asymmetric Information   347
  10.1 Games of Incomplete Information   347
  10.2 Refinements of Bayesian Nash Equilibrium   360
  10.3 Games with Unobservable Strategies and Public Signals 373

11 Incentive Compatibility and Mechanism Design   382
  11.1 Incentive Compatibility   382
  11.2 Information Revelation, Adverse Selection, and Signaling 396
  11.3 Mechanism Design   411

12 Auctions and Public Goods   436
  12.1 Auctions   436
  12.2 Revenue Equivalence Theorem   451

12.3 Optimal Auctions   456
12.4 Designing an Efficient Mechanism   462
12.5 Trade-Off between Efficiency and Designer Profit   474
12.6 Efficient Production and Exchange with Private Values
      and Costs   480

Appendix A: Mathematical Foundations   491
A.1 Is It Really True?   491
A.2 Mappings of a Single Variable   495
A.3 Derivatives and Integrals   500
A.4 Optimization   507
A.5 Sufficient Conditions for a Maximum   513

Appendix B: Mappings of Vectors   521
B.1 Vectors and Sets   521
B.2 Functions of Vectors   526
B.3 Transformations of Vectors   544
B.4 Systems of Linear Difference Equations   555

Appendix C: Optimization   567
C.1 Maximization with Two Variables   567
C.2 Unconstrained Optimization   570
C.3 Implicit Function Theorem   573
C.4 Constrained Maximization   578
C.5 Supporting Hyperplanes   584
C.6 Taylor Expansion   586

Answers to Odd-Numbered Exercises   593

Index   691

Preface

Although proving a theorem is always a special joy, finding a convincing way to understand why theorems are true has always been a major fascination. I often learn much more from an informal graphical argument or from a well-thought-out example than from the formal analysis. Perhaps that is why I have always enjoyed teaching so much. It is very satisfying to take a major idea in economic theory and explain it in a way that gives students a new and deeper understanding.

I have written this text with the core goal of answering the question "Why?" in a clear and convincing manner. Some texts try to be encyclopedic. This one does not. Instead it explores the most important contributions of both price theory and game theory with the objective of developing strong insights as to why the results are true.

People learn in different ways. I remember once excitedly showing Roy Radner a diagrammatic explanation of a paper he had written with Joe Stiglitz. Roy listened patiently, then smiled and said, "Very good, John, but I never did understand a graphical argument!" Despite this disappointment, most people do find a clear diagram very helpful. There are a lot of them in this text. Yet looking at a graph only takes learning so far. There is no substitute for learning by doing. For this reason there is a strong focus on exercises. Many of the exercises are illustrative examples, but many others provide opportunities for a student to prove something related to the theorems presented in the text. Answers to all of the questions are provided. Half are in the text, and the rest can be found on the Web site, http://www.essentialmicroeconomics.com.

I have learned from many remarkable economists. My earliest inspiration and mentor was Bert Brownlie at the University of Canterbury. In addition, two very early and profoundly different teachers were Joe Stiglitz, who presented a freshly written paper in every class, and Gerard Debreu, whose teaching discipline and clarity were stunning. At MIT my approach to both teaching and research was deeply influenced by Bob Solow. Then, as a junior colleague at UCLA, I taught my first classes on the economics of uncertainty with my most important mentor, Jack Hirshleifer. Our teaching styles were very different but complementary. Among my recent colleagues at UCLA, Christian Hellwig and William Zame have been especially influential. Of course I have learned much from coauthors, in particular from Eric Maskin.

Synopsis of the Text

Essential Microeconomics is designed to help students deepen their understanding of the core theory of microeconomics. Unlike other texts, this book focuses on the most important ideas and does not attempt to be encyclopedic.

Two-thirds of the book focuses on price theory. As well as taking a new look at standard equilibrium theory, there is an extensive examination of equilibrium under uncertainty, the capital asset pricing model, and arbitrage pricing theory. Choice over time is also given extensive coverage and includes a basic introduction to continuous time models (control theory).

The final third of the book, on game theory, has an extensive introduction to models with asymmetric information. Topics such as auctions, signaling, and mechanism design are made very accessible to students who have a basic rather than a deep understanding of mathematics.

There is extensive use of examples and diagrams to illustrate the essence of an issue, as well as formal derivations. Readers have a choice of whether to go beyond the core ideas to the underlying mathematics of the model.

Problem solving is crucial to developing a deep understanding of a topic. Therefore the book contains a large number of exercises (all with answers available). Most provide the reader with opportunities to apply economic principles. Other questions ask the reader to extend the formal theory.

There is also a Web-based self-learning course to help students review the mathematics that is used in the text.

Approach of the Text and Summary of Chapters and Appendixes

In contrast to most economics textbooks, which typically hide all the "required mathematics" in an appendix, this book opens with a discussion of the theory of maximization. To be an effective economic theorist it is essential to develop the ability to look at a problem from both a mathematical and an economics perspective. To use a language metaphor, a student needs to be able to think not only in the language of mathematics but also like an economist. Developing that bilingual skill is the goal of the first chapter.

It is very important to read Chapter 1 carefully and thoroughly. Then, in working through the next four chapters, the reader will develop both a high comfort level with the principles of maximization and an appreciation of the role that prices play in allocating resources.

Although a large part of modern research is game theoretic, the core of economic theory is price theoretic. Therefore anyone who wants to be an effective economics practitioner needs to understand both the power of price theory and its limitations. Chapter 2 examines price-taking behavior by a consumer. In contrast with traditional texts, it focuses on extracting insights about the elasticity of demand with respect to prices and income. The timeless model is then generalized to incorporate choice over time. In a formal sense this is a direct reinterpretation of the timeless model. However, this mathematical viewpoint glosses over the role of futures markets, future spot markets, and market intermediaries like banks.

In Chapter 3 the two great welfare theorems are examined in a simple economy in which consumers exchange their endowments of commodities. In such an economy the theorems are quite easily proved. However, to develop a real appreciation of the theorems it is extremely helpful to consider them in the context of examples with two commodities and two consumers. These "Edgeworth box" economies are examined in detail.

Chapter 4 on firms begins by examining cost minimization by a single firm that is a price taker in input markets and then studies the relationship between local returns to scale and minimized average cost. The chapter then

xv

focuses on how costs influence the equilibrium price of output if there are many competing firms. Introductory textbooks study market equilibrium if firms are price takers in the output market as well as input markets. Given the deeper analysis of the relationship between input prices and cost, the focus here is on how changes in input prices affect each firm's cost and hence the equilibrium output price.

Under the assumption of increasing returns to scale it is efficient for industry output to be produced by a single firm. The final topic of the chapter is monopoly pricing. A monopoly firm profits from raising output price above marginal cost. If resale is costly, a monopoly also has an incentive to price a commodity differently for different groups of buyers. In addition, it has an incentive to vary the price per unit with the number of units purchased. One simple way to do so is to introduce two-part pricing. Each buyer is charged a monthly fee for access to the product or service and also pays a price for each unit purchased. Legal restrictions typically prohibit firms from excluding classes of consumers. However a monopoly still has an incentive to offer a menu of different two-part pricing schemes. The chapter concludes with a discussion of how to choose the profit-maximizing two-part pricing scheme.[1]

Chapter 5 adds firms to the simple exchange economy of Chapter 3, and also examines the conditions under which there exist prices at which all markets clear. The market equilibrium model is then generalized to incorporate public goods and choice over time. Finally the chapter considers equilibrium in an economy that exhibits constant returns to scale at the market level. In such an environment the price of outputs is determined by costs and hence by technology. This makes it possible to draw strong conclusions about the way technology affects equilibrium prices.

Most texts give short shrift to choice over time. Chapter 6 redresses the balance. With a finite number of periods a model with time is mathematically indistinguishable from a timeless model. However, to derive useful economic insights it is necessary to make strong assumptions about the linkages between periods, for both preferences and technology. As a modeling simplification it is often easier to assume that there is no last period. Instead the number of periods is infinite. The goal of this chapter is to provide an understanding both of why simplifying assumptions are made and of the tight connection between models with a large but finite number of periods and infinite horizon models. Another modeling choice is between models in which there are discrete time periods and those where time is a continuous variable. A further goal is to introduce the reader to the continuous model.

---

[1] The goal is to give the reader insights into "mechanism design" without having to worry about the subtleties.

First it is examined as the limit of the discrete time model. Then Pontryagin's Maximum Principle for continuous time models is derived.

Chapter 7 introduces uncertainty. A commodity is no longer defined only by its characteristics and time of delivery but also by the state of the world (or more simply "state"). For example, an insurance company contracts to supply funds for surgery if the state of the world is "malfunctioning heart." Aversion to risk is central to decision making under uncertainty. This chapter examines how to model differences in risk aversion. It also studies the conditions under which different risky prospects can be ranked regardless of a consumer's aversion to risk.

Chapter 8 extends the basic equilibrium model to financial markets. Typically texts focus on the Arrow-Debreu "complete market" equilibrium in which every commodity can be traded in every contingency. Such equilibrium is a direct extension of the standard timeless model. This chapter takes the complete market equilibrium as a starting point and then examines equilibrium when there are more limited trading opportunities. The chapter first provides conditions under which trading only in securities markets achieves complete market equilibrium outcomes. It then examines models when trading in financial markets offers more limited risk-spreading opportunities. Both the capital asset pricing model and arbitrage pricing model are examined.

Chapter 9 introduces the reader to the basic concepts in game theory. The strategies of the players in a game are Nash equilibrium strategies if they are mutual best responses. To play such a strategy requires that players share a deep understanding of the game being played. The chapter discusses in detail this critical but controversial assumption (the "common knowledge" assumption).

Chapter 10 takes up the subtleties of game theory when players have private information. Typically such games have multiple Nash equilibria or even a continuum of equilibria. The assumption that all players know which equilibrium is being played stretches the common knowledge assumption even further. As an alternative, game theorists have sought ways to refine the definition of equilibrium to yield a unique refined equilibrium. Commonly used refinements are examined. The final section examines an infinitely repeated game in which strategies are private but all players observe a public signal that is correlated with the actions taken.

Chapter 11 further develops the theory of games with private information. Different types of player typically take different actions. If each player is taking his or her equilibrium action there can be no advantage in switching to the strategy of some other type. Strategies for which this is true are said to be incentive compatible. At the core of successful modeling of private information is an assumption about preferences (the "single crossing property") that greatly simplifies the constraints imposed by incentive compatibility. The implications of single crossing are examined and then applied to the theory of signaling. The chapter next introduces mechanism design under the single crossing property. To develop insights into solution methods, the chapter then examines the design of selling schemes by a monopolist facing buyers with different demand functions.

Chapter 12 applies the principles of mechanism design to the theory of auctions and public good provision. It explores major results in ranking different types of auctions. The method of analysis is then used to examine efficient public good provision. In contrast with the auction environment in which the efficient mechanism generates revenue to the mechanism designer, the efficient provision of public goods generates a loss to the designer. The reasons for the different results are examined, and it is shown that an auction is only efficient and profitable if the reservation price of the seller is public information.

The three appendixes cover the mathematics that is essential to any graduate course in microeconomics. Appendix A examines the foundations of calculus with a single variable and also introduces concave and quasi-concave functions. Appendix B focuses on mappings of vectors and includes an introduction to difference equations. Appendix C provides the foundations of multivariable constrained optimization.

Thoughts on Teaching Microeconomic Theory

Economics is built on two fundamental ideas: each agent in a population makes choices based on the agent's underlying preferences, and the outcome for the population is an equilibrium outcome. So a student who really understands individual optimizing behavior and notions of price and game theoretic equilibria is ready to do research in any field of economics. Therefore the key to successful teaching is to give each student a deep understanding of these two ideas.

Doing so means presenting the big theorems and proving a version of the theorems that is appropriate to the mathematical preparation of the class. Yet this is only the beginning. It is even more important to breathe life into the theorems by showing how they can be applied to generate useful insights. Thus I believe that a significant fraction of class time should be spent on applications and examples.

Consider, for example, the Walrasian equilibrium. Understanding the two great welfare theorems and how to prove existence using a fixed point theorem is important. Yet it is only through the study of the special cases of Edgeworth box and representative agent models that a student gets a sense of how general equilibrium influences economic outcomes. One great example is the constant returns to scale model of international trade theory with two inputs and two outputs. There is so much to learn from this model. A second example is equilibrium risk sharing through trading in contingent and security markets. At a formal level it is simply a matter of showing that the new model is mathematically equivalent. Therefore all the theorems without uncertainty generalize. The important step is helping students develop an understanding of how risk is shared in a Walrasian equilibrium using simpler models such as the capital asset pricing model.

To further develop the ability to draw insights from and apply theory, homework should be devoted almost entirely to examples and applications. Of course, the teaching assistant must first offer help where the instructor has left students mystified, but after this is done, the focus should be on examples and applications.

The text offers many practice exercises, and there are more on the Web site. If you are willing to share exercises that you have found helpful, send them to me, and I will add a selection to the site and acknowledge your help. The Web site also contains a set of slides for each chapter and the appendixes. I am never satisfied with my presentations so I cannot say that the slides represent the way I would next teach the material. However, to a first approximation, they represent the way I recently thought the topics should be presented.

Web Site

The Web site www.essentialmicroeconomics.com complements the text. One critical challenge for a teacher of a first-year graduate class is the wide variation in students' mathematical backgrounds. To ameliorate these problems the Web site offers a two-part approach. First, there is a Web page containing a set of calculus and linear algebra review modules that students can work through to check their level of preparedness. Each module provides problem sets (primarily on optimization) and lots of hints to help a student work through each problem. Second, there is a Web page containing a set of slides on "Mathematical Foundations." These cover most of the topics in the three appendices. At UCLA these lectures are offered to entering graduate students in a two-week intensive "Summer Math Camp." Any student who has successfully worked through both the modules and the topics covered in the slides will be fully prepared.

The Web site also provides a set of slides for each chapter. These are designed to help an instructor or teaching assistant prepare lectures and also to provide students with a summary of material covered. Although half of the answers to the problems sets are in the textbook, the other half are accessible only from the Web site. Especially for the later chapters there are also notes on topics not covered in the text, additional exercises, and links to other Web-based material. Suggestions as to additional helpful links are welcome.

Finally the student has access to the UCLA Auction House. This Web site is designed to introduce the reader to competitive bidding. For a series of different auction environments, students have the opportunity to bid against one or more "robot" bidders who follow theoretical equilibrium strategies. Instructors are welcome to suggest additional auctions.

1

Prices and Optimization

1.1 Supporting Prices

Key ideas: convex and non-convex production sets, price-based incentives, Supporting Hyperplane Theorem

The pursuit of self-interest is central to economics. Thus a deep understanding of the theory of maximization is essential to effective theorizing. In particular, the theory of constrained maximization is so crucial that we explore it in this first chapter.[1] In contrast to a purely mathematical exposition, the emphasis here is on prices.

Our first topic is the role of *supporting prices*. We explore the issue of how prices can be used to provide incentives for an economic agent to make a desired choice. In addition to being of direct importance, supporting prices are central to the theory of constrained maximization. Section 1.2 explores this point, emphasizing the intuition behind the formal mathematics. Section 1.3 then examines how the maximized payoff of an agent is affected by a change in the environment (a *parametric* change.) Section 1.4 contains a formal proof of the necessary conditions for a constrained maximum. An example showing how to apply the necessary conditions is presented in Section 1.5.

Consider a production plant or firm that can produce as many as n different outputs $q = (q_1, \ldots, q_n)$ using up to m different inputs $z = (z_1, \ldots, z_m)$. A production plan is then an input-output vector (z, q). The manager of the plant must choose from different feasible plans. Let $Y \subset \mathbb{R}_+^{m+n}$ be the set of all feasible plans. This is the plant's production set.

It turns out to be helpful to treat inputs as negative numbers and define a *production vector* $y = (y_1, \ldots, y_{n+m}) = (-z_1, \ldots, -z_m, q_1, \ldots, q_n)$. In vector notation, $y = (-z, q)$. In this new notation the firm's production set is the set $\mathcal{Y} \subset \mathbb{R}^{m+n}$.

---

[1] Other mathematical topics can be found in the Appendixes.

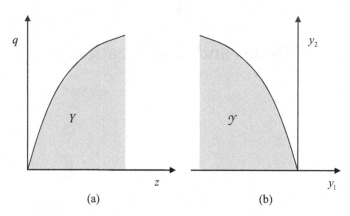

Figure 1.1-1. (a) Production set. (b) Production set.

Given a price vector $p = (p_1, \ldots, p_{m+n})$, the total revenue of the plant is $\sum_{i=m+1}^{m+n} p_i y_i$ and the total cost is $\sum_{i=1}^{m} p_i z_i = \sum_{i=1}^{m} p_i(-y_i)$. Thus the profit of the plant can be written succinctly as

$$\pi = \sum_{i=m+1}^{m+n} p_i y_i - \sum_{i=1}^{m} p_i z_i = p \cdot y.$$

Example: Production Function and Production Set
A plant has a production function $q = 4z^{1/2}$. That is, given input z, the maximum output that the plant can produce is $q = 4z^{1/2}$. Therefore output must satisfy the constraint $q \leq 4z^{1/2}$. The production set Y is the set of feasible plans so

$$Y = \{(z, q) | z \geq 0, q \leq 4z^{1/2}\}.$$

This set is depicted in Figure 1.1-1a.

Equivalently the production set is the set $Y = \{(z, q) | 16z - q^2 \geq 0\}$.[2] If we treat inputs as negative then a feasible plan is a production vector $(y_1, y_2) = (-z, q)$ and the production set is $\mathcal{Y} = \{(y_1, y_2) | -16y_1 - y_2^2 \geq 0\}$. This set is depicted in Figure 1.1-1b.

Production Efficiency

A production plan y is wasteful if there is another plan in the production set for which outputs are larger and inputs are smaller. Non-wasteful plans are said to be production efficient. Formally the plan $\bar{y}$ is production efficient if there is no $y \in \mathcal{Y}$ such that $y > \bar{y}$.[3]

---

[2] Note that in this reformulation $z \geq q^2/16$. Because the right-hand side is positive, this constraint implies that $z \geq 0$.

[3] For a vector, our convention is that if $y_j \geq \bar{y}_j$ for all j we write $y \geq \bar{y}$. If, in addition, the inequality is strict for some j we write $y > \bar{y}$ and if the inequality is strict for all j we write $y \gg \bar{y}$.

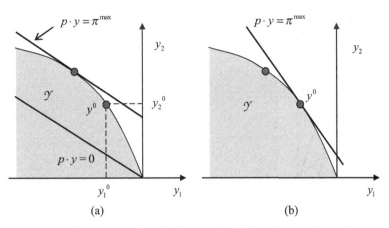

Figure 1.1-2. (a) Transfer price too high. (b) Optimal transfer price.

We begin by asking whether prices and profit maximizing can provide appropriate incentives for all efficient production plans. Mathematically, we seek prices that "support" an efficient production plan.

To illustrate, consider a plant that uses a single input to produce a single output. The input can be purchased at a price p_1. Suppose that the production set $\mathcal{Y}$ (the plant's set of feasible plans) is as depicted in Figure 1.1-2a.

For each input level y_1, the maximum feasible output is the point on the boundary of the plant's production set. As shown in Figure 1.1-2, the plant exhibits diminishing marginal productivity; each additional unit of input produces less additional output. As a result, the production set $\mathcal{Y}$ is convex. That is, for any pair of production vectors y^0, y^1 in the set $\mathcal{Y}$, every convex combination

$$y^\lambda = (1 - \lambda)y^0 + \lambda y^1, \quad 0 < \lambda < 1$$

is also a feasible plan.

Suppose, furthermore, that the plant is part of a large firm and has been given the target of producing y_2^0 units of output. This output is an intermediate product, to be sent to another "downstream" plant within the firm. From Figure 1.1-2a, it is clear that the best choice of the plant manager is to purchase $z_1 = -y_1^0$ units of the input. With any less input, the output target is not feasible, and with any more, the plant has excess capacity. A critical question is how to provide the plant manager with an appropriate incentive to make the right choice. Suppose that the firm introduces a *transfer price* p_2, paid for each unit delivered to the downstream division. The plant manager's bonus will be based on the profit

$$\pi(y) = p_1 y_1 + p_2 y_2.$$

Two contour sets of $\pi(y)$ or *iso-profit* lines are depicted in Figure 1.1-2a. The steepness of any such line is the input-output price ratio p_1/p_2. As shown,

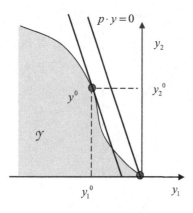

Figure 1.1-3. No optimal transfer price.

the ratio is too low because profit is maximized at a point to the north-west of y^0. However, with the transfer price lowered appropriately, as in Figure 1.1-2b, the optimal production plan is achieved. The correct transfer price thus provides the manager with the appropriate incentive.

Unfortunately, this approach does not always work. Consider Figure 1.1-3 and suppose, once again, that the output target is y_2^0 units.

Examine the line $\{y|p \cdot y = p \cdot y^0\}$ drawn touching the boundary of the production set at y^0. As depicted, the profit of the plant producing at (y_1^0, y_2^0) is greater than the profit associated with all production plans that are sufficiently close to this plan. But the line lies to the left of the zero profit line $p \cdot y = 0$, so the profit of the plant is negative. Thus the manager now maximizes profit by choosing to purchase no inputs and hence produce no output.

The key difference between the two cases is that the production set is convex in the first but not in the second. This suggests that using prices to guide production decisions works well, as long as production sets are *convex sets*. This is indeed correct.

Proposition 1.1-1: Supporting Hyperplane Theorem
Suppose $\mathcal{Y} \subset \mathbb{R}^n$ is non-empty and convex and y^0 lies on the boundary of $\mathcal{Y}$. Then there exists $p \neq 0$ such that (i) for all $y \in \mathcal{Y}$, $p \cdot y \leq p \cdot y^0$ and (ii) for all $y \in \text{int } \mathcal{Y}$, $p \cdot y < p \cdot y^0$.

For a general proof see Appendix C. Here we consider the special case in which the convex set $\mathcal{Y}$ is an upper contour set; that is,

$$\mathcal{Y} = \{y | g(y) \geq g(y^0)\}.$$

As long as the gradient vector is non-zero at y^0, the linear approximation of g at y^0 is

$$\overline{g}(y) = g(y^0) + \frac{\partial g}{\partial y}(y^0) \cdot (y - y^0).$$

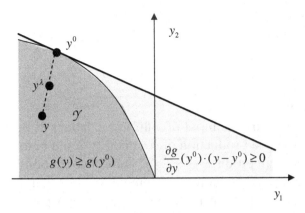

Figure 1.1-4. Supporting hyperplane.

In two dimensions, the contour set of the linear approximation is the tangent plane as depicted in Figure 1.1-4.

If the upper contour set $\mathcal{Y} = \{y | g(y) \geq g(y^0)\}$ is convex as depicted, all the points in $\mathcal{Y}$ lie in the upper contour set of $\bar{g}$ (i.e. the lightly and heavily shaded areas.) In mathematical terms,

$$g(y) \geq g(y^0) \Rightarrow \frac{\partial g}{\partial y}(y^0) \cdot (y - y^0) \geq 0. \tag{1.1-1}$$

Formally, we have the following lemma.

Lemma 1.1-2: If $\mathcal{Y} = \{y | g(y) \geq g(y^0)\}$ is convex then

$$y \in \mathcal{Y} \Rightarrow \frac{\partial g}{\partial y}(y^0) \cdot (y - y^0) \geq 0.$$

Proof: Pick any y in $\mathcal{Y}$. Because $\mathcal{Y}$ is convex, all convex combinations of y^0 and y lie in $\mathcal{Y}$. That is, for all $\lambda \in (0, 1)$,

$$g(y) - g(y^0) \geq 0 \Rightarrow g(y^\lambda) - g(y^0) \geq 0 \quad \text{where} \quad y^\lambda = (1 - \lambda)y^0 + \lambda y.$$

Define $h(\lambda) \equiv g(y^\lambda) = g((1 - \lambda)y^0 + \lambda y) = g(y^0 + \lambda(y - y^0))$. Then

$$\frac{h(\lambda) - h(0)}{\lambda} = \frac{g(y^0 + \lambda(y^1 - y^0)) - g(y^0)}{\lambda} \geq 0, \quad \text{for all} \quad \lambda \in (0, 1).$$

Note that the limit of the left-hand side as $\lambda \to 0$ is the derivative of $h(\lambda)$ evaluated at $\lambda = 0$. Therefore $h'(0) \geq 0$. Differentiating $h(\lambda)$ we obtain

$$\frac{dh}{d\lambda}(\lambda) = \frac{\partial g}{\partial y}(y^0 + \lambda(y - y^0)) \cdot (y - y^0).$$

Setting $\lambda = 0$ it follows that

$$\frac{\partial g}{\partial y}(y^0) \cdot (y - y^0) \geq 0. \qquad \square$$

To prove Proposition 1.1-1, note that for any y^0 on the boundary of the contour set we can choose $p = -\frac{\partial g}{\partial y}(y^0)$. Then, appealing to the lemma,

$$p \cdot y \leq p \cdot y^0 \quad \text{for all} \quad y \in \mathcal{Y}.$$

Example: Firm with Two Outputs

Let z be the single variable input of a firm (e.g. labor). If the firm allocates z_2 units of labor to the production of commodity 2 and z_3 to the production of commodity 3 it can produce $y_2 = 2z_2^{1/2}$ units of commodity 2 and $y_3 = z_3^{1/2}$ units of commodity 3. The input requirement for y_2 is therefore $\frac{1}{4}y_2^2$ and for y_3 is y_3^2. Thus the total input requirement for the output vector (y_2, y_3) is $\frac{1}{4}y_2^2 + y_3^2$. Define $y_1 = -z$. The set of feasible plans is therefore the set

$$\mathcal{Y} = \left\{ y | g(y) = -y_1 - \tfrac{1}{4}y_2^2 - y_3^2 \geq 0 \right\}.$$

The point $y^0 = (-25, 8, 3)$ is on the boundary of this set, and the gradient vector at this point is $\frac{\partial g}{\partial y}(y^0) = (-1, -\tfrac{1}{2}y_2^0, -2y_3^0) = (-1, -4, -6)$. Because the function $g(y)$ is the sum of three concave functions, it is concave (and hence quasi-concave).

Define $p = -\frac{\partial g}{\partial y}(y^0) = (1, 4, 6)$. Then by the lemma, the plane $\{y | p \cdot y = p \cdot y^0\}$, is a supporting plane.

We can easily check this directly. Given the price vector $p = (1, 4, 6)$, the profit of the firm is

$$\pi(z) = -z_2 - z_3 + 4\left(2z_2^{1/2}\right) + 6z_3^{1/2}.$$

It is readily confirmed that profit is maximized at $(\bar{z}_2, \bar{z}_3) = (16, 9)$. Then the profit-maximizing production vector is $\bar{y} = (-25, 8, 3)$.

The Supporting Hyperplane Theorem has a direct economic interpretation if we can further establish that the vector p is non-negative. Consider once more the plant with a production set $\mathcal{Y}$. In addition to assuming convexity we need another assumption.

Free Disposal For any feasible production plan $y \in \mathcal{Y}$ and any $\delta > 0$, the production plan $y - \delta$ is also feasible.

Note that $y - \delta$ is a plan with a smaller output vector and a larger input vector. Thus one way to achieve the alternative plan $y - \delta$ is to operate according to the plan y, purchase the additional vector of inputs δ, and dispose of these inputs. Then the net production vector is $y - \delta$. Hence this assumption is immediately satisfied if commodities can be disposed of freely.

We assume that the production set is closed so that it contains all its boundary points. A plan $y^0 \in \mathcal{Y}$ is production efficient if there is no other feasible plan y such that $y > y^0$. That is, y^0 must lie on the boundary of the production set. Appealing to the Supporting Hyperplane Theorem, there exists a vector $p \neq 0$ such that $p \cdot (y^0 - y) \geq 0$ for all $y \in \mathcal{Y}$. By free disposal, $y^1 = y^0 - \delta \in \mathcal{Y}$ for all vectors $\delta > 0$. Hence

$$p \cdot (y^0 - y^1) = p \cdot \delta = \sum_{i=1}^{n} p_i \delta_i \geq 0.$$

This holds for all $\delta > 0$. Setting $\delta_j = 0$ for all $j \neq i$ and $\delta_i = 1$, it follows that $p_i \geq 0$ for each $i = 1, \ldots, n$.

If in addition $0 \in \mathcal{Y}$, then, by the Supporting Hyperplane Theorem $p \cdot y^0 \geq p \cdot 0 = 0$. We thus have the following result.

Proposition 1.1-3: Supporting Prices
If y^0 is a boundary point of a convex set $\mathcal{Y}$ and the free disposal assumption holds, then there exists a price vector $p > 0$ such that $p \cdot y \leq p \cdot y^0$ for all $y \in \mathcal{Y}$. Moreover, if $0 \in \mathcal{Y}$, then $p \cdot y^0 \geq 0$.

Thus price-guided production decisions can always be used to achieve any efficient production plan if the set of feasible plans is convex.

Linear Model

We now examine the special case of a linear technology. As will become clear, understanding this model is the key to deriving the necessary conditions for constrained optimization problems.

A firm produces a single output q using m inputs $(z_1, \ldots, z_m)$. The firm has n plants. If plant j operates at activity level x_j it can produce $a_{0j}x_j$ units of output using $a_{ij}x_j$ units of input $i, i = 1, \ldots, m$. Summing over the n plants, total output is $\sum_{j=1}^{n} a_{0j}x_j$ and the total input i requirement is $\sum_{j=1}^{n} a_{ij}x_j$. The production vector $y = (-z, q)$ is then feasible if it is in the following set:

$$\mathcal{Y} = \{(-z, q) | x \geq 0, q \leq a_0 \cdot x, Ax \leq z\}. \tag{1.1-2}$$

Note that, because all the constraints are linear, the production set $\mathcal{Y}$ is convex. Note also that if $(-z, q) \in \mathcal{Y}$, then for any $\delta_0 \geq 0$ and $\delta = (\delta_1, \ldots, \delta_n) \geq 0$, $(-z - \delta, q - \delta_0) \in \mathcal{Y}$. That is, the free disposal assumption holds.

The production set for the special case of two inputs and two plants is depicted in Figure 1.1-5.

As we see later, each crease in the boundary of the production set is a production plan in which only one plant is operated. For all the points on the plane between the two creases, both plants are in operation. Note that

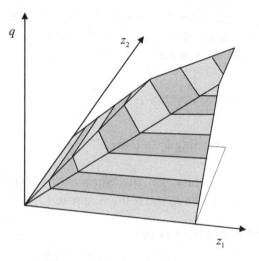

Figure 1.1-5. Production set.

each point on the boundary lies on one or more planes. Thus there is a supporting plane for every such boundary point. We now show that supporting prices exist for the general linear model and then characterize the mapping from the input vector $\bar{z}$ to the efficient output $\bar{q}$.

Existence of Supporting Prices

For any input vector $\bar{z}$, let $\bar{q}$, be the maximum possible output.[4] Formally,

$$\bar{q} = \underset{x}{\mathrm{Max}}\{q = a_0 \cdot x \,|\, \mathbf{A}x \leq \bar{z}, x \geq 0\}. \tag{1.1-3}$$

Thus $(-\bar{z}, \bar{q})$ is a boundary point of the production set $\mathcal{Y}$. Because the production set $\mathcal{Y}$ is convex and the free disposal assumption holds, there exists a positive supporting price vector (r, p) such that

$$p\bar{q} - r \cdot \bar{z} \geq pq - r \cdot z \quad \text{for all} \quad (-z, q) \in \mathcal{Y}. \tag{1.1-4}$$

With the following mild assumption we show that the supporting output price, p, must be strictly positive.

Assumption: The Feasible Set Has a Non-Empty Interior
There exists some $\hat{x} \gg 0$ such that $\hat{z} \equiv \mathbf{A}\hat{x} \ll \bar{z}$.

Define $\hat{q} = a_0 \cdot \hat{x}$. Given the preceding assumption $\{-\hat{z}, \hat{q}\} \in \mathcal{Y}$. Therefore by the Supporting Hyperplane Theorem

$$p\bar{q} - r \cdot \bar{z} \geq p\hat{q} - r \cdot \hat{z}. \tag{1.1-5}$$

---

[4] Because all the constraints are weak inequality constraints, X is closed. We assume that the feasible set $X = \{x \,|\, x \geq 0, \mathbf{A}x \leq \bar{z}\}$ is bounded. Then X is a compact set. Thus the maximum exists.

We have already argued that $p \geq 0$. To prove that it is strictly positive, we suppose that $p = 0$ and obtain a contradiction. First note that, if $p = 0$ it follows from equation (1.1-5) that

$$r \cdot \overline{z} \leq r \cdot \hat{z}.$$

Also, because $(r, p) > 0$, if $p = 0$ then $r > 0$. Therefore, because $\hat{z} \ll \overline{z}$, $r \cdot \hat{z} < r \cdot \overline{z}$.

But this contradicts our previous conclusion. Thus p cannot be zero after all. Then, dividing by p and defining the supporting input price vector $\lambda = r/p \geq 0$, condition (1.1-4) can be rewritten as follows:

$$\overline{q} - \lambda \cdot \overline{z} \geq q - \lambda \cdot z \quad \text{for all} \quad (-z, q) \in \mathcal{Y}. \tag{1.1-6}$$

Characterization of the Activity Vector

Appealing to the Supporting Hyperplane Theorem, we have shown that there exists a positive vector $(r, p) = (\lambda_1, \ldots \lambda_m, 1)$ such that the boundary point $(-\overline{z}, \overline{q})$ is profit maximizing. We now use this result to characterize the efficient output $\overline{q}$ given an input vector $\overline{z}$.

Proposition 1.1-4: Necessary Conditions for a Production Plan to Be on the Boundary of the Production Set

Let $(-\overline{z}, \overline{q})$ be a point on the boundary of the linear production set. That is $\overline{q} = a_0 \cdot \overline{x}$ where $\overline{x} \in \text{arg Max}_x\{a_0 \cdot x | \mathbf{A}x \leq \overline{z}, x \geq 0\}$. Then, if the interior of the feasible set is non-empty, there exists a supporting price vector $\lambda \geq 0$ such that

$$a_0' - \lambda'\mathbf{A} \leq 0 \tag{1.1-7}$$

where $\overline{x}$ and λ satisfy the following *complementary slackness* conditions.

$$\text{(i) } (a_0' - \lambda'\mathbf{A})\overline{x} = 0 \quad \text{and} \quad \text{(ii) } \lambda'(\overline{z} - \mathbf{A}\overline{x}) = 0.$$

Proof: Rewriting (1.1-6) in matrix notation,

$$q - \overline{q} - \lambda'(z - \overline{z}) \leq 0 \quad \text{for all} \quad (-z, q) \in \mathcal{Y}. \tag{1.1-8}$$

Consider the change in the activity vector $x - \overline{x}$. The associated change in input requirements is $z - \overline{z} = \mathbf{A}(x - \overline{x})$, and the change in output is $q - \overline{q} = a_0'(x - \overline{x})$.

Substituting into (1.1-8),

$$a_0'(x - \overline{x}) - \lambda'\mathbf{A}(x - \overline{x}) = (a_0' - \lambda'\mathbf{A}) \cdot (x - \overline{x}) \leq 0. \tag{1.1-9}$$

Next set all the changes in x except the jth component equal to zero. Inequality (1.1-9) then becomes

$$\left(a_{0j} - \sum_{i=1}^{m} \lambda_i a_{ij} \right) (x_j - \overline{x}_j) \leq 0. \tag{1.1-10}$$

If $\overline{x}_j > 0$ this inequality must hold regardless of the sign of $x_j - \overline{x}_j$. Therefore

$$a_{0j} - \sum_{i=1}^{m} \lambda_i a_{ij} = 0.$$

If $\overline{x}_j = 0$ this inequality (1.1-10) must hold if $x_j - \overline{x}_j$ is positive. Therefore

$$a_{0j} - \sum_{i=1}^{m} \lambda_i a_{ij} \leq 0.$$

Summarizing these results,

$$a_{0j} - \sum_{i=1}^{m} \lambda_i a_{ij} \leq 0 \quad \text{and} \quad \left(a_{0j} - \sum_{i=1}^{m} \lambda_i a_{ij} \right) \overline{x}_j = 0.$$

An identical argument holds for each component of $\overline{x}$. Therefore we can write the necessary conditions as follows.

$$a_0' - \lambda' \mathbf{A} \leq 0 \quad \text{and} \quad (a_0' - \lambda' \mathbf{A}) \overline{x} = 0.$$

We must now prove the second complementary slackness condition. By construction

$$\overline{q} = \underset{x \geq 0}{\text{Max}} \{ q = a_0 \cdot x \mid \mathbf{A}x \leq \overline{z} \}$$

and

$$\overline{x} \in \arg \underset{x \geq 0}{\text{Max}} \{ q = a_0 \cdot x \mid \mathbf{A}x \leq \overline{z} \}.$$

Define $z^* = \mathbf{A}\overline{x}$. Because the activity vector $\overline{x}$ is feasible, $\overline{z} - A\overline{x} = \overline{z} - z^* \geq 0$.

From the Supporting Hyperplane Theorem

$$\overline{q} - \lambda' z^* \leq \overline{q} - \lambda' \overline{z}.$$

Rearranging this inequality, $\lambda'(\overline{z} - z^*) \leq 0$. But $\overline{z} - z^* \geq 0$ and $\lambda \geq 0$ so $\lambda'(\overline{z} - z^*) \geq 0$. Combining these inequalities, it follows that

$$\lambda'(\overline{z} - A\overline{x}) = \lambda'(\overline{z} - z^*) = 0. \qquad \square$$

Example: Two Plants and Two Inputs

Consider the following two-plant example. If plant 1 operates at the unit activity level it produces $a_{01} = \frac{1}{3}$ units of output and has an input requirement vector of $(1, 1)$. If plant 2 operates at the unit activity level it produces $a_{02} = \frac{1}{2}$ units of output and has an input requirement of $(4, 1)$. Then given the vector x of activity levels, total input requirements are

$$\mathbf{A}x = \begin{bmatrix} 1 & 4 \\ 1 & 1 \end{bmatrix} \begin{bmatrix} x_1 \\ x_2 \end{bmatrix}.$$

Maximum output with activity vector x is $q = a_0 \cdot x = \frac{1}{3}x_1 + \frac{1}{2}x_2$.

Suppose that the vector of available inputs is $\bar{z} = (11, 5)$. What is the maximum output of the firm?

Note that to produce an additional unit of output requires increasing the activity level of plant 1 by three so that the input requirement vector for each unit of output is

$$\hat{z}_1 = \begin{bmatrix} 1 & 4 \\ 1 & 1 \end{bmatrix} \begin{bmatrix} 3 \\ 0 \end{bmatrix} = \begin{bmatrix} 3 \\ 3 \end{bmatrix}.$$

Similarly, for plant 2 the unit input requirement vector is

$$\hat{z}_2 = \begin{bmatrix} 1 & 4 \\ 1 & 1 \end{bmatrix} \begin{bmatrix} 0 \\ 2 \end{bmatrix} = \begin{bmatrix} 8 \\ 2 \end{bmatrix}.$$

These two input vectors are depicted in Figure 1.1-6.

Using convex combinations of these two input vectors also yields one unit of output. Thus the line joining $\hat{z}^1$ and $\hat{z}^2$ is a line of equal quantity or *isoquant*. Because the constraints are all linear, the production set must therefore be as depicted in Figure 1.1-5.

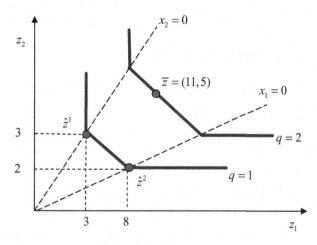

Figure 1.1-6. Isoquants.

The input-output vector $(\overline{z}, \overline{q})$ lies on the boundary of the production set. Because the set is convex there are supporting prices. That is, for some output price $p \geq 0$ and input price vector $r \geq 0$, and any feasible vector (z, q), $pq - r \cdot z \leq p\overline{q} - r \cdot \overline{z}$.

To support the production plan of plant 1 the marginal profit of increasing the activity level of the plant by 1 must be zero. That is,

$$MR(x_1) - MC(x_1) = p\frac{1}{3} - (r_1 1 + r_2 1) = 0.$$

Similarly,

$$MR(x_2) - MC(x_2) = p\frac{1}{2} - (r_1 4 + r_2 1) = 0.$$

Dividing by p we can therefore rewrite these equations as follows:

$$MR_1 - MC_1 = \tfrac{1}{3} - (\lambda_1 1 + \lambda_2 1) = 0.$$
$$MR_2 - MC_2 = \tfrac{1}{2} - (\lambda_1 4 + \lambda_2 1) = 0.$$

Solving, $\lambda_1 = \frac{1}{18}$ and $\lambda_2 = \frac{5}{18}$.

Because both supporting prices are strictly positive, the complementary slackness property implies that $\overline{z} - \mathbf{A}\overline{x} = 0$; that is,

$$\overline{z} - \mathbf{A}x = \begin{bmatrix} 11 \\ 5 \end{bmatrix} - \begin{bmatrix} 1 & 4 \\ 1 & 1 \end{bmatrix} \begin{bmatrix} \overline{x}_1 \\ \overline{x}_2 \end{bmatrix} = \begin{bmatrix} 0 \\ 0 \end{bmatrix}.$$

The solution to this system of equations is $\overline{x} = (3, 2)$. Then the maximum output is $\overline{q} = a_0 \cdot \overline{x} = 2$.

Exercises

Exercise 1.1-1: Supporting Hyperplane

(a) Show that the function $U(x) = \sum_{i=1}^{n} \alpha_i \ln x_i$ is quasi-concave for all $x > 0$.
(b) For any $\overline{x} > 0$ obtain an expression for the supporting hyperplane of the upper contour set through $\overline{x}$.
(c) For $n = 2$ depict this in a neat figure.

Exercise 1.1-2: Supporting Hyperplane for CES Preferences

(a) For $\sigma > 1$ show that the CES utility function $U(x) = (x_1^{1-\frac{1}{\sigma}} + x_1^{1-\frac{1}{\sigma}})^{\frac{1}{1-\frac{1}{\sigma}}}$ is strictly quasi-concave. HINT: Show that the utility function $u(x) = f(U(x))$ is concave, where $f(U) = U^{1-\frac{1}{\sigma}}$.
(b) Show that this is true for $\sigma < 1$. HINT: Consider the mapping $f(U) = -U^{1-\frac{1}{\sigma}}$.
(c) For any $\overline{x} > 0$ obtain an expression for the supporting hyperplane of the upper contour set through $\overline{x}$.

Exercise 1.1-3: Supporting Prices
A firm has the following production set:

$$\mathcal{Y} = \{(-z, q) | q \leq F(z) = z_1^{1/3} z_2^{2/3}, z \geq 0\}.$$

(a) The Cobb-Douglas function $F(z) = z_1^{\alpha_1} z_2^{\alpha_2}$, $z \geq 0$, $\alpha \gg 0$ is concave if $\alpha_1 + \alpha_2 \leq 1$.[5] Use this to establish that the production set is convex.

(b) Confirm that $(z, q) = (1, 1, 1)$ lies on the boundary of $\mathcal{Y}$.

(c) Solve for the supporting price vector.

(d) Suppose instead that the production set is

$$\mathcal{Y} = \left\{ y | g(y) = y_1 y_2^2 + y_3^3 \leq 0, \ y_1, y_2 \leq 0, \ y_3 \geq 0 \right\}.$$

Compare this with the previous production set and show that $y^0 = (-1, -1, 1)$ lies on the boundary of this set. What price vector supports this production plan?

Exercise 1.1-4: Robinson Crusoe Economy Robinson Crusoe lives alone on an island off the coast of New Zealand. He has a production set $\mathcal{Y} = \{(-z_1, y_2) | y_2 \leq 16 z_1^{1/3}, \ z_1 \geq 0\}$ and an endowment vector $\omega = (32, 0)$. His preferences are represented by the utility function $U(x) = \ln x_1 + \ln x_2$.

(a) Solve for his optimal choice of input and hence his optimal production plan and consumption plan x^*.

(b) Depict the production set and the set $\mathcal{Y} + \omega$ in a neat figure and indicate the optimal production and consumption plans. Explain what it means for the optimal production plan to be supported by a price vector $p = (p_1, p_2)$.

(c) Solve for the price vector that supports the optimal production plan.

(d) Depict this supporting price line, Crusoe's budget set and indifference curve through x^*.

(e) Hence explain why the supporting price vector is a Walrasian equilibrium price vector if Robinson Crusoe is a price-taker.

Exercise 1.1-5: Robinson Crusoe Economy with Three Commodities Robinson Crusoe has a production set $\mathcal{Y} = \{(-z, y_3) | y_3 \leq z_1^{1/3} z_2 2^{1/3}, \ z \geq 0\}$ and an endowment vector $\omega = (32, 160, 0)$. His preferences are represented by the utility function $U(x) = \ln x_1 + \ln x_2 + \ln x_3$.

(a) Solve for his optimal choice of inputs and hence his optimal production plan and consumption plan x^*.

(b) Solve for the price vector that supports the optimal production plan.

(c) At these prices what is Crusoe's budget set? Confirm that x^* is the optimal point in this budget set.

(d) Hence explain why the supporting prices are equilibrium prices.

Exercise 1.1-6: Robinson Crusoe Economy with Four Commodities Robinson Crusoe has a production set $\mathcal{Y} = \{(-z, y_3) | y_3 \leq z_1^{1/3} z_2^{2/3}, \ z \geq 0\}$ and an endowment vector $\omega = (32, 160, 0, 16)$. His preferences are represented by the utility function $U(x) = \sum_{j=1}^{4} \ln x_j$.

(a) Solve for the optimal production plan and hence the optimal consumption vector x^*.

---

[5] See Appendix B.

(b) Obtain a price vector (p_1, p_2, p_3), where $p_2 = 1$, that supports the optimal production plan.

(c) What must be the price of commodity 4 if x^* is Crusoe's optimal consumption bundle in his budget set? HINT: There is only one consumer so Crusoe must consume his endowment.

Exercise 1.1-7: Linear Technology A firm has two plants and produces a single output using two inputs. If plant 1 operates at level x_1, it produces x_1 units of output and utilizes $4x_1$ units of input 1 and $2x_1$ units of input 2. If plant 2, operates at level x_2 it produces x_2 units of output and utilizes $3x_2$ units of input 1 and $4x_2$ units of input 2. Let z_1 be the level of input 1 and z_2 be the level of input 2.

(a) Depict the set of inputs (z_1, z_2) that yields an output of at least one unit.
(b) Suppose that the input vector is $z^0 = (14, 12)$. Explain why the maximum output is

$$q^0 = \underset{x}{\mathrm{Max}}\{x_1 + x_2 | x \geq 0, 4x_1 + 3x_2 \leq 14, 2x_1 + 4x_2 \leq 12\}.$$

(c) Solve for the maximum output.
(d) Let (λ_1, λ_2) be supporting prices. Use the fact that profit at each plant must be zero to solve for these prices.

1.2 Shadow Prices

Key ideas: shadow prices, Kuhn-Tucker conditions, linearized maximization problem, constraint qualification, necessary and sufficient conditions for a maximum

Before examining the formalities of constrained optimization, we consider necessary conditions from an economic perspective. Consider the following maximization problem:

$$\underset{x}{\mathrm{Max}}\{f(x) | x \geq 0, b - g(x) \geq 0\}.$$

We interpret this mathematical problem as the decision problem of a profit maximizing firm. This firm can produce any vector of outputs x that satisfies the non-negativity constraint, $x \geq 0$ and a resource constraint

$$g(x) \leq b.$$

A simple example is a linear constraint. Each unit of x_j requires a_j units of resource b. Then $a \cdot x = \sum_{j=1}^{n} a_j x_j \leq b$.

Suppose that $\overline{x}$ solves the optimization problem. If the firm increases x_j, there is a direct effect, $\frac{\partial f}{\partial x_j}$, on the firm's profit. However, the increase in x_j also uses additional resources so that there must be offsetting changes in other commodities. The extra resource requirement is $\frac{\partial g}{\partial x_j}$. If these resources were to be purchased at a market price r, the additional cost for the firm would be $r\frac{\partial g}{\partial x_j}$. In the absence of such a market, we introduce a *shadow price* $\lambda \geq 0$ to reflect the opportunity cost of using the additional resources. Multiplying the extra resource requirement $\frac{\partial g}{\partial x_j}$ by the shadow price of the resource gives the opportunity cost of increasing x_j. The net gain to increasing x_j is therefore

$$\frac{\partial f}{\partial x_j}(\overline{x}) - \lambda \frac{\partial g}{\partial x_j}(\overline{x}).$$

If this net gain is strictly positive, the firm gains by increasing x_j. Thus a necessary condition for $\overline{x}_j$ to be optimal is

$$\frac{\partial f}{\partial x_j}(\overline{x}) - \lambda \frac{\partial g}{\partial x_j}(\overline{x}) \leq 0.$$

If $x_j > 0$ and the net gain is strictly negative, the firm gains by reducing x_j. Thus a further necessary condition for $\overline{x}_j$ to be optimal is

$$\frac{\partial f}{\partial x_j}(\overline{x}) - \lambda \frac{\partial g}{\partial x_j}(\overline{x}) \geq 0, \quad \text{when} \quad \overline{x}_j > 0.$$

Thus the marginal net gain is zero at the optimum unless the optimum is zero.

Summarizing,

$$\frac{\partial f}{\partial x_j}(\overline{x}) - \lambda \frac{\partial g}{\partial x_j}(\overline{x}) \leq 0, \quad \text{with equality if } \overline{x}_j > 0.$$

Because $\overline{x}$ must be feasible, $b - g(\overline{x}) \geq 0$. Moreover, we have defined λ to be the opportunity cost of additional resource use. Then, if not all of the resource is used, λ must be zero. Summarizing,

$$b - g(\overline{x}) \geq 0, \quad \text{with equality if } \lambda > 0.$$

There is a convenient way to remember these conditions. First, write the constraint in the form $h(x) \geq 0$. Thus in our example we write the constraint as $b - g(x) \geq 0$. Second, introduce the *Lagrange multiplier* or shadow price λ. Then the Lagrangian for the maximization problem is

$$\mathcal{L}(x, \lambda) = f(x) + \lambda h(x).$$

The first-order conditions are then all restrictions on the partial derivatives of $\mathcal{L}(x, \lambda)$.

(i) $\dfrac{\partial \mathcal{L}}{\partial x_j} = \dfrac{\partial f}{\partial x_i} + \lambda \dfrac{\partial h}{\partial x_j} \leq 0$,   with equality if $\overline{x}_j > 0, j = 1, \ldots, n$.

(ii) $\dfrac{\partial \mathcal{L}}{\partial \lambda} = h(\overline{x}) \geq 0$,   with equality if $\lambda > 0$.

Multiple Constraints

Although we have thus far considered only a single constraint, exactly the same intuitive argument holds if there are m constraints of the form $h_i(x) \geq 0$. The Lagrangian becomes

$$\mathcal{L}(x, \lambda) = f(x) + \lambda \cdot h(x),$$

where $\lambda = (\lambda_1, \ldots, \lambda_m)$ is the vector of shadow prices for the m constraints and $h(x) = (h_1(x), \ldots, h_m(x))$ is the vector of constraint functions. Differentiating the Lagrangian yields the following first-order conditions (FOC):

(i) $\dfrac{\partial \mathcal{L}}{\partial x_j} = \dfrac{\partial f}{\partial x_j} + \lambda \cdot \dfrac{\partial h}{\partial x_j} \leq 0,$ with equality if $\overline{x}_j > 0, j = 1, \ldots, n$

(ii) $\dfrac{\partial \mathcal{L}}{\partial \lambda_i} = h_i(x) \geq 0,$ with equality if $\lambda_i > 0, i = 1, \ldots, m.$

Concave Maximization Problems

Maximization problems are especially easy to solve if the problem is concave; that is, the objective function and each of the constraint functions are all concave. Then we have the following proposition.

Proposition 1.2-1: Sufficient Conditions for a Maximum
If $f(\cdot)$ and $h_i(\cdot), i = 1, \ldots, m$ are all concave and there exists a shadow price vector λ and $\overline{x}$, both non-negative and satisfying the FOC, then $\overline{x}$ solves $\text{Max}_{x \geq 0}\{f(x)|h(x) \geq 0\}$.

Proof: Given the concavity of f and h, the Lagrangian $\mathcal{L}(x, \lambda) = f(x) + \lambda \cdot h(x)$ is a concave function of x. It follows that the tangent hyperplane at any $\overline{x}$ lies above the graph of the function; that is,

$$\mathcal{L}(x, \lambda) \leq \mathcal{L}(\overline{x}, \lambda) + \frac{\partial \mathcal{L}}{\partial x}(\overline{x}, \lambda) \cdot (x - \overline{x}). \qquad (1.2\text{-}1)$$

Suppose that $(\overline{x}, \lambda)$ satisfies the FOC. If $\overline{x}_j > 0$ then $\frac{\partial \mathcal{L}}{\partial x_j}(\overline{x}, \lambda) = 0$ and if $\overline{x}_j = 0$ then $\frac{\partial \mathcal{L}}{\partial x_j}(\overline{x}, \lambda) \leq 0$. Together these results imply that for all $x_j \geq 0$

$$\frac{\partial \mathcal{L}}{\partial x_j}(\overline{x}, \lambda)(x_j - \overline{x}_j) \leq 0.$$

Because this is true for $j = 1, \ldots, n$ it follows that

$$\frac{\partial \mathcal{L}}{\partial x}(\overline{x}, \lambda) \cdot (x - \overline{x}) \leq 0.$$

Moreover, either the ith constraint is binding or the associated shadow price is zero. Therefore $\mathcal{L}(\overline{x}, \lambda) = f(\overline{x}) + \lambda \cdot h(\overline{x}) = f(\overline{x})$.

Substituting these results into (1.2-1) it follows that

$$\mathcal{L}(x, \lambda) = f(x) + \lambda \cdot h(x) \leq f(\overline{x}).$$

For any feasible x, $h(x) \geq 0$. Moreover the shadow price vector is positive. Therefore for any feasible x, $f(x) \leq f(\overline{x})$. Thus any $\overline{x}$ satisfying the FOC is optimal. ☐

This result makes it easy to solve a concave optimization problem. First write down the FOC. Make some assumption about which constraints are binding and which components of $\overline{x}$ are positive and see if all the FOC hold. If so, $\overline{x}$ solves the optimization problem.

Example 1

$$\underset{x}{\text{Max}} \{ f(x) = \ln(1 + x_1) + \ln(1 + x_2) | x \geq 0, h(x) = 2 - x_1 - x_2 \geq 0 \}.$$

Note that the second derivative of $\ln(1 + x)$ is negative. Because the sum of strictly concave functions is strictly concave, then it follows that f is strictly concave. Thus if we can find some $(\overline{x}, \lambda)$ satisfying the FOC we are done.

The Lagrangian for the problem is

$$\mathcal{L}(x, \lambda) = \ln(1 + x_1) + \ln(1 + x_2) + \lambda(2 - x_1 - x_2).$$

Because f is an increasing function the constraint will be binding at the maximum. As a first pass assume that $\overline{x} \gg 0$. If so, the FOC are as follows:

$$\frac{\partial \mathcal{L}}{\partial x_1} = \frac{1}{1 + x_1} - \lambda = 0,$$

$$\frac{\partial \mathcal{L}}{\partial x_2} = \frac{1}{1 + x_2} - \lambda = 0,$$

$$\frac{\partial \mathcal{L}}{\partial \lambda} = 2 - x_1 - x_2 = 0.$$

From the first two of these conditions $\overline{x}_1 = \overline{x}_2$. Substituting into the constraint, $\overline{x} = (1, 1)$.

The feasible set and contour set for f through $\overline{x} = (1, 1)$ are depicted in Figure 1.2-1.

As the next example shows, if the optimization problem is not concave, our informal arguments leading to the FOC are not quite complete. In this second problem the feasible set and maximand are exactly the same as in example 1, so the solution is again $\overline{x} = (1, 1)$. However the FOC do not hold at the maximum.

Example 2 Consider the following problem.

$$\underset{x \geq 0}{\text{Max}} \left\{ f(x) = \ln(1 + x_1) + \ln(1 + x_2) | h(x) = (2 - x_1 - x_2)^3 \geq 0 \right\}.$$

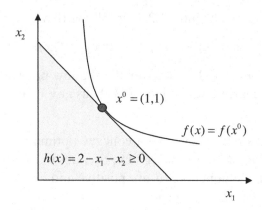

Figure 1.2-1. Constrained maximum.

The Lagrangian is

$$\mathcal{L}(x, \lambda) = \ln(1 + x_1) + \ln(1 + x_2) + \lambda(2 - x_1 - x_2)^3.$$

Differentiating by x_j,

$$\frac{\partial \mathcal{L}}{\partial x_j} = \frac{1}{1 + x_j} - 3\lambda(2 - x_1 - x_2)^2 = \frac{1}{2} \text{ at } \overline{x} = (1, 1).$$

Thus the informally derived FOC does not hold at the maximum.

Our intuitive argument breaks down because $\frac{\partial h}{\partial x}$, the gradient of the constraint function, is zero at the maximum. Thus the partial derivatives of h no longer reflect the opportunity cost of the scarce resource.

More formally, suppose the ith constraint is binding at $\overline{x}$ so that $h_i(\overline{x}) = 0$. The linear approximation of the constraint at $\overline{x}$ is

$$h_i(\overline{x}) + \frac{\partial h_i}{\partial x}(\overline{x}) \cdot (x - \overline{x}) = \frac{\partial h_i}{\partial x}(\overline{x}) \cdot (x - \overline{x}) = 0.$$

This only approximates the constraint if the gradient vector is non-zero.

There is a second (though highly unlikely) situation in which the linear approximations fail. Consider the following problem:

$$\text{Max}_x \left\{ f(x) = 12x_1 + x_2 | h(x) = (2 - x_1)^3 - x_2 \geq 0, x \geq 0 \right\}.$$

The feasible set is the shaded region in Figure 1.2-2a.

Also depicted in Figure 1.2-2a is the contour set for f through $\overline{x} = (2, 0)$. From the figure it is clear that f takes on its maximum at $\overline{x} = (2, 0)$. However,

$$\frac{\partial \mathcal{L}}{\partial x_1}(\overline{x}) = 12 - 3\lambda(\overline{x}_1 - 2)^2 = 12.$$

Thus again the FOC do not hold at the maximum.

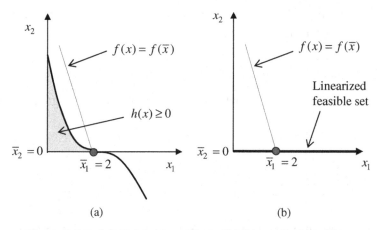

Figure 1.2-2. (a) Original problem. (b) Linearized problem.

This time the problem occurs because the feasible set, after taking a linear approximation of the constraint function, looks nothing like the original feasible set. At $\overline{x}$, the gradient vector $\frac{\partial h}{\partial x}(x) = (0, -1)$. Thus the linear approximation of the constraint $h(x) \geq 0$ through $\overline{x}$ is

$$\frac{\partial h}{\partial x}(\overline{x}) \cdot (x - \overline{x}) = \frac{\partial h}{\partial x_1}(\overline{x})(x_1 - 2) + \frac{\partial h}{\partial x_2}(\overline{x})x_2 = -x_2 \geq 0.$$

Because x must be non-negative, the only feasible value of x_2 is $x_2 = 0$. In Figure 1.2-2b the linearized feasible set is therefore the horizontal axis. Then the solution to the linearized problem is not the solution to the original problem.

Note that this example is very special because the feasible set for the linearized constraints has no interior. In Section 1.4 we show that the intuitive development of the first-order conditions is correct as long as the linearized feasible set has a non-empty interior.

Suppose we replace each constraint that is binding at $\overline{x}$ by its linear approximation at $\overline{x}$. Let $\overline{h}_i(x)$ be the linear approximation for the ith constraint; that is,

$$\overline{h}_i(x) = h_i(\overline{x}) + \frac{\partial h_i}{\partial x}(\overline{x}) \cdot (x - \overline{x}).$$

Then the linearized constraint is

$$\overline{h}_i(x) = h_i(\overline{x}) + \frac{\partial h_i}{\partial x}(\overline{x}) \cdot (x - \overline{x}) \geq 0. \tag{1.2-2}$$

Let B be the set of constraints that are binding at $\overline{x}$; that is,

$$B = \{i \,|\, i = 1, \ldots, m, h_i(\overline{x}) = 0\}.[6]$$

[6] This is known as an index set.

For such constraints $h_i(\bar{x}) = 0$. Appealing to (1.2-2), the linearized constraint can be rewritten as follows:

$$\frac{\partial h_i}{\partial x}(\bar{x}) \cdot (x - \bar{x}) \geq 0, i \in B.$$

Note that for this to be a constraint we require that the gradient vector $\frac{\partial h_i}{\partial x}(\bar{x}) \neq 0$.

We define $\bar{X}$ to be the set of non-negative vectors satisfying these linearized binding constraints; that is,

$$\bar{X} \equiv \left\{ x \mid x \geq 0 \quad \text{and} \quad \frac{\partial h_i}{\partial x} \cdot (x - \bar{x}) \geq 0, i \in B \right\}.$$

Definition: Constraint Qualification Define X to be the set of feasible vectors; that is,

$$X = \{x \mid x \geq 0, h_i(x) \geq 0, i = 1, \ldots, m\}.$$

The constraint qualification is said to hold at $\bar{x} \in X$ if

(i) for each constraint that is binding at $\bar{x}$, the associated gradient vector $\frac{\partial h_i}{\partial x}(\bar{x}) \neq 0$ and

(ii) $\bar{X}$, the set of non-negative vectors satisfying the linearized binding constraints, has a non-empty interior.

As long as the constraint qualification holds, the intuitively derived conditions are indeed necessary conditions. This is summarized in Proposition 1.2-2.

Proposition 1.2-2: Kuhn-Tucker Conditions (First-Order Conditions)
Suppose $\bar{x}$ solves the following problem

$$\underset{x}{\text{Max}}\{ f(x) \mid x \in X\} \quad \text{where} \quad X = \{x \mid x \geq 0, h_i(x) \geq 0, i = 1, \ldots, m\}.$$

If the Constraint Qualification holds at $\bar{x}$ then there exists a vector of shadow prices $\lambda \geq 0$ such that

$$\left. \begin{array}{l} \dfrac{\partial \mathcal{L}}{\partial x_j}(\bar{x}, \lambda) \leq 0, j = 1, \ldots, n \text{ with equality if } \bar{x}_j > 0 \\[1em] \text{and} \\[1em] \dfrac{\partial \mathcal{L}}{\partial \lambda}(\bar{x}, \lambda) \geq 0, i = 1, \ldots, m \text{ with equality if } \lambda_i > 0 \end{array} \right\} \begin{array}{l} \text{Kuhn-Tucker} \\ \text{conditions} \end{array}$$

Because Kuhn and Tucker were the first to characterize a constraint qualification, the first-order conditions (FOC) are often called the Kuhn-Tucker conditions.

Remark

Because $\bar{x} \geq 0$ and $\lambda \geq 0$ the Kuhn-Tucker conditions can be rewritten as follows:

$$\frac{\partial \mathfrak{L}}{\partial x_j} \leq 0 \quad \text{and} \quad \bar{x}_j \frac{\partial \mathfrak{L}}{\partial x_j}(\bar{x}, \lambda) = 0, \quad j = 1, \ldots, n$$

and

$$\frac{\partial \mathfrak{L}}{\partial \lambda_i}(\bar{x}, \lambda) \geq 0 \quad \text{and} \quad \lambda_i \frac{\partial \mathfrak{L}}{\partial \lambda_i}(\bar{x}, \lambda) = 0, \quad i = 1, \ldots, m.$$

Expressed in vector notation, the Kuhn-Tucker conditions are therefore

$$\frac{\partial \mathfrak{L}}{\partial x}(\bar{x}, \lambda) \leq 0 \quad \text{and} \quad \bar{x} \cdot \frac{\partial \mathfrak{L}}{\partial x}(\bar{x}, \lambda) = 0$$

and

$$\frac{\partial \mathfrak{L}}{\partial \lambda}(\bar{x}, \lambda) \geq 0 \quad \text{and} \quad \lambda \cdot \frac{\partial \mathfrak{L}}{\partial \lambda}(\bar{x}, \lambda) = 0.$$

The Constraint Qualification is especially easy to check if, for every binding constraint, the constraint function is quasi-concave. If so, then the tangent hyperplanes are supporting hyperplanes. As shown earlier, let B be the index set of binding constraints. By Lemma 1.1-2, as long as $\frac{\partial h_i}{\partial x}(\bar{x}) \neq 0$, for $i \in B$, the set of vectors satisfying each binding constraint

$$X = \{x | x \geq 0, h_i(x) \geq 0, i \in B\}$$

is a subset of the vectors satisfying the linearized constraint. That is,

$$X \subset \overline{X} = \{x | x \geq 0, \frac{\partial h_i}{\partial x}(\bar{x}) \cdot (x - \bar{x}) \geq 0, i \in B\}.$$

We summarize this in Lemma 1.2-3.

Lemma 1.2-3: If, for each of the constraints that are binding at $\bar{x}$, h_i is quasi-concave and $\frac{\partial h_i}{\partial x}(\bar{x}) \neq 0$ then $X \subset \overline{X}$.

It follows that if X has a non-empty interior then so does the linearized set $\overline{X}$. Hence we have the following result.

Proposition 1.2-4: Constraint Qualification with Convex Constraint Sets
Suppose that the feasible set $X = \{x | x \geq 0, h_i(x) \geq 0, i = 1, \ldots, m\}$ has a non-empty interior. If for each of the constraints that are binding at $\bar{x}$, the constraint function h_i is quasi-concave and $\frac{\partial h_i}{\partial x}(\bar{x}) \neq 0$ then the Constraint Qualification is satisfied at $\bar{x}$.

For many economic applications, it is fairly easy to check that the conditions of this proposition are satisfied.

Finally we note that the Kuhn-Tucker conditions are only necessary conditions for a maximum. We have seen that for concave problems they are both necessary and sufficient. As we show in Section 1.4, they are also necessary and sufficient if the objective function and constraint functions are quasi-concave.

Proposition 1.2-5: Necessary and Sufficient Conditions for a Maximum
If f and $h_i, i = 1, \ldots, m$ are quasi-concave, the Kuhn-Tucker conditions hold at $\bar{x}$ and for each binding constraint, $\frac{\partial h_i}{\partial x}(\bar{x}) \neq 0$, then $\bar{x}$ solves

$$\underset{x}{\text{Max}}\{f(x)|x \geq 0, h_i(x) \geq 0, i = 1, \ldots, m\}.$$

Exercises

Exercise 1.2-1: How Many Goods Should She Consume? Bev has the following optimization problem

$$\underset{x}{\text{Max}}\{U(x) = \ln(a + x_1) + \ln x_2 | 4x_1 + x_2 \leq 20\}.$$

Solve if (i) $a = 0$, (ii) $a = 6$.

Exercise 1.2-2: Consumer Choice A consumer with income I has a utility function $U(x) = x_1^{\alpha_1} \ldots x_n^{\alpha_n}, \alpha > 0$ and faces the price vector p.

(a) Find an increasing function f such that $u(x) = f(U(x))$ is concave and hence quasi-concave.
(b) By Proposition 1.2-4 the FOC for the modified problem are both necessary and sufficient. Hence solve for the consumer's optimal choice.

Exercise 1.2-3: Multi-Plant Firm A firm produces a single product at n different plants. The cost of producing q_j units of output at plant j is $C_j(q_j) = \frac{1}{2\alpha_j}q_j^2, \alpha_j > 0, j = 1, \ldots, n$. The firm's objective is to produce a total of q units at minimum cost.

(a) Write down the optimization problem and form the Lagrangian. Hence show that the first-order condition is $q_j = \alpha_j \lambda$.
(b) Show that $\lambda = \frac{q}{n\bar{\alpha}}$, where $\bar{\alpha} = \frac{1}{n}\sum_{j=1}^{n}\alpha_j$.
(c) Solve for the total cost of production at each plant and hence solve for the minimized total cost for the firm.
(d) Confirm that the marginal cost for the firm is $MC(q) = \frac{q}{n\bar{\alpha}}$.
(e) Is it a coincidence that the answers to parts (b) and (d) are the same?

Exercise 1.2-4: Satisfying the Constraint Qualification with a Single Constraint There is a single constraint $g(x) \geq g(\bar{x})$ and $\bar{x} \cdot \frac{\partial g}{\partial x}(\bar{x}) < 0$.

(a) Show that the linearized set at $\bar{x}$ has a non-empty interior.
(b) Hence show that the constraint qualifications hold at $\bar{x}$.

1.3 The Envelope Theorem

Key ideas: direct and indirect effects on the maximum as a parameter changes

When the economic environment of an optimizing agent changes, the agent adapts by re-optimizing. As a result, there is both a direct effect on the agent's payoff and an indirect effect resulting from the re-optimization. This suggests that evaluating the total effect of a change in the agent's environment is typically complex. Indeed this is true for any finite change. However, it is much easier to derive strong conclusions about the rate of change of the maximized payoff. Suppose the change in the environment can be represented by a change $\Delta\alpha$ in a parameter α. As we see later, although the direct effect on the agent's objective is of order $\Delta\alpha$, the indirect effect is of order $(\Delta\alpha)^2$. Thus for small changes in the parameter, the indirect effects can be ignored. To illustrate why this must be the case, we first consider a simple example.

Example: Profit-Maximizing Firm

A firm with cost function $C(q)$ can sell as much output as it wishes at the fixed price p. Profit is therefore $\pi = pq - C(q)$. Initially we assume that output $q \in Q = \{0, q_1, q_2\}$. That is, output must be one of three levels.

Figure 1.3-1 depicts the graph of the profit as a function of the output price. If $q = 0$ the profit is zero for all prices. If $q > 0$, profit $\pi = pq - C(q)$ is a line with intercept $-C(q)$ and slope q. For prices below p' the profit-maximizing output is zero. For prices $p \in [p', p'']$ the profit-maximizing output is q_1. For all higher prices the profit-maximizing output is q_2. Maximized profit is indicated by the heavy line segments. This is known as the *upper envelope* of the profit functions.

Figure 1.3-2 shows the upper envelope when there are twice as many profit lines. Intuitively, in the limit, as the difference between the possible outputs

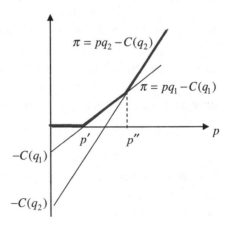

Figure 1.3-1. Upper envelope.

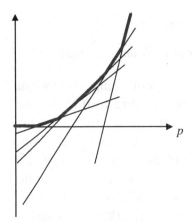

Figure 1.3-2. Upper envelope.

approaches zero, the envelope becomes a smooth curve. Each point on the smooth envelope is also on one of the output-constant profit lines. Thus as output price changes, marginal profit is equal to marginal profit if output is held fixed.

Consider next the case when output can be any real number. The profit-maximizing output $q^*(p)$ solves

$$\text{Max}_q\{\pi = pq - C(q)\}.$$

Let $\Pi(p)$ be maximized profit. That is,

$$\Pi(p) = pq^*(p) - C(q^*(p)).$$

Suppose that the output price is initially p^0 and so output is $q^*(p^0)$ and profit is $\Pi(p^0)$. Consider the effect on profit of a price change if output is held constant. For every dollar increase in price, the change in profit is $q^*(p^0)$. Thus profit with output constant is

$$\pi = \Pi(p^0) + (p - p^0)q^*(p^0).$$

The graph of this expression is a line of slope $q^*(p^0)$ through the point $(p^0, \pi(p^0))$. This is depicted in Figure 1.3-3.

Also depicted is the graph of maximized profit $\Pi(p)$. Clearly the firm cannot be worse off if it is free to vary quantity. Thus $\Pi(p)$ cannot be anywhere below the constrained profit line. It follows that if $\Pi(p)$ is smooth, then the curve and line must have the same slope at p^0. That is,

$$\frac{\partial \Pi}{\partial p}(p^0) = q^*(p^0);$$

Thus, in evaluating the first-order effect of a parameter change on profit, we need only consider the direct effect, holding the maximizer (output) constant. Intuitively, because the marginal profit from increasing output is zero

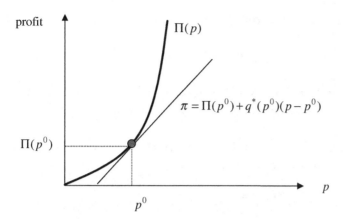

Figure 1.3-3. Direct and total effects.

at the maximum, the indirect effect of the output change is small relative to the direct price effect and becomes infinitesimally small in the limit. In the language of mathematics, the price effect is of first order and the output effect of second order.

There is one other piece of geometry that is helpful. Figure 1.3-4 depicts the marginal cost curve of the firm. Because the firm is a price-taker, marginal revenue is given by the horizontal line $p = p^0$. Suppose the output price rises to $p^1 = p^0 + \Delta p$. Let the new optimal output be $q^1 = q^*(p^1)$. The increase in profit is the shaded area to the left of the marginal cost curve. This is larger than the change in profit if output is held constant, $q^0 \Delta p$. Moreover it is smaller than $q^1 \Delta p$. The actual profit increase (the area above the marginal cost curve) thus satisfies the following bounds:

$$q^0 \Delta p \le \Delta \Pi \le q^1 \Delta p = q^0 \Delta p + \Delta q \Delta p.$$

Note that the difference between the bounds is $\Delta q \Delta p$. Because both Δq and Δp are small, this is a second-order difference.

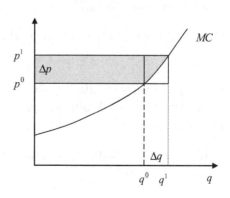

Figure 1.3-4. Bounding the change in profit.

Dividing the above inequalities by Δp we have

$$q^0 \leq \frac{\Delta \Pi}{\Delta p} \leq q^0 + \Delta q.$$

Taking the limit, it follows that as long as maximized output varies continuously with p, the rate of change of maximized profit is just the direct effect $q^0 = q^*(p^0)$.

We now turn to a formal discussion of the Envelope Theorem. Consider the optimization problem $\text{Max}_x \{ f(x, \alpha) | x \in X \subset \mathbb{R}^n \}$ and define

$$F(\alpha) = \text{Max}_x \{ f(x, \alpha) | x \in X \subset \mathbb{R}^n \}.$$

The function $F(\alpha)$ is the maximized value of the function $f(x, \alpha)$. We refer to $F(\alpha)$ more simply as the value function. It is intuitively clear that this function must be continuous as long as f is a continuous function. Consider two individuals with parameters α and α'. If these parameters are very similar the first individual can achieve almost the same value as the second by mimicking the choice of the second and vice versa.

Proposition 1.3-1: Continuity of the Value Function
If X is compact[7] and f is continuous, then $F(\alpha) = \text{Max}_{x \in X} \{ f(x, \alpha) \}$ is continuous.

Proof: Let $x(\alpha^1)$ be optimal for α^1 and let $x(\alpha^2)$ be optimal for α^2. Then

$$F(\alpha^2) = f(x(\alpha^2), \alpha^2) \geq f(x(\alpha^1), \alpha^2) \quad \text{and} \quad F(\alpha^1) = f(x(\alpha^1), \alpha^1)$$

and so

$$F(\alpha^2) - F(\alpha^1) \geq f(x(\alpha^1), \alpha^2) - f(x(\alpha^1), \alpha^1).$$

By the same argument,

$$F(\alpha^1) - F(\alpha^2) \geq f(x(\alpha^2), \alpha^1) - f(x(\alpha^2), \alpha^2).$$

Combining these inequalities,

$$f(x(\alpha^1), \alpha^2) - f(x(\alpha^1), \alpha^1) \leq F(\alpha^2) - F(\alpha^1)$$
$$\leq f(x(\alpha^2), \alpha^2) - f(x(\alpha^2), \alpha^1). \quad (1.3\text{-}1)$$

As long as f varies continuously with α it follows that the left- and right-hand expressions in this double inequality approach zero as $\alpha^2 \to \alpha^1$. Thus $F(\alpha)$ is continuous.   □

If there is a unique optimum for each α, we have the following further important result.

---

[7] A set is compact if it is both closed and bounded.

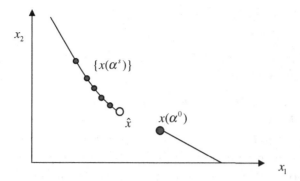

Figure 1.3-5. Continuity of the optimum.

Proposition 1.3-2: Continuity of the Optimum[8]

If X is compact, f is continuous and the problem $\text{Max}_{x \in X}\{f(x, \alpha)\}$ has a unique maximizer then $x(\alpha)$ is continuous.

Proof: Consider the sequence $\{\alpha^t\}$ with limit α^0 and sequence of optimal choices $\{x(\alpha^t)\}$. Because X is bounded, there must be some convergent subsequence $\{x(\alpha^s)\}$. Let the limit point be $\hat{x}$. This is depicted in Figure 1.3-5.

Suppose that there is a discontinuity at α^0 so that $\hat{x} \neq x(\alpha^0)$. By Proposition 1.3-1, F is continuous, therefore

$$F(\alpha^s) \to F(\alpha^0) = f(x(\alpha^0), \alpha^0).$$

Also, $F(\alpha^s) = f(x(\alpha^s), \alpha^s)$ and because $(x(\alpha^s), \alpha^s) \to (\hat{x}, \alpha^0)$,

$$F(\alpha^s) \to f(\hat{x}, \alpha^0).$$

Therefore $f(\hat{x}, \alpha^0) = f(x(\alpha^0), \alpha^0)$. However, this is impossible because, by hypothesis $x(\alpha^0)$ is the unique maximizing value of x. $\qquad \square$

From these two propositions we have the following result that plays a central role in economic theory.

Proposition 1.3-3: Envelope Theorem I

If X is compact, f is continuously differentiable and $x(\alpha) = \arg\text{Max}_{x \in X}\{f(x, \alpha)\}$ is unique, then the value function $F(\alpha) = \text{Max}_{x \in X}\{f(x, \alpha)\}$ is differentiable and

$$\frac{dF}{d\alpha} = \frac{\partial f}{\partial \alpha}(x(\alpha), \alpha).$$

Proof: Appealing to inequality (1.3-1)

$$\frac{f(x(\alpha), \alpha') - f(x(\alpha), \alpha)}{\alpha' - \alpha} \leq \frac{F(\alpha') - F(\alpha)}{\alpha' - \alpha} \leq \frac{f(x(\alpha'), \alpha') - f(x(\alpha'), \alpha)}{\alpha' - \alpha}.$$

Taking the limit as α' approaches α, $\frac{dF}{d\alpha} = \frac{\partial f}{\partial \alpha}(x(\alpha), \alpha)$. $\qquad \square$

[8] This is a special case of the Theorem of the Maximum. See Appendix C.

Note that this result is somewhat restrictive in that only the maximand is affected by the parameter change. Under slightly stronger assumptions we have a similar result when both the maximand and the constraints are affected by the parameter change.

Proposition 1.3-4: Envelope Theorem II

Define $F(\alpha) = \text{Max}_x\{f(x, \alpha) | h(x, \alpha) \geq 0, x \geq 0\}$ and $\mathcal{L}(x, \lambda, \alpha) = f(x, \alpha) + \lambda h(x, \alpha)$, where f and h are continuously differentiable. Let $x(\alpha)$, $\lambda(\alpha)$ be the unique solution to this maximization problem and suppose the Constraint Qualification holds. Suppose also that the implicit function theorem applies so that $x(\alpha)$ and $\lambda(\alpha)$ are continuously differentiable at α^0 ; then

$$\frac{\partial F}{\partial \alpha}(\alpha^0) = \frac{\partial \mathcal{L}}{\partial \alpha}(x(\alpha^0), \lambda(\alpha^0), \alpha^0).$$

Proof: At the optimum for parameter α, either $h_i(x(\alpha), \alpha) = 0$, or, if the constraint is not binding $\lambda_i(\alpha) = 0$. Hence

$$\lambda(\alpha) \cdot h(x(\alpha), \alpha) = 0$$

and so

$$\mathcal{L}(x(\alpha), \lambda(\alpha), \alpha) = f(x(\alpha), \alpha) + \lambda(\alpha) \cdot h(x(\alpha), \alpha)$$
$$= f(x(\alpha), \alpha) \equiv F(\alpha).$$

Let $B = \{i | h_i(x(\alpha^0), \alpha^0) = 0\}$. For any $i \notin B$, $h_i(x(\alpha^0), \alpha^0) > 0$. Because $x(\alpha)$ is continuous it follows that for some delta neighborhood of α^0, $h_i(x(\alpha), \alpha) > 0$. From the Kuhn-Tucker conditions it follows that in this neighborhood $\lambda_i(\alpha) = 0$. Then in this neighborhood the Lagrangian can be rewritten as follows:

$$\mathcal{L}(x(\alpha), \lambda(\alpha), \alpha) = f(x(\alpha), \alpha) + \sum_{i \in B} \lambda_i h_i(x, \alpha).$$

Therefore

$$\frac{\partial F}{\partial \alpha}(\alpha^0) = \sum_{j=1}^{n} \frac{\partial \mathcal{L}}{\partial x_j} \frac{\partial x_j}{\partial \alpha} + \sum_{i \in B} \frac{\partial \mathcal{L}}{\partial \lambda_i} \frac{\partial \lambda_i}{\partial \alpha} + \frac{\partial \mathcal{L}}{\partial \alpha}.$$

Because for each $i \in B$, $\frac{\partial \mathcal{L}}{\partial \lambda_i} = h_i(x(\alpha^0), \alpha^0) = 0$ the second summation on the right-hand side is zero. For each j, either $\frac{\partial \mathcal{L}}{\partial x_j} = 0$ or $\frac{\partial \mathcal{L}}{\partial x_j}(x(\alpha^0), \lambda(\alpha^0), \alpha^0) < 0$. Because $x(\alpha)$ and $\lambda(\alpha)$ are continuous it follows that if the latter is true for x_j then for some delta neighborhood of α^0

$$\frac{\partial \mathcal{L}}{\partial x_j}(x(\alpha), \lambda(\alpha), \alpha) < 0.$$

Appealing to the Kuhn-Tucker conditions $x_j(\alpha) = 0$ in this delta neighborhood and so $\frac{\partial x_j}{\partial \alpha}(\alpha^0) = 0$. Thus either $\frac{\partial \mathcal{L}}{\partial x_j}(x(\alpha^0), \lambda(\alpha^0), \alpha^0) = 0$ or $\frac{\partial x_j}{\partial \alpha}(\alpha^0) = 0$ and so

$$\frac{\partial F}{\partial \alpha} = \sum_{j \in J} \frac{\partial \mathcal{L}}{\partial x_j} \frac{\partial x_j}{\partial \alpha} + \frac{\partial \mathcal{L}}{\partial \alpha} = \frac{\partial \mathcal{L}}{\partial \alpha}. \tag{1.3-2}$$

$\square$

Exercises

Exercise 1.3-1: Price Elasticity of Profit A price-taking, profit-maximizing firm faces a price $p_1 = 10$ and produces $q_1 = 100$ units. Total cost is \$600.

(a) What is the elasticity of profit with respect to price $\mathcal{E}(\Pi, p_1) = \frac{p_1}{\Pi} \frac{\partial \Pi}{\partial p_1}$ if output is held fixed?
(b) What is the price elasticity of profit if the firm responds optimally to the price change?
(c) The firm sees a new opportunity and sells 50 units of product 2, which is priced at $p_2 = 20$. Production of product 1 drops to 80. Total cost rises to \$1,000. Are there enough data to compute $\mathcal{E}(\Pi, p_1) = \frac{p_1}{\Pi} \frac{\partial \Pi}{\partial p_1}$?

Exercise 1.3-2: Illustrating the Envelope Theorem To produce q units of output, a profit-maximizing firm requires $\frac{1}{2} q^2$ units of the single input. The price of the output is p and the price of the input is r.

(a) Write down an expression for profit $\pi(q, p, r)$.
(b) Solve for the profit-maximizing output q^* and hence show that maximized profit is

$$\Pi(p, r) = \pi(q^*(p, r), p, r) = \frac{1}{2} \frac{p^2}{r}.$$

(c) Confirm that $\frac{\partial \Pi}{\partial p} = \frac{\partial \pi}{\partial p}(q^*, p, r)$ and $\frac{\partial \Pi}{\partial r} = \frac{\partial \pi}{\partial r}(q^*, p, r)$.

Exercise 1.3-3: Cross Price Effects The production set of a firm is $\mathcal{Y} = \{(-z, q) | h(z, q) \geq 0\}$. The firm is a price taker. Given an input price vector r and output price vector p, maximized profit is $\Pi(p, r)$.

(a) Appeal to the Envelope Theorem to show that $\frac{\partial \Pi}{\partial p_j} = q_j^*$.
(b) Hence show that cross output price effects are symmetric; that is, $\frac{\partial q_i^*}{\partial p_j} = \frac{\partial q_j^*}{\partial p_i}$.
(c) Is there a parallel result for input price changes?

Exercise 1.3-4: Envelope Theorem with a Corner Solution A consumer has a utility function $U(x) = \ln(\alpha + x_1) + \ln x_2$, income I and faces a price vector $p = (p_1, p_2) \gg 0$.

(a) Show that if she consumes both commodities, her optimal consumption bundle is

$$x(p, I, \alpha) = \left(\frac{I - p_1\alpha}{2p_1}, \frac{I + p_1\alpha}{2p_2} \right).$$

(b) Hence write down an expression for maximized utility $F(\alpha) = U(x(p, I, \alpha))$ and show that

$$\frac{dF}{d\alpha} = \frac{2p_1}{I + \alpha p_1}.$$

(c) Explain why, for large α, $F(\alpha) = \ln \alpha + \ln(I/p_2)$ and confirm that F is continuously differentiable for all $\alpha \geq 0$.

1.4 Foundations of Constrained Optimization[9]

Key ideas: Fundamental Theorem of Linear Programming, reducing a maximization problem to a linear problem, shadow prices as supporting prices

In Section 1.1 we saw how prices support efficient plans given a convex technology. In Section 1.2 we explored the role of shadow prices in obtaining necessary conditions for a maximum. In this section we use the Supporting Hyperplane Theorem to provide the mathematical underpinnings of constrained optimization.

Linear Optimization

As a first step we consider linear optimization problems (linear programming problems). In the second step we then obtain necessary and sufficient conditions for general problems by examining the linearized approximation of the original problem.

Consider the following linear maximization problem.

$$\underset{x}{\text{Max}}\{q = a_0 \cdot x | x \in X \subset \mathbb{R}^n\} \quad \text{where} \quad X = \{x | x \geq 0, \mathbf{A}x \leq \bar{z}\},$$

$\mathbf{A}$ is an $m \times n$ matrix. We assume that X is bounded. Thus by the extreme value theorem there exists a solution $\bar{x}$. We also assume that X has a non-empty interior.

We now prove the following result.

---

[9] How important is it to really understand the theory underlying the Kuhn-Tucker necessary conditions for a maximum? As an analogy, suppose you have been given a toolkit containing a saw and blades capable of cutting steel. If all you will be doing is cut steel, the optimal short-run strategy is to learn how to use the saw without knowing anything about the underlying technology. But, in the long run, if you are going to want to cut other materials (such as glass), it becomes important to have a good general understanding of how the saw actually works. For this reason this section focuses on explaining the underlying theory.

Proposition 1.4-1: Fundamental Theorem of Linear Programming

Suppose that $\bar{x}$ solves $\underset{x}{\text{Max}}\{a_0 \cdot x | x \in X \subset \mathbb{R}^n\}$ where $X = \{x | x \geq 0, \mathbf{A}x \leq \bar{z}\}$ is bounded and has a non-empty interior. Then there exists a shadow price vector $\lambda \geq 0$ such that

$$a_0' - \lambda'\mathbf{A} \leq 0, \tag{1.4-1}$$

and the following "complementary slackness" conditions hold:

$$\text{(i) } (a_0' - \lambda'\mathbf{A})\bar{x} = 0 \quad \text{and} \quad \text{(ii) } \lambda'(\bar{z} - \mathbf{A}\bar{x}) = 0.$$

Moreover, these conditions are not only necessary but sufficient. That is, if $A\bar{x} \leq \bar{z}$, $a_0 - \lambda'\mathbf{A} \geq 0$, and the complementary slackness conditions hold, then $\bar{x}$ is the solution to the linear optimization problem.

Necessity follows directly from Proposition 1.1-4. That is, although we interpreted the linear model as an activity model of a firm with n plants, the formal analysis applies to any linear constrained optimization problem. Moreover, because the problem is linear it is concave. Then by Proposition 1.2-1, any $\bar{x}$ satisfying the necessary conditions is a solution to the maximization problem. That is, the necessary conditions are also sufficient.

Non-Linear Optimization Problems

As a first step we consider an optimization problem with linear constraints and a nonlinear objective function. Because the constraints are linear, the feasible set X is convex.

$$P : \underset{x}{\text{Max}}\{f(x) | x \in X\}.$$

Suppose that $\bar{x} \in \arg\underset{x}{\text{Max}}\{f(x) | x \in X\}$. We assume that $\frac{\partial f}{\partial x}(\bar{x}) \neq 0$. To establish that the Kuhn-Tucker conditions are necessary conditions we show that if $\bar{x}$ solves the problem P, then it must also solve the following linear maximization problem:

$$\bar{P} : \underset{x}{\text{Max}}\left\{\frac{\partial f}{\partial x}(\bar{x}) \cdot x | x \in X\right\}.$$

If not there is some $x^1 \in X$ such that $\frac{\partial f}{\partial x}(\bar{x}) \cdot x^1 > \frac{\partial f}{\partial x}(\bar{x}) \cdot \bar{x}$; that is,

$$\frac{\partial f}{\partial x}(\bar{x}) \cdot (x^1 - \bar{x}) > 0.$$

This is depicted in Figure 1.4-1. Consider all the convex combinations of $\bar{x}$ and x^1; that is,

$$x^\mu = (1 - \mu)\bar{x} + \mu x^1 = \bar{x} + \mu(x^1 - \bar{x}).$$

These are the points on the dotted line segment in the figure.

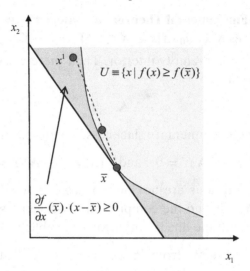

Figure 1.4-1. Upper contour sets of f and $\frac{\partial f}{\partial x}$.

The hyperplane $\frac{\partial f}{\partial x}(\overline{x}) \cdot (x - \overline{x}) = 0$ is tangent to the upper contour set $U \equiv \{x \mid f(x) \geq f(\overline{x})\}$. Because x^1 satisfies $\frac{\partial f}{\partial x}(\overline{x}) \cdot (x^1 - \overline{x}) > 0$ it is intuitively clear that, for sufficiently small μ, the convex combination x^μ must lie in the interior of U.

We establish this in the following lemma.

Lemma 1.4-2: If $f \in \mathbb{C}^1$ and $\frac{\partial f}{\partial x}(\overline{x}) \cdot (x^1 - \overline{x}) > 0$ then for all convex combinations x^μ of $\overline{x}$ and x^1, sufficiently close to $\overline{x}$, $f(x^\mu) > f(\overline{x})$.

Proof: Define the function

$$g(\mu) \equiv f(x^\mu) = f((1 - \mu)\overline{x} + \mu x^1) = f(\overline{x} + \mu(x^1 - \overline{x})).$$

Note that $g(0) = f(\overline{x})$ and $g(1) = f(x^1)$. We wish to prove that for $\mu > 0$ and sufficiently small $g(\mu) > g(0)$. To do so we show that $g'(0) > 0$. From the definition of g,

$$g'(\mu) = \frac{\partial f}{\partial x}(x^\mu) \cdot (x^1 - \overline{x}).$$

Setting $\mu = 0$, $g'(0) = \frac{\partial f}{\partial x}(\overline{x}) \cdot (x^1 - \overline{x})$. By hypothesis this is strictly positive. $\qquad\square$

We have therefore shown that there exists a convex combination of $\overline{x}$ and x^1 such that $f(x^\mu) > f(\overline{x})$. By construction $x^1 \in X$ and the optimizing $\overline{x} \in X$. Because the feasible set is convex it follows that $x^\mu \in X$. Yet this is impossible for it contradicts the hypothesis that $\overline{x}$ solves the optimization problem P.

The General Non-Linear Optimization Problem[10]

Now consider the general non-linear problem

$$P : \operatorname*{Max}_{x}\{ f(x)|x \in X\} \quad \text{where} \quad X = \left\{ x \in \mathbb{R}^n_+ | h_i(x) \geq 0, i = 1, \ldots, m \right\}.$$

We assume throughout that all functions are continuously differentiable. Suppose that $\overline{x} \in \arg \operatorname{Max}_x\{ f(x)|x \in X\}$. If $\frac{\partial f}{\partial x}(\overline{x}) = 0$, the Kuhn-Tucker conditions (see Proposition 1.2-2) necessarily hold because we can set the vector of shadow prices equal to zero.

Henceforth suppose that $\frac{\partial f}{\partial x}(\overline{x}) \neq 0$. To establish that the Kuhn-Tucker conditions are necessary conditions we show that if $\overline{x}$ solves the problem P, then it must also solve the following linear maximization problem:

$$\overline{P} : \operatorname*{Max}_{x} \left\{ \frac{\partial f}{\partial x}(\overline{x}) \cdot x | x \in \overline{X} \right\}$$

$$\text{where} \quad \overline{X} = \left\{ x \in \mathbb{R}^n_+ | \frac{\partial h_i}{\partial x}(\overline{x}) \cdot (x - \overline{x}) \geq 0, i \in B \right\},$$

where B is the set of nonlinear constraints that are binding at $\overline{x}$.

The Kuhn-Tucker conditions are then obtained by applying the Fundamental Theorem of Linear Programming to this linearized problem.

Proposition 1.4-3: Necessary Conditions
Suppose that $\overline{x}$ solves $P : \operatorname{Max}_x\{ f(x)|x \in X\}$ and the following constraint qualifications hold. (i) $\operatorname{int}\overline{X}$ is non-empty and (ii) $\frac{\partial h_i}{\partial x}(\overline{x}) \neq 0, i \in B$, where B is the set of binding constraints. Define $\overline{X} = \{ x \in \mathbb{R}^n_+ | \frac{\partial h_i}{\partial x}(\overline{x}) \cdot (x - \overline{x}) \geq 0, i \in B \}$. Then $\overline{x}$ solves

$$\overline{P} : \operatorname*{Max}_{x} \left\{ \frac{\partial f}{\partial x}(\overline{x}) \cdot x | x \in \overline{X} \right\}$$

Proof: Consider Figure 1.4-2. Suppose that the ith constraint is binding. Then the set of vectors satisfying the ith linearized constraint is $\overline{X}_i = \{ x \in \mathbb{R}^n_+ | \frac{\partial h_i}{\partial x}(\overline{x}) \cdot (x - \overline{x}) \geq 0 \}$, and the upper contour set of the linearized maximand through $\overline{x}$ is $\overline{U} = \{ x \in \mathbb{R}^n_+ | \frac{\partial f}{\partial x}(\overline{x}) \cdot (x - \overline{x}) \geq 0 \}$. We suppose that proposition is false and seek a contradiction. If the proposition is false there must be some $\hat{x}$ in both $\overline{X}_i$ and $\operatorname{int}\overline{U}$. This is depicted in Figures 1.4-2a and 1.4-2b.

Consider the left-hand diagram. Because the linearized feasible set has a non-empty interior there is some $x^0 \in \operatorname{int}\overline{X}_i$. Because $\overline{X}_i$ is convex it follows that for every convex combination $\hat{\hat{x}} = (1 - \mu)x^0 + \mu\hat{x} \in \operatorname{int}\overline{X}_i$ as depicted.

The convex combinations $x^\lambda = (1 - \lambda)\overline{x} + \lambda\hat{\hat{x}}$ of $\hat{\hat{x}}$ and $\overline{x}$ are also depicted. Because $\hat{\hat{x}} \in \operatorname{int}\overline{X}_i$ and $\overline{x} \in \overline{X}_i$ it follows that for all $\lambda \in (0, 1)$, $x^\lambda \in \operatorname{int}\overline{X}_i$.

---

[10] The formal derivation is similar to that for the special case of linear constraints but does require the repeated use of Lemma 1.4-1. The proof may be safely skipped on a first reading.

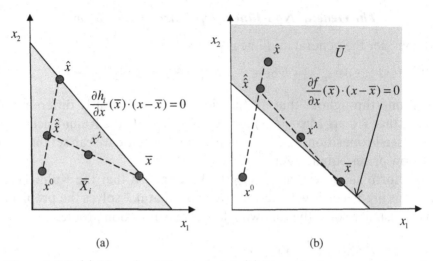

Figure 1.4-2. (a) Linearized *i*th constraint. (b) Linearized upper contour set.

Appealing to Lemma 1.4-2, it follows that for all λ sufficiently small, $h_i(x^\lambda) > h(\overline{x}) = 0$. Exactly the same argument holds for each binding constraint.

Suppose instead that the *i*th constraint is not binding so that $h_i(\overline{x}) > 0$. Appealing to the continuity if h_i it follows that for all λ sufficiently small, $h_i(x^\lambda) > 0$. We have therefore established that for all λ sufficiently small,

$$x^\lambda \in X = \{x \in \mathbb{R}_+^n | h_i(x) \geq 0, i = 1, \ldots, m\}.$$

We next argue that for some μ and λ, $f(x^\lambda) > f(\overline{x})$. Consider the right hand diagram. Because $\hat{x} \in \text{int}\overline{U}$ and $\overline{U}$ is convex it follows that for μ sufficiently close to 1, $\hat{\hat{x}} = (1 - \mu)x^0 + \mu\hat{x} \in \text{int}\overline{U}$. Again by the convexity of $\overline{U}$ it follows that for all $\lambda \in (0, 1)$ $x^\lambda = (1 - \lambda)\overline{x} + \lambda\hat{\hat{x}} \in \text{int } \overline{U}$.

Appealing to Lemma 1.4-2, it follows that for λ sufficiently small, $f(x^\lambda) > f(\overline{x})$.

We have already shown that for λ sufficiently small $x^\lambda \in X$. Yet $\overline{x} \in \arg\text{Max}_x\{f(x)|x \in X\}$ so we have a contradiction. Thus there can be no such $\hat{x}$. $\square$

Appealing to the Fundamental Theorem of Linear Programming we have the following proposition.[11]

Proposition 1.4-4: Kuhn-Tucker Conditions
Suppose that $\overline{x}$ solves $\text{Max}_x\{f(x)|x \in X\}$ where

$$X \equiv \{x | x \geq 0, h_i(x) \geq 0, i = 1, \ldots, m\}.$$

---

[11] This is a restatement of Proposition 1.2-2.

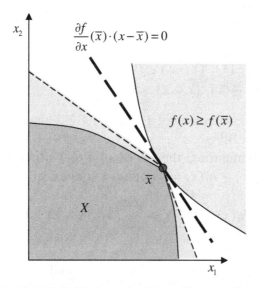

Figure 1.4-3. Sufficient conditions for a maximum.

Let $\overline{X}$ be the set of linearized binding constraints at $\overline{x}$. If (i) the interior of $\overline{X}$ is non-empty and (ii) for each binding constraint $\frac{\partial h_i}{\partial x}(\overline{x}) \neq 0$, then the Kuhn-Tucker conditions must hold at $\overline{x}$.

When Are the Necessary Conditions Sufficient?

Finally we establish conditions under which the Kuhn-Tucker conditions are sufficient.

Proposition 1.4-5: Sufficient Conditions for a Maximum
Suppose that the Constraint Qualifications and Kuhn-Tucker conditions hold at $\overline{x}$. If each of the binding constraints bounds a convex set and the upper contour set $\{x \mid f(x) \geq f(\overline{x})\}$ is convex, then $\overline{x}$ is optimal.

Consider the two constraint case depicted in Figure 1.4-3.

Because $\overline{x}$ satisfies the Kuhn-Tucker conditions and Constraint Qualification, then by the Fundamental Theorem of Linear Programming $\overline{x}$ is the solution of the linearized problem $\overline{P}$. Given the convexity of the constraint functions, the linearized constraint set, $\overline{X}$, contains the original set X. Given the convexity of the upper contour set of f, it follows that the line tangent to the contour set of f through $\overline{x}$ is a separating line. Thus the intersection of the set $\{x \mid f(x) > f(\overline{x})\}$ and X is empty.

To prove the proposition we make use of the following mathematical lemma.

Lemma 1.4-6: If the upper contour set $\{x|g(x) \geq g(\overline{x})\}$ is convex, $g \in \mathbb{C}^1$ and $\frac{\partial g}{\partial x}(\overline{x}) \neq 0$ then

(i) $g(x) \geq g(\overline{x}) \Rightarrow \frac{\partial g}{\partial x}(\overline{x}) \cdot (x - \overline{x}) \geq 0$ and

(ii) $g(x) > g(\overline{x}) \Rightarrow \frac{\partial g}{\partial x}(\overline{x}) \cdot (x - \overline{x}) > 0$.

Condition (i) is a restatement of Lemma 1.1-2. Condition (ii) is formally proved in Appendix B.[12]

With these preliminaries, the proof of Proposition 1.4-5 is short. By Lemma 1.4-6, if $h_i(x) \geq h_i(\overline{x}) = 0$ bounds a convex set and $\frac{\partial h_i}{\partial x}(\overline{x}) \neq 0$, then

$$h_i(x) \geq h_i(\overline{x}) \Rightarrow \frac{\partial h_i}{\partial x}(\overline{x}) \cdot (x - \overline{x}) \geq 0. \tag{1.4-2}$$

Thus $X \subset \overline{X}$.

Suppose that the Kuhn-Tucker conditions hold at $\overline{x}$. Consider the linearized problem at $\overline{x}$. Because the Kuhn-Tucker conditions are both necessary and sufficient for this linear optimization problem, it follows that $\overline{x}$ solves $\text{Max}_x\{\frac{\partial f}{\partial x}(\overline{x}) \cdot x | x \in \overline{X}\}$. Because $X \subset \overline{X}$ it follows that $\overline{x}$ solves $\text{Max}_x(\{\frac{\partial f}{\partial x}(\overline{x}) \cdot x | x \in X\}$. By Lemma 1.4-5 (ii), because $\{x|f(x) \geq f(\overline{x})\}$ is convex, $f(x) > f(\overline{x}) \Rightarrow \frac{\partial f}{\partial x}(\overline{x}) \cdot x > \frac{\partial f}{\partial x}(\overline{x}) \cdot \overline{x})$ Thus $\overline{x}$ solves $\text{Max}_x(\{f(x)|x \in X\}$.

Exercises

Exercise 1.4-1: Sufficient Conditions for a Unique Maximum If the assumptions of Proposition 1.4-2 hold and f is strictly quasi-concave, show that if $\overline{x}$ satisfies the necessary conditions, it is the unique optimum. HINT: Suppose that both $\overline{x}^0$ and $\overline{x}^1$ satisfy the necessary conditions. Show that all convex combinations are feasible.

Exercise 1.4-2: Generalization of the Kuhn-Tucker Conditions

(a) Suppose that

$$\overline{x} = \arg \underset{x}{\text{Max}}\{a_0 \cdot x | Ax \leq \overline{z}, x \in \overline{\mathbb{R}}\}$$

where $\overline{\mathbb{R}} \equiv \{x|x_j \in \mathbb{R}_+ \ j \in I, x_j \in \mathbb{R} \ j \in J, x_j \in \mathbb{R}_-, j \in K\}$.
exists and that the interior of the feasible set is non-empty. Modify the proof of Proposition 1.1-5 to obtain new necessary conditions.

(b) Suppose that

$$\overline{x} = \arg \underset{x}{\text{Max}}\{f(x)|h_i(x) \geq 0, i = 1, \ldots, m, x \in \overline{\mathbb{R}}\}.$$

Explain how Proposition 1.4-3 must be restated.

[12] See Corollary B.2-11.

Exercise 1.4-3: Dual Linear Programming Problem Suppose $\bar{x} = \arg \text{Max}_x$ $\{a_0 \cdot x | x \geq 0, \mathbf{A}x \leq \bar{z}\}$. Let the supporting price vector be $\bar{\lambda}$. Define the set $\Lambda \equiv \{\lambda \in \mathbb{R}^m | \lambda \geq 0, \lambda' \mathbf{A} - a_0 \geq 0\}$.

(a) Show that for all $\lambda \in \Lambda$, $\lambda' \bar{z} \geq \lambda' \mathbf{A} \bar{x} \geq a_0' \bar{x}$.
(b) Appeal to complementary slackness to show that

$$\lambda' \bar{z} \geq \bar{\lambda}' \bar{z}, \lambda \in \Lambda.$$

Hence

$$\bar{\lambda} = \arg \underset{\lambda}{\text{Min}} \{\lambda' \bar{z} | \lambda \in \Lambda\}.$$

This is known as the dual linear programming problem.
(c) Consider the following linear programming problem.

$$\underset{x}{\text{Max}} \{5x_1 + 4x_2 + 10x_3 | x \in X\},$$

where $X = \{x \in \mathbb{R}^3 | x \geq 0, x_1 + x_1 + 4x_3 \leq 30, 2x_1 + x_2 + x_3 \leq 10\}$.

Write down the dual problem. Solve it graphically and show that $\bar{\lambda} = (2, 2)$. Which dual constraint is not binding? Finally appeal to complementary slackness to solve the original problem.

1.5 Application – Monopoly Pricing with Joint Costs

Key ideas: extracting insights from necessary conditions, the economic margins for a multi-product firm

In economic theorizing, asking the right question (or at least an interesting question) is the first and most critical step. The second step is to write down a model simple enough to make mathematical analysis possible. As my thesis advisor Robert Solow[13] liked to say, "Start with a model so simple that it looks almost too easy to solve." Assuming the model is of a maximizing agent, the third and easiest step is to write down the necessary conditions for a maximum. The final step is to glean insights from these conditions. To do so requires some inspiration as well as perspiration and perhaps a bit of luck. The following example provides a good illustration of this final step.

Although simple models of monopoly assume that a firm produces a single product, almost all firms produce a menu of products. Typically there is some "jointness" in the production of these products (such as a common factory building or marketing department.) Consider, for example, the production of electricity by an unregulated monopolist. We divide the time unit of analysis (day, week, year) into n periods. Define $q = (q_1, \ldots, q_n)$ to be the output

---

[13] He would continue, "If you never succeed in writing a successful paper, at least you will have a good problem set for your graduate students!"

vector. The cost of supplying electricity in any of the periods depends on the cost of operating the plant and on the production capacity of the plant. Let this capacity be q_0. Then output in each period is limited by the capacity constraint,

$$q_j \leq q_0, \, j = 1, \ldots, n.$$

To simplify the discussion we assume that marginal costs are constant so that total cost is as follows:

$$C(q_0, q) = F + c_0 q_0 + c \cdot q.$$

Note that there is a marginal cost of adding production capacity c_0 and, in each period, a marginal cost of producing additional electricity (the marginal operating cost). The former cost includes the interest cost associated with the purchase of capital equipment (e.g., gas turbines) and time-related maintenance costs. The latter cost includes energy and labor costs.

Let the demand price function in period j be $p_j(q)$. In general we would expect demand prices to depend on consumption in other periods so q is the output vector. Let $R(q) = p \cdot q$ be total revenue. We assume that $R(q) \in \mathbb{C}^2$. Moreover, to rule out functions with no maximum we assume that $R(q)$ takes on its maximum at $\hat{q}$. Any output vector greater than $\hat{q}$ has a lower revenue than $R(\hat{q})$ and a strictly greater cost. Thus profit is maximized at some $\bar{q} \leq \hat{q}$.

The monopolist then maximizes profit subject to the capacity constraints:

$$\underset{q_0, q}{\text{Max}} \{ R(q) - F - c_0 q_0 - c \cdot q | q_0 - q_j \geq 0, \, j = 1, \ldots, n \}.$$

Note that $(q_0, q_1, \ldots, q_n) = (2, 1, \ldots, 1)$ is in the interior of the feasible set. Because the constraints are all linear, it follows that the linearized feasible set has a non-empty interior as well. Moreover the gradient vector of each constraint function is non-zero. Thus the constraint qualifications are all satisfied. Then the Kuhn-Tucker conditions are necessary conditions for a maximum. We will assume that it is optimal to supply a positive quantity in each subperiod.

We form the Lagrangian and hence obtain the first-order conditions:

$$\mathcal{L}(q_0, q) = R(q) - F - \sum_{j=1}^{n} c_j q_j - c_0 q_0 + \sum_{j=1}^{n} \lambda_j (q_0 - q_j)$$

$$= R(q) - \sum_{j=1}^{n} (c_j + \lambda_j) q_j + \left(\sum_{j=1}^{n} \lambda_j - c_0 \right) q_0 - F$$

$$\frac{\partial \mathcal{L}}{\partial q_j} = MR_j - c_j - \lambda_j = 0, \quad j = 1, \ldots, n \qquad (1.5\text{-}1)$$

$$\frac{\partial \mathcal{L}}{\partial q_0} = \sum_{j=1}^{n} \lambda_j - c_0 = 0 \tag{1.5-2}$$

$$\frac{\partial \mathcal{L}}{\partial \lambda_j} = q_0 - q_j \geq 0, \quad \text{with equality if } \lambda_j > 0. \tag{1.5-3}$$

What can we learn from these conditions? First we note from (1.5-2) that the sum of the shadow prices is strictly positive. Then at least one must be strictly positive. From (1.5-3), in any such period output is at capacity.[14] Also, from (1.5-3), in any period operating below capacity ("off-peak") the shadow price is zero.

Then, from (1.5-1),

$$\overline{q}_j < \overline{q}_0 \Rightarrow MR_j(\overline{q}) = c_j.$$

Thus in any period where output is off-peak, marginal revenue is equal to the marginal operating cost in that period.

Define $I = \{j | \overline{q}_j = \overline{q}_0\}$ to be the index set of periods where output is at capacity.

For each such period

$$MR_j(\overline{q}) = c_j + \lambda_j.$$

Summing over the capacity periods,

$$\sum_{j \in I} (MR_j(\overline{q}) - c_j) = \sum_{j \in I} \lambda_j.$$

Finally, appealing to (1.5-2),

$$\sum_{j \in I} (MR_j(\overline{q}) - c_j) = c_0. \tag{1.5-4}$$

Thus in each peak period marginal revenue exceeds marginal operating cost, and the sum of the differences must be equal to the marginal of capacity.

What are the economic insights to be gleaned from this analysis? At heart they are insights into the marginal decisions facing the decision maker. Suppose that the current capacity/output vector is $(q_0, q_1, \ldots, q_n)$. Output in an off-peak period can be increased without affecting anything other than the operating cost in that period. The firm can therefore increase profit unless the marginal revenue in that period is equal to the marginal operating cost. For the peak periods output can only be increased by also increasing capacity. The true marginal decision is the choice of whether to increase capacity.

---

[14] Having selected an output vector, capacity can be reduced to the maximum output without affecting revenue so this is obvious.

As long as the sum of the marginal revenues from all the peak periods exceeds the marginal operating costs by enough to cover the cost of additional capacity, capacity should be increased.

Example: Joint Costs with Two Periods

Suppose that the cost parameters are $c_0 = 40, c_1 = c_2 = 20$ and demand prices are $p_1(q) = 200 - 2q_1 - q_2$ and $p_2(q) = 150 - q_1 - 2q_2$. Total revenue is therefore

$$R(q) = 200q_1 + 150q_2 - 2q_1^2 - 2q_1q_2 - 2q_2^2. \qquad (1.5\text{-}5)$$

Note that $R(q)$ is concave and total cost is linear. Therefore profit is a concave function. Also the constraint functions are linear and hence concave. Thus the first-order conditions are both necessary and sufficient for a maximum. This makes the solution of the problem especially easy. For if we find a solution to the necessary conditions then we have solved the problem.

From (1.5-5),

$$MR_1(q) = 200 - 4q_1 - 2q_2 \quad \text{and} \quad MR_2(q) = 150 - 2q_1 - 4q_2.$$

We first see if there is a solution with output equal to capacity in both periods.

Letting $q_1 = q_2 = q_0$ in (1.5-4),

$$(MR_1 - c_1) + (MR_2 - c_2) = 310 - 12q_0 = c_0 = 40.$$

Thus $q_0 = q_1 = q_2 = 22\frac{1}{2}$.

Appealing to (1.5-1).

$$\lambda_1 = MR_1 - c_1 = 180 - 6q_1 = 45.$$
$$\lambda_2 = MR_2 - c_2 = 130 - 6q_2 = -5.$$

Yet this is impossible because both shadow prices must be non-negative. Because the shadow price in period 1 is positive, this seems likely to be the peak period. We therefore consider a possible solution in which period 1 is the peak period and period 2 is off-peak. From the first-order conditions,

$$MR_1 - c_1 = 180 - 4q_1 - 2q_2 = c_0 = 40.$$
$$MR_2 - c_2 = 130 - 2q_1 - 4q_2 = 0.$$

By solving these two equations it follows that $q_1^M = 25$ and $q_2^M = 20$. Note that output in period 2 is off-peak as hypothesized. Therefore this is the monopoly solution.

Exercises

Exercise 1.5-1: Multi-Product Firm and Joint Costs Consider a vertically integrated firm. The "upstream" division of the company is a logging operation. Raw materials (trees in the forest) are cut down and the logs are debarked. The cost of processing q_0 logs is $C_0(q_0) = 30q_0$. The resulting timber and bark are delivered to two "downstream" divisions. Division 1 converts logs to newsprint. Each log yields one unit of newsprint at a cost of $10 per unit. Division 2 converts the bark into chipboard. One log yields one unit of chipboard at a cost of $4 per unit. That is, newsprint and chipboard are jointly produced from logs.

Demand prices for newsprint $p_1(q_1)$ and chipboard $p_2(q_2)$ are given as follows:

$$p_1 = 100 - \tfrac{1}{2}q_1, \ p_2 = 25 - \tfrac{1}{4}q_2.$$

(a) Solve for the profit-maximizing number of logs assuming that all logs are converted into both chipboard and newsprint.
(b) Show that the firm is losing money on marginal units of chipboard.
(c) Solve for the profit-maximizing sale of chipboard and newsprint.
(d) Solve for the social optimum.
(e) What is the new solution if the demand price for product 2 rises to $p_2 = 35 - \tfrac{1}{4}q_2$?

Exercise 1.5-2: Multi-Product Firm with Joint Costs A firm produces two products. The production function for product j, $j = 1, 2$ is $F_j(K_j, L_j) = \sqrt{K_j L_j}$. Capital equipment can be used in the production of either or both products. Thus if K_0 units of capital are rented, the capital use constraints are $K_j \leq K_0$, $j = 1, 2$. The unit cost of labor is $2 and the unit cost of capital is $10.

(a) Explain why the Lagrangian for minimizing the total cost of producing (q_1, q_2) can be written as follows:

$$\mathfrak{L}(q, K) = -\frac{2q_1^2}{K_1} - \frac{2q_2^2}{K_2} - 10K_0 + \lambda_1(K_0 - K_1) + \lambda_2(K_0 - K_2).$$

(b) Hence show that all the capital equipment will be used for the production of both products.
(c) Solve for the minimized total cost.
(d) Fix q_2 and depict the marginal cost of producing commodity 1.

Exercise 1.5-3: Electricity Supply A firm produces q_t units of electricity in period t. The firm has the same production function as the firm in the previous exercise. However the cost of production is different. Now the interest cost of capital is 6 per unit. There is also a maintenance cost of $2 per unit of capital utilized in the day and $2 per unit of capital utilized during the night. Thus the cost of production is $2(L_1 + L_2) + 2(K_1 + K_2) + 6K_0$. We consider cost minimization when $q_1 \leq q_2$.

(a) Write down the new Lagrangian.

For the next three parts assume that $q_1 < q_2$.

(b) Solve for the minimized cost when outputs are similar.
(c) Hence show that if the ratio of output levels is sufficiently far from 1, capital will no longer be fully utilized in the low-demand period.
(d) Solve for the minimized cost when outputs are very different.
(e) Fix q_2 and depict the marginal cost of producing commodity 1.

References and Selected Historical Reading

Koopmans, Tjalling C. (1957). "Essay I." In Tjalling Koopmans (ed.), *Three Essays in the State of Economic Science*. New York: McGraw Hill.

Kuhn, Harold W. and Tucker, A. W. (1951). "Nonlinear Programming." *Proceedings of 2nd Berkeley Symposium*. Berkeley: University of California Press, pp. 481–92.

2

Consumers

2.1 Theory of Choice

Key ideas: ordering consumption bundles, axioms of choice, utility representation of preferences

Anyone who has taken more than an introductory class in economics has become thoroughly familiar with the idea that consumers maximize "utility." In mathematical terms, preferences are represented by the contour sets of a function U defined over some set of consumption bundles, X. Take any consumption bundle x^0 in this set. The upper contour set of this function $\{x | U(x) \geq U(x^0), x \in X\}$ is the set of consumption vectors for which the consumer would be willing to trade away x^0. Equivalently, the upper contour set is the set of bundles that the consumer weakly prefers to x^0.

At heart, a theory of choice is a theory of how alternatives are ordered. Thus a more fundamental theory of choice begins with ordering axioms. Formally, for consumer (or household) h we define the binary relation $\underset{h}{\succsim}$. If the consumer orders bundle x^1 at least as highly as bundle x^2 we write $x^1 \underset{h}{\succsim} x^2$.

In general orders are not defined over all consumption vectors. Consider for example the weak inequality order ($\geq$). That is, a consumer prefers x^1 over x^2 if and only if $x^1 \geq x^2$. In this case the probability that any two randomly chosen bundles of dimension n can be ranked is $1/2^{n-1}$ so such an order is clearly unsatisfactory. For a strong theory we require that a consumer can compare all bundles in the consumption set X.

Order is Complete[1] For any consumption bundles $x^1, x^2 \in X$, either $x^1 \underset{i}{\succsim} x^2$ or $x^2 \underset{h}{\succsim} x^1$.

Next we require that there is a consistency across pair-wise rankings.

---

[1] Note that this includes the statement that $x \underset{h}{\succsim} x$. Mathematicians call such an ordering reflexive.

43

Order Is Transitive For any bundles $x^1, x^2, x^3 \in X$, if $x^1 \succsim_h x^2$ and $x^2 \succsim_h x^3$ then $x^1 \succsim_h x^3$.

Given the first axiom, consider any two consumption bundles x^1 and x^2. We can distinguish three cases:

(i) $x^1 \succsim_h x^2$ and $x^2 \succsim_h x^1$ (ii) $x^1 \succsim_h x^2$ and $x^2 \not\succsim_h x^1$ (iii) $x^2 \succsim_h x^1$ and $x^1 \not\succsim_h x^2$.

In case (i) where both bundles are ordered weakly ahead of the other we say that the consumer is indifferent between the two bundles and write $x^1 \sim_h x^2$. In case (ii) where the weak ordering goes one way but not the other, we say that x^1 is strictly preferred to x^2 and write $x^1 \succ_h x^2$. Case (iii) is the reverse of case (ii) so $x^2 \succ_h x^1$.

Note that both the indifference order and the strict preference order satisfy the transitivity axiom. However neither is a total order.

We now argue that these two axioms taken together are not enough. Consider the following example.

Example: The "Not-Less-Than" Order
$x^1 \succsim_h x^2$ if and only if $x^1 \not< x^2$.

This order is both complete and transitive. Consider the two consumption bundles x^a and x^b on the horizontal line in Figure 2.1-1. We first argue that $x^a \succ_h x^b$. For if not, then $x^b \succsim_h x^a$ and so $x^b \not< x^a$. But this is false. Next consider any consumption bundle y^t in the interior of the shaded region. Because $y_2^t > x_2^a$, it follows that $y^t \succsim_h x^a$. Since $x_1^a > y_1^t$, it also follows that $x^a \succsim_h y^t$. Then $y^t \sim_h x^a$.

To see why there is something rather unsatisfactory about such preferences, consider the sequence of consumption bundles $\{y^t\}_{t=1}^{\infty}$ in the interior of the shaded region that converges to x^b. For each y^t in the sequence

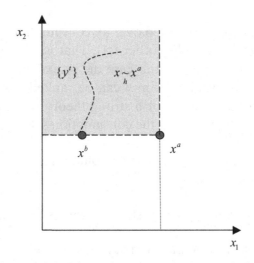

Figure 2.1-1. Discontinuous preference ordering.

$y^t \underset{h}{\sim} x^a$. However, for the limiting consumption x^b, we have $x^a \underset{h}{\succ} x^b$. Suppose there were a utility representation of these preferences. Then for all y^t in the sequence approaching x^b, $U(y^t) = U(x^a) > U(x^b)$. Thus the utility function could not be continuous.

To rule such oddities out we introduce a third axiom.

Order Is Continuous Let x^0 be the limit point of a sequence of consumption bundles $\{x^t\}_{t=1,2...}$.

$$\text{If for all } t, x^t \underset{i}{\succsim} y \text{ then } x^0 \underset{i}{\succsim} y. \text{ If for all } t, y \underset{i}{\succsim} x^t \text{ then } y \underset{i}{\succsim} x^0.$$

These postulates are entirely uncontroversial for frequent purchases. Suppose shoppers are evaluating two large shopping baskets full of goods. Although they may hesitate for a while, surely each shopper would eventually choose between them. And for anyone who strictly prefers the first shopping basket, making a tiny change in items in the basket should not change the ranking.

However, the supermarket is a familiar place. A customer has likely walked the aisles dozens of times and has a good idea about the vast majority of products available for purchase. Yet take that same person into an open-air market in a faraway country and fill up two shopping carts with exotic produce. Then the consumer is likely to be much less confident about making a choice. The postulates are therefore most reasonable when the choices are between familiar commodities.

Further complicating the selection of the shopping basket is the reality that the current choice is not independent of prior choices or of choices planned in the future. Major decisions like choosing a job, or where to live, or family size, or how much to invest for retirement depend very much on future consumption plans. Suppose that our consumer will live for T periods. Let $x_t = (x_{1t}, \ldots, x_{nt})$ be her period t consumption bundle. Then she must rank each $T \times n$ dimensional consumption bundle $x = (x_{11}, \ldots, x_{nT})$. The higher dimensionality of the choice problem adds to its complexity. Moreover, just as in the open-air market in a faraway country, there is considerable uncertainty about the complete consumption bundle.

As long as the consumer is able to assign probabilities to different outcomes then this uncertainty can be incorporated as well. To illustrate, suppose that there are just two periods and the consumer's health will be either good or bad in the next period. Let (x_1, x_2^g) be consumption over the two periods if her health is good and let (x_1, x_2^b) be consumption if her health is bad. (In the extreme, bad health might result in her death before she can enjoy any second-period consumption.) Let π^g be the probability that her health will be good and let π^b be the probability that her health will be bad. Then we can characterize the consumer's consumption plan as a "prospect" $(x_1, x_2^g, x_2^b; \pi^g, \pi^b)$. The preference ranking now involves different prospects.

Much of the controversy about this extended consumer choice model hinges on whether or not consumers assess probabilities consistently.

In later chapters we consider choice under uncertainty, but initially we focus on a world of full information. The ordering postulates alone say nothing about the desirability of commodities. Note, in particular, that an individual who is indifferent between all consumption bundles satisfies all the postulates. To incorporate unbounded "wants" into the choice model, we add the assumption that whatever bundle a consumer receives, there is always another similar bundle that is strictly preferred.

Local Non-Satiation For any consumption bundle $x \in X \subset \mathbb{R}^n$ and any δ – neighborhood $N(x, \delta)$ of x, there is some bundle $y \in N(x, \delta)$ such that $y \underset{h}{\succ} x$.

Especially when analyzing consumption of commodity groups (food, clothing, housing, etc.) it is natural to make the stronger assumption that more is always strictly preferred.

Strict Monotonicity If $y > x$ then $y \underset{h}{\succ} x$.

The final postulate reflects the idea that individuals have a preference for variety.

Preferences Are Convex Let X be a convex subset of $\mathbb{R}^n$. Preferences are convex on X if, for any consumption bundle $y \in X$, the set of bundles (weakly) preferred to y is convex. That is, for any $x^0, x^1 \in X$, if $x^0 \underset{h}{\succsim} y$ and $x^1 \underset{h}{\succsim} y$ then the convex combination $x^\lambda = (1 - \lambda)x^0 + \lambda x^1 \underset{h}{\succsim} y, 0 < \lambda < 1$.

Two examples of convex preferences are illustrated in Figure 2.1-2. The shaded set in each diagram depicts the sets of bundles preferred over y, holding constant the consumption of all the other commodities. The first case

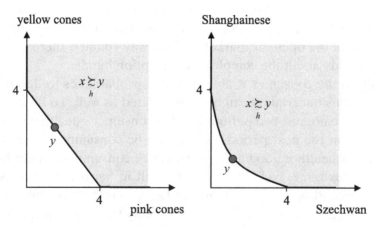

Figure 2.1-2. Convex preferences.

shows the limiting case where there is no strict preference for diversity. The consumer is indifferent between four pink cones of ice-cream per week and four yellow cones of ice-cream or any convex combination. In the second case the individual is indifferent between eating out an average of four times a month at a Szechwan restaurant and four times a month at a Shanghainese restaurant but strictly prefers convex combinations of these two bundles.

If this strict preference for diversity holds for all bundles we can strengthen the convexity axiom as follows.

Preferences Are Strictly Convex Suppose that x^0, x^1 and $y \in X$, where X is a convex subset of $\mathbb{R}^n$.

$$\text{If } x^0 \underset{h}{\succsim} y \quad \text{and} \quad x^1 \underset{h}{\succsim} y \quad \text{then} \quad x^\lambda \underset{h}{\succ} y, \quad 0 < \lambda < 1.$$

These basic postulates are a sufficiently strong foundation for a very general theory of market equilibrium. However for the study of specific markets, we typically add further structure to the preference rankings of consumers. To do so we give a consumer a ranking function (or utility function) $U(x)$ and impose restrictions on the nature of this function. The following theorem establishes that there is no inconsistency between this approach and the general axiomatic approach.

Proposition 2.1-1: Utility Function Representation of Preferences
If preferences are complete, reflexive, transitive and continuous, on the consumption set $X \subset \mathbb{R}^n$, they can be represented by a function $U(x)$ that is continuous over X.[2]

Although we do not provide a general proof, it is reasonably easy to see why this proposition must be true if preferences are strictly monotonic. Pick any consumption bundles x^0 and $x^1 \in X$ such that $x^1 > x^0$. If preferences are strictly monotonic, then $x^1 \underset{h}{\succ} x^0$. Consider all the consumption bundles in the set $T = \{x \in X | x^1 \underset{h}{\succsim} x \underset{h}{\succsim} x^0\}$. Define the convex combination $x^\lambda = (1 - \lambda)x^0 + \lambda x^1$. We will argue that for any $y \in T$ there must be some weighting factor λ such that $y \underset{h}{\sim} x^\lambda$ and that the mapping $\lambda(y)$ from T onto the unit interval must be continuous.

The intuition is straightforward. Consider Figure 2.1-3. Along the line joining x^0 and x^1, $x^\lambda = x^0 + \lambda(x^1 - x^0)$ is a strictly increasing function of λ, because $x^1 > x^0$. Thus $x^\lambda \succ x^\mu$ if and only if $\lambda > \mu$. Because preferences are continuous and $x^1 \underset{h}{\succsim} y \underset{h}{\succsim} x^0$ it is intuitively clear that there must be some weight $\hat{\lambda}$ such that $y \underset{h}{\sim} x^{\hat{\lambda}}$. To find this weight we can follow a step-by-step approach. First, if either $y \underset{h}{\sim} x^0$ or $y \underset{h}{\sim} x^1$ then we are finished. If not,

---

[2] The converse is also true. See Exercise 2.1-7.

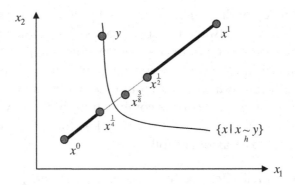

Figure 2.1-3. Constructing a utility function.

consider the convex combination $x^{\frac{1}{2}}$. If $y \underset{h}{\sim} x^{\frac{1}{2}}$, then we are done. If, as in Figure 2.1-3, $x^{\frac{1}{2}} \underset{h}{\succ} y$ then we can rule out any $\lambda \geq \frac{1}{2}$.

Now split the remaining interval $[0, \frac{1}{2}]$ and try $\lambda = \frac{1}{4}$. The figure shows $y \underset{h}{\succ} x^{\frac{1}{4}}$ so we can rule out any weight $\lambda \leq \frac{1}{4}$. Again split the remaining interval $[\frac{1}{4}, \frac{1}{2}]$ and try $\lambda = \frac{3}{8}$. Continuing in this way, either there is some step at which we find a weight $\lambda(y)$ such that $y \underset{h}{\sim} x^{\lambda(y)}$, or the weights converge to some limit point $\lambda(y)$.

We now formalize this intuition to prove the existence of such a utility function.[3] Define decreasing and increasing sequences $\{v_t\}_{t=0,1,\dots}$ and $\{\mu_t\}_{t=0,1,\dots}$ as follows:

$$\lambda_{t+1} = \frac{1}{2}(v_t + \mu_t) \quad \text{where} \quad (v_0, \mu_0) = (1, 0).$$

From this equation it follows that $\lambda_1 = \frac{1}{2}$. At step t, if $y \underset{h}{\sim} x^{\lambda_t}$ we are done. If $x^{\lambda_t} \underset{i}{\succ} y$, then define $(v_{t+1}, \mu_{t+1}) = (\lambda_{t+1}, \mu_t)$. If $y \underset{i}{\succ} x^{\lambda_t}$, then define $(v_{t+1}, \mu_{t+1}) = (v_t, \lambda_{t+1})$.

The first three steps of this process are depicted in Figure 2.1-4 for the preferences shown in Figure 2.1-3. Note that the sequences are constructed so that, at each step,

$$x^{v_t} \underset{h}{\succsim} x \underset{h}{\succsim} x^{\mu_t}.$$

If the process does not stop, we define $\hat{\lambda}$ to be the limit point of the decreasing sequence $\{v_t\}_{t=0}^{\infty}$. At each step the difference between the decreasing and increasing sequences is halved. Thus $\hat{\lambda}$ must also be the limit point of the increasing sequence $\{\mu_t\}_{t=0}^{\infty}$. Because for all t, $y \underset{h}{\succ} x^{\mu_t}$ it follows from the continuity of preferences that $y \underset{h}{\succsim} x^{\hat{\lambda}}$. Moreover, because for all t, $x^{v_t} \succ y$. It follows from the continuity axiom that $x^{\hat{\lambda}} \underset{h}{\succsim} y$ and so $x^{\hat{\lambda}} \underset{h}{\sim} y$.

---

[3] See Exercise 2.1-2 for an outline of how to prove continuity.

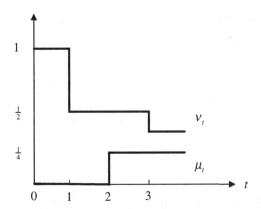

Figure 2.1-4. Monotonic sequences.

We now show that the assumption that preferences are convex is equivalent to the assumption that the utility representation of these preferences is quasi-concave.

Definition: Quasi-Concave Function[4] U is quasi-concave on X if, for any $x^0, x^1 \in X$ and convex combination $x^\lambda = (1 - \lambda)x^0 + \lambda x^1, 0 < \lambda < 1$, $U(x^\lambda) \geq \text{Min}\{U(x^0), U(x^1)\}$.

Suppose that preferences are convex on X and can be represented by a utility function U. For any $x^0, x^1 \in X$, either (i) $x^1 \succsim x^0$ or (ii) $x^0 \succ x^1$. If (i) holds then $U(x^1) \geq U(x^0)$. Because preferences are convex, for any convex combination x^λ, $U(x^\lambda) \geq U(x^0)$. Combining these results it follows that $U(x^\lambda) \geq \text{Min}\{U(x^0), U(x^1)\}$.

If (ii) holds, an almost identical argument leads to this same conclusion. Thus if preferences are convex, the utility function is quasi-concave.

To prove the converse, suppose that $x^0 \succsim y$ and $x^1 \succsim y$. Then $U(x^0) \geq U(y)$ and $U(x^1) \geq U(y)$. If U is quasi-concave, it follows that $U(x^\lambda) \geq \text{Min}\{U(x^0), U(x^1)\} \geq U(y)$. Therefore $x^\lambda \succsim y$.

Exercises

Exercise 2.1-1: Transitivity

(a) Show that the transitivity axiom implies that if $x \underset{h}{\succ} y$ and $y \underset{h}{\succ} z$, then $x \underset{h}{\succ} z$. HINT: Appealing to the transitivity axiom, $x \underset{h}{\succsim} z$. Suppose that $x \underset{h}{\sim} z$ then appeal to transitivity to establish that $z \underset{h}{\succsim} y$.

(b) Is it also the case that if $x \underset{h}{\succ} y$ and $y \underset{h}{\succsim} z$, then $x \underset{h}{\succ} z$? HINT: Again assume that $x \underset{h}{\sim} z$ and seek a contradiction.

---

[4] U is strictly quasi-concave if the inequality is always strict.

Exercise 2.1-2: Continuity of the Utility Function Let $\lambda(x)$ be the monotonic utility function defined in the proof of existence of a utility function.

(a) Show that if $\lambda(\cdot)$ is discontinuous at y there must be some $\hat{\varepsilon}$ and sequence of consumption bundles $\{y^t\}_{t=1}^{\infty}$ approaching y such that $\left|\lambda(y^t) - \lambda(y)\right| > \hat{\varepsilon}$.
(b) Consider the subsequence $\{y_+^t\}_{t=1}^{\infty}$ such that $\lambda(y^t) - \lambda(y) > \hat{\varepsilon}$ and a second subsequence $\{y_-^t\}_{t=1}^{\infty}$ consisting of all the remaining bundles in the sequence $\{y^t\}_{t=1}^{\infty}$ such that $\lambda(y^t) - \lambda(y) < -\hat{\varepsilon}$. At least one must be an infinite sequence. Suppose that it is the former. Appeal to the continuity of preferences to establish a contradiction.

Exercise 2.1-3: Sufficient Condition for Convex Preferences Let $U(x)$ be a utility function and let $f(\cdot)$ be an increasing function.

(a) If $u(x) = f(U(x))$ is concave, show that preferences are convex.
(b) If u is strictly concave show that preferences are strictly convex.
(c) If f is strictly concave are preferences strictly convex?

Exercise 2.1-4: Sufficient Condition for Convex Preferences Let $U(x)$ be a utility function. If there is some increasing function f such that

$$f(U(x)) = \sum_{j=1}^{m} u_j(x), \text{ where } u_j(x), \ j = 1, \ldots, m \text{ is concave}$$

show that preferences are convex.

Exercise 2.1-5: Strictly Convex Preferences Consider strictly convex preferences defined on the consumption set $X = \mathbb{R}_+^2$.

(a) Suppose Alex has a utility function $U(x) = (1 + x_1)(1 + x_2)$. Show that his preferences are convex. Are his preferences strictly convex?
(b) Bev has a utility function $U(x) = x_1 x_2$. Are her preferences (i) convex or (ii) strictly convex?

Exercise 2.1-6: Strictly Convex Preferences and Strict Quasi-Concave Utility

(a) Show that if U is strictly quasi-concave on X, preferences are strictly convex on X.
(b) Prove the converse.

Exercise 2.1-7: Quasi-Linear Preferences Write the $n + 1$-dimensional consumption vector x as (y, z) where y is a scalar and z is an n-dimensional consumption vector. A utility function $U(x)$ is quasi-linear if it can be written as follows $U(x) = \alpha y + V(z)$. The consumption set $X = \mathbb{R}_+^{n+1}$.

(a) Show that if V is concave, U is quasi-concave.

(b) Show that if U is quasi-concave, V is concave. HINT: Suppose that for some x^0, x^1, x^λ, concavity fails; that is, $V(x^\lambda) < (1 - \lambda)V(x^0) + \lambda V(x^1)$. Choose y^0, y^1 such that $U(x^0) = U(x^1)$ and show that $U(x^\lambda) < U(x^0)$.

2.2 Budget-Constrained Choice with Two Commodities

Key ideas: continuity of demand, quasi-linear, Cobb-Douglas and CES preferences, expenditure function, income and substitution effects, elasticity of substitution, determinants of demand elasticity

In this section we focus on the effects of income and price changes on a consumer's choice. Consider the simplest two-commodity choice problem of a consumer with income I facing prices p_1 and p_2,

$$\underset{x}{\text{Max}} \left\{ U(x) | p \cdot x \leq I, x \in \mathbb{R}_+^2 \right\}. \tag{2.2-1}$$

We assume that the local non-satiation assumption holds and that the utility function is continuous and strictly quasi-concave on $\mathbb{R}_+^2$. The local non-satiation assumption ensures that the consumer spends all his or her income and strict quasi-concavity ensures that there is a unique solution $x^0 = x(p, I)$.[5] Given uniqueness and continuity of preferences, it is intuitively plausible that the implied demand function $x(p, I)$ must be continuous. This is an important result and follows from the following mathematical theorem.[6]

Proposition 2.2-1: Theorem of the Maximum (I)
Consider the maximization problem $\text{Max}_x\{f(x, \alpha)|x \in X(\alpha), \alpha \in A\}$ where $X(\alpha) = \{x \in \mathbb{R}_+^n, h_i(x, \alpha) \geq 0, i = 1, \ldots, m\}$.
  If f and $X(\alpha)$ are continuous[7] and, for all α, there is a unique solution $\bar{x}(\alpha)$, then $\bar{x}(\alpha)$ is continuous.

For the most general propositions about consumers (and firms as well) continuity is all that we need. However, to simplify modeling, it is convenient to assume some degree of differentiability as well. Then the necessary conditions for a maximum are restrictions on the gradient vector of the maximand and constraint functions.

For the rest of this section we assume that the utility function is continuously differentiable on $\mathbb{R}_+^2$. Initially we also assume that for all $x \in \mathbb{R}_+^2$, $\frac{\partial U}{\partial x}(x) \gg 0$ so that preferences are strictly increasing. Finally, whenever

---

[5] Suppose x^0 and x^1 are both solutions. Then $U(x^0) = U(x^1)$ and because U is strictly quasi-concave it follows that for any convex combination x^λ, $U(x^\lambda) > U(x^0)$ Finally, because $p \cdot x^0 \leq I$ and $p \cdot x^1 \leq I$, then $p \cdot x^\lambda \leq I$ Thus x^λ is feasible and strictly preferred.

[6] See Appendix C.

[7] The mapping from a parameter to a set is called a correspondence. For a formal definition of a continuous correspondence see Appendix A.

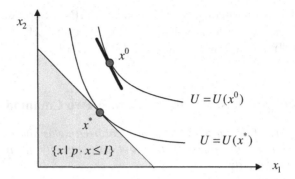

Figure 2.2-1. Budget-constrained choice.

we wish to avoid the possibility of corner solutions we also assume that $\lim_{x_j \to 0} \frac{\partial U}{\partial x_j} = \infty$, $j = 1, 2$.

Forming the Lagrangian for the maximization problem,

$$\mathcal{L} = U + \lambda(I - p \cdot x).$$

The first-order conditions (FOC) for a maximum are then as follows:

$$\frac{\partial \mathcal{L}}{\partial x_j} = \frac{\partial U}{\partial x_j}(x^*) - \lambda p_j = 0, \quad j = 1, 2.$$

Note that because marginal utility is strictly positive, the shadow price (or marginal utility of income) must be strictly positive.

Moreover, rearranging the FOC,

$$\frac{\frac{\partial U}{\partial x_1}}{p_1} = \frac{\frac{\partial U}{\partial x_2}}{p_2} = \lambda. \tag{2.2-2}$$

Intuitively, a maximizing consumer will equate the marginal value of spending on each commodity. One extra dollar spent on commodity 1 yields $\frac{1}{p_1}$ additional units thus the marginal value per dollar spent on commodity 1 is $\frac{1}{p_1}\frac{\partial U}{\partial x_1}$. Spending on commodity 1 is increased until this is equal to the marginal value of spending an additional dollar on commodity 2.

We can also rewrite the FOC as follows:

$$\text{MRS}(x^*) = \frac{\frac{\partial U}{\partial x_1}}{\frac{\partial U}{\partial x_2}} = \frac{p_1}{p_2}.$$

That is, the slope of the indifference curve must equal the slope of the budget line in Figure 2.2-1.

Income Effects

Figure 2.2-2 shows the path of the consumer's choice $x^* = x(p, I)$ as income increases. As shown, this Income Expansion Path is initially positively

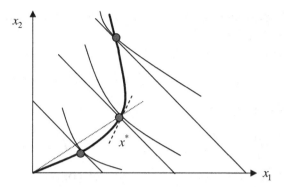

Figure 2.2-2. Income expansion path.

sloped (i.e., $\frac{\partial x_1}{\partial I}$ and $\frac{\partial x_2}{\partial I}$ are both positive). In this case the commodities are said to be normal in the neighborhood of the optimum. However, as depicted, for higher incomes consumption of commodity 1 declines as income increases. In this case commodity 1 is "inferior" in the neighborhood of the optimum.

To facilitate comparisons across commodities, it is helpful to consider the proportional effects on demand as income changes; in other words, the income elasticity of demand:

$$\mathcal{E}(x_j, I) = \frac{I}{x_j} \frac{\partial x_j}{\partial I}.$$

In Figure 2.2-2 the slope of the Income Expansion Path at $x^* = x(p, I)$ is steeper than the line joining x^* and the origin; that is,

$$\frac{dx_2}{dx_1}\bigg|_{IEP} = \frac{\frac{\partial x_2}{\partial I}}{\frac{\partial x_1}{\partial I}} > \frac{x_2^*}{x_1^*}.$$

Rearranging this inequality,

$$\mathcal{E}(x_2, I) = \frac{I}{x_2^*} \frac{\partial x_2}{\partial I} > \frac{I}{x_1^*} \frac{\partial x_1}{\partial I} = \mathcal{E}(x_1, I).$$

Appealing to the following lemma, the income elasticities weighted by their expenditure shares must sum to 1. Thus, in Figure 2.2-2, the income elasticity of demand for commodity 2 exceeds 1 and for commodity 1 is less than 1.

Lemma 2.2-2: Income Elasticities Weighted by Expenditure Shares Sum to 1

$$k_1 \mathcal{E}(x_1^*, I) + k_2 \mathcal{E}(x_2^*, I) = 1,$$

where $k_j = \frac{p_j x_j^*}{I}$ is the expenditure share for commodity j.

Proof: To establish this proposition, we substitute the consumer's choice into the budget constraint and differentiate by I.

$$p_1 \frac{\partial x_1^*}{\partial I} + p_2 \frac{\partial x_2^*}{\partial I} = 1.$$

Rearranging the left-hand side,

$$\left(\frac{p_1 x_1^*}{I}\right) \frac{I}{x_1^*} \frac{\partial x_1^*}{\partial I} + \left(\frac{p_2 x_2^*}{I}\right) \frac{I}{x_2^*} \frac{\partial x_2^*}{\partial I} = k_1 \mathcal{E}(x_1^*, I) + k_2 \mathcal{E}(x_2^*, I) = 1. \qquad \square$$

We now examine income elasticities for three commonly used utility functions.

Example 1: Quasi-Linear Convex Preferences

If preferences are quasi-linear so that $U(x) = v(x_1) + \alpha x_2$, the marginal rate of substitution (MRS) at x^* is

$$\left. \frac{dx_2}{dx_1} \right|_{U=U(x^*)} = \frac{\frac{\partial U}{\partial x_1}}{\frac{\partial U}{\partial x_2}} = \frac{v'(x_1^*)}{\alpha}.$$

The MRS is independent of commodity 2 which means that the indifference curves are vertically parallel. As depicted in Figure 2.2-3, it follows that the Income Expansion Path is first horizontal and then vertical.

Over the range in which both commodities are consumed, it follows that the income elasticity of commodity 1 is zero. Given Lemma 2.2-2, the income elasticity of commodity 2 is the inverse of the expenditure share.

Example 2: Cobb-Douglas Preferences

$$U(x) = x_1^{\alpha_1} x_2^{\alpha_2}, \alpha_1, \alpha_2 > 0.$$

Differentiating by x_1, $\frac{\partial U}{\partial x_1} = \alpha_1 x_1^{\alpha_1-1} x_2^{\alpha_2} = \frac{\alpha_1 U}{x_1}$. Similarly, $\frac{\partial U}{\partial x_2} = \frac{\alpha_2 U}{x_2}$.

At the maximum the FOC must be satisfied, hence

$$\frac{\frac{\partial U}{\partial x_1}}{p_1} = \frac{\frac{\partial U}{\partial x_2}}{p_2} = \lambda.$$

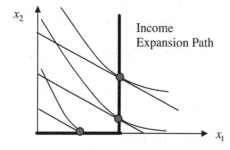

Figure 2.2-3. Quasi-linear preferences.

Substituting and then dividing by U,

$$\frac{\alpha_1}{p_1 x_1} = \frac{\alpha_2}{p_2 x_2} = \frac{\lambda}{U} \equiv \mu, \quad \text{hence} \quad p_j x_j = \frac{\alpha_j}{\mu}.$$

We then solve for μ by substituting back into the budget constraint.

$$p_1 x_1 + p_2 x_2 = \frac{\alpha_1 + \alpha_2}{\mu} = I, \quad \text{hence} \quad \mu = \frac{\alpha_1 + \alpha_2}{I}.$$

Demand for commodity j is therefore

$$x_j(p, I) = \frac{I}{p_j} \frac{\alpha_j}{\alpha_1 + \alpha_2}.$$

Finally, substituting back into the utility function, maximized utility is

$$U(x(p, I)) = \left(\frac{\alpha_1}{p_1}\right)^{\alpha_1} \left(\frac{\alpha_2}{p_2}\right)^{\alpha_2} \left(\frac{I}{\alpha_1 + \alpha_2}\right)^{\alpha_1 + \alpha_2}.$$

Example 3: CES Preferences

$$U(x) = \left(\alpha_1 x_1^{1-\frac{1}{\theta}} + \alpha_2 x_2^{1-\frac{1}{\theta}}\right)^{\frac{1}{1-\frac{1}{\theta}}}, \alpha_1, \alpha_2, \theta > 0, \theta \neq 1.$$

From the definition of U,

$$U(x)^{1-\frac{1}{\theta}} = \alpha_1 x_1^{1-\frac{1}{\theta}} + \alpha_2 x_2^{1-\frac{1}{\theta}}.$$

Differentiating by x_j,

$$(1 - \tfrac{1}{\theta}) U^{-\frac{1}{\theta}} \frac{\partial U}{\partial x_j} = (1 - \tfrac{1}{\theta}) \alpha_j x_j^{-\frac{1}{\theta}}.$$

Hence $\frac{\partial U}{\partial x_j} = \frac{\alpha_j U^{\frac{1}{\theta}}}{x_j^{\frac{1}{\theta}}}$.

We follow the same steps as for Example 2.
Substituting into the FOC and then dividing by $U^{\frac{1}{\theta}}$,

$$\frac{\alpha_1}{p_1 x_1^{\frac{1}{\theta}}} = \frac{\alpha_2}{p_2 x_2^{\frac{1}{\theta}}} = \frac{\lambda}{U^{\frac{1}{\theta}}} \equiv \mu. \tag{2.2-3}$$

Hence $x_j = (\frac{\alpha_j}{p_j \mu})^{\theta}$ and so $p_j x_j = \frac{\alpha_j^{\theta} p_j^{1-\theta}}{\mu^{\theta}}$.

We then solve for μ^{θ} by substituting back into the budget constraint:

$$p_1 x_1 + p_2 x_2 = \frac{1}{\mu^{\theta}} \left(\alpha_1^{\theta} p_1^{1-\theta} + \alpha_2^{\theta} p_2^{1-\theta}\right) = I, \quad \text{hence} \quad \frac{1}{\mu^{\theta}} = \frac{I}{\alpha_1^{\theta} p_1^{1-\theta} + \alpha_2^{\theta} p_2^{1-\theta}}.$$

Demand for commodity j is therefore

$$x_j(p, I) = \frac{I}{p_j}\left(\frac{\alpha_j^\theta p_j^{1-\theta}}{\alpha_1^\theta p_1^{1-\theta} + \alpha_2^\theta p_2^{1-\theta}}\right). \qquad (2.2\text{-}4)$$

Substituting $x(p, I)$ into the utility function and collecting terms,

$$U(x(p, I)) = \frac{I}{(\alpha_1^\theta p_1^{1-\theta} + \alpha_2^\theta p_2^{1-\theta})^{\frac{1}{1-\theta}}}.$$

Note that the demand functions given by (2.2-4) reduce to the Cobb-Douglas demand functions if $\theta = 1$.

Dual Optimization Problem:[8] *Expenditure Minimization*

Given the very weak assumption of local non-satiation, for any budget-constrained utility maximization problem there is a "dual" optimization problem. As we shall see, this dual problem is very useful in understanding the determinants of demand.

Suppose that x^* is a solution to a consumer's maximization problem. That is,

$$x^* \in \arg\underset{x}{\text{Max}}\{U(x)|x \geq 0, p \cdot x \leq I\}.$$

Such a consumption bundle is depicted in Figure 2.2-4.

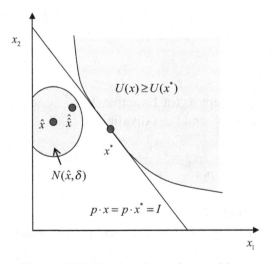

Figure 2.2-4. Dual optimization problem.

---

[8] The "dual" is the second member of a pair of items, in this case a pair of related optimization problems.

Consider any consumption bundle $\hat{x}$ such that $p \cdot \hat{x} < I$. If δ is sufficiently small the neighborhood $N(\hat{x}, \delta)$ lies in the budget set. If the local non-satiation property holds, then there exists some $\hat{\hat{x}}$ in this neighborhood that is strictly preferred to $\hat{x}$. Then $\hat{x}$ cannot be optimal. Hence

$$p \cdot x < I \Rightarrow U(x) < U(x^*).$$

Equivalently,

$$U(x) \geq U(x^*) \Rightarrow p \cdot x \geq p \cdot x^*.$$

Thus, x^* is expenditure minimizing, among all consumption bundles that are preferred to x^*. We summarize this result as follows.

Lemma 2.2-3: Duality Lemma If the local non-satiation assumption holds and $x^* \in \arg \text{Max}_x\{U(x)|x \geq 0, p \cdot x \leq I\}$, then $U(x) \geq U(x^*) \Rightarrow p \cdot x \geq p \cdot x^*$ and so $x^* \in \arg \text{Min}_x\{p \cdot x|x \geq 0, U(x) \geq U(x^*)\}$.

For any level of utility, $\overline{U}$ and price vector p we define the expenditure function $M(p, \overline{U})$ to be the minimum expenditure needed to achieve the utility level $\overline{U}$.

Definition: Expenditure Function

$$M(p, \overline{U}) = \text{Min}_x\{p \cdot x|U(x) \geq \overline{U}\}.$$

Although it is not difficult to solve for the expenditure function, it is often more convenient to solve first for the maximized utility

$$V(p, I) = \text{Max}_x\{U(x)|p \cdot x \leq I\}.$$

Given local non-satiation, the consumer spends his entire income. Moreover the higher his income the greater is his utility. Thus maximized utility $V(p, I)$ is a strictly increasing function of income. This is depicted in Figure 2.2-5.

For any utility $\overline{U}$ there is a unique income level M such that $\overline{U} = V(p, M)$. Note that for any lower income, maximized utility is less than $\overline{U}$. Thus the

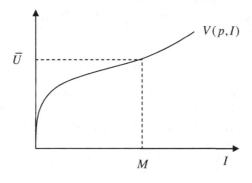

Figure 2.2-5. Maximized utility as a function of income.

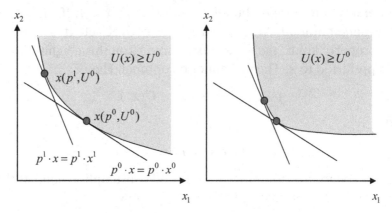

Figure 2.2-6. Substitution effect.

income level M is the minimized expenditure. For any utility level $\overline{U}$, we can therefore solve for $M(p, \overline{U})$ by inverting the equation $\overline{U} = V(p, M)$.

Compensated Demand

Let $x^c(p, \overline{U})$ be the solution to the dual problem, that is $x^c(p, \overline{U})$ solves

$$M(p, \overline{U}) = \underset{x}{\text{Min}}\{p \cdot x | U(x) \geq \overline{U}\}.$$

This is known as the consumer's compensated demand. Consider the effect on compensated demand of an increase in the price of commodity 1. This is depicted in Figure 2.2-6 for price vectors p^0 and p^1. As the price of commodity 1 rises, the consumer is compensated so that he is just able to maintain the utility level U^0. The following useful property of the expenditure function is an immediate implication of the Envelope Theorem[9]

$$\frac{\partial M}{\partial p} = x^c(p, U^0).$$

Informally, if the price of commodity j rises and the consumer maintains his consumption plan, his extra expenditure is x_j^*. This is the direct effect. The indirect effect associated with adjusting to the change in the price is of the second order.

Substitution Effect

The effect on demand of a compensated price change is called the substitution effect. As Figure 2.2-6 illustrates, the size of this effect depends critically on the curvature of the indifference curve. In the left diagram, as the price

---

[9] See Exercise 2.2-2. Converting the expenditure minimization problem to a maximization problem, $\mathcal{L} = -p \cdot x + \lambda(U(x) - \overline{U})$ so $-\frac{\partial M}{\partial p_j} = \frac{\partial \mathcal{L}}{\partial p_j} = -x_j$.

ratio changes, the consumption ratio $\frac{x_2^c(p,U^0)}{x_1^c(p,U^0)}$ changes a lot. That is, the substitution effect is large.

In the right diagram a price change has a small effect on the consumption ratio so the substitution effect is small. As we shall see, the elasticity of the consumption ratio with respect to the price ratio is a very useful measure of price sensitivity.

Definition: Elasticity of Substitution

$$\sigma = \mathcal{E}\left(\frac{x_2^c}{x_1^c}, \frac{p_1}{p_2}\right).$$

Example: CES Utility Function
From equation (2.2-3),

$$\frac{x_2^c}{x_1^c} = \frac{\alpha_2^\theta p_1^\theta}{\alpha_1^\theta p_2^\theta}.$$

Taking the logarithm,

$$\ln\left(\frac{x_2^c}{x_1^c}\right) = \theta \ln\left(\frac{p_1}{p_2}\right) + \text{constant}.$$

As is readily confirmed, $\mathcal{E}(y, x) = x\frac{d}{dx}\ln y$. Hence,

$$\mathcal{E}\left(\frac{x_2^c}{x_1^c}, \frac{p_1}{p_2}\right) = \theta.$$

Hence, for the CES utility function, the parameter θ is the elasticity of substitution.

We now show that there are several equivalent definitions of the elasticity of substitution. Lemma 2.2-4 is a direct implication of the following property of elasticity.

$$\mathcal{E}(\alpha z, \beta y) = \mathcal{E}(z, y) = y\frac{d}{dy}\ln z.$$

Lemma 2.2-4[10]

$$\sigma = \mathcal{E}\left(\frac{x_2^c}{x_1^c}, \frac{p_1}{p_2}\right) = \mathcal{E}(x_2^c, p_1) - \mathcal{E}(x_1^c, p_1)$$

The properties in Lemma 2.2-4 hold for any ratio. Two further useful results hold for compensated demand.

---

[10] In Exercise 2.2-3 you are asked to prove this Lemma.

Proposition 2.2-5: Elasticity of Substitution and Compensated Own Price Elasticity

$$\sigma = \frac{\mathcal{E}(x_2^c, p_1)}{k_1} \quad \text{where} \quad k_1 \equiv \frac{p_1 x_1}{p \cdot x}$$

and

$$\mathcal{E}(x_1^c, p_1) = -(1 - k_1)\sigma.$$

Proof: To demonstrate equivalence, first note that around the indifference curve as p_1 rises we have

$$\frac{\partial U}{\partial x_1}\frac{\partial x_1^c}{\partial p_1} + \frac{\partial U}{\partial x_2}\frac{\partial x_2^c}{\partial p_1} = 0.$$

Also, from the first-order condition, the marginal utility of each commodity is proportional to its price. Hence

$$p_1\frac{\partial x_1^c}{\partial p_1} + p_2\frac{\partial x_2^c}{\partial p_1} = 0. \tag{2.2-5}$$

Dividing by x_1^c and rearranging this equation,

$$\frac{p_1}{x_1^c}\frac{\partial x_1^c}{\partial p_1} = -\frac{p_2}{x_1^c}\frac{\partial x_2^c}{\partial p_1} = -\left(\frac{p_2 x_2^c}{p_1 x_1^c}\right)\frac{p_1}{x_2^c}\frac{\partial x_2^c}{\partial p_1}$$

$$= -\frac{k_2}{k_1}\frac{p_1}{x_2^c}\frac{\partial x_2^c}{\partial p_1}, \quad \text{where} \quad k_j = p_j x_j^c / p \cdot x^c.$$

Therefore

$$\mathcal{E}(x_1^c, p_1) = -\frac{k_2}{k_1}\mathcal{E}(x_2^c, p_1). \tag{2.2-6}$$

From Lemma 2.2-4,

$$\sigma = \mathcal{E}(x_2^c, p_1) - \mathcal{E}(x_1^c, p_1).$$

Substituting for the second term,

$$\sigma = \mathcal{E}(x_2^c, p_1) + \frac{k_2}{k_1}\mathcal{E}(x_2^c, p_1) = \frac{1}{k_1}\mathcal{E}(x_2^c, p_1).$$

Substituting this expression into (2.2-6),

$$\mathcal{E}(x_1^c, p_1) = -k_2\sigma = -(1 - k_1)\sigma. \qquad \square$$

Note that the compensated own price elasticity, $\mathcal{E}(x_1^c, p_1) = -(1 - k_1)\sigma$, is bounded from below by the elasticity of substitution. Moreover, if the expenditure share is small, the elasticity of substitution is a good approximation for the compensated own price elasticity.

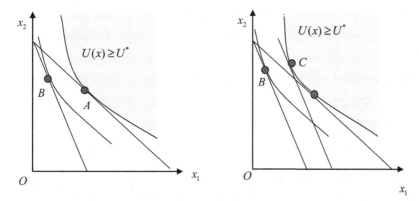

Figure 2.2-7. Decomposition of the price effect into income and substitution effects.

Decomposition of Price Effects

To understand the impact of a price change it proves helpful to decompose it into two parts: a compensated price effect and an income effect. Consider Figure 2.2-7. The left-hand diagram illustrates the effect of an increase in the price of commodity 1.

Suppose next that the individual is fully compensated as the price rises. In the right-hand diagram in Figure 2.2-7 the consumer moves along his indifference curve from A to C substituting commodity 2 for commodity 1. This is the substitution effect of the price increase. In the second step, the extra compensation is taken away and the budget line is pulled in toward the origin. The consumer then moves from C to B. Note that if, as depicted, commodity 1 is a normal good, both the substitution and income effects are negative. That is, the bigger (i.e., the more negative) the substitution effect and the bigger the income effect, the greater will be the total effect on demand for commodity 1.

For commodity 2, with constant prices, the income and substitution effects on demand are offsetting in the normal good case. Although there is substitution of x_2 into the consumption bundle around the indifference curve, the income effect is to reduce expenditure on all commodities. In Figure 2.2-7, the substitution effect dominates.

Returning to the own price effect, suppose that commodity 1 is an inferior good. Then the income effect offsets rather than reinforces the substitution effect. Thus the price sensitivity of inferior goods is typically lower for such commodities. Figure 2.2-8 illustrates the extreme situation in which the income effect dominates.

Although there is no convincing evidence of "Giffen goods" at the market level, it is easy to think of examples in which a commodity is a Giffen good for some consumers. Suppose Alex lives in the Arizona Desert and the price

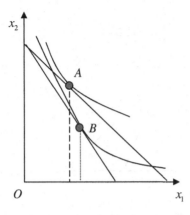

Figure 2.2-8. Giffen good (demand rises with price).

of electricity soars. The air-conditioning bill rises so much that Alex can no longer afford to spend his summer in New Zealand. Instead he stays home and, as a result, his demand for electricity rises.

Slutsky Equation

We now consider the decomposition of the price effect in mathematical terms. If $M(p, \overline{U})$ is minimized total expenditure at utility level $\overline{U}$, and $x_1(p, I)$ is the consumer's demand for commodity 1, the compensated demand is $x_1^c = x_1(p, M(p, \overline{U}))$. Differentiating by p_1, the slope of the compensated demand curve is

$$\frac{\partial x_1^c}{\partial p_1} = \frac{\partial x_1}{\partial p_1} + \frac{\partial x_1}{\partial I}\frac{\partial M}{\partial p_1}.$$

Yet we have seen that $\frac{\partial M}{\partial p_1} = x_1$. Substituting into the above expression and rearranging,

$$\underbrace{\frac{\partial x_j}{\partial p_1}}_{\substack{\text{total price} \\ \text{effect}}} = \underbrace{\frac{\partial x_j^c}{\partial p_1}}_{\substack{\text{compensated} \\ \text{price effect}}} \underbrace{-x_1\frac{\partial x_j}{\partial I}}_{\substack{\text{income} \\ \text{effect}}}. \quad \text{Slutsky equation}$$

In particular, the Slutsky decomposition of the "own price effect" is as follows:

$$\frac{\partial x_1}{\partial p_1} = \frac{\partial x_1^c}{\partial p_1} - x_1\frac{\partial x_1}{\partial I}. \tag{2.2-7}$$

Determinants of Demand Price Elasticity

Using the Slutsky equation, we can develop insights into the determinants of demand elasticity. Converting (2.2-7) into elasticity form,

$$\frac{p_1}{x_1}\frac{\partial x_1}{\partial p_1} = \frac{p_1}{x_1}\frac{\partial x_1^c}{\partial p_1} - \frac{p_1 x_1}{I}\frac{I}{x_1}\frac{\partial x_1}{\partial I},$$

where $x_1^c = x_1^c(p, \overline{U})$ is the compensated demand for commodity 1. Hence

$$\mathcal{E}(x_1, p_1) = \mathcal{E}(x_1^c, p_1) - k_1 \mathcal{E}(x_1, I). \tag{2.2-8}$$

From Proposition 2.2-5, $\mathcal{E}(x_1^c, p_1) = -(1 - k_1)\sigma$.

Substituting for $\mathcal{E}(x_1^c, p_1)$ in equation (2.2-8) we have the following proposition.

Proposition 2.2-6: Decomposition of Own Price Elasticity
$$\mathcal{E}(x_1, p_1) = -(1 - k_1)\sigma - k_1 \mathcal{E}(x_1, I).$$

We have therefore established that the own price elasticity must lie between the income elasticity and the elasticity of substitution. Holding the expenditure share constant, the higher the elasticity of substitution or the income elasticity, the more negative is the own price elasticity. Moreover, the higher the expenditure share of commodity 1, the greater the weight on the income elasticity. Intuitively, a higher share means that a price rise requires a bigger change in income for the individual to be compensated. Thus the income effect on the change in demand is greater.

Exercises

Exercise 2.2-1: Consumer Choice A consumer has a utility function $U(\cdot)$. He has an income of y and faces a price vector $p = (p_1, p_2)$. In each of the following cases, solve for the consumer's optimal choice under the assumption that he will consume a strictly positive amount of both commodities.

(a) $U(x) = \beta \ln x_1 + x_2$, (ii) $U(x) = \alpha \ln(1 + x_1) + x_2$ and (iii) $U(x) = \ln(1 + x_1) + \ln(1 + x_2)$.

In each case, demand for both commodities $x(p, I)$, is strictly positive for some prices but not for others. Analyze each case in turn and find the shape in Figure 2.2-9 that depicts the set of price vectors for which $x(p, I) \gg 0$.

Exercise 2.2-2: Compensated Demand Show that the price effect on compensated demand $\frac{\partial M}{\partial p_j}(p, U^0) = x_j^c(p, U^0)$.

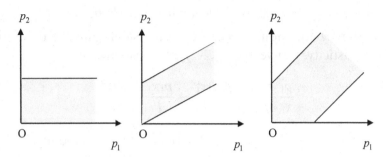

Figure 2.2-9. Price space.

HINT: Converting the minimization problem to the standard form, the compensated demand solves

$$-M(p, U^0) = \underset{x}{\text{Max}}\{-p \cdot x | U(x) - U^0 \geq 0\}.$$

Write down the Lagrangian and appeal to the Envelope Theorem.

Exercise 2.2-3: Elasticity of Substitution

(a) Show that $\mathcal{E}(y(x), z(x)) = \frac{\frac{d}{dx}\ln y}{\frac{d}{dx}\ln z}$.

(b) Use this to show that $\mathcal{E}(\frac{1}{y}, \frac{1}{x}) = \mathcal{E}(y, x)$ and that $\mathcal{E}(y_2/y_1, x) = \mathcal{E}(y_2, x) - \mathcal{E}(y_1, x)$.

(c) Use these results to prove Lemma 2.2-3.

Exercise 2.2-4: CES Preferences ($\sigma < 1$) A consumer has a CES utility function $U(x) = (x_1^{1-\frac{1}{\sigma}} + x_2^{1-\frac{1}{\sigma}})^{\frac{1}{1-\frac{1}{\sigma}}}, 0 < \sigma < 1$.

(a) If $\sigma = \frac{1}{2}$ write down the indifference curve in the form $x_2 = f(x_1)$ and hence show that the indifference curve through (a, a) has an asymptote $x_2 = \frac{a}{2}$.

(b) What is the other asymptote?

(c) Repeat the analysis if $\sigma = \frac{1}{4}$.

(d) Show that as $\sigma \to 0$ the horizontal asymptote approaches $x_2 = a$.

(e) Hence show that in the limit the indifference curve becomes L-shaped.

Exercise 2.2-5: CES Preferences ($\sigma > 1$) An individual has a symmetric CES utility function $U(x) = (x_1^{1-\frac{1}{\sigma}} + x_2^{1-\frac{1}{\sigma}})^{\frac{1}{1-\frac{1}{\sigma}}}, \sigma > 1$.

(a) If $\sigma = 2$ write down the indifference curve in the form $x_2 = f(x_1)$ and hence show that the indifference curve through (a, a) has endpoints $(0, 4a)$ and $(4a, 0)$.

(b) What is the marginal rate of substitution at these points?

(c) Show that as σ increases the intercept with the axes $b(\sigma)$ decreases.

(d) Depict the limiting indifference curve as $\sigma \to \infty$.

Exercise 2.2-6: Parallel Income Expansion Paths A consumer has a utility function $U(x) = \sum_{i=1}^{2} -\alpha_i e^{-Ax_i}$. She has an income I and faces a price vector p.

(a) Show that her optimal consumption bundle satisfies a condition of the following form:

$$x_2 - x_1 = a + b \ln \frac{p_1}{p_2}.$$

(b) Depict her Income Expansion Paths in a neat figure.

2.3 Consumer Choice with *n* Commodities

Key ideas: indirect utility function, homothetic preferences, the representative agent, elasticity of substitution

For a budget-constrained consumer there are no completely general propositions about the effect of price changes on consumption. As we have seen in the previous section, the magnitude and direction of price effects depend upon the relative size of income and substitution effects. We can, however, say a lot about compensated price changes. We therefore begin by analyzing the dual consumer problem

$$M(p, U^*) = \underset{x}{\text{Min}}\{p \cdot x | U(x) \geq U^*\}.$$

Proposition 2.3-1:
For compensated price changes the product of the price and quantity changes is negative ($\Delta p \cdot \Delta x \leq 0$).

Proof: Let x^0 be expenditure minimizing when the price vector is p^0 and x^1 be expenditure minimizing when the price vector is p^1. Both x^0 and x^1 satisfy the constraint $U(x) \geq U^*$. Therefore

$$p^0 \cdot x^0 \leq p^0 \cdot x^1 \text{ (because } x^0 \text{ is cost minimizing at } p^0)$$

and

$$p^1 \cdot x^1 \leq p^1 \cdot x^0 \text{ (because } x^1 \text{ is cost minimizing at } p^1).$$

Rearranging, it follows that

$$-p^0 \cdot (x^1 - x^0) \leq 0 \quad \text{and} \quad p^1 \cdot (x^1 - x^0) \leq 0.$$

Adding these two inequalities,

$$\Delta p \cdot \Delta x = (p^1 - p^0) \cdot (x^1 - x^0) \leq 0. \qquad \square$$

Special Case of a Single Price Change

Note that if only the price of commodity j changes it follows that $\Delta p_j \Delta x_j \leq 0$; therefore the compensated own price effect $\frac{\partial x_j^c}{\partial p_j}$ is negative.

Writing the dual problem as a maximization problem, we have

$$-M(p, U^*) = \underset{x}{\text{Max}}\{-p \cdot x | U(x) \geq U^*\}.$$

The Lagrangian of this maximization problem is $\mathcal{L} = -p \cdot x + \lambda(U(x) - U^*)$. Appealing to the Envelope Theorem,

$$-\frac{\partial M}{\partial p_j} = \frac{\partial \mathcal{L}}{\partial p_j} = -x_j^c.$$

Therefore

$$\frac{\partial}{\partial p_i}\frac{\partial M}{\partial p_j} = \frac{\partial x_j^c}{\partial p_i}. \tag{2.3-1}$$

Setting $i = j$ in this equation, it follows that the expenditure function is a concave function of each price taken separately. We now prove a stronger result.

Proposition 2.3-2:
The expenditure function $M(p, U^*)$ is a concave function of the price vector, that is, for any p^0, p^1,

$$M(p^\lambda, U^*) \geq (1 - \lambda)M(p^0, U^*) + \lambda M(p^1, U^*). \tag{2.3-2}$$

Proof: The method of proof is similar to the proof of Proposition 2.3-1. For the three prices p^0, p^1 and p^λ let x^0, x^1 and x^λ be the expenditure-minimizing consumption vectors. Because $M(p, U^*)$ is minimized expenditure we start with the terms on the right-hand side of inequality (2.3-2). Because x^λ is feasible,

$$M(p^0, U^*) = p^0 \cdot x^0 \leq p^0 \cdot x^\lambda \quad \text{and} \quad M(p^1, U^*) = p^1 \cdot x^1 \leq p^1 \cdot x^\lambda.$$

Hence

$$(1 - \lambda)M(p^0, U^*) \leq (1 - \lambda)p^0 \cdot x^\lambda \quad \text{and} \quad \lambda M(p^1, U^*) \leq \lambda p^1 \cdot x^\lambda.$$

Adding these two inequalities,

$$(1 - \lambda)M(p^0, U^*) + \lambda M(p^1, U^*) \leq (1 - \lambda)p^0 \cdot x^\lambda + \lambda p^1 \cdot x^\lambda$$

$$= p^\lambda \cdot x^\lambda = M(p^\lambda, U^*). \qquad \square$$

Special Case $M(p, U) \in \mathbb{C}^2$

Assuming $M(p, U^*)$ is twice differentiable, it is concave in p if and only if the matrix of second derivatives is negative semi-definite. Appealing to equation (2.3-1) it follows that

$$\left[\frac{\partial^2 M}{\partial p_i \partial p_j} \right] = \left[\frac{\partial x_j^c}{\partial p_i} \right]$$

is negative semi-definite.

Indirect Utility Function

Let $x^* = x(p, I)$ be the n commodity consumption bundle chosen by a consumer with utility function $U(\cdot)$ and income I facing a price vector p. Define $V(p, I)$ to be maximized utility, that is,

$$V(p, I) = \underset{x}{\text{Max}}\{U(x) | p \cdot x \le I, x \ge 0\} = U(x^*(p, I)).$$

The maximized utility function $V(p, I)$ is known as the indirect utility function.

Forming the Lagrangian for this problem,

$$\mathcal{L}(x, \lambda) = U(x) + \lambda(I - p \cdot x).$$

By the Envelope Theorem,

$$\frac{\partial V}{\partial I} = \frac{\partial \mathcal{L}}{\partial I}(x^*, \lambda^*) = \lambda^*$$

and

$$\frac{\partial V}{\partial p_j} = \frac{\partial \mathcal{L}}{\partial p_j}(x^*, \lambda^*) = -\lambda^* x_j^*(p, I).$$

Combining these results yields the following simple rule.

Proposition 2.3-3: Roy's Identity

$$x_j^*(p, I) = -\frac{\partial V}{\partial p_j} \bigg/ \frac{\partial V}{\partial I}.$$

Thus we can always recover the consumer's demand functions from the indirect utility function.

Example: Cobb-Douglas Preferences

Consider the indirect utility function[11] $V(p, I) = \times_{i=1}^n (\frac{\alpha_i I}{p_i})^{\alpha_i}$, where $\sum_{i=1}^n \alpha_i = 1$.

---

[11] We use the shorthand $\times_{i=1}^n a_i$ to denote $a_1 \times \cdots \times a_n$, the product of the components of the n dimensional vector a. Mathematicians typically prefer to use the notation $\Pi_{i=1}^n a_i$ However, in economics, the Greek letter pi has a host of different uses.

Taking the logarithm,

$$\ln V = \ln I - \sum_{i=1}^{n} \alpha_i \ln p_i + \sum_{i=1}^{n} \alpha_i \ln \alpha_i.$$

Then $\dfrac{\partial}{\partial I} \ln V = \dfrac{1}{V} \dfrac{\partial V}{\partial I} = \dfrac{1}{I}$ and $\dfrac{\partial}{\partial p_i} \ln V = \dfrac{1}{V} \dfrac{\partial V}{\partial p_i} = -\dfrac{\alpha_i}{p_i}.$

Appealing to Roy's Identity,

$$x_i(p, I) = \frac{\alpha_i I}{p_i}.$$

Finally, substituting this back into the indirect utility function,

$$U(x(p, I)) \equiv V(p, I) = \mathop{\times}_{i=1}^{n} x_i(p, I)^{\alpha_i}.$$

Therefore

$$U(x) = \mathop{\times}_{i=1}^{n} (x_i)^{\alpha_i}.$$

Thus we can retrieve not only the demand functions but also the original Cobb-Douglas utility function.

For this example demand is proportional to income. We now introduce a family of utility functions that have this property.

Definition: Homothetic Preferences A function $U(x)$ is homothetic if, for any x^0, x^1 and $\theta > 0$ $U(x^0) \geq U(x^1) \Rightarrow U(\theta x^0) \geq U(\theta x^1).$

Note that if an individual with homothetic preferences is indifferent between the two bundles x^0 and x^1 then $U(x^0) \geq U(x^1)$ and $U(x^1) \geq U(x^0)$. Therefore, if preferences are homothetic, $U(\theta x^0) \geq U(\theta x^1)$ and $U(\theta x^1) \geq U(\theta x^0)$ so $U(\theta x^0) = U(\theta x^1)$. It follows also that if $U(x^0) > U(x^1)$, then $U(\theta x^0) > U(\theta x^1)$.

Proposition: 2.3-4:
If preferences are homothetic and x^* is optimal given income I, then θx^* is optimal given income θI.

Proof: Let x^{**} be optimal given income θI. Because $\frac{1}{\theta} x^{**}$ is feasible with budget I, and x^* is optimal,

$$U(x^*) \geq U\left(\frac{1}{\theta} x^{**}\right).$$

By homotheticity, it follows that

$$U(\theta x^*) \geq U(x^{**}).$$

Because x^{**} is optimal with income θI and θx^* is feasible,

$$U(x^{**}) \geq U(\theta x^*).$$

Together these last two inequalities imply that $U(x^{**}) = U(\theta x^*)$. Therefore θx^* is also optimal with income θI. □

Lemma 2.3-5: Homogeneous Functions Are Homothetic If $U(\lambda x) = \lambda^k U(x)$, then preferences are homothetic.

Proof: A function U is homogeneous of degree k if $U(\lambda x) = \lambda^k U(x)$. Suppose $U(x) \geq U(y)$. Then

$$U(\lambda x) = \lambda^k U(x) \geq \lambda^k U(y) = U(\lambda y). \qquad □$$

In fact, as we now establish, if preferences are homothetic, there is no loss in generality if it is assumed that the utility function is homogeneous of degree 1.

Proposition 2.3-6:
If preferences are homothetic and strictly increasing, they can be represented by a utility function that is homogeneous of degree 1.

Proof: Let **e** be the unit vector $(1, \ldots, 1)$. Because preferences are strictly increasing, for any consumption vector $\hat{x}$, there must be some number $\hat{u}$ such that $\hat{x} \sim \hat{u}\mathbf{e}$. This is depicted in Figure 2.3-1 for the two-commodity case. The number $\hat{u}$ is chosen so that the indifference curve through $\hat{x}$ also passes through the point $\hat{u}\mathbf{e}$ on the 45° line.

Because for each $\hat{x}$ there exists a number $\hat{u}$, the mapping $g : x \to u$ is a utility function. In particular, $g(\hat{x}) = \hat{u}$. Appealing to homotheticity, because $\hat{x} \sim \hat{u}\mathbf{e}$, it follows that $\lambda\hat{x} \sim (\lambda\hat{u})\mathbf{e}$, that is $g(\lambda\hat{x}) = \lambda\hat{u}$. Because $g(\hat{x}) = \hat{u}$ it follows that $g(\lambda\hat{x}) = \lambda g(\hat{x})$. □

Example:
$U(x) = a_1 x_1^{\alpha} + a_2 x_2^{\alpha}, 0 < \alpha \leq 1$. Note first that $U(\lambda x) = a_1(\lambda x_1)^{\alpha} + a_2(\lambda x_2)^{\alpha} = \lambda^{\alpha} U(x)$. Thus the utility function is homogeneous of degree α and

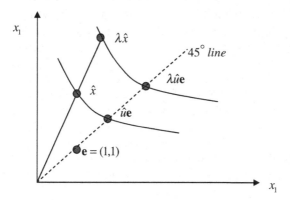

Figure 2.3-1. Homothetic preferences.

is therefore homothetic. Define $u(x) = U(x)^{\frac{1}{\alpha}}$. Then $u(\lambda x) = U(\lambda x)^{\frac{1}{\alpha}} = (\lambda^{\alpha} U(x))^{\frac{1}{\alpha}} = \lambda U(x)^{\frac{1}{\alpha}} = \lambda u(x)$. Thus preferences can be represented by the homogenous of degree 1 utility function $u(x)$.

Representative Preferences

If a group of consumers has identical homothetic preferences, it is especially easy to sum individual demands to solve for the aggregate demand. As the following proposition reveals, what matters is the total income of the group, and not its distribution among the members. Thus there is no loss in generality if it is assumed that all the income is in the hands of one "representative" member of the group.

Proposition 2.3-7: Representative Preferences
Define $x(p, I) = \arg \text{Max}_x \{U(x)|p \cdot x \le I\}$. If U is homothetic then

$$\sum_{h=1}^{H} x(p, I^h) = x(p, I^R) \quad \text{where} \quad I^R = \sum_{h=1}^{H} I^h.$$

Proof: Define $x(p, 1) = \arg \text{Max}_x \{U(x)|p \cdot x \le 1\}$. Because U is homothetic,

$$x(p, I^h) = I^h x(p, 1)$$

and so

$$\sum_{h=1}^{H} x(p, I^h) = \sum_{h=1}^{H} I^h x(p, 1) = I^R x(p, 1) = x(p, I^R). \qquad \square$$

Elasticity of Substitution with n *Commodities (a Two-Stage Approach)*

To analyze the effects of a price change, there is a second "indirect" utility function that will prove to be helpful. Suppose that the consumer breaks his choice problem down into two stages. At the first stage he fixes his consumption of commodity j and asks how he should best spend a budget of y on the other n-1 commodities. Let $u(x_j, y)$ be the resulting indirect utility, that is,

$$u(x_j, y) = \text{Max}_{x_{-j}} \left\{ U(x)| \sum_{\substack{i=1 \\ i \ne j}}^{n} p_i x_i \le y \right\}.$$

Because we are interested in the effect of a change in the price of commodity j we have suppressed the dependence of the indirect utility on $p_{-j} \equiv (p_1, \ldots, p_{j-1}, p_{j+1}, \ldots, p_n)$.

In stage 2 our consumer decides how to allocate his budget between commodity j and spending for the other goods,

$$\max_{x_j, y}\{u(x_j, y)|p_j x_j + y \le I\}.$$

This second-stage problem is precisely the problem studied in the previous section. In particular we can define the elasticity of substitution for commodity j as follows.

Definition: Elasticity of Substitution

$$\sigma_j = \frac{\mathcal{E}(y^c, p_j)}{k_j}, \quad \text{where} \quad k_j = \frac{p_j x_j}{I}.$$

Having reduced the n commodity problem to an equivalent two-commodity problem, we can appeal to Section 2.2. In particular, from Proposition 2.2-2, the own price elasticity can be decomposed as follows:

$$\mathcal{E}(x_j, p_j) = -(1 - k_j)\sigma_j - k_j \mathcal{E}(x_j, I). \tag{2.3-3}$$

Thus again the own price elasticity is a weighted average of the elasticity of substitution and the income elasticity.

Remark: One popular model of imperfect substitutes assumes that preferences are in the CES family and that the elasticity of substitution is independent of the number of commodities. Suppose that the number of commodities is large and the share of any one commodity is small; that is $k_j \approx 0$, $j = 1, \ldots, n$. It follows from the decomposition formula that $\mathcal{E}(x_j, p_j) \approx -\sigma$. Thus the own price elasticity of each commodity is independent of the number of substitutes. For most markets this seems likely to be at odds with the facts!

The elasticity of substitution is a measure of the overall substitutability of a product. Intuitively it must be some average of the substitutability of the product with each of the other products. We define this pair-wise elasticity of substitution as follows.[12]

Definition: Elasticity of Substitution between Pairs of Products

$$\sigma_{ij} = \frac{\mathcal{E}(x_i^c, p_j)}{k_j} = \frac{\mathcal{E}(x_j^c, p_i)}{k_i} = \sigma_{ji}$$

At first sight it is surprising that for any pair of commodities we can pick any one commodity and the price of the other commodity to compute this

---

[12] Note that this definition is only equal to the elasticity of the consumption ratio $\mathcal{E}(x_i/x_j, p_j)$ in the two-commodity case.

pairwise elasticity of substitution. To see why this must be the case note that from equation (2.3-1)

$$\frac{\partial x_j^c}{\partial p_i} = \frac{\partial}{\partial p_i}\frac{\partial M}{\partial p_j} \quad \text{and} \quad \frac{\partial x_i^c}{\partial p_j} = \frac{\partial}{\partial p_j}\frac{\partial M}{\partial p_i}.$$

Because the order in which M is differentiated does not matter, the cross partial derivatives are equal. Multiplying both sides by the two prices yields the following result.

$$p_j x_j^c \left(\frac{p_i}{x_j^c}\frac{\partial x_j^c}{\partial p_i} \right) = p_i p_j \frac{\partial x_j^c}{\partial p_i} = p_j p_i \frac{\partial x_i^c}{\partial p_j} = p_i x_i^c \left(\frac{p_j}{x_i^c}\frac{\partial x_i^c}{\partial p_j} \right).$$

Rearranging, it follows that $\sigma_{ij} = \sigma_{ji}$.

The next result follows directly from the elasticity of substitution definitions.

Proposition 2.3-8:

$$(1 - k_j)\sigma_j = \sum_{\substack{i=1 \\ i \neq j}}^{n} k_i \sigma_{ij}, \quad \text{where} \quad k_i = \frac{p_i x_i}{p \cdot x}.$$

Because $\sum_{\substack{i=1 \\ i \neq j}}^{n} k_i = 1 - k_j$ it follows that the elasticity of substitution is the

expenditure share weighted average of the pair-wise elasticities of substitution.

Exercises

Exercise 2.3-1: Expenditure Function with Cobb-Douglas Preferences Suppose that $U(x) = \times_{j=1}^{n} x_j^{\alpha_j} \equiv x_1^{\alpha_1} \ldots x_n^{\alpha_n}$, $\sum_{j=1}^{n} \alpha_j = 1$.

(a) Solve for the indirect utility function $V(p, I)$.
(b) Explain why you can "invert" your result to obtain the expenditure function.
(c) Hence solve for the expenditure function.

Exercise 2.3-2: Quasi-Linear Concave Preferences and Multi-Valued Demand Bev has a utility function $U(x) = \sqrt{x_1 x_2} + x_3$.

(a) Suppose that she allocates y toward the purchase of commodities 1 and 2 and purchases x_3 units of commodity 3. Show that her resulting utility will be $U^*(x_3, y) = \frac{y}{2\sqrt{p_1 p_2}} + x_3$.
(b) Given this preliminary optimization problem has been solved, her budget constraint is $p_3 x_3 + y \leq I$. Solve for her optimizing values of x_3 and y.
(c) Under what conditions, if any, is she strictly worse off if she is told that she can consume at most two of the three available commodities?

(d) Is this two-stage approach to optimization equivalent to solving directly for the optimal consumption bundle? Explain.

Remark: Note that for one price ratio, the individual is indifferent between a range of possible consumption bundles. Thus there is no demand function. Such multi-valued mappings are known as demand correspondences.

Exercise 2.3-3: Consuming Pairs of Commodities A consumer has concave utility function $U(x) = \sqrt{x_1 x_2} + \sqrt{x_3 x_4}$. Solve for the consumer's choice as a function of his income and prices. HINT: You may wish to try breaking the problem down into two smaller problems, as in the previous question.

Exercise 2.3-4: Slutsky Equation with Endowments Suppose that an individual has an endowment of commodities $\bar{x}$ as well as an income of I.

(a) Show that the Slutsky equation for this individual is
(b) $\frac{\partial x_i}{\partial p_j} = \frac{\partial x_i^c}{\partial p_j} - (x_j - \bar{x}_j)\frac{\partial x_i}{\partial I}$.
(c) If all h individuals in an economy have an endowment and no other income and each has the same marginal propensity to consume out of income ($\frac{\partial x_i^h}{\partial I} = \alpha, h = 1, \ldots, H$), show that if markets clear, the slope of the market demand curve and the slope of the compensated market demand curves are identical.
(d) Returning to part (a) can you interpret one commodity as leisure time? If so examine the effect of a wage increase on demand for leisure and hence on the supply of labor.

Exercise 2.3-5: Compensated Price Elasticities Appeal to the convexity of the expenditure function to show that for any pair of commodities x_i and x_j compensated price elasticities must satisfy the following inequality

$$\mathcal{E}(x_i^c, p_i)\mathcal{E}(x_j^c, p_j) \geq \mathcal{E}(x_i^c, p_j)\mathcal{E}(x_j^c, p_i).$$

2.4 Consumer Surplus and Willingness to Pay

Key ideas: willingness to pay, compensating variation, equivalent variation

Suppose the price of a commodity falls. How much better off is a consumer? A simplified answer is as follows. Let $B(q)$ be the benefit measured in dollars if consumption is q. If the unit price is p the net benefit is $B(q) - pq$. The consumer then makes purchases until the marginal benefit $B'(q)$ is equal to the price. Because this is true for each price, the mapping from quantities to market-clearing prices (or "demand price function") is

$$p(q) = B'(q).$$

Then the total benefit of q units is $B(q) = \int_0^q p(x)dx$.
The marginal benefit function is depicted in Figure 2.4-1.

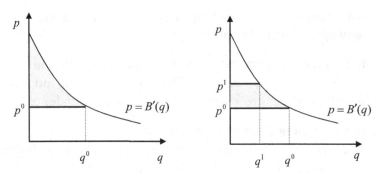

Figure 2.4-1. Consumer surplus.

At the price p^0 the consumer purchases q^0 units. The gross consumer benefit

$$B(q^0) = \int_0^{q^0} B'(q)dq$$

is the area under the demand price function. The net consumer benefit or consumer surplus is

$$B(q^0) - p^0q^0 = \int_0^{q^0} (B'(q) - p^0)dq.$$

This is the shaded area in the left-hand diagram in Figure 2.4-1. It follows that if the price rises to p^1, the change in the consumer surplus is the shaded area in the right-hand diagram in Figure 2.4-1; that is, the area to the left of the demand price function.

Left unexplained in this argument is the origin of the consumer's "benefit function." In general benefit it is not well defined because the marginal benefit of consuming a particular commodity depends on how much of the other commodities are consumed. However there is another way to proceed. We can ask how much an individual would need to be compensated to be no worse off after the price increase. For a price decrease, we can ask how much the consumer would be willing to pay for the change.

Compensating Variation

Consider a consumer with income I facing a price vector p^0. Let U^0 be maximized utility. That is, $U^0 = \text{Max}_x\{U(x)|p \cdot x \leq I\}$. Then I is the minimized income of the dual problem,

$$I = M(p^0, U^0) = \underset{x}{\text{Min}}\{p \cdot x|U(x) \geq U^0\}.$$

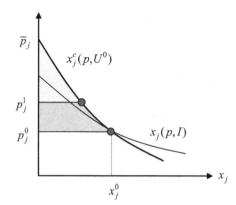

Figure 2.4-2. Compensating variation.

The compensating variation (CV) in income is defined as the extra income that the consumer needs to be fully compensated when the price changes from p^0 to p^1.

$$CV = M(p^1, U^0) - I = M(p^1, U^0) - M(p^0, U^0).$$

Suppose that the price of commodity j rises. By the Envelope Theorem, the rate at which income must rise with p_j is the compensated demand. That is,

$$\frac{\partial M}{\partial p_j} = x_j^c(p, U^0).$$

Integrating this expression,

$$CV \equiv M(p^1, U^0) - M(p^0, U^0) = \int_{p_j^0}^{p_j^1} \frac{\partial M}{\partial p_j} dp_j = \int_{p_j^0}^{p_j^1} x_j^c(p, U^0) dp_j.$$

Thus the total compensation needed to maintain the initial utility is the area behind the compensated demand curve. Figure 2.4-2 depicts the ordinary demand curve $x_j(p, I)$ and the compensated demand curve $x_j^c = x_j^c(p, U^0)$ under the assumption that commodity j is a normal good. Then, as the price of commodity j rises and the consumer is compensated with additional income, consumption of the commodity is greater. The compensated demand curve must therefore be steeper. The compensating variation for the price increase is the more heavily shaded region behind the compensated demand curve.

The entire shaded area is the compensation required if the price rises above $\overline{p}_j$ so that the consumer is squeezed out of the market for commodity j completely. Thus consumer surplus, as measured by the area to the left

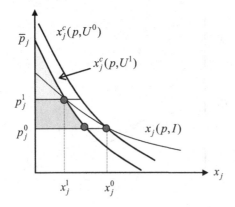

Figure 2.4-3. Equivalent variation.

of the ordinary (uncompensated) demand curve, is an underestimate of the compensating variation in income.

Equivalent Variation

Another way of measuring the loss to the consumer due to a price increase is to evaluate compensation *after* the price increase has taken place. With the price increasing to p^1, the consumer has a new maximized utility $U^1 = \text{Max}_x\{U(x)|p^1 \cdot x \leq I\}$. The question now becomes, how much income would the consumer be willing to give up to be offered the old price vector?

Let $x_j^1 = x_j(p^1, I)$ be the consumption of commodity j after the price increase. This is depicted in Figure 2.4-3.

The equivalent variation (EV) is the amount of income that must be taken away to leave the consumer's utility constant as the price is returned to its initial level, that is,

$$EV = M(p^1, U^1) - M(p^0, U^1).$$

Again appealing to the Envelope Theorem we can rewrite this as follows:

$$EV = \int_{p_j^0}^{p_j^1} \frac{\partial M}{\partial p_j} dp_j = \int_{p_j^0}^{p_j^1} x_j^c(p, U^1) dp_j.$$

Thus the equivalent variation is the area to the left of the demand curve $x_j^c(p, U^1)$. As long it is a normal good, demand for commodity j is lower at the lower utility level U^1. Thus this measure is smaller than the compensating variation.

Note also that the area to the left of the ordinary (uncompensated) demand curve must lie between *CV* and *EV*. As Figure 2.4-3 suggests, the difference between the two "true measures" of compensation and consumer surplus will be small, unless the price change is very large. Thus in practice, estimates of welfare gains are typically based on estimates of ordinary rather than compensated demand curves.

Applied economists have tried to use estimates of compensating and equivalent variation to determine upper and lower bounds on the social cost of un-priced commodities such as pollution. For example, the EV group of individuals might be shown two photos depicting different levels of pollution and asked how much they would be willing to pay to live in the less polluted environment. The CV group might be asked how much money they would need to be paid to live in the more polluted environment. Unfortunately the answers are several orders of magnitude apart.[13] Thus any such estimate is very imprecise. For this reason economists typically try to find some way of indirectly inferring estimating costs using market demand analysis.

Measuring Benefits with Multiple Price Changes

Suppose that we wish to measure the cost associated with raising the price of two commodities. What is the generalization of the area behind the demand curve depicted in Figure 2.4-3? Consider the case of changes in the prices of commodities 1 and 2. Let p_1^0 and p_2^0 be current prices and let (p_1^1, p_2^1) be a pair of higher prices.

Arguing as before, the compensating variation is

$$
\begin{aligned}
CV &= M(p^1, U^0) - M(p^0, U^0) \\
&= M(p_1^1, p_2^1, U^0) - M(p_1^1, p_2^0, U^0) + M(p_1^1, p_2^0, U^0) - M(p_1^0, p_2^0, U^0) \\
&= \int_{p_2^0}^{p_2^1} \frac{\partial}{\partial p_2} M(p_1^1, p_2, U^0) dp_2 + \int_{p_1^0}^{p_1^1} \frac{\partial}{\partial p_1} M(p_1, p_2^0, U^0) dp_1 \\
&= \int_{p_2^0}^{p_2^1} x_2^c(p_1^1, p_2, U^0) dp_2 + \int_{p_1^0}^{p_1^1} x_1^c(p_1, p_2^0, U^0) dp_1
\end{aligned}
$$

This is the sum of the areas to the left of the two compensated inverse demand curves.

---

[13] Presumably those surveyed are suspicious and fear that if they say they are willing to pay a lot might also be charged a lot. And if the government is going to give money out, why not get back some of those taxes you paid but felt were wasted!

Exercises

Exercise 2.4-1: Consumer Surplus, Compensated Variation, and Equivalent Variation

(a) Depict indifference curves for the derived utility function $u(x_j, y)$. Show the individual's choice before and after an increase in the price of commodity j from p_j to p'_j. Draw the budget line that keeps the individual at his initial utility level.
(b) Mark the two points where the budget lines meet the vertical axis as A and B. Explain why AB is the compensating variation.
(c) Either in a second figure (or in the same one if it is not too messy!) show the equivalent variation on the vertical axis.

Exercise 2.4-2: Compensating Variation for Consumers with Different Incomes A consumer with utility function $U(x, y) = x^\alpha y^{1-\alpha}$ has a budget constraint $p^0 x + y \leq I$.

(a) Solve for his maximized utility $U^0(p, I)$ and hence show that if the price of x rises to p^1, his income must rise to $M = I(\frac{p^1}{p^0})^\alpha$ to be fully compensated.
(b) Obtain expressions for both the change in the consumer surplus and the compensating variation as a function of price and income.
(c) Use a spreadsheet to compute the percentage difference between the consumer surplus and CV for different price ratios p^1/p^0.
(d) How would your answer to part (a) change if the utility function was $U(x, y) = \alpha \ln x + (1 - \alpha) \ln y$?

2.5 Choice over Time

Key ideas: interest rate, lifetime budget constraint, futures prices, and future spot prices

The one-period model can be readily adapted to analyze the savings decision of a consumer. To focus on intertemporal choice, we begin by assuming that there is a single consumption good in each period. A consumer has an income in period t of y_t and consumption is c_t. Her utility is $U(c) = U(c_1, \ldots, c_T)$. The consumer can borrow or save in period t at the interest rate r. Assuming period 1 assets are zero, the consumer can accumulate assets by saving some of her period 1 income and earning the period 1 interest rate. Her period 2 asset level is

$$K_2 = (1 + r)(y_1 - c_1).$$

In period 2 the consumer has the assets she has previously accumulated plus his current income. She consumes some part of her wealth and earns interest on the remainder. Her period 3 asset level is therefore

$$K_3 = (1 + r)(K_2 + y_2 - c_2).$$

Similarly in period t, the consumer must decide how much to consume and how much to save. The consumer then chooses a consumption stream $\{c_t\}_{t=1}^T$ to maximize lifetime utility subject to T asset accumulation constraints.

Lifetime Budget Constraint

To analyze this choice problem we first show that the T constraints can be reduced to a single lifetime budget constraint. Consider the period 1 asset accumulation constraint. Dividing by $1 + r$ to put everything in "present value" terms,

$$\frac{K_2}{1+r} = y_1 - c_1.$$

Similarly expressing the period 2 constraint in present value terms,

$$\frac{K_3}{(1+r)^2} = \frac{K_2}{(1+r)} + \frac{y_2 - c_2}{(1+r)}.$$

Substituting for K_2,

$$\frac{K_3}{(1+r)^2} = y_1 - c_1 + \frac{y_2 - c_2}{1+r}.$$

Repeating this for all T periods,

$$\frac{K_{T+1}}{(1+r)^T} = y_1 - c_1 + \cdots + \frac{y_T - c_T}{(1+r)^{T-1}}.$$

Because the consumer cares only about her consumption vector, she will never want to leave assets behind so $K_{T+1} \leq 0$. Moreover, no financial intermediary will agree to a loan that will never be repaid; thus $K_{T+1} \geq 0$. To satisfy both inequalities $K_{T+1} = 0$. Rearranging the previous equation yields the following lifetime budget constraint:

$$PV\{c\} = c_1 + \frac{c_2}{1+r} \cdots + \frac{c_T}{(1+r)^{T-1}} = y_1 + \frac{y_2}{1+r} \cdots + \frac{y_T}{(1+r)^{T-1}} = PV\{y\}.$$

The consumer's choice problem is therefore to maximize lifetime utility $U(c_1, \ldots, c_T)$, subject to the constraint that the present value of consumption cannot exceed the present value of income.

Two Periods

We analyze this problem in detail in Chapter 6. Here we focus on the simplest two-period case. The solution to the two-period optimization problem

$$\underset{c}{\text{Max}} \left\{ U(c) | c_1 + \frac{c_2}{1+r} \leq y_1 + \frac{y_2}{1+r} \right\}$$

is depicted in Figure 2.5-1 and Figure 2.5-2.

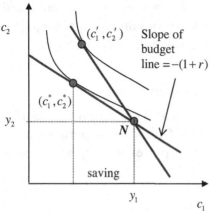

Figure 2.5-1. Optimal saving.

In Figure 2.5-1 the consumer saves part of her first-period income for period 2 when she is semi-retired and her income is lower. In Figure 2.5-2 a young consumer borrows in period 1 and plans to repay it in period 2 when her income will be higher.

From these figures we can glean some insights into the effects of an increase in the interest rate on aggregate saving and borrowing. In each case the substitution effect is around the indifference curve toward period 2 consumption. The higher interest rate lowers the present dollars needed to purchase a unit of future consumption. That is. it lowers the relative price of future consumption. However, the income effect is different for savers and borrowers. Holding period 1 consumption constant, the increased interest rate raises the future assets of savers so they achieve a higher utility level. Assuming that consumption goods are normal goods, the higher wealth leads to greater first-period consumption. That is, for first-period consumption, the income effect works against the substitution effect. This strongly suggests that the net effect on first-period consumption is likely to be small. But then the net effect on saving must also be small.

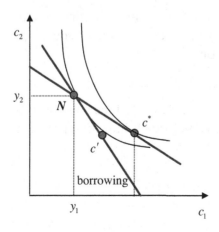

Figure 2.5-2. Optimal borrowing.

For borrowers, the higher interest rate makes it more costly to repay debt so they are worse off. The income effect on first-period consumption reinforces the consumption effect and so borrowing falls.

These observations fit the macro data well. Increases in interest rates do reduce consumer borrowing but have only small effects on aggregate consumer saving.

Futures and Future Spot Prices

We now extend the model to multiple commodities. For the key insight, it is enough to consider a two-period model. Let $x_t = (x_{t1}, \ldots, x_{tn})$, $t = 1, 2$ be the consumer's consumption bundle in period t. We consider an endowment economy. The consumer has a period t endowment of $\omega_t = (\omega_{t1}, \ldots, \omega_{tn})$. Her lifetime utility $U(x_1, x_2)$ is a function of her entire consumption bundle. To optimally trade in period 1, the consumer needs to know her trading opportunities in period 2.

Initially we assume that in period 1, there are markets both for commodities to be delivered in the current period and for commodities to be delivered in period 2. The latter are called "futures markets." (A wide variety of agricultural commodities are traded in such markets.) Given that there are prices for all $2n$ commodities, the consumer's endowment has a value of $W_1 = p_1 \cdot \omega_1 + p_2 \cdot \omega_2$. She then solves the following optimization problem:

$$\underset{x}{\text{Max}}\{U(x_1, x_2) | p_1 \cdot x_1 + p_2 \cdot x_2 \leq W_1\}.$$

From a mathematical perspective, this optimization problem is no different from a one-period problem in which the commodities have been partitioned into two disjoint subsets. However, from an economics perspective, clearly something is missing. All decisions are made in period 1 and all transactions are completed. Thus all stores can close their doors at the end of the first period!

Future Spot Markets and a Financial Intermediary

This is not the fatal flaw that it appears to be. Rather than introduce futures markets, suppose that there are no such markets. The consumer can trade in period 1 and knows that she can trade again in period 2. Her consumption choice is thus dependent upon the current prices (spot prices) and the prices that will prevail in the future (future spot prices). In the two-period model we let the future spot price vector be p_2^s. To move wealth between the two periods, the consumer utilizes a financial intermediary (the banking system). Let r be the interest rate offered by banks. As in the one-commodity case, if the value of the consumer's first period endowment $p_1 \cdot \omega_1$ exceeds the value of her consumption, she accumulates assets in period 2 of

$$K_2 = (1 + r)(p_1 \cdot \omega_1 - p_1 \cdot x_1).$$

Expressing this in present value terms,

$$\frac{K_2}{1+r} = p_1 \cdot \omega_1 - p_1 \cdot x_1.$$

In period 2, the consumer has both the value of her second period endowment and her assets to spend. Thus her future spot market budget constraint is

$$p_2^s \cdot x_2 \leq K_2 + p_2^s \cdot \omega_2.$$

Expressing this in present value terms and substituting for K_2,

$$p_1 \cdot x_1 + \frac{p_2^s}{1+r} \cdot x_2 \leq p_1 \cdot \omega_1 + \frac{p_2^s}{1+r} \cdot \omega_2$$

We now compare this with the budget constraint when it is possible to trade in spot and futures markets in period 1. This budget constraint is

$$p_1 \cdot x_1 + p_2 \cdot x_2 \leq p_1 \cdot \omega_1 + p_2 \cdot \omega_2.$$

Note that if $p_2^s = (1+r)p_2$, the two budget constraints are identical. Thus trading in futures markets can always be replicated by trading in spot and future spot markets. Resources are moved from one period to another by borrowing or lending.

There is one important difference between the two models. If all markets open in period 1, the equilibrating forces of the marketplace determine the prices at which commodities are traded. If only spot markets open, consumers (and firms) must form beliefs about the future spot prices in order to know how much to save or invest. If changes in a particular market are small, future spot prices will typically be similar to the current prices so forecasting is straightforward. However, if a market is subject to big shocks (such as drought or flood) the futures market plays an important role in price determination.

Exercises

Exercise 2.5-1: Choice over Time with Many Commodities A consumer has a quasi-concave utility function $U(x_1, \ldots, x_T)$, where x_t is the consumption vector in period t. Define

$$U^*(c_1, \ldots, c_T) = \underset{x}{\text{Max}}\{U(x) | p_t \cdot x_t \leq c_t, t = 1, \ldots, T\}.$$

(a) Show that $U^*(c_1, \ldots, c_T)$ is quasi-concave.
(b) Hence explain how the multi-commodity model can be analyzed as a one-commodity model.
(c) Suppose that $U(x) = \sum_{t=1}^{T} \delta^{t-1} u(x_t)$, where $u(x) = \sum_{j=1}^{n} \alpha_j \ln x_j$. Show that the indirect utility function $U^*(c) = \sum_{t=1}^{T} \delta^{t-1} \ln c_t + $ terms independent of c. Hence

explain why the individual's expenditure vector $(c_1^*, \ldots, c_T^*)$ is independent of future spot prices.

(d) Write down the life-cycle expenditure budget constraint. Then use the Lagrange method to show that $c_{t+1} = (1+r)^t \delta^t c_1$.

(e) Hence show that $c_1^* = \frac{1-\delta}{1-\delta^T} W_1$, where W_1 is the present value of the consumer's lifetime endowments.

Exercise 2.5-2: All-or-Nothing Consumer A consumer has utility function $U(x) = x_{11}^\alpha x_{12}^{1-\alpha} + \delta x_{21}^\beta x_{22}^{1-\beta}, 0 < \alpha, \beta < 1.$

(a) Solve for the indirect utility function if the consumer must spend c_t in period t.

(b) Hence show that this consumer is always happiest only consuming in one period.

(c) Modify the utility function so ensure that it is strictly quasi-concave. Given your modification, would the consumer ever buy only one commodity in any period? Might the consumer still consume only in one period?

Exercise 2.5-3: Saving and Borrowing in an Exchange Economy with a Continuum of Consumers Consumers have Cobb-Douglas preferences $U(x, \alpha) = \alpha \ln x_1 + (1 - \alpha) \ln x_2$, where x_t is consumption in period t. Consumers vary in their preference parameter α. We will refer to a consumer with parameter α as a type α consumer. There is a single commodity. Types are distributed continuously over the interval $[0, 1]$. Type α has density $f(\alpha) = 1$ over this interval so that the total mass of types is 1. Each type has the same income in each of two periods.

(a) If the interest rate is r, which types will be savers and which will be borrowers.

(b) Show that type α has a net saving of $s(\alpha) = \omega(1 - \frac{2+r}{1+r}\alpha)$.

(c) Solve for the total saving $S(r)$ by all types who save and the total borrowing $B(r)$ by all types who borrow. Depict $S(r)$ and $B(r)$ in a neat figure.

Exercise 2.5-4: Futures and Future Spot Prices A consumer has the two-period utility function

$$U(x_1, x_2) = \ln x_{11} + 2 \ln x_{21} + \delta(\ln x_{12} + 2 \ln x_{22}).$$

The period 1 (spot) market price vector is $p_1 = (p_{11}, p_{21})$ and the futures market price vector is $p_2 = (p_{12}, p_{22})$.

(a) Show that expenditure on each of the first- and second-period commodities is as follows.

$$(p_{11}x_{11}^*, p_{21}x_{21}^*, p_{12}x_{12}^*, p_{22}x_{22}^*) = \frac{p \cdot \omega}{3(1+\delta)}(1, 2, \delta, 2\delta)$$

(b) Obtain an expression for total spending in period 1.

(c) Hence show that the consumer will save if and only if $\frac{p_2 \cdot \omega_2}{p_1 \cdot \omega_1} < \delta$.

References and Selected Historical Reading

Blume, L. and Easley, D. (2008). "Rationality." In *The New Palgrave Dictionary of Economics* (2nd edition). New York: Palgrave/Macmillan.

Hicks, John. (1939). *Value and Capital*. Oxford: Clarendon Press.

Samuelson, Paul A. (1947). *Foundations of Economic Analysis*. Cambridge, MA: Harvard University Press.

3

Equilibrium and Efficiency in an Exchange Economy

3.1 The 2 × 2 Exchange Economy

Key ideas: Pareto efficiency, Edgeworth Box diagram, first and second welfare theorems

In this chapter the focus shifts from the individual agent to the market. Specifically we examine the allocation that results if all economic agents are price takers and prices adjust until markets clear. Rather than attempt to bring firms and consumers into the analysis all at once, we focus here on equilibrium in which there is no production. Consumers have endowments of commodities that they may exchange. As we see later, the ideas developed here extend very directly to economies with production.

Even though this chapter focuses on equilibrium outcomes, it is helpful to keep in mind a possible adjustment process that might lead to equilibrium. Suppose that there is an auctioneer who calls out prices for each of the commodities. Consumers and firms respond with the demands that they would make at these prices. The auctioneer lowers prices in markets where there is excess supply and raises them in markets where there is excess demand. At a price-taking (Walrasian) equilibrium, all markets clear.

The central results are the two welfare theorems. The First welfare theorem formalizes Adam Smith's argument about the "invisible hand" of the market place. Under extremely weak assumptions we establish that a Walrasian equilibrium (WE) is efficient. The Second welfare theorem establishes that in a convex economy, any efficient allocation can be supported as a WE with appropriate lump-sum transfers.

In this first section we focus on a simple exchange economy in which there are two consumers, A (Alex) and B (Bev). The set $H = \{A, B\}$ is then the set of consumers. Each consumer has an endowment of two commodities. Commodities are private. That is, each consumer cares only about his or her

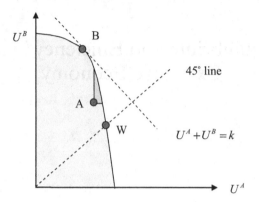

Figure 3.1-1. Utility possibility set.

own consumption. Consumer h, $h \in \mathsf{H}$ has an endowment ω^h, a consumption set $X^h = \mathbb{R}^2_+$ and a utility function $U^h(x^h)$ that is strictly monotonic.

Pareto Efficiency

With more than one consumer, the social ranking of allocations requires weighing the utility of one individual against that of another. Suppose that the set of possible utility pairs (the "utility possibility set") associated with all possible allocations of the two commodities is the shaded area depicted in Figure 3.1-1.

Setting aside the question of measuring utility, one philosophical approach to social choice places each individual behind a "veil of ignorance." Not knowing which consumer you are going to be, it is natural to assign a probability of $\frac{1}{2}$ to each possibility. If individuals are neutral toward risk while behind the veil of ignorance, they will prefer allocations with a higher expected utility

$$\tfrac{1}{2}U^A + \tfrac{1}{2}U^B.$$

This is equivalent to maximizing the sum of utilities, a proposal first put forth by Jeremy Bentham. In Figure 3.1-1, the Benthamite criterion picks the point B.

A more recent philosophical argument developed by John Rawls argues that behind the veil of ignorance consumers will be infinitely averse to risk and thus will place all weight on the worst possible outcome. The social criterion then become the Max Min criterion. Maximizing the minimum utility is achieved by moving out along the 45° line to the utility possibility frontier: the point W in the figure.

Economists tend to be agnostic when it comes to theorizing about social choice rankings. Instead they focus on minimizing unnecessary waste. The utility allocation A in Figure 3.1-1 is wasteful or "inefficient" because there are alternative allocations of goods that would make both individuals better off. Both the Benthamite and the Rawlsian allocations are said to be Pareto efficient (or simply "efficient") because the only way to raise the utility of one individual is by reducing the utility of the other. Generalizing to more than two individuals we have the following definition.

Pareto Efficient Allocation A feasible allocation of commodities is Pareto efficient (PE) if there is no other feasible allocation that is strictly preferred by at least one consumer and is weakly preferred by all consumers.

For the special 2 × 2 case, Alex and Bev must share the aggregate endowment $\omega = (\omega_1, \omega_2)$. Let $\hat{x}^B$ be the allocation to Bev and let $\hat{B}$ be the set of allocations that Bev prefers over $\hat{x}^B$. This is depicted in Figure 3.1-2. For any $x^B \in \hat{B}$, the allocation to Alex is $x^A = \omega - x^B$. Thus the best possible allocation to Alex that leaves Bev no worse off is Alex's utility maximizing allocation in $\hat{B}$.

Figure 3.1-3 shows Figure 3.1-2 rotated 180°. This depiction of the preferences of both consumers in a rectangle is called an *Edgeworth box* diagram. Note that at the bottom left corner Bev consumes the entire endowment. Therefore this is the zero consumption point for Alex. Also shown is the indifference curve for Alex through $\hat{x}^A = \omega - \hat{x}^B$. Any point in the

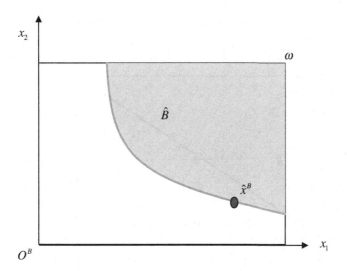

Figure 3.1-2. Bev's upper contour set.

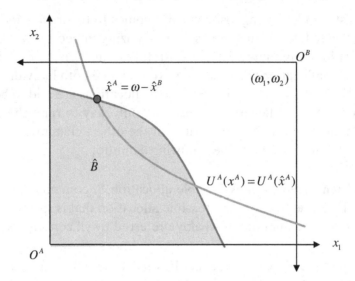

Figure 3.1-3. Edgeworth box diagram.

intersection of $\hat{B}$ and Alex's upper contour set $\{x|U^A(x^A) \geq U^A(\hat{x}^A)\}$ is strictly preferred by both Alex and Bev. Then the allocation depicted $\{\hat{x}^A, \hat{x}^B = \omega - \hat{x}^A\}$ is not PE.

For efficiency, there can be no such mutually preferred alternative. One such allocation is depicted in Figure 3.1-4. As long as an allocation $\{\hat{x}^A, \hat{x}^B = \omega - \hat{x}^A\}$ is in the interior of the Edgeworth box, a necessary condition for the allocation to be PE is that the slopes of the two indifference curves must be

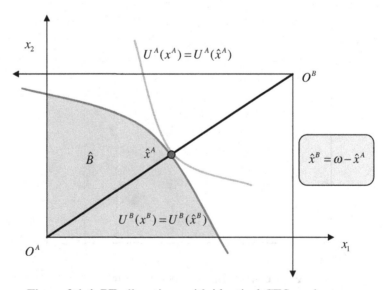

Figure 3.1-4. PE allocations with identical CES preferences.

equal. Thus the graph of the PE allocations is the set of allocations to Alex (and hence Bev) satisfying

$$\text{MRS}^A(\hat{x}^A) = \frac{\frac{\partial U^A}{\partial x_1}(\hat{x}^A)}{\frac{\partial U^A}{\partial x_2}(\hat{x}^A)} = \frac{\frac{\partial U^B}{\partial x_1}(\hat{x}^B)}{\frac{\partial U^B}{\partial x_2}(\hat{x}^B)}, \quad \text{where } \hat{x}^B = \omega - \hat{x}^A.$$

Mathematically, an allocation is Pareto efficient if

$$\hat{x}^A = \omega - \hat{x}^B \in \arg\max_{x^A, x^B} \left\{ U^A(x^A) | U^B(x^B) \geq U^B(\hat{x}^B), x^A + x^B \leq \omega \right\}.$$

Example: Identical Constant Elasticity of Substitution (CES) Preferences
If preferences are CES with elasticity of substitution σ, both consumers have a marginal rate of substitution, $\text{MRS}^h(x^h) = k(\frac{x_2^h}{x_1^h})^{1/\sigma}$. If a PE allocation is in the interior of the Edgeworth box, the indifference curves of the two consumers must have the same slope; that is,

$$\left(\frac{x_2^A}{x_1^A}\right)^{1/\sigma} = \left(\frac{x_2^B}{x_1^B}\right)^{1/\sigma} \quad \text{hence} \quad \frac{x_2^A}{x_1^A} = \frac{x_2^B}{x_1^B}.$$

Appealing to the Ratio Rule[1] and then setting demand equal to supply,

$$\frac{x_2^A}{x_1^A} = \frac{x_2^B}{x_1^B} = \frac{x_2^A + x_2^B}{x_a^A + x_1^B} = \frac{\omega_2}{\omega_1}.$$

Thus, in a PE allocation each consumer is allocated a fraction of the aggregate endowment. It follows that for each consumer the marginal rate of substitution is

$$\text{MRS}^h(\hat{x}^h) = k \left(\frac{\omega_2}{\omega_1}\right)^{1/\sigma}. \tag{3.1-1}$$

The PE allocations are depicted in Figure 3.1-4.

Walrasian Equilibrium for an Exchange Economy

In a WE each consumer is a price taker. We write the set of consumers as H so in the two-person economy $H = \{A, B\}$. Consumer $h \in H$, with endowment ω^h has preferences represented by the utility function $U^h(x^h)$ where x^h is the private consumption of consumer h. The value of the consumer's endowment is $p \cdot \omega^h$ and so the consumer chooses a bundle of goods, $x^h(p, \omega^h)$, that solves

$$\max_x \{U^h(x) | p \cdot x \leq p \cdot \omega^h\}.$$

---

[1] If $\frac{a_1}{a_2} = \frac{b_1}{b_2} = k$ then $a_1 = ka_2$ and $b_1 = kb_2$ and so $a_1 + b_1 = k(a_2 + b_2)$. Hence $\frac{a_1+b_1}{a_2+b_2} = k$.

Let $p \geq 0$ be a price vector of this exchange economy. Define $\omega = \sum_{h \in H} \omega^h$ to be the vector of total endowments in the economy and $x(p) = \sum_{h \in H} x^h(p, \omega^h)$ to be total (or "market") demand. Then the vector of excess demands is

$$z(p) = x(p) - \omega.$$

A market clears if either excess demand is zero or it is negative and the price of the commodity is zero.

Definition: Market-Clearing Prices Let $z_j(p)$ be the excess demand for commodity j at the price vector $p \geq 0$. The market for commodity j clears if $z_j(p) \leq 0$ and $p_j z_j(p) = 0$.

Walras' Law

We assume that the preferences of each consumer satisfy the local non-satiation axiom (discussed in Chapter 2). Given this axiom, each consumer must spend all of his income. To see this, we suppose instead that consumer h spends less than the value of his endowment and seek a contradiction. If the consumer's optimal consumption bundle x^h satisfies $p \cdot x^h < p \cdot \omega^h$, then for $\delta > 0$ and sufficiently small, the $\delta-$ neighborhood $N(x^h, \delta)$ lies in the budget set. Yet by local non-satiation, there must be some consumption bundle in $N(x^h, \delta)$ that is strictly preferred to x^h. However, if this is true, x^h cannot be optimal after all so we have a contradiction.

We now show that for any price vector p the market value of excess demands must be zero. First note that

$$p \cdot z(p) = p \cdot (x - \omega) = p \cdot \left(\sum_{h \in H} (x^h - \omega^h) \right) = \sum_{h \in H} (p \cdot x^h - p \cdot \omega^h).$$

Because all consumers spend their entire wealth the right-hand expression is zero. Hence

$$p_1 z_1(p) + p_2 z_2(p) = 0.$$

This is known as Walras' Law. Suppose that the first market clears, that is $p_1 z_1(p) = 0$. Then $p_2 z_2(p) = 0$ so market 2 must clear as well.[2] Note also that if one market does not clear, the other cannot clear either.

Definition: Walrasian Equilibrium The price vector $p \geq 0$ is a WE price vector if all markets clear.

For our two-commodity model, it follows from Walras' Law that we need to consider market clearing in only one market. Take any price vector

---

[2] With H consumers and n commodities an identical argument establishes that $p \cdot z(p) = 0$. Thus if $n - 1$ markets clear, then the remaining market must also clear.

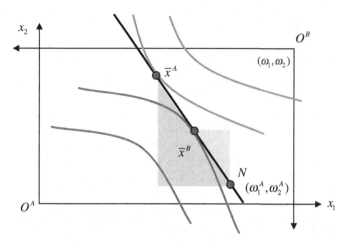

Figure 3.1-5. Excess supply of commodity 1.

$p = (p_1, p_2)$. Given an endowment allocation $\{\omega^A, \omega^B\}$, each consumer chooses his utility-maximizing consumption bundle.

It is helpful to depict trades in the Edgeworth box diagram. However there is one important caveat. From the viewpoint of each consumer, the budget set is the set of non-negative consumption bundles between the origin and the budget line. Consumers know nothing about the size of the Edgeworth box. In equilibrium all markets must clear. However, the demands of an individual consumer do not take into account aggregate supply constraints. For this reason, each side of the Edgeworth box is depicted as an axis for either Alex or Bev and indifference curves are depicted extending outside the box.

As depicted, in Figure 3.1-5, Alex wants to trade from the endowment point N to his most preferred desired consumption $\overline{x}^A$, whereas Bev wishes to trade from N to $\overline{x}^B$. Thus, there is excess supply of commodity 1.

By lowering the price of commodity 1 (relative to commodity 2) the budget line becomes less steep until eventually supply equals demand. The Walrasian equilibrium E is depicted in Figure 3.1-6.

Equilibrium and Efficiency

In Figure 3.1-6 the Walrasian equilibrium (WE) allocation is in the interior of the Edgeworth box. Thus the marginal rates of substitution must both be equal to the price ratio:

$$\text{MRS}^A(\overline{x}^A) = \frac{\frac{\partial U^A}{\partial x_1}(\overline{x}^A)}{\frac{\partial U^A}{\partial x_2}(\overline{x}^A)} = \frac{p_1}{p_2} = \frac{\frac{\partial U^B}{\partial x_1}(\overline{x}^B)}{\frac{\partial U^B}{\partial x_2}(\overline{x}^B)} = \text{MRS}^B(\overline{x}^B), \quad \text{where } \overline{x}^B = \omega - \overline{x}^A.$$

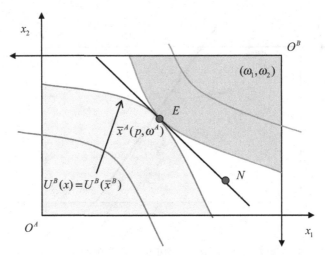

Figure 3.1-6. Walrasian equilibrium.

Comparing this condition with the necessary condition for an allocation to be PE, it follows that the WE allocation must be PE.

To prove that this result holds very generally, we appeal to the Duality Lemma. In Section 2.2 we argued that if the local non-satiation property holds, then the utility-maximizing bundle is cost minimizing among all preferred consumption bundles. Formally, if

$$\overline{x}^h = \arg \max_{x^h} \{ U^h(x^h) | p \cdot x^h \le p \cdot \omega^h \},$$

then

$$p \cdot \overline{x}^h = \min_{x^h} \{ p \cdot x^h | U^h(x^h) \ge U^h(\overline{x}^h) \}.$$

With this observation, the proof that a WE is Pareto efficient is short and simple.

Proposition 3.1-2: First Welfare Theorem for an Exchange Economy
If preferences satisfy local non-satiation, a WE allocation in an exchange economy is PE.

Proof: Let $\{\overline{x}^h\}_{h \in H}$ be a WE allocation for the exchange economy with endowments $\{\omega^h\}_{h \in H}$. Let $p \ge 0$ be the WE price vector. Because $\overline{x}^h$ maximizes consumer h's budget constrained utility, any strictly preferred bundle x^h must cost strictly more, that is $p \cdot x^h > p \cdot \overline{x}^h$. Moreover, by the Duality Lemma (Lemma 2.2-3) any weakly preferred bundle x^h must cost at least as much as $\overline{x}^h$; that is $p \cdot x^h \ge p \cdot \overline{x}^h$.

Consider any allocation $\{x^h\}_{h\in H}$ that is Pareto-preferred to $\{\bar{x}^h\}_{h\in H}$. Because none of the consumers can be worse off in the Pareto-preferred allocation, it follows that

$$p \cdot x^h - p \cdot \bar{x}^h \geq 0, \quad h \in H.$$

Moreover at least one consumer must be strictly better off. Thus

$$p \cdot x^h - p \cdot \bar{x}^h > 0 \quad \text{for some } h.$$

Summing over consumers,

$$p \cdot \left(\sum_{h\in H} x^h - \sum_{h\in H} \bar{x}^h \right) > 0.$$

Also all markets clear in a Walrasian equilibrium. Therefore

$$p \cdot \left(\sum_{h\in H} \bar{x}^h - p \cdot \sum_{h\in H} \omega^h \right) = 0.$$

Combining these results yields

$$p \cdot \left(\sum_{h\in H} x^h - \sum_{h\in H} \omega^h \right) > 0.$$

Because $p \geq 0$, it follows that there must be some commodity j such that $\sum_{h\in H} x_j^h - \sum_{h\in H} \omega_j^h > 0$. Thus all Pareto-preferred allocations are infeasible.[3] □

Clearly consumers' WE allocations depend on their initial endowments. Thus the outcome will change if a government intervenes and redistributes income. We now argue that, as long as preferences are convex, any PE allocation is also a WE allocation with the appropriate redistribution of resources.

We first sketch the argument for the two commodity case. Consider the PE allocation $\hat{x}^A, \hat{x}^B = \omega - \hat{x}^A$ in Figure 3.1-7. The indifference curves are tangential at $\hat{x}^A$, that is,

$$\frac{\frac{\partial U^A}{\partial x_1}(\hat{x}^A)}{\frac{\partial U^A}{\partial x_2}(\hat{x}^A)} = \frac{\frac{\partial U^B}{\partial x_1}(\hat{x}^B)}{\frac{\partial U^B}{\partial x_2}(\hat{x}^B)}.$$

Therefore, for some θ.

$$\frac{\partial U^A}{\partial x}(\hat{x}^A) = \theta \frac{\partial U^B}{\partial x}(\hat{x}^B).$$

---

[3] Note that the proof does not appeal to the assumption that the set of consumers is $H = \{A, B\}$. It holds for any number of consumers.

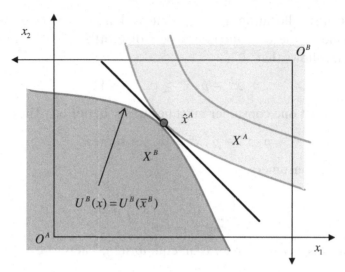

Figure 3.1-7. PE allocation $\{\hat{x}^A, \hat{x}^B = \omega - \hat{x}^A\}$.

Since the upper contour set $X^A = \{x^A | U^A(x^A) \geq U^A(\hat{x}^A)\}$ is convex, it follows from Lemma 1.1-2 that

$$U^A(x^A) \geq U^A(\hat{x}^A) \Rightarrow \frac{\partial U^A}{\partial x}(\hat{x}^A) \cdot (x^A - \hat{x}^A) \geq 0.$$

Making the same argument for Bev,

$$U^B(x^B) \geq U^B(\hat{x}^B) \Rightarrow \frac{\partial U^B}{\partial x}(\hat{x}^B) \cdot (x^B - \hat{x}^B) \geq 0.$$

Choose $p = \frac{\partial U^B}{\partial x}(\hat{x}^B)$. Then $\frac{\partial U^A}{\partial x}(\hat{x}^A) = \theta p$ and so

$$U^A(x^A) \geq U^A(\hat{x}^A) \Rightarrow p \cdot x^A \geq p \cdot \hat{x}^A$$

and

$$U^B(x^B) \geq U^B(\hat{x}^B) \Rightarrow p \cdot x^B \geq p \cdot \hat{x}^B.$$

Suppose that $U^A(x^A) > U^A(\hat{x}^A)$ and $p \cdot x^A = p \cdot \hat{x}^A$. Then, since U is strictly increasing and continuous, there exists $\delta \gg 0$ and sufficiently small such that $U^A(x^A - \delta) > U^A(\hat{x}^A)$ and $p \cdot (x^A - \delta) < p \cdot \hat{x}^A$. However, we have just argued that $U^A(x^A) \geq U^A(\hat{x}^A) \Rightarrow p \cdot x^A \geq p \cdot \hat{x}^A$, so this is impossible. Therefore

$$U^A(x^A) - U^A(\hat{x}^A) > 0 \Rightarrow p \cdot x^A > p \cdot \hat{x}^A.$$

Hence no allocation that Alex strictly prefers is in his budget set $\{x^A | p \cdot x^A \leq p \cdot \hat{x}^A\}$.

An identical argument holds for Bev. Because demand equals supply for each individual, all markets clear. Therefore, the vector p is a WE price vector.

Define the transfer payment $T^h = p \cdot (\hat{x}^h - \omega^h), h \in \mathsf{H}$.

Because $\sum_{h\in H} \hat{x}^h = \sum_{h\in H} \omega^h$ the sum of these transfers is zero so this is a feasible redistribution of wealth. The budget constraint $p \cdot x^h \le p \cdot \hat{x}^h$ can be rewritten as follows:

$$p \cdot x^h \le p \cdot \omega^h + T^h.$$

Then given transfers $T^h, h \in H$, the price vector p is a WE price vector.

This argument holds for PE allocations in which consumer $h \in H$ has an allocation $\hat{x}^h \gg 0$. We now prove a more general result.

Proposition 3.1-3: Second Welfare Theorem for an Exchange Economy
In an exchange economy with endowments $\{\omega^h\}_{,h\in H}$, suppose that $U^h(x)$, is continuously differentiable, quasi concave on $\mathbb{R}_+^2$ and that $\frac{\partial U^h}{\partial x^h}(x^h) \gg 0, h \in$ H. Then any PE allocation $\{\hat{x}^h\}_{h\in H}$ where $\hat{x}^h \ne 0, h \in H$, can be supported by a price vector $p \gg 0$.

Proof: We prove this for the two-person exchange economy.[4] If $\hat{x}^A, \hat{x}^B = \omega^A + \omega^B - \hat{x}^A$ is a PE allocation then

$$\hat{x}^A \in \arg \underset{x^A,x^B}{\text{Max}} \left\{ U^A(x^A) | x^A + x^B \le \omega^A + \omega^B, U^B(x^B) \ge U^B(\hat{x}^B) \right\}. \quad (3.3\text{-}2)$$

Let the aggregate endowment be ω. We begin by examining the feasible set of this optimization problem. Consider $\overline{x}^A = \delta \gg 0$ and $\overline{x}^B = \omega - \delta$. Because $U^B(\cdot)$ is strictly increasing and $0 < \hat{x}^B < \omega$, there exists some sufficiently small δ such that $U^B(\hat{x}^B) < U^B(\overline{x}^B) < U^B(\omega)$. Thus the feasible set has a non-empty interior. Because $U^B(\cdot)$ is quasi-concave the feasible set is convex. Also none of the constraint functions has a zero gradient. Thus by Proposition 1.2-4 the Constraint Qualification is satisfied. Then the Kuhn-Tucker conditions are necessary conditions.

The Lagrangian for the optimization problem (3.1-2) is

$$\mathcal{L} = U^A(x^A) + v(\omega^A + \omega^B - x^A - x^B) + \mu(U^B(x^B) - U^B(\hat{x}^B)).$$

Differentiating we obtain the following Kuhn-Tucker conditions:

$$\frac{\partial \mathcal{L}}{\partial x^A} = \frac{\partial U^A}{\partial x^A}(\hat{x}^A) - v \le 0, \quad \text{where} \quad \hat{x}^A \left(\frac{\partial U^A}{\partial x^A}(\hat{x}^A) - v \right) = 0.$$
$$(3.1\text{-}3)$$

$$\frac{\partial \mathcal{L}}{\partial x^B} = \mu \frac{\partial U^B}{\partial x^A}(\hat{x}^B) - v \le 0, \quad \text{where} \quad \hat{x}^B \left(\mu \frac{\partial U^B}{\partial x^B}(\hat{x}^B) - v \right) = 0.$$
$$(3.1\text{-}4)$$

$$\frac{\partial \mathcal{L}}{\partial v} = \omega^A + \omega^B - \hat{x}^A - \hat{x}^B \ge 0, \quad \text{where} \quad v(\omega^A + \omega^B - \hat{x}^A - \hat{x}^B) = 0.$$
$$(3.1\text{-}5)$$

---

[4] The reader is left to check that the proof extends directly to an exchange economy with more than two consumers and more than two commodities.

Because $\frac{\partial U^A}{\partial x^A} \gg 0$ it follows from (3.1-3) that $\nu \gg 0$. From (3.1-5) it then follows that

$$\omega^A + \omega^B - \hat{x}^A - \hat{x}^B = 0. \qquad (3.1\text{-}6)$$

Because $\hat{x}^B > 0$ and $\frac{\partial U^B}{\partial x^B} \gg 0$ it follows from (3.1-4) that $\mu > 0$.

Now consider an economy with endowments $\hat{\omega}^h = \hat{x}^h, h \in \mathsf{H}$ and consider the price vector $p = \nu$. Consumer h chooses

$$\bar{x}^h = \arg \underset{x^h}{\mathrm{Max}} \{ U^h(x^h) | \nu \cdot x^h \le \nu \cdot \hat{x}^h \}.$$

The FOC for this optimization problem is

$$\frac{\partial \mathcal{L}}{\partial x^h} = \frac{\partial U^h}{\partial x^h}(\bar{x}^h) - \lambda^h \nu \le 0, \quad \text{where} \quad \bar{x}^h \left(\frac{\partial U^h}{\partial x^h}(\bar{x}^h) - \lambda^h \nu \right) = 0.$$

Moreover, because $U^h(\cdot)$ is quasi-concave the FOC is also sufficient. Choose $\lambda^A = 1$ and $\lambda^B = 1/\mu$. Then, appealing to (3.1-3) and (3.1-4), the FOC hold at $\bar{x}^h = \hat{x}^h, h \in \mathsf{H}$.

Thus at the price $p = \nu$ no consumer wishes to trade. Therefore supply equals demand and so the price vector is a WE price vector.

Finally define transfers $T^h = \nu \cdot (\hat{x}^h - \omega^h)$. Appealing to (3.1-6), the sum of these transfers is zero. Consumer h's budget constraint with these transfers is

$$\nu \cdot x^h \le \nu \cdot \omega^h + T^h = \nu \cdot \hat{x}^h.$$

Thus the PE allocation is achievable as a WE with the appropriate transfer payments among consumers. $\qquad \square$

Example: Quasi-Linear Preferences

Alex has a utility function $U^A = x_1^A + \ln x_2^A$ whereas Bev has a utility function $U^B = x_1^B + 2 \ln x_2^B$.

At a PE allocation in the interior of the Edgeworth box the marginal rates of substitution must be equal. In this special case $\mathrm{MRS}^A = x_2^A$ and $\mathrm{MRS}^B = \frac{1}{2} x_2^B$. Thus, for an interior allocation in the Edgeworth box to be PE, it must be the case that $x_2^A = \frac{1}{2} x_2^B$.

Also total consumption $x_2^A + x_2^B = \omega_2$. Solving these two equations, it follows that for an allocation in the interior of the Edgeworth box to be PE, $x_2^A = \frac{1}{3} \omega_2$ and $x_2^B = \frac{2}{3} \omega_2$.

The Pareto efficient allocations are shown as heavy horizontal line segments in Figure 3.1-8. For any efficient allocation in the interior of the box, the marginal rate of substitution $\mathrm{MRS}^A(x^A) = x_2^A = \frac{1}{3} \omega_2$. Thus the supporting prices are the same for all these allocations.

Consider the Pareto efficient allocation $(\hat{x}_1^A, \hat{x}_2^A)$ on the boundary of the Edgeworth box. Suppose that this is also the endowment point. From the

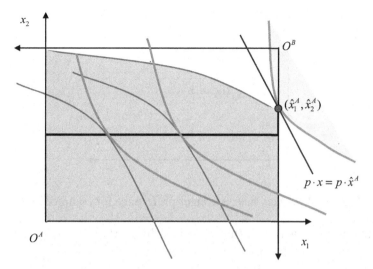

Figure 3.1-8. PE allocations with quasi-linear preferences.

First welfare theorem, if there is a Walrasian equilibrium then it must be PE. Thus the only possible equilibrium is a no-trade equilibrium. Consider the budget line through $\hat{x}^A = (\hat{x}_1^A, \hat{x}_2^A)$. This is in the interior of Alex's consumption set thus it must be tangential to his indifference curve. This determines the equilibrium price ratio.

The two welfare theorems offer a useful indirect way to analyze equilibrium. Often it is easier to characterize the PE allocations of an economy than to compute Walrasian equilibria. To illustrate this, we examine the effects on WE prices of a change in the distribution of wealth.

Homothetic Preferences

Suppose that the two individuals in the economy (Alex and Bev) have different convex and homothetic preferences. At the aggregate endowment, (ω_1, ω_2), Alex has a stronger preference for commodity 1 than Bev. That is, Alex is willing to give up more units of commodity 2 than Bev in exchange for an additional unit of commodity 1.

Assumption: Intensity of Preferences
At the aggregate endowment, Alex has a stronger preference for commodity 1 than Bev

$$\text{MRS}_A(\omega_1, \omega_2) = \frac{\partial U^A}{\partial x_1} \Big/ \frac{\partial U^A}{\partial x_2} > \frac{\partial U^B}{\partial x_1} \Big/ \frac{\partial U^B}{\partial x_2} = \text{MRS}_B(\omega_1, \omega_2). \quad (3.1\text{-}7)$$

This is depicted in Figure 3.1-9.

We now explore the implications of this assumption on the Pareto efficient allocations. Consider the Edgeworth box diagram shown in Figure 3.1-10.

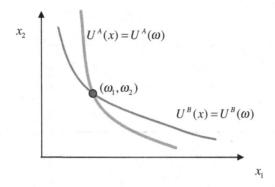

Figure 3.1-9. Alex has a stronger preference for commodity 1.

First note that along the dotted diagonal line $(x_1^h, x_2^h) = \theta^h \omega$. By hypothesis, preferences are homothetic. Because Alex places a higher value on commodity 1,

$$\text{MRS}_A(\theta^A \omega) > \text{MRS}_B(\theta^A \omega) = \text{MRS}_B(\theta^B \omega).$$

It follows that the Pareto efficient allocations must lie below the diagonal.

Let C be an efficient allocation and C' be a second such allocation preferred by Alex. In Figure 3.1-10, C' must lie to the northeast of C. Intuitively, because Alex's consumption is higher and Bev's is lower at C', the marginal rate of substitution at C' will be higher, reflecting the greater influence of Alex's stronger preference for commodity 1.

To confirm this, let the MRS at C be m. Given homothetic preferences, for any point above the line $O_A D$, $\text{MRS}^A(x_1, x_2) > m$. Also, for any point above the line $O_B F$, $\text{MRS}^B(x_1, x_2) < m$. Hence in the upper shaded region

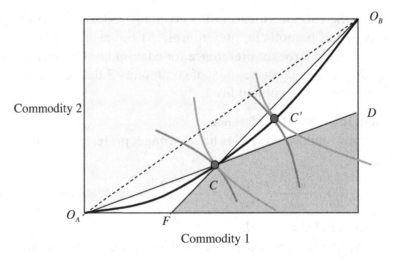

Figure 3.1-10. Pareto efficient.

Alex has a MRS exceeding m, while Bev has a MRS less than m. It follows that no such point can be Pareto efficient. A symmetric argument establishes that allocations in the lower shaded region are also not Pareto efficient.

Consider the efficient allocation C' to the northeast of C. Because this point lies below $O_A D$ and above $O_B F$, it follows that

$$\left.\frac{x_2^h}{x_1^h}\right|_C < \left.\frac{x_2^h}{x_1^h}\right|_{C'}, \quad h \in \mathsf{H}, \tag{3.1-8}$$

and

$$\mathrm{MRS}^h(C') > m = \mathrm{MRS}^h(C), \quad h \in \mathsf{H}. \tag{3.1-9}$$

It follows that, on the map of Pareto efficient allocations between C to C', the marginal rate of substitution increases. Hence the supporting prices must have the property that the relative price of commodity 1 rises. Thus the greater the wealth of Alex relative to Bev, the higher will be the relative price of commodity 1. Because we refer to these results later, we summarize them below.

Proposition 3.1-4: Pareto Efficient Allocations with Homothetic Preferences
In the 2×2 exchange economy, suppose both consumer A and B have homothetic preferences. Suppose also that at the aggregate endowment, consumer A has a stronger preference for commodity 1. Then at any interior efficient allocation,

$$\frac{x_2^A}{x_1^A} < \frac{x_2^B}{x_1^B}.$$

Moreover, along the locus of efficient allocations, as consumer A's utility rises, the consumption ratio x_2^h/x_1^h and marginal rate of substitution of x_1 for x_2 of both consumers rise.

Exercises

Exercise 3.1–1: Prices with Quasi-Linear Preferences Consider a two-person economy in which the aggregate endowment is $(\omega_1, \omega_2) = (100, 200)$ and both have the same quasi-linear utility function $U(x^h) = x_1^h + \sqrt{x_2^h}$.

(a) Solve for the Walrasian equilibrium price ratio under the assumption that the equilibrium consumption of commodity 1 is positive for both individuals.
(b) What is the range of possible equilibrium price ratios in this economy?

Exercise 3.1-2: Pareto Efficient Allocations

(a) If U^A and U^B are strictly increasing, explain why the allocation $\{\hat{x}^A, \hat{x}^B\} = \{\omega^A + \omega^B, 0\}$ is a PE and WE allocation.

Suppose that $U^A = x_1^A + 10 \ln x_2^A$ and $U^B = \ln x_1^B + x_2^B$. The aggregate endowment is $\omega = (20, 10)$.

(b) Show that the PE allocations in the interior of the Edgeworth box can be expressed in the form $\hat{x}_2^A = f(\hat{x}_1^A)$.

(c) Suppose that $\omega_2^A = f(\omega_1^A)$. How does the equilibrium price ratio change as ω_1^A increases along this curve?

(d) Which allocations on the boundary of the Edgeworth box are PE allocations?

Exercise 3.1-3: Walrasian equilibrium Suppose half the population (the Biggs) each have an endowment $(24, 8)$ and the other half (the Littles) each have an endowment $(20, 10)$. Each Mr. Bigg has a utility function

$$U^B = \ln x_1^B + \ln x_2^B.$$

Each Ms. Little has a utility function

$$U^L = \ln\left(4 + x_1^L\right) + \ln\left(6 + x_2^L\right).$$

(a) By solving for and then aggregating individual demands, solve for the equilibrium price ratio.

(b) Solve also for the contract curve and depict it in a neat Edgeworth box diagram showing the bottom left-hand corner as the zero consumption point for a representative Ms. Little and the top right-hand corner as the zero consumption point for a representative Mr. Bigg.

(c) Explain carefully why the equilibrium price will not change if endowments are reallocated in favor of the Biggs.

(d) What will be the equilibrium price ratio if the Littles have an endowment of $(8, 0)$ while the Biggs have an endowment of $(36, 18)$?

(e) What if the Littles have an endowment of $(2, 0)$ and the Biggs have an endowment of $(42, 18)$?

Exercise 3.1-4: Linear Preferences Consider a 2 person economy in which Alex's preferences are represented by the utility function $U^A(x) = 2x_1 + x_2$, while Bev's preferences are represented by the utility function $U^B(x) = x_1 + 2x_2$. The total endowment is $(30, 20)$.

(a) Characterize the PE allocations and depict them in an Edgeworth box.

Show that if Alex has a sufficiently large fraction of the total endowment the equilibrium price ratio $p_1/p_2 = 2$. What if Bev has a large fraction of the total endowment?

(b) For what endowments will the price ratio lie between these two extremes? Characterize the Walrasian equilibrium.

(c) Show that for some endowments a transfer of wealth from Alex to Bev has no effect on prices. Also show that for other endowments there is no effect on the Walrasian equilibrium allocation.

Exercise 3.1-5: More on the Biggs and Littles Suppose that the Biggs only like commodity 1, whereas the Littles only like commodity 2. Depict the PE allocations in a neat Edgeworth box diagram. Is there a Walrasian equilibrium? If so depict it.

Exercise 3.1-6: Market Excess Demand Consider the following two-person exchange economy. Alex and Bev each has a consumption set $X = \{x | x \geq (2, 2)\}$. Alex has a consumption utility function $U^A = (x_1^A - 2)^5(x_2^A - 2)$ and endowment $\omega^A = (7 + \alpha, 1 - \alpha)$. Bev has a utility function $U^B = (x_1^B - 2)(x_2^B - 2)^5$ and endowment $\omega^B = (1 - \alpha, 7 + \alpha)$. The parameter $\alpha \in [0, 1]$.

(a) Show that for both consumers to be able to purchase a bundle in their consumption sets the price ratio must satisfy

$$\frac{5 + \alpha}{1 + \alpha} \geq \frac{p_1}{p_2} \geq \frac{1 + \alpha}{5 + \alpha}.$$

(b) Solve for each consumer's demand for commodity 1.
(c) Hence show that the market excess demand function for commodity 1 is

$$z_1(p) = -\frac{\alpha}{3}\left(\frac{p_2}{p_1} - 1\right).$$

(d) For what values of α does the excess demand for commodity 1 increase as the price of commodity 1 increases? Provide some intuition for this paradoxical result. HINT: Consider the income effects of an increase in p_1.
(e) If $\alpha = 0$ characterize the Walrasian equilibrium prices and allocations.

3.2 The Fundamental Welfare Theorems

Key ideas: Walrasian equilibrium, First and Second welfare theorems

We now consider an exchange economy with an arbitrary number of commodities and consumers. As we see, the insights gleaned from the two-person two-commodity economy generalize. Commodities are private, that is, consumer $h \in \mathsf{H} = \{1, \ldots, H\}$ has preferences over his own consumption vector $x^h = (x_1^h, \ldots, x_n^h)$ and not over those of other consumers. Let $X^h \subset \mathbb{R}^n$ be the consumption set of consumer h. That is, preferences are defined over X^h. We assume that consumer h has an endowment vector $\omega^h \in X^h$. A consumption allocation in this economy $\{x^h\}_{h \in \mathsf{H}}$ is an allocation of consumption bundles $x^h \in X^h, h \in \mathsf{H}$. The aggregate consumption in the economy is the sum of the individual consumption vectors $x = \sum_{h \in H} x^h$. Similarly the aggregate endowment is $\omega = \sum_{h \in H} \omega^h$.

Feasible Allocation

An allocation is feasible if the sum of the consumption vectors of all the consumers does not exceed the aggregate endowment

$$x - \omega \leq 0.$$

Pareto Efficient Allocation

A feasible plan for the economy, $\{\hat{x}^h\}_{h \in H}$, is Pareto efficient if there is no other feasible plan that is strictly preferred by at least one consumer and weakly preferred by all consumers.

Price Taking

Let $p \geq 0$ be the price vector. Consumers are price takers. Consumer h has an endowment ω^h.

She chooses a consumption bundle $\bar{x}^h$ in her budget set $\{x^h \in X^h | p \cdot x^h \leq p \cdot \omega^h\}$.

Walrasian Equilibrium

Consumer h chooses a most preferred consumption plan $\bar{x}^h$ in her budget set. That is,

$$U^h(\bar{x}^h) \geq U^h(x^h), \quad \text{for all} \quad x^h \text{ such that } p \cdot x^h \leq p \cdot \omega^h.$$

Let $\bar{x} = \sum \bar{x}^h$ be the total consumption of the consumers. Excess demand is then

$$\bar{z} = \bar{x} - \omega.$$

Definition: Walrasian Equilibrium Prices The price vector $p \geq 0$ is a Walrasian equilibrium price vector if there is no market in excess demand ($\bar{z} \leq 0$) and $p_j = 0$ for any market in excess supply ($\bar{z}_j < 0$).

Welfare Theorems

The proof of the First welfare theorem is exactly the same as for the two-commodity case examined in Section 3.1. In the proof of the Second welfare theorem for the two-person exchange economy we assumed quasi-concavity and differentiability of utility functions and appealed to the Kuhn-Tucker conditions. Here we drop the differentiability assumption and appeal directly to the Supporting Hyperplane Theorem.[5]

The allocation $\{\hat{x}^h\}_{h \in H}$ is PE if there is no alternative allocation that increases the utility of consumer 1 without lowering the utility of at least one other agent. Thus $\{\hat{x}^h\}_{h \in H}$ must solve the following optimization problem:

$$\underset{\{x^h\}_{h \in H}}{\text{Max}} \left\{ U^1(x^1) | U^h(x^h) \geq U^h(\hat{x}^h), h = 2, \ldots, H, \sum_{h \in H} (\omega^h - x^h) \geq 0, x^h \in \mathbb{R}^n_+ \right\}.$$

Define $V^1(x)$ to be the maximum utility for consumer 1 given an aggregate supply of x, that is,

$$V^1(x) = \underset{\{x^h\}_{h=1}^H}{\text{Max}} \left\{ U^1(x^1) | U^h(x^h) \geq U^h(\hat{x}^h), \right.$$
$$\left. h = 2, \ldots, H, x - \sum_{h=1}^H x^h \geq 0 \right\}. \tag{3.2-1}$$

Note that $\{\hat{x}^h\}_{h \in H}$ solves this optimization problem if $x = \omega$.

Lemma 3.2-1: Quasi-Concavity of $V^1(\cdot)$ If $U^h, h \in H$ is quasi-concave then so is the indirect utility function $V^1(\cdot)$.

Proof: Consider the aggregate endowments a and b. We must show that for any convex combination $c = (1 - \lambda)a + \lambda b$, $V^1(c) \geq \text{Min}\{V^1(a), V^1(b)\}$. Suppose that the allocation $\{a^h\}_{h \in H}$ solves the optimization problem (3.2-1), with aggregate endowment a and that $\{b^h\}_{h \in H}$ solves the optimization problem when the aggregate endowment is b. Then $V^1(a) = U^1(a^1)$ and $V^1(b^1) = U^1(b^1)$. We must then show that $V^1(c) \geq \text{Min}\{V^1(a), V^1(b)\}$.

Because $\{a^h\}_{h \in H}$ is feasible with a and $\{b^h\}_{h=1}^H$ is feasible with b, the convex combination $\{c^h\}_{h \in H}$ is feasible with aggregate endowment $c = (1 - \lambda)a + \lambda b$. Then $V^1(c) \geq U^1(c^1)$.

Appealing to quasi-concavity, $U^1(c^1) \geq \text{Min}\{U^1(a^1), U^1(b^1)\}$. Combining the last two inequalities, $V^1(c) \geq \text{Min}\{U^1(a^1), U^1(b^1)\} = \text{Min}\{V^1(a), V^1(b)\}$.

$\square$

Proposition 3.2-2: Second Welfare Theorem for an Exchange Economy
Consumer $h \in H$ has an endowment $\omega^h \in \mathbb{R}^n_+$. The consumption set for each individual X^h is the positive orthant $\mathbb{R}^n_+$. Suppose also that utility functions $U^h(\cdot), h \in H$ are continuous, quasi-concave and strictly increasing. If $\{\hat{x}^h\}_{h \in H}$

---

[5] As we see in Chapter 5, this proof can be easily modified to include production.

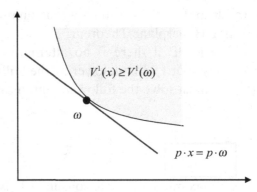

Figure 3.2-1. Supporting hyperplane.

where $\hat{x}^h \neq 0,$[6] $h \in \mathsf{H}$ is a PE allocation, then there exists a price vector $p > 0$ such that

$$U^h(x^h) > U^h(\hat{x}^h) \Rightarrow p \cdot x^h > p \cdot \hat{x}^h, \quad h \in \mathsf{H}.$$

Proof: Define

$$V^1(x) = \underset{\{x^h\}_{h=1}^H}{\text{Max}} \left\{ U^1(x^1) | U^h(x^h) \geq U^h(\hat{x}^h), h = 2, \dots, H, x - \sum_{h=1}^H x^h \geq 0 \right\}.$$

Appealing to Lemma 3.2-1, $V^1(\cdot)$ is quasi-concave. Also $V^1(\cdot)$ is strictly increasing because $U^1(\cdot)$ is strictly increasing and any increment in the aggregate supply can be allocated to the first consumer.

We have already noted that $\{\hat{x}^h\}_{h \in \mathsf{H}}$ is the solution of this optimization problem if $x = \omega$.

Moreover, because $U^1(\cdot)$ is strictly increasing,

$$\sum_{h=1}^H \hat{x}^h = \omega. \tag{3.2-2}$$

Because ω is on the boundary of the set $\{x | V^1(x) \geq V^1(\omega)\}$, it follows from the Supporting Hyperplane Theorem that there is a vector $p \neq 0$, such that

$$V^1(x) > V^1(\omega) \Rightarrow p \cdot x > p \cdot \omega \quad \text{and} \quad V^1(x) \geq V^1(\omega) \Rightarrow p \cdot x \geq p \cdot \omega. \tag{3.2-3}$$

The supporting line through the aggregate endowment vector is depicted in Figure 3.2-1.

---

[6] If there are M consumers with a zero allocation, we set these aside and appeal to the theorem for the H-M consumers with non-zero allocations. Because all feasible allocations are strictly preferred to the zero allocation, the theorem then extends immediately.

We now argue that the vector p must be positive. If not, define $\delta = (\delta_1, \ldots, \delta_n) > 0$ such that $\delta_j > 0$ if and only if $p_j < 0$. Then $V^1(\omega + \delta) > V^1(\omega)$ and $p \cdot (\omega + \delta) < p \cdot \omega$. But this contradicts (3.2-3) so p must be positive after all.

From (3.2-3) and the definition of the indirect utility function,

$$U^h(x^h) \geq U^h(\hat{x}^h), \quad h = 1, \ldots, H \Rightarrow p \cdot x = p \cdot \sum_{h=1}^{H} x^h \geq p \cdot \omega. \quad (3.2\text{-}4)$$

Substituting for ω from (3.2-2) it follows that

$$U^h(x^h) \geq U^h(\hat{x}^h), \quad h = 1, \ldots, H \Rightarrow p \cdot \sum_{h=1}^{H} x^h \geq p \cdot \sum_{h=1}^{H} \hat{x}^h.$$

Setting $x^k = \hat{x}^k$, $k \neq h$, we may then conclude that for consumer h,

$$U^h(x^h) \geq U^h(\hat{x}^h) \Rightarrow p \cdot x^h \geq p \cdot \hat{x}^h. \quad (3.2\text{-}5)$$

It remains to show that any strictly preferred bundle costs strictly more. Suppose instead that $U^h(x^h) > U^h(\hat{x}^h)$ and $p \cdot x^h = p \cdot \hat{x}^h$. Then for all $\lambda \in (0, 1)$, $p \cdot \lambda x^h < p \cdot \hat{x}^h$. Also because $U^h(\cdot)$ is continuous, for all λ sufficiently close to 1, $U^h(\lambda x^h) > U^h(\hat{x}^h)$. But these two inequalities contradict (3.2-5). Hence

$$U^h(x^h) > U^h(\hat{x}^h) \Rightarrow p \cdot x^h > p \cdot \hat{x}^h. \qquad \square$$

Exercise 3.2-1: Walrasian Equilibrium with Identical Homothetic Preferences Suppose each consumer has a consumption set $\mathbb{R}^n_+$ and the same strictly increasing, quasi-concave, homothetic utility function $U \in \mathbb{C}^1$. Characterize Walrasian equilibrium prices.

References and Selected Historical Reading

Edgeworth, Francis Y. (1881). *Mathematical Psychics: An Essay on the Application of Mathematics to the Moral Sciences*. London: C. K. Paul.

Pareto, Vilfredo. (1909). *Manuele di economia politica*. Trans. Augustus M. Kelley, 1971.

Rawls, John. (1971). *A Theory of Justice*. Cambridge, MA: Belknap Press.

Walras, Leon. (1874). *Éléments d'économie politique pure, ou théorie de la richesse sociale*. Lausanne: F. Rouge Editeur.

4

Firms

4.1 What Is a Firm?

Key ideas: firm as a transformer of inputs into outputs, production sets, production functions, net supply and net demand

In this chapter the focus switches to the transformation of commodities by firms. Within a firm, raw materials and other commodity inputs are processed by labor and managerial inputs to produce goods and services. These outputs may be for consumption (final products) or for sale as inputs to other firms (intermediate products). The amount of output that can be produced depends on the technology (machinery, buildings, etc.) held by the firm.

This is relatively straightforward. Consider, for example, a newsprint manufacturer. It transforms the primary raw materials of lumber, energy, and labor into giant rolls of paper ready for delivery to daily newspapers, using an array of machines. However, from a broader perspective, the machines are also inputs. In addition to purchasing labor inputs and raw materials, the firm can purchase additional capital equipment (for the same plant or to build a new plant) and so alter the set of available outputs. From this perspective, the technology of a firm is a set of blueprints for the transformation of commodities.

Even this is an incomplete view. Rather than purchase additional equipment, the firm might purchase another firm, or maybe all the other firms in the economy! Do regulatory constraints determine the number of firms, or are there some other natural factors that limit the scope for the agglomeration of firms into super-firms? These very important and controversial questions lie at the heart of modern industrial organization. Here we simply take the boundary of each firm (or its set of blueprints) as a given.

If there were no economies of scale there would be no technological rationale for economic agents to work together as partners or in an employer–employee relationship. Thus, gains to specialization are a core explanation for the existence of firms. However, once there is an agglomeration of human and non-human inputs, another critical issue concerns the effective utilization of these inputs. In particular, the performance of workers must be monitored. In very small firms the owner bears this cost directly. In larger firms the monitoring of workers requires the recruiting of managers. In turn, the managers are monitored by the owners as represented by a board of directors. Thus, in either case the ultimate monitoring cost is a cost borne by the owners.[1]

In this chapter we abstract from such issues and ignore the cost of monitoring the utilization of inputs to carry out the plan selected by the owners of a firm.[2] These owners receive dividends based on their shareholdings. The higher the profit of the firm the higher is the dividend stream. Thus the owners seek to maximize the profit of the firm.

Consider a firm that can produce m possible outputs $q = (q_1, \ldots, q_m)$ using n inputs $z = (z_1, \ldots, z_n)$. The $m + n$ dimensional vector $(z, q) \geq 0$ is a feasible plan of firm f if the output vector q is feasible given the input vector z.

Let Y^f be the set of feasible input-output vectors for firm f. This is the firm's *production set*. For any input vector z, let $Q(z)$ be the set of feasible output vectors. An output vector q is output efficient for the firm if it is not possible to increase the output of one commodity without decreasing the output of some other commodity. Mathematically, for a given input vector z, an output vector is output-efficient if it lies on the boundary of $Q(z)$.

In the special case in which there is only a single output, the efficient output $q = F(z)$ is the maximum feasible output. The function $F(\cdot)$ is then referred to as the firm's *production function*.

Example 1: Cobb-Douglas Production Function

$$q = A \overset{n}{\underset{j=1}{\times}} z_j^{\alpha_j} = A z_1^{\alpha_1} \ldots z_n^{\alpha_n}, A, \alpha > 0.$$

Example 2: CES Production Function

$$q = \left(\sum_{j=1}^{n} a_j z_j^{\frac{\sigma-1}{\sigma}} \right)^{\frac{\sigma}{\sigma-1}}, a, \sigma > 0, \sigma \neq 1.$$

With more than one output, it is often convenient to characterize the production set as the set of input-output vectors (z, q) that satisfy certain inequality constraints. That is,

$$\mathcal{Y}^f = \{(z, q) | h_k(z, q) \geq 0, k = 1, \ldots, K\}.$$

---

[1] In reality top managers are offered bonuses and other incentives. Thus a key role of the owners is to design effective incentive schemes. We return to this in Chapter 7.

[2] Monitoring costs can be added without affecting the analysis in any significant way if these costs are independent of the production plan. Then we simply have an additional fixed cost.

The characteristics of the production set thus depend on the characteristics of the constraint functions. For example, if each of the constraint functions is quasi-concave (so that it has a convex upper-contour set), then the production set is convex.

Example 3: Multi-Product Production Set

$$\mathcal{Y}^f = \{(z_1, q_1, q_2)|z_1 - q_1^2 - q_2^2 \geq 0, (z, q) \geq 0\}.$$

In this case the constraint function is the sum of three concave functions and is therefore concave so the production set is convex. Note that for any input z_1 the set of feasible output vectors $Q(z) = \{q|q_1^2 + q_2^2 \leq z_1\}$. This is a quarter-circle with radius $\sqrt{z_1}$.

At the level of the individual firm, the focus is often on the cost of the inputs and the revenue from the output. However, when the focus is on markets as a whole, this approach is not so useful. One reason is that the outputs of one firm are very often the inputs of another firm. A second reason is that, as relative prices change, a firm can switch from being a net demander of some commodity (such as electricity) to being a net supplier.

A more general approach focuses on the net supply of commodities by each firm. Firm f is a net supplier of commodity j if $y_j^f \geq 0$ and it is a net demander of commodity j if $y_j^f < 0$. In this case $-y_j^f$ is the firm's input demand.

Given a price vector p, the total revenue of the firm is $R^f = \sum_{j, y_j \geq 0} p_j y_j^f$ and the total cost is $C^f = \sum_{j, y_j < 0} p_j(-y_j^f)$. The profit of the firm is therefore

$$R^f - C^f = \underbrace{\sum_{j, y_j > 0} p_j y_j^f}_{\text{revenue}} - \underbrace{\sum_{j, y_j \leq 0} p_j(-y_j^f)}_{\text{cost}} = p \cdot y^f.$$

Thus, there is a third important reason for this alternative approach. It is far more convenient from a mathematical perspective. The set of feasible plans $\mathcal{Y}^f$ is the firm's production set,[3] and any vector $y^f \in \mathcal{Y}^f$ is a feasible production vector. To satisfy the interests of its shareholders, the firm chooses its most profitable feasible production vector.

4.2 Decision Making by Price-Taking Firms

Key ideas: input prices and marginal cost, laws of firm demand and supply, short-versus long-run response to a price change

---

[3] If the production vector is $(z^f, q^f) \geq 0$ where z^f and q^f are the input and output vectors then we write the production set as Y^f. When y^f is a firm's net supply we write the production set as $\mathcal{Y}^f$.

Initially we assume that the firm is a price taker in all input markets. A necessary condition for profit maximization is that, given the output choice q, the cost of the inputs should be minimized. This minimized cost of production is known as the cost function of the firm.

Cost Function

Let Y be the production set of firm f and let r be the vector of input prices. Then the cost function is

$$C(r, q) \equiv \underset{z}{\text{Min}}\{r \cdot z | (z, q) \in Y\}.$$

If the firm has a single output we define $F(z)$ to be the maximum output given the input vector z. This is called the firm's production function. In this case the cost function is

$$C(r, q) \equiv \underset{z}{\text{Min}}\{r \cdot z | F(z) - q \geq 0\}.$$

Note that from a mathematical perspective, if there is a single output, then the cost function of the firm is identical in structure to the expenditure function of the consumer. Thus, all of our analysis of the expenditure function carries over directly. In particular, the cost function is a concave function of the input price vector. We have the following further result.

Lemma 4.2-1: Gradient of the Cost Function If the cost-minimizing input vector $z(q, r)$ is a continuous function of input prices, then

$$\frac{\partial C}{\partial r_i}(r, q) = z_i(r, q) \, i = 1, \ldots, n. \tag{4.2-1}$$

This is readily proved by appealing to the Envelope Theorem. However it is best understood by making a direct argument. Suppose that input vector z^0 is optimal with input price vector r^0 and that z^1 is optimal with price vector r^1. When the input price vector changes from r^0 to r^1 one option is for the firm to produce the output vector q using the same input vector. Thus $C(r^1, q) \leq r^1 \cdot z^0$ and so we have the following upper bound for the change in cost:

$$C(r^1, q) - C(r^0, q) \leq (r^1 - r^0) \cdot z^0.$$

Also, starting from input price vector r^1, the change in minimized cost has the following upper bound:

$$C(r^0, q) - C(r^1, q) \leq (r^0 - r^1) \cdot z^1.$$

Combining these results,

$$(r^1 - r^0) \cdot z^1 \leq C(r^1, q) - C(r^0, q) \leq (r^1 - r^0) \cdot z^0. \qquad (4.2\text{-}2)$$

Suppose only the *i*th input price changes. Then (4.2-2) can be rewritten as follows

$$z_i(r^1, q) \leq \frac{C(r^1, q) - C(r^0, q)}{r_i^1 - r_i^0} \leq z_i(r^0, q).$$

Then if the input demand function $z(r, q)$ is continuous $\lim_{r^1 \to r^0} z(r^1, q) = z(r^0, q)$.

Therefore, in the limit the lower and upper bounds converge and so $\frac{\partial C}{\partial r_i} = z_i(r^0, q)$.

Output Effect of an Input Price Increase

With this simple result, we can gain insight into the response of a firm to an input price increase. The price-taking firm chooses output so that price equals marginal cost. It is tempting to believe that an increase in r_j will raise the marginal cost of producing each commodity. Thus, as depicted in Figure 4.2-1, the output of each commodity will fall. However, as we now demonstrate, this intuition is incorrect. We assume that $z(r, q) \in \mathbb{C}^1$. Then differentiating equation (4.2-1),

$$\frac{\partial^2 C}{\partial q_i \partial r_j} = \frac{\partial z_j}{\partial q_i}.$$

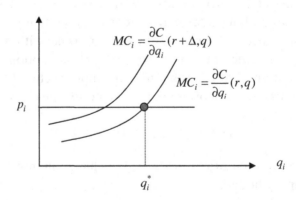

Figure 4.2-1. The normal case.

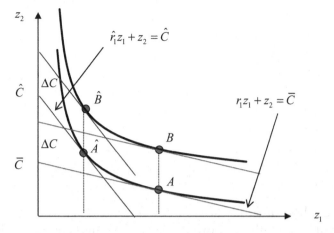

Figure 4.2-2. Isoquants are vertical translations.

The order of partial differentiation is immaterial. Moreover, $\partial C/\partial q_i$ is the marginal cost of producing commodity i. Thus,

$$\frac{\partial}{\partial r_j} MC_i = \frac{\partial}{\partial r_j} \frac{\partial C}{\partial q_i} = \frac{\partial}{\partial q_i} \frac{\partial C}{\partial r_j} = \frac{\partial z_j}{\partial q_i}. \qquad (4.2\text{-}3)$$

The partial derivative $\partial z_j/\partial q_i$ is the rate at which the jth input rises when the output of commodity i rises. If this rate is positive, the input is called a normal input. If not, the input is said to be an inferior input. We therefore have the following result.

Proposition 4.2-2: Effect of Input Price Change on Marginal Cost
A rise in the price of input j raises the marginal cost of commodity i if and only if z_j is a normal input.

It seems paradoxical that marginal cost could remain constant or decline with an increase in an input price. However this result is readily illustrated.[4] Consider the production function $q = F(z) = G(h(z_1) + z_2)$, where $h(\cdot)$ is an increasing concave function and $G(\cdot)$ is increasing. For such a production function, the marginal rate of technical substitution (*MRTS*) is

$$MRTS(z_1, z_2) = \frac{\partial F}{\partial z_1} \Big/ \frac{\partial F}{\partial z_2} = h'(z_1).$$

Note that the *MRTS* is independent of z_2 so that isoquants are vertical translations of one another as depicted in Figure 4.2-2.

Setting the price of input 2 equal to unity, the iso-cost line, $r_1 z_1 + z_2 = \overline{C}$ intersects the vertical axis at $\overline{C}$. With the price of input 1 equal to r_1, the

---

[4] See also Exercise 4.2-4.

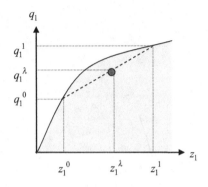

Figure 4.2-3. Convex production set.

lowest cost method of producing q units of output is given by the point A and the lowest cost method of producing $q + \Delta q$ units of output is given by the point B. The extra cost of the additional Δq units is thus the vertical distance $\Delta C = AB$.

Next suppose that the price of input 1 rises to $\hat{r}_1$ and that the new cost minimizing method of producing q units is the point $\hat{A}$. As depicted, the iso-quants are vertical translations. Therefore, the lowest cost method of pro-ducing $q + \Delta q$ units is the point $\hat{B}$, which is located directly above $\hat{A}$.

Moreover, because the isoquants are vertical translations, the distance $\hat{A}\hat{B}$ is equal to the distance AB. However $\hat{A}\hat{B}$ is the extra cost ΔC of producing the additional Δq units. Thus in this particular case a change in input price has no effect on marginal cost.

Convexity of the Production Set and Increasing Marginal Cost

Consider a firm that produces a single output using a single input. If the pro-duction set is convex, as depicted in Figure 4.2-3, the extra output produced using an additional unit of input declines with output. Thus, the marginal cost of producing an additional unit of output rises with output. The follow-ing proposition generalizes this result.

Proposition 4.2-3: Convex Costs
If the production set of a firm is convex, then the cost function of the firm is a convex function of outputs.

Proof: Let z^0 be cost minimizing given an input price vector r and output q^0. Also let z^1 be cost minimizing when the output vector is q^1. Given convexity of the production set, the production vector (z^λ, q^λ), $0 < \lambda < 1$ is feasible. Then the minimized cost of output vector q^λ satisfies

$$C(q^\lambda, r) \leq r \cdot z^\lambda. \tag{4.2-4}$$

By construction, $C(q^0, r) = r \cdot z^0$ and $C(q^1, r) = r \cdot z^1$. Therefore,

$$(1 - \lambda)C(q^0, r) + \lambda C(q^1, r) = (1 - \lambda)r \cdot z^0 + \lambda r \cdot z^1$$
$$= r \cdot ((1 - \lambda)z^0 + \lambda z^1) = r \cdot z^{\lambda}.$$

Substituting from (4.2-4) it follows that

$$C(q^{\lambda}, r) \le (1 - \lambda)C(q^0, r) + \lambda C(q^1, r), 0 < \lambda < 1. \qquad \square$$

First Laws of Firm Supply and Demand

We now extend the price-taking assumption to output prices. So far we have denoted the outputs of a firm as a positive vector q and the inputs as a positive vector z.

To simplify the mathematics we now switch to the alternative formulation in which a production plan is simply a vector $y^f = (y_1^f, \ldots, y_n^f)$. All the positive components of this plan are net outputs, and all the negative components are net inputs. The profit of a firm choosing the production vector y is

$$p \cdot y = \underbrace{\sum_{j,\, y_j \ge 0} p_j y_j}_{\text{revenue}} - \underbrace{\sum_{j,\, y_j < 0} p_j(-y_j)}_{\text{cost}}.$$

The firm chooses from among the set of possible plans or blueprints $\mathcal{Y}^f$. The profit-maximizing firm then chooses a plan $\bar{y}^f$ that solves the following problem:

$$\Pi(p) = \operatorname*{Max}_{y}\{p \cdot y \mid y \in \mathcal{Y}^f\}.$$

The maximized profit $\Pi(p)$ is known as the profit function. The following result also has its parallel in Section 2.3.

Proposition 4.2-4: Effect of Price Changes on Inputs and Outputs
Let p^0 and p^1 be two different price vectors and let y^0 and y^1 be profit maximizing production plans at these prices. Then $(p^1 - p^0) \cdot (y^1 - y^0) \ge 0$.

It follows immediately that if only the price of commodity j changes, then

$$\Delta p_j \Delta y_j \ge 0.$$

If the jth commodity is an output ($y_j > 0$), it follows that

$$\frac{\Delta y_j}{\Delta p_j} \ge 0. \text{ first law of supply}$$

If the jth commodity is an input ($y_j < 0$), then $-y_j$ is the number of inputs purchased and

$$\frac{-\Delta y_j}{\Delta p_j} \leq 0. \text{ first law of input demand}$$

Proof: The proof follows directly from the profit-maximization hypothesis. Because y^1 is profit maximizing at p^1,

$$\Pi(p^1) = p^1 \cdot y^1 \geq p^1 \cdot y, \quad \text{for all } y \in \mathcal{Y}^f. \tag{4.2-5}$$

In particular, this must be true for $y = y^0$. Hence,

$$p^1 \cdot (y^1 - y^0) \geq 0.$$

Also, because y^0 is profit maximizing at p^0,

$$\Pi(p^0) = p^0 \cdot y^0 \geq p^0 \cdot y, \quad \text{for all } y \in \mathcal{Y}^f.$$

Hence,

$$- p^0 \cdot (y^1 - y^0) = p^0 \cdot (y^0 - y^1) \geq 0. \tag{4.2-6}$$

Adding these inequalities,

$$(p^1 - p^0) \cdot (y^1 - y^0) \geq 0. \qquad \square$$

We actually have a stronger result. Let p^λ be a convex combination of the two price vectors. That is, $p^\lambda = (1 - \lambda)p^0 + \lambda p^1, 0 < \lambda < 1$. Also let y^* be profit maximizing at p^λ. From (4.2-5),

$$\Pi(p^1) \geq p^1 \cdot y^*. \quad \text{Hence } \lambda \Pi(p^1) \geq \lambda p^1 \cdot y^*.$$

From (4.2-6),

$$\Pi(p^0) \geq p^0 \cdot y^*. \quad \text{Hence } (1 - \lambda)\Pi(p^0) \geq (1 - \lambda)p^0 \cdot y^*.$$

Adding these inequalities yields

$$\lambda \Pi(p^1) + (1 - \lambda)\Pi(p^0) \geq ((1 - \lambda)p^0 + \lambda p^1) \cdot y^* = p^\lambda \cdot y^* = \Pi(p^\lambda).$$

We thus have the following result.

Proposition 4.2-5: Convexity of the Profit Function
$\Pi(p) \equiv \text{Max}_y\{p \cdot y | y \in \mathcal{Y}^f\}$ is a convex function.

Short-Run and Long-Run Adjustments to a Price Change

Suppose that a price-taking firm has a profit-maximizing production plan y^0 given the price vector p^0. Then the price of one of its inputs or outputs unexpectedly changes. A full analysis of the firm's response to this change

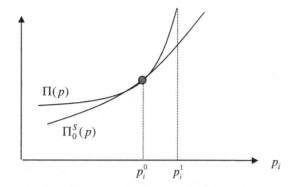

Figure 4.2-4. Short run versus long run.

would require a model of the dynamics of costly adjustment. As a first simple step toward such a model, we suppose that the firm is more limited in its feasible alternatives over the short run than over the long run.[5] Let $\mathcal{Y}$ be the set of feasible long-run plans. Starting from y^0 let $\mathcal{Y}^s(y^0)$ be those production plans that are feasible in the short run. Then $\mathcal{Y}^s(y^0) \subset \mathcal{Y}$.

Proposition 4.2-6: Le Chatelier Principle
Own price effects are larger in the long-run than in the short-run.

Proof: Let $\Pi(p)$ and $\Pi_0^S(p)$ be the long-run and short-run profit functions of the firm, starting from the long-run profit-maximizing plan at p^0. The additional short-run constraints bind more tightly so that for all price vectors $p \neq p^0$,

$$\Pi_0^S(p) < \Pi(p).$$

This is depicted in Figure 4.2-4 when it is the price of the ith commodity that changes.

Note that the additional short-run constraints bind only if the firm *changes* its production plan. Hence $\Pi_0^S(p^0) = \Pi(p^0)$. We further assume that the profit-maximizing production vector $y(p) \in \mathbb{C}^1$. Suppose that the price vector changes from p^0 to p^1. Because $y(p^0)$ is most profitable at the price vector p^0,

$$\Pi(p^1) - \Pi(p^0) = p^1 \cdot y(p^1) - p^0 \cdot y(p^0) \leq p^1 \cdot y(p^1) - p^0 \cdot y(p^1).$$

Similarly, because $y(p^1)$ is most profitable at the price vector p^1,

$$\Pi(p^1) - \Pi(p^0) = p^1 \cdot y(p^1) - p^0 \cdot y(p^0) \geq p^1 \cdot y(p^0) - p^0 \cdot y(p^0).$$

---

[5] This is a generalization of the traditional definition of the short run as a period over which some subset of the inputs is fixed.

Combining these results,

$$(p^1 - p^0) \cdot y(p^1) \geq \Pi(p^1) - \Pi(p^0) \geq (p^1 - p^0) \cdot y(p^0).$$

Suppose that only the ith price changes. Then

$$y_i(p^1) \geq \frac{\Pi(p^1) - \Pi(p^0)}{p_i^1 - p_i^0}) \geq y_i(p^0).$$

Taking the limit,

$$\frac{\partial \Pi}{\partial p_i} = y_i(p) \quad \text{and so} \quad \frac{\partial^2 \Pi}{\partial p_i^2} = \frac{\partial y_i}{\partial p_i}.$$

An identical argument for the short-run profit function establishes that

$$\frac{\partial \Pi_0^S}{\partial p_i} = y_i^S(p) \quad \text{and} \quad \frac{\partial^2 \Pi_0^S}{\partial p_i^2} = \frac{\partial y_i^S}{\partial p_i}.$$

Thus the two profit functions have the same slope at p^0. Because $\Pi(p) \geq \Pi_0^S(p)$ it follows that $\frac{\partial^2 \Pi}{\partial p_i^2}(p^0) \geq \frac{\partial^2 \Pi_0^S}{\partial p_i^2}(p^0)$ and hence $\frac{\partial y_i}{\partial p_i} \geq \frac{\partial y_i^S}{\partial p_i}$.   □

Exercises

Exercise 4.2-1: Cost Minimization

(a) Prove that the cost function is a concave function of the input price vector.
(b) Assuming that the cost-minimizing input vector $z^*(r, q)$ is continuously differentiable, show that $\partial z_i^*/\partial r_j = \partial z_j^*/\partial r_i$.

Exercise 4.2-2: Cost Function of a Cobb-Douglas Firm What is the cost function of a firm with a Cobb-Douglas production function?

Exercise 4.2-3: CES Production Function A firm has a production function $q = z_1^{\frac{1}{2}} + z_2^{\frac{1}{2}}$.

(a) Show that minimized cost is

$$C(r, q) = \frac{q^2}{\frac{1}{r_1} + \frac{1}{r_2}}.$$

(b) Solve for the cost function if the production function is instead $q = (z_1^{\frac{1}{2}} + z_2^{\frac{1}{2}})^2$.

Exercise 4.2-4: Quasi-Linear Production Function Output q is produced according to the following production function:

$$q = z_1 + 10\sqrt{z_2}.$$

(a) Show that for q sufficiently large

$$C(r, q) = r_1 q - 25r_1^2/r_2.$$

(b) Show that $C(r, q)$ is proportional to q^2 for sufficiently small q.
(c) Depict $C(r, q)$ for $q \geq 0$ in a neat figure.
(d) In a second figure depict marginal cost as a function of q for two different values of r_2.
(e) If the output is sold by a monopolist, describe the effect on output of an increase in r_2. Does it make a difference whether the profit-maximizing output q^* is large or small?

Exercise 4.2-5: Marginal Cost Independent of an Input Price Consider the production function $q = F(h(z_1) + z_2) \in C^2$ where $F(\cdot)$ is increasing, $h(\cdot)$ is an increasing concave function, $h'(0) = \infty$, and $h'(\infty) = 0$.

(a) Given an input price vector r, show that for large enough outputs, $z_2(r, q)$, the cost-minimizing level of z_2 must be strictly positive. Henceforth assume that $z_2(r, q) > 0$.
(b) Write down total cost as a function of $F^{-1}(q)$ and z_1. Hence show that the optimal input of commodity 1, $z_1(r, q)$ is independent of q.
(c) Show that marginal cost is independent of r_1.

Exercise 4.2-6: Properties of Firm Input Demand and Output Supply Let $z^*(r)$ be the profit-maximizing input vector for a monopolist producing outputs $(q_1, \ldots, q_m)$ using inputs $(z_1, \ldots, z_n)$. The firm is a price taker in input markets. Let r be the input price vector.

(a) Assume that $z^*(r)$ is continuously differentiable and show that the matrix $\left[\frac{\partial z_i}{\partial r_j} \right]$ is negative semi-definite.
(b) If the firm is also a price taker in output markets, what can be said about the $m \times m$ matrix $\left[\partial q_i^* / \partial p_j \right]$?

Exercise 4.2-7: Short Run versus Long Run Suppose a firm is a price taker in its inputs but has monopoly power in its output markets. Does the Le Chatelier Principle still hold for inputs?

4.3 Returns to Scale

Key ideas: global and local returns to scale, implications for average and marginal cost

In the previous section we examined the implications of price-taking behavior by firms. The plausibility of the price-taking hypothesis depends, to a great extent, on whether it is technologically advantageous for a firm to be

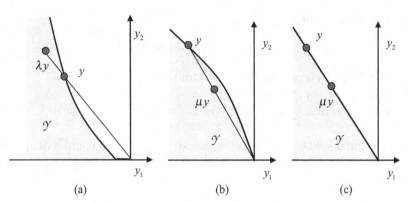

Figure 4.3-1. (a) Increasing returns to scale. (b) Decreasing returns to scale. (c) Constant returns to scale.

large. If, as a result of increasing inputs by some factor λ, outputs are scaled up by the same factor λ, then the technology exhibits constant returns to scale. If outputs are smaller than λ times the original output vector, then the technology exhibits decreasing returns to scale. If outputs exceed λ times the original output vector, then the technology exhibits increasing returns to scale. When there are decreasing returns to scale, it is hard for a large firm to compete with smaller firms, and so the number of firms in the market is likely to be relatively large. It is in such situations that a firm is most likely to lose much of its sales when it raises prices and hence the price-taking assumption is most plausible.

Definition: Returns to Scale[6] The production set $\mathcal{Y} \subset \mathbb{R}^n$ exhibits constant returns to scale if, for all $y \in \mathcal{Y}$, and any $\lambda > 0$, $\lambda y \in \mathcal{Y}$. The production set exhibits increasing returns to scale if, for any $y \in \mathcal{Y}$, such that $y_j \neq 0$, $j = 1, \ldots, n$ and any $\lambda > 1$, $\lambda y \in \text{int} \mathcal{Y}$. The production set exhibits decreasing returns to scale if, for any $y \in \mathcal{Y}$ such that $y_j \neq 0$, $j = 1, \ldots, n$ and any $\mu \in (0, 1)$, $\mu y \in \text{int} \mathcal{Y}$.

We begin by showing that this definition yields the familiar definitions for a firm producing a single output.

Increasing Returns to Scale Production Function

Consider a firm with a production function $F(\cdot)$. Suppose that the production set exhibits increasing returns to scale (IRS; see Figure 4.3-1a). With input vector z the maximum feasible output is $F(z)$. With input vector λz the maximum output is $F(\lambda z)$. From the definition of IRS, for any $\lambda > 1$ the input-output vector $(\lambda z, \lambda q) = (\lambda z, \lambda F(z))$ lies in the interior of the

---

[6] If $y \in \mathcal{Y}$ and y is not a boundary point, then y is called an interior point, and we write $y \in \text{int } \mathcal{Y}$.

production set. Thus, with the input λz the maximum output must be greater than $\lambda F(z)$. Therefore, for any $z > 0$,

$$\lambda > 1 \Rightarrow F(\lambda z) > \lambda F(z). \tag{4.3-1}$$

Decreasing Returns to Scale Production Function

If the production function exhibits decreasing returns to scale (DRS), then for any $\mu \in (0, 1)$, $(\mu z, \mu F(z))$ is in the interior of the production set (see Figure 4.3-1)b. Therefore, with the input μz the maximum output $F(\mu z)$ is greater. Thus

$$\mu \in (0, 1) \Rightarrow F(\mu z) > \mu F(z), \forall z > 0. \tag{4.3-2}$$

This holds for all $z > 0$. Hence, for any λ it holds for λz. That is,

$$\mu \in (0, 1) \Rightarrow F(\mu \lambda z) > \mu F(\lambda z), \lambda > 1.$$

Choose $\lambda > 1$ and $\mu = 1/\lambda$. Then $F(z) > \frac{1}{\lambda} F(\lambda z), \lambda > 1$.
Rearranging this inequality we have the standard definition for DRS.

$$\lambda > 1 \Rightarrow F(\lambda z) < \lambda F(z), \forall z > 0. \tag{4.3-3}$$

Constant Returns to Scale Production Function

If a firm exhibits constant returns to scale (CRS) any input-output vector can be scaled up or down. Therefore, as depicted in Figure 4.3-1c, any scaled version of a boundary point must also be a boundary point. To demonstrate this, consider a CRS firm with a production function $F(\cdot)$. With input vector z the maximum feasible output is $F(z)$. Because $(z, F(z))$ is feasible, the CRS assumption implies that $(\lambda z, \lambda F(z))$ is feasible. With input vector λz the maximum output is $F(\lambda z)$. Thus

$$F(\lambda z) \geq \lambda F(z).$$

Moreover, because $(\lambda z, F(\lambda z))$ is feasible the CRS assumption implies that $\frac{1}{\lambda}(\lambda z, F(\lambda z)) = (z, \frac{1}{\lambda} F(\lambda z))$ is also feasible. However, with input vector z, $F(z)$ is maximum output. Therefore

$$\frac{1}{\lambda} F(\lambda z) \leq F(z).$$

Combining the two inequalities it follows that

$$F(\lambda z) = \lambda F(z).$$

Remark: Suppose that the total supply of inputs to an industry is z and that the allocation to firm k is $z^k = \theta^k z$. If technology exhibits CRS and can be freely replicated, then

$$\sum_{k=1}^{n} F(z^k) = \sum_{k=1}^{n} F(\theta^k z) = \sum_{k=1}^{n} \theta^k F(z) = F(z).$$

It follows that any industry output $q = F(z)$ can be equally well produced by a single firm or many firms. As a result the number of firms is indeterminate.

We now consider some important properties of CRS production functions. We begin by showing that the gradient vector of the production function is constant along a ray.

Proposition 4.3-1:
Suppose F exhibits constant returns to scale and is differentiable for all $z \gg 0$. Then for all $z \gg 0$, $\frac{\partial F}{\partial z}(\lambda z) = \frac{\partial F}{\partial z}(z)$.

Proof: Given CRS, for any $\hat{z}$ and $\lambda > 0$, $F(\lambda \hat{z}) = \lambda F(\hat{z})$. Differentiating this equation by $\hat{z}_j$ we obtain

$$\lambda \frac{\partial F}{\partial z_j}(\lambda \hat{z}) = \lambda \frac{\partial F}{\partial z_j}(\hat{z}). \qquad \square$$

The following proposition is a restatement of results derived in Appendix B.[7]

Proposition 4.3-2: Constant Returns to Scale and Concavity
If the function F is strictly quasi-concave and exhibits CRS, then for any z^0, z^1 and $\lambda \in (0, 1)$

$$F((1 - \lambda)z^0 + \lambda z^1) \geq (1 - \lambda)F(z^0) + \lambda F(z^1).$$

Moreover, the inequality is strict unless z^0 and z^1 are linearly dependent.

Returns to Scale and the Scale Elasticity of Output

Define $q(\lambda) = F(\lambda z)$. Then the proportional increase in maximum output as the scale parameter rises from 1 to λ is

$$\frac{1}{q(1)} \frac{q(\lambda) - q(1)}{\lambda - 1} = \frac{1}{F(z)} \frac{F(\lambda z) - F(z)}{\lambda - 1}.$$

Taking the limit yields the scale elasticity of output

$$\mathcal{E}(q(\lambda), \lambda)\Big|_{\lambda=1} = \frac{\lambda}{F(z)} \frac{\partial}{\partial \lambda} F(\lambda z)\Big|_{\lambda=1}.$$

---

[7] See Proposition B.2-9 and Corollary B.2-10.

With DRS, it follows from inequalities (4.3-2) and (4.3-3), that for all $\lambda > 0$, $\lambda \neq 1$,

$$\frac{1}{F(z)} \frac{F(\lambda z) - F(z)}{\lambda - 1} < \frac{1}{F(z)} \frac{\lambda F(z) - F(z)}{\lambda - 1} = 1.$$

Taking the limit as $\lambda \to 1$ we obtain the following result

$$\text{DRS} \ \Rightarrow \ \mathcal{E}(F(\lambda z), \lambda)\big|_{\lambda=1} \leq 1.$$

A similar argument establishes that

$$\text{IRS} \ \Rightarrow \ \mathcal{E}(F(\lambda z), \lambda)\big|_{\lambda=1} \geq 1.$$

Local Returns to Scale

The assumption of (global) increasing or decreasing returns is a very strong one. Typically firms exhibit increasing returns at low output levels because of indivisibilities in entrepreneurial setup and monitoring costs. As output grows large, the costs of monitoring a large managerial work force and providing appropriate work incentives typically rise more rapidly than output. These cost increases can more than offset any purely technological advantages to greater scale.

It is therefore helpful to consider returns to scale locally. Local returns are increasing at the input vector z if a small proportional increase in z leads to a larger proportional increase in output. Local returns are decreasing if the proportional increase in inputs leads to a smaller proportional increase in output.

Because the point elasticity $\mathcal{E}(y, x) \equiv \frac{x}{y} \frac{\partial y}{\partial x}$, it follows that

$$\mathcal{E}(q(\lambda), \lambda) = \frac{\lambda}{F(\lambda z)} \frac{\partial}{\partial \lambda} F(\lambda z) = \frac{z \cdot \frac{\partial F}{\partial z}(\lambda z)}{F(\lambda z)}.$$

Hence the scale elasticity at z can be expressed as

$$\mathcal{E}(q(\lambda), \lambda)\big|_{\lambda=1} = \frac{z \cdot \frac{\partial F}{\partial z}(z)}{F(z)}, \quad \text{where } q(\lambda) \equiv F(\lambda z).$$

Definition: Local Returns to Scale If the production function $F(\cdot)$ has scale elasticity $\mathcal{E}(q(\lambda), \lambda)\big|_{\lambda=1} = z \cdot \frac{\partial F}{\partial z}/F(z)$, greater than 1 then $F(\cdot)$ exhibits increasing returns at z. If the scale elasticity is less than 1 then $F(\cdot)$ exhibits decreasing returns at z.

In the exercises that follow, you are asked to establish that if a production function exhibits local increasing returns to scale everywhere, it exhibits (global) increasing returns.

We next show that average cost exceeds marginal cost if and only if local returns are increasing.

Proposition 4.3-3: Average and Marginal Cost
If z is cost minimizing for output q, then

$$\frac{AC(q)}{MC(q)} = \frac{z \cdot \frac{\partial F}{\partial z}}{F(z)} = \mathcal{E}\left(q(\lambda), \lambda\right)\big|_{\lambda=1}. \qquad (4.3\text{-}4)$$

Proof: Given the input price vector r, the cost function is

$$C(q, r) = \underset{z}{\text{Min}}\{r \cdot z \,|\, q \leq F(z)\}.$$

Converting this to a maximization problem, the associated Lagrangian is

$$\mathcal{L} = -r \cdot z + \lambda(F(z) - q).$$

By the Envelope Theorem,

$$MC(q) = \frac{\partial C}{\partial q} = \lambda.$$

Moreover the necessary conditions for an interior maximum are

$$\frac{\partial \mathcal{L}}{\partial z_i} = -r_i + \lambda \frac{\partial F}{\partial z_i} \leq 0, \; i = 1, \ldots, n \text{ with equality if } z_i > 0.$$

Multiplying this inequality by $z_i \geq 0$, it follows that $-r_i z_i + \lambda z_i \frac{\partial F}{\partial z_i} = 0$.
  Then total cost is

$$C(q, r) = r \cdot z = \lambda z \cdot \frac{\partial F}{\partial z}. \qquad (4.3\text{-}5)$$

Thus the average cost of production is

$$AC(q) = \frac{C(q)}{q} = \lambda \frac{z \cdot \frac{\partial F}{\partial z}}{F(z)} = MC(q) \frac{z \cdot \frac{\partial F}{\partial z}}{F(z)}. \qquad \square$$

Note next that

$$MC(q) = \frac{\partial}{\partial q} C(q) = \frac{\partial}{\partial q}(q\,AC(q)) = AC(q) + q \frac{\partial AC}{\partial q}.$$

With local increasing returns, average cost is greater than marginal cost and therefore $AC(q)$ is a decreasing function of q. With local decreasing returns, on the other hand, $AC(q)$ is an increasing function of q.

Exercises

Exercise 4.3-1: Increasing Returns to Scale If the strictly increasing production function $F(\cdot)$ exhibits IRS show that for all $z \neq 0$ and $\mu \in (0, 1)$, $F(\mu z) < \mu F(z)$.

Exercise 4.3-2: Returns to Scale and Average Cost Prove that if a firm exhibits increasing/decreasing returns to scale then average cost must decrease/increase with output.

Exercise 4.3-3: Local and Global Returns to Scale

(a) Show that if a production function $F(z)$ exhibits local increasing returns to scale everywhere, then the scale elasticity $\mathcal{E}(F(\mu z), \mu) > 1$ for all z and all $\mu > 0$.
(b) Hence show that $\frac{\partial}{\partial \mu} \ln F(\mu z) > \frac{1}{\mu}$.
(c) Show that for any $\lambda > 1$,

$$\ln \frac{F(\lambda z)}{F(z)} = \int_1^\lambda \frac{\partial}{\partial \mu} \ln F(\mu z) d\mu.$$

Then appeal to part (b) to establish that the production function exhibits (global) IRS.

Exercise 4.3-4: Modified Cobb-Douglas Production Function The production function of a firm is defined implicitly as follows:

$$q = K^{\frac{\alpha}{q}} L^{\frac{\beta}{q}}, \alpha, \beta > 0.$$

(a) Given input prices (r, w), show that the cost-minimizing input demands satisfy

$$\frac{\alpha}{rK} = \frac{\beta}{wL} = \frac{\alpha + \beta}{C(q)}.$$

(b) Hence or otherwise obtain an expression for the firm's cost function.
(c) If $\alpha + \beta = 1$, show that the average cost function is U-shaped, with a minimum at $q = 1$.
(d) Does a change in an input price have any effect on the cost-minimizing output?

4.4 Firm and Industry Analysis

Key ideas: optimality of marginal cost pricing, equilibrium with free entry, scale of competitive firms

It is efficient for an agglomeration of inputs to be organized together in a firm if and only if there are gains to specialization in some part of the production process. If the gains to specialization persist as the firm grows, it is efficient to have all production within a single firm – a "natural monopoly." This

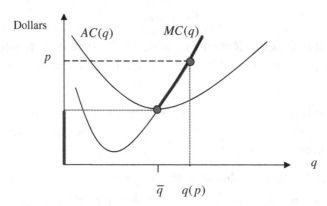

Figure 4.4-1. A firm's supply curve.

is considered in the next section. Here we consider an industry where the returns to specialization occur only at output levels that are small relative to the market. At higher output levels, large firms are less efficient, and thus we would expect to see competition between several or many small firms in such a market.

Consider a firm that produces a single output. The production function of the firm exhibits local increasing returns to scale (local IRS) at output levels below $\bar{q}$ and local decreasing returns to scale (local DRS) at higher output levels. Then the average and marginal cost curves must be as depicted in Figure 4.4-1. For $q < \bar{q}$, MC is less than AC and so AC is decreasing. For $q > \bar{q}$, MC is greater than AC and so AC is increasing.

Suppose that firm j is small enough relative to the market to make the assumption of price taking plausible. If the output price is strictly below the minimum average cost, the firm must lose money regardless of its level of production and therefore the profit-maximizing output is zero. If the price exceeds the minimum average cost, profit is maximized at the output $q_j(p)$ where marginal cost is equal to price. Thus for $p > AC(\bar{q})$, the marginal cost curve is the firm's supply curve.

The Social Optimum

Suppose there are n price-taking firms in an industry. Let $p(Q)$ be the market demand price function. The aggregate supply at the equilibrium price p must equal aggregate demand. Moreover, for each firm, marginal cost is equal to price. Thus,

$$p(Q) = MC_j(q_j), \ j = 1, \ldots, n, \ \text{where} \quad Q = \sum_{j=1}^{n} q_j. \qquad (4.4\text{-}1)$$

Define $C(Q)$ to be the minimized cost of producing the aggregate output Q. That is,

$$C(Q) = \underset{q}{\text{Min}} \left\{ \sum_{j=1}^{n} C_j(q_j) \mid \sum_{j=1}^{n} q_j \geq Q \right\}.$$

For all firms that produce a positive output, the first-order condition for minimizing the industry cost of production is

$$MC_j(q_j) = \lambda(Q), \quad \text{where} \quad Q = \sum_{j=1}^{n} q_j.$$

Note that this is exactly the same condition as for each of the n price-taking firms. It follows that, given our price taking assumption, total industry cost is minimized. Hence for any aggregate output Q, the industry cost is the aggregate cost function $C(Q)$.

For any industry supply $\hat{Q}$ the demand price $p(\hat{Q})$ is the market-clearing price. Therefore it is the marginal willingness to pay or "marginal social benefit."

Next define $B(\hat{Q})$ to be the area under the market demand curve. That is,

$$B(\hat{Q}) = \int_{0}^{\hat{Q}} p(q)dq.$$

This integral of marginal social benefit is the total social benefit.[8]

We can also write total cost as the integral of the industry marginal cost:

$$C(\hat{Q}) = \int_{0}^{\hat{Q}} MC(q)dq.$$

Social surplus is then

$$S(\hat{Q}) = B(\hat{Q}) - C(\hat{Q}) = \int_{0}^{\hat{Q}} [p(q) - MC(q)]dq.$$

Social surplus is the area between the industry demand curve and the industry marginal cost curve. This is the dotted area depicted in Figure 4.4-2.

---

[8] See Chapter 2 for a discussion of the limitations of this measure of social benefit.

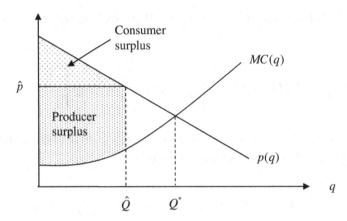

Figure 4.4-2. Social surplus.

For an output of $\hat{Q}$, demand equals supply at the price $\hat{p} = p(\hat{Q})$. It is sometimes helpful to divide the social surplus into the gains to consumers and the gains to firms:

$$S = \underbrace{B(\hat{Q}) - \hat{p}\hat{Q}}_{\text{consumer surplus}} + \underbrace{\hat{p}\hat{Q} - C(\hat{Q})}_{\text{producer surplus}}.$$

Consumer surplus is the lightly dotted region between the demand price function and the market-clearing price line. Producer surplus is the heavily dotted region between the industry marginal cost curve and the market-clearing price line.

From Figure 4.4-2, social surplus is maximized by choosing an industry output Q^* such that $p(Q^*) = MC(Q^*)$. Thus, marginal cost pricing is socially optimal.

Industry Supply with Free Entry

We now apply our methods of analysis to an industry consisting of a large number of identical firms with free entry and exit. Suppose that each firm produces a single product and that marginal cost rises with output. Furthermore, assume that there are fixed costs of production. Marginal and average costs are then as depicted in Figure 4.4-3.

With the price of output equal to p^o, each firm maximizes profit by choosing output q^o such that price equals marginal cost. As depicted, $AC(q^0) < p^o$ and thus there is an incentive for additional firms to enter the market. Entry then increases aggregate supply and so the market-clearing price must fall. Because this argument holds for any price above $\overline{p}$, industry equilibrium is

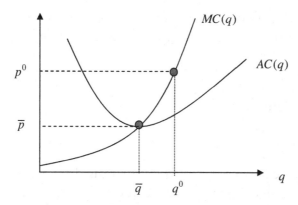

Figure 4.4-3. AC and MC.

only reached when the price is $\bar{p}$. In the long run, the industry supply curve is therefore a horizontal line.[9]

We now explore how a change in an input price affects the equilibrium output price. Suppose that the cost share of input j is k_j. A naïve answer might go as follows. A 1 percent increase in the cost of input j has a 1 percent effect on the cost of the input. Because input j's cost share is only a fraction k_j of the total input cost, the latter will rise by k_j per cent. Yet, if total cost rises by k_j percent then average cost will rise by k_j percent. In a competitive industry with free entry $p = AC$ and thus the equilibrium price must also rise by k_j percent.

This argument is clearly incomplete in that it ignores both the substitution effect on input as an input price rises and the change in the average cost-minimizing output. Despite this, the answer is correct!

Proposition 4.4-1:
In an industry with free entry of identical firms, the elasticity of the equilibrium output price with respect to an input price change is equal to the input cost share.

Proof: Given the assumption of free entry of identical firms the equilibrium output price is equal to the minimum average cost. Appealing to the Envelope Theorem, $\frac{\partial C}{\partial r_j}(q,r) = z_j$. Hence, $\frac{\partial}{\partial r_j}AC(q,r) = \frac{z_j}{q}$ and so the elasticity of average cost is

$$\mathcal{E}(AC, r_j) \equiv \frac{r_j}{AC}\frac{\partial}{\partial r_j}AC(q,r) = \frac{r_j z_j}{qAC} = \frac{r_j z_j}{C(q,r)} = \frac{r_j z_j}{r \cdot z}.$$

Thus, holding output constant, $\mathcal{E}(AC(q,r), r_j) = \frac{r_j z_j}{r \cdot z}$. As we will see later, the average cost-minimizing output may rise or fall when an input price

[9] This is not quite true. With m firms in the market each may be profitable, whereas with $m + 1$ firms the market-clearing price may drop below the minimum average cost. Then, the equilibrium number of firms is m and equilibrium profit is small but positive. However, unless m is small the statement is a useful practical approximation.

changes. However, at the point of minimum average cost $\overline{q}(r)$, $\frac{\partial}{\partial q} AC(q, r) = 0$. Recalling that the equilibrium price is equal to minimized average cost,

$$dp = dAC(\overline{q}(r), r_j) = \frac{\partial}{\partial q} AC(\overline{q}, r)d\overline{q} + \frac{\partial}{\partial r_j} AC(\overline{q}, r)dr_j = \frac{\partial}{\partial r_j} AC(\overline{q}, r)dr_j.$$

Converting this into an elasticity,

$$\mathcal{E}(p, r_j) = \frac{r_j}{p}\frac{\partial p}{\partial r_j} = \frac{r_j}{p}\frac{\partial AC}{\partial r_j} = \mathcal{E}(AC, r_j), \quad \text{since } p = AC. \qquad \square$$

Why is the naive answer correct? First, as argued in Section 4.2, the substitution effect on input demand is a second-order effect because competitive firms are cost minimizers. (This is the Envelope Theorem at work.) Second, although it is true that the cost-minimizing output changes, equilibrium output is where average cost is minimized and is therefore where the slope of the AC curve is zero. Thus, the change in output has only a second-order effect on minimized average cost.

An input price increase results in an output price increase and so leads to a reduction in aggregate output. Yet what happens to the output of the firms remaining in the industry? An instinctive guess would probably be that each firm would cut output as well. However, the new equilibrium output is at the intersection of the MC and AC curves. Thus, output of a surviving firm falls if and only if MC cost rises more than AC when the input price rises. We have seen that there are cases when MC is not affected by an input price change; then MC lies below AC cost at the initial output level and, with a price increase, output must rise until MC and AC are equated. Figure 4.4-4 depicts the case in which both MC and AC rise but the former rises less, so again output of the surviving firms must rise.

We conclude by providing the necessary and sufficient conditions for the output of surviving firms to rise.

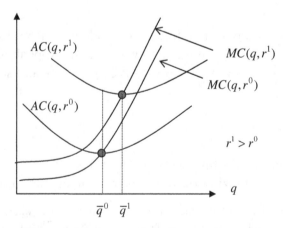

Figure 4.4-4. Input price effect on firm scale.

Proposition 4.4-2: Scale of Competitive Firms

If all firms have the same technology, an increase in the price of an input increases the output of firms remaining in a competitive industry (with free entry) if and only if the output elasticity of the demand for the input is less than unity.

Proof: From Section 4.2 we know that $(i) \frac{\partial C}{\partial r_j} = z_j$ and $(ii) \frac{\partial}{\partial r_j} MC = \frac{\partial}{\partial r_j} \frac{\partial C}{\partial q} = \frac{\partial z_j}{\partial q}$. Because $AC = C/q$, it follows that $(iii) \frac{\partial}{\partial r_j} AC = \frac{z_j}{q}$. Combining (ii) and (iii),

$$\frac{\partial}{\partial r_j} MC = \mathcal{E}(z_j, q) \frac{\partial}{\partial r_j} AC.$$

Suppose that at the initial lower input prices, the average cost-minimizing output is $\overline{q}^0$. At this output, average and marginal costs are equal. Suppose also that $\mathcal{E}(z_j, q) < 1$. Then, holding output constant, MC rises less than AC when an input price rises. Then $AC(\overline{q}^0, r^1) > MC(\overline{q}^0, r^1)$ and so AC is declining at $\overline{q}^0$. Then the new AC-minimizing output $\overline{q}^1$ exceeds $\overline{q}^0$.

□

Exercises

Exercise 4.4-1: The Social Optimum Firm j has a cost function $C_j(q_j) j = 1, \ldots, n$. The demand price function is $p(Q)$.

(a) Write down the social surplus optimization problem. Then form the Lagrangian and hence obtain the first-order conditions.

(b) Show that for the social optimum,

$$\frac{dB}{dQ} \leq MC_j(q_j) j = 1, \ldots, n \text{ with equality if } q_j > 0.$$

(c) Hence establish the optimality of the marginal cost pricing rule.

Exercise 4.4-2: Marginal Cost Pricing with Many Commodities A consumer has utility function $U(q, x, x_0) = B(q_1, q_2) + F(x) + x_0$. Let $p = (p_1, p_2)$ be the price vector for q and let r be the price vector for $x = (x_1, \ldots, x_n)$. Normalize so that the price of x_0 is 1. Assume throughout that income I is large enough for demand for this commodity, $x_0(p, r, I)$ to be strictly positive.

(a) Show that demand for all the other commodities is independent of income.
    Assume, henceforth, that for all p above some upper bound $\overline{p}$, $q(p) = 0$.

(b) Explain why indirect utility is

$$V(p, r, I) = B(q(p)) + f(x(r)) + x_0(p, r, I), \ p < \overline{p}$$

and

$$V(p, r, I) = f(x(r)) + x_0(p, r, I), \ p \geq \overline{p}.$$

(c) Hence explain why the gain in utility from a price $p < \bar{p}$ can be written as follows:

$$\Delta V = \int_0^{q_1(p)} \frac{\partial B}{\partial q_1}(q_1, 0)dq_1 + \int_0^{q_2(p)} \frac{\partial B}{\partial q_2}(q_1(p), q_2)dq_1.$$

(d) Let $p_i(q), i = 1, 2$ be the demand price functions. Appeal to the FOC to show that

$$\Delta V = \int_0^{q_1(p)} p_1(q_1, 0)dq_1 + \int_0^{q_2(p)} p_2(q_1(p), q_2)dq_1.$$

Exercise 4.4-3: Scale of Competitive Firms There is free entry into an industry of firms with the same U-shaped AC curve.

(a) Show that for each firm $MC = \sum_{j=1}^n \frac{r_j z_j}{q} \mathcal{E}(z_j, q)$. Hence show that, at the average cost-minimizing output,

$$1 = \sum_{j=1}^n k_j \mathcal{E}(z_j, q), \quad \text{where } k_j = \frac{r_j z_j}{r \cdot z}.$$

(b) Hence in the two-input case show that if

$$\mathcal{E}(z_2, q) > \mathcal{E}(z_1, q), \quad \text{then} \quad \mathcal{E}(z_2, q) > 1 > \mathcal{E}(z_1, q).$$

(c) A firm has production function $F(z) = (z_1 - a)^\alpha z_2^\beta, z_1 \geq a > 0, z_2 \geq 0$. The input price vector is r. Show that along the output expansion path $r_2 z_2 = \frac{\beta}{\alpha}(r_1 z_1 - ar_1)$. Hence show that along the output expansion path, $\mathcal{E}(z_2, q) > 1 > \mathcal{E}(z_1, q)$.

(d) Hence show that the scale of the active firms will rise if one of the input prices rises and the scale will fall if the other rises.

4.5 Monopoly Pricing

Key ideas: natural monopoly, price discrimination, indirect price discrimination

If there are enough firms in a market, the influence of any one firm's decisions on the market equilibrium price is small. Thus, the price-taking assumption of the Walrasian equilibrium is a good first approximation. If AC rises with output, a small firm is more efficient than a large firm, and so monopolization of a market is impossible (without government regulation or collusion). Conversely, if average cost decreases with higher output, a firm can cut prices to the point where the profit of any smaller competitor is negative. Thus, if increasing returns are in effect up to market output levels, then monopoly is natural.

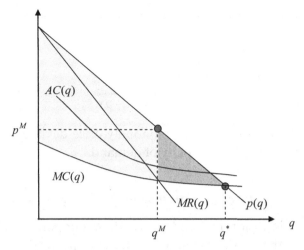

Figure 4.5-1. Social optimum with decreasing AC.

From a cost perspective, production by a natural monopoly is efficient. To maximize profit, the monopoly minimizes its costs, and given increasing returns to scale, these costs are lower than the costs of producing the same level of output by two or more firms. However, on the demand side, the monopolist is not a price taker; as it increases its output the market-clearing price falls. Thus, the marginal revenue from an output increase is less than the market price.

The profit-maximizing firm equates MR and MC. As we have seen, social surplus is maximized if the demand price (marginal social benefit) and marginal cost are equated. Thus, the profit-maximizing monopolist reduces social surplus by undersupplying the market.

The social optimum and the monopoly outcome are depicted in Figure 4.5-1. The social benefit from producing q units is the area under the demand price function. The total cost is the area under the marginal cost function. Thus, the social surplus is

$$S(q^M) = B(q^M) - C(q^M) = \int_0^{q^M} p(q)dq - \int_0^{q^M} MC(q)dq.$$

This is the lightly shaded region in the figure. The social cost of a monopoly is the extra surplus generated by increasing to q^* and is represented by the more heavily shaded area.

Note that

$$MR(q) = \frac{d}{dq}(p(q)q) = p(q) + q\frac{dp}{dq} = p(q)\left(1 + \frac{q}{p}\frac{dp}{dq}\right)$$
$$= p(q)\left(1 + \frac{1}{\varepsilon(q,p)}\right),$$

where $\mathcal{E}(q, p)$ is the price elasticity of demand. Hence, the profit-maximizing price is

$$p(q) = \frac{MC(q)}{1 + \dfrac{1}{\mathcal{E}(q, p)}}.$$

Therefore the degree to which the monopoly price deviates from marginal cost depends on the market elasticity of demand.[10]

Price Discrimination by Group

Implicit in this discussion is the idea that the monopolist can charge only a single price. If the cost of reselling by market intermediaries is low, this is a reasonable assumption. However, for many commodities, the cost of resale is significant, and a monopolist can charge different prices to different groups of customers.[11] Shipping costs are one example of a barrier to resale. If a firm locates outlets in two disparate locations and shipping costs by consumers (or middlemen) are sufficiently high, a monopoly firm can charge different prices in each location. Let $p_i(q_i)$ be the demand price function for group i. If there are n groups, the monopoly chooses output for each group to solve

$$\underset{q}{\text{Max}} \left\{ \sum_{i=1}^{n} p_i(q_i)q_i - C(q_1 + \cdots + q_n) \right\}.$$

From the first-order conditions,

$$MR_i = p_i \left(1 + \frac{1}{\mathcal{E}_i(q_i, p_i)} \right) = MC.$$

Hence

$$p_i = \frac{MC}{1 + \dfrac{1}{\mathcal{E}_i(q_i, p_i)}}.$$

Thus, the more negative is the price elasticity of group i, the lower is the price set by the monopoly.

---

[10] Obviously this condition fails if the elasticity of demand lies between 0 and −1. However, in this case higher prices increase revenue so a monopolist always increases price until the elasticity of demand, $\mathcal{E}(q, p)$, is less than −1.

[11] Seniors and students are offered price "discounts" on all sorts of commodities. Certainly seniors can buy any number of cheap movie tickets, but they and their companions must present plausible IDs at the entrance to prove that they all qualify.

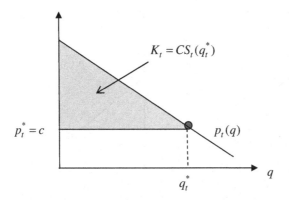

Figure 4.5-2. Extracting all the surplus.

Price Discrimination by Buyer Type

In the previous discussion, price discrimination is possible because of sufficiently high resale costs between groups. The implicit assumption is that resale is easy within groups. A buyer who is offered the low price can go on the Internet and cheaply resell to those who are precluded from direct purchase at the low price.

However, for many commodities, the cost of resale is high between all pairs of consumers. Commodities that are flows of services (such as electricity, phone services, or satellite TV) are particularly difficult to resell. In such cases a monopoly has a much more powerful incentive to price discriminate, because it can personalize both the services offered and the fees that it charges to each consumer. Let $p_t(q)$ be the demand price function for the t th type of consumer. For simplicity, suppose that the marginal cost of production is a constant, c. Then social surplus is maximized at output q_t^* where price $p_t(q_t^*) = c$ as depicted in Figure 4.5-2.

The very best that the monopoly can do is to extract the entire buyer surplus. This is the shaded region in the figure. Consider the following two-part pricing plan. Each type t buyer is charged both a use fee equal to p_t and an access fee K_t. The total cost of purchasing q units is then $K_t + p_t q$. If the monopoly charges a use fee equal to marginal cost, it induces the efficient output q_t^*. Then, by charging an access fee equal to the total buyer surplus, the monopoly profit is equal to the maximized total surplus.

Indirect Price Discrimination (Two-Part Pricing)

The previous argument is rather extreme for two reasons. First, governments often legislate against pricing policies that discriminate by personal characteristics. Second, even if the monopoly knows that there are "big buyers" and "little buyers" in its market, it may not be easy to identify them in

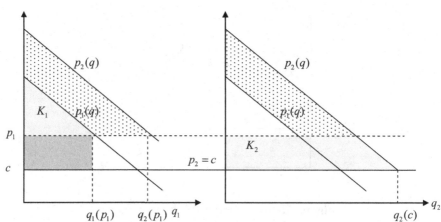

Figure 4.5-3. Price discrimination by type.

advance. Despite these barriers, a monopoly still has a powerful incentive to price discriminate. Instead of offering a single plan to each customer type, it is profitable to offer multiple plans and let each consumer choose between them. Intuitively, by carefully designing the different plans, the monopoly can give each consumer type an incentive to choose the plan designed for it.

Consider the simplest case of two consumer types: low demanders (type 1) and high demanders (type 2). Suppose that the monopolist offers a plan with a use fee p_1 intended for type 1 buyers. Consider the left-hand diagram in Figure 4.5-3. If both types of buyer choose plan 1 their demands are $q_1(p_1)$ and $q_2(p_1)$. The consumer surplus for the low demanders is the lightly shaded area. For the high demanders it is the sum of the lightly shaded and dotted areas. The entire surplus for the low demanders, $S_1(p_1)$ can be extracted by charging an access fee K_1 equal to the lightly shaded area.

The total profit on each type 1 consumer is the sum of the access fee and the profits made from the use fee $(p_1 - c)q_1(p_1)$, that is,

$$\Pi_1(p_1) = S_1(p_1) = CS_1(p_1) + (p_1 - c)q_1(p_1).$$

This is the sum of the heavily and lightly shaded regions.

Suppose then that the monopoly offers this access and use fee so that the total payment for q units is $K_1 + p_1 q$. A type 2 (high) demander who was to select this plan would purchase $q_2(p_1)$ units. Type 2's consumer surplus is then the sum of the lightly shaded and dotted regions in the left-hand diagram. Because all customers pay an access fee K_1 on this plan, each high-demand consumer has a net payoff equal to the dotted area.

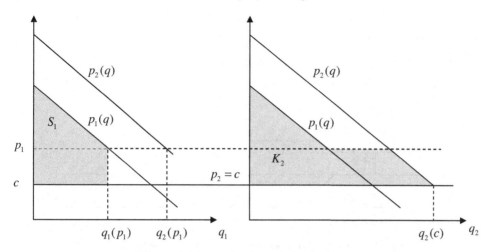

Figure 4.5-4. Profit on each buyer type.

These observations are crucial. Whereas the monopolist is able to extract all of the social surplus from low demanders, it cannot do so for high demanders because they have the option of switching to the low plan. The dotted area in the left-hand diagram is therefore an upper bound on the consumer surplus that the monopoly can extract from high demanders.

In the right-hand diagram of Figure 4.5-3, the maximum possible gain to buyer and seller is the sum of the shaded and dotted regions (maximized social surplus). The monopoly induces a purchase by each high demander equal to $q_2(c)$ by setting the use fee in plan 2 equal to marginal cost. Each high demander is better off switching to plan 1 unless offered a net gain at least equal to the dotted area. Thus, profit is maximized by choosing an access fee K_2 that extracts all the rest of the consumer surplus (the shaded region in the right-hand diagram). Because the use fee is equal to marginal cost, the shaded region is also the profit made by the firm from each high demander. The total profit made on each buyer type is therefore the sum of the shaded regions depicted in Figure 4.5-4.

This leaves open the question of what use fee, p_1, to set in the first plan. Suppose that p_1 is raised to $\hat{p}_1$ as shown in Figure 4.5-5.

At the new higher price, the reduction in low demander total surplus and hence the reduction in profit from low demanders, ΔS_1, is the heavily shaded region in the left diagram. The unshaded region in the right diagram is the surplus to high demanders if they switch to plan 1. Comparing this with the dotted region of the right diagram in Figure 4.5-4, the surplus associated with switching has been reduced by the heavily shaded region. Thus, the monopoly can increase its access fee in plan 2 by this heavily shaded region

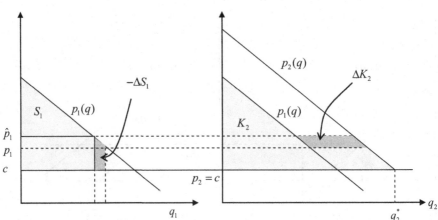

Figure 4.5-5. Choosing the use fee for plan 1.

without giving the high demanders an incentive to switch to plan 1. Thus the increase in profit from high demanders is ΔK_2.

Note that when p_1 is close to c, the heavily shaded region in the left diagram is small relative to the heavily shaded region in the right diagram. Thus when p_1 is raised, the loss in profit ΔS_1, from each low demander is small relative to the gain in profit ΔK_2, from each high demander. Therefore, regardless of the number of buyers of each type, the monopoly is better off setting the plan 1 price, p_1, higher than c. Just as with simple monopoly pricing, indirect price discrimination is inefficient in that it undersupplies the low demanders.

As we see in the discussion of "mechanism design" in Chapter 11, this is a general principle. The basic idea is that to extract more consumer surplus from the high demanders, the monopoly makes the alternative option (plan 1) less attractive. It does so by raising the price offered on plan 1. The larger the proportion of high demanders, the greater the incentive to extract surplus from them and thus the higher is the price offered on plan 1. Moreover, if the ratio of high to low demanders is sufficiently high, the low demanders are squeezed from the market completely.

Example: Linear Demands
Suppose that $p_i(q) = a_i - q, i = 1, 2$, and that the fraction of type i buyers is f_i. Because the slope of the demand price functions is -1, $\Delta q_1 = -\Delta p_1$, $\Delta S_1 = (p_1 - c)\Delta q_1 = -(p_1 - c)\Delta p_1$. Moreover, for any p_1, the difference in demand by the two types of buyer if they both choose plan 1 is $a_2 - a_1$. Thus, $\Delta K_2 = (a_2 - a_1)\Delta p_1$. The total change in profit is therefore

$$\Delta \Pi = f_1(\Delta S_1) + f_2 \Delta K_2 = [-f_1(p_1 - c) + f_2(a_2 - a_1)]\Delta p_1.$$

Dividing both sides by Δp_1 and taking the limit,

$$\frac{d\Pi}{dp_1} = -f_1(p_1 - c) + f_2(a_2 - a_1) = f_1\left(c + \frac{f_2}{f_1}(a_2 - a_1) - p_1\right).$$

Case (i) $c + \frac{f_2}{f_1}(a_2 - a_1) \le a_1$. Setting $\frac{d\Pi}{dp_1} = 0$, yields the optimal price

$$p_1^* = c + \frac{f_2}{f_1}(a_2 - a_1).$$

Case (ii) $c + \frac{f_2}{f_1}(a_2 - a_1) > a_1$. Then $\frac{d\Pi}{dp_1} > 0$, $p_1 \le a_1$ and thus the profit-maximizing price drives low demanders out of the market. The monopolist then extracts the entire surplus from type 2 buyers by setting a price $p_1 \ge a_2$. This is equivalent to dropping plan 1 and only offering plan 2.

Exercises

Exercise 4.5-1: Price Discrimination by Region In region 1 the market demand price function is $p_1 = a_1 - q$ whereas in region 2 it is $p_2 = a_2 - q$, where $a_2 > a_1$. There are equal numbers in each region. The unit cost of production is c.

(a) Solve for the profit-maximizing prices if firms can price discriminate across regions.
(b) Suppose such price discrimination is impossible. Compare the profit-maximizing price with the prices in part (a) if a_1 and a_2 are sufficiently close for it to be optimal to sell to both regions. Show also that if a_2 is sufficiently large relative to a_1, region 1 buyers are priced out of the market completely. Is there a discontinuity in the profit-maximizing price function $p^*(a_2)$?

Exercise 4.5-2: Indirect Price Discrimination There are two types of buyers. Each type 1 buyer has a low demand price function $p_1 = a_1 - q$, whereas each type 2 buyer has a high demand price function $p_2 = a_2 - q$. The number of type t buyers is n_t. The unit cost of production is c.

(a) Explain why, if it is most profitable to sell only to the high demanders, the profit-maximizing two-part pricing plan is $(p_2, F_2) = (c, \frac{1}{2}(a_2 - c)^2)$.
(b) Alternatively, the monopolist offers two plans and serves both types (so $p_1 < a_1$). Show that the gain to a type 1 buyer who purchases plan 1 is $U_1 = \frac{1}{2}(a_1 - p_1)^2 - F_1$.
(c) Hence show that if the monopoly extracts the entire surplus from type 1 buyers, the access fee is $\frac{1}{2}(a_1 - p_1)^2$ and so the profit from a type 1 buyer is $(p_1 - c)(a_1 - p_1) + \frac{1}{2}(a_1 - p_1)^2$. Show also that with this access fee, type 2 buyers have a gain of $U_{21} = (a_2 - a_1)(a_1 + a_2 - 2p_1)$ if they choose plan 1.
(d) Explain why the maximum profit that the monopoly can extract from type 2 is $\frac{1}{2}(a_2 - c)^2 - \frac{1}{2}(a_2 - a_1)(a_1 + a_2 - 2p_1)$.

(e) Appeal to your answers to (c) and (d) to obtain an expression for the total profit. Then solve for the profit-maximizing price p_1.

(f) Confirm that as the number of type 2 buyers increases, the plan 1 use fee rises.

References and Selected Historical Reading

Debreu, G. (1959). *Theory of Value*. Cowles Foundation Monograph. New York: John Wiley & Sons.

Marshall, A. (1920). *Principles of Economics*. New York: Macmillan.

5

General Equilibrium

5.1 The Robinson Crusoe Economy

Key ideas: Walrasian equilibrium allocation, optimal allocation, invisible hand at work

In Chapter 3 we studied equilibrium and efficiency in exchange economies. In this chapter we add firms to the economy and show how the welfare theorems generalize. In this introductory section we consider the simplest such economy – the one-person economy. To introduce trade, we assume that the single individual Robinson Crusoe is schizophrenic, making his decisions as a manager and a consumer separately. His decisions are guided by market prices. In Section 5.2 we examine a general equilibrium model with production and extend the two welfare theorems.

The power of the first theorem hinges critically on the assumption that a Walrasian equilibrium exists. This is addressed in Section 5.3. In the basic model all goods are private. In Sections 5.4 and 5.5 we show how the basic model can be extended to incorporate multiple time periods and public goods.

Although the two welfare theorems are both elegant and fundamental, they yield little insight into how underlying tastes and technology affect prices. For this we need to look at much simpler general equilibrium models. We illustrate this approach in Section 5.6 where we examine a two-commodity model with constant returns to scale.

As a first example, we consider an economy in which there are two commodities and each consumer has the same homothetic utility function $U(x^h), h = 1, \ldots, H$. Commodity 1 is consumption of hours (leisure time) and commodity 2 is corn. Each consumer has an endowment of hours and corn. Consumers must decide how many hours to consume and how many hours to sell in the labor market. From the discussion of consumers in Chapter 2, we know that with identical homothetic preferences market demand is

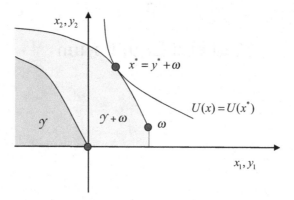

Figure 5.1-1. The optimum.

equal to the demand of a single consumer who holds the aggregate endowment $\omega = \sum_{h=1}^{H} \omega^h$. We call this representative agent Robinson Crusoe. There is a single firm in the economy and it has a convex production set $\mathcal{Y}$. Commodity 1 is an input in the production of commodity 2. Thus, as depicted in Figure 5.1-1, y_1 is negative and y_2 is positive.

At any point in time, Robinson Crusoe wears only one hat. As Robinson he wears his manager hat, deciding how much output to produce. As Crusoe he wears his consumer hat, deciding how many hours to work and how much of commodity 2 to consume, given his endowment and the dividends of the firm. Market prices then guide his consumption and production choices.

The Optimum

If Robinson Crusoe, with endowment vector ω, chooses the production plan y, his consumption vector of leisure and corn is $x = y + \omega$. The set of feasible consumption bundles is therefore the set $\mathcal{Y} + \omega$. This set is also depicted in Figure 5.1-1. Robinson Crusoe then chooses the consumption bundle x^* that maximizes his utility from the bundles in the set $\mathcal{Y} + \omega$. Formally, x^* solves the following maximization problem:

$$\text{Max}_{x}\{U(x)|x \in \mathcal{Y} + \omega\}.$$

Example:

$$\mathcal{Y} = \left\{(y_1, y_2)|y_1 \leq 0, \ y_2^2 + y_1 \leq 0\right\}, \quad U(x) = \ln x_1 + \ln x_2, \quad \omega = (144, 3).$$

We substitute for $x = y + \omega$ and write utility as $U(y + \omega) = \ln(\omega_1 + y_1) + \ln(\omega_2 + y_2)$. Because utility is increasing, the optimum must be on the boundary of the production set so that $y_1 = -y_2^2$. Substituting for ω and y_1, $U = \ln(144 - y_2^2) + \ln(3 + y_2)$.

FOC:

$$\frac{dU}{dy_2} = \frac{-2y_2}{144 - y_2^2} + \frac{1}{3 + y_2} = \frac{144 - 6y_2 - 3y_2^2}{(144 - y_2^2)(3 + y_2)} = \frac{3(6 - y_2)(8 + y_2)}{(144 - y_2^2)(3 + y_2)} = 0$$

Note that the slope is positive for $y_2 < 6$ and negative for $y_2 > 6$. Thus U takes on its maximum at $y_2 = 6$. Hence, $y^* = (-36, 6)$ and $x^* = y^* + \omega = (108, 9)$.

Walrasian Equilibrium

Robinson the Price-Taking Manager

Let us now consider what Robinson would do as a price-taking manager of the firm. Given the price vector p the profit of the firm is then $p \cdot y$. The profit is distributed to shareholders in proportion to their ownership shares. The larger the dividend, the better off are all the shareholders, so the owners' interests are best served if profit is maximized.

Robinson then chooses a production plan $y(p)$ such that

$$\Pi(p) = p \cdot y(p) = \underset{y}{\text{Max}}\{p \cdot y | y \in \mathcal{Y}^f\}.$$

The profit-maximizing production plan $y(p)$ is depicted in Figure 5.1-2.

Example (continued):
Robinson the manager solves the following maximization problem: $\underset{y}{\text{Max}}\{p \cdot y | y \in \mathcal{Y}\}$, that is,

$$\underset{y}{\text{Max}}\{p \cdot y | y_1 \leq 0, \; y_1 + (y_2)^2 \leq 0\}.$$

For an optimum the constraint must be binding. Then substituting for y_1, profit is

$$\pi(y_2) = -p_1(y_2)^2 + p_2 y_2.$$

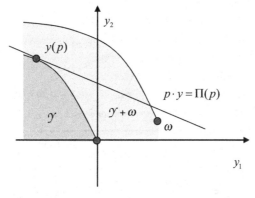

Figure 5.1-2. Profit maximization.

Solving for the profit-maximizing output we obtain, $y_2(p) = \frac{1}{2}\frac{p_2}{p_1}$. Thus $y_1(p) = -y_2(p)^2 = -\frac{1}{4}(\frac{p_2}{p_1})^2$ and maximized profit is $\Pi(p) = p \cdot y(p) = \frac{(p_2)^2}{4p_1}$.

Crusoe the Price-Taking Consumer

Next consider the choice of Crusoe the consumer. The value of his endowment is $p \cdot \omega$. In addition, as the single shareholder in the economy he collects all the dividends $\Pi(p) = p \cdot y(p)$. His spending on corn is therefore constrained as follows: $p \cdot x \leq p \cdot \omega + \Pi(p)$.

He therefore solves the following maximization problem:

$$\underset{x \geq 0}{\text{Max}}\{U(x) | p \cdot x \leq p \cdot \omega + \Pi(p)\}.$$

This is depicted in Figure 5.1-3 with Crusoe's optimal choice $x(p)$.

As shown, $x_1(p) > y_1(p) + \omega_1$ and $x_2(p) < y_2(p) + \omega_2$. That is, there is excess demand for leisure and excess supply of commodity 2. Thus the Walrasian auctioneer raises the price of commodity 1 and lowers the price of commodity 2. The relative price of commodity 1 rises so the profit and budget lines become steeper.

The Walrasian equilibrium (WE) is depicted in Figure 5.1-4.

Comparing Figure 5.1-1 and Figure 5.1-4 it is clear that the Walrasian equilibrium coincides with the optimum. Thus the price-taking behavior of the schizophrenic Robinson Crusoe, along with market clearing, guides him to the optimum. This is a simple illustration of Adam Smith's famous "invisible hand" at work.

Example (concluded):
Crusoe the consumer solves the following problem:

$$\underset{x}{\text{Max}}\{\ln x_1 + \ln x_2 | p \cdot x \leq \Pi(p) + \omega\}.$$

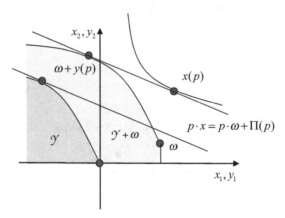

Figure 5.1-3. Utility maximization by Crusoe.

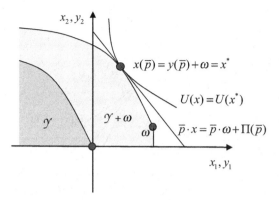

Figure 5.1-4. Walrasian equilibrium.

Because utility is strictly increasing, the budget constraint must be satisfied with equality at the maximum. From the FOC, and appealing to the Ratio Rule,

$$\frac{\frac{\partial U}{\partial x_1}}{p_1} = \frac{\frac{\partial U}{\partial x_2}}{p_2} \Rightarrow \frac{1}{p_1 x_1} = \frac{1}{p_2 x_2} = \frac{2}{p_1 x_1 + p_2 x_2} = \frac{2}{p \cdot \omega + \Pi(p)}.$$

Therefore $x_2(p) = \frac{1}{2}(\frac{\Pi(p) + p \cdot \omega}{p_2})$. We have already seen that

$$y_2^*(p) = \frac{1}{2}\frac{p_2}{p_1} \quad \text{and} \quad \Pi(p) = \frac{(p_2)^2}{4 p_1}.$$

Therefore demand for commodity 2 is $x_2(p) = \frac{1}{2}(\frac{p_2}{4 p_1} + 144 \frac{p_1}{p_2} + 3)$.
  It follows that excess demand for commodity 2 is

$$z_2(p) = x_2(p) - y_2(p) - 3 = \frac{1}{2}\left(144 \frac{p_1}{p_2} - \frac{3}{4}\frac{p_2}{p_1} - 3\right)$$

$$= \frac{1}{2}\frac{p_1}{p_2}\left(12 - \frac{p_2}{p_1}\right)\left(12 + \frac{3}{4}\left(\frac{p_2}{p_1}\right)\right)$$

$$= 0 \quad \text{at} \quad \frac{p_2}{p_1} = 12.$$

In Section 5.3 we ask what conditions are sufficient to guarantee existence of a Walrasian equilibrium. We conclude here by showing the problem that can arise if the production set is not convex. Consider the example depicted in Figure 5.1-5 in which there is a fixed cost that has to be incurred before any output is produced. For simplicity there is a zero endowment of commodity 2 so the endowment vector is on the horizontal axis.

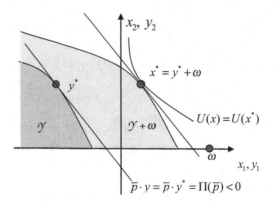

Figure 5.1-5. No Walrasian equilibrium with large fixed costs.

The optimal production plan is y^* and the optimal consumption plan is $x^* = y^* + \omega$. For this plan to be an equilibrium allocation, we draw the budget line through x^* tangential to the set $\mathcal{Y} + \omega$ and the parallel profit line through y^* tangential to the production set. Note that the profit line lies to the left of the origin. Yet then the optimum cannot be a Walrasian equilibrium because the firm is strictly better off producing nothing and making a profit of zero.

Exercises

Exercise 5.1-1: Equilibrium Robinson has a utility function $U(x_1, x_2) = x_1 x_2$. His endowment of hours is 147. He can produce coconuts according to the production function $y_2 = 2\sqrt{-y_1}$.

(a) Solve for his optimum.
(b) If the price of commodity 2 is one, what wage will induce Robinson, acting as a profit-maximizing manager, to demand the optimal labor input.
(c) Depict the production set, preferences, and separating plane in a neat figure.

Exercise 5.1-2: Walrasian Equilibrium with CRS Suppose that Robinson can produce coconuts using labor according to the production function $y_2 = -2y_1$. He has an endowment of β units of commodity 2 and an endowment of γ units of time. Preferences are represented by the utility function $U(x_1, x_2) = \ln x_1 + \ln(\alpha + x_2)$, where x_1 is leisure.

(a) Depict the production set $\mathcal{Y}$ in a neat figure and also the set $\mathcal{Y} + \omega$.
(b) Solve for the optimal number of working hours for all values of α, β and γ. Under what conditions is it optimal for Robinson not to work at all?
(c) Explain why equilibrium profit must be zero.
(d) If the optimum labor supply is zero, show that there is an interval of Walrasian equilibrium "real wage rates" p_1/p_2.

Exercise 5.1-3: Existence with a Non-Convexity Suppose that Robinson Crusoe can produce coconuts (y_2) using labor ($-y_1$). The production set $\mathcal{Y} = \hat{\mathcal{Y}} \cup \{0\}$ where $\hat{\mathcal{Y}} = \{(y_1, y_2) | y_1 \leq -\gamma, y_1 + \gamma + \frac{1}{8} y_2^2 \leq 0\}$. His utility function is $U(x) = x_1 + \ln x_2$. He has an endowment of 2γ units of time.

(a) Depict the production set in a neat figure.
(b) Show that the optimal output of coconuts is 2.
(c) Solve for the firm's supply curve for coconuts as a function of the "real wage" p_1/p_2.
(d) Solve for the consumer's demand curve for coconuts.
(e) Hence or otherwise show that if there is a WE, the WE price ratio $p_2/p_1 = \frac{1}{2}$.
(f) Compute the implied equilibrium profit as a function of γ.
(g) Hence obtain the values of γ for which there exists a WE.

5.2 Equilibrium and Efficiency with Production

Key ideas: Walrasian equilibrium, First and Second welfare theorems

We now consider an economy with an arbitrary number of commodities, consumers, and firms.

Firms

There are F firms in the economy. Firm f has a set of feasible production plans $\mathcal{Y}^f \subset \mathbb{R}^n$ and chooses a production vector $y^f = (y_1^f, \ldots, y_n^f) \in \mathcal{Y}^f$. A production plan for the economy $\{y^f\}_{f=1}^F$ is a plan for each of the firms. The aggregate production plan for the economy is the sum of all the individual plans

$$y = \sum_{f=1}^F y^f.$$

The set of all feasible aggregate production plans, $\mathcal{Y}$, is the aggregate production set.

Consumers

Commodities are private, that is, consumer h has preferences over her own consumption vector $x^h = (x_1^h, \ldots, x_n^h)$ and not those of other consumers. Let $X^h \subset \mathbb{R}^n$ be the consumption set of consumer h, $h = 1, \ldots, H$. That is, preferences are defined over X^h. We assume that consumer h has an endowment vector $\omega^h \in X^h$. A consumption allocation in this economy $\{x^h\}_{h=1}^H$ is an allocation of consumption bundles $x^h \in X^h$, $h = 1, \ldots, H$. The aggregate consumption in the economy is the sum of the individual consumption vectors $x = \sum_{h=1}^{H} x^h$. Similarly the aggregate endowment is $\omega = \sum_{h=1}^{H} \omega^h$.

Shareholdings

Firms are owned by consumers. Consumer h has an ownership share in firm f of θ^{hf}. Ownership shares must sum to 1, that is,

$$\sum_{h=1}^{H} \theta^{hf} = 1, \quad f = 1, \ldots, F.$$

Feasible Allocation

Given the aggregate demand x, endowment ω and supply y, define excess demand $z = x - \omega - y$. An allocation is feasible if aggregate excess demand is negative:

$$z = x - \omega - y \leq 0.$$

Pareto Efficient Allocation

A feasible plan for the economy $\{\hat{x}^h\}_{h=1}^{H}$, $\{\hat{y}^f\}_{f=1}^{F}$ is Pareto efficient (PE) if there is no other feasible plan $\{x^h\}_{h=1}^{H}$, $\{y^f\}_{f=1}^{F}$ that is strictly preferred by at least one consumer and weakly preferred by all consumers.

Price Taking

Let $p > 0$ be the price vector. Consumers and firms are price takers. Thus if firm f chooses the production plan y^f it has a profit of $p \cdot y^f$. Consumer h receives her share of the profit as a dividend payment. The total dividend payment received by consumer h is therefore $\sum_{f} \theta^{hf} p \cdot y^f$. Adding the value of her endowment, consumer h has a wealth

$$W^h = p \cdot \omega^h + \sum_{f} \theta^{hf} p \cdot y^f.$$

She then chooses a consumption bundle $\bar{x}^h$ in her budget set

$$\{x^h \in X^h | p \cdot x^h \leq W^h\}.$$

Note that her budget set is largest if wealth is maximized. Thus, as a shareholder, consumer h's interests are best served by firm managers who maximize profit.

Walrasian Equilibrium

Given the price vector p, let $\overline{y}^f$, $f = 1, \ldots, F$, be a production plan that maximizes the profit of firm f. That is,

$$p \cdot \overline{y}^f \geq p \cdot y^f, \quad \text{for all} \quad y^f \in \mathcal{Y}^f, f = 1, \ldots, F. \tag{*}$$

Also, let $\overline{x}^h$ be a most preferred consumption plan in consumer h's budget set. That is,

$$U^h(\overline{x}^h) \geq U^h(x^h), \quad \text{for all } x^h \text{ such that } p \cdot x^h \leq W^h. \tag{**}$$

The aggregate excess demand vector is then $\overline{z} = \overline{x} - \omega - \overline{y}$.

Definition: Walrasian Equilibrium Prices The price vector $p \geq 0$ is a WE price vector if for some $\{\overline{y}^f\}_{f=1}^F$ satisfying (*) and $\{\overline{x}^h\}_{h=1}^H$ satisfying (**), the excess demand vector is negative ($\overline{z} \leq 0$). Moreover $p_j = 0$ for any market in which excess demand is strictly negative ($\overline{z}_j < 0$).

The Adam Smith Theorem

The proof of the First welfare theorem follows closely that for the exchange economy. The proof of the Second welfare theorem parallels the proof for the two-person exchange economy. However there are some additional subtleties.

Proposition 5.2-1: First Welfare Theorem
If the preferences of each consumer satisfy the local no-satiation postulate, the Walrasian equilibrium allocation is Pareto efficient.

Proof: First we note that because $\overline{x}^h$ maximizes utility over consumer h's budget set, any strictly preferred bundle x^h must cost strictly more than the equilibrium allocation. That is,

$$U^h(x^h) > U^h(\overline{x}^h) \Rightarrow p \cdot x^h > p \cdot \omega^h + p \cdot \sum_{f=1}^{F} \theta^{hf} \overline{y}^f. \tag{5.2-1}$$

Moreover, appealing to the Duality Lemma (Lemma 2.2-3), any weakly preferred bundle x^h must cost at least as much. That is,

$$U^h(x^h) \geq U^h(\overline{x}^h) \Rightarrow p \cdot x^h \geq p \cdot \omega^h + p \cdot \sum_{f=1}^{F} \theta^{hf} \overline{y}^f. \tag{5.2-2}$$

Suppose that the allocation $\{x^h\}_{h=1}^H$, $\{y^f\}_{f=1}^F$ is feasible and Pareto preferred to the WE allocation. We now show, by contradiction, that no such allocation exists.

For feasibility, excess demands must be negative so $z = x - \omega - y \leq 0$. Then, because the Walrasian equilibrium price vector is positive,

$$p \cdot (x - \omega - y) \leq 0. \tag{5.2-3}$$

Because all consumers must be at least as well off as in the PE allocation, inequality (5.2-2) must hold for all h. Moreover at least one consumer must be strictly better off so inequality (5.2-1) must hold for some h. Summing over consumers,

$$p \cdot \sum_h x^h > p \cdot \sum_h \omega^h + p \cdot \sum_h \sum_f \theta^{hf} \overline{y}^f = p \cdot \sum_h \omega^h + p \cdot \sum_f \overline{y}^f \sum_h \theta^{hf}.$$

Because shares sum to 1, this can be rewritten as follows:

$$p \cdot \sum_h x^h > p \cdot \omega + \sum_f p \cdot \overline{y}^f.$$

Also $\overline{y}^f$ is profit maximizing over Y^f. Hence $p \cdot \overline{y}^f \geq p \cdot y^f$. Therefore

$$p \cdot (x - \omega - y) \geq p \cdot \left(\sum_h x^h - \omega - \sum_f \overline{y}^f \right) > 0.$$

Yet this contradicts (5.2-3). Thus there is no Pareto preferred feasible allocation. □

Decentralization Theorem

Next we consider the Second welfare theorem with production. We follow the same line of argument as in the proof for the exchange economy. However we no longer assume that consumption bundles are necessarily positive. Thus consumers may supply commodities (e.g., labor services), and production vectors have both positive components (outputs) and negative components (inputs.)

Proposition 5.2-2: Second Welfare Theorem with Production
Let $\{\hat{x}^h\}_{h=1}^H$, $\{\hat{y}^f\}_{f=1}^F$ be a Pareto efficient allocation. Suppose

(a) consumption vectors are private,
(b) consumption sets X^h, $h = 1, \ldots, H$ are convex,
(c) utility functions are continuous, and quasi-concave and satisfy the local non-satiation property,
(d) for each h there is some $\underline{x}^h \in X^h$ such that $\underline{x}^h < \hat{x}^h$, and
(e) production sets $\mathcal{Y}^f$, $f = 1, \ldots, F$ are convex and satisfy the free disposal property.

Then there exists a price vector $p > 0$ such that

$$x^h \underset{h}{\succ} \hat{x}^h \Rightarrow p \cdot x^h > p \cdot \hat{x}^h, \quad h = 1, \ldots, H$$

$$y^f \in \mathcal{Y}^f \Rightarrow p \cdot y^f \leq p \cdot \hat{y}^f.$$

Proof: Let $\{\hat{x}^h\}_{h=1}^H$, $\{\hat{y}^f\}_{f=1}^F$ be a PE allocation. As in the pure exchange economy we introduce the indirect utility function

$$V^1(x) = \underset{\{x^h\}_{h=1}^H}{\text{Max}} \left\{ U^1(x^1) \mid \sum_{h=1}^H x^h \leq x, \quad U^h(x^h) \geq U^h(\hat{x}^h), \quad h = 2, \ldots, H \right\}.$$

As argued in Chapter 3, $V^1(x)$ is quasi-concave. Also because U^1 has the local non-satiation property, so does V^1.

We also define the set of feasible aggregate consumption vectors $\{\omega\} + \mathcal{Y}$. This is depicted in Figure 5.2-1 for a two-commodity example in which some of the initial endowment of commodity 1 is transformed into commodity 2. Note that because production sets are convex, so is the aggregate production set.

Consider the following optimization problem:

$$\underset{\{x^h\},\{y^f\}}{\text{Max}} \{ V^1(x) \mid x \in \{\omega + \mathcal{Y}\}. \tag{5.2-4}$$

Because $\{\hat{x}^h\}_{h=1}^H$, $\{\hat{y}^f\}_{f=1}^F$ is Pareto efficient, $U^1(\hat{x}^1)$ is the highest feasible utility for consumer 1, given that no other consumer is made worse off than in the PE allocation. Thus $\{\hat{x}^h\}_{h=1}^H$, $\{\hat{y}^f\}_{f=1}^F$ solves this maximization problem and so $V^1(\hat{x}) = U^1(\hat{x}^1)$. The solution is depicted in Figure 5.2-1.

Given local non-satiation, the maximizing aggregate consumption vector $\hat{x} = \omega + \hat{y}$ must lie on the boundary of $\{\omega\} + \mathcal{Y}$. Because the preferred set

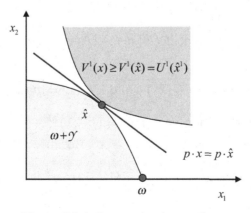

Figure 5.2-1. Supporting hyperplane.

$\hat{X} \equiv \{x \mid V^1(x) \geq V^1(\hat{x})\}$ and $\mathcal{Y}$ are both convex, the set $\hat{X} - \{\omega\} - \mathcal{Y}$ is convex. Moreover $\hat{x} - \omega - \hat{y} = 0$ is a boundary point of this set. Appealing to the Supporting Hyperplane Theorem there exists a vector $p \neq 0$ such that

$$p \cdot (x - \omega - y) \geq p \cdot (\hat{x} - \omega - \hat{y}) = 0, \quad \forall x \in \hat{X} \text{ and } \forall y \in \mathcal{Y}.$$

Setting $x = \hat{x}$,

(i) $p \cdot (\hat{x} - \omega - y) = p \cdot (\hat{y} - y) \geq 0, \quad \forall y \in \mathcal{Y}.$

Setting $y = \hat{y}$,

(ii) $p \cdot (x - \omega - \hat{y}) = p \cdot (x - \hat{x}) \geq 0, \quad \forall x \in \hat{X}.$

We now argue that the vector p must be positive. We suppose that some components of p are negative and show that this yields to a contradiction of (i). Define $\delta = (\delta_1, \ldots, \delta_n) > 0$ such that $\delta_j > 0$ if and only if $p_j < 0$. Then $p \cdot \delta < 0$. Consider an aggregate production vector $y = \hat{y} - \delta$. Then $p \cdot (\hat{y} - y) = p \cdot \delta < 0$. Because $\delta > 0$ it follows by free disposal that y is feasible. But then condition (i) is violated. Thus $p > 0$ after all.

Next note that we can rewrite conditions (i) and (ii) as follows:

(i) $y \in \mathcal{Y} \Rightarrow \sum_{f=1}^{F} p \cdot y^f \leq \sum_{f=1}^{F} p \cdot \hat{y}^f$

(ii) $V^1(x) \geq V^1(\hat{x}) \Rightarrow \sum_{h=1}^{H} p \cdot x^h \geq \sum_{h=1}^{H} p \cdot \hat{x}^h.$

Setting $y^j = \hat{y}^j$, $j \neq f$ in (i) it follows that

(i)' $y^f \in \mathcal{Y}^f \Rightarrow p \cdot y^f \leq p \cdot \hat{y}^f, \quad f = 1, \ldots, F.$

Thus $\hat{y}^f$ is profit maximizing for firm f.

Similarly, setting $x^i = \hat{x}^i$, $i \neq h$ in (ii) it follows that[1]

(ii)' $U^h(x^h) \geq U^h(\hat{x}^h) \Rightarrow p \cdot x^h \geq p \cdot \hat{x}^h.$

The final step is to show that if $U^h(x^h) > U^h(\hat{x}^h)$ then $p \cdot x^h > p \cdot \hat{x}^h$. Suppose instead that

$$U^h(x^h) > U^h(\hat{x}^h) \quad \text{and} \quad p \cdot x^h = p \cdot \hat{x}^h.$$

Consider the consumption vector $\check{x}^h = (1 - \lambda)x^h + \lambda \underline{x}^h$, where $\lambda \in (0, 1)$. Because $\underline{x}^h \in X^h$ and X^h is convex, $\check{x}^h \in X^h$. Because $\underline{x}^h < \hat{x}^h$,

$$p \cdot \check{x}^h = (1 - \lambda)p \cdot x^h + \lambda p \cdot \underline{x}^h < (1 - \lambda)p \cdot x^h + \lambda p \cdot \hat{x}^h = p \cdot \hat{x}^h.$$

---

[1] From the definition of the indirect utility function $U^h(x^h) \geq U^h(\hat{x}^h)$, $h = 2, \ldots, H$. Also $U^1(x^1) = V^1(x) \geq V^1(\hat{x}) = U^1(\hat{x}^1)$.

Also, given the continuity of preferences, $U^h(\bar{x}^h) > U^h(\hat{x}^h)$ for λ sufficiently close to 1. However, this is impossible because condition (ii)$'$ is violated.

$\square$

The two welfare theorems lie at the heart of arguments in favor of free trade as opposed to intervention by the state. They also lie at the heart of arguments for such intervention! At issue is the relevance of the assumptions that underpin the theorems. First there is the assumption of price-taking behavior. If economic agents are able to form cartels and exploit their monopoly power, they have an incentive to do so.[2] Second, and equally important, the theorems require that goods be private. That is, individuals care about their own consumption only. When this is not the case (whether the concern is noisy neighbors, industrial pollution, or a city park) the theorems fail.

However, whether or not intervention can be justified is a complex matter. The beauty of the First welfare theorem is that no economic agent has to know anything about anyone else's preferences. Any intervention requires an evaluation of costs and benefits that are often difficult to measure because agents have an incentive to misrepresent the truth.

Exercises

Exercise 5.2-1: Cobb-Douglas Economy All consumers have the same Cobb-Douglas utility function $U^h(x^h) = \sum_{j=1}^{2} a_j \ln x_j^h$, $h = 1, \ldots, H$. There are two inputs. The aggregate endowment of input i is ω_i, $i = 1, 2$. The production set of any firm producing commodity j is

$$\mathcal{Y}_j^f = \left\{ \left(z_j^f, q_j^f\right) \mid q_j^f \leq \left(z_{1j}^f\right)^{\alpha_j} \left(z_{2j}^f\right)^{1-\alpha_j} \right\}.$$

(a) Show that the industry production set is

$$\mathcal{Y}_j = \left\{ \left(z^f, q_j^f\right) \mid q_j \leq (z_{1j})^{\alpha_j} (z_{2j})^{1-\alpha_j} \right\}.$$

(b) Show that the optimal allocation of input 1 is

$$(z_{11}^*, z_{12}^*) = \left(\frac{a_1 \alpha_1 \omega_1}{a_1 \alpha_1 + a_2 \alpha_2}, \frac{a_2 \alpha_2 \omega_1}{a_1 \alpha_1 + a_2 \alpha_2} \right).$$

Solve also for the optimal allocation of input 2.

HINT: This is an economy with identical homothetic preferences.

(c) Appeal to part (a) to solve for WE input prices.

---

[2] It was for this reason that Adam Smith argued in favor of placing restrictions on the collusive activities of manufacturing associations, thus allowing the invisible hand to do its work.

(d) Show that the associated WE output price vector is

$$p_j = \left(\frac{r_1}{\alpha_j}\right)^{\alpha_j} \left(\frac{r_2}{1-\alpha_j}\right)^{1-\alpha_j}.$$

HINT: Marginal cost is independent of output in this economy. Why is this?

Exercise 5.2-2: Robinson Meets Friday Suppose that Robinson owns the firm but is unable to work. Friday has 32 units of potential labor hours and a utility function $U(x) = \ln x_1 + \ln x_2$. The production function is $y_2 = 4(-y_1)^{1/2}$, equivalently, $y_1 + y_2^2/16 \leq 0$.

(a) Solve for Friday's labor supply curve.
(b) Solve for the firm's demand for labor. Hence, solve for the Walrasian equilibrium.
(c) Draw the production set $\mathcal{Y}$ and the set $\mathcal{Y} + \omega$ in a neat figure. Show Friday's equilibrium budget constraint and the firm's profit-maximizing profit line.
(d) Suppose that Friday receives a lump-sum subsidy (and Robinson pays a lump-sum tax.) Show that at the no tax Walrasian equilibrium prices, Friday's supply of labor falls so that there is excess demand for labor. Hence draw a conclusion as to how the WE price ratio changes.
(e) Hence or otherwise comment on the price effect if Friday is given shareholdings in the firm.

Exercise 5.2-3: Robinson and Friday Suppose that Robinson owns the firm. Friday and Robinson have equal endowments of time to be allocated between leisure and work. The total endowment of time is ω_1 so each has an endowment of $\frac{1}{2}\omega_1$ units of time. Each has a utility function $U(x) = \ln x_1 + 2a \ln x_2$. The production function is $y_2 = (z_1)^{1/2}$.

(a) Treat this as a representative agent problem and show that the optimal total supply of labor is $z_1^* = \frac{a\omega_1}{1+a}$. Hence

$$x^* = \left(\frac{\omega_1}{1+a}, \left(\frac{a\omega_1}{1+a}\right)^{1/4}\right).$$

(b) Consider the consumer optimization problem (remembering that the representative agent has an endowment of time and dividend income) and hence solve for the WE prices.
(c) Show that Friday's demand for leisure is $x_1^F = \frac{\omega_1}{2(1+4a)}$. Market demand for leisure is given in part (a). Hence solve for Robinson's equilibrium demand for leisure. Show that this exceeds his time available if a is strictly positive and sufficiently small. Thus the simple representative agent approach needs modifying.
(d) What is the equilibrium in this case?

5.3 Existence of Equilibrium

Key ideas: Fixed point theorems, continuity of excess demand functions, and correspondences

As we saw in the Robinson Crusoe economy of Section 5.1, continuity is the key to proving a general existence result. We first consider an exchange economy.

Proposition 5.3-1: Existence of a WE in an Exchange Economy
Suppose $U^h(x^h)$ $h = 1, \ldots, H$ is strictly increasing and strictly quasi-concave over $X^h = \mathbb{R}^n_+$ and consumer h has endowment $\omega^h \in X^h$. Then there exists a WE.

Regardless of prices, a consumer with an endowment of zero has a zero consumption and thus an excess demand of zero. Thus we can ignore all such individuals and assume that $\omega^h > 0, h = 1, \ldots, H$. Because only relative prices matter, there is no loss in generality in normalizing and considering only price vectors $p \geq 0$ such that $\sum_{i=1}^n p_i = 1$. (The set of non-negative vectors summing to 1 is called the unit simplex.) In the two-commodity case, proving the existence of a WE is straightforward. For any $p \gg 0$ the budget set is compact so there is a solution to consumer h's maximization problem. Given the strict quasi-concavity hypothesis the solution is unique. Thus there exists a unique excess demand function $z^h(p)$. By the Theorem of the Maximum $z^h(p)$ is continuous. Summing over individuals, $z(p) = \sum_{h=1}^H z^h(p)$ is continuous.

By hypothesis, $U^h(x)$ is strictly increasing. Thus, as the price of commodity 1 declines toward zero (and $p_2 \to 1$), demand for commodity 1 rises without bound. Furthermore, because $U^h(\cdot)$ is strictly increasing, the consumer's choice $x^h(p)$ will satisfy his budget constraint with equality. Therefore his excess demand $z^h(p)$ satisfies

$$p \cdot z^h(p) = p \cdot (x^h(p) - \omega^h) = 0.$$

Summing over all consumers,

$$p \cdot z(p) = p_1 z_1(p) + p_2 z_2(p) = 0. \tag{5.3-1}$$

For p_1 sufficiently small there is excess demand for commodity 1. Appealing to (5.3-1) there is excess supply of commodity 2.

By the same argument, for p_1 sufficiently close to 1 (and so for p_2 sufficiently close to zero) there is excess demand for commodity 2 and so excess supply of commodity 1.

Given the continuity of the market demand function it follows that there is some price pair $\overline{p} = (\overline{p}_1, 1 - \overline{p}_1)$ such that $z_1(\overline{p}) = 0$. Appealing to (5.3-1) it follows immediately that $z_2(\overline{p}) = 0$. Thus the price vector $\overline{p} = (\overline{p}_1, 1 - \overline{p}_1)$ is a WE price vector.

With more than two commodities we appeal to the following theorem.

Brouwer's Fixed Point Theorem Let $S \subset \mathbb{R}^n$ be closed and bounded and suppose that the continuous function $g(x) = (g_1(x), \ldots, g_n(x))$ maps each element of S into a point in S. Then for some $\overline{x} \in S$, $g(\overline{x}) = \overline{x}$.

Proof of Proposition 5.3-1 As in the two-commodity case, let Δ be the unit simplex; that is,

$$\Delta \equiv \left\{ p | p \geq 0, \sum_{j=1}^{n} p_j = 1 \right\}.$$

We choose a mapping $g(p)$ that raises the price of every commodity for which there is excess demand and lowers every other price. Consider the following mapping:

$$g(p) = \frac{p + z^+(p)}{1 + \sum\limits_{j=1}^{n} z_j^+(p)} \quad \text{where } z_j^+(p) = \text{Max}\{z_j(p), 0\}.$$

Note that $\hat{p}_j = p_j + z_j^+(p)$ is a price that is strictly larger than p_j for each market in which there is excess demand and is equal to p_j in a market for which there is excess supply. Note also that

$$\sum_{j=1}^{n} \hat{p}_j = 1 + \sum_{j=1}^{n} z^+(p).$$

Thus $g(p)$ is in the unit simplex.

At points in the interior of the unit simplex (so that $p \gg 0$) the excess demand function is continuous. However, the mapping is not defined at boundary points because excess demand is infinite. Thus we cannot appeal directly to the fixed point theorem. To deal with this problem we constrain each consumer's optimization problem to lie in a compact set. We define

$$\Omega = \{x^h | 0 \leq x^h \leq k\omega, k > 1\}$$

and consider the following modified maximization problem for consumer $h = 1, \ldots, H$:

$$\text{Max}_{x^h} \{U^h(x^h) | p \cdot x^h \leq p \cdot \omega^h, x^h \in \Omega\}.$$

Because the feasible set is compact for all $p \in \Delta$, a maximum for this modified problem exists. Given strict quasi-concavity, this maximum is unique. Thus for each h there is a unique excess demand $z^h(p)$. By the Theorem of the Maximum, this mapping is continuous. Hence the mapping $g(p)$ is continuous. Appealing to Brouwer's Fixed Point Theorem, there is some $\overline{p} \in \Delta$ such that

$$g(\overline{p}) \equiv \frac{\overline{p} + z^+(\overline{p})}{1 + \sum\limits_{j=1}^{n} z_j^+(\overline{p})} = \overline{p}. \tag{5.3-2}$$

We now argue that $\overline{p} \gg 0$. Suppose instead that $\overline{p}_j = 0$. At this price the upper bound for consumption of commodity j is $k\omega_j$. Because utility is strictly increasing $x_j^h(\overline{p}) = k\omega_j$. Thus for each consumer there is excess demand and so $z_j^+(\overline{p}) > 0$. Yet then

$$g_j(\overline{p}) = \frac{z_j^+(\overline{p})}{1 + \sum\limits_{j=1}^{n} z_j^+(\overline{p})} > 0 = \overline{p}_j.$$

This violates (5.3-2).

Let I be the index set of commodities for which excess demand is positive. By Walras' Law, $\overline{p} \cdot z(\overline{p}) = 0$ so this cannot be true of all markets. Therefore

$$\sum_{i \in I} \overline{p}_i < 1 \tag{5.3-3}$$

From (5.3-2)

$$\overline{p}_i + z_i^+(\overline{p}) = \overline{p}_i \left(1 + \sum_{j=1}^{n} z_j^+(\overline{p}) \right), \quad \text{for all } i \in I.$$

Summing over $i \in I$,

$$\sum_{i \in I} z_i^+(\overline{p}) = \left(\sum_{i \in I} \overline{p}_i \right) \left(\sum_{j=1}^{n} z_j^+(\overline{p}) \right).$$

But $z_j^+(\overline{p}) = 0$ for $j \notin I$. Therefore $\sum_{i \in I} \overline{p}_i = 1$, contradicting (5.3-3).

Therefore there is no market in which there is excess demand. It follows immediately from Walras' Law that there can be no market in which there is excess supply. Thus $z(\overline{p}) = \sum_{h=1}^{H} x^h(\overline{p}) - \omega = 0$. It follows that $x^h(\overline{p}) \le \omega$, $h = 1, \ldots, H$. Then for each consumer the constraint $x^h \le k\omega$ is not binding, and so the price vector remains a Walrasian equilibrium price vector for any consumption set containing Ω. In particular, this holds if the consumption set is $\mathbb{R}_+^n$. $\qquad\square$

If demand is not continuous, it is easy to see why there may be no Walrasian equilibrium. Figure 5.3-1 illustrates the problem. Suppose that each consumer has the same endowment vector and preferences. Thus, the Walrasian equilibrium allocation must be the no trade allocation. Note that the

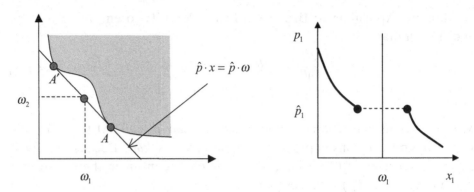

Figure 5.3-1. No Walrasian equilibrium.

budget constraint $\hat{p} \cdot x = \hat{p} \cdot \omega$ touches the indifference curve at A and A' ; thus there are two equilibrium demands at the price vector p. At any higher price ratio p_1/p_2 there is excess demand for commodity 2, and for any lower price ratio there is excess demand for commodity 1. Thus there is no equilibrium.

An Economy with Production

Although the production vector of a firm may include positive and negative elements (outputs and inputs) we will continue to assume that the consumption set $X^h \subset \mathbb{R}^n_+$. This may seem restrictive because a consumer may supply labor services. However, such services are readily incorporated by giving consumers initial endowments. Then consumers sell some of their labor endowments but their consumption remains positive.

We assume that $\mathcal{Y}^f$, $f = 1, \ldots, F$ is closed, strictly convex, and bounded from above and that $0 \in \mathcal{Y}^f$. Then the aggregate production set $\mathcal{Y}$ is closed and bounded from above. That is, for some $\overline{y}$, $y \leq \overline{y}$ for all $y \in \mathcal{Y}$. Define z to be the supply of all firms other than firm f. That is $y = y^f + z$. For feasibility, the aggregate production plus endowment $y^f + z + \omega$ must exceed aggregate demand by consumers x. Therefore

$$y^f \geq x - \omega - z.$$

Because $x \geq 0$ it follows that $y^f \geq -\omega - z$. Because $0 \in \mathcal{Y}^f$, $z \in \mathcal{Y}$. Then $z \leq \overline{y}$ and so $-z \geq -\overline{y}$.

It follows that $y^f \geq -\omega - \overline{y}$.

Consider then production vectors in the set $\overline{\mathcal{Y}}^f = \{y^f \in \mathcal{Y}^f | y^f \geq -\alpha\omega - \overline{y}, \alpha > 1\}$. Because $\overline{\mathcal{Y}}^f$ is compact and strictly convex there is a unique continuous profit-maximizing aggregate supply $y^f(p) \in \overline{\mathcal{Y}}^f$. It follows immediately that the profit function is continuous; hence the total dividends for each consumer are continuous and so the consumer demand functions are continuous as well. Thus excess demand functions are continuous. Arguing exactly as in the proof of Proposition 5.3-1, it follows that a WE exists for the economy with the modified production sets.

Finally we note that because the equilibrium allocation for the modified economy must be feasible, the lower bound in each production set cannot be binding. Thus the WE of the modified economy is also a WE of the original economy.

Proposition 5.3-2: Existence of WE with Bounded Production
Suppose $U^h(x^h)$ $h = 1, \ldots, H$ is strictly quasi-concave over $X^h \subset \mathbb{R}_+^n$ and consumer h has endowment $\omega^h \in X^h$. Suppose also that the production sets $\mathcal{Y}^f$ $f = 1, \ldots, F$ are closed, strictly convex and bounded from above and $0 \in \mathcal{Y}^f$. Then there exists a Walrasian equilibrium.

One limitation of this proposition is that it appeals to the strict convexity of both preferences and production sets. Although this is a reasonable assumption for preferences, it excludes the possibility of a linear technology in which inputs and outputs can be simply scaled up, at least over some range. Fortunately, the assumption of strict convexity can be replaced by (weak) convexity. Although the formal mathematics becomes a little more complicated, the basic ideas are similar.

Consider a two-commodity world and a single firm with a production set as depicted in Figure 5.3-2.

We normalize so that the price of commodity 1 is 1. For low output prices, the profit-maximizing output is zero. If the price of commodity 2 is between $1/a$ and $1/b$ the profit-maximizing output is a. For higher prices of commodity 2 the profit-maximizing output is $a + b$. Note also that, at the two critical prices of commodity 1, there is a set of profit-maximizing production vectors. Thus we no longer have a production function but a set-valued production correspondence $y_2(p_2)$. This correspondence is also depicted in Figure 5.3-2.

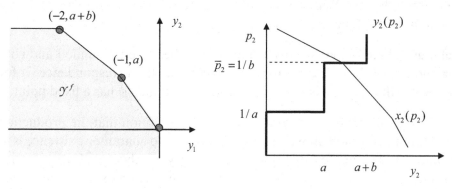

Figure 5.3-2. Supply correspondence.

Suppose that this is the only firm and that preferences are strictly convex. Because maximized firm profit $\Pi(p)$ is a continuous function of the price vector, it follows that the aggregate demand function is also continuous. It follows that the supply correspondence and demand functions intersect at some price $\bar{p}_2$.

For the case of strict convexity we appealed to the continuity of the excess demand function in order to prove existence. With convexity we appeal to the following smoothness property of supply and demand correspondences.

Definition: Upper Hemi-Continuous Correspondence The correspondence ϕ is upper hemi-continuous at x^0 if $\{x^t\} \to x^0$, $\{y^t \in \phi(x^t)\} \to y^0$ implies $y^0 \in \phi(x^0)$.

Consider the supply correspondence $y_2(p_2)$ depicted in Figure 5.3-2. Note that $y_2(\bar{p}_2) = [a, a + b]$. For the increasing sequence $\{p_2^t\} \to \bar{p}_2$, $y_2(p_2^t) \to a$, and for the decreasing sequence $\{p_2^t\} \to \bar{p}_2$, $y_2(p_2^t) \to a + b$. Thus the correspondence is upper hemi-continuous at $\bar{p}_2$.

Although we do not derive it here, Proposition 5.3-3 can be proved using arguments paralleling those in the proof of continuity for a strictly convex economy.

Proposition 5.3-3: Upper Hemi-Continuity of the Excess Demand Correspondence
Suppose $U^h(x^h)$ $h = 1, \ldots, H$ is quasi-concave and continuous over $X^h \subset \mathbb{R}_+^n$ and consumer h has endowment $\omega^h \in X^h$. Suppose also that the production sets $\mathcal{Y}^f f = 1, \ldots, F$ are closed, strictly convex, and bounded from above and $0 \in \mathcal{Y}^f$. Then for the modified economy in which each consumption set is bounded from above and each production set is bounded from below, the excess demand correspondence $z(p)$ is upper hemi-continuous and convex.

The final step is to first appeal to the following fixed point theorem and then argue that the Walrasian equilibrium of the modified economy is also an equilibrium of the unmodified economy.

Kakutani's Fixed Point Theorem Let $S \subset \mathbb{R}^n$ be closed, bounded and convex and let $\phi : S \to S$ be an upper hemi-continuous correspondence. If for each $x \in S$ the set $\phi(x)$ is non-empty and convex, then ϕ has a fixed point.

A limitation of the proof of existence is the assumption that the production sets are bounded from above. An alternative way to guarantee existence is to assume that demand for at least one commodity is unbounded when a price approaches zero. We begin by "trimming" the unit simplex to eliminate any price less than ε and apply the fixed point theorem to the trimmed simplex

$\Delta(\varepsilon)$. We then let ε approach zero and show that for sufficiently small ε, the fixed point is in the interior of $\Delta(\varepsilon)$.

Proposition 5.3-4: Existence of Walrasian Equilibrium with Unbounded Excess Demand[3]

Let $z(p)$ be a continuous excess demand mapping from the unit simplex $\Delta \in \mathbb{R}^n \to \mathbb{R}^n$, where (1) $z(p)$ is bounded from below, (2) $p \cdot z(p) = 0$, and (3) $p \to bdy\Delta \Rightarrow \|z(p)\| \to \infty$.

Then there exists $\overline{p} \in \Delta$ such that $z(\overline{p}) = 0$.

Proof: Define P to be the unit hyperplane (i.e., $P = \{p| \sum_{i=1}^n p_i = 1\}$) and consider the mapping

$$F : \Delta \to \mathbb{R}^n,$$

where

$$F_i(p) = \frac{p_i + \frac{z_i(p)}{1+\|z(p)\|}}{1 + \sum_{i=1}^n \frac{z_i(p)}{1+\|z(p)\|}}, \quad i = 1, \ldots, n. \tag{5.3-4}$$

Note that $F(p) \in P$. If we can find a fixed point of F we are done. For then

$$p = F(p) = \frac{p + \frac{z(p)}{1+\|z(p)\|}}{1 + \sum_{i=1}^n \frac{z_i(p)}{1+\|z(p)\|}}. \tag{5.3-5}$$

Appealing to (2) in the statement of the proposition,

$$p \cdot p = \frac{p \cdot p + \frac{p \cdot z(p)}{1+\|z(p)\|}}{1 + \sum_{i=1}^n \frac{z_i(p)}{1+\|z(p)\|}} = \frac{p \cdot p}{1 + \sum_{i=1}^n \frac{z_i(p)}{1+\|z(p)\|}}$$

and so $\sum_{i=1}^n \frac{z_i(p)}{1+\|z(p)\|} = 0$.

Substituting this into (5.3-5), $p = p + \frac{z(p)}{1+\|z(p)\|}$; hence $z(p) = 0$.

The difficulty is that $F : \Delta \to P$ so that we cannot apply Brouwer's Fixed Point Theorem directly. The first step in dealing with this difficulty is to define the trimmed unit simplex

$$\Delta(\varepsilon) = \{p \in \Delta | p_i \geq \varepsilon > 0, i = 1, \ldots, n\}.$$

Let $G \circ F(p)$ be the point in $\Delta(\varepsilon)$ closest to $F(p)$, as illustrated in Figure 5.3-3. The heavily shaded line segment is the trimmed unit simplex and the dashed line is the unit line. For any p in the trimmed unit simplex there is

---

[3] The proof is for the mathematically inclined. A similar proof applies if $z(p)$ is an upper hemi-continuous correspondence.

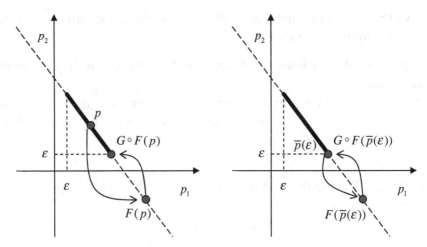

Figure 5.3-3. Mapping from trimmed simplex.

some $F(p)$ on the unit line. If, as depicted in the left diagram, $F(p) \notin \Delta(\varepsilon)$, then the closest point $G \circ F(p)$ is one of the boundary points of $\Delta(\varepsilon)$.

The compound mapping $G \circ F : \Delta(\varepsilon) \to \Delta(\varepsilon)$ is continuous and so has a fixed point $\overline{p}(\varepsilon)$. This is depicted in the right diagram. But note that in the case depicted $F(\overline{p}) \neq \overline{p}$. To complete the proof we show that in the limit, as the trimming goes to zero, this cannot be the case.

Consider any sequence of trimmed unit simplexes $\{\Delta(\varepsilon^s)\}$ where $\{\varepsilon^s\} \to 0$ and define $\overline{p}^s = \overline{p}(\varepsilon^s)$. Because $\overline{p}^s \in \Delta(\varepsilon^s) \subset \Delta$, $\{\overline{p}^s\}$ is bounded. Thus there exists a convergent subsequence

$$\{\overline{p}^t\} = \{\overline{p}(\varepsilon^t)\} \to \overline{p} \in \Delta.$$

We will argue that, for sufficiently large t, $F(\overline{p}^t) \in \Delta(\varepsilon^t)$; thus $G \circ F(\overline{p}^t) = F(\overline{p}^t)$. But $\overline{p}^t$ is a fixed point of $G \circ F : \Delta(\varepsilon^t) \to \Delta(\varepsilon^t)$. So then $\overline{p}^t = G \circ F(\overline{p}^t) = F(\overline{p}^t)$ and, by our earlier argument, we are done.

Suppose instead that

$$F(\overline{p}^t) \notin \Delta(\varepsilon^t), \quad \text{for all large } t. \tag{5.3-6}$$

Then $G \circ F(\overline{p}^t) \in bdy\Delta(\varepsilon^t)$ and so $G \circ F(\overline{p}) \in bdy\Delta$. If follows that $\overline{p}_i = 0$ for some i and so $\|z(\overline{p}^t)\| \to \infty$.

The next step is to show that this implies that $F(\overline{p}) \in \Delta$.

$$F(\overline{p}^t) = \frac{N^t}{D^t},$$

where

$$D^t = 1 + \sum_{i=1}^{n} \frac{z_i(\overline{p}^t)}{1 + \|z(\overline{p}^t)\|} \quad \text{and} \quad N^t = \overline{p}^t + \frac{z(\overline{p}^t)}{1 + \|z(\overline{p}^t)\|}.$$

Let I be the index set of commodities for which $z_i(\overline{p}^t) \to \infty$. Because $z(p)$ is bounded from below it follows that

$$\overline{D} - 1 = \lim_{t \to \infty} D^t - 1 = \lim_{t \to \infty} \sum_{i=1}^{n} \frac{z_i(\overline{p}^t)}{1 + \|z(\overline{p}^t)\|}$$

$$= \lim_{t \to \infty} \sum_{i=1}^{n} \frac{\frac{z_i(\overline{p}^t)}{\|z(\overline{p}^t)\|}}{1 + \frac{1}{\|z(\overline{p}^t)\|}} = \lim_{t \to \infty} \sum_{i \in I} \frac{z_i(\overline{p}^t)}{\|z(\overline{p}^t)\|}.$$

For t sufficiently large $z_i(\overline{p}^t) \geq 0$, $i \in I$. Hence

$$\overline{D} - 1 \geq \underset{z \geq 0}{\text{Min}} \left\{ \frac{\sum_{i \in I} z_i}{\|z\|} \right\} = 1.[4]$$

For $i \in I$, $N_i^t = \overline{p}_i^t + \frac{z_i(\overline{p}^t)}{1 + \|z(\overline{p}^t)\|} > 0$ for t sufficiently large because $z_i(\overline{p}^t) \to \infty$.

For $i \notin I$, $z_i(\overline{p}^t)$ is bounded and so $N_i^t \to \overline{p}_i \geq 0$. Therefore $F(\overline{p}) \geq 0$. Because $F(\overline{p}) \in H$ it follows that $F(\overline{p}) \in \Delta$. Then

$$\overline{p} = \lim_{t \to \infty} \overline{p}^t = \lim_{t \to \infty} G \circ F(\overline{p}^t) = G \circ F(\overline{p}) = F(\overline{p}). \qquad (5.3\text{-}7)$$

Finally we note that, because $\overline{p} \in \Delta$, $\overline{p}_j > 0$ for some j.

Because $z(p)$ is bounded from below there exists some $\alpha > 0$ such that $z(p) > -\alpha$. Also, because $p \cdot z(p) = 0$,

$$\overline{p}_j^t z_j(\overline{p}^t) = \sum_{i \neq j} \overline{p}_i^t \cdot (-z_i(\overline{p}^t)) \leq \alpha \sum_{i \neq j} \overline{p}_i^t \leq \alpha.$$

Then the sequence $\{z_j(\overline{p}^t)\}$ is bounded. It follows that

$$F_j(\overline{p}) = \lim_{t \to \infty} \frac{\overline{p}_j^t + \frac{z_t(\overline{p}^t)}{1 + \|z(\overline{p}^t)\|}}{D^t} = \frac{\overline{p}_j}{\overline{D}} \leq \tfrac{1}{2}\overline{p}_j.$$

Therefore $F(\overline{p}) \neq \overline{p}$. But this contradicts (5.3-7). Hence (5.3-6) cannot be true. $\qquad \square$

Exercises

Exercise 5.3-1: Continuity of the Supply Function Show that if a firm's production set is closed, bounded, and strictly convex, then the profit-maximizing supply $y(p)$ is continuous. HINT: Appeal to arguments in section 4 of Appendix C.

Exercise 5.3-2: Supply and Demand Correspondences Suppose that each firm's production set is compact and convex.

---

[4] To confirm this show that $k = \underset{z \geq 0}{\text{Min}}\{\sum_{j=1}^{n} z_j \mid \sum_{j=1}^{n} z_j^2 = k^2\}$.

(a) Appeal to any theorems you like to show that each firm's profit function is continuous and supply correspondence $y^f(p)$ is upper hemi-continuous.

(b) Show that for any $p \gg 0$ the budget set of consumer h, $B^h(p)$ is a continuous correspondence at p. Hence show that the demand correspondence $x^h(p)$ is upper hemi-continuous at p.

Exercise 5.3-3: Existence and Non-Existence with a Minimum Consumption Threshold

(a) Consumer h, $h \in \{A, B\}$ has a consumption set $X^h = \mathbb{R}^2_+$ and a utility function $U^h = x_1^{\alpha^h} x_2^{\beta^h}$, where $\alpha^h + \beta^h = 1$ and $\alpha^A > \alpha^B$. The aggregate endowment of each commodity is ω. Depict the PE allocations in a neat figure and explain carefully why, in this economy, WE price ratios satisfy

$$\frac{\alpha^B}{\beta^B} \le \frac{p_1}{p_2} \le \frac{\alpha^A}{\beta^A}.$$

Henceforth assume that consumer h, $h \in \{A, B\}$ has a consumption set $X^h = \{x \,|\, x_1 \ge \gamma, x_2 \ge \gamma\}$ where $2\gamma < \omega$. His utility function is $U^h = (x_1 - \gamma)^{\alpha^h} (x_2 - \gamma)^{\beta^h}$, where $\alpha^h + \beta^h = 1$ and $\alpha^A > \alpha^B$.

(b) Depict the Edgeworth Box and indicate the inner box where allocations are in both consumption sets.

(c) Define $\hat{x}_i^h = x_i^h - \gamma$ and $\hat{\omega}_i^h = \omega_i^h - \gamma$ then show that, using these redefined variables, it is possible to analyze the problem exactly as in part (a). Depict the PE allocations in an Edgeworth Box diagram and show that the range of possible WE prices is the same as in part (a).

(d) Depict the budget lines for the two extreme PE allocations and then shade in the region of the Edgeworth Box for which there is a WE.

Exercise 5.3-4: Continuum of Equilibria and Utility-Reducing Transfers

(a) For the utility functions used in part (b) of the previous exercise, show that

$$x_1^h(p) - \gamma = \alpha^h \left[(\omega_1^h - \gamma) + \frac{p_2}{p_1} (\omega_2^h - \gamma) \right].$$

(b) Setting market demand equal to supply show that

$$\beta^A (\omega_1^A - \gamma) + \beta^B (\omega_1^B - \gamma) = \frac{p_2}{p_1} \left[\alpha^A (\omega_2^A - \gamma) + \alpha^B (\omega_2^B - \gamma) \right].$$

Henceforth assume that $\alpha^A = \beta^B = \frac{1}{3}$, $\gamma = 2$ and $\omega^A = (4, 1)$ and $\omega_2^B = (1, 4)$.

(c) Show that the market clears for all possible price ratios on the interval $[\frac{1}{2}, 2]$.

(d) Shade in the cone of WE budget lines in a neat Edgeworth Box diagram. Explain why, for any other endowment in this cone, equilibrium is unique. (Thus the WE is "generically" unique.)

(e) If the endowment is in the cone to the northwest of $(4, 1)$ explain why a transfer of endowment from Bev to Alex will raise Alex's utility and the relative price of commodity 1.

(f) What happens to Alex's utility if the endowment point is in the shaded cone to the southeast of $(4, 1)$?

Exercise 5.3-5: Continuum of Equilibria with No Consumption Threshold

Consumer h, $h \in \{A, B\}$ has consumption set $X^h = \mathbb{R}_+^2$ and a utility function

$$U^h(x_1, x_2) = \begin{cases} \text{Min}\{x_1 - \gamma, x_2 - \gamma\} & \text{if Min}\{x_1, x_2\} \leq \gamma \\ (x_1 - \gamma)^{\alpha^h}(x_2 - \gamma)^{\beta^h}, & \text{otherwise} \end{cases}$$

where $\alpha^h + \beta^h = 1$.

(a) Solve for consumer h's demand for commodity 1 for all price ratios and show that his demand function is continuous.
(b) Characterize the PE allocations and possible WE price ratios if all parameter values are as in the previous exercise. HINT: Appeal extensively to the answer to the previous exercise.

5.4 Public Goods

Key ideas: non-rivalrous consumption, joint products, personalized prices, Lindahl equilibrium

In the basic economic model, individuals have private wants. Holding production fixed, every time my wants are satisfied by an increase in my allocation of some commodity, there is an equal reduction in the allocation of this good to everyone else. Commodities are thus fully *rivalrous*. However, for some commodities, an individual's consumption has little or no such offset. National defense and warning beacons are two extreme examples in which consumption is completely non-rivalrous. My consumption does not reduce yours at all. For many other commodities the degree of rivalry is small. If I utilize a public park I might make your visit somewhat less enjoyable if you are seeking solitude, but you can certainly still get a lot of enjoyment. To a first approximation park consumption is thus completely non-rivalrous.

Private Non-Rivalrous Goods (Joint Products)

In this section we add commodities that are perfectly non-rivalrous to the private goods model. Before discussing "public goods" like national defense or city parks, we consider commodities that are private in consumption but non-rivalrous in production.

Suppose that, in addition to the production of N regular commodities $(y_1, \ldots, y_N)$, an economy produces y_0 units of electricity capacity. This capacity is sold to electricity distributors who offer to supply electricity at different times of the day. We divide the day into T periods and define $(x_{N+1}^h, \ldots, x_{N+T}^h)$ to be the electricity consumption by individual h. Consumer h's full consumption vector of the other N commodities and electricity is therefore $x^h = (x_1^h, \ldots, x_{N+T}^h)$. Then aggregate demand for electricity in period t is

$$x_{N+t} = \sum_{h=1}^{H} x_{N+t}^h.$$

For consumers, electricity is private. Thus for aggregate feasibility $x_{N+t} - y_0 \le 0, t = 1, \ldots, T$.

For the distributor who purchases the electricity capacity, the situation is very different. Once the capacity is purchased, its use in one period does not reduce its potential use in each of the other periods. For the sake of concreteness, think of the capacity as hydroelectric capacity. If we ignore the cost of maintaining the turbines, the cost of the electricity is the same, regardless of how much is actually sold in each period. Let y_{N+t}^d be distributor d's output of electricity in period t. If this is less than capacity, an increase in period t output has no effect on the ability of the firm to produce in other periods and no effect on total cost. In the electricity distribution sector electricity capacity is an input. We adopt the convention that inputs are negative. Thus the capacity constraint of an electricity distributor is

$$y_{N+t}^d + y_0^d \le 0, \quad t = 1, \ldots, T.$$

Distributor d has input $y_0^d < 0$ and output vector $y_{N+1}^d, \ldots, y_{N+T}^d$. Thus distributor d's production vector is $y^d = (y_0^d, 0 \ldots, 0, y_{N+1}^d, \ldots, y_{N+T}^d)$. The production set of this distributor is therefore

$$\mathcal{Y}^d = \{y^d | y_n^d = 0, \quad n = 1, \ldots, N, \quad y_{N+t}^d + y_0^d \le 0, \quad t = 1, \ldots, T\}.$$

Because the constraints are linear this production set is convex. Thus, as long as the technology of all the other firms and the consumers satisfy the standard convexity properties, the two welfare theorems continue to hold.

Consider, in particular, the dth electricity distributor. Suppose that its equilibrium production vector is $\bar{y}^d$. Let C be the index set of periods in which the WE price of electricity is strictly positive. Because the cost of producing electricity is zero, the firm maximizes profit by producing at capacity. Thus the marginal revenue of increasing capacity is $\sum_{t \in C} p_{N+t}$. In equilibrium this must equal the marginal cost of an additional unit of electricity capacity; that is, p_0. Hence, for a WE, it must be the case that

$\sum_{t \in C} p_{N+t} = p_0$. But for all other periods the price of electricity is zero. Thus

$$\sum_{t=1}^{T} p_{N+t} = p_0.$$

That is, the sum of the prices of electricity in the T periods must equal the market price of an additional unit of capacity.

Public Goods

We now argue that this private goods model can be reinterpreted as a public goods model. We do this in stages. Suppose first that there are as many periods of the day as consumers ($H = T$.) Suppose next that only consumer h enjoys consuming electricity in period h. That is the utility of consumer h can be written as $U^h(x^h) = U^h(x_1^h, \ldots, x_N^h, x_{N+h}^h)$. From the viewpoint of consumer preferences, this can be seen as a special case of the previous model, where all $N + T$ commodities potentially enter every utility function.

Suppose that consumer h has a consumption that is below capacity. Because she is the only person purchasing this commodity, it follows that market supply exceeds demand and thus the Walrasian equilibrium price of commodity $N + h$, p_{N+h} must be zero. For all other consumers demand is equal to capacity and arguing as before, the sum of the equilibrium prices satisfies

$$\sum_{h=1}^{H} p_{N+h} = p_0.$$

Lindahl Equilibrium

Now consider the conversion of land from housing to a public park. Ignoring any congestion effects of park utilization we can reinterpret y_0 as the size of the park. Consumption is non-rivalrous so consumption of the park by consumer h, x_{N+h}^h has no effect on the potential consumption by other consumers. For every consumer, however, park consumption is limited by the aggregate supply constraint

$$x_{N+h}^h \leq y_0.$$

This is precisely the model described earlier. Thus we have almost effortlessly extended the basic general equilibrium model to incorporate public goods. The one importance difference between this equilibrium and the standard WE is that, with the public goods, there is a different price of the public good for each consumer. Commodities and prices are personalized.

Thus the buyer in each market is a monopolist and so the usual rationale for the price-taking assumption does not apply. For this reason a WE with personalized prices is usually referred to as a *Lindahl equilibrium*.

Given the absence of markets underlying the personalized prices, what are the alternatives? If numbers are small, an outcome may be negotiated by the participants. For example if the public good is street lighting on a neighborhood block, those directly concerned can meet and attempt to reach a decision that is in the interest of each homeowner. Similarly, for a lighthouse, shipping lines may be able to negotiate a mutually agreeable outcome. However, when numbers are large, such negotiations are not feasible. The alternative is an imposed solution. In principle, the government could introduce a user fee p_h for each consumer. With full information about preferences this could mimic the market equilibrium. Realistically, however, the best the government can do is impose a more arbitrary fee system, perhaps based on property value or income.

Excludable Public Goods

For some public goods like national defense, every person receives the commodity or service whether they want it or not. However for something like a park, it may be economical to surround it with a fence and exclude those unwilling to pay for its use. In the absence of any information about willingness to pay, the user fee is necessarily the same for everyone or is based on some observable characteristic (such as age). Whether such a scheme closely approximates an efficient outcome then depends on how much the user fees deviate from the theoretical Lindahl equilibrium personalized prices. Viewed in this way, the Lindahl equilibrium is a standard against which real solutions can be compared.

Exercises

Exercise 5.4-1: A Public "Bad" Consider a one-consumer, one-firm economy (or equivalently an economy with many identical consumers and firms.) There are two private commodities. The firm also produces a level of pollution b. The production set of the firm is the convex set $\mathcal{Y} = \{(y_1, y_2, b) | G(y, b) \leq 0\}$, where $G(\cdot)$ is strictly increasing in its first two arguments and strictly decreasing in b. Thus by increasing pollution, the firm can produce more output (or use less input). The consumer has a concave utility function $U(x_1, x_2, b)$ that is also increasing in its first two arguments and decreasing in b.

(a) Write down the first-order conditions for the optimal production plan and pollution level.

(b) Write down the first-order conditions for profit maximization and utility maximization if there is a pollution tax t on each unit of pollution produced and the firm and consumers are price takers.

(c) Confirm that by choosing the tax appropriately, the optimal level of pollution is produced.

(d) Add a second firm with a different production function. Now the consumers observe a pollution level $b = b^1 + b^2$. Show that the optimum can still be achieved by the imposition of a tax.

(e) Suppose that the optimal pollution level is b^*. Suppose that the government announces that it will sell b^* "rights" to pollute. Will the tax rate emerge as the equilibrium market-clearing price?

(f) Finally add more consumers and show that the arguments generalize.

5.5 Equilibrium Futures Prices

Key ideas: reinterpreting the timeless model, equilibrium spot, futures and future spot market prices

In the baseline general equilibrium model, time plays no role. Goods are all transformed instantaneously by firms and then consumed. In this section we show that, by simply reinterpreting commodities and prices, the analysis continues to apply when the time dimension is added.

Consider a WE. Firms choose an input vector to maximize profit and consumers maximize utility subject to their budget constraints. Let $y^f(p)$ be the production vector of firm f, given a price vector p. Therefore

$$y^f(p) \text{ solves } \underset{y}{\text{Max}}\{p \cdot y^f | y^f \in Y^f\}, \quad f = 1, \dots, F.$$

Maximized profit $\Pi^f(p) = p \cdot y^f(p)$ is distributed as dividends. Then consumer h, with shareholdings θ^{hf}, $f = 1, \dots, F$ has consumption vector $x^h(p)$, where

$$x^h(p) \text{ solves } \text{Max} \left\{ U^h(x^h) | p \cdot x^h \leq p \cdot \omega^h + \sum_{f=1}^{F} \theta^{hf} \Pi^f \right\}, \quad h = 1, \dots, H.$$

In the earlier sections, the WE was interpreted as a one-period or "static" model. However the WE also has a dynamic interpretation. Although we examine here the simplest two-period case, the argument is completely general. If there are n commodities, the production plan for firm f, is $y^f = (y_1^f, y_2^f)$, where

$$y_t^f = \left(y_{t1}^f, \dots, y_{tn}^f \right), \quad t = 1, 2.$$

We similarly define the consumption vectors of each agent as $x^h = (x_1^h, x_2^h)$ and the price vector as $p = (p_1, p_2)$.

Note that in this interpretation, all agents trade all $2n$ commodities in period 1. The commodity vector x_1^h is purchased for delivery "on the spot" and traded at the spot price vector $p_1 = (p_{11}, \ldots, p_{1n})$. The period 2 or "future" commodities are traded at the "futures" price vector p_2. Because firms are able to sell today all goods delivered in the future, they can pay dividends on the spot. Similarly, because consumers can contract to deliver their labor in the future they can be paid in advance and then choose a life-time consumption plan utilizing their income from all future periods.

Clearly this is a very fanciful story, and one that deviates dramatically from the way markets actually operate. However, as noted in Chapter 2, it is possible to reinterpret this model as one in which agents trade only in spot markets, and transfer wealth between periods by borrowing and lending. Let r be the market rate of interest and define p_2^s to be the period 2 spot price vector. That is, once period 2 arrives, an agent will be able to trade commodity j at the price p_{2j}^s. Thus unlike spot and futures prices, this is the price at which the commodity is anticipated to trade. Let d_t^f be the dividend paid in period t. If the first-period dividend exceeds first-period profit, the firm borrows B_1^f and then is able to pay a dividend of

$$d_1^f = p_1 \cdot y_1^f + B_1^f.$$

Then, in period 2, the anticipated dividend is the profit remaining after paying back the loan, that is,

$$d_2^f = p_2^s \cdot y_2^f - B_1^f(1 + r).$$

Dividing the period 2 equation by $1 + r$ and then adding the two equations, the present value of the dividend stream is

$$PV\left\{d_1^f, d_2^f\right\} = d_1^f + \frac{d_2^f}{1 + r} = p_1 \cdot y_1^f + \frac{1}{1 + r}p_2^s \cdot y_2^f. \qquad (5.5\text{-}1)$$

Note that as long as $p_2^s = (1 + r)p_2$, the present value of the dividend stream is

$$p_1 \cdot y_1^f + p_2 \cdot y_2^f = \Pi^f(p).$$

Thus a firm using spot and futures prices to maximize profit maximizes the present value of the dividend stream.

Next consider consumer h. In period 1 he receives dividends of $\sum_{f=1}^F \theta^{hf} d_1^f$. If he saves S_1^h, his budget constraints in the two periods are as follows:

$$p_1 \cdot x_1^h \leq p_1 \cdot \omega_1^h + \sum_{f=1}^{F} \theta^{hf} d_1^f - S_1^h$$

$$p_2^s \cdot x_2^h \leq p_2^s \cdot \omega_2^h + \sum_{f=1}^{F} \theta^{hf} d_2^f + (1+r)S_1^h.$$

Expressing the second constraint in present value terms and then adding the two constraints,

$$p_1 \cdot x_1^h + \frac{1}{1+r} p_2^s \cdot x_2^h \leq p_1 \cdot \omega_1^h + \frac{1}{1+r} p_2^s \cdot \omega_2^h + \sum_{f=1}^{F} \theta^{hf} \left[d_1^f + \frac{d_2^f}{(1+r)} \right]$$

$$= p_1 \cdot \omega_1^h + \frac{1}{1+r} p_2^s \cdot \omega_2^h + \sum_{f=1}^{F} \theta^{hf} \Pi^f(p), \quad \text{substituting from (5.5-1).}$$

Again, this is exactly the same as the budget constraint with futures prices as long as the present value of the anticipated future spot price vector is the same as the futures price vector $\frac{p_2^s}{1+r} = p_2$.

Rational Expectations

Three cautionary remarks need to be emphasized. First, to be able to make the correct choices in the first period, all economic agents need to be able to correctly forecast the equilibrium future spot prices. Economists call this the assumption of rational expectations. It is rational in the sense that if everyone believes that the future spot price vector will be p_2^s and makes optimizing trades based on such belief, then this price vector is indeed a WE price vector. However only the spot markets open in period 1. There is no market guide as to how consumers and firms should form beliefs about prices in markets that will reopen in the future. (See the example immediately following.) The most positive spin on this uncomfortable truth is that the problem is less likely to be severe if there are experts who do understand the economy and act as arbitrageurs whenever spot prices are inconsistent with the multi-period equilibrium prices.

A second difficulty is that it is not enough for a consumer or firm to correctly predict future prices. Consumers desiring to spend more than their income when young must borrow based on their future income. Because consumers can choose bankruptcy, they do not always have the incentive to live up to promises made when young. Knowing this, potential lenders will be more reluctant to lend than the equilibrium model suggests.

Finally, these problems are exacerbated by uncertainty about future preferences and technology. As we see in Chapter 7, the formal equilibrium model can be further extended to incorporate uncertainty. In addition to markets for different commodities to be delivered at different dates, we introduce commodities where the delivery is contingent on uncertain future events. The weakness of this approach is that it stretches even further the underlying implicit assumptions that promises made can be cheaply monitored by the judicial system.

An Example

Suppose that consumers all have the same logarithmic preferences,

$$U = u(x_1) + \tfrac{1}{2}u(x_2) \quad \text{where} \quad x_t = (x_{t1}, x_{t2}) \quad \text{and} \quad u(x_t) = 2\ln x_{t1} + \ln x_{t2}.$$
$$(5.5\text{-}2)$$

The period 1 endowment is $\omega_1 = (120, 120)$. There is no period 2 endowment.

In period 1 there are two commodities that can be either consumed or invested. Each unit of commodity 1 invested yields two units of commodity 1 in period 2. Each unit of commodity 2 invested yields four units of commodity 2 in period 2. Let z_{1i} be the input of commodity i in period 1 and let q_{2i} be period 2 output, $i = 1, 2$. The production functions can then be written as

$$q_{21} = 2z_{11} \quad \text{and} \quad q_{22} = 4z_{12}.$$

Because preferences are homothetic, it follows that we can analyze equilibrium as if there were a single aggregate individual, holding all the endowment and shares.

Let $x_t = (x_{t1}, x_{t2})$ be period t consumption. Then

$$x_{11} = \omega_{11} - z_{11}, \quad x_{12} = \omega_{12} - z_{12}, \quad x_{21} = 2z_{11}, \quad \text{and} \quad x_{22} = 4z_{12}. \quad (5.5\text{-}3)$$

Substituting (5.5-3) into (5.5-2) we obtain

$$U = 2\ln(120 - z_{11}) + \ln(120 - z_{12}) + \ln 2z_{11} + \tfrac{1}{2}\ln 4z_{12}.$$

We can then solve for the optimal period 1 investments. It is readily confirmed that the utility-maximizing input vector is $(z_{11}^*, z_{12}^*) = (40, 40)$ and hence that the optimal consumption vector is $\bar{x} = (80, 80, 80, 160)$.

Because the technology and preferred sets are convex, we know that there are Walrasian equilibrium prices (Lagrange multipliers) that support this optimum. Let the prices for delivery in period 1 be p_1 and the prices for delivery in period 2 (futures prices) be p_2. Then if the value of the consumer's wealth is W, she chooses her consumption vector x to solve

$$\underset{x}{\text{Max}}\{U(x)|p \cdot x = p_1 \cdot x_1 + p_2 \cdot x_2 = W\}.$$

The first-order conditions are as follows:

$$\frac{\frac{\partial U}{\partial x_{11}}}{p_{11}} = \frac{\frac{\partial U}{\partial x_{12}}}{p_{12}} = \frac{\frac{\partial U}{\partial x_{21}}}{p_{21}} = \frac{\frac{\partial U}{\partial x_{22}}}{p_{22}} = \lambda.$$

For our example, with logarithmic preferences, this can be rewritten as

$$\frac{2}{p_{11}80} = \frac{1}{p_{12}80} = \frac{1}{p_{21}80} = \frac{\frac{1}{2}}{p_{22}160} = \lambda.$$

Then for the representative consumer to choose the (Pareto) optimum $\bar{x} = (80, 80, 80, 160)$, we require

$$\frac{2}{p_{11}80} = \frac{1}{p_{12}80} = \frac{1}{p_{21}80} = \frac{\frac{1}{2}}{p_{22}160}.$$

Suppose we make commodity 1 in period 1 the numeraire commodity; that is, $p_{11} = 1$. Then the equilibrium price vector is

$$p = (p_{11}, p_{12}, p_{21}, p_{22}) = \left(1, \tfrac{1}{2}, \tfrac{1}{2}, \tfrac{1}{8}\right). \tag{5.5-4}$$

Note once again that these prices are all period 1 prices. The vector $p_1 = (p_{11}, p_{12}) = (1, \tfrac{1}{2})$ is the vector of prices for immediate delivery ("spot prices"), whereas the vector $p_2 = (p_{21}, p_{22}) = (\tfrac{1}{2}, \tfrac{1}{8})$ is the vector of prices for delivery in the future ("futures prices").

Suppose we make commodity 1 the numeraire commodity in each period and set the spot price of commodity 1 equal to 1 in each period, that is $p_1 = p_{21}^s = 1$. From (5.5-4), $p_{22}/p_{21} = 1/4$. Thus the future spot price vector is $p_2^s = (1, \tfrac{1}{4})$.

Let the market interest rate be r. An arbitrageur can sell a unit of commodity 1 in the futures market for a price of $p_{21} = \tfrac{1}{2}$ and earn interest so that he has $p_{21}(1 + r)$ dollars in period 2. He can then buy the commodity back at the future spot price, p_{21}^s. Thus he makes a profit of $p_{21}(1 + r) - p_{21}^s$ on each unit traded. Then the arbitrageur's period 2 demand is unbounded if $p_{21}(1 + r) > p_{21}^s$. If the inequality is reversed, the arbitrageur makes a profit by buying commodity 1 in the futures market and selling again in the future spot market. Thus demand in the spot market is unbounded. Therefore market clearing requires that $p_{21}(1 + r) = p_{21}^s$. For the example with $p_{21} = \tfrac{1}{2}$ and $p_{21}^s = 1$ it follows that $1 + r = 2$ so that the nominal interest rate is 1.

Exercises

Exercise 5.5-1: Robinson Crusoe Economy Robinson Crusoe has a two-period utility function $U = \sqrt{x_1 x_2}$ where x_t is corn consumption in period t. The farm has a current crop of 108 units of corn. If Robinson plants z_1 units of corn, his second-period output is $y_2 = 12\sqrt{z_1}$. His first-period consumption is then $x_1 = 108 - z_1$.

(a) Solve for Robinson Crusoe's optimal first- and second-period consumption of corn.
(b) If the spot and futures price are $p = (p_1, p_2)$, show that the profit-maximizing demand for input on the spot market is $z_1(p) = 36(\frac{p_2}{p_1})^2$.
(c) Show that $\bar{p} = (1, 1)$ is a WE price vector.
(d) Suppose that there is no spot or futures market. However individuals can save or borrow at the interest rate r. Write down the new optimization problem of the firm and hence confirm that the equilibrium interest rate is zero.

Exercise 5.5-2: Two Commodities and Two Periods Continuing with the example discussed in this section, suppose that commodity 1 is the "numeraire commodity" with a spot price of 1 and that the market rate of interest is zero.

(a) Consider a representative firm maximizing profit with spot and futures markets and another representative firm maximizing the *PV* of the firm and show that these firms will do the same if the future spot price vector $p_2^{2f} = (1 + r)p_2$.
(b) Consider the representative consumer in these two pricing regimes and show that his optimization problem will also be the same.
(c) What must the interest rate be if the future spot price and spot price of the numeraire commodity are both 1?
(d) The "own rate of return" on a commodity is the number of units that can be consumed in period 2 if a consumer withholds a unit of consumption in period 1. What is the equilibrium own rate of return on each commodity?
(e) There is no "real" interest rate in this economy. True or false? Explain.

Exercise 5.5-3: Rational Expectations Equilibrium Suppose that the example discussed in this section is modified so that each consumer has an endowment of $(\omega_{21}, \omega_{22}) = (120, 120)$ in period 2 as well as in period 1. There is a banking sector but there are no futures markets.

(a) Solve for the new utility-maximizing input vector z_1^*
(b) Suppose that the representative consumer can trade in spot and futures markets. If $p_{11} = 1$ what are the WE prices?
(c) If the interest rate is zero, what are the equilibrium spot prices in each period?

Exercise 5.5-4: Worthless Technology? Suppose that the example is modified so that the second-period endowment $\omega_2 = (600, 600)$. In period 1 there are both spot and futures markets for each commodity.

(a) If the technology is disabled so that only the endowments remain, what will be the equilibrium prices?
    Henceforth assume that the technology is enabled.
(b) At these prices is it profitable for the firm to produce?
(c) Does it immediately follow that zero production is optimal? Explain.
(d) For what period 2 endowments is the technology unprofitable? For what period 2 endowments is the technology worthless?

Exercise 5.5-5: WE in a Two-Period Model All individuals have identical Cobb-Douglas preferences $U^h(x) = u(x_1^h) + \delta u(x_2^h)$, where $u(x_t) = \ln x_{t1} + 2 \ln x_{t2}$. The aggregate endowment is $\omega = (\omega_{11}, \omega_{12}, \omega_{21}, \omega_{22}) = (2, 2, 1, 1)$.

(a) If commodities are not storable, what is the WE of this economy?
(b) Show that there is an equilibrium in which the future spot prices and spot prices are identical. What is the WE interest rate in this economy?
(c) Next suppose that there are firms that can store at no cost. That is, each firm has a production set $Y^f = \{y^f | y_{2j}^f \leq -y_{1j}^f, j = 1, 2\}$. Assuming that storage takes place, what are the WE spot and futures prices. HINT: Consider the behavior of the firms.
(d) Under what conditions will there be storage?

5.6 Equilibrium with Constant Returns to Scale

Key ideas: mapping between input and output price is invertible and independent of input endowment

We can gain further powerful insights into the relationship between endowments, technology, and prices if we are willing to make the additional assumption that an economy exhibits constant returns to scale (CRS). In this section we consider an economy that produces commodities A and B using two inputs z_1 and z_2. The total supply of input i is fixed and equal to $\bar{z}_i$.

Although the assumption of constant returns to scale is very strong at the level of the individual firm, it is a natural starting point for analysis at a more aggregate level. In particular, if there is free entry into an industry and all firms have access to the same technology, CRS emerges at the industry level as long as average cost curves have the usual U-shape.

Let $q_i = F_i(z_{1i}, z_{2i})$ be the aggregate production function for commodity i, $i = A, B$. We make the further weak assumption that the production function is strictly quasi-concave. That is, for any z^0, z^1 and convex combination z^λ, $F_i(z^1) \geq F_i(z^0) \Rightarrow F_i(z^\lambda) > F_i(z^0)$. In particular, this implies that for any isoquant $F_i(z) = k$, and any input price vector r, there is a unique cost-minimizing input vector. Finally we label commodities so that if a firm uses inputs in proportion to the aggregate endowment, the marginal value of input 1 is higher for commodity A.

Assumption: Production of Commodity A Is More Input 1 Intensive
At the aggregate endowment of inputs, the marginal rate of technical substitution is higher for commodity A than for commodity B; that is,

$$\text{MRTS}_A(\bar{z}) > \text{MRTS}_B(\bar{z}).$$

In an exact parallel to the definition of Pareto efficiency for an exchange economy, we define production efficiency for this economy.

Production Efficiency A production plan for the economy is production efficient if it is not possible to increase the output of one commodity without reducing the output of the other.

Formally, a production plan is efficient if, for some output q_B^0, it solves the following problem:

$$\underset{z_A, z_B}{\text{Max}}\{q_A = F_A(z_A) | F_B(z_B) \geq q_B^0, \ z_A + z_B \leq \bar{z}\}.$$

The production-efficient allocations are depicted in an Edgeworth Box diagram in Figure 5.6-1.

Given the CRS assumption, we can provide a strong characterization of the locus of efficient input allocations. First we note that a function exhibiting constant returns to scale is homothetic. Thus, all the results of Section 3.1 for exchange economies with homothetic preferences carry over immediately.

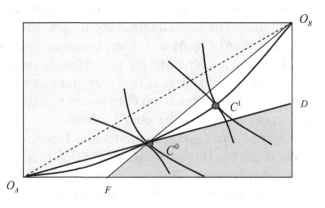

Figure 5.6-1. Production efficiency.

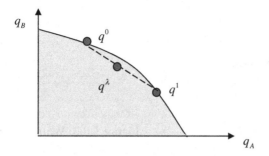

Figure 5.6-2. The production possibility set.

Hence we have the following proposition:

Proposition 5.6-1:
At any interior production-efficient allocation, $\frac{z_{A2}}{z_{A1}} < \frac{z_{B2}}{z_{B1}}$. Moreover, along the locus of production efficient inputs, as output of commodity A increases, both of these input-ratios z_{i2}/z_{i1}, $i = A, B$ increase, as does the marginal rate of technological substitution.

All these results are illustrated in Figure 5.6-1.
We refer to the set of feasible output vectors as the production possibility set. We now prove that the boundary of this set is strictly "bowed out" as depicted in Figure 5.6-2.

Proposition 5.6-2:
If q^0 and q^1 are feasible output vectors, no convex combination q^λ is production efficient.

Proof: Let z_A^0 and z_B^0 be the input vectors at q^0 and let z_A^1 and z_B^1 be the input vectors at q^1. Define $z_A^\lambda = (1 - \lambda)z_A^0 + \lambda z_A^1$ and $z_B^\lambda = (1 - \lambda)z_B^0 + \lambda z_B^1$. The input allocation z_A^λ, z_B^λ is feasible because

$$z_A^\lambda + z_B^\lambda = (1 - \lambda)(z_A + z_B) + \lambda(z_A' + z_B') \leq \bar{z}.$$

Appealing to Proposition 4.3-2, $F_A(z)$ is concave. Moreover by Proposition 5.6-1, z_A^0 and z_A^1 are linearly independent, so from Proposition 4.3-2 it follows that

$$\hat{q}_A \equiv F_A\left((1 - \lambda)z_A^0 + \lambda z_A^1\right) > (1 - \lambda)F_A\left(z_A^0\right) + \lambda F_A\left(z_A^1\right)$$
$$= (1 - \lambda)q_A^0 + \lambda q_A^1 = q_A^\lambda.$$

A symmetrical argument for commodity B establishes that

$$\hat{q}_B \equiv F_B((1 - \lambda)z_B^0 + \lambda z_B^1) > (1 - \lambda)q_B^0 + \lambda q_B^1 = q_B^\lambda.$$

Thus there exists a feasible output pair to the northeast of q^λ in Figure 5.6-3.
$\square$

Let r and p be WE input and output price vectors and let $q(p)$ be a WE output vector. Note that at all points on the frontier, all inputs are utilized

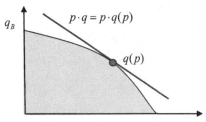

Figure 5.6-3. Walrasian equilibrium.

so total cost is $r \cdot \bar{z}$. Total profit must be maximized at $q(p)$. Because total cost is the same at all points on the production possibility frontier, it follows that total revenue is maximized at $q(p)$. Thus, unless $q(p)$ is at a corner, the slope of the equal revenue line must be equal to the slope of the production possibility frontier. This is depicted in Figure 5.6-3.

Appealing to Proposition 5.6-2, it follows that the WE output vector $q(p)$ is unique.

Also, for any good that is produced, cost minimization implies that

$$\frac{r_2}{r_1} = \mathrm{MRTS}_i(z_i).$$

It follows that the higher the output price ratio p_A/p_B, the greater is the output of commodity A and hence (by Proposition 5.6-1), the greater is the input price ratio r_1/r_2. We summarize this as follows.

Proposition 5.6-3: Equilibrium Input and Output Prices
If the production of commodity A is more input 1 intensive at the aggregate endowment and both commodities are produced, there is a strictly increasing one-to-one mapping between the equilibrium output price ratio p_A/p_B and the input price ratio r_1/r_2.

A further important feature of the CRS economy is that if both commodities are produced, the relationship between input and output prices is independent of the aggregate input vector. To understand this, consider the cost function for a commodity $C(q, r)$. Under CRS cost rises proportionally with output so that the cost function can be written as follows:

$$C(q, r) = qC(1, r).$$

The function $C(1, r)$ is the cost of producing one unit or average cost $AC(r)$. Because equilibrium profit is zero, the equilibrium price of each output must equal its average cost. Thus, as long as both goods are produced, the relationship between input and output prices is independent of the aggregate supply of inputs.

The next result follows immediately from Proposition 5.6-3.

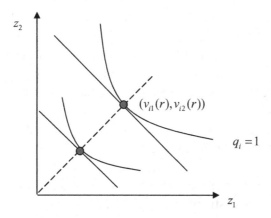

Figure 5.6-4. Ray expansion path.

Proposition 5.6-4: Input Price Equalization
Suppose two countries have the same technology. Suppose also that at the aggregate endowment for each country, commodity A is more input 1 intensive. Then if the two countries trade at the same world prices and both commodities are produced, the WE input prices are also the same.

It is useful to next define the cost-minimizing unit input requirements $v_i(r)$, given input prices r. Because of the strict quasi-concavity of the production functions, $(v_{i1}(r), v_{i2}(r))$ is uniquely defined. This is depicted in Figure 5.6-4. Unit cost is minimized at the point where the unit isoquant is tangential to the iso-cost line.

The average cost of commodity i is

$$AC_i(r) = r_1 v_{i1}(r) + r_2 v_{i2}(r).$$

Equilibrium output prices are therefore as follows:

$$p_i = AC_i(r) = r_1 v_{i1}(r) + r_2 v_{i2}(r), \quad i = A, B.$$

Because a CRS production function is homothetic, output expansion paths are rays. Moreover, given constant returns to scale, it follows that if output is scaled up by a factor of θ, the cost-minimizing input vector is also scaled up by this same factor. Then for an output vector (q_A, q_B), the aggregate demand for inputs is $v_A(r)q_A + v_B(r)q_B$. Thus we can rewrite the equilibrium conditions for input markets as follows:[5]

$$v_A(r)q_A + v_B(r)q_B = \bar{z}. \tag{5.6-1}$$

---

[5] This result provides a simple way to solve for each point on the production possibility frontier. First choose an input price vector and solve for the unit input demands. Then appeal to the linear equation system to solve for (q_A, q_B).

Thus far we have not tried to close the model on the demand side. For some applications, the natural simplification is to assume that consumer preferences can be represented by a single representative consumer. The second alternative is to assume that the economy is small and trades freely in world markets at fixed world prices p. For the rest of this section we take the latter approach.

We next consider the effect of an increase in an output price on input prices. Because the value of total output rises, the total value of the two inputs must rise. Thus the price of at least one input must rise. The following result establishes that one input price necessarily falls. Thus changes in world prices have important distributional effects.

Proposition 5.6-5: Stolper-Samuelson Theorem
Suppose that at the aggregate endowment, commodity A is more input 1 intensive. Then an increase in the price of commodity A results in an increase in the price of input 1 and a decrease in the price of input 2.

Proof: As p_A increases, x_A increases. By Proposition 5.6-3, r_1/r_2 increases. But

$$p_B = AC_B(r_1, r_2) \tag{5.6-2}$$

where $AC_B(r)$ is an increasing function. A k percent increase in all input prices has no effect on the cost-minimizing input vector; thus average cost also rises by k percent. That is, $AC_B(r)$ is homogeneous of degree 1, and so we can rewrite this expression as

$$p_B = r_2 AC_B(r_1/r_2, 1). \tag{5.6-3}$$

Because r_1/r_2 rises r_2 must fall. From (5.6-2) it then follows that r_1 must rise.
□

We next ask how the boundary of the aggregate production set shifts with an increase in the aggregate supply of one of the inputs. As the following proposition shows, if we fix the slope before and after an increase in the supply of input 1, each point on the old frontier shifts to the southeast. This is depicted in Figure 5.6-5.

Proposition 5.6-6: Rybczynski Theorem
Suppose that at the aggregate endowment, commodity A is more input 1 intensive and remains so as the endowment of input 1 rises. Then at constant output prices, output of commodity A rises and output of commodity B falls.

Proof: Because output prices are fixed, unit input requirements are fixed. From Proposition 5.6-1, we know that $v_{B2}/v_{B1} > v_{A2}/v_{A1}$. Also,

$$q_A v_{A1} + q_B v_{B1} = \bar{z}_1 \quad \text{and} \quad q_A v_{A2} + q_B v_{B2} = \bar{z}_2. \tag{5.6-4}$$

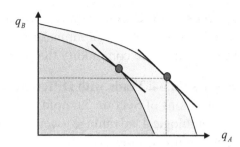

Figure 5.6-5. Effect of increasing the supply of input 1.

Hence

$$\begin{bmatrix} v_{A1} & v_{B1} \\ v_{A2} & v_{B2} \end{bmatrix} \begin{bmatrix} dq_A \\ dq_B \end{bmatrix} = \begin{bmatrix} d\bar{z}_1 \\ 0 \end{bmatrix}. \tag{5.6-5}$$

Applying Cramer's Rule

$$dq_B = \begin{vmatrix} v_{A1} & d\bar{z}_1 \\ v_{A2} & 0 \end{vmatrix} \bigg/ \begin{vmatrix} v_{A1} & v_{B1} \\ v_{A2} & v_{B2} \end{vmatrix}$$

$$= \frac{-v_{A2}d\bar{z}_1}{v_{A1}v_{B2} - v_{B1}v_{A2}}.$$

$$< 0 \text{ because } \frac{v_{A2}}{v_{A1}} < \frac{v_{B2}}{v_{B1}}.$$

$\square$

Exercises

Exercise 5.6-1: Market Adjustment Consider an economy with land and labor inputs and two outputs. It trades at fixed international prices p_A and p_B. The supply of land is fixed although the supply of labor is increasing. Commodity A is more labor intensive. As the supply of labor increases, simple economic intuition tells us that the price of labor will fall. Is this correct? If not, try to describe the likely adjustment process in the economy.

Exercise 5.6-2: Output Price Effect on Input Prices Suppose there is a decrease in the price of the commodity that is less input 1 intensive (commodity B).

(a) Show that the price of input 1 will rise and the price of input 2 will fall.
(b) Suppose p_A rises and p_B falls. Is it still the case that r_1 will rise and r_2 will fall?

Exercise 5.6-3: Corollary of the Rybczynski Theorem Show that a 1-percent increase in the supply of input 1 results in more than a 1-percent increase in the output of the commodity that is more input 1 intensive.

Exercise 5.6-4: Trade with Differences in Technology Suppose all the assumptions of Section 5.6 hold for two countries. However, country U has a technological advantage over country C. In country C the production function for commodity i is

$$G_i(z_1, z_2) = F_i(\alpha_1 z_1, \alpha_2 z_2), \quad \text{where} \quad \alpha_i < 1, i = A, B.$$

Suppose both countries are price takers and trade at the same world prices. Suppose in addition that both countries produce both commodities. Show that

$$\left(r_1^C, r_2^C\right) = \left(\alpha_1 r_1^U, \alpha_2 r_2^U\right).$$

HINT: Create comparable inputs by introducing "efficiency units" $\hat{z}_j = \alpha_j z_j$ for country C. Then appeal to Proposition 5.6-4.

Exercise 5.6-5: Which Input Prices? Production functions are as follows:

$$F_A(z) = \tfrac{1}{8}\text{Min}\{z_{A1}, z_{A2}\}, \quad F_B(z) = \tfrac{1}{40}\sqrt{z_{B1} z_{B2}}.$$

The output price vector is $p = (1, 1)$.

(a) Show that if the input price vector is $r = (\tfrac{1}{10}, \tfrac{1}{40})$, the unit output vectors are $v_A = (8, 8)$ and $v_B = (5, 20)$ and confirm that unit profit is zero for both commodities.
(b) Depict the unit cost line and unit isoquants in a neat figure.
(c) Appeal to the symmetry of the problem to show that there is another possible equilibrium input price vector $r\prime = (\tfrac{1}{40}, \tfrac{1}{10})$.
(d) Which of these input price vectors is the equilibrium price vector if $\bar{z} = (100, 200)$?
(e) What if instead $\bar{z} = (200, 100)$?

References and Selected Historical Reading

Arrow, K. and Debreu, G. (1951). "An Extension of the Basic Theorems of Classical Welfare Economics." *Proceedings of the Second Berkeley Symposium on Mathematical Statistics and Probability* (J. Nayman, ed.). Berkeley: University of California Press, pp. 507–32.

Arrow, K. and Debreu, G. (1954). "Existence of Equilibrium for a Competitive Economy." *Econometrica* **22**: 265–90.

Debreu, G. (1959). *Theory of Value*. Cowles Foundation Monograph. New York: John Wiley & Sons.

Kirman, A. and Hildenbrand, W. (1988). *Equilibrium Analysis: Variations on Themes by Edgeworth and Walras*. Amsterdam: North Holland.

Lindahl, E. (1919). *Die Gerechtigkeit der Besteuring*. Lind: Gleerup. Translated in *Classics in the Theory of Public Finance* (R. Musgrave and T. Peacock, eds.). London: Macmillan, 1958.

Samuelson, P. (1948). "International Trade and the Equalization of Factor Prices." *Economic Journal* (June): 163–84.

Stolper, W. and Samuelson, P. A. (1941). "Protection and Real Wages." *Review of Economic Studies* **9**(1): 58–73.

6

Dynamic Optimization

6.1 Life-Cycle Consumption and Wealth

Key ideas: lifetime budget constraint, limiting solution as the time horizon grows large

Our basic model of optimization by firms or consumers is static. However, as we have seen in the general equilibrium discussion, a simple reinterpretation of commodities allows an immediate generalization to environments where time plays a central role. However, to extract strong predictions about the way changes in preferences or technology affects dynamic decisions, we need to make major simplifications. We begin our analysis by considering choices facing a single consumer who has T periods to live. As our first simplification we assume that there is a single consumption good. Then the consumer's choice is a consumption sequence $\{x_t\}_{t=1}^{T}$. For our example we show that the current consumption choice x_1 approaches a limit as the "time horizon" tends to infinity. This suggests that it should not have any practical significance whether the problem is one with a very long finite horizon or an infinite horizon. Thus the choice of horizon becomes simply a modeling decision. For some models, it is easier to avoid "terminal conditions" and work with an infinite time horizon.

Because the necessary and sufficient conditions for a maximum assume a finite commodity space, it is necessary to find a way to apply these methods indirectly. In Section 6.2 we consider a class of models in which the solution of long finite horizon versions of the model converges to the infinite horizon solution. We then consider several applications.

Consider an individual with preferences over the consumption sequence $\{x_t\}_{t=1}^{T}$. Our first key simplification is the assumption that preferences can be expressed as an additively separable concave utility function:

$$U(x_1, \ldots, x_T) = \sum_{t=1}^{T} u_t(x_t) \text{ where } u_t(x_t) = \delta^{t-1} u(x_t), \ u'(\cdot) > 0 \text{ and } u''(\cdot) < 0.$$

We assume that δ lies in the interval $[0, 1]$, reflecting the observation that consumers are typically more focused on immediate concerns than on those in the distant future. Unless otherwise noted, it is assumed that $u'(0) = \infty$, thereby ensuring that consumption in all periods is strictly positive.

The assumption that preferences can be represented by an additively separable function ensures that the marginal rate of substitution (MRS) of period t for period $t + 1$ consumption depends only on consumption in these two periods. This greatly simplifies the analysis. Another strong simplification that we shall sometimes make is that preferences are in the CES family. Then the marginal rate of substitution depends only on the ratio of consumption levels in the two periods:

$$\text{MRS}(x_t, x_{t+1}) \equiv \frac{\frac{\partial U}{\partial x_t}}{\frac{\partial U}{\partial x_{t+1}}} = \frac{u'(x_t)}{\delta u'(x_{t+1})} = \frac{1}{\delta} \left(\frac{x_{t+1}}{x_t} \right)^{1/\sigma}, \quad \sigma > 0. \quad (6.1\text{-}1)$$

The higher the elasticity of substitution σ, the more slowly the marginal rate of substitution changes as the consumption ratio increases. The individual is therefore more willing to substitute consumption between any two periods.

For our first example we assume that preferences are in the CES family. We assume that the individual can borrow or lend at the same rate r in each period. Suppose that the individual has an initial capital of k_1. He lives for T periods, and over his lifetime his income sequence is $\{y_t\}_{t=1}^{T}$. We wish to characterize the capital accumulation sequence $\{k_t\}_{t=1}^{T}$. Given a period t consumption of x_t, the individual saves $y_t - x_t$ out of his current income so that his capital increases to $k_t + y_t - x_t$. This capital earns interest at the rate r. Thus his capital in period $t + 1$ must satisfy the following capital accumulation constraint:

$$CA_t : k_{t+1} \leq (1 + r)(k_t + y_t - x_t).$$

For period 1 we can rewrite this as follows:

$$\frac{k_2}{1 + r} \leq x_1 + y_1 - k_1.$$

Similarly, for period 2,

$$\frac{k_3}{(1 + r)^2} \leq \frac{k_2}{1 + r} + \frac{y_2}{1 + r} - \frac{x_2}{1 + r},$$

and for period t,

$$\frac{k_{t+1}}{(1 + r)^t} \leq \frac{k_t}{(1 + r)^{t-1}} + \frac{y_t}{(1 + r)^{t-1}} - \frac{x_t}{(1 + r)^{t-1}}.$$

Summing these inequalities and noting that the terms in $k_2, \ldots, k_T$ all cancel each other out, we have

$$\frac{k_{T+1}}{(1+r)^T} \leq k_1 + \sum_{t=1}^{T} \frac{y_t}{(1+r)^{t-1}} - \sum_{t=1}^{T} \frac{x_t}{(1+r)^{t-1}}.$$

In the absence of a bequest motive the consumer will not wish to leave any capital. Moreover no lender will knowingly allow him to die in debt; therefore $k_{T+1} = 0$. We can therefore rewrite the life-cycle budget constraint as

$$\sum_{t=1}^{T} \frac{x_t}{(1+r)^{t-1}} \leq k_1 + \sum_{t=1}^{T} \frac{y_t}{(1+r)^{t-1}}.$$

The left-hand side is the present value of the consumption stream. It cannot exceed his initial wealth plus the present value of his future income stream. Because utility is strictly increasing in period t consumption, this constraint will be satisfied with equality. Writing the current total wealth as W_t, the life-cycle constraint becomes

$$\sum_{t=1}^{T} \frac{x_t}{(1+r)^{t-1}} = W_1, \qquad (6.1\text{-}2)$$

where $W_1 \equiv k_1 + \sum_{t=1}^{T} \frac{y_t}{(1+r)^{t-1}}$.

We now write the optimization problem in standard form:

$$\text{Max}_{\{x_t\}} \left\{ \sum_{t=1}^{T} \delta^{t-1} u(x_t) \,|\, W_1 - \sum_{t=1}^{T} \frac{x_t}{(1+r)^{t-1}} \geq 0 \right\}.$$

Because the maximand is concave and the constraint is linear, the Kuhn-Tucker conditions are both necessary and sufficient. We form the Lagrangian

$$\mathcal{L} = \sum_{t=1}^{T} \delta^{t-1} u(x_t) + \mu \left(W_1 - \sum_{t=1}^{T} \frac{x_t}{(1+r)^{t-1}} \right),$$

and obtain the Kuhn-Tucker conditions,

$$\frac{\partial \mathcal{L}}{\partial x_t} = \delta^{t-1} u'(x_t) - \frac{\mu}{(1+r)^{t-1}} = 0 \quad \text{and} \quad \frac{\partial \mathcal{L}}{\partial x_{t+1}} = \delta^t u'(x_{t+1}) - \frac{\mu}{(1+r)^t} = 0.$$

Eliminating the shadow price from these two equations yields the following necessary condition for a maximum:

$$\frac{u'(x_t)}{u'(x_{t+1})} = (1+r)\delta.$$

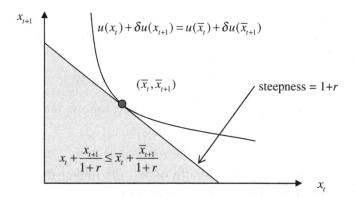

Figure 6.1-1. Necessary condition.

There is an even more basic way to see that this must be the FOC. Suppose that the optimal consumption stream is $\{\bar{x}_t\}_{t=1}^T$. Consider consumption streams in which only consumption in periods t and $t+1$ vary. Because the present value of the two consumption streams must be the same,

$$x_t + \frac{x_{t+1}}{1+r} = \bar{x}_t + \frac{\bar{x}_{t+1}}{1+r}.$$

This is depicted in Figure 6.1-1. At the optimum $(\bar{x}_t, \bar{x}_{t+1})$ the steepness of the constraint must equal the marginal rate of substitution. Appealing to (6.1-1)

$$\mathrm{MRS}(x_t, x_{t+1}) \equiv \frac{1}{\delta}\frac{u'(x_t)}{u'(x_{t+1})} = 1+r.$$

For the CES case, $\frac{u'(x_t)}{u'(x_{t+1})} = (\frac{x_{t+1}}{x_t})^{1/\sigma}$. Substituting this into the above expression and rearranging,

$$\frac{x_{t+1}}{x_t} = (\delta(1+r))^\sigma. \qquad (6.1\text{-}3)$$

Initially we will assume that $(1+r)\delta > 1$. Thus consumption grows at the constant rate $((1+r)\delta)^\sigma$.

It is of particular importance whether the consumption growth rate is faster or slower than the gross interest rate. From (6.1-3),

$$\frac{x_{t+1}}{x_t} = (\delta(1+r))^\sigma = (1+r)\alpha \quad \text{where} \quad \alpha = \delta((1+r)\delta)^{\sigma-1}.$$

Note that $\ln\alpha = \ln\delta + (\sigma-1)\ln((1+r)\delta)$. Thus as σ increases, so does $\ln\alpha$ and hence α. Moreover, if $\sigma \le 1$, then $\alpha \le \delta < 1$. However, because $(1+r)\delta > 1$, α exceeds 1 for sufficiently large σ.

Initially we will assume that $\alpha < 1$ so that the growth rate of consumption is lower than $1 + r$. Substituting the consumption growth equation back into the life-cycle budget constraint, we find that

$$x_1 + \alpha x_1 + \alpha^2 x_1 + \cdots + \alpha^{T-1} x_1 = W_1.$$

Appealing to the formula for a geometric sum, it follows that

$$x_1 = \frac{(1-\alpha)W_1}{1-\alpha^T}. \tag{6.1-4}$$

Note that, given an initial total wealth of W_1, the longer the time horizon, the smaller is first-period (current) consumption.

As a prelude to our later analysis, it is useful to also examine the evolution of the individual's wealth $\{W_t\}_{t=1}^{T}$. If the utility of the entire consumption sequence is maximized, it must also be the case that, holding first-period consumption constant, utility is maximized beginning in period 2. Then, appealing to the previous argument, it must also be the case that $x_2 = \frac{(1-\alpha)W_2}{1-\alpha^{T-1}}$ and for period t,

$$x_t = \frac{(1-\alpha)W_t}{1-\alpha^{T-t+1}}. \tag{6.1-5}$$

Note that the denominator is smaller for higher t. Thus the consumption-wealth ratio increases over the life cycle. In the final period the individual consumes her wealth so the ratio is 1.

Consider also the consumer's T-1 period optimization problem. Arguing exactly as in the T period optimization problem, the life-cycle constraint becomes

$$\sum_{t=2}^{T} \frac{x_t}{(1+r)^{t-2}} = W_2.$$

Dividing by $1 + r$, this condition becomes $\sum_{t=2}^{T} \frac{x_t}{(1+r)^{t-1}} = \frac{W_2}{1+r}$. Substituting this into (6.1-2), the full life-cycle constraint, we obtain,

$$x_1 + \frac{W_2}{1+r} = W_1, \quad \text{or equivalently,} \quad W_2 = (1+r)(W_1 - x_1).$$

Exactly the same argument holds for all t so total wealth accumulates according to the accumulation constraint

$$W_{t+1} = (1+r)(W_t - x_t). \tag{6.1-6}$$

There is a simple intuition for this constraint. Remember that W_t is the total value of financial plus human capital. Suppose that an individual borrows using all of his future income as collateral. Then the total in his checking account is W_t. If the interest rate is r and he consumes x_t, the amount in his checking account increases to $(1+r)(W_t - x_t)$ next period.

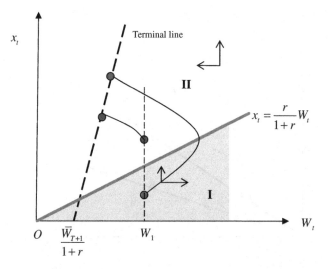

Figure 6.1-2. Consumption-wealth phase diagram with $(1 + r)\delta > 1$.

Subtracting W_t from both sides of (6.1-6),

$$W_{t+1} - W_t = rW_t - (1+r)x_t.$$

Thus wealth increases if and only if period t consumption lies below the line

$$x_t = \frac{r}{1+r} W_t.$$

This line is depicted in Figure 6.1-2. Below this boundary line wealth is increasing and above it wealth is decreasing. This is indicated by the horizontal arrows. Given our assumption that the discount factor is not too small so that $\delta(1+r) > 1$, consumption increases over the life cycle, as indicated by the vertical arrows. This figure is known as a phase diagram because the wealth-consumption dynamics can be separated into two phases.

If there is no bequest motive, the individual maximizes by leaving no wealth in period $T + 1$. More generally, we can allow for a bequest motive by seeking the optimal consumption path that leaves a period $T + 1$ wealth of $\overline{W}_{T+1}$. Then, in period T, consumption must satisfy the accumulation constraint:

$$\overline{W}_{T+1} = (1+r)(W_T - x_T).$$

Rearranging this expression, (x_T, W_T) must lie on the "terminal line"

$$x_T = W_T - \frac{\overline{W}_{T+1}}{1+r}.$$

This last period constraint is depicted as the heavy dashed line in Figure 6.1-2.

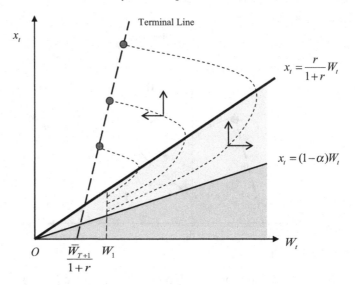

Figure 6.1-3. Phase diagram for the CES case.

From (6.1-5),

$$\frac{x_t}{W_t} = \frac{(1-\alpha)}{1 - \alpha^{T-t+1}}. \tag{6.1-7}$$

At time t, the number of periods remaining (or time horizon) is $T - t$. Thus, holding t constant, the longer the time horizon, the larger the denominator. Therefore the ratio x_t/W_t decreases with longer T. For short horizons the starting point is above the phase boundary and so wealth is decreasing in each period. For long horizons the time path goes through two phases. In phase I wealth rises. Then in phase II wealth declines until the terminal line is reached.

Finally, under the assumption that $\alpha < 1$, we consider what happens as the time horizon grows large. From (6.1-7), because the denominator is an increasing function of T, the consumption wealth ratio x_t/W_t falls with age and life-span and, in the limit, approaches $1 - \alpha$. Moreover, for very large $T - t$,

$$x_t \approx (1 - \alpha)W_t.$$

Thus for long horizons the sequence $\{x_t, W_t\}$ must lie close to this line, whenever t is small relative to T. This is depicted in Figure 6.1-3.

This leads to a very important observation. There is a class of problems (such as this one) for which the impact of the time horizon on optimal choices in the early periods diminishes to zero as the time horizon grows long. Thus, for long finite horizons, we can approximate the optimal path by taking the limit and letting the horizon approach infinity.

In such cases it is tempting to conjecture that the limiting sequence $\{x_t, W_t\}$ satisfying

$$x_t = (1 - \alpha)W_t$$

is the solution to the infinite horizon optimization problem

$$\underset{\{x_t, W_t\}}{\text{Max}} \left\{ \sum_{t=1}^{\infty} \delta^{t-1} u(x_t) \mid W_{t+1} = (1+r)(W_t - x_t) \right\}.$$

As we shall see, this conjecture is correct. Looked at this way, introducing the infinite horizon is a modeling simplification that avoids the extra step of taking the limit of the solution to the long finite horizon problem.

Infinite Horizon Problems with No Solution

From (6.1-3), $\frac{x_{t+1}}{x_t} = (\delta(1+r))^\sigma$. Suppose that $\delta(1+r) > 1$. Then for a sufficiently large elasticity of substitution parameter σ, the growth rate exceeds $1 + r$. Therefore the growth equation for consumption is $\frac{x_{t+1}}{x_t} = (1+r)\alpha$ where $\alpha > 1$. Then from (6.1-5),

$$x_t = \frac{(\alpha - 1)W_t}{\alpha^{T-t+1} - 1}.$$

Note that the denominator increases without bound as $T \to \infty$. Therefore for any t, $x_t \to 0$ as $T \to \infty$. Thus the limit of the finite horizon solution is for the consumer to delay consumption indefinitely! Clearly this is not optimal because the consumer would be strictly better off consuming all his or her wealth in the first period.

Thus argument suggests strongly that there is no solution to the infinite horizon problem. Although we do not provide a formal argument, this intuition is correct. To strengthen the intuition, suppose that preferences are linear so that the T period optimization problem is

$$\underset{\{x_t, W_t\}}{\text{Max}} \left\{ \sum_{t=1}^{\infty} \delta^{t-1} x_t \mid W_{t+1} = (1+r)(W_t - x_t) \right\}.$$

As long as $(1+r)\delta > 1$, it is easily checked that it is optimal to defer all consumption until period T. Because there is no last period in the infinite horizon problem, there is no optimal solution.

Exercises

Exercise 6.1-1: Optimal Wealth Accumulation Consider the basic wealth accumulation problem

$$\underset{x}{\text{Max}} \left\{ \sum_{t=1}^{T} \delta^{t-1} u(x_t) \,|\, W_{t+1} = (1+r)(W_t - x_t) \right\}.$$

(a) Draw the phase diagram and show that if x_1 is small, total wealth grows initially.
(b) Explain why there is a unique sequence $\{x_t\}$ satisfying the growth equation, the FOC and the terminal condition $x_{T'} = W_T$. Explain also why this must be the solution.
(c) Suppose income is y in each period until the retirement age R and is zero thereafter. Use the phase diagram to compare the optimal path of wealth and capital with $R = T$ and $R < T$. In particular compare (i) first period consumption and wealth and (ii) last period consumption and wealth for the different values of R.

Exercise 6.1-2: Optimal Saving with More Than One Commodity Alex has a T period utility function $U(x) = \sum_{t=1}^{T} \delta^{t-1} u(x_t)$ where $x_t = (x_{1t}, \ldots, x_{nt})$ and $u(\cdot)$ is strictly concave. The spot price vector is p in each period and the one-period interest rate is r. His initial total wealth is W_1. Let c_t be total spending in period t and let $v(p, c_t)$ be the indirect utility function in period t.

(a) Prove that $v(p, c_t)$ is a strictly concave function of c_t.
(b) Write down the optimization problem using the indirect utility function. Hence show that total spending will rise over time if and only if $(1 + r)\delta > 1$.
(c) What additional assumptions (if any) are needed for the optimal consumption sequence $\{\overline{x}_t\}$ to be strictly increasing?

Exercise 6.1-3: Optimal Saving with More Than One Commodity and Logarithmic Preferences Bev has a T period utility function $\sum_{t=1}^{T} \delta^{t-1} u(x_t)$ where $u(x_t) = \sum_{j=1}^{n} \alpha_j \ln x_{jt}$ and $\sum_{j=1}^{n} \alpha_j = 1$. The spot price vector in period t is p_t and the one-period interest rate is r. Her initial total wealth is W_1. Let c_t be total spending in period t and let $v(p_t, c_t)$ be the indirect utility function in period t.

(a) Write down the optimization problem using the indirect utility function. Hence show that optimal total spending in period t is independent of prices.
(b) Solve for the optimal expenditure sequence $\{\overline{c}_t\}_{t=1}^{T}$ and hence the optimal consumption sequence $\{\overline{x}_t\}_{t=1}^{T}$.
(c) Suppose that $(1 + r)\delta > 1$. For any initial wealth W_1 and any $\hat{x}$, show that if spot prices are constant, then $\overline{x}_t > \hat{x}$ for any t sufficiently large.

Exercise 6.1-4: Optimal Saving with Bounded Consumption Alex has a T period utility function $\sum_{t=1}^{T} \delta^{t-1} u(x_t)$ where $u(x_t) = \sum_{j=1}^{2} \alpha_j \ln x_{jt}$ and

$\sum_{j=1}^{2} \alpha_j = 1$. The spot price vector in period t is p and the one-period interest rate is r. His initial total wealth is W_1. Assume that $(1+r)\delta > 1$. Consumption of commodity 2 in each period is bounded from above by $\hat{x}_2$.

(a) Appeal to your answer to Exercise 6.1-3 to show that, for any given T, $\overline{x}_t < \hat{x}$, $t = 1, \ldots, T$ as long as initial wealth is sufficiently small. Thus the upper bound is never binding.

(b) By considering how the unconstrained solution $\{\overline{x}_t(W_1)\}_{t=1}^{T}$ changes with wealth, explain why, for large enough W_1, the constrained optimum is $x_{2t}^* < \hat{x}_2, t \le S$ and $x_{2t}^* = \hat{x}_2, t > S$.

(c) Optimal total spending in period t is $c_t^* = px_t^*$. Explain why $\{c_t^*\}_{t=1}^{T}$ must solve

$$\underset{c}{\text{Max}} \left\{ \sum_{t=1}^{S} \delta^{t-1} \ln c_t + \frac{\alpha_1}{\alpha_1 + \alpha_2} \sum_{t=S+1}^{T} \delta^{t-1} \ln c_t \,\middle|\, W_{t+1} = (1+r)(W_t - c_t) \right\}.$$

(d) Use this conclusion to explain why $\overline{c}_1 < c_1^*$.

(e) Suppose that the consumer has no initial financial capital. Every period he has an endowment of $\omega = (0, \hat{x}_2)$ where $\hat{x}_2$ is the number of hours in each period. Interpret x_{2t} as consumption of leisure in period t and use your answer to (b)–(d) to show that if the time horizon is sufficiently long, the consumer will choose to retire late in life.

6.2 A Family of Dynamic Optimization Problems

Key Ideas: value function, Malinvaud Condition, sufficient conditions for a maximum

The wealth accumulation problem examined in the previous section is a member of the following family of capital accumulation problems:

$$\underset{\{x_t, k_{t+1}\}_{t=1}^{T}}{\text{Max}} \left\{ \sum_{t=1}^{T} \delta^{t-1} u(x_t, k_t), \, |k_{t+1} \le g_t(x_t, k_t), \, (x_t, k_{t+1}) \ge 0, \right.$$

$$\left. t = 1, \ldots, T \quad \text{and} \quad k_{T+1} = \overline{k}_{T+1} \right\}.$$

As in the previous section we refer to the constraint $k_{t+1} \le g_t(x_t, k_t)$ as the period t capital accumulation constraint. The initial capital stock is $\overline{k}_1$.

For many applications there is no obvious terminal date so it is natural to seek a solution to the infinite horizon optimization problem:

$$\underset{\{x_t, k_{t+1}\}_{t=1}^{\infty}}{\text{Max}} \left\{ \sum_{t=1}^{\infty} u_t(x_t, k_t), \, |k_{t+1} \le g_t(x_t, k_t), \, (x_t, k_{t+1}) \ge 0, \, \forall t \right\}.$$

Suppose that $\{\overline{z}_t\}_{t=1}^{\infty} \equiv \{\overline{x}_t, \overline{k}_t\}_{t=1}^{\infty}$ solves this problem. Fix $k_{T+1} = \overline{k}_{T+1}$. Then $\{\overline{x}_t, \overline{k}_t\}_{t=1}^{T}$ must solve

$$\underset{\{x_t, k_t\}}{\text{Max}} \left\{ \sum_{t=1}^{T} u_t(x_t, k_t) | k_{t+1} \leq g(x_t, k_t), k_{T+1} = \overline{k}_{T+1} \right\}.$$

Thus the FOC for the finite horizon problem must hold for all $t \leq T$. Because this is true for all T it follows that the FOC for a finite time horizon must hold for all t in the infinite horizon problem.

For any x_1 the FOC and growth equation map out a sequence $\{x_t, k_t\}_{t=1}^{\infty}$. Suppose that there is a sequence $\{\overline{x}_t, \overline{k}_t\}_{t=1}^{\infty}$ satisfying the FOC, the capital accumulation constraints, and the non-negativity constraints for all t. We show that if the problem is concave and the shadow value of the capital stock $\lambda_t \overline{k}_{t+1}$, has a limiting value of zero, then this path is indeed an optimal path.

Proposition 6.2-1: Malinvaud Condition[1]
Suppose that $u_t(\cdot)$ and $g_t(\cdot), t = 1, \ldots$ are concave functions and $\{\overline{z}_t\}_{t=1}^{\infty} \equiv \{\overline{x}_t, \overline{k}_t\}_{t=1}^{\infty}$ satisfies the Kuhn-Tucker conditions and feasibility constraints. If the value of the capital stock approaches zero, that is $\{\lambda_t \overline{k}_{t+1}\} \to 0$, then for any other feasible sequence $\{\overline{z}_t\}_{t=1}^{\infty} \equiv \{x_t, k_t\}_{t=1}^{\infty}$ and any $\varepsilon > 0$ there exists a $\hat{T}$ such that for all $T > \hat{T}$

$$\sum_{t=1}^{T} u_t(z_t) \leq \sum_{t=1}^{T} u_t(\overline{z}_t) + \varepsilon.$$

Note that the sums on both sides need not converge to a limit as T gets large.

Proof: Define $\overline{z} = (\overline{z}_1, \ldots, \overline{z}_T)$ to be the solution of the finite horizon optimization problem with final capital $\overline{k}_{T+1}$. Let $z = (z_1, \ldots, z_T)$ be any other feasible sequence with final capital k_{T+1}. Then we need to compare the sequences $(\overline{z}, \overline{k}_{T+1})$ and (z, k_{T+1}).

The Lagrangian for the optimization problem is

$$\mathcal{L}(z, k_{T+1}, \lambda) = \sum_{t=1}^{T} u_t(z_t) + \sum_{t=1}^{T} \lambda_t(g_t(z_t) - k_{t+1}).$$

Because $\mathcal{L}(z, k_{T+1}, \lambda)$ is a concave function of (z, k_{T+1}),

$$\mathcal{L}(z, k_{T+1}, \lambda) \leq \mathcal{L}(\overline{z}, \overline{k}_{T+1}, \lambda).$$
$$+ \frac{\partial \mathcal{L}}{\partial z}(\overline{z}, \overline{k}_{T+1}, \lambda) \cdot (z - \overline{z}) + \frac{\partial \mathcal{L}}{\partial k_{T+1}}(\overline{z}, \overline{k}_{T+1}, \lambda)(k_{T+1} - \overline{k}_{T+1}). \quad (6.2\text{-}1)$$

---

[1] This condition is also known as the Transversality Condition.

Because $k_{T+1} \geq 0$ and $\frac{\partial \mathcal{L}}{\partial k_{T+1}}(\bar{z}, \overline{k}_{T+1}, \lambda) = -\lambda_T \leq 0$ it follows that

$$\frac{\partial \mathcal{L}}{\partial k_{T+1}}(\bar{z}, \overline{k}_{T+1}, \lambda)(k_{T+1} - \overline{k}_{T+1}) = -\lambda_t k_{T+1} + \lambda_T \overline{k}_{T+1} \leq \lambda_T \overline{k}_{T+1}.$$

Then, from inequality (6.2-1)

$$\mathcal{L}(z, k_{T+1}, \lambda) \leq \mathcal{L}(\bar{z}, \overline{k}_{T+1}, \lambda) + \frac{\partial \mathcal{L}}{\partial z}(\bar{z}, \overline{k}_{T+1}, \lambda) \cdot (z - \bar{z}) + \lambda_T \overline{k}_{T+1}. \quad (6.2\text{-}2)$$

Because $\bar{z}$ solves the finite horizon optimization problem it must satisfy the following Kuhn-Tucker conditions.

$$\frac{\partial \mathcal{L}}{\partial z_j}(\bar{z}, \overline{k}_{T+1}, \lambda) \leq 0 \quad \text{with equality if} \quad \bar{z}_j = 0, \forall j.$$

Therefore either $\frac{\partial \mathcal{L}}{\partial z_j}(\bar{z}, \overline{k}_{T+1}, \lambda) = 0$ or $\frac{\partial \mathcal{L}}{\partial z_j}(\bar{z}, \overline{k}_{T+1}, \lambda) < 0$ and $\bar{z}_j = 0$. Because $z_j \geq 0$, in both cases it follows that $\frac{\partial}{\partial z_j}(\bar{z}, \overline{k}_{T+1}, \lambda)(z_j - \bar{z}_j) \leq 0$.

Because this is true for all j

$$\frac{\partial \mathcal{L}}{\partial z}(\bar{z}, \overline{k}_{T+1}, \lambda) \cdot (z - \bar{z}) \leq 0.$$

Therefore from inequality (6.2-2),

$$\mathcal{L}(z, k_{T+1}, \lambda) \leq \mathcal{L}(\bar{z}, \overline{k}_{T+1}, \lambda) + \lambda_T \overline{k}_{T+1}.$$

That is,

$$\sum_{t=1}^{T} u_t(z_t) + \sum_{t=1}^{T} \lambda_t(g_t(z_t) - k_{t+1})$$

$$\leq \sum_{t=1}^{T} u_t(\bar{z}_t) + \sum_{t=1}^{T} \lambda_t(g_t(\bar{z}_t) - \overline{k}_{t+1}) + \lambda_T \overline{k}_{T+1}.$$

From the Kuhn-Tucker conditions the second sum on the right-hand side is zero. For feasibility, $g_t(z_t) - k_{t+1} \geq 0$ so the second sum on the left-hand side is positive. Therefore

$$\sum_{t=1}^{T} u_t(z_t) \leq \sum_{t=1}^{T} u_t(\bar{z}_t) + \lambda_T \overline{k}_{T+1}.$$

If the value of the capital stock has a limit of zero it follows that for any ε there exists a $\hat{T}$ such that for all $T > \hat{T}$

$$\sum_{t=1}^{T} u_t(z_t) \leq \sum_{t=1}^{T} u_t(\bar{z}_t) + \varepsilon.$$

$\square$

There is a second way to derive this result that is also revealing. For any terminal capital stock k_{T+1} define

$$U^*(k_{T+1}) = \underset{z \geq 0}{\text{Max}} \left\{ \sum_{t=1}^{T} u_t(z_t) | g_t(z_t) - k_{t+1} \geq 0 \right\}, \quad \text{where} \quad z_t = (x_t, k_t).$$

We begin by establishing that $U^*(\cdot)$ is concave. Suppose that $\{z_t^0\}_{t=1}^{T}$ is optimal for terminal capital k_{T+1}^0 and that $\{z_t^1\}_{t=1}^{T}$ is optimal for terminal capital k_{T+1}^1. Because g is concave the convex combination $\{z_t^\lambda\}_{t=1}^{T}$ is feasible with terminal capital k_{T+1}^λ. Because u is concave $u_t(z_t^\lambda) \geq (1 - \lambda)u_t(z_t^0) + \lambda u_t(z_t^1)$. Therefore

$$U^*(k_{T+1}^\lambda) \geq (1 - \lambda)U^*(k_{T+1}^0) + \lambda U^*(k_{T+1}^1)$$

The graph of this function is depicted in Figure 6.2-1.

Suppose that $\{\bar{z}_t\}_{t=1}^{\infty} = \{\bar{x}_t, \bar{k}_t\}_{t=1}^{\infty}$ satisfies the necessary conditions and growth equation. Then $\{\bar{z}_t\}_{t=1}^{T}$ is the solution to the finite horizon problem with terminal capital $\bar{k}_{T+1}$. Given the concavity of $U^*(\cdot)$

$$U^*(k_{T+1}) \leq U^*(\bar{k}_{T+1}) + (k_{T+1} - \bar{k}_{T+1})\frac{dU^*}{dk_{T+1}}(\bar{k}_{T+1})$$

$$\leq U^*(\bar{k}_{T+1}) - \bar{k}_{T+1}\frac{dU^*}{dk_{T+1}}(\bar{k}_{T+1}) \quad \text{because} \quad k_{T+1} \geq 0.$$

As argued earlier, $\frac{\partial \mathcal{L}}{\partial k_{T+1}}(\bar{z}, \bar{k}_{T+1}, \lambda) = -\lambda_T$. Appealing to the Envelope Theorem,

$$\frac{dU^*}{dk_{T+1}}(\bar{k}_{T+1}) = \frac{\partial \mathcal{L}}{\partial k_{T+1}}(\bar{z}, \bar{k}_{T+1}, \lambda) = -\lambda_T$$

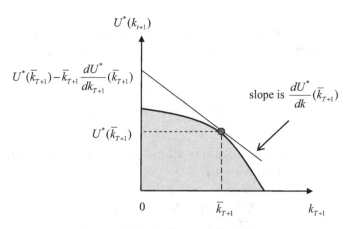

Figure 6.2-1. Malinvaud Condition.

and so

$$U^*(k_{T+1}) \leq U^*(\overline{k}_{T+1}) + \lambda_T \overline{k}_{T+1}.$$

Therefore for any alternative feasible sequence $\{z_t\}_{t=1}^T = \{x_t, k_t\}_{t=1}^T$

$$\sum_{t=1}^T u_t(x_t, k_t) \leq \sum_{t=1}^T u_t(\overline{x}_t, \overline{k}_t) + \lambda_T \overline{k}_{T+1}.$$

An Example: Optimal Wealth Accumulation

As an illustration, consider the finite horizon wealth accumulation problem

$$\underset{\{x_t, W_t\}_{t=1}^T}{\text{Max}} \left\{ \sum_{t=1}^T \delta^{t-1} u(x_t) | W_{t+1} \leq (1+r)(W - x_t), W_{T+1} \geq \overline{W}_{T+1} \right\}$$

and its infinite horizon counterpart

$$\underset{\{x_t, W_t\}_{t=1}^\infty}{\text{Max}} \left\{ \sum_{t=1}^\infty \delta^{t-1} u(x_t) | W_{t+1} \leq (1+r)(W - x_t) \right\}.$$

The Lagrangian for the finite horizon problem is

$$\mathcal{L} = \sum_{t=1}^T \delta^{t-1} u(x_t) + \sum_{t=1}^T \lambda_t ((1+r)(W_t - x_t) - W_{t+1}) + \mu(W_{T+1} - \overline{W}_{T+1}).$$

For any $W_{t+1} > 0$, $\frac{\partial \mathcal{L}}{\partial W_{t+1}} = \lambda_{t+1}(1+r) - \lambda_t = 0$. Thus

$$\frac{\lambda_{t+1}}{\lambda_t} = \frac{1}{1+r}.$$

In Section 6.1 we saw that the necessary conditions for a maximum yield the constant growth equation

$$\frac{x_{t+1}}{x_t} = (1+r)\alpha.$$

Moreover, for the T period problem the optimal first-period consumption is

$$x_t = \frac{(1-\alpha)W_t}{1 - \alpha^{T-t+1}}.$$

This suggests that for the infinite horizon problem, first-period consumption is

$$c_1 = (1-\alpha)W_1.$$

If so, second-period wealth is

$$W_2 = (1+r)(W_1 - x_1) = (1+r)\alpha W_1$$

Then both consumption and wealth grow at the same rate $(1+r)\alpha$ and so $x_2 = (1-\alpha)W_2$

Exactly the same argument holds for all t so the equal growth path $x_t = (1-\alpha)W_t$ satisfies both the necessary condition and the feasibility constraints for all t.

Note that along this constant growth path wealth grows at the rate $(1+r)\alpha$ while the shadow prices follow the growth path $\frac{\lambda_{t+1}}{\lambda_t} = \frac{1}{1+r}$. Therefore if $\alpha < 1$ then $\lambda_t W_{t+1} \to 0$ and so the Malinvaud Condition is satisfied.

Exercises

Exercise 6.2-1: Linear Utility Consider the finite horizon wealth accumulation problem with no bequest motive. Suppose that $u(x_t) = x_t$ and $\delta(1+r) > 1$.

(a) What is the optimal consumption and wealth accumulation sequence in the finite horizon optimization problem?
(b) Is there a solution to the infinite horizon problem? Explain.
(c) What if $\delta(1+r) < 1$?

Exercise 6.2-2: Infinite Horizon When x_t is a Vector An infinitely lived consumer has utility $\sum_{t=1}^{\infty} \delta^{t-1} u(x_t)$ where $u(x_t) = \sum_{j=1}^{n} \alpha_j \ln x_{jt}$ and $\sum_{j=1}^{n} \alpha_j = 1$. The sequence of future spot prices is $\{p_t\}_{t=1}^{\infty}$ and the interest rate is r. Initial wealth is W_1.

(a) Convert the period t utility into the indirect utility $v(p_t, c_t)$ where $c_t = p_t \cdot x_t$ is total spending in period t. Then solve for the optimal spending sequence $\{\bar{c}_t\}_{t=1}^{\infty}$.
   HINT: First show that $(W_{t+1}, c_{t+1}) = (1+r)\delta(W_t, c_t)$ satisfies the FOC and growth equation for all t.
(b) Hence solve for the optimal consumption sequence $\{\bar{x}_t\}_{t=1}^{\infty}$.
(c) Compare the solution to the solution of the finite horizon optimization problem.

6.3 The Ramsey Problem

Key ideas: representative agent model of optimal growth, stationary state, shadow prices and futures prices

In Section 6.1 we examined the optimal wealth accumulation decision of a single individual facing a fixed interest rate. We now extend this analysis to examine aggregate capital accumulation in an economy. We consider a single representative individual who lives forever and has utility function $\sum_{t=1}^{\infty} \delta^{t-1} u(x_t)$. To avoid the possibility of corner solutions we assume that $u'(0) = \infty$. At time t the capital stock is k_t. This yields an output of $q(k_t)$, where $q(\cdot)$ is a strictly increasing and strictly concave function. The consumer must decide how much of this output to invest and how much to consume. Let i_t be period t investment. Then

$$x_t + i_t = q(k_t).$$

Capital depreciates at a rate θ. Thus with gross investment i_t, the capital stock next period is

$$k_{t+1} = (1 - \theta)k_t + i_t = (1 - \theta)k_t + q(k_t) - x_t.$$

We write this more simply as

$$k_{t+1} = F(k_t) - x_t \quad \text{where} \quad F(k_t) = (1 - \theta)k_t + q(k_t). \quad (6.3\text{-}1)$$

Because we have assumed that the gross output function $q(\cdot)$ is strictly concave, the net output function $F(\cdot)$ is also strictly concave. For simplicity we also assume that $F(\cdot)$ is strictly increasing.

To solve the representative agent's optimization problem, we begin by using the Lagrange method to obtain necessary conditions for the finite horizon version of the problem

$$\mathcal{L} = \sum_{t=1}^{T} \delta^{t-1} u(x_t) + \lambda_t (F(k_t) - k_{t+1} - x_t).$$

Ignoring the possibility of a boundary solution, the first-order conditions are

$$\frac{\partial \mathcal{L}}{\partial x_t} = \delta^{t-1} u'(x_t) - \lambda_t = 0, \quad (6.3\text{-}2)$$

and

$$\frac{\partial \mathcal{L}}{\partial k_t} = \lambda_t F'(k_t) - \lambda_{t-1} = 0. \quad (6.3\text{-}3)$$

Combining these conditions yields the necessary condition

$$\text{MRS}(x_{t-1}, x_t) = \frac{u'(x_{t-1})}{\delta u'(x_t)} = F'(k_t), \quad t = 2, \dots. \quad (6.3\text{-}4)$$

To draw the phase diagram we first note that, from (6.3-4), $u'(x_{t-1}) = \delta F'(k_t) u'(x_t)$. Thus $u'(x_{t-1}) > u'(x_t)$ if and only if $\delta F'(k_t) > 1$. Because $u(\cdot)$ is strictly concave, it follows that

$$x_t > x_{t-1} \quad \text{if and only if} \quad \delta F'(k_t) > 1.$$

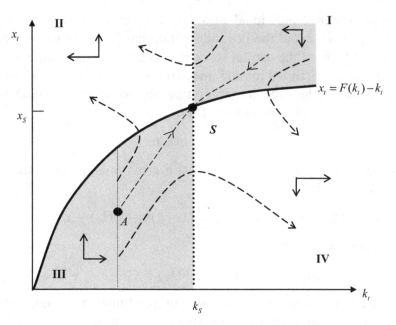

Figure 6.3-1. Phase diagram.

Suppose that for some capital stock k_S, $\delta F'(k_S) = 1$. Because $F(\cdot)$ is strictly concave there can be at most one such capital stock. Then consumption is increasing if and only if $k_t < k_S$. The vertical consumption arrows are therefore as depicted in the phase diagram in Figure 6.3-1.

Next consider capital accumulation. The accumulation constraint (6.3-1) can be rewritten as follows:

$$k_{t+1} - k_t = F(k_t) - x_t - k_t.$$

Thus capital is increasing if and only if (x_t, k_t) lies below the phase boundary

$$x_t = F(k_t) - k_t.$$

The phase diagram is then as depicted in Figure 6.3-1. Consumption increases if and only if the economy is in phases II or III. Capital grows if and only if the economy is in phases III or IV.

Starting from a low capital stock, there is a sequence $\{x_t, k_t\}_{t=1}^{\infty}$ in phase III that approaches the stationary point S. This is depicted in the figure as the curve AS. Note that, because the consumption path approaches x_S, it follows directly from (6.3-2) that the sequence of shadow prices approaches zero. Also the limiting capital stock is finite. Thus the value of the capital stock $\lambda_t k_{t+1}$ approaches zero so the Malinvaud Condition holds. Given the concavity of the production function and utility function, it follows that the sequence $\{x_t, k_t\}_{t=1}^{\infty}$ is optimal.

Supporting Prices

For the finite horizon economy, we know from the Second welfare theorem that the efficient outcome can be supported as a Walrasian equilibrium. Thus with a single commodity and T periods there is a sequence $\{p_t\}_{t=1}^{T}$ of supporting futures prices. Indeed the supporting prices are the Lagrange multipliers; that is for some $\kappa > 0$, $\{p_t\}_{t=1}^{T} = \{\kappa \lambda_t\}_{t=1}^{T}$. We now show that this is the case for the infinite horizon problem as well.

Let $\{p_t\}_{t=1}^{\infty}$ be a sequence of futures prices. First for the consumer, the infinite horizon budget constraint is

$$\sum_{t=1}^{\infty} p_t x_t = W_1,$$

where W_1 is the value of the future dividend stream.

The Lagrangian for this optimization problem is

$$\mathcal{L} = \sum_{t=1}^{\infty} \delta^{t-1} u(x_t) + \mu \left(W_1 - \sum_{t=1}^{\infty} p_t x_t \right).$$

It is readily confirmed that the first-order conditions are as follows:

$$\text{MRS}(x_{t-1}, x_t) = \frac{u(x_{t-1})}{\delta u'(x_t)} = \frac{p_{t-1}}{p_t}.$$

These conditions satisfy (6.3-2) if and only if, for some $\kappa > 0$, $\{p_t\}_{t=1}^{T} = \{\kappa \lambda_t\}_{t=1}^{T}$.

Next consider the decision of a profit-maximizing price-taking firm manager. In period t the firm manager purchases k_{t+1} units of capital for next period's production of output. Gross output in period $t + 1$ is $q(k_{t+1})$. The manager can also sell the undepreciated capital stock. His profit is therefore

$$p_{t+1} q(k_{t+1}) + p_{t+1}(1 - \theta)k_{t+1} - p_t k_{t+1} = p_{t+1} F(k_{t+1}) - p_t k_{t+1}.$$

The FOC for profit maximization is therefore

$$p_{t+1} F'(k_{t+1}) - p_t = 0.$$

If $\{p_t\}_{t=1}^{T} = \{\kappa \lambda_t\}_{t=1}^{T}$ this satisfies (6.3-3).

Note finally that the one-period interest rate at time t is the price ratio $p_t/p_{t+1} = \lambda_t/\lambda_{t+1}$. Thus the profit-maximizing firm chooses to accumulate capital so that in each period the marginal product of capital is equal to the interest rate. We have seen that, starting from a low capital stock, capital increases steadily, approaching in the limit the stationary level k_S. Because the production function is concave, it follows that the one-period interest rate declines over time. In the limit, the gross return $1 + r_t$ approaches the steady state gross marginal product of capital $F'(k_S)$.

Exercises

Exercise 6.3-1: Optimal Rate of Investment A firm with capital k_t that hires z_t units of inputs at spot price vector r can produce output $q(k_t, z_t)$. The demand price function is $p(q)$. Period t revenue is therefore

$$R(k_t, z_t) = q(k_t, z_t)p(q(k_t, z_t)).$$

You should assume that $R(\cdot)$ is strictly increasing and strictly concave. Capital depreciates at the rate θ ; thus the growth equation is $k_{t+1} = (1 - \theta)k_t + x_t$. The firm can add new capital x_t at time t at a cost of $C(x_t)$, where $C(\cdot)$ is strictly convex and $C'(0) = 0$. The firm has an infinite horizon and discounts the future using the interest rate r.

(a) Maximized period t net revenue is

$$N(k_t) = \underset{z_t}{\text{Max}}\{R(k_t, z_t) - r \cdot z_t\}.$$

Show that $N(\cdot)$ is strictly concave.
HINT: Let z^0 be optimal with capital k^0 and let z^1 be optimal with capital k^1 and show that $N(k^\lambda) \geq R(k^\lambda, z^\lambda) - r \cdot z^\lambda$.
(b) Write down the firm's optimization problem.
(c) Depict the capital phases in a neat figure with k_{t+1} on the horizontal and x_t on the vertical axis.
(d) Assuming that investment is positive in each period, show that the local FOC can be expressed as follows:

$$\frac{1}{1+r}N'(k_t) - C'(x_{t-1}) + \frac{1-\theta}{1+r}C'(x_t) = 0.$$

Hence explain why $x_t > x_{t-1}$ if and only if (k_t, x_t) lies above the phase boundary implicitly defined by the following equation:

$$N'(k_t) = (r + \theta)C'(x_t).$$

(e) Draw in all the arrows depicting the evolution of (k_t, x_t).
(f) Starting with a small capital stock, characterize the profit-maximizing investment strategy.

Exercise 6.3-2: Advertising and Reputation Demand for a firm's product in period t is a function of the price that the firm charges and of the reputation of the product k_t

$$p_t = p(q_t, k_t) = q_t^{-\alpha} k_t^{\beta}, \quad 0 < \beta < \alpha < 1.$$

The cost of production is c per unit.

(a) Show that maximized profit at time t, $\Pi(k_t) = \underset{q_t}{\text{Max}}\{p_t q_t - c q_t\}$ is an increasing concave function of K_t.

Reputation depreciates over time and is increased via advertising expenditures according to

$$k_{t+1} - k_t = f(a_t) - v k_t,$$

where a_t is advertising in period t and $f(\cdot)$ is concave.

(b) Write down the optimization problem for the firm, assuming an interest rate of r and an infinite time horizon.

(c) Show that $\{a_t, k_t\}$ must satisfy

$$\frac{1+r}{f'(a_t)} = \Pi'(k_{t+1}) + \frac{1-v}{f'(a_{t+1})}.$$

Hence show that $a_t > a_{t+1}$ if and only if $\Pi'(k_t) < \frac{r+v}{f'(a_t)}$.

(d) Draw the phase diagram for this problem. Hence show that the optimal rate of advertising declines over time as the firm builds up its reputation.

(e) Suppose the firm is at its steady-state reputation level. If the interest rate suddenly falls and it is believed that it will remain forever at this new lower level, what will be the firm's advertising policy?

Exercise 6.3-3: Comparative Dynamics of Optimal Investing Consider the optimal investment problem in Exercise 6.3-1. Suppose that the firm begins at its steady-state capital stock. Describe as best you can, the effect on gross investment and the capital stock if (a) the cost of investment goods rises from $C(\cdot)$ to $(1 + \kappa) C(\cdot)$ (b) the interest rate rises, and (c) the depreciation rate falls.

6.4 Dynamic Programming Reformulation

Key ideas: value function, backward induction, Bellman equation

In Section 6.2 we considered the following class of optimization problems:

$$V_1(\overline{k}_1) = \underset{\{x_t, k_t\}_{t=1}^{T}}{\text{Max}} \left\{ \sum_{t=1}^{T} \delta^{t-1} u(x_t, k_t) | k_{t+1} \leq g_t(x_t, k_t), k_{T+1} \geq \overline{k}_{T+1} \right\}.$$

The subscript 1 on the value function $V_1(\cdot)$ indicates the period at which the optimization takes place. For any k_2, the remaining optimization problem at time 2 is

$$V_2(k_2) = \max_{\{x_t, k_t\}_{t=2}^T} \left\{ \sum_{t=2}^T \delta^{t-1} u(x_t, k_t) | k_{t+1} \le g_t(x_t, k_t), k_{T+1} \ge \overline{k}_{T+1} \right\}.$$

We can then break the problem down into two stages. First we imagine solving the optimization problem with T-1 periods to go for all possible levels of the capital stock K_2. The second step is then a simple two-period optimization problem:

$$V_1(\overline{k}_1) = \max_{\{x_1, k_2\}} \{ u(k_1, k_2) + \delta V_2(k_2) | k_2 \le g_1(x_1, k_1) \}.$$

Of course the problem with T-1 period remaining can be similarly broken down into two stages. Thus for all $t = 1, \ldots, T$,

$$V_t(k_t) = \max_{x_t, k_{t+1}} \{ u(x_t, k_t) + \delta V_{t+1}(k_{t+1}) | k_{t+1} \le g_t(x_t, k_t) \}. \quad (6.4\text{-}1)$$

This is known as the Bellman equation.

As an alternative method of solution, suppose we consider the following simple two-period optimization problem at time t. The value function at time $t+1$ is $V_{t+1}(k_{t+1})$. Thus utility is $u(c_t, k_t) + \delta V_{t+1}(k_{t+1})$. Given a period t capital stock k_t, the consumer chooses consumption and capital for the next period to satisfy the capital accumulation constraint, $k_{t+1} \le g_t(x_t, k_t)$.

To obtain the necessary conditions we form the Lagrangian,

$$\mathcal{L} = u(x_t, k_t) + \delta V_{t+1}(k_{t+1}) + \mu_t [g_t(k_t, x_t) - k_{t+1}].$$

The first-order conditions are therefore

$$\frac{\partial \mathcal{L}}{\partial x_t} = \frac{\partial u}{\partial x_t} + \mu_t \frac{\partial g_t}{\partial x_t} = 0 \quad \text{and} \quad (6.4\text{-}2)$$

$$\frac{\partial \mathcal{L}}{\partial x_{t+1}} = \delta V'_{t+1}(k_{t+1}) - \mu_t = 0. \quad (6.4\text{-}3)$$

Also, by the Envelope Theorem,

$$V'_t(k_t) = \frac{\partial \mathcal{L}}{\partial k_t} = \frac{\partial u}{\partial k_t} + \mu_t \frac{\partial g_t}{\partial k_t}. \quad (6.4\text{-}4)$$

Conditions (6.4-2), (6.4-3), (6.4-4), and the terminal condition completely characterize the optimal path. Note that we can eliminate the shadow price μ_t and rewrite conditions (6.4-3) and (6.4-4) as follows:

$$\begin{cases} \delta^{t-1}\frac{\partial u}{\partial x_t} - \delta^t V'_{t+1}(k_{t+1})\frac{\partial g_t}{\partial x_t} = 0, \\ \delta^{t-1}\frac{\partial u}{\partial k_t} + \delta^t V'_{t+1}(k_{t+1})\frac{\partial g_t}{\partial k_t} - \delta^{t-1} V'_t(k_t) = 0. \end{cases}$$

Comparing these two conditions with condition (6.3-2), it follows that

$$\lambda_t = \delta^t V'_{t+1}(k_{t+1})\frac{\partial g_t}{\partial x_t}.$$

The slope of the value function reflects the marginal value of capital at time $t+1$. Moreover, if the function $g_t(\cdot)$ is linear in x, then the slope of the value function is exactly the marginal value of capital at time $t+1$. Thus, discounting this to the present yields the present shadow value of capital at time $t+1$.

For the special case in which the function $g_t(\cdot)$ is independent of t and the horizon is infinite we can simplify the Bellman equation further. Now the optimization problem from time $t+1$ has exactly the same form as the optimization problem from time t. Then the time subscript is no longer necessary and we can rewrite the Bellman equation as follows:

$$V(k_t) = \underset{x_t, k_{t+1}}{\text{Max}}\{u(x_t, k_t) + \delta V(k_{t+1}) | k_{t+1} \le g(x_t, k_t)\}.$$

Note that $V'(k_t)$ is the marginal value of capital at time t. Thus $\delta^{t-1} V'(k_t)$ is the discounted marginal value of capital. Thus the Transversality Condition is the requirement that $\delta^{t-1} V'(k_t) k_t \to 0$.

Our earlier results suggest a simple way of solving for the value function. Consider the finite horizon "approximation":

$$V_1(k_1) = \underset{\{x_t, k_t\}_{t=1}^T}{\text{Max}} \left\{ \sum_{t=1}^T \delta^{t-1} u(x_t, k_t) | k_{t+1} \le g(x_t, k_t), k_{T+1} \ge 0 \right\}.$$

We know that if the Malinvaud Condition holds, the solution to this problem must converge to the solution when the horizon is infinite.

In some special cases, this method yields an analytical solution for the value function. Consider the simple growth model of Section 6.3. The capital accumulation constraint is reproduced here:

$$k_{t+1} = F(k_t) - x_t.$$

Suppose $F(k_t) = k_t^\alpha$. Then

$$V(k_1) = \underset{\{x_t, K_t\}_{t=1}^\infty}{\text{Max}} \left\{ \sum_{t=1}^\infty \delta^{t-1} \ln x_t \,|\, x_t + k_{t+1} \le k_t^\alpha \right\}.$$

First we solve the finite approximation with one period remaining.

$$V_T(k_T) = \underset{x_T, k_{T+1}}{\text{Max}} \{\ln x_T \,|\, k_{T+1} = k_T^\alpha - x_T \ge 0\}.$$

The solution is $x_T^* = k_T^\alpha$, so $V_T(k) = \ln k^\alpha = \alpha \ln k$.

Appealing to the Bellman equation,

$$V_{T-1}(k_{T-1}) = \underset{x_{T-1}, k_T}{\text{Max}} \{\ln x_{T-1} + \delta V_T(k_T) \,|\, k_T = k_{T-1}^\alpha - x_{T-1}\}.$$

Substituting for the one-period value function, the optimization problem can be rewritten as

$$V_{T-1}(k_{T-1}) = \underset{x_{T-1}}{\text{Max}} \{\ln x_{T-1} + \alpha\delta \ln(k_{T-1}^\alpha - x_{T-1})\}.$$

The first-order conditions can be written as follows:[2]

$$\frac{1}{x_{T-1}} = \frac{\alpha\delta}{k_{T-1}^\alpha - x_{T-1}} = \frac{1 + \alpha\delta}{k_{T-1}^\alpha}.$$

Thus, $V_{T-1}(k) = \alpha(1 + \alpha\delta) \ln k + \text{constant terms}$.

It is easily checked that

$$V_{T-1}(k) = \alpha(1 + \alpha\delta + \alpha^2\delta^2) \ln k + \text{constant terms}$$

and so on. As long as $\alpha\delta < 1$ we can take the limit to obtain

$$V(k) = \frac{\alpha}{1 - \alpha\delta} \ln k + \text{constant terms}.$$

Having solved for the value function, we can easily solve for the optimal consumption rule:

$$V(k_s) = \underset{x_s}{\text{Max}} \{\ln x_s + \delta V(k_s^\alpha - x_s)\} = \underset{x_s}{\text{Max}} \left\{ \ln x_s + \frac{\alpha\delta}{1 - \alpha\delta} \ln(k_s^\alpha - x_s) \right\}.$$

Solving as earlier, it follows that $x_s = (1 - \alpha\delta)k_s^\alpha$. Thus the optimal consumption rule is to consume a constant fraction $(1 - \alpha\delta)$ of net output.

---

[2] The second equality follows by the Ratio Rule.

Exercises

Exercise 6.4-1: Solving for the Value Function Consider the following problem:

$$V(k_1) = \max_{\{x_t, k_t\}_{t=1}^T} \left\{ \sum_{t=1}^{\infty} \delta^{t-1} \ln x_t | x_t + k_{t+1} \le k_t^{\alpha} \right\}.$$

As shown in this section, the value function for the one-period approximation is $V_1(k) = \alpha \ln k$. This suggests a trial-and-error approach. Try the value function $V(k) = \beta \ln k$.

(a) Solve the following optimization problem:

$$V(k_1) = \max_{x_1} \{\ln x_1 + \delta \beta \ln(k_1^{\alpha} - x_1)\}.$$

(b) Hence show that $V(k_1) = (\alpha + \alpha \delta \beta) \ln k_1 + \text{constant terms}$.
(c) Solve for β and hence show that $x_t = \frac{1 - \alpha \delta}{1 - \alpha \delta(1-\alpha)} k_t^{\alpha}$.

Exercise 6.4-2: A-K Model with Anticipated Shocks Consider the following problem:

$$V(k_1) = \max_{\{x_t, k_t\}_{t=1}^{\infty}} \left\{ \sum_{t=1}^{\infty} u_t(x_t) | k_{t+1} \le A(k_t + \mu_t) - x_t, x_t \ge 0 \right\}, \quad \text{where } \{\mu_t\}_{t=1}^{\infty}$$

is a sequence of known (i.e. fully anticipated) shocks.

(a) Define $W_t = k_t + \sum_{s=t}^{\infty} \frac{\mu_s}{A^{t-s}}$. Show that the dynamic programming problem can be rewritten as follows:

$$V(W_t) = \max_{x_t, W_{t+1}} \{u_t(x_t) + \delta V(W_{t+1}) | W_{t+1} \le AW_t - x_t, x_t \ge 0\}.$$

(b) Hence draw a conclusion as to how the size of the shocks affects the optimal consumption sequence.

Exercise 6.4-3: Solving the A-K Model An economy with capital stock k_t has the following growth equation:

$$k_{t+1} = Ak_t - x_t, \quad \text{where} \quad A > 1.$$

Preferences of consumers are represented by a single infinitely lived agent with utility function $\sum_{t=1}^{\infty} u_t(x_t)$ where $u_t(x_t) = (\frac{\sigma}{\sigma-1}) \delta^{t-1} x_t^{1-1/\sigma}$, $\sigma \ne 1$, $\delta < 1$, and $A\delta > 1$.

(a) Consider the finite horizon version of the problem with no final capital stock. Appeal to the growth equation to show that the consumption plan must satisfy the following constraint:

$$x_1 + \frac{x_2}{A} + \cdots + \frac{x_T}{A^{T-t-1}} = Ak_1.$$

(b) Hence show that consumption must grow at some constant rate γ, that is, $x_{t+1} = (1 + \gamma)x_t$.

(c) Consider the remaining optimization problem at time t and confirm that period t consumption satisfies the following condition:

$$x_t \left(1 + \frac{1 + \gamma}{A}\right) + \cdots + \left(\frac{1 + \gamma}{A}\right)^{T-t-1} = A K_t.$$

Hence show that

$$x_t = \frac{1 - \frac{1 + \gamma}{A}}{1 - \left(\frac{1+\gamma}{A}\right)^{T-t}} A K_t.$$

(d) Show that if $\sigma < 1$, $x_t \to (A - 1 - \gamma)k_t$ as $T \to \infty$. Show also that if σ is sufficiently large, then x_t approaches zero as $T \to \infty$.

Henceforth assume that $\sigma < 1$.

(e) For the infinite horizon problem, we seek a value function such that

$$V(k_t) = \underset{x_t, k_{t+1}}{\text{Max}} \{u_t(x_t) + \delta V(k_{t+1}) | k_{t+1} + x_t = A k_t\}.$$

Show that the limit of the finite horizon problem is the constant growth path $(x_{t+1}, k_{t+1}) = (1 + \gamma)(x_t, k_t)$. Show also that in the limit $u_{t+1} = \left(\frac{1+\gamma}{A}\right)u_t$. Hence show that $\sum_{t=1}^{T} u_t$ converges as $T \to \infty$. Thus $V(k_1) = \lim_{t \to \infty} \sum_{t=1}^{\infty} u_t$.

6.5 Optimal Control[3]

Key ideas: short time intervals, continuous model, state and control variables, small variations, Hamiltonian, Maximum Principle

Consider the following class of optimization problems:

$$\underset{\{x_t, k_{t+1}\}}{\text{Max}} \left\{ \sum_{t=1}^{T} U_t(k_t, x_t) + V_{T+1}(k_{T+1}) | k_{t+1} - k_t \leq F_t(k_t, x_t) \right\}.$$

In the language of control theory, the vector k_t is the state variable in period t. The decision maker controls the growth rate of this vector by deciding the level of a vector of control variables x_t.

Example: Life-Cycle Capital Accumulation
An individual with initial capital k_1 has a discounted lifetime utility of

$$U = \sum_{t=1}^{T} \delta^t u(x_t) + \delta^T v(k_{T+1}),$$

---

[3] This section was inspired by Lawrence Evans' discussion of optimal control. For a more comprehensive introduction go on the web to http://math.berkeley.edu/~evans/control.course.pdf.

where the final term is her utility from her bequest k_{T+1}. Financial capital k_t has a gross return of $1 + r$. The individual's period t wage is w_t. Therefore if she consumes x_t her capital next period is $k_{t+1} = (1 + r)k_t + w_t - x_t$.

The Lagrangian of this optimization problem is

$$\mathcal{L} = \sum_{t=1}^{T} U_t(k_t, x_t) + \delta^T V_T(k_{T+1}) + \lambda_t (F_t(k_t, x_t) - k_{t+1} + k_t).$$

Assuming an interior solution we have the following first-order conditions:

$$\frac{\partial \mathcal{L}}{\partial x_t} = \frac{\partial U_t}{\partial x_t} + \lambda_t \frac{\partial F_t}{\partial x_t} = 0, \quad t = 1, \ldots, T \qquad (6.5\text{-}1)$$

$$\frac{\partial \mathcal{L}}{\partial k_t} = \frac{\partial U_t}{\partial k_t} + \lambda_t \left(\frac{\partial F_t}{\partial k_t} + 1 \right) - \lambda_{t-1} = 0, \quad t = 1, \ldots, T, \qquad (6.5\text{-}2)$$

$$\frac{\partial \mathcal{L}}{\partial k_{T+1}} = \delta^T \frac{\partial V_T}{\partial k_{T+1}} - \lambda_T = 0. \qquad (6.5\text{-}3)$$

Rearranging the second condition, we obtain the following expression for the evolution of the shadow prices

$$\lambda_t - \lambda_{t-1} = - \left(\frac{\partial U_t}{\partial k_t} + \lambda_t \frac{\partial F_t}{\partial k_t} \right), \quad t = 1, \ldots, T. \qquad (6.5\text{-}4)$$

Reducing the Time between Periods

It is often more convenient to model decisions as continuous variables. The decision maker chooses the level of the control variables to determine the rate of accumulation of the state variables. We look at this in two ways. First we modify the discrete time model by introducing an interval Δt between decision points and consider the necessary conditions as Δt approaches zero.

To modify the discrete model we redefine decision point t to be the decision made after t periods of length Δt have elapsed. We let x_t be the level of the control variable between decision point t and $t + 1$. The rate at which the state variable grows over this interval is $f_t(k_t, x_t)$. Then the change in the state variable between decision points is

$$k_{t+1} - k_t = F_t(k_t, x_t) \equiv f_t(k_t, x_t)\Delta t.$$

The function $u_t(k_t, x_t)$ is now the flow of utility to the consumer. Total utility is therefore

$$\sum_{t=1}^{T} U_t(k_t, x_t) = \sum_{t=1}^{T} u_t(k_t, x_t)\Delta t.$$

Appealing to the first-order conditions (6.5-1) and (6.5-4)

$$\frac{\partial \mathcal{L}}{\partial x_t} = \left(\frac{\partial u_t}{\partial x_t} + \lambda_t \frac{\partial f_t}{\partial x_t} \right) \Delta t = 0, \quad t = 1, \ldots, T$$

and

$$\lambda_t - \lambda_{t-1} = -\Delta t \left(\frac{\partial u_t}{\partial k_t} + \lambda_t \frac{\partial f_t}{\partial k_t} \right), \quad t = 1, \ldots, T.$$

Dividing both conditions by Δt and defining $\Delta \lambda = \lambda_t - \lambda_{t-1}$, the first-order conditions become

$$\frac{\partial u_t}{\partial x_t} + \lambda_t \frac{\partial f_t}{\partial x_t} = 0 \quad \text{and,} \quad \frac{\Delta \lambda}{\Delta t} = -\left(\frac{\partial u_t}{\partial k_t} + \lambda_t \frac{\partial f_t}{\partial k_t} \right) \quad t = 1, \ldots, T. \quad (6.5\text{-}5)$$

There is an easy way to write down these conditions. We define the "Hamiltonian" of the problem as

$$H_t(k_t, x_t) \equiv u_t(k_t, x_t) + \lambda_t f_t(k_t, x_t).$$

The necessary conditions (6.5-5) can then be written succinctly as follows:

$$\frac{\partial H_t}{\partial x_t} = 0, \quad \frac{\Delta \lambda}{\Delta t} = -\frac{\partial H_t}{\partial k_t}. \quad (6.5\text{-}6)$$

Finally, taking the limit as $\Delta t \to 0$, these arguments strongly suggest the following necessary conditions for the continuous time version of the model:

$$\frac{\partial H}{\partial x} = 0, \quad \frac{d\lambda}{dt} = -\frac{\partial H}{\partial k}. \quad (6.5\text{-}7)$$

As we shall see, these are indeed the necessary conditions for an interior solution.

Continuous Model

In the continuous time version of the model, the vector of n state variables is $k(t) = (k_1(t), \ldots, k_n(t))$ and the vector of m control variables is $x(t) = (x_1(t), \ldots, x_m(t))$. The total payoff is the integral of the flow payoff $u(k(t), x(t), t)$ over the time interval $[0, T]$ plus the terminal value of the state variables $V(k(T), T)$:

$$U = \int_0^T u(k(t), x(t), t)dt + V(K(T), T). \quad (6.5\text{-}8)$$

The rate of change of the state vector $k(t)$ satisfies

$$\frac{dk}{dt} = f(k(t), x(t), t).$$

The set of feasible control variables is the convex set X.

Consider the following continuous time maximization problem:

$$\underset{x(t)\in X}{\text{Max}}\left\{\int_0^T u(k(t), x(t), t)dt + V(k(T), T)|\frac{dk}{dt} = f(k, x, t)\right\}. \quad (6.5\text{-}9)$$

Suppose that $(k^*(t), x^*(t)), t \in [0, T]$ is a solution to this optimization problem. Paralleling the discrete time model, it is convenient to introduce a vector, $\lambda(t)$, of shadow prices for the n state variables and define the Hamiltonian

$$H(k, x, t) = u(k, x, t) + \lambda \cdot f(k, x, t),$$

where

$$\frac{d\lambda}{dt} = -\frac{\partial H}{\partial k} \quad \text{and} \quad \lambda(T) = \frac{\partial V}{\partial k}(k^*(T), T). \quad (6.5\text{-}10)$$

We then have the following elegant theorem.

Proposition 6.5-1: Pontryagin's Maximum Principle
If $x^*(t)$ solves the maximization problem (6.5-9), and the functions u and f are both continuously differentiable, then there exists a shadow price function $\lambda(t) : [0, T] \to \mathbb{R}^n$ satisfying (6.5-10) such that

$$x^*(t) = \arg\underset{x\in X}{\text{Max}} H(k^*(t), x(t), t).$$

Proof:[4]

Step 1: Conversion to a terminal value problem
It is easiest to analyze the necessary conditions for a maximum if the maximand is simply a function of the terminal vector of state variables $k(T)$. We can do so by introducing the new state variable

$$k_0(t) = \int_0^t f_0(k(\tau), x(\tau), \tau)d\tau, \quad \text{where} \quad f_0(k, x, \tau) \equiv u(k, x, \tau).$$

Then $\frac{dk_0}{dt} = f_0(k(t), x(t), t)$ and $k_0(T) = \int_0^T f_0(k(t), x(t), t)dt = \int_0^T u(k(t), x(t), t)dt$.

Finally define a new terminal value function $\overline{V}(k(T), T) = k_0(T) + V(k(T), T)$. Then, we can rewrite the optimization problem as follows:

$$\underset{x(t)\in X}{\text{Max}}\left\{U = \overline{V}(k(T), T)|\frac{dk_i}{dt} = f_i(k, x, t), i = 0, \ldots, n\right\}.$$

---

[4] The proof is long but it is a beautiful and important theorem, and if you like mathematics, you will find it well within your reach.

Note that the new Hamiltonian is

$$\overline{H} = \sum_{i=0}^{n} \lambda_i f_i.$$

Associated with the new state variable is a new shadow price $\lambda_0(t)$. This must evolve according to

$$\frac{d\lambda_0}{dt} = -\frac{\partial \overline{H}}{\partial k_0}.$$

Because k_0 is not an argument of $\overline{H}$, $\frac{d\lambda_0}{dt} = 0$. Also $\lambda_0(T) = \frac{\partial \overline{V}}{\partial k_0} = 1$. Then $\lambda_0(t) = 1, t \in [0, T]$ and so

$$\overline{H} = \sum_{i=0}^{n} \lambda_i f_i = u + \sum_{i=1}^{n} \lambda_i f_i = H.$$

It is convenient to introduce the row vector of shadow prices $\lambda(t)' = (\lambda_0(t), \ldots \lambda_n(t))$. Then the Hamiltonian can be rewritten as follows:

$$H = \overline{H} = \lambda(t)' f(k(t), x(t), t). \qquad (6.5\text{-}11)$$

Step 2: Variation of the control
Consider a variation in the control variables over some small sub-interval $[s - \varepsilon, s]$ of $[0, T]$. Over this interval the optimal control vector $x^*(t)$ is replaced by $x \in X$. That is,

$$x(t, \varepsilon) = \begin{cases} x , & t \in [s - \varepsilon, s] \\ x^*(t), & t \notin [s - \varepsilon, s] \end{cases}.$$

The variation is depicted in Figures 6.5-1a and 6.5-1b.

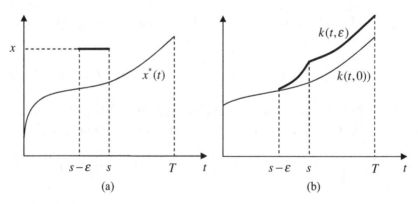

Figure 6.5-1. (a) Variation of the control. (b) Variation of the state.

We first examine how the variation in the control variables affects the state at time s and then ask how this changed state variable evolves after time s.

With control $x(t, \varepsilon)$ the value of the maximand is

$$U(\varepsilon) = \overline{V}(k(T, \varepsilon)), \quad \text{where} \quad \frac{\partial k}{\partial t}(t, \varepsilon) = f(k(t, \varepsilon), x(t, \varepsilon), t). \quad (6.5\text{-}12)$$

A necessary condition for $(k^*(t), x^*(t))$ to be a maximum is that $U(\varepsilon)$ should have a local maximum at $\varepsilon = 0$. It proves convenient to introduce the following shorthand,

$$k_\varepsilon(t, \varepsilon) \equiv \frac{\partial}{\partial \varepsilon} k(t, \varepsilon).$$

Because $\varepsilon \geq 0$, the first-order condition is

$$\frac{dU}{d\varepsilon}(0) = \frac{\partial \overline{V}}{\partial k}(k(T), T)' k_\varepsilon(T, 0) = \lambda(T)' k_\varepsilon(T, 0) \leq 0. \quad (6.5\text{-}13)$$

In step 3 we show that the right-hand side of this equation is time independent over the time interval $[s, T]$. Therefore the FOC can be rewritten as follows:

$$\frac{dU}{d\varepsilon}(0) = \lambda(s)' k_\varepsilon(s, 0) \leq 0 \quad (6.5\text{-}14)$$

To compute this derivative we need to know how $k(s, \varepsilon)$ varies with ε in the neighborhood of $\varepsilon = 0$. Because the variation in the control begins at $s - \varepsilon$,

$$k(s - \varepsilon, \varepsilon) = k(s - \varepsilon, 0) \equiv k^*(s - \varepsilon). \quad (6.5\text{-}15)$$

Over the interval $[s - \varepsilon, s]$,

$$\frac{dk^*}{dt} = f(k^*(t), x^*(t), t) = f(k^*(s), x^*(s), s) + o(\varepsilon)$$

Integrating over this interval,

$$k^*(s) - k^*(s - \varepsilon) = f(k^*(s), x^*(s), s)\varepsilon + o(\varepsilon^2). \quad (6.5\text{-}16)$$

Similarly, over the interval $[s - \varepsilon, s]$,

$$\frac{\partial k}{\partial t}(t, \varepsilon) = f(k(t, \varepsilon), x, t) = f(k^*(s), x, s) + o(\varepsilon).$$

Integrating over this interval

$$k(s, \varepsilon) - k(s - \varepsilon, \varepsilon) = f(k^*(s), x, s)\varepsilon + o(\varepsilon^2). \quad (6.5\text{-}17)$$

Appealing to (6.5-15)–(6.5-17) it follows that

$$k(s, \varepsilon) - k^*(s) = (f(k^*(s), x, s) - f(k^*(s), x^*(s), s))\varepsilon + o(\varepsilon^2).$$

Dividing both sides by ε and taking the limit

$$k_\varepsilon(s, 0) = f(k^*(s), x, s) - f(k^*(s), x, s).$$

Substituting this into (6.5-14), the FOC is as follows:

$$\frac{dU}{d\varepsilon}(0) = \lambda(s)' f(k^*(s), x, s) - \lambda(s)' f(k^*(s), x^*(s), s) \leq 0$$

From (6.5-11), the FOC can be rewritten as follows:

$$\frac{dU}{d\varepsilon}(0) = \overline{H}(k^*(s), x, s) - \overline{H}(k^*(s), x^*(s), s)$$
$$= H(k^*(s), x, s) - H(k^*(s), x^*(s), s) \leq 0.$$

Thus at each time s,

$$x^*(s) = \arg \underset{x \in X}{\text{Max}} \{ H(k^*(s), x, s) \}.$$

Step 3: Time Independence of $\lambda(t)'k_\varepsilon(t, 0)$
It remains to show that $\lambda(t)'k_\varepsilon(t, 0)$ is time independent. Over the interval $[s, T]$, both $k(t, 0)$ and $k(t, \varepsilon)$ are solutions of the same ordinary differential equation system

$$\frac{\partial k}{\partial t} = f(k, x, t).$$

Differentiating the ith element in this vector by ε,

$$\frac{\partial}{\partial \varepsilon} \left(\frac{\partial k_i}{\partial t} \right) = \frac{\partial f_i}{\partial k}(k(t, \varepsilon), x^*(t), t) \cdot k_\varepsilon(k(t, \varepsilon), t),$$

because $x(t, \varepsilon) = x^*(t), \forall t > s$.

Define $z(t) = k_\varepsilon(t, 0)$. Setting $\varepsilon = 0$ and reversing the order of differentiation,

$$\frac{dz_i}{dt} = \frac{\partial}{\partial t}\frac{\partial}{\partial \varepsilon} k_i(t, 0) = \frac{\partial}{\partial \varepsilon}\frac{\partial}{\partial t} k_i(t, 0) = \frac{\partial f_i}{\partial k}(k^*(t), x^*(t), t)' z(t).$$

Note that this is a system of ordinary differential equations for the vector $z(t)$.

Define the matrix $\mathbf{A}(t) = [\frac{\partial f_i}{\partial k_j}(k^*(t), x^*(t), t)]$. Then this system of ordinary differential equations can be rewritten in matrix form as follows:

$$\frac{dz}{dt} = \mathbf{A}z(t). \qquad (6.5\text{-}18)$$

We wish to establish that $\lambda(t)'k_\varepsilon(t, 0) = \lambda(t)'z(t)$ is time independent over $[s, T]$.

$$\frac{d}{dt}\lambda(t)'z(t) = \frac{d\lambda'}{dt}z(t) + \lambda(t)'\frac{dz}{dt}.$$

Substituting from (6.5-18),

$$\frac{d}{dt}\lambda(t)'z(t) = \frac{d\lambda'}{dt}z(t) + \lambda(t)'\mathbf{A}z(t). \qquad (6.5\text{-}19)$$

From (6.5-10),

$$\frac{d\lambda_j}{dt} = -\frac{\partial H}{\partial k_j}$$

$$= -\frac{\partial \overline{H}}{\partial k_j}, \quad \text{because} \quad \overline{H} = H$$

$$= -\lambda'\frac{\partial f}{\partial k_j}.$$

Writing this in matrix form,

$$\frac{d}{dt}\lambda(t)' = -\lambda'\left[\frac{\partial f_i}{\partial k_j}\right] = -\lambda'\mathbf{A}.$$

Substituting this back into (6.5-19)

$$\frac{d}{dt}\lambda(t)'z(t) = -\lambda'\mathbf{A}z(t) + \lambda'\mathbf{A}z(t) = 0.$$

$\square$

Fixed Endpoint Problems

The analysis is more complicated if the final state $k(T)$ is fixed. The problem is that the simple perturbation over an interval $[s - \varepsilon, s]$ changes the state variable from $k(t, 0)$ to $k(t, \varepsilon)$ for all $t > s$. Thus the fixed final endpoint constraint is violated. A formal analysis requires more complicated variations over multiple small intervals. Here we provide some intuition. Suppose that at time $\hat{T} < T$ the state variable is $k(\hat{T})$. Define

$$V^*(k(\hat{T}), \hat{T}) \equiv \underset{x(t) \in X}{\text{Max}} \left\{ \int_{\hat{T}}^{T} u(k(t), x(t), t)dt \,\middle|\, \frac{dk}{dt} = f(k, x, t), k(T) = \overline{K} \right\}.$$

We can then rewrite the fixed endpoint problem as follows:

$$\underset{x(t)\in X}{\text{Max}} \left\{ \int_0^{\hat{T}} u(k(t), x(t), t)dt + V^*(k(\hat{T}), \hat{T}) \Big| \frac{dk}{dt} = f(k, x, t) \right\}.$$

Thus we have turned the fixed endpoint problem into a free endpoint problem. If we are willing to assume that the function V^* is continuously differentiable, we can appeal to the Maximum Principle for the free endpoint problem, and thus the necessary conditions are exactly the same.

Application: Lifetime Consumption with Different Lending and Borrowing Rates

A consumer with a wage rate w, initial financial capital $k(0) = 0$, and consumption path $x(t)$ has lifetime utility

$$\int_0^T e^{-\delta t} u(x(t))dt.$$

We assume that $u' > 0$, $u'' < 0$, and $u'(0) = \infty$. The last assumption ensures that optimal consumption is strictly positive.

If at time t $k(t)$, her financial capital is positive she can invest it at a rate r. The growth rate of her assets thus satisfies

$$\frac{dk}{dt} = rk(t) + w - x(t).$$

If she is in debt she can borrow at a rate ρ and so her asset growth rate is

$$\frac{dk}{dt} = \rho k(t) + w - x(t).$$

We consider the case where $r < \delta < \rho$; that is, the consumer's discounts rate lies between her return on investing and her cost of borrowing. Let the lifetime utility-maximizing profile be $(k^*(t), x^*(t))$. Consider any time interval $[t_1, t_2]$ over which $k^*(t) > 0$. Then $(k^*(t), x^*(t))$ must solve the following fixed endpoint problem:

$$\underset{x(t)\geq 0}{\text{Max}} \left\{ \int_{t_1}^{t_2} e^{-\delta t} u(x(t))dt \Big| \frac{dk}{dt} = rk(t) + w - x(t), k(t_i) = k^*(t_i), i = 1, 2 \right\}.$$

The consumer will never leave a strictly positive capital stock because she could always do better by spending more. Thus $k^*(T) \leq 0$. Moreover, lenders will never lend money that cannot be paid back; thus $k^*(T) \geq 0$. Therefore this is a fixed endpoint problem.

We write down the Hamiltonian

$$H = e^{-\delta t} u(x) + \lambda(rk + w - x).$$

Then

$$\frac{d\lambda}{dt} = -\frac{\partial H}{\partial k} = -r\lambda \quad \text{and} \tag{6.5-20}$$

$$\frac{\partial H}{\partial x} = e^{-\delta t} u'(x) - \lambda = 0. \tag{6.5-21}$$

From (6.5-20), $\lambda(t) = \lambda(0)e^{-rt}$. Substituting into (6.5-21),

$$u'(x(t)) = e^{(\delta - r)t}\lambda(0).$$

Thus marginal utility increases over time. Because $u''(x) < 0$ it follows that consumption increases with t. Financial capital increases if $\frac{dk}{dt} = rk(t) + w - x(t) > 0$. Thus the phase diagram is as depicted on Figure 6.5-2.

To be in the interior of phase II at time t, the capital stock must be positive. However, initial capital is zero. Thus to get to phase II the consumer must first have been in phase I. But note that if the consumer is ever in phase I, capital must grow thereafter. Then, the terminal condition cannot be satisfied. Therefore the consumer can never be in the interior of phase I or phase II.

We can similarly study sub-intervals $[t_1, t_2]$ over which the consumer is in debt. It is left to the reader to confirm that the new phase diagram is as shown in Figure 6.5-3. Arguing as earlier, to be in the interior of phase IV, the consumer must have first been in phase III. But consumption and debt increase in phase III so any such path cannot enter phase IV. We can therefore conclude that there is no such time interval $[t_1, t_2]$. It follows that capital can never be positive or negative. Thus the optimal consumption profile is $x(t) = w$.

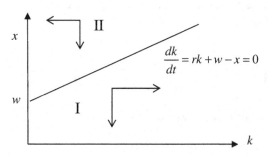

Figure 6.5-2. Phase diagram (lending).

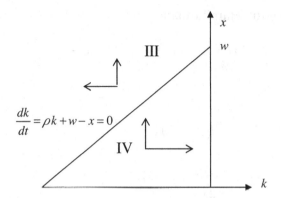

Figure 6.5-3. Phase diagram (borrowing).

Exercises

Exercise 6.5-1: Maximum Indebtedness Consider the continuous version of the life-cycle model. Suppose that $\delta > r$, wage income is w in each period and the time horizon is very long.

(a) Characterize as completely as you can the optimal consumption and capital stock sequences. HINT: Even with an infinite horizon, what is the most that any creditor would lend to this individual?
(b) With a very long finite horizon, is it necessarily the case that the individual spends most of the time in debt?

Exercise 6.5-2: A Debtor Who Saves for Retirement Suppose an individual earns an income at the rate w over $[0, T_w]$ and must then retire. He lives off his savings over the interval $[T_w, T]$. He discounts the future at the rate δ, and the interest rate for borrowing and lending is r where $r < \delta$. Use a phase diagram for both $t < T_w$ and $t > T_w$ to describe his lifetime path of consumption and asset accumulation.

HINT: Assume that he wishes to begin his retirement with asset level $K(T_w) = \hat{K}$. Analyze the interval $[0, T_w]$ with this terminal condition. Then appeal to the earlier discussion to characterize the path for $t > T_w$.

Exercise 6.5-3: Bequest Motive Consider the saving-borrowing model described at the end of this chapter. That is,

$$\operatorname*{Max}_{x(t)} \left\{ \int_0^T e^{-\delta t} u(x_t) + e^{-\delta T} V(k(T)) \Big| \frac{dk}{dt} = rk(t) + w \right\}.$$

The individual has no initial capital and T is large.

(a) Characterize the optimal consumption path if $\rho > r > \delta$.
(b) Characterize the optimal consumption path if $\rho < r < \delta$.

References and Selected Historical Reading

Bellman, R. (1953). *An Introduction to the Theory of Dynamic Programming.* Santa Monica, CA: RAND Corporation. http://www.rand.org/pubs/reports/R245.

Evans, L. (1983). An Introduction to Mathematical Optimal Control Theory. Berkeley: Department of Mathematics, UC Berkeley.

Malinvaud, E. (1953). "Capital Accumulation and Efficient Allocation of Resources." *Econometrica* 21: 223–68.

Pontryagin, L., Boltyanski, V., Gamkrelidze, R., and Mishchenko, E. (1962). The Mathematical Theory of Optimal Processes. New York: Interscience.

Ramsey, F. (1928). "A Mathematical Theory of Saving." *Economic Journal* 38: 543–49.

7

Uncertainty

7.1 Risky Choices

Key ideas: prospects, compound prospects, independence axiom, expected utility, paradoxes

We now extend the choice model to deal with uncertainty. We begin with an axiomatic development of expected utility theory. Because risk lovers are likely doomed to rapid ruin as they take huge gambles, agents that survive and thrive in the marketplace are almost surely either neutral or averse towards risk. Section 7.2 explores various ways of thinking about risk aversion and its consequences. In Section 7.3 we examine different ways of characterizing a change in beliefs that makes an agent "more optimistic" and explore their implications for the decisions that the agent makes.

A key assumption in the basic model of decision making under uncertainty is that all uncertainty faced by individuals contracting with one another is resolved eventually. Thus, any contract can be readily enforced. However, if one of the parties to a contract takes actions that are hidden, the ability to write contracts is constrained. We take up this important issue in Section 7.4.

If an economic agent is uncertain as to the consequences of his or her action, we can extend the basic choice model as long as the consumer is able to characterize fully the set of possible consequences and assign a probability to each. Historically, there has been much debate about whether individuals are always able to assign probabilities. It is surely true that probabilities can be assigned more easily if there is a body of experimental data. For example, if a coin has been tossed 1,000 times and heads has come up almost exactly half the time, most people would be willing to assign a probability of 0.5 to the event that the next outcome will be heads. However, even in this case, if there is a lot riding on the outcome and the choice is between calling heads and declining to participate, some might be suspicious that the person tossing the coin will use sleight of hand to switch the coin. Thus it is very difficult to find cases in which a probability is believed to be truly objective. Instead, there are usually some subjective elements involved.

This does not mean that the strength of beliefs is unimportant. Suppose that you are to play a game in which a coin is to be tossed 10 times. If you have tossed it 100 times in advance and the fraction of heads is close to one-half, a sequence of four tails will not be influential. However if you have just looked at the coin, you will be much more suspicious that the coin is loaded in favor of tails and will strictly prefer to call "tails." Generally, the weaker the information before the game, the more you will be influenced by the outcome of the game as play continues.

Initially we consider decisions when the number of possible outcomes or "states" is finite. The decision maker then assigns a probability to each state. Suppose that in state s the consequence is x_s. Let π_s be the probability that the individual assigns to this state. Then a complete description of the uncertain outcome or "prospect" is the $2 \times S$ vector

$$(\pi; x) = ((\pi_1, \ldots, \pi_S); (x_1, \ldots, x_S)).$$

Under the axioms of consumer choice, there exists a continuous utility function $U(\pi, x)$ over prospects. Because our focus is initially on the choice over probabilities, it is convenient to fix the S consequences and simply write the prospect as the probability vector π. For the case of three states, preferences over prospects $\pi = (\pi_1, \pi_2, \pi_3)$ are illustrated in Figure 7.1-1.

We assume that $x_1 \prec x_2 \prec x_3$. Figure 7.1-1 shows only the probabilities of the best and worst states. If $\pi_1 = 1$, the outcome is x_1 with probability 1. If $\pi_3 = 1$, the outcome is x_3 with probability 1. Because probabilities add up to 1, the set of possible probability pairs (π_1, π_3) is the shaded region in each diagram. In particular, at the origin $\pi_1 = \pi_3 = 0$, so this is the certain outcome x_2.

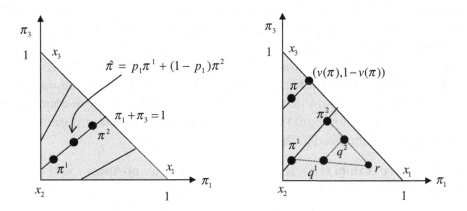

Figure 7.1-1. Preferences over lotteries.

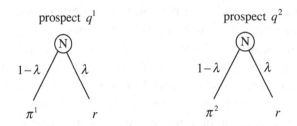

Figure 7.1-2. Tree diagrams of compound prospects.

Suppose you must choose between two prospects π^1 and π^2. You are about to choose one of them when you are offered the opportunity to randomize. If you accept, a spinner will be used that will select prospect 1 with probability p_1 and prospect 2 with probability $p_2 = 1 - p_1$. We write this new *compound prospect* as follows:

$$\hat{\pi} = (p; \pi^1, \pi^2) = \left((p_1, p_2); \left(\pi_1^1, , , .\pi_S^1\right), \left(\pi_1^2, , , .\pi_S^2\right)\right).$$

Note that the probability of state s in this compound lottery is $\hat{\pi}_s = p_1\pi_s^1 + p_2\pi_s^2$. Thus, $\hat{\pi} = p_1\pi^1 + (1 - p_1)\pi^2$ is a convex combination of π^1 and π^2. In Figure 7.1-1, this is a point on the line joining the two prospects π^1 and π^2.

Suppose you are indifferent between the prospects π^1 and π^2. How will you feel about randomizing between them? When asked this question, respondents overwhelmingly indicate that they will be indifferent between all three prospects. Formally,

$$\pi^1 \sim \pi^2 \Rightarrow \pi^1 \sim \left(p_1, p_2; \pi^1, \pi^2\right), \quad \text{where} \quad p_1, p_2 > 0 \quad \text{and} \quad p_1 + p_2 = 1.$$

It follows that indifference curves must be linear as depicted.

For the indifference curves to be parallel, as depicted in the right-hand diagram, we need a further assumption. Consider the prospect $q^1 = (1 - \lambda, \lambda; \pi^1, r)$, a convex combination of π^1 and some alternative prospect r. Similarly define $q^2 = (1 - \lambda, \lambda; \pi^2, r)$. These compound prospects can also be depicted in tree diagrams as shown in Figure 7.1-2.

Suppose you prefer π^1 to π^2. You are then asked to choose between q^1 and q^2. When asked what they will do, respondents overwhelmingly conclude that they would prefer q^1 over q^2. Intuitively, because the outcome r is an independent event that occurs with probability λ in both compound prospects, the ranking should be the same whether λ is zero or positive.

This idea is formalized in the following axiom.

Independence Axiom (IA) If $\pi^1 \succsim \pi^2$, then for any prospect r and probabilities $p_1, p_2 > 0$ where $p_1 + p_2 = 1$,

$$q^1 = (p_1, p_2 : \pi^1, r) \succsim (p_1, p_2 : \pi^2, r) = q^2.$$

From the geometry of the right-hand diagram in Figure 7.1-1, it follows that indifference curves are parallel.

Expected Utility

Consider the right-hand diagram in Figure 7.1-1. Note that for every feasible prospect π, there is a prospect $(v(\pi), 0, 1 - v(\pi))$ on the line $\pi_1 + \pi_3 = 1$ such that

$$\pi \sim (v(\pi), 0, 1 - v(\pi)).$$

This is a prospect in which there is positive probability on only the best and worst outcomes. Thus, one possible utility representation of the consumer's preferences is the win probability $v(\pi)$ in this extreme lottery.

For the certain consequence x_1 the win probability $v(x_1) = 1$ and for x_3, the win probability is $v(x_3) = 0$. For the intermediate consequence x_2 the win probability $v(x_2)$ lies between zero and one. This is true for any consequence x such that $x_1 \precsim x \precsim x_3$. Thus the probability $v(x)$ is a utility representation of preferences over certain consequences. The great advantage of using this utility function is that for any prospect $(x; p) = (x_1, \ldots, x_S; p_1, \ldots, p_S)$, the consumer is indifferent between p and playing the extreme lottery with a win probability of

$$\sum_{s=1}^{S} p_s v(x_s).$$

Thus, we can represent the consumer's preferences in terms of expected win probabilities in the extreme lotteries, or expected utility.

Expected Utility Rule Preferences over prospects $(x; p) = (p_1, \ldots, p_S; x_1, \ldots, x_S)$ can be represented by the von Neumann-Morgenstern utility function $u(p, x) = \sum_{s=1}^{S} p_s v(x_s)$.

To prove this result we appeal to the following restatement of the Independence Axiom.

Independence Axiom (IA′) If $\pi^m \succsim \hat{\pi}^m, m = 1, \ldots, M$, then for any probability vector $p = (p_1, \ldots, p_M)$

$$(p_1, \ldots, p_M : \pi^1, \ldots, \pi^M) \succsim (p_1, \ldots, p_M : \hat{\pi}^1, \ldots, \hat{\pi}^M).$$

Clearly **IA′** implies **IA**.[1]

---

[1] In Exercise 7.1-1 you are asked to show that the converse is also true.

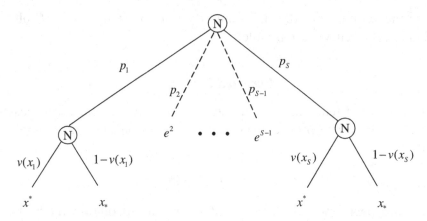

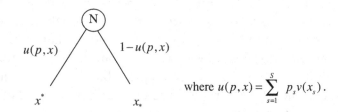

$$\text{where } u(p,x) = \sum_{s=1}^{S} p_s v(x_s).$$

Figure 7.1-3. Deriving the expected utility rule.

To derive the expected utility rule, consider any S consequences where x^* is the most preferred and x_* the least. For each consequence there must be some probability $v(x_s)$ of winning in the extreme lottery. That is,

$$x_s \sim e^s \equiv (v(x_s), 1 - v(x_s) : x^*, x_*).$$

By **IA′**, it follows that $(p : c) \sim (p_1, \ldots, p_S : e^1, \ldots, e^S)$. The compound prospect is depicted in the tree diagram in Figure 7.1-3. Although there are $2S$ terminal nodes, each of these is either x^* or x_*. Thus the big tree and the little tree in Figure 7.1-3 are equivalent.

That is,

$$(p : x) \sim (p_1, \ldots, p_S : e^1, \ldots, e^S) \sim (u(p, x), 1 - u(p, x) : x^*, x_*).$$

Although the assumptions underlying this rule seem plausible, experiments show that there are systematic deviations from the rule. Perhaps the most famous is an example of Allais.

Allais Paradox

In Figure 7.1-4 the payoff in state 1 is zero, in state 2 it is $1 million, and in state 3 it is $5 million. A prospect is a point in the triangle. Consider the four prospects A, B, C and D. Note that the slope of the line CD is

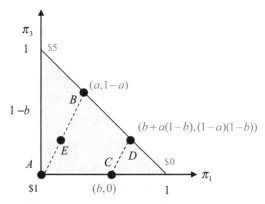

Figure 7.1-4. The Allais paradox.

$(1-a)(1-b)/a(1-b) = (1-a)/a$. This is also the slope of the line AB. We have seen that the Independence Axiom implies that indifference curves are parallel lines. Thus, if $D \succ C$, then expected utility must be rising along the line AB in the direction of B. Conversely, if $D \prec C$, then expected utility must be decreasing along the line AB.

Suppose $a = 0.9$ and $b = 0.1$. Then the four prospects are as follows:

$$A = (0, 1, 0) \quad B = (0.1, 0, 0.9) \quad C = (0.9, 0.1, 0) \quad D = (0.91, 0, 0.09).$$

When asked to choose between a guaranteed $1 million (prospect A) and a 90 percent chance of $5 million (prospect B) most people will choose A. However, when offered a 10 percent chance of $1 million (prospect C) or a 9 percent chance of $5 million (prospect D), these same people indicate that they would prefer D, violating an implication of the expected utility postulates. Subsequent experiments confirm the robustness of this result.[2]

Given such inconsistencies, there have been many attempts to provide alternatives to the Independence Axiom. One such approach proposed by Machina (1982) allows for indifference curves to be linear but replaces the parallel indifference lines with indifference lines that fan out as depicted in Figure 7.1-5. Note that with fanning, it is no longer inconsistent for an individual to prefer D to C and A to B.

A second famous paradox is due to Ellsberg.

Ellsberg Paradox

An urn has 30 black balls and 60 other balls, some of which are red and some green. An individual is invited to choose black or green and will be paid $100 if the ball drawn is that color. Typically individuals choose black. A second

---

[2] In his original experiment, Allais used the convex combination $E = (0.1, 0.9; A, B)$ rather than B. (Adding up probabilities, it is readily checked that $E = (0.01, 0.9, 0.09)$).

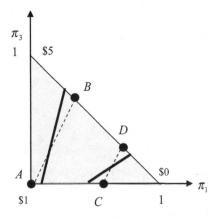

Figure 7.1-5. Non-expected utility resolution of the Allais paradox.

experiment offers individuals the chance to pick red and one other color. If the ball drawn is one of the colors selected, the individual wins $50. Typically individuals choose red and green.

If the experiment is conducted with different individuals, it is easy to see why these outcomes might occur. In the first experiment an individual may think that the experimenter will try to minimize the expected loss by having very few green balls. The individual thus chooses black. In the second experiment the same logic leads to the red-green choice because this guarantees 60 balls. However if the same individual is offered both experiments, the pattern is much harder to explain. For regardless of the number of green balls, if the individual's probability assessment leads him to choose black in the first experiment, he must believe that there are at least as many red balls as green. Hence he must believe that there are at least 30 red balls. Because there are 30 black balls it follows that he must believe that there are at least 60 balls colored either red or black. Then in the second experiment red-black is at least as good as red-green.

The Ellsberg experimental results are robust. However, when I conduct such experiments and then point out that the participants' behavior violates the Independence Axiom, I find most people are quick to change their choices. Thus the result seems to reflect the inexperience of the participants. If so, the Ellsberg paradox is much less likely to occur when the stakes are higher and the participants are experienced.

"Soft" and "Hard" Probabilities

A "hard" probability can be determined by direct observation. A "soft" probability requires some inference. Following Frank Knight, some have argued that a distinction should be made between "soft" and "hard" probabilities and that individuals prefer the latter. This next example illustrates the point. Suppose three urns each contain 100 balls. Urn 1 is Greek and has 60 yellow balls. Urns 2 and 3 are identical Egyptian urns. One has 75 yellow balls and the other has 25 yellow balls. Urns 2 and 3 are shuffled and one is removed. You will win a prize if you draw a yellow ball. You are given a choice between the Greek and remaining Egyptian urn. Before you decide, a ball is drawn at random from the Egyptian urn and it is yellow.[3] What should you do?

The information that the ball is yellow makes it more likely that the unlabelled urn is the "good" one with 75 yellow balls, rather than the "bad" one with 25 yellow balls. As a careful Bayesian you compute the probability that the state is good, given the information that the ball is yellow (represented as the event I). The two possible events are (I, G) and (I, B). The conditional probability that the urn is good is therefore

$$\Pr\{G|I\} = \frac{\Pr\{I, G\}}{\Pr\{I, G\} + \Pr\{I, B\}}$$

$$= \frac{\Pr\{I|G\}\Pr\{G\}}{\Pr\{I|G\}\Pr\{G\} + \Pr\{I|B\}\Pr\{B\}}$$

$$= \frac{\frac{3}{4} \times \frac{1}{2}}{\frac{3}{4} \times \frac{1}{2} + \frac{1}{4} \times \frac{1}{2}} = \frac{3}{4}.$$

Because the only other possibility is bad, $\Pr\{B|I\} = \frac{1}{4}$.

The probability of drawing a yellow ball is then

$$\Pr\{Y|I\} = \Pr\{Y|G\}\Pr\{G|I\} + \Pr\{Y|B\}\Pr\{B|I\}$$

$$= \frac{3}{4}\frac{3}{4} + \frac{1}{4}\frac{1}{4} = 0.625.$$

Because there are 60 yellow balls in the Greek urn, the probability of winning is 0.6 if the contestant chooses this urn. The good Bayesian thus chooses the Egyptian urn.

In reality many participants choose the Greek urn. The application of Bayes' Rule is subtle and people are wary of making mistakes. The problem is that inexperienced respondents do not trust their ability to utilize the information and therefore discount it. The key insight is not that individuals dislike "soft" probabilities, but that soft probabilities create a demand for information and experts who can process this information reliably.

Game Show Paradox

The winning contestant in a game show must select one of three curtains. Behind each is a prize. However, there is only one grand prize. Behind each

---

[3] The ball is then replaced.

of the other two curtains is a beach towel. The contestant knows that after she has picked a curtain, the game-show host (who knows where the grand prize is hidden) will open one of the other curtains and offer her the chance to pick again. Should she do so?

Most contestants choose to stick with their "hunch." However, by doing so they are making a big mistake. The contestant's probability of picking the correct curtain is 1/3. Thus, the probability that the grand prize is behind one of the other two curtains is 2/3. If one of the curtains is opened revealing a beach towel, the probability that the grand prize is behind the other curtain is 2/3. Thus the contestant doubles her win probability by switching.

Try this on your friends. You will find that they are suspicious at first and may need to hear the logic several times before they become convinced. The point is that individuals do often make instinctive decisions, and it is possible to characterize the direction of the bias when they do. However, in an environment where the same kinds of decisions are being made repeatedly, Bayes' Rule is much more likely to be correctly applied.

Rabin Paradox

Experimenters typically find that individuals exhibit much more aversion to risk in the laboratory than in the marketplace. Moreover it is easy to construct examples in which subjects' choices are inconsistent with the standard expected utility model. Suppose you are offered the opportunity to draw a ball at random from an urn containing 100 balls, some green and some red. The payoff when a green ball is drawn is in the left column of Table 7.1-1, and the payoff for a red ball is in the right column. Each of the shaded cells indicates a different gamble. For example in the top left cell you win 100 with probability 0.52; otherwise you lose 100. Would you accept or reject this gamble?

Note that the probability of winning rises as you move to the right along each row. Thus an individual accepting any particular gamble would also accept any other gamble to the right of the accepted gamble.

Consider the first row. Which of these five gambles would you accept? Then look at the other gambles in these same columns. Would you be willing

Table 7.1-1. *Acceptable Gambles*

Payoff if Green Ball	Number of Green Balls (out of 100)					Payoff if Red Ball
100	52	55	60	66	70	− 100
1,000	13	20	33	48	57	− 100
5,000	7	18	33	48	57	− 100
25,000	7	18	33	48	57	− 100

to accept any of these? For most subjects, there are more acceptable gambles in the bottom rows than in the top rows. Yet expected utility theory implies that this should not be the case.

Let the win probability be p, let the winning payoff be g, and let the agent's wealth be w. If the first-row gamble is rejected, it follows that

$$v(w) \geq (1-p)v(w-g) + pv(w+g). \tag{7.1-1}$$

This inequality can be rewritten as follows:

$$v(w+g) - v(w) \leq \frac{1-p}{p}(v(w) - v(w-g)). \tag{7.1-2}$$

We also assume that there is a range of higher wealth levels over which the ranking would not change. For someone whose wealth is $w' > w$, it follows that

$$v(w'+g) - v(w') \leq \frac{1-p}{p}(v(w') - v(w'-g)).$$

Setting $w' = w + g$,

$$v(w+2g) - v(w+g) \leq \frac{1-p}{p}(v(w+g) - v(w)).$$

Substituting from (7.1-2), if follows that

$$v(w+2g) - v(w+g) \leq \left(\frac{1-p}{p}\right)^2 (v(w) - v(w-g)). \tag{7.1-3}$$

Define

$$s(n, p) = 1 + \frac{1-p}{p} + \left(\frac{1-p}{p}\right)^2 + \cdots \left(\frac{1-p}{p}\right)^n.$$

Adding (7.1-2) and (7.1-3), it follows that

$$v(w+2g) - v(w-g) \leq s(2, p)(v(w) - v(w-g)).$$

Rearranging this expression it follows that

$$v(w) \geq \frac{1}{s(2, p)}v(w+2g) + \left(1 - \frac{1}{s(2, p)}\right)v(w-g).$$

We can repeat this argument n times to show that

$$v(w) \geq \frac{1}{s(n, p)}v(w+ng) + \left(1 - \frac{1}{s(n, p)}\right)v(w-g).$$

As is readily checked, each term in the table is $100/s(n, p)$. Thus, for example, any individual rejecting the gamble $(100, -100; 0.55, 0.45)$ should also reject the gamble $(25000, -100; 0.18, 0.82)$.

Continuous Probability Distributions

In the previous discussion the number of states is finite. The decision maker assigns a probability π_s to each of the states in $S = \{1, , \ldots, S\}$. An alternative modeling strategy is to assume that the set of states are points in some closed set $S = [\alpha, \beta]$. We define the increasing cumulative distribution function (c.d.f.) $F(t) = \Pr\{s \le t\}$ where $F(\alpha) = 0$ and $F(\beta) = 1$. The probability of being in any sub-interval $C = [s, s']$ is then $\pi(C) = F(s') - F(s)$. This is known as the probability measure of C. The laws of probability then apply to the intersection and union of these closed intervals.

If for every neighborhood $N(x, \delta)$ of x, $\pi(N(x, \delta)) > 0$, the point x is said to be in the support of the distribution. Suppose for example that $S = [1, 3]$ and

$$F(s) = \begin{cases} \frac{1}{2}\theta, & 0 \le \theta \le 1 \\ \frac{1}{2}, & 1 < \theta < 2 \\ \frac{1}{2}(\theta - 1), & 2 \le \theta \le 3 \end{cases}.$$

Then $F(\theta)$ is strictly increasing on the sub-intervals $[0, 1]$ and $[2, 3]$ so the support of the distribution is the union of these intervals.

The continuous model is easily generalized to higher dimensions. Let C be a closed convex hypercube in $\mathbb{R}^n$. The decision maker then assigns a probability measure over all closed hyper cubes in C.

There are some mathematical subtleties when using infinite state spaces to prove theorems. Despite this, as a modeling strategy, it is often more convenient to work with continuous distributions than with finite state spaces.

Exercises

Exercise 7.1-1: Equivalence of the Independence Axioms For $M = 2$ show that **IA** implies **IA'**.

(a) Complete the proof by induction. That is, show that if the proposition holds for $M = k - 1$, then it must also hold for $M = k$.

Exercise 7.1-2: Allais Paradox

(a) Draw a tree diagram showing that the prospect C can be represented as a compound gamble between A and (1,0,0). Draw another tree diagram showing that the prospect D can be represented as a compound gamble between B and (1,0,0), where the probability of (1,0,0) is the same.
(b) Show that the ranking of A and B must be the same as the ranking of C and D. Hence establish the original version of the Allais paradox; that is $C \succsim D \Leftrightarrow A \succsim E$.

Table 7.1-2. *Acceptable Gambles*

Payoff if Green Ball	Number of Green Balls (out of 100)					Payoff if Red Ball
200	52	55	60	66	70	0
1,100	13	20	33	48	57	0
5,100	7	18	33	48	57	0
25,100	7	18	33	48	57	0

Exercise 7.1-3: Linear and Monotonic Transformations

(a) Show that if preferences can be represented by the von Neumann utility function $v(\cdot)$, they can also be represented by any affine transformation $Av(\cdot) + B$, $A > 0$.

(b) Alex has an expected utility function $u(p, x) = \sum_{s=1}^{S} p_s \ln x_s$. Bev has a utility function $U(p, x) = x_1^{p_1} x_2^{p_2} \ldots x_S^{p_S}$. Is she an expected utility maximizer? Do her preferences satisfy the Independence Axiom?

Exercise 7.1-4: Rabin Paradox You are offered either a guaranteed $100 or one of the risky alternatives shown in Table 7.1-2. Which would you accept?

Compare your answers to the answers you gave in the discussion of the Rabin paradox. Are the differences consistent with expected utility maximization?

7.2 Attitudes toward Risk

Key ideas: risk aversion, acceptable gambles, measures of risk aversion, Jensen's Inequality, trading in state claims

Consider an individual choosing over prospects $(\pi_1, \ldots, \pi_S; x_1, \ldots, x_S)$, where $x_s \in \mathbb{R}$. Holding the consequences fixed, we now examine more systematically choices over probability distributions. We begin by considering changes to the probabilities of three outcomes. We re-label the S outcomes so that the first three are the ones with changing probabilities and let x_1 be the lowest outcome, x_2 be the intermediate outcome, and x_3 be the highest outcome. First consider an individual whose expected utility function is

$$U^0(x) = \sum_{s=1}^{S} \pi_s x_s.$$

This individual is said to be risk neutral in that he is indifferent between prospects that have the same expected value, even though one may be much riskier than another. Suppose that the initial and final probability vectors are $\hat{\pi}$ and $\pi = \hat{\pi} + \Delta\pi$. Then the change in the expected payoff is

$$\Delta U^0 = \sum_{s=1}^{3} \Delta\pi_s x_s.$$

Also, because probabilities only change for the first three states $\sum_{s=1}^{3} \hat{\pi}_s = \sum_{s=1}^{3} \pi_s$ and so

$$\sum_{s=1}^{3} \Delta\pi_s = 0.$$

Using this equation to substitute for $\Delta\pi_2$, we can write the change in expected payoff as follows:

$$\Delta U^0 = \Delta\pi_3(x_3 - x_2) - \Delta\pi_1(x_2 - x_1).$$

Indifference lines are depicted in Figure 7.2-1. Note that the slope of each indifference line is

$$m^0 = \frac{\Delta\pi_3}{\Delta\pi_1} = \frac{x_2 - x_1}{x_3 - x_2}.$$

Consider the indifference curve through the origin. At O, both π_1 and π_3 are zero so this is the certain consequence x_2. All the points in the shaded region on or above the indifference line have a positive expected payoff. Suppose that the individual begins with x_2. Then the shaded region G^0 is the set of acceptable risky outcomes or "acceptable gambles" for a risk-neutral individual. We define a risk-averse individual to be one who will accept fewer gambles than a risk-neutral individual.

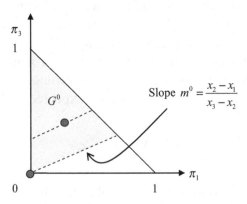

Figure 7.2-1. Acceptable gambles for a risk-neutral individual.

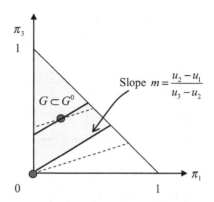

Figure 7.2-2. Acceptable gambles for a risk-averse agent.

Let $u_s = u(x_s)$ be the von Neumann Morgenstern utility function of a risk-averse agent. Arguing as earlier, if the probability vector changes from $\hat{\pi}$ to π, the change in expected utility is

$$\Delta U = \sum_{s=1}^{S} (\pi_s - \hat{\pi}_s) u_s = \Delta \pi_3 (u_3 - u_2) - \Delta \pi_1 (u_2 - u_1).$$

Along an indifference line the slope is

$$m = \frac{\Delta \pi_3}{\Delta \pi_1} = \frac{u_2 - u_1}{u_3 - u_2}.$$

This is depicted in Figure 7.2-2. The set of acceptable gambles G is the set of points on or above the indifference line through the origin. Thus $G \subset G^0$ and $G \neq G^0$ if and only if $m > m^0$, that is,

$$m = \frac{u_2 - u_1}{u_3 - u_2} > \frac{x_2 - x_1}{x_3 - x_2} = m^0.$$

Rearranging, $G \subset G^0$ and $G \neq G^0$ if and only if

$$\frac{u_2 - u_1}{x_2 - x_1} > \frac{u_3 - u_2}{x_3 - x_2}. \tag{7.2-1}$$

Lemma 7.2-1: Strictly Concave Function[4] $u(x), x \in \mathbb{R}$ is strictly concave if and only if for any $x_2 \in (x_1, x_3)$,

$$\frac{u(x_2) - u(x_1)}{x_2 - x_1} > \frac{u(x_3) - u(x_2)}{x_3 - x_2}.$$

This is illustrated in Figure 7.2-3.

The function $u(\cdot)$ is strictly concave if and only if for all $x_2 \in (x_1, x_3)$, the point A_2 lies above the chord $A_1 A_3$. Equivalently, the slope of the chord $A_1 A_2$ exceeds the slope of the chord $A_2 A_3$. This illustrates an important

---

[4] You are asked to provide a formal proof in Exercise 7.2-6.

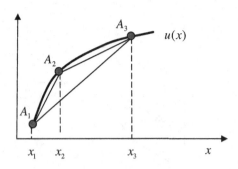

Figure 7.2-3. Strictly concave function.

result. An expected utility-maximizing individual is risk averse if and only
the utility function is concave.

Greater Aversion to Risk

Next consider two individuals, Victor and Ursula, with utility functions $v(\cdot)$
and $u(\cdot)$, respectively. Suppose that the former is a strictly concave transformation of the latter; that is, $v = g(u)$ where g is an increasing strictly concave
function. We now argue that Victor must have a smaller set of acceptable
gambles. In other words, Victor is more risk averse than Ursula.

Appealing to Lemma 7.2-1, the function g is strictly concave if and only if,
for all $x_1, x_3 > x_1$ and convex combinations x_2,

$$\frac{g(u_2) - g(u_1)}{g(u_3) - g(u_2)} > \frac{u_2 - u_1}{u_3 - u_2},$$

That is,

$$m^v = \frac{v_2 - v_1}{v_3 - v_2} > \frac{u_2 - u_1}{u_3 - u_2} = m^u.$$

Measures of Absolute Risk Aversion

As we have just argued, Victor is everywhere more risk averse than Ursula if
his utility function is a strictly increasing concave transformation of Ursula's.
For any pair of increasing functions $v(x)$ and $u(x)$ there is some increasing
mapping $v = g(u)$. Then

$$v'(x) = g'(u(x))u'(x).$$

Taking logs, $\ln v'(x) = \ln g'(u(x)) + \ln u'(x)$.

Differentiating again and rearranging,

$$-\frac{v''(x)}{v'(x)} = -\frac{g''(u)}{g'(u)} - \frac{u''(x)}{u'(x)}.$$

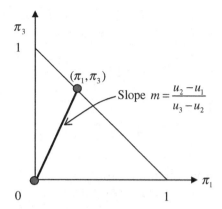

Figure 7.2-4. Shifting the odds.

Note that because g is strictly increasing and concave, the first term on the right-hand side is positive. Thus, Victor is more risk averse if and only if

$$A^v(x) \equiv -\frac{v''(x)}{v'(x)} \geq -\frac{u''(x)}{u'(x)} = A^u(x).$$

This ratio is known as the degree of absolute risk aversion.

Small Risks

Consider the special case in which $(x_1, x_2, x_3) = (w, w + z, w + 2z)$. Suppose the probabilities are chosen so that the individual is indifferent between $(\pi_1, 0, \pi_3)$ and $(0, 1, 0)$. That is, the individual is indifferent between receiving z for sure and receiving 0 with probability π_1 and $2z$ with probability π_3 This is depicted in Figure 7.2-4.

The individual is indifferent between the origin and the gamble (π_1, π_3). Thus the slope of the indifference line is

$$m(z) \equiv \frac{u_2 - u_1}{u_3 - u_2} = \frac{\pi_3}{\pi_1}.$$

If the individual is risk neutral,

$$\frac{\pi_3}{\pi_1} = m^0(z) = \frac{u(w + z) - u(w)}{u(w + 2z) - u(w + z)} = \frac{(w + z) - (w)}{(w + 2z) - (w + z)} = 1.$$

Thus for any risk-averse individual, the odds must exceed 1. As a measure of aversion to small risks we ask how rapidly the odds that an individual will accept increase as the size of the gamble increases from zero.

Define $n(z) = u_2 - u_1$ and $d(z) = u_3 - u_2$.
Then

$$m(z) = \frac{u(w + z) - u(w)}{u(w + 2z) - u(w + z)} = \frac{n(z)}{d(z)}$$

As z approaches zero both numerator and denominator approach zero. Appealing to l'Hôpital's Rule,[5]

$$m(0) = \lim_{x \to 0} \frac{n'(z)}{d'(z)} = \lim_{x \to 0} \frac{u'(w + z)}{2u'(w + 2z) - u'(w + z)} = 1.$$

Then

$$\frac{m(z) - m(0)}{z} = \frac{m(z) - 1}{z} = \frac{2u(w + z) - u(w) - u(w + 2z)}{z(u(w + 2z) - u(w + z))}.$$

Both the numerator and the denominator and their first derivatives are zero at $z = 0$. By l'Hôpital's Rule the limit of the right-hand side is the ratio of the second derivatives. The limit of the left hand side is the derivative of m. Differentiating and collecting non-zero terms,

$$m'(0) = -\frac{u''(w)}{u'(w)}.$$

Thus, for any small z the odds π_3/π_1 needed for the individual to accept the gamble must be

$$m(z) \approx m(0) + m'(0)z = 1 + A(w)z.$$

Therefore $A(w) = -u''(w)/u'(w)$ is a measure of aversion to a small absolute risk.

Economists are often interested in responses to changes in proportional or "relative" risk, rather than absolute risk. We can use our results to get a measure of aversion to such risk. Suppose that the gamble is over a fraction θ of the individual's wealth; that is $x = \theta w$. For each fraction θ, let $m_R(\theta)$ be the slope of the indifference line (the acceptable odds).

Then $m_R(\theta) = m(\theta w)$. Differentiating by θ, $m'_R(\theta) = wm'(\theta w)$. Hence,

$$m'_R(0) = -w\frac{u''(w)}{u'(w)} \equiv R(w).$$

Thus, $R(w)$ is a measure of aversion to relative risk and is called the degree of relative risk aversion.

State Claims

Thus far, our focus has been on the ranking of probability vectors. We now switch our attention to the choice of consumption bundles. It is helpful to think about a prospect as being Nature's choice of one of the S states (e.g., inches of rainfall). The probability of state s is π_s. In state s the individual's

---

[5] Using Taylor's Expansion we can write the ratio as follows: $\frac{n(z)}{d(z)} = \frac{n(0) + zn'(z_1)}{d(0) + zd'(z_2)}$ where z_1 and $z_2 \in [0, z]$. Taking the limit, $m'(0) = \lim_{z \to 0} \frac{zn'(z_1)}{zd'(z_2)} = \lim_{z \to 0} \frac{n'(z_1)}{d'(z_2)} = \frac{n'(0)}{d'(0)}$.

consumption is x_s. Thus our focus shifts from varying the probabilities of the different states to varying the consumption in these states.

We first compare a risky prospect $(\pi_1, \ldots, \pi_S; x_1, \ldots, x_S)$ with its expectation $\bar{x} = \sum_{s=1}^{S} \pi_s x_s$. Intuitively, an individual who is risk averse (or equivalently has a concave utility function) will strictly prefer the certain expectation $\bar{x}$ over the risky prospect.

Jensen's Inequality If $u(\cdot)$ is strictly concave, then $\sum_{s=1}^{S} \pi_s u(x_s) \leq u(\sum_{s=1}^{S} \pi_s x_s)$ and the inequality is strict unless $x_1 = \cdots = x_S$.

Proof: Re-label states so that $x_1 \neq x_2$. Then for $S = 2$, Jensen's Inequality is a restatement of the definition of a strictly concave function. We appeal to concavity to show that the proposition holds for $S = 3$.

From the strict concavity of $u(\cdot)$,

$$\frac{\pi_1}{\pi_1 + \pi_2} u(x_1) + \frac{\pi_2}{\pi_1 + \pi_2} u(x_2) < u\left(\frac{\pi_1 x_1 + \pi_2 x_2}{\pi_1 + \pi_2}\right).$$

Again appealing to the concavity of $u(\cdot)$,

$$(\pi_1 + \pi_2) u\left(\frac{\pi_1 x_1 + \pi_2 x_2}{\pi_1 + \pi_2}\right) + \pi_3 u(x_3) \leq u\left((\pi_1 + \pi_2)\left(\frac{\pi_1 x_1 + \pi_2 x_2}{\pi_1 + \pi_2}\right) + \pi_3 x_3\right)$$

$$= u(\pi_1 x_1 + \pi_2 x_2 + \pi_3 x_3).$$

Multiplying the first inequality by $\pi_1 + \pi_2$ and adding the two inequalities, it follows that

$$\pi_1 u(x_1) + \pi_2 u(x_2) + \pi_3 u(x_3) < u(\pi_1 x_1 + \pi_2 x_2 + \pi_3 x_3).$$

Thus, the theorem holds for the three-outcome case. An inductive argument extends this to the S-outcome case. □

Trading in Markets for State Claims

Suppose Bev will have a higher income in state 1 (Republican candidate wins) than state 2 (Democrat wins). That is, her state-contingent income vector is (ω_1, ω_2) where $\omega_1 > \omega_2$. Before the election she can trade in the Iowa Presidential futures market.[6] Let p_1 be the current price of 1 unit of consumption if the Republican candidate wins and let p_2 be the corresponding price if the Democrat wins. Her budget constraint is

$$p_2(x_2 - \omega_2) = p_1(\omega_1 - x_1), \quad \text{or rearranging,} \quad p_1 x_1 + p_2 x_2 = p_1 \omega_1 + p_2 \omega_2.$$

Her budget set is depicted in Figure 7.2-5.

[6] You can place a modest bet at http://www.biz.uiowa.edu/iem/.

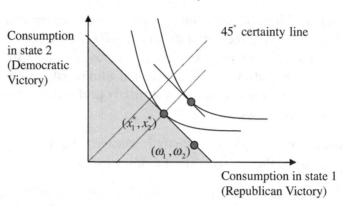

Figure 7.2-5. Partial insurance against a Democratic victory.

The steepness of the indifference curve on the certainty line is equal to Bev's odds of a Republican victory. Thus, if the market price ratio is equal to her subjective odds, Bev will choose a bet that moves her to the 45° line. In other words, Bev will trade in the presidential futures market in order to completely insure herself against the unfavorable outcome (victory by the Democratic Party candidate). As depicted, the price is less favorable so Bev partially insures against a Democratic victory.

How would the riskiness of her optimal consumption bundle change if her wealth were to increase? As we see, this depends on how her degree of absolute risk aversion changes with wealth. If it is constant, then her new consumption point is on the dotted line parallel to the certainty line. Thus she chooses the same absolute risk. If it declines as x increases, then Bev will take on greater absolute risk.

Consider the effect on the marginal rate of substitution as consumption rises from (x_1, x_2) to $(x_1 + z, x_2 + z)$, a point on the line parallel to the 45° line. The MRS is

$$M(x_1 + z, x_2 + z) = \frac{\pi_1}{\pi_2} \frac{v'(x_1 + z)}{v'(x_2 + z)}.$$

Therefore $\ln M(x_1 + z, x_2 + z) = \ln v'(x_1 + z) - \ln v'(x_2 + z) + \ln (\pi_1/\pi_2)$. Hence,

$$\frac{1}{M} \frac{\partial M}{\partial z} = \frac{v''(x_1 + z)}{v'(x_1 + z)} - \frac{v''(x_2 + z)}{v'(x_2 + z)}.$$

It follows immediately that if the degree of absolute risk aversion is constant, then the marginal rate of substitution is unchanged. If the degree of absolute risk aversion decreases with x, then below the 45° certainty line

$$A(x_1 + z) = -\frac{v''(x_1 + z)}{v'(x_1 + z)} < -\frac{v''(x_2 + z)}{v'(x_2 + z)} = A(x_2 + z).$$

Thus, in this case the marginal rate of substitution increases and the optimal consumption bundle is farther from the certainty line. Therefore greater wealth leads to a consumption bundle exhibiting greater absolute risk.

Finally, we consider a simple portfolio decision. Ursula must decide how much to invest in a riskless asset that has a gross yield of $1 + r_1$ and how much to invest in a risky asset (or mutual fund) with a gross yield $1 + r_2$. Intuitively, if Ursula is risk averse she will need to be paid some premium to invest in the risky asset. That is, unless the expected yield for the risky asset is sufficiently greater than that for the riskless asset, she will choose not to take on any risk. As we see, this intuition is not quite correct.

Converting to the state claim formulation, let the gross yield of the risky asset be $1 + r_{2s}$ in state s, and the probability of state s be $\pi_s, s = 1, \ldots, S$. Suppose that Ursula invests q dollars in the risky asset and her remaining wealth $W - q$ in the riskless asset. Her final consumption in state s is then

$$x_s = (W - q)(1 + r_1) + q(1 + r_{2s}) = W(1 + r_1) + q\theta_s \quad \text{where} \quad \theta_s = r_{2s} - r_1.$$
(7.2-2)

Substituting from (7.2-2), Ursula has an expected utility of

$$U(q) = \sum_{s=1}^{S} \pi_s u(x_s) = \sum_{s=1}^{S} \pi_s u(W(1 + r_1) + q\theta_s).$$

Then her marginal gain from increasing q is

$$U'(q) = \sum_{s=1}^{S} \pi_s u'(W(1 + r_1) + q\theta_s)\theta_s = \sum_{s=1}^{S} \pi_s u'(x_s)\theta_s. \quad (7.2\text{-}3)$$

Differentiating again, it is easily checked that the second derivative is negative and so there is a single turning point. Moreover, at $q = 0$,

$$U'(0) = u'(W(1 + r_1)) \sum_{s=1}^{S} \pi_s \theta_s > 0 \Leftrightarrow \sum_{s=1}^{S} \pi_s \theta_s > 0.$$

Thus unless Ursula is infinitely risk averse, she will purchase some of the risky asset.

To understand why this must be the case, consider equation (7.2-3). Ursula weights her marginal claims in state s by her marginal utility in that state and then takes the expectation of marginal utilities. But when she is taking no risk, each of the marginal utility weights is the same. Thus, the decision whether to invest at all is the same as the decision of a risk-neutral individual. Of course, for any positive investment in the risky asset, the marginal utility weights change. Intuitively, the marginal utility weights change more if the degree of risk aversion is greater.

We now show that this intuition is correct. If a second individual, Victor, is everywhere more risk averse, he will invest less in the risky asset.

We have seen that if Victor is more risk averse than Ursula, then his utility function $v(x)$ is a concave function of Ursula's utility function; that is $v(x) = g(u(x))$, where $g(\cdot)$ is an increasing strictly concave function. Let z^* be optimal for Ursula and define $x_s^* = W(1 + r_s) + \theta_s q^*$. Then

$$U'(q^*) = \sum_{s=1}^{S} \pi_s u'(x_s^*)\theta_s = 0.$$

We show that if Victor chooses the same portfolio his expected marginal utility of increasing q is negative at q^*. Thus Victor invests less of his wealth in the risky asset. Suppose we order states so that $\theta_1 > \theta_2 > \cdots > \theta_S$. Let t be the largest state for which θ_s is positive. Then $u(x_s^*) \geq u(x_t^*)$, $s = 1, \ldots, t$, and $u(x_s^*) < u(x_t^*)$, $s = t + 1, \ldots, S$.

Define $V(q) = \sum_{s=1}^{S} \pi_s v(x_s)$. Then

$$V'(q^*) = \sum_{s=1}^{S} \pi_s v'(x_s^*)\theta_s = \sum_{s=1}^{S} \pi_s g'(u(x_s^*))u'(x_s^*)\theta_s$$

$$= \sum_{s=1}^{t} \pi_s g'(u(x_s^*)u'(x_s^*)\theta_s - \sum_{s=t+1}^{S} \pi_s g'(u(x_s^*))u'(x_s^*)(-\theta_s).$$

Each term in the two summations is non-negative. For each of the terms in the first summation, the strict concavity of $g(\cdot)$ implies that $g'(u(x_s^*)) \leq g'(u(x_t^*))$ and the inequality is strict for $s = 1$ (otherwise there is no risk.). For each of the terms in the second summation, $g'(u(x_s^*)) \geq g'(x(x_t^*))$.

Hence,

$$V'(q^*) < \sum_{s=1}^{t} \pi_s g'(u(x_t^*))u'(x_s^*)\theta_s - \sum_{s=t+1}^{S} \pi_s g'(u(x_t^*))u'(x_s^*)(-\theta_s)$$

$$= g'(u(x_t^*)) \sum_{s=1}^{S} \pi_s u'(x_s^*)\theta_s = g'(u(x_t^*))U'(q^*) = 0.$$

Exercises

Exercise 7.2-1: Risk Aversion and Trading in State Claims Markets   Alex and Bev have the same wealth and both trade in state claims markets. For the two-state case, show that if Bev has a higher degree of absolute risk aversion than Alex, her final consumption bundle will lie closer to the certainty line.

Exercise 7.2-2: Relative Risk Aversion The degree of relative risk aversion $R(x) = -xv''(x)/v'(x)$.

(a) Show that if an individual exhibits constant relative risk aversion, his marginal rate of substitution $M(x_1, x_2)$ is constant along a ray from the origin. Assuming that he can trade in claims to each state, show that the risk he will take on rises proportionally with his wealth.

(b) Show that if $v'(x) = x^{-1/\sigma}$, $\sigma > 0$, the individual exhibits constant relative risk aversion. Hence solve for the constant relative risk aversion utility functions.

(c) It is usually argued that individuals exhibit increasing relative risk aversion and decreasing absolute risk aversion. What does this imply about the shape of wealth expansion paths?

Exercise 7.2-3: Risky Choices with Two Commodities A consumer purchases commodities x and y. If her von Neumann Morgenstern expected utility is $v(x, y) = x^\alpha y^\beta$, solve for the consumer's indirect utility function $V(p, I)$.

(a) Under what assumptions is the consumer's utility function concave in income (so that the marginal utility of income decreases with income)?

(b) Under what assumptions is utility convex in prices?

(c) Does it follow that in an economy with Cobb-Douglas preferences, all individuals would favor price uncertainty over mean-preserving price stabilization?

Exercise 7.2-4 Wealth Effects An individual with wealth W must decide how much to invest in a riskless asset with yield $1 + r_1$ and in a risky asset with yield $1 + \tilde{r}_2$ where $E\{\tilde{r}_2\} > r_1$.

(a) If the individual exhibits constant absolute risk aversion, show that her investment in the risky asset is independent of her wealth.

(b) If the individual exhibits decreasing absolute risk aversion, show that she will invest more as her wealth increases.

Exercise 7.2-5: Wealth Effects on Asset Shares Suppose that the individual invests a fraction z of his wealth in the risky asset.

Show that expected utility can be written as

$$U(z) = E\left\{V\left(W(1 + r_1) + Wz\tilde{\theta}_s\right)\right\}.$$

(a) Assume constant relative risk aversion and show that the asset share is independent of wealth.

(b) Show that if relative risk aversion increases with wealth, the asset share z^* will decline with wealth.

Exercise 7.2-6: Concave Function A function $u(c)$ where $c \in \mathbb{R}$ is strictly concave if for any c_1 and $c_3 > c_1$

$$c_2 = (1 - \lambda)c_1 + \lambda c_3, \quad 0 < \lambda < 1 \Rightarrow u(c_2) > (1 - \lambda)u(c_1) + \lambda u(c_3).$$

(a) Rearrange these two expressions and hence show that $u(c)$ is concave if

$$\lambda(c_3 - c_2) - (1 - \lambda)(c_2 - c_1), \quad 0 < \lambda < 1 \Rightarrow \lambda(u(c_3) - u(c_2))$$
$$- (1 - \lambda)(u(c_2) - u(c_1)) < 0.$$

(b) Hence show that the concavity of $u(c)$ is equivalent to the statement that for all c_1 and $c_3 > c_1$ and $c_2 \in (c_1, c_3)$

$$\frac{c_2 - c_1}{c_3 - c_2} < \frac{u(c_2) - u(c_1)}{u(c_3) - u(c_2)}. \quad \text{That is,} \quad \frac{u(c_2) - u(c_1)}{c_2 - c_1} > \frac{u(c_3) - u(c_2)}{c_3 - c_2}.$$

7.3 Comparing Risky Alternatives

Key ideas: first- and second-order stochastic dominance, conditional stochastic dominance, monotone likelihood ratio, mean-preserving spread, responses to an increase in risk

A choice under uncertainty is a ranking of different risky prospects. Therefore, an individual's attitude toward risk is a crucial factor in such rankings. However, some prospects can be ranked regardless of risk aversion. To take a simple example, suppose that prospect A is $(\pi_1, \pi_2, \pi_3; c_1, c_2, c_3)$ and prospect B is $(\pi_1 - \delta_1, \pi_2 + \delta_1 - \delta_3, \pi_3 + \delta_3; c_1, c_2, c_3)$, where $c_1 < c_2 < c_3$. Starting with prospect A, we can first shift probability mass from state 1 to state 2 so that the new prospect is $(\pi_1 - \delta_1, \pi_2 + \delta_1, \pi_3; c_1, c_2, c_3)$. As long as utility is increasing in c, the second prospect is strictly preferred. Next shift mass from state 2 to state 3. Again the shift is strictly preferred. Therefore, prospect B can be obtained from prospect A by a sequence of rightward shifts in probability mass. In this case, prospect B is said to exhibit (first-order) stochastic dominance over A. Any such shift in probability mass will be strictly preferred, regardless of an individual's aversion to risk.

Definition: First-Order Stochastic Dominance Let $\tilde{c}^A$ and $\tilde{c}^B$ be two random variables with realizations in $C \subset \mathbb{R}^n$. If for each $c \in C$, $\Pr\{\tilde{c}^B \leq c\} \leq \Pr\{\tilde{c}^A \leq c\}$, then $\tilde{c}^B$ exhibits (first-order) stochastic dominance over $\tilde{c}^A$.

For the three-state example, we now show formally that if utility is increasing and two prospects can be ranked by first-order stochastic dominance, then the dominating distribution will be preferred. First note that

$$\pi_1 u_1 + \pi_2 u_2 = -\pi_1(u_2 - u_1) + (\pi_1 + \pi_2)u_2$$
$$= -\pi_1(u_2 - u_1) - (\pi_1 + \pi_2)(u_3 - u_2) + (\pi_1 + \pi_2)u_3.$$

Then

$$\pi_1 u_1 + \pi_2 u_2 + \pi_3 u_3 = -\pi_1(u_2 - u_1) - (\pi_1 + \pi_2)(u_3 - u_2) + (\pi_1 + \pi_2 + \pi_3)u_3.$$

Because probability mass must sum to 1, the third term is the same for any pair of distributions. It follows immediately that if distribution B stochastically dominates distribution A so that $\pi_1^B \le \pi_1^A$ and $\pi_1^B + \pi_2^B \le \pi_1^A + \pi_2^A$, then

$$\pi_1^B u_1 + \pi_2^B u_2 + \pi_3^B u_3 \ge \pi_1^A u_1 + \pi_2^A u_2 + \pi_3^A u_3.$$

In the exercises you are asked to prove the following generalization of this result.

Proposition 7.3-1:
If $u(\cdot)$ is increasing and the prospect $(\pi^B; c)$ exhibits first-order stochastic dominance over the prospect $(\pi^A; c)$ (so there is a smaller probability in every left tail), then prospect B is preferred to prospect A.

Note that we have not yet made any assumption about aversion to risk. To do so we continue with our three-state example but make the further assumption that $(c_1, c_2, c_3) = (w, w + \delta, w + 2\delta)$, where $\delta > 0$.

As argued in Section 7.2, the slope of an indifference curve in probability space is

$$m = \frac{u_2 - u_1}{u_3 - u_2} = \frac{u(w + \delta) - u(w)}{u(w + 2\delta) - u(w + \delta)}.$$

If the individual is risk neutral the right-hand side of this equation is 1 and for a strictly risk-averse individual it exceeds 1.

Now consider shifting an equal mass from both tails to the center. That is, suppose that $\pi_1^A - \pi_1^B = \pi_3^A - \pi_3^B > 0$ so that $\frac{\pi_3^B - \pi_3^A}{\pi_3^B - \pi_1^A} = 1$.

This is depicted in Figure 7.3-1. Because the slope of the indifference line exceeds 1, it follows that the individual strictly prefers the new gamble with less weight in the tails.

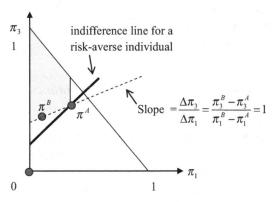

Figure 7.3-1. Preferred gambles for a risk-averse individual.

Holding π_1 constant, expected utility rises as π_3 increases (and π_2 decreases). Thus, a risk-averse individual prefers all points in the shaded region in the figure. We may conclude that, as long as $\Delta\pi_1 < 0$ and $\Delta\pi_1 - \Delta\pi_3 \leq 0$, a risk-averse individual strictly prefers prospect B over A. Equivalently, because $\Delta\pi_3 = -(\Delta\pi_1 + \Delta\pi_2)$, as long as $\Delta\pi_1 \leq 0$ and $\Delta\pi_1 + (\Delta\pi_1 + \Delta\pi_2) \leq 0$, a risk averse individual will strictly prefer prospect B.

Note that the sufficient condition is expressed in terms of sums of probabilities in the left tails. If these sums are all smaller for distribution B than distribution A, the former is said to exhibit second-order stochastic dominance over the latter.

Definition: Second-Order Stochastic Dominance Let $\pi^B = (\pi_1^B, \ldots, \pi_S^B)$ and $\pi^A = (\pi_1^A, \ldots, \pi_S^A)$ be two probability distributions. Let Π_S^B and Π_S^A be the associated cumulative probabilities or left tail probabilities. Distribution B exhibits second order stochastic dominance over A if

$$\sum_{\tau=1}^{s} \Pi_\tau^B \leq \sum_{\tau=1}^{s} \Pi_\tau^A, \quad s = 1, \ldots, S.$$

We have shown that in the three-state case, any risk-averse individual strictly prefers distribution B over distribution A as long as B exhibits second-order stochastic dominates over A. The proof can be readily generalized.[7]

Proposition 7.3-2:
Suppose that $u(c)$ is increasing and concave and that $c_{s+1} - c_s = \delta$. If π^B exhibits second-order stochastic dominance over π^A then the prospect (c, π^B) is preferred over (c, π^A).

Other Dominance Relations

For many applications, the assumption of first-order stochastic dominance needs to be strengthened to achieve unambiguous analytical results. We now consider two stronger assumptions.

Conditional Stochastic Dominance

For any pair of probability distributions $\pi^A = (\pi_1^A, \ldots, \pi_S^A)$ and $\pi^B = (\pi_1^B, \ldots, \pi_S^B)$, suppose we truncate the distributions at t and consider the left tail distributions. The c.d.f.'s of these left tail distributions are

$$\frac{\Pi_s^A}{\Pi_t^A} \quad \text{and} \quad \frac{\Pi_s^B}{\Pi_t^B} \quad \forall s \leq t.$$

---

[7] See Exercise 7.3-2.

The probability distribution π^B exhibits conditional stochastic dominance over π^A if the first-order stochastic dominance property holds for every left tail distribution.

Definition: Conditional Stochastic Dominance The probability distribution π^B exhibits conditional stochastic dominance (CSD) over π^A if, for every left tail distribution the first-order stochastic dominance relation holds. That is,

$$\frac{\Pi_s^B}{\Pi_t^B} \le \frac{\Pi_s^A}{\Pi_t^A}, \forall t \quad \text{and} \quad \forall s < t.$$

Note that an implication of CSD is that

$$\frac{\pi_t^B}{\Pi_t^B} = 1 - \frac{\Pi_{t-1}^B}{\Pi_t^B} \ge 1 - \frac{\Pi_{t-1}^A}{\Pi_t^A} = \frac{\pi_t^A}{\Pi_t^A}.$$

Thus the CSD relation implies that each truncated distribution of π has more weight in the extreme right tail. We now show that the converse is also true.

Proposition 7.3-3: Conditional Stochastic Dominance[8]
The probability distribution π^B exhibits CSD over π^A if and only if

$$\frac{\pi_t^B}{\Pi_t^B} \ge \frac{\pi_t^A}{\Pi_t^A}, \forall s.$$

Proof: We begin by rewriting the condition $\frac{\pi_t^B}{\Pi_t^B} \ge \frac{\pi_t^A}{\Pi_t^A}$ as $\frac{\Pi_t^A}{\Pi_t^B} \ge \frac{\pi_t^A}{\pi_t^B}$.

Define $k = \frac{\Pi_t^A}{\Pi_t^B}$. Then $\Pi_t^A = k\Pi_t^B$ and $\pi_t^A \le k\pi_t^B$ and so $\Pi_t^A - \pi_t^A \ge k(\Pi_t^B - \pi_t^B)$. Therefore

$$\frac{\Pi_{t-1}^A}{\Pi_{t-1}^B} = \frac{\Pi_t^A - \pi_t^A}{\Pi_t^B - \pi_t^B} \ge k = \frac{\Pi_t^A}{\Pi_t^B}.$$

Because this argument holds for all t it follows that

$$\frac{\Pi_s^A}{\Pi_s^B} \ge \frac{\Pi_t^A}{\Pi_t^B} \forall t \quad \text{and} \quad \forall s < t.$$

Rearranging this inequality,

$$\frac{\Pi_s^A}{\Pi_t^A} \ge \frac{\Pi_s^B}{\Pi_t^B} \forall t \quad \text{and} \quad \forall s < t. \qquad \square$$

---

[8] The direct proof for the continuous case is somewhat different. See Exercise 7.3-4.

Monotone Likelihood Ratio Property

Two probability distributions are said to satisfy the monotone likelihood property if for some ordering of states

$$\frac{\pi_s^A}{\pi_s^B} \geq \frac{\pi_t^A}{\pi_t^B}, \quad s < t.$$

Intuitively if the ratio of the probabilities (the *likelihood ratio*) is decreasing across states, then there must be more weight in the left tails of the distribution of π^A. In fact we prove a stronger result. Let Π_s^A and Π_s^B be the cumulative probabilities, that is, $\Pi_t^A = \sum_{s=1}^{t} \pi_s^A$ and $\Pi_t^B = \sum_{s=1}^{t} \pi_s^B$.

Proposition 7.3-4:
The monotone likelihood ratio property implies conditional stochastic dominance.

Proof: Appealing to the monotone likelihood ratio property,

$$\pi_s^B \leq \left(\frac{\pi_t^B}{\pi_t^A}\right) \pi_s^A, \forall t \quad \text{and} \quad \forall s \leq t \quad \text{so that}$$

$$\Pi_t^B = \sum_{s=1}^{t} \pi_s^B \leq \left(\frac{\pi_t^B}{\pi_A^t}\right) \sum_{s=1}^{t} \pi_s^A = \left(\frac{\pi_t^B}{\pi_A^t}\right) \Pi_s^A, \forall t.$$

Rearranging this inequality,

$$\frac{\pi_t^B}{\Pi_t^B} \geq \frac{\pi_t^A}{\Pi_t^A}, \forall t.$$

Appealing to Proposition 7.3-3 the conditional stochastic dominance relation holds. □

Continuous Distributions

For completeness, we now show how to establish these same results if consequences are continuously distributed. Suppose that both $\tilde{c}_A$ and $\tilde{c}_B$ have supports (possibly different) within the interval $[\alpha, \beta]$ and probability density functions $f_j(c)$, $j \in \{A, B\}$. We write the c.d.f of distribution j as $F_j(c)$ and the integrals of the c.d.f. as $T_j(c) = \int_\alpha^c F_j(\theta)d\theta$. These integrals are the continuous equivalents of the sums of left tails.

Then

$$E\{v(\tilde{c}_B)\} - E\{v(\tilde{c}_A)\} = \int_\alpha^\beta v(c)f_B(c)dc - \int_\alpha^\beta v(c)f_A(c)dc.$$

Integrating by parts and noting that $F_A(\alpha) = F_B(\alpha) = 0$ and $F_A(\beta) = F_B(\beta) = 1$,

$$E\{v(\tilde{c}_B)\} - E\{v(\tilde{c}_A)\} = \int_\alpha^\beta -v'(c)F_B(c)dc - \int_\alpha^\beta -v'(c)F_A(c)dc.$$

Hence,

$$E\{v(\tilde{c}_B)\} - E\{v(\tilde{c}_A)\} = \int_\alpha^\beta v'(c)[F_A(c) - F_B(c)]dc. \qquad (7.3\text{-}1)$$

Thus, if v is increasing and $\tilde{c}^B$ exhibits first-order stochastic dominance over $\tilde{c}^A$, then $E\{v(\tilde{c}^B)\} - E\{v(\tilde{c}^A)\} \geq 0$. This is Proposition 7.3-1.

Integrating again,

$$E\{v(\tilde{c}_B)\} - E\{v(\tilde{c}_A)\} = v'(\beta)[T_A(\beta) - T_B(\beta)] - \int_\alpha^\beta v''(c)[T_A(c) - T_B(c)]dc.$$

Thus, if $v(\cdot)$ is increasing and concave and the left tail sums are smaller for distribution B than A, then $E\{v(\tilde{c}_B)\} \geq E\{v(\tilde{c}_A)\}$. This is Proposition 7.3-2.

We next seek conditions under which two distributions have the same mean. Setting $v(c) = c$ in equation (7.3-1),

$$E\{\tilde{c}_B\} - E\{\tilde{c}_A\} = \int_\alpha^\beta [F_A(c) - F_B(c)]dc = T_A(\beta) - T_B(\beta).$$

Hence, we have the following proposition.

Proposition 7.3-5:
The distributions $\tilde{c}_A$ and $\tilde{c}_B$ with supports in $[\alpha, \beta]$ have the same mean if $\int_\alpha^\beta F_A(c)dc = \int_\alpha^\beta F_B(c)dc$, that is, the areas under each c.d.f. are the same.

Consider the first of the two diagrams in Figure 7.3-2. If the two shaded areas are equal, then the areas under each c.d.f. are equal. Note that the slope of $F_A(c)$ is decreasing to the left of γ while the slope of $F_B(c)$ is increasing. That is, the density of $\tilde{c}_A$ is decreasing and the density of $\tilde{c}_B$ is increasing. The opposite is true to the right of γ.

The probability density functions must therefore be as depicted. Note also that for any $c < \beta$,

$$T_A(c) = \int_\alpha^c F_A(x)dx > \int_\alpha^c F_B(x)dx = T_B(c).$$

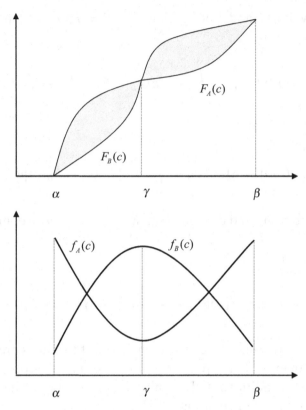

Figure 7.3-2. Mean-preserving spread.

Because the two distributions have the same mean, it is natural to describe $\tilde{c}_A$, with its greater weight in the tails, as a mean-preserving spread of $\tilde{c}_B$.

Definition: Mean-Preserving Spread Suppose that $\tilde{c}_A$ and $\tilde{c}_B$ are random variables with supports in $[\alpha, \beta]$. The random variable $\tilde{c}_A$ is a mean-preserving spread of $\tilde{c}_B$ if for all $c \in [\alpha, \beta]$

$$T_B(c) = \int_\alpha^c F_B(x)dx \leq \int_\alpha^c F_A(x)dx = T_A(c) \quad \text{and} \quad T_B(\beta) = T_A(\beta).$$

From (7.3-1),

$$E\{v(\tilde{c}_B)\} - E\{v(\tilde{c}_A)\} = \int_\alpha^\beta v'(c)[F_A(c) - F_B(c)]dc.$$

Integrating again by parts,

$$E\{v(\tilde{c}_B)\} - E\{v(\tilde{c}_A)\} = v'(c)[T_A(c) - T_B(c)]|_\alpha^\beta - \int_\alpha^\beta v''(c)[T_A(c) - T_B(c)]dc.$$

Appealing to the definition of a mean-preserving spread, we have the following proposition.

Proposition 7.3-6:
If $\tilde{c}_A$ is a mean-preserving spread of $\tilde{c}_B$, and $v(\cdot)$ is concave, then $E\{v(\tilde{c}_B)\} \geq E\{v(\tilde{c}_A)\}$. If $v(\cdot)$ is convex then $E\{v(\tilde{c}_B)\} \leq E\{v(\tilde{c}_A)\}$.

Application: The Savings Decision

An individual has current income y_1, future income $\tilde{y}_2$ and strictly concave utility $u = v_1(c_1) + \delta v_2(c_2)$. The interest rate is r. Thus an individual who saves S has a consumption bundle of $(c_1, \tilde{c}_2) = (y_1 - S, \tilde{y}_2 + (1 + r)S)$ and hence an expected utility of

$$U(S) = v_1(y_1 - S) + E\delta v_2(\tilde{y}_2 + (1 + r)S). \tag{7.3-2}$$

It is left as an exercise to confirm that the strict concavity of u implies that $U(S)$ is a strictly concave function. We also assume that the individual exhibits decreasing absolute aversion to risk. Hence

$$\frac{d}{dc}\left(-\frac{v_2''(c)}{v_2'(c)}\right) = -\frac{v_2'''v_2' - (v_2'')^2}{(v_2')^2} < 0.$$

Note that a necessary condition for this inequality to hold is $v_2'''(c_2) > 0$. Thus the function $v_2'(c)$ is decreasing and convex.

Suppose two individuals, A and B, have the same current income and preferences but face different uncertain future incomes $\tilde{y}^A$ and $\tilde{y}^B$. Suppose also that the latter first-order stochastically dominates the former. By Proposition 7.3-1, individual A has a lower expected utility. Because this is true for all S, the two expected lifetime indirect utility functions must be as depicted in Figure 7.3-3.

As shown the optimal savings under $\tilde{y}_2^A$ is S^A. Note that the picture is drawn so that the slope of $U^A(S)$ is strictly positive at S^B. Thus, individual A saves more.

Proposition 7.3-7: Saving and Risk Suppose that individuals with the same current income and preferences have different uncertain future incomes $\tilde{y}^A$ and $\tilde{y}^B$. If preferences exhibit decreasing absolute risk aversion and $\tilde{y}^B$ first-order stochastically dominates $\tilde{y}^A$, then individual A saves more or borrows less.

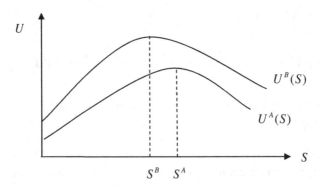

Figure 7.3-3. Optimal saving as risk increases.

Proof: Differentiate (7.3-2) to obtain

$$\frac{dU}{dS} = -v_1'(y_1 - S) + \delta(1 + r)E\{v_2'(\tilde{y}_2 + (1+r)S)\}$$

Because $v_2'(c)$ is a decreasing function, it follows from Proposition 7.3-2 that $E\{v_2'(\tilde{c}^B)\} \leq E\{v_2'(\tilde{c}^A)\}$. Hence $\frac{dU^A}{dS}(S) \geq \frac{dU^B}{dS}(S)$ and so $\frac{dU^A}{dS}(S^B) \geq \frac{dU^B}{dS}(S^B)$.
$\square$

The intuition for this result is clearest when all the realizations under $\tilde{c}^A$ are less than all the possible realizations under $\tilde{c}^B$. This is an extreme case of first-order stochastic dominance. If second-period income is lower with probability 1, then the consumer will save more to offset the decline in second-period income.

Finally suppose that the new income distribution is a mean-preserving spread of the old distribution. We know that $v_2'(c)$ is a convex function. Thus, appealing to Proposition 7.3-6, expected marginal utility is higher under $\tilde{y}_2^A$. Again we have that $\frac{dU^A}{dS} \geq \frac{dU^B}{dS}$ and so saving is higher when future income is riskier.

Exercises

Exercise 7.3-1: Portfolio Choice A risk-averse individual with wealth w must choose a portfolio containing quantities of a riskless and risky asset.

(a) Let x be the individual's spending on the risky asset. For simplicity you may assume that the net return on the riskless asset is zero and on the risky asset is $\tilde{\theta}$. Show that the expected utility can be written as follows:

$$U(x) = E\{u(x, \tilde{\theta})\} = E\{v(w + x\tilde{\theta})\}.$$

(b) Write down the FOC.
(c) Show that $\frac{\partial^2 u}{\partial x \partial \theta} = v'(1 - R(x, \theta) - A(x, \theta))$.
(d) Suppose that the individual exhibits decreasing absolute risk aversion, and increasing relative risk aversion and that relative risk aversion is less than 1.

Show that a mean-preserving increase in risk will lead to a smaller investment in the risky asset.

Exercise 7.3-2: First-Order Stochastic Dominance

(a) For $S = 2$ and $S = 3$ confirm the following identity:

$$\sum_{s=1}^{S} \pi_s u_s = u_S - \sum_{t=1}^{S} \Pi_t(u_{t+1} - u_t) \quad \text{where} \quad \Pi_t \equiv \sum_{s=1}^{t} \pi_s. \qquad (7.3\text{-}3)$$

Prove by induction that the identity holds for all S.

Consider the two consequences $(\pi^A; c)$, $(\pi^B; c)$ where $c_{s+1} > c_s$. Suppose that the second probability distribution stochastically dominates the first so that there is less weight in the left tails, that is

$$\Pi_s^B \leq \Pi_s^A, \quad s = 1, \ldots, S.$$

(b) If $u(\cdot)$ is an increasing function, show that the individual prefers B over A.
(c) Suppose that $c_{s+1} - c_s = \delta > 0$. Define $\Delta u_t = u_{t+1} - u_t$. Appeal to the identity in (a) to show that

$$\sum_{t=1}^{S} \Pi_t \Delta u_t = \sum_{t=1}^{S} \Pi_t - \sum_{s=1}^{S} \left(\sum_{t=1}^{s} \Pi_t \right) (\Delta u_{t+1} - \Delta u_t).$$

Substitute this expression into (7.3-3), hence proving Proposition 7.3-2.

Exercise 7.3-3 Mean Utility-Preserving Increase in Risk

Consider the portfolio choice problem of Exercise 7.3-1. Let $\theta = h(u)$ be the inverse of the mapping $u = v(w + x\theta)$. Define $G(u) = F(h(u))$. This is the c.d.f. of u.

(a) Show that $xh'(u)v'(w + x\theta) = 1$.
(b) Explain why expected utility can be written as $U(x) = \int v(w + xh(u))dG(u)$.
(c) Differentiate and appeal to (a) to show that

$$\frac{\partial}{\partial u} \frac{\partial}{\partial x} v(w + xh(u)) = \frac{1}{x} \left(1 + xh \frac{v''(w + xh)}{v'(w + xh)} \right)$$

$$= \frac{1}{x}(1 - R(w + xh) + wA(w + xh)).$$

(d) Hence show that under decreasing absolute risk aversion and increasing relative risk aversion, $\frac{\partial}{\partial x} v(w + xh(u))$ is a concave function of u.
(e) Appeal to Proposition 7.3-6 to show that under these assumptions, a mean utility-preserving increase in risk (i.e., $G_A(u)$ is a mean-preserving spread of $G_B(u)$,) and will lead to a smaller investment in the risky asset.

Exercise 7.3-4 Equivalent Definition of Conditional Stochastic Dominance

Suppose F_A and F_B are continuously differentiable over support $[\alpha, \beta]$. Then F_B exhibits conditional stochastic dominance over F_A if and only if $\frac{F_B(s)}{F_B(t)} \leq \frac{F_A(s)}{F_A(t)}$, $\forall t$ and $\forall s < t$.

(a) If this condition holds confirm that

$$\frac{F_B(t) - F_B(s)}{(t-s)F_B(t)} \geq \frac{F_A(t) - F_A(s)}{(t-s)F_A(t)}, \ \forall t \quad \text{and} \quad \forall s < t.$$

Hence establish that

$$\frac{F_B'(t)}{F_B(t)} \geq \frac{F_A'(t)}{F_A(t)}, \ \forall t.$$

(b) For any $y > x$ show that the CSD requirement can be rewritten as follows:

$$\ln\left(\frac{F_B(t)}{F_A(t)} \bigg/ \frac{F_B(s)}{F_A(s)}\right) = \ln\left(\frac{F_B(t)}{F_A(t)}\right) - \ln\left(\frac{F_B(s)}{F_A(s)}\right) \geq 0.$$

(c) Show that this condition can be rewritten as

$$\int_s^t \frac{d}{d\theta} \ln\left(\frac{F_B(\theta)}{F_A(\theta)}\right) d\theta \geq 0.$$

(d) Hence show that the requirement for conditional stochastic dominance can be written as follows:

$$\int_s^t \left(\frac{F_B'(\theta)}{F_B(\theta)} - \frac{F_A'(\theta)}{F_A(\theta)}\right) d\theta \geq 0.$$

Thus the condition $\frac{F_B'(\theta)}{F_B(\theta)} \geq \frac{F_A'(\theta)}{F_A(\theta)}, \ \forall t$ is both necessary and sufficient for conditional stochastic dominance.

Exercise 7.3-5 Simple Mean-Preserving Spread If (i) the distributions $\tilde{\theta}_A$ and $\tilde{\theta}_B$ have support $[\alpha, \beta]$ and the same mean and (ii) there is some $\hat{\theta}$ such that

$$(F_A(\theta) - F_B(\theta))(\theta - \hat{\theta}) \leq 0,$$

then $\tilde{\theta}_A$ is a simple mean-preserving spread of $\tilde{\theta}_B$.

Suppose that (i) holds and for some θ^*, $\left(\frac{F_A'(\theta)}{F_A(\theta)} - \frac{F_B'(\theta)}{F_B(\theta)}\right)(\theta - \theta^*) > 0, \theta \neq \theta^*$.

(a) Show that $\ln \frac{F(\theta_2)}{F(\theta_1)} = \int_{\theta_1}^{\theta_2} \frac{F'(x)}{F(x)} dx$
(b) Hence show that $F_B(\theta) > F_A(\theta), \forall \theta \in [\theta^*, \beta)$.
(c) Show that there can be no interval $[\underline{\theta}, \hat{\theta}]$ where $\alpha < \underline{\theta} < \hat{\theta} < \theta^*$ such that the c.d.f.'s are equal at $\underline{\theta}$ and $\hat{\theta}$ and $F_A(\theta) - F_B(\theta) > 0$ on $(\underline{\theta}, \hat{\theta})$.
(d) Hence show that $\tilde{\theta}_A$ is a simple mean-preserving spread of $\tilde{\theta}_B$.

7.4 Principal-Agent Problem

Key ideas: contracting with hidden actions, incentive constraints, insurance with moral hazard

In all the analysis thus far, there is no difficulty in writing contracts to optimally allocate risk. Implicitly, every contingent outcome or "state of the world" can be costlessly verified. This is a reasonable assumption for many contingencies that are exogenous from the perspective of each agent. However, if an individual directly determines or influences the nature of the contingencies, this individual is likely to have an informational advantage over those with whom he or she is contracting. In such situations, a full contingent contract is unverifiable and so the contract must be designed to give the informed agent a direct incentive to perform.

To illustrate, suppose that the owner of a firm (the "principal") wishes to hire an agent to manage a plant. The output of the plant and hence its revenue are uncertain. We assume that there are S possible revenue levels $(y_1, \ldots, .y_S)$, where $y_1 < \cdots < y_S$. Let $X = \{x_1, \ldots, x_n\}$ be the set of possible actions of the agent. Although both the principal and agent observe the revenue of the firm, only the agent knows his own action. His cost of taking action $x \in X$ is $C(x)$. Higher indexed actions are more costly.

We define $\pi_s(x)$ to be the probability of outcome s given action x. The greater the effort of the agent, the more favorable is the probability distribution over these S outcomes. For any outcome state s and pair of actions x and $x' > x$ we define the likelihood ratio as

$$L(s, x, x') = \frac{\pi_s(x')}{\pi_s(x)}.$$

To reflect the idea that choosing a higher action results in a more favorable output distribution, we assume that the likelihood ratio is an increasing function of s. That is, the greater the output, the more likely it is that the agent chose the more favorable action x' rather than x.

Suppose that the von Neumann Morgenstern (VNM) utility function of the firm owner (the "principal") is $u(\cdot)$ and the utility of the agent is $v(\cdot) - C(x)$. Then if the agent chooses action x and the principal pays the agent a wage w_s in state s, the expected utilities of the principal and agent are as follows:

$$U_P = \sum_{s=1}^{S} \pi_s(x)u(y_s - w_s), \quad U_A = \sum_{s=1}^{S} \pi_s(x)v(w_s) - C(x).$$

Efficient Contract with Full Information

As a preliminary to studying contracts with asymmetric information, we first characterize efficient contracts when the principal does observe the agent's action. To do so we fix the expected utility of one of the two contracting parties and then solve for the action and payments that maximize the expected utility of the other. When both the action of the agent and the output are observable, we can proceed as follows. First choose an action $x \in X$ and thus the probability of state s, $\pi_s(x)$. Second, for each possible expected utility of

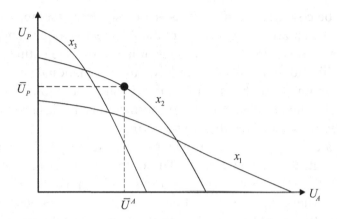

Figure 7.4-1. Pareto-efficient outcomes with three actions.

one of the two contracting parties, solve for the expected utility-maximizing contract for the other. In this way it is possible to map out the Pareto frontier as depicted in Figure 7.4-1. Then repeat this with each of the n possible actions. The outer envelopes of the Pareto frontiers for each $x \in X$ are the Pareto efficient outcomes.

Formally, we can fix the principal's expected payoff and solve the following optimization problem for each possible action as follows:

$$\underset{x,w}{\text{Max}} \left\{ \sum_{s=1}^{S} \pi_s(x)v(w_s) - C(x) \middle| x \in X, \sum_{s=1}^{S} \pi_s(x)u(y_s - w_s) \geq \overline{U}_P \right\}. \quad (7.4\text{-}1)$$

In the figure there are three possible actions. Given an expected utility of $\overline{U}_P$ for the principal, the efficient action is x_2.

We next consider two special cases that are of direct interest and also shed light on the solution to the general problem.

Risk-Neutral Principal

Suppose that the principal is risk neutral and the agent is risk averse. From our earlier discussion, we know that for the final allocation to be efficient, the principal must bear all the risk. That is, the agent is offered a fixed wage w and the principal receives the residual $y_s - w$. To characterize the efficient allocations we pick some utility for the agent $\overline{U}_A = v(w) - C(x)$ and choose the action that maximizes the expected payoff to the principal

$$\underset{x,w}{\text{Max}} \left\{ \sum_{s=1}^{S} \pi_s(x)y_s - w \middle| x \in X, v(w) - C(x) \geq \overline{U}_A \right\}.$$

At the optimum the constraint must be binding. Hence $v(w) = \overline{U}_A + C(x)$. Let $v^{-1}(\cdot)$ be the inverse function; that is, w must satisfy $w = v^{-1}(\overline{U}_A + C(x))$. Then the maximization problem of the principal can be rewritten as follows:

$$\underset{x,w}{\text{Max}} \left\{ \sum_{s=1}^{S} \pi_s(x) y_s - v^{-1}(\overline{U}_A + C(x)) \right\},$$

that is,

$$\underset{x,w}{\text{Max}} \left\{ \sum_{s=1}^{S} \pi_s(x) y_s - C_P(x) \right\}, \quad \text{where} \quad C_P(x) \equiv v^{-1}(\overline{U}_A + C(x)).$$

We can think of the function $C_P(x)$ as the virtual cost function for the principal. The efficient contract thus maximizes expected revenue less the virtual cost. Consider two actions x and $x' > x$. Define

$$\Delta C_P \equiv C_P(x') - C_P(x).$$

This is the marginal cost of paying the agent to take the more costly action x'. It is the increase in the wage needed to compensate the agent so that the payoff remains at $\overline{U}_A$. Next suppose that the agent's payoff is increased to $\overline{U}_A + \Delta U$. Because v is concave, the marginal utility of the agent is lower at the higher utility level. Thus the dollar compensation needed to pay for the more costly action is higher. That is, the marginal cost of providing a big enough incentive for the agent to take a more costly action rises with the utility level of the agent. Therefore, the higher the expected utility of the agent, the lower will be the efficient action. This is the case depicted in Figure 7.4-1. As the expected utility of the agent rises, the efficient action changes first from the highest cost action x_3 to x_2 and then from x_2 to the lowest cost action x_1.

Risk-Neutral Agent

Suppose next that the principal is risk averse and the agent is risk neutral. For efficiency all the risk is born by the agent so that the payment to the principal must be independent of the state. In this case, having selected some action, efficiency requires that the agent should bear all the risk. That is, the principal receives a fixed rent r and the agent receives the residual $w_s = y_s - r$. To satisfy the constraint in (7.4-1), this rent must be chosen so that

$$\sum_{s=1}^{S} \pi_s(x) u(y_s - w_s) = u(r) = \overline{U}_P.$$

The choice of a Pareto efficient contract therefore reduces to the following problem.

$$\text{Max}_x \left\{ \sum_{s=1}^{S} \pi_s(x)(y_s - r) - C(x) | x \in X \right\}.$$

Thus the optimal action x^* maximizes the expected profit $\sum_{s=1}^{S} \pi_s(x) y_s - C(x)$.

Hidden Actions

In the analysis thus far, both parties have full information about the output state and the action taken. The contract then provides for payments in each output state contingent on the agent performing the contracted action. We have already argued that there are environments in which the principal will be less well informed. But, even if this informational asymmetry does not exist, there is a further problem. Unless the contract can be enforced by a court or other third party, the principal can simply claim that the agent has taken a cheaper action and pay him accordingly. To be enforced, the action must therefore be verifiable by this third party. We now consider contracting when such verification is prohibitively costly.

There is one special case where designing such a contract is easy. Suppose that the agent is risk neutral. As we have seen, the optimal contract with observable action is achievable with a rental contract. The optimal action then maximizes the expected payoff of the agent. It follows that there is no reason for the principal to observe the action. She simply collects the rent and the agent chooses the efficient output by maximizing his expected payoff.

Incentive Compatibility

Suppose instead that the principal is risk neutral and the agent is risk averse. The full-information efficient contract is a wage payment to the agent that is independent of the state. But if the principal does not observe the agent's action, such a contract provides the agent no incentive to take any action other than his lowest cost action x_1. The efficient contract with hidden actions must therefore be designed to provide the agent with the incentive to take the appropriate action. As a first stage, we fix the expected utility of the agent, pick some arbitrary action $\bar{x}$, and solve for the contract that maximizes the expected payoff of the principal, under the constraint that the agent has an incentive to take the action, $\bar{x}$. That is,

$$U_A(x, w) \le U_A(\bar{x}, w), x \in X. \text{ Incentive Constraints (IC)}$$

Only contracts that satisfy each of these constraints are incompatible with the objective of inducing the action $\bar{x}$. Thus the constraints are known as the incentive constraints.

The best contract for the principal, given the selection of action $\bar{x}$, thus solves the following optimization problem:

$$\underset{w}{\text{Max}}\{U_P|U_A(\bar{x}, w) \geq \overline{U}_A, \quad U_A(\bar{x}, w) \geq U_A(x, w), x \in X\}. \quad (7.4\text{-}2)$$

Let the maximized payoff for the principal be $U_P^*(\bar{x})$. In principle this can be computed for each possible action. The efficient action is then the one that yields the highest expected utility for the principal. Formally, the efficient action x^* solves the following maximization problem:

$$\underset{x}{\text{Max}}\{U_P^*(x)|x \in X\}.$$

Although we will not solve this second-stage problem, we can further characterize the efficient wage payments by considering the first stage. Arguing as earlier, to induce the optimal action x^*, the efficient state-contingent wage $w^* = (w_1^*, \ldots, w_S^*)$ must solve the first-stage optimization problem (7.4-2). That is, w^* solves

$$\underset{w}{\text{Max}}\{U_P|U_A(x^*, w) \geq \overline{U}_A, U_A(x^*, w) \geq U_A(x, w), x \in X\}. \quad (7.4\text{-}3)$$

Intuitively the contract must be designed to stop the agent from choosing any action x that is less costly for him ($x < x^*$). Suppose that in fact there is a single binding constraint.[9] The optimization problem can then be rewritten more simply as follows:

$$\underset{w}{\text{Max}}\{U_P|U_A(x^*, w) \geq \overline{U}_A, \quad U_A(x^*, w) \geq U_A(x, w), \quad \text{for some} \quad x < x^*\}.$$

The Lagrangian of this optimization problem is

$$\begin{aligned}
\mathcal{L} &= U_P + \lambda(U_A(x^*, w) - \overline{U}_A) + \mu(U_A(x^*, w) - U_A(x, w)) \\
&= U_P + (\lambda + \mu)(U_A(x^*, w) - \mu U_A(x, w)) + \text{a constant} \\
&= \sum_{s=1}^{S} \pi_s(x^*)(y_s - w_s) + (\lambda + \mu)\sum_{s=1}^{S} \pi_s(x^*)v(w_s) \\
&\quad - \mu\sum_{s=1}^{S} \pi_s(x)v(w_s) + \text{a constant}
\end{aligned}$$

---

[9] It is not important that there be one binding constraint, but only that the binding constraints are all associated with lower cost actions. Generally sufficient conditions to ensure this are quite stringent. However, for numerical examples it is typically the "downward" constraints that are binding.

The first-order conditions are therefore

$$\frac{\partial \mathfrak{L}}{\partial w_s} = -\pi_s(x^*) + (\lambda + \mu)\pi_s(x^*)v'(w_s^*) - \mu\pi_s(x)v'(w_s^*) = 0, \quad s = 1, \dots, S.$$

Hence

$$\frac{1}{v'(w_s^*)} = \lambda + \mu - \mu\frac{\pi_s(x)}{\pi_s(x^*)}, \quad \text{where} \quad x < x^*.$$

By hypothesis, the likelihood ratio $\frac{\pi_s(x^*)}{\pi_s(x)}$ is increasing in the output state s. Thus the right-hand side of this expression increases with s. Therefore, because $v(\cdot)$ is concave, w_s is increasing in s. Thus for efficiency, the higher the output, the higher is the payment to the agent.

Application: Insurance with Moral Hazard

An individual's house burns down with probability $\pi_1(x)$, where x is the effort the owner makes to avoid such a catastrophe. The house can be rebuilt at a cost of L. Given an income y^0 the state-contingent income of the homeowner is $(y_1, y_2) = (y^0 - L, y^0)$. Operating via the law of large numbers the insurance company (the principal) is approximately risk neutral. If the insurance company observes the homeowner's action, the optimal action x^* is selected and then, because only the homeowner is risk averse, the efficient insurance contract is for the homeowner to be charged a fixed insurance premium θ^*. The insurance company then bears all the risk. The state-contingent outcome for the insurance company is $(-L + \theta^*, \theta^*)$ and for the homeowner is $(y^0 - \theta^*, y^0 - \theta^*)$. Finally, to cover its expected payment, the insurance company must be paid a premium $\theta^* \geq \pi(x^*)L$.

If the insurance company does not observe the homeowner's action but the home owner is perfectly moral, he tells the truth and the efficient contract is unaffected. However if a homeowner is not so trustworthy, the insurance company faces a *moral hazard problem*. With full coverage the incentive to take care is eliminated so the homeowner's best choice is the cheapest action x_1. To give the homeowner the incentive to take appropriate care the homeowner must be offered a contract in which he is sufficiently penalized in the loss state. That is, for efficiency the insurance company charges a premium $\bar{\theta}$ and also introduces a deductible $\bar{d}$. The homeowner's state-contingent net income is therefore $(y^0 - \bar{\theta} - \bar{d}, y^0 - \bar{\theta})$.

Exercises

Exercise 7.4-1: Increasing Likelihood Ratio and Stochastic Dominance
Suppose that the likelihood ratio $L(s, x, x') = \frac{\pi_s(x')}{\pi_s(x)}$ increases with s.

(a) Show that $\pi_s(x') < \left(\frac{\pi_t(x')}{\pi_t(x)}\right)\pi_s(x), s = 1, \ldots, t-1$ and hence that,

$$\frac{\sum\limits_{s=1}^{t} \pi_s(x')}{\sum\limits_{s=1}^{t} \pi_s(x)} \leq \frac{\pi_t(x')}{\pi_t(x)}.$$

(b) Hence show that the probability distribution for output given that the agent chooses action a' first-order stochastically dominates the probability distribution for output given action a. HINT: Appeal to Proposition 7.3-5.

Exercise 7.4-2: Pareto Efficiency and Monotonicity with More Than One Binding Incentive Constraint Extend the analysis to show that as long as all the binding constraints are associated with less costly actions, the efficient wage is higher in states where output is higher.

Exercise 7.4-3: Principal's Virtual Cost Function Suppose that the principal is risk neutral and the action is observable. Consider action x_1 and the more costly action x_2. The agent has utility function $u = v(w) - C(x)$ and reservation utility $\overline{U}_A$. To induce action x therefore costs the principal $w(x) = f(U_A + C(x)) = v^{-1}(U_A + C(x))$.

(a) Show that the extra payment needed to induce the higher action (the marginal cost of the principal) can be written as

$$w(x_2) - w(x_1) = \int_{x_1}^{x_2} f'(\overline{U}_A + C(x))C'(x)dx = \int_{x_1}^{x_2} \frac{C'(x)}{v'(w(x))}dx.$$

(b) Hence, show that as $\overline{U}_A$ increases, the marginal cost of inducing a higher action $w(x_2) - w(x_1)$ increases.

References and Selected Historical Reading

Allais, M. (1953. "Le comportement de l'homme rationnel devant le risqué." *Econometrica* **21**.

Arrow, K. (1965). "The Theory of Risk Bearing." In *Aspects of the Theory of Risk Bearing*. Helsinki: Yrjo Jahnssonin Saatio. Republished in *Essays in the Theory of Risk Bearing*. Chicago: Markham, 1971.

Diamond, P. and Stiglitz, J. (1974). "Increases in Risk and in Risk Aversion." *Journal of Economic Theory* **8**: 337–60.

Grossman, S. and Hart, O. (1983). "An Analysis of the Principal–Agent Problem." *Econometrica* **51**: 7–45.

Jewitt, I. (1988). "Justifying the First-Order Approach to Principal–Agent Problems." *Econometrica* **56**: 1177–90.

Machina, M. (1982). "A Stronger Characterization of Declining Risk Aversion." *Econometrica* **50**: 1069–80.

Rabin, M. (1998). "Psychology and Economics." *Journal of Economic Literature* **36**: 11–46.

Rothschild, M. and Stiglitz, J. (1971a). "Increasing Risk I: A Definition." *Journal of Economic Theory* **2**: 225–43.

Rothschild, M. and Stiglitz, J. (1971b). "Increasing Risk II: Its Economic Consequences." *Journal of Economic Theory* **3**: 66–84.

Neumann von, J. and Morgenstern, O. (1944). *Theory of Games and Economic Behavior*. Princeton NJ: Princeton University Press.

8

Equilibrium in Financial Markets

8.1 Arrow-Debreu Equilibrium

Key ideas: trading in state-contingent markets to spread risk security markets as a substitute for state-contingent markets

In the last chapter we extended the core consumer choice model to uncertain environments. We now examine market equilibria under uncertainty. As a first step in developing general principles, consider a very simple two-person economy. Alex owns a coconut plantation to the east and Bev owns one to the west of a volcano. The volcano will erupt and one of the plantations will be damaged. In state 1 the ash will damage Alex's plantation and in state 2 Bev's plantation. Thus each consumer has an endowment of coconuts that is state dependent. Let $\omega^h = (\omega_1^h, \omega_2^h)$, $h \in \{A, B\}$ be the endowment of agent h. Initially we assume that the loss is the same in each state, that is, $\omega_1^A = \omega_2^A - L$ and $\omega_2^B = \omega_1^B - L$.

Clearly the aggregate endowment is the same in each state. Let the probability of state s be π_s. Then, if consumer h has a von Neumann Morgenstern (VNM) utility function $v^h(\cdot)$ and is allocated a final consumption bundle $x^h = (x_1^h, x_2^h)$, the consumer's expected utility is

$$U^h(x^h) = \sum_{s=1}^{2} \pi_s v^h\left(x_s^h\right), \quad h \in \{A, B\}.$$

Consumer h thus has a marginal rate of substitution (MRS)

$$MRS^h(x_1, x_2) = \frac{\partial U^h/\partial x_1^h}{\partial U^h/\partial x_2^h} = \frac{\pi_1 v_h'\left(x_1^h\right)}{\pi_2 v_h'\left(x_2^h\right)} = \frac{\pi_1}{\pi_2} \text{ along the } 45° \text{ line.}$$

With no aggregate uncertainty, the Edgeworth Box is as depicted in Figure 8.1-1.

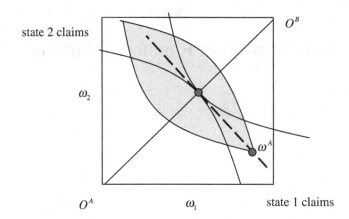

state 2 claims

Figure 8.1-1. Efficiency with no aggregate risk.

Note that the diagonal is the 45° line for each consumer. Thus, the indifference curves are tangential along this line. It follows that the Pareto efficient (PE) allocations must lie along the diagonal. As long as each consumer is holding risk, both gain from shedding some of that risk. Setting this in a market context, Alex would like to trade away some of his state 2 endowment for additional claims in state 1. In contrast, Bev would like to trade some of her state 1 endowment for additional claims in state 2. Each seeks to insure against the possible loss.

Suppose that insurance companies offer units of coverage in state 1 at a price per unit of r' in state 2. This is an opportunity to trade state claims at an implicit price ratio of r'. Similarly, if the insurance companies offer units of coverage in state 2 at a price per unit of r'' in state 1, this is an opportunity to trade at an implicit price ratio of $\frac{1}{r''}$. Unless these two implicit prices are equal there is an opportunity for a sure gain. Then, in a Walrasian equilibrium (WE), there is a unique implicit price ratio $\frac{p_1}{p_2} = r' = \frac{1}{r''}$.

Buying insurance against the possibility of loss is therefore equivalent to trading in state claims markets at prices $p = (p_1, p_2)$. If individual h trades these claims, she seeks to solve the following problem:

$$\underset{x^h}{\text{Max}} \left\{ \sum_{s=1}^{2} \pi_s v_h \left(x_s^h \right) \mid p \cdot x^h \le p \cdot \omega^h \right\}.$$

Except for the interpretation, this problem is completely standard. By the First welfare theorem, the WE must be a PE allocation. But we have just argued that for efficiency $x_1^h = x_2^h$. Thus the equilibrium price ratio is

$$\frac{p_1}{p_2} = \frac{\pi_1 v_h' \left(x_1^h \right)}{\pi_2 v_h' \left(x_2^h \right)} = MRS^h(x^h) = \frac{\pi_1}{\pi_2}.$$

That is, the equilibrium price ratio is equal to the probability ratio or "odds."

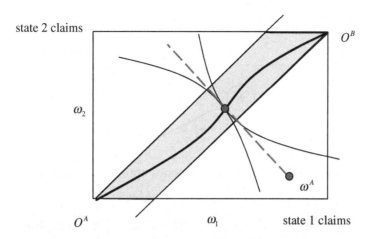

Figure 8.1-2. Efficient allocations with aggregate risk.

Suppose next that the loss is bigger in state 2. Then the aggregate endowment is larger in state 1. This is depicted in Figure 8.1-2. Note that below Alex's certainty line, $MRS^A(x) < \frac{\pi_1}{\pi_2}$, and below Bev's certainty line $MRS^B(x) > \frac{\pi_1}{\pi_2}$. Thus, no efficient allocation lies below both certainty lines. An identical argument establishes that no efficient allocation lies above both certainty lines. Thus the efficient allocations lie in the shaded region depicted in Figure 8.1-2, between the certainty lines.

There are two immediate implications. First, at any efficient allocation, both Alex and Bev are allocated more state 1 claims than state 2 claims. Thus, the aggregate risk is shared. Second, it follows that for all efficient allocations,

$$MRS^h(x^h) = \frac{\pi_1 v'_h\left(x^h_1\right)}{\pi_2 v'_h\left(x^h_2\right)} < \frac{\pi_1}{\pi_2}.$$

Hence, the market equilibrium price of state claims $\frac{p_1}{p_2} = MRS^h(\overline{x}^h) = \frac{\pi_1 v'_h(\overline{x}^h_1)}{\pi_2 v'_h(\overline{x}^h_2)} < \frac{\pi_1}{\pi_2}$. Thus the market prices of state claims reflect the relative shortage of state 2 output.

Arrow-Debreu Equilibrium

We now consider a general economy of H consumers, F firms, and S states. At each date and in each state there are L commodities. We extend the basic equilibrium model by indexing each commodity by the date of its delivery and the state in which it is delivered. For simplicity we consider a two-period world. Consumer h has a date zero consumption vector of $x^h_0 = (x^h_{01}, \ldots, x^h_{0L})$. Uncertainty is resolved after date 0 and before date

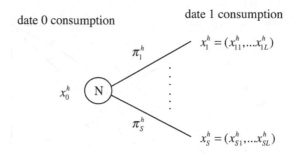

date 0 consumption   date 1 consumption

Figure 8.1-3. State-contingent consumption by consumer h.

1. If state s is realized, consumer h has a date 1 consumption vector of $x_s^h = (x_{s1}^h, \ldots, x_{sL}^h)$. Figure 8.1-3 depicts the uncertain consumption vectors of consumer h in tree form.

At date 0 and in each of the S states at date 1 there are L commodities; thus there are $L + SL = (S+1)L$ commodities in this economy. We write the entire consumption vector as $x^h = (x_0^h, x_1^h, \ldots, x_S^h) \in X^h \subset \mathbb{R}^{(S+1)L}$. Similarly we write consumer h's endowment vector as $\omega^h = (\omega_0^h, \omega_1^h, \ldots, \omega_S^h)$.

Let y_0^f be the period 1 production vector of firm f and let y_s^f be the period 2 production vector in state s of firm f. Thus the production vector of the firm is $y^f = (y_0^f, y_1^f, \ldots, y_S^f)$ where each component is itself an L vector, that is $y^f \in \mathbb{R}^{(S+1)L}$. Firm f has a production set $\mathcal{Y}^f$.

Given the Independence Axiom plus the basic axioms of consumer choice, there exists a continuous utility function $u^h(x_0^h, x_s^h)$ such that preferences over these risky prospects can be expressed in the following separable expected utility form:

$$U^h(x^h) = \sum_{s=1}^{S} \pi_s^h u^h\left(x_0^h, x_s^h\right).$$

We assume that utility is strictly increasing in at least one commodity. Finally let θ^{hf} be consumer h's shareholding of firm f.

An allocation $\{x^h \in X^h\}_{h=1}^{H}, \{y^f \in \mathcal{Y}^f\}_{f=1}^{F}$ is feasible if

$$\sum_{h=1}^{H} x^h \leq \sum_{h=1}^{H} \omega^h + \sum_{f=1}^{F} y^f.$$

A WE of this economy can then be defined in the usual way. That is, we introduce markets for each of the $(S+1)L$ commodities. The allocation $\{x^h \in X^h\}_{h=1}^{H}, \{y^f \in \mathcal{Y}^f\}_{f=1}^{F}$ is a WE allocation if for some $p > 0$,

(i) $p \cdot x^h \leq p \cdot \omega^h + \sum_{f=1}^{F} \theta^{hf} p \cdot y^f$

consumption allocations are in budget sets

(iia) $p \cdot \hat{y}^f > p \cdot y^f \Rightarrow \hat{y}^f \notin \mathcal{Y}^f$

the profit of each firm is maximized

(iib) $U^h(\hat{x}^h) > U^h(x^h) \Rightarrow p \cdot \hat{x}^h > p \cdot x^h$

no strictly preferred allocation is in a consumer's budget set

(iii) $\sum_{h=1}^{H} x^h = \sum_{h=1}^{H} \omega^h + \sum_{f=1}^{F} y^f.$

markets clear

The two welfare theorems then apply immediately. An Arrow-Debreu (A-D) equilibrium allocation is PE, and given convex preferences and production sets, any PE allocation can be achieved as an A-D equilibrium via an appropriate redistribution of income.

Example: A-D Equilibrium with Production

Alex owns a firm with a state-contingent output of $(140, 80)$. Bev owns a firm with non-contingent production set $Y = \{(z, q) | q \leq 80 - z^2, z \geq 0\}$. The two states are equally likely. Each individual has a VNM utility function

$$U^h \left(x_1^h, x_2^h \right) = \pi_1 \ln \left(x_1^h \right) + \pi_2 \ln \left(x_2^h \right).$$

In principle we could solve this problem as follows. First, solve for Bev's profit-maximizing outputs given state claims prices $p = (p_1, p_2)$. This yields the aggregate supply vector $y(p)$. Second, compute Bev's profit and the value of Alex's endowment at these prices. We can then solve for the consumption choice of each consumer at these prices and hence solve for aggregate demand $x(p)$. Finally, choose a price ratio that equates supply and demand.

Instead there is a convenient short-cut. We note that Alex and Bev have the same homothetic preferences. Then we can treat the economy as a Robinson Crusoe economy with just one individual. Aggregate supply is $(220 - z^2/20, 80 + z)$, $z \geq 0$. The expected utility of the representative consumer is therefore

$$U^R = \tfrac{1}{2} \ln(220 - z^2/20) + \tfrac{1}{2} \ln(80 + z).$$

It is readily checked that this is maximized at $z^* = 20$ and hence that aggregate supply is $(200, 100)$. To solve for the equilibrium prices we seek prices such that z^* is indeed the profit-maximizing plan. Iso-profit lines and the production possibility frontier of Bev's firm are depicted in Figure 8.1-4. Along

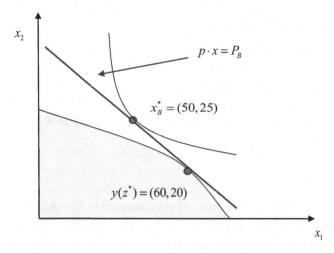

Figure 8.1-4. Bev's optimal production and consumption plan.

the frontier we have $(y_1(z), y_2(z)) = (80 - z^2/20, z)$. Thus, the slope of the frontier at z^* is

$$\frac{dy_2}{dy_1} = \frac{y_2'(z^*)}{y_1'(z^*)} = -\frac{10}{z^*} = -\frac{1}{2}.$$

Thus, the slopes of the iso-profit line and the frontier are equal at z^* if the price ratio $p_1/p_2 = 1/2$.

Suppose we set the price of state 1 claims equal to 1. Then $p_2 = 2$. The value of Alex's firm is $P^A = (1, 2) \cdot (140, 80) = 300$, and the value of Bev's firm is $P^B = p \cdot y(z) = 100$.

Thus far we have focused on trading in state claims markets. Suppose instead that the two individuals trade shares in the two firms. Given her initial shareholding of 100% of the shares in firm 2, Bev's wealth is 100. If she does no trading, her final consumption is the output of the firm (60, 20). Alternatively, she could sell her firm and buy a fraction 100/300 =1/3 of firm 1, thus giving her one-third of the total dividend stream from firm 1. The consumption bundles associated with these two non-diversified portfolios are depicted in Figure 8.1-5.

A third alternative is to purchase one-quarter of the shares of firm 1 at a cost of 75. This leaves Bev holding shares worth 25 in firm 2; that is, a 25% holding. Her final dividend is then one-quarter of the total output in each state; that is, (50, 25). Thus, by trading in the asset markets, Bev is able to achieve the same outcome as she would have by trading in state claims markets.

As this example suggests, in certain circumstances trading in security markets achieves the same allocation achieved in an Arrow-Debreu equilibrium

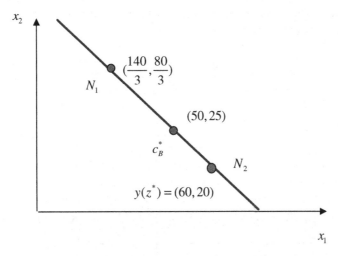

Figure 8.1-5. Bev's portfolio choice.

in which consumers trade directly in contingent claims markets. We explore this issue in the next section.

Comparing the Price of a Riskless Bond and Risky Assets with the Same Expected Dividends

Consider an economy in which consumers have the same beliefs and identical homothetic utility function $U = \sum_{s=1}^{S} \pi_s u(x_s^i)$. Each individual begins with a share of each of the real assets in the economy. As we have seen, the A-D equilibrium prices are the no-trade prices for a single representative agent. Hence, with an aggregate endowment of dividends $\bar{d} = (\bar{d}_1, \ldots, \bar{d}_S)$ all markets clear at the state claims price vector:

$$p = (\pi_1 u'(\bar{d}_1), \ldots, \pi_S u'(\bar{d}_S)).$$

The value of the market portfolio is then

$$P_M = \sum_{s=1}^{S} p_s \bar{d}_s = \sum_{s=1}^{S} \pi_s u'(\bar{d}_s)\bar{d}_s.$$

The expected dividend yield from the market portfolio is $E_s\{\bar{d}_s\} = \sum_{s=1}^{S} \pi_s \bar{d}_s$. Therefore the value of a share of the market portfolio with an expected dividend of 1 is

$$\frac{P_M}{E\{\bar{d}_s\}} = \frac{\sum\limits_{s=1}^{S} \pi_s u'(\bar{d}_s)\bar{d}_s}{\sum\limits_{s=1}^{S} \pi_s \bar{d}_s}.$$

We wish to compare this with the value of a riskless bond, that is, a security paying off $1 in every state:

$$P_B = \sum_{s=1}^{S} p_s = \sum_{s=1}^{S} \pi_s u'(\bar{d}_s).$$

We define

$$\hat{\pi}_s \equiv \frac{\pi_s u'(\bar{d}_s)}{\sum_{s=1}^{S} \pi_s u'(\bar{d}_s)}. \tag{8.1-1}$$

Then

$$\frac{\dfrac{P_M}{E\{\bar{d}_s\}}}{P_B} = \left(\frac{\sum_{s=1}^{S} \pi_s u'(\bar{d}_s)\bar{d}_s}{\sum_{s=1}^{S} \pi_s u'(\bar{d}_s)} \right) \frac{1}{\sum_{s=1}^{S} \pi_s \bar{d}_s} \equiv \frac{\sum_{s=1}^{S} \hat{\pi}_s \bar{d}_s}{\sum_{s=1}^{S} \pi_s \bar{d}_s}.$$

Note that the components of the vector $\hat{\pi}$ sum to 1. Therefore we can interpret the numerator as the expected value of all the dividends using not the true probabilities but the adjusted probabilities.

Henceforth suppose we label the states so that the market dividend is higher in higher numbered states. We show that the adjusted probabilities place more weight on every left tail of the distribution. That is, the true beliefs exhibit first-order stochastic dominance over the adjusted beliefs. It follows immediately that the expected dividend payoff is lower under the adjusted beliefs, and so the price of the "riskless" bond is higher than the risky security with the same expected value. From (8.1-1),

$$\frac{\hat{\pi}_s}{\hat{\pi}_t} = \frac{\pi_s u'(\bar{d}_s)}{\hat{\pi}_t u'(\bar{d}_t)} > \frac{\pi_s}{\hat{\pi}_t}, \quad s < t$$

because, by hypothesis, $\bar{d}_s < \bar{d}_t$ and hence $u'(\bar{d}_s) > u'(\bar{d}_t)$.

Rearranging this inequality,

$$\frac{\hat{\pi}_s}{\pi_s} > \frac{\hat{\pi}_t}{\pi_t}, \quad s < t.$$

Thus the ratio of the probabilities (the *likelihood ratio*) is monotonically decreasing. Appealing to Proposition 7.3-4 it follows that the conditional stochastic dominance property holds. Then π exhibits first-order stochastic dominance over $\hat{\pi}$. Because dividends are higher in higher numbered states, it follows from Proposition 7.3-1 that $\sum_{s=1}^{S} \hat{\pi}_s \bar{d}_s < \sum_{s=1}^{S} \pi_s \bar{d}_s$. Therefore

$$\frac{P_M}{E\{\bar{d}_s\}} < P_B.$$

Thus the equilibrium price of a riskless bond exceeds the value of risky equity with the same expected payoff.

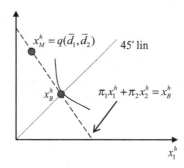

Figure 8.1-6. Pricing the market portfolio.

To understand this result, consider a consumer who could purchase q units of the market portfolio. That is the portfolio $\xi_M = (0, q)$ lies on her portfolio constraint $P'\xi = W^h$. Then one feasible consumption bundle is the point $x_M^h = q(\bar{d}_1, \bar{d}_2)$ depicted in Figure 8.1-6.

Consider a riskless bond with the same expected dividend. If the price of this bond P_B is the same as the price of the market portfolio, then the portfolio $\xi_B = (q, 0)$ also lies on her portfolio constraint. Then a second feasible consumption bundle is the point $x_B^h = q(E\{\bar{d}_s\}, E\{\bar{d}_s\})$. This lies on the 45° line. Since the expected value of the two consumption bundles is the same, it follows that the set of feasible consumption bundles is bounded by the line

$$\pi_1 x_1^h + \pi_2 x_2^h = x_B^h.$$

Note that the slope of this line is the same as the slope of the indifference curve at x_B^h because this point lies on the 45° line. Therefore the consumer's optimal portfolio is $\xi_B = (q, 0)$. Note finally that the same argument holds for all consumers. Thus if the price of the market portfolio and the bond are the same, aggregate demand for the market portfolio is zero. It follows that the equilibrium relative price of the risky asset P_M/P_B must be less than 1.

Exercises

Exercise 8.1-1: Uncertainty in an Economy with CES Preferences Each individual in an economy in which there are two states has expected utility function

$$u^h(x^h, \pi) = \pi_1 v(x_1) + \pi_2 v(x_2) = \pi_1(1 - \tfrac{1}{\sigma})x_1^{1-1/\sigma} + \pi_2(1 - \tfrac{1}{\sigma})x_2^{1-1/\sigma}, \sigma \neq 1.$$

The aggregate endowment vector is (ω_1, ω_2), where $\omega_1 > \omega_2$.

(a) Show that these preferences are homothetic. Hence solve for the equilibrium state claims prices.
(b) What is the degree of relative risk aversion in this economy?

(c) How does the equilibrium price ratio vary with the degree of risk aversion?

(d) What happens as the degree of risk aversion goes to infinity? Explain this result.

Exercise 8.1-2: Variations on a Logarithmic Theme Suppose consumer $h, h = 1, \ldots, H$ has a logarithmic utility function

$$u(x) = \sum_{i=1}^{n} \alpha_i \ln x_i.$$

(a) Show that if this is an endowment economy with aggregate endowment $(\omega_1, \ldots, \omega_n)$, the price vector

$$p = \left(\frac{\alpha_1}{\omega_1}, \cdots, \frac{\alpha_n}{\omega_n} \right), \quad i = 2, \ldots, n$$

  is a WE price vector.

(b) Consider a T-period economy where there is one commodity and the lifetime utility function of a representative individual is

$$U(x) = \sum_{t=1}^{T} \delta^{t-1} \ln x_t.$$

The aggregate endowment in period t is $\omega_t = (1 + \gamma)^{t-1} \omega_1$. There is no storage. Solve for the WE prices. Hence show that the equilibrium one-period gross interest rate $1 + r_t$ is the same in each period.

(c) Consider a two-period economy. The endowment in period 1 is ω_1. In period 2 there are two states. In state 1 (the good state) the endowment increases to $\omega_{12} = (1 + \theta)\omega_1$ and in state 2 (the bad state) the endowment declines to $\omega_{22} = (1 - \gamma)\omega_1$.

The two states are equally likely so that each individual has a VNM utility function

$$U(x) = \ln x_1 + \delta \sum_{s=1}^{2} \tfrac{1}{2} \ln x_{s2}.$$

Let p_1 be the spot price and let p_{s2} be the price of claims to state s in period 2. Solve for WE prices.

(d) Explain why the price of non-contingent delivery of a unit of the commodity in state 2 is $p_{12} + p_{22}$. Hence obtain an expression for the riskless gross interest rate $1 + r$. How does this vary with θ?

(e) Suppose that storage is costless. Under what conditions would there be no storage in the WE?

Exercise 8.1-3: Time, Uncertainty, and Production Preferences for each individual in a two-period, two-state model are as follows:

$$U(x_0, x_{11}, x_{12}) = \ln x_0 + \delta(\pi_1 \ln x_{11} + \pi_2 \ln x_{12}).$$

The aggregate endowment in period 1 is ω_1. In period 2 the endowment is ω_{21} if state 1 (rain) occurs; otherwise it is ω_{22}.

(a) Solve for the equilibrium spot and contingent futures prices. Henceforth assume that $\delta = 1$.
(b) Suppose that there is also a linear production technology. Each unit of input of the commodity in period 1 yields two units in period 2 if it rains, otherwise it yields a half-unit. That is, the production vector is $(-z, 2z, 0.5z)$. For simplicity suppose that the first-period endowment is 100, and the second-period endowment is 0 in both states. If the price of the commodity in period 1 is 1, what can be said about p_{21} and p_{22}?

HINT: Use the representative individual and the fact that his expected utility is $U(x) = \ln(100 - z) + \pi_1 \ln 2z + \pi_2 \ln(0.5z)$ and then solve for the optimal z and hence the optimal supply in each state. Equilibrium prices must equate supply and demand.

Exercise 8.1-4: Equilibrium Gambling UCLA fans think that the Bruins will beat the USC Trojans with probability 0.9. Trojan fans think that the Bruins only have an equal chance of winning. The preference scaling function of each fan is logarithmic; that is, $v(x) = \ln x$. If the total wealth of UCLA and Trojan fans is the same, show that the equilibrium state claims price ratio will be 7/3. How much would a fan with a wealth W actually bet?

8.2 Security Market Equilibrium

Key ideas: trading financial assets, complete security markets, incomplete security markets, implicit state claims prices

In the previous section we examined equilibrium when consumers trade directly in state-contingent markets. Here we examine equilibrium when consumers trade in asset markets. Initially we consider a one-good exchange economy in which there are S states.

Consumer $h, h = 1, \ldots, H$ has a state-contingent endowment $\omega^h = (\omega_1^h, \ldots, \omega_S^h)$. Let $x^h = (x_1^h, \ldots, x_S^h)$ be his consumption vector. We assume that consumer h has a strictly increasing expected utility function

$$U^h(x^h) = \sum_{s=1}^{S} \pi_s^h u^h(x_s^h).$$

Arrow-Debreu Equilibrium

As a preliminary we summarize the A-D equilibrium in which consumers trade directly in state claims markets. The one-good exchange economy is a special case of the economy examined in the previous section. We introduce markets for each of the S commodities. The allocation $\{x^h \in X^h\}_{h=1}^H$ is an A-D equilibrium allocation if for some $p \gg 0$,

(i) $p \cdot x^h \le p \cdot \omega^h + \sum_{f=1}^F \theta^{hf} p \cdot y^f$

   consumption allocations are in budget sets
(ii) $U^h(\hat{x}^h) > U^h(x^h) \Rightarrow p \cdot \hat{x}^h > p \cdot x^h$

   no strictly preferred allocation is in a consumer's budget set
(iii) $\sum_{h=1}^H x^h = \sum_{h=1}^H \omega^h + \sum_{f=1}^F y^f$.

   markets clear

Security Market (SM) Equilibrium

Suppose that individuals do not trade state-contingent commodities but instead trade financial assets. Asset a, $a = 1, \ldots, A$ has a price P_a and a state-contingent dividend $d_a = (d_{1a}, \ldots, d_{Sa})$. Consumer h can transfer wealth across states by buying and selling assets. Let ξ_a^h be the number of units of asset a held by consumer h. Then his portfolio of asset holdings is $\xi^h = (\xi_1^h, \ldots, \xi_A^h)$. Because consumers begin with no financial assets, the market value of this portfolio cannot be positive. Given our assumption that utility is strictly increasing the market value of the portfolio cannot be negative. Then the portfolio constraint is

$$\sum_{a=1}^A P_a \xi_a^h = 0.$$

Given such a portfolio, consumer h has a final consumption of

$$x^h = \omega^h + \sum_{a=1}^S d_a \xi_a^h.$$

Because we have placed no restriction on the sign of the dividends, an asset price may be positive or negative. An equilibrium allocation is then defined in essentially the same way as the A-D equilibrium. The only differences are that consumption bundles can only be achieved by trading assets and that both the commodity and asset markets must clear.

Definition: SM Equilibrium An allocation $\{x^h \in X^h \subset \mathbb{R}^S, \xi^h \in \mathbb{R}^S\}_{h=1}^H$ where $x^h = \omega^h + \sum_{a=1}^A d_a \xi_a^h$ is a (Walrasian) security market equilibrium allocation if for some $P = (P_1, \ldots, P_A)$,

(i) $\sum_{a=1}^A P_a \xi_a^h = 0 \quad h = 1, \ldots, H$

consumption allocations are in budget sets

(ii) $U^h(\omega^h + \sum_{a=1}^A d_a \hat{\xi}_a^h) > U^h(x^h) \Rightarrow P \cdot \hat{\xi}^h > 0$

no strictly preferred allocation is in a consumer's budget set

(iii) $\sum_{h=1}^H x^h = \sum_{h=1}^H \omega^h$, and $\sum_{h=1}^H \xi^h = 0$.

markets clear

Except in some special cases, if there are fewer assets than states, the wealth transfers across states via asset trades are more limited then wealth transfers in an A-D equilibrium. However, suppose that there are at least as many assets as states and that the dividend vectors $\{d_a\}_{a=1}^A$ span $\mathbb{R}^S$. Without loss of generality, we may re-label the assets so that the dividend vectors of the first S assets are linearly independent. Then, any allocation in $\mathbb{R}^S$ can be expressed as a linear combination $\sum_{a=1}^S \xi_a d_a$ of the first S assets. It follows that for every h there is some portfolio ξ^h such that

$$x^h - \omega^h = \sum_{a=1}^S d_a \xi_a^h. \tag{8.2-1}$$

Proposition 8.2-1:
An A-D equilibrium is a SM equilibrium if the asset dividends span $\mathbb{R}^S$.

Proof: Let $\{x^h \in X^h\}_{h=1}^H$ be an A-D equilibrium with equilibrium price p. It follows from (8.2-1) that

$$p \cdot x^h - p \cdot \omega^h = \sum_{a=1}^S p \cdot d_a \xi_a^h.$$

Define $P_a = p \cdot d_a$, $a = 1, \ldots, A$. Then $p \cdot x^h - p \cdot \omega^h = \sum_{a=1}^S P_a \xi_a^h$. An A-D allocation must lie in individual h's budget set. Therefore $\sum_{a=1}^S P_a \xi_a^h = p \cdot x^h - p \cdot \omega^h \leq 0$. Thus the portfolio constraints are satisfied. Summing (8.2-1) over h,

$$\sum_{h=1}^H x^h - \omega^h = \sum_{h=1}^H \sum_{a=1}^A d_a \xi_a^h = \sum_{a=1}^A d_a \sum_{h=1}^H \xi_a^h = \mathbf{D} \sum_{h=1}^H \xi_a^h,$$

where $\mathbf{D}$ is a matrix of the S column vectors of dividends. In the A-D equilibrium markets clear, thus

$$\mathbf{D}\sum_{h=1}^{H}\xi_a^h = \sum_{h=1}^{H}x^h - \omega^h = 0.$$

Because the columns of $\mathbf{D}$ are linearly independent it follows that $\mathbf{D}$ is invertible and so $\sum_{h=1}^{H}\xi_a^h = 0$. Thus asset markets clear.

Finally let $\hat{x}^h = \sum_{a=1}^{A}d_a\hat{\xi}_a^h + \omega^h$ be strictly preferred to x^h. Because x^h is a A-D equilibrium with state-contingent price vector p, it follows that $\hat{x}^h$ must cost strictly more. That is,

$$p\cdot\hat{x}^h - p\cdot\omega^h = \sum_{a=1}^{A}p\cdot d_a\hat{\xi}_a^h = \sum_{a=1}^{A}P_a\hat{\xi}_a^h > 0.$$

It follows that any strictly preferred portfolio violates the portfolio budget constraint. Then the allocation $\{x^h, \xi^h\}_{h=1}^{H}$ is an SM equilibrium allocation with asset prices $P_a = p\cdot d_a, a = 1, \ldots, A$.

We now prove the converse. The proof is similar. We begin with an SM equilibrium in which the dividends of the A assets span the complete state space $\mathbb{R}^S$. Given completeness we can define implicit prices for each state. We then show that this implicit price vector is an A-D equilibrium.   □

Proposition 8.2-2:
An SM equilibrium is an A-D equilibrium if the asset dividends span $\mathbb{R}^S$.

Proof: Let $\{x^h \in X^h \subset \mathbb{R}^S, \xi^h \in \mathbb{R}^S\}_{h=1}^{H}$ where $x^h = \omega^h + \sum_{a=1}^{A}d_a\xi_a^h$ be an SM equilibrium allocation, and let $P = (P_1, \ldots, P_A)$ be the equilibrium vector of security prices. Re-label the assets so that the dividend vectors of the first S assets are linearly independent. As in the proof of the previous propositions define $\mathbf{D}$ to be the matrix of columns of dividend vectors. Because these columns are independent, there exists a unique state-contingent p such that

$$p'\mathbf{D} = P'. \tag{8.2-2}$$

Also, for each s, there exists some portfolio $\xi_s = (\xi_{1s}, \ldots, \xi_{Ss})$ such that $\mathbf{D}\xi_s = \mathbf{1}_s$. This portfolio must have a strictly positive price; otherwise consumption in state s is unbounded. Thus $P'\xi_s > 0, s = 1, \ldots, S$. Rewriting these results in matrix form,

$$\mathbf{D}[\xi_1, \ldots, \xi_S] = \mathbf{I} \quad \text{and} \quad P'[\xi_1, \ldots, \xi_S] > 0.$$

Substituting from (8.2-2),

$$p'\mathbf{D}[\xi_1, \ldots, \xi_S] = p'\mathbf{I} = p' \gg 0.$$

Thus the vector p is strictly positive.

The rest of the proof parallels that of the previous proposition. Suppose that individual h strictly prefers $\hat{x}^h$ over the SM equilibrium allocation x^h. Because the asset markets are complete there is some portfolio $\hat{\xi}^h$ such that $\hat{x}^h - \omega^h = \mathbf{D}\hat{\xi}^h$. From the definition of an SM equilibrium, this cannot satisfy the individual's portfolio constraint. Therefore $P'\hat{\xi}^h > 0$ and so

$$p \cdot (x^h - \omega^h) = p'\mathbf{D}\hat{\xi}^h = P'\hat{\xi}^h > 0.$$

Thus no strictly preferred consumption bundle is feasible if the price vector is p. It follows that the allocation is an A-D equilibrium at the price vector $p > 0$. $\qquad\square$

Multiple Periods, States, and Commodities

Thus far we have focused on trading in security markets with a single commodity. We now consider an economy with production and L commodities delivered at each date and in each state. To simplify the exposition we assume that there are two dates, date 0 and date 1. Let y_0^f be the date 0 production vector of firm f and let y_s^f be the date 1 production vector in state s of firm f. We write the production vector of firm f as $y^f = (y_0^f, y_1^f, \ldots, y_S^f)$. Firm f has a production set $\mathcal{Y}^f$. That is, $y^f \in \mathcal{Y}^f$. Consumer h has a consumption vector $x^h \in \mathbb{R}^{(S+1)L}$ and von Neumann expected utility function

$$U^h(x^h) = \sum_{s=1}^{S} \pi_s^h u^h(x_0^h, x_s^h).$$

Finally let θ^{hf} be consumer h's shareholding of firm f and let ω^h be consumer h's endowment vector.

Trading in Future Spot Markets

The A-D equilibrium of this economy is an allocation $\{x^h\}_{h=1}^{H}, \{y^f\}_{f=1}^{F}$ and price vector $p > 0$ satisfying market clearing and individual rationality given each consumer's budget constraint (see Section 7.4). In that equilibrium, markets for all $(S+1)L$ commodities are open at date 0. Thus consumers can make all of their trades in the first period. There is no need for any market to reopen in later periods. But suppose that state s occurs and the L commodity markets unexpectedly reopen. Setting $\hat{y}_{s'}^h = y_{s'}^h$ for all h and all

$s' \neq s$, define $\mathcal{Y}_s^f$ to be the feasible production plans in state s. Conditions (i)–(iii) for an A-D equilibrium become

$$\text{(i)}' \ p_s \cdot \hat{y}_s^f > p_s \cdot y_s^f \Rightarrow \hat{y}_s^f \notin \mathcal{Y}_s^f$$

$$\text{(ii)}' \ p_s \cdot x_s^h = p_s \cdot \omega_s^h + \sum_{f=1}^{F} \theta^{hf} p_s \cdot y_s^f$$

$$\text{(iii)}' \ u^h(\hat{x}_s^h) > u^h(x_s^h) \Rightarrow p_s \cdot \hat{x}_s^h > p_s \cdot x_s^h.$$

Also

$$\sum_{h=1}^{H} x_s^h = \sum_{h=1}^{H} \omega_s^h + \sum_{f=1}^{F} y_s^h.$$

Condition (iii)′ reveals that if the state s spot price vector p_s^1 is equal to the date 0 contingent price vector p_s, no consumer will wish to trade again at date 1. Thus the future spot markets all clear in period 1. Of course any multiple of this price vector is a WE as well. Then for any number $r_s > -1$ the price vector $p_s^1 = (1 + r_s)p_s$ is a WE future spot price vector. Equivalently

$$p_s = \frac{p_s^1}{1 + r_s}.$$

Thus the A-D state s spot price is the present value of the future spot price where the interest rate r_s is state dependent. Because it will be useful later, note that because p_s^1 dollars in state s have a date 0 value (i.e. present value) of $p_s = \frac{p_s^1}{1+r_s}$, one dollar in state s has a present value of $\frac{1}{1+r_s}$.

Next suppose that individuals anticipate that markets will reopen. Now consumer h can purchase a unit of commodity l in state s in the A-D market at date 0 or place p_{sl} dollars in a bank, earn interest r_s, and thus have $p_{sl}(1 + r_s) = p_{sl}^1$ in state s. Thus there is no arbitrage opportunity, and consumers are indifferent as to whether they trade in the A-D market or trade first with a financial intermediary and then in the future spot markets.

Replacing A-D State-Contingent Markets by Trades in Security Markets

If it seems far-fetched to imagine being able to trade in state-contingent markets in all commodities, you are right! We now argue that there is a simple way to economize on the number of markets. Instead of trading in every commodity, all that is necessary is for an individual to be able to move wealth across time and states and then trade in future spot markets.

Let W_s^h be the extra wealth in state s that individual h needs to finance his purchases, that is,

$$W_s^h = p_s \cdot x_s^h - p \cdot \omega_s^h - \sum_{f=1}^{F} \theta^{hf} p_s \cdot y_s^f, \quad s = 1, \ldots, S. \qquad (8.2\text{-}3)$$

Summing over the consumers

$$\sum_{h=1}^{H} W_s^h = \sum_{h=1}^{H} \left(p_s \cdot x_s^h - p \cdot \omega_s^h \right) - \sum_{h=1}^{H} \sum_{f=1}^{F} \theta^{hf} p_s \cdot y_s^f$$

$$= \sum_{h=1}^{H} \left(p_s \cdot x_s^h - p \cdot \omega_s^h \right) - \sum_{h=1}^{H} \theta^{hf} \sum_{f=1}^{F} p_s \cdot y_s^f$$

$$= \sum_{h=1}^{H} p_s \cdot \left(x_s^h - \omega_s^h - \sum_{f=1}^{F} y_s^f \right), \quad \text{because shareholdings must sum to 1}$$

$$= 0 \quad \text{because supply equals demand in an A-D equilibrium.}$$

This must be true because there can be no aggregate transfer of wealth in or out of state s, even though individuals can shift wealth across time and states.

Similarly let W_0^h be the date 0 wealth needed to finance these trades; that is[1]

$$W_0^h = p_0 \cdot \omega_0^h + \sum_{f=1}^{F} \theta^{hf} p_0 \cdot y_0^f - p_0 \cdot x_0^h. \qquad (8.2\text{-}4)$$

The A-D lifetime budget constraint is

$$p_0 \cdot x_0^h + \sum_{s=1}^{S} p_s \cdot x_s^h = p_0 \cdot \omega_0^h + \sum_{s=1}^{S} p_s \cdot \omega_s^h + \sum_{f=1}^{F} \theta^{hf} \left(p_0 \cdot y_0^f + \sum_{s=1}^{S} p_s \cdot y_s^f \right).$$

That is, the value of consumption equals the value of the endowments plus the value of the profits in each period (distributed as dividends). This budget constraint can be written as follows: $\sum_{s=1}^{S} p_s \cdot (x_s^h - \omega_s^h - \sum_{f=1}^{F} \theta^{hf} y_s^f) + p_0 \cdot (x_0^h - \omega_0^h - \sum_{f=1}^{F} \theta^{hf} y_0^f) = 0.$

Substituting from (8.2.3) and (8.2.4),

$$\sum_{s=1}^{S} W_s = W_0^h.$$

---

[1] Note that we are assuming that shareholder h has a first-period dividend of $k^{hf} p_0 \cdot y_0^f$ from firm f. Alternatively, if this is negative, shareholder h is responsible for financing his share of the cost of the firm's date 0 inputs.

Thus instead of trading in the state claims markets, individual h simply needs some way of transferring wealth across time and states.

SM Equilibrium with Multiple Dates

Suppose that individuals can trade financial assets where asset a, $a = 1, \ldots, A$ has a state s, and date 1 dividend of d^1_{sa}. The date 0 price of this asset is P_a. Let $d^1_a = (d^1_{1a}, \ldots, d^1_{Sa})$ be the vector of date 1 dividends. Note that dividend vectors are now "nominal"; that is, they are denominated in dollars rather than date 1 commodities. We assume that the production plans of the F firms, $\{y^f\}^F_{f=1}$ are the same as in the A-D equilibrium.

An SM allocation $\{x^h, \xi^h\}^H_{h=1}$ is feasible if commodity markets clear and if financial markets clear; that is,

$$\sum_{h=1}^{H} \xi^h_a = 0, \quad a = 1, \ldots, A.$$

Consider some feasible SM allocation $\{x^h, \xi^h\}^H_{h=1}$, commodity prices $p^0, p^1_1, \ldots, p_S > 0$, and asset price vector P. The allocation is an SM equilibrium allocation if, for any $\hat{x}^h$ such that

$$U^h(\hat{x}^h) > U^h(x^h) \quad \text{and} \quad p_0 \cdot \hat{x}^h_0 + P \cdot \xi^h = p_0 \cdot \omega^h_0 + \sum_{f=1}^{F} \theta^{hf} p \cdot y^f_0$$

the date 1 budget constraints are violated in at least one state. That is, for some s,

$$p^1_s \cdot \hat{x}^h_s > d^1 \cdot \xi^h + p_s \cdot \omega^h_s + \sum_{f=1}^{F} \theta^{hf} p_s \cdot y^f_s.$$

Proposition 8.2-3: Replicating the A-D Equilibrium Allocation as an SM Equilibrium

The A-D equilibrium allocation can be achieved simply by trading in asset markets, as long as the state-contingent dividend vectors associated with these assets span $\mathbb{R}^S$.

Proof: We begin by valuing the financial assets in an A-D equilibrium.

Earlier we argued that a dollar in state s has a present value of $\frac{1}{1+r_s}$. Then the date 0 vector of values of each component of this future dividend vector is

$$d_a = \left(\frac{d^1_{1a}}{1 + r_1}, \ldots, \frac{d^1_{Sa}}{1 + r_S} \right).$$

In the A-D equilibrium, the value of asset a is simply the sum of the present value of the dividends. That is

$$P_a = \sum_{s=1}^{S} d_{sa} = \sum_{s=1}^{S} \frac{d_{sa}^1}{1 + r_s}.$$

Because the date 0 dividend vectors span $\mathbb{R}^S$ we re-label the assets so that the first S is linearly independent. Then there exists $\xi^h = (\xi_1^h, \ldots, \xi_S^h)$ such that

$$\sum_{a=1}^{S} d_{sa} \xi_a^h = W_s^h, \quad s = 1, \ldots, S.$$

Step 1: Portfolio constraints are satisfied.

Summing over the states

$$\sum_{a=1}^{S} \xi_a^h \sum_{s=1}^{S} d_{sa} = \sum_{s=1}^{S} W_s^h.$$

But $\sum_{s=1}^{S} d_{sa} = P_a$ and $\sum_{s=1}^{S} W_s^h = W_0^h$. Therefore

$$\sum_{a=1}^{S} P_a \xi_a^h = W_0^h.$$

Thus the portfolio ξ^h is feasible.

Step 2: All financial markets clear.

By construction

$$\sum_{a=1}^{S} d_a \xi_a^h = x^h - \omega^h - \sum_{f=1}^{F} \theta^{hf} y^f.$$

Summing over h and defining the matrix $\mathbf{D}$ to be the matrix of the S column vectors of dividends,

$$\mathbf{D} \sum_{h=1}^{H} \xi_a^h = \sum_{a=1}^{S} d_a \sum_{h=1}^{H} \xi_a^h = \sum_{h=1}^{H} \sum_{a=1}^{S} d_a \xi_a^h = \sum_{h=1}^{H} \left(x^h - \omega^h - \sum_{f=1}^{F} \theta^{hf} y^f \right)$$

$$= \sum_{h=1}^{H} x^h - \sum_{h=1}^{H} \omega^h - \sum_{f=1}^{F} y^f$$

$$= 0, \quad \text{because A-D markets all clear.}$$

Because the columns of $\mathbf{D}$ are linearly independent it follows that $\sum_{h=1}^{H} \xi_a^h = 0$.

Step 3: No consumer has a strictly preferred allocation satisfying the portfolio constraints.

Suppose that $U^h(\hat{x}^h) > U^h(x^h)$ where

$$\hat{x}^h = \sum_{a=1}^{A} d_{as}\hat{\xi}_a^h + \omega^h + \sum_{f=1}^{F} \theta^{hf}y^f. \tag{8.2-5}$$

It follows from the definition of an A-D equilibrium that the A-D budget constraint must be violated, that is,

$$p \cdot \hat{x}^h - p \cdot \omega^h - \sum_{f=1}^{F} \theta^{hf} p \cdot y^f > 0. \tag{8.2-6}$$

Also in an A-D equilibrium the value of asset a is $P_a = p \cdot d_a$. Then

$$\sum_{a=1}^{A} P_a\hat{\xi}_a^h = \sum_{a=1}^{A} p \cdot d_a\hat{\xi}_a^h$$

$$= p \cdot \left(\hat{x}^h - \omega^h + \sum_{f=1}^{F} \theta^{hf}y^f \right), \text{ appealing to (8.2-5)}.$$

Appealing to (8.2-6),

$$\sum_{a=1}^{A} P_a\hat{\xi}_a^h > 0.$$

We have therefore established that there exists a securities market equilibrium that replicates the A-D allocation. Thus no individual has an incentive to trade in the A-D state claims markets as well as the security markets. We can therefore close the state claims markets and achieve the A-D equilibrium allocation by trading only in the A financial assets. □

Stock Market Equilibrium

Thus far we have not considered trading in stock markets. If the date 0 value of the date 1 dividends of the F firms span $\mathbb{R}^S$, then the previous arguments apply directly. By trading in the stock markets and commodity markets, the stock market equilibrium replicates the A-D equilibrium. The date 0 market value of the firm is simply its date 0 value in the A-D equilibrium, that is, $P^f = p \cdot y^f$.

Perfect Foresight

At first blush it appears that we have eliminated a host of markets at no cost. Rather than trade at date 0 in all future contingencies, it is equivalent to defer many trades to later periods by moving wealth across dates via trade in securities markets. Because markets are not costless to operate, it is tempting to conclude that trading in security markets dominates trading in state-contingent markets. However, there is one very important qualification. In the A-D equilibrium, consumers and firms observe the price of every contingent commodity. However, in the SM equilibrium, individuals trading at date 0 do not observe the prices of commodities in the future spot markets. Thus what we have really established is that the SM equilibrium replicates the A-D equilibrium if every consumer correctly forecasts these future spot prices. This is obviously a very strong assumption. However, it is not as preposterous as it may seem. For many commodities aggregate shocks tend to be highly correlated across markets. Thus relative price changes are small. For commodities whose relative prices do vary widely across states, there is an incentive for financial intermediaries to create new financial instruments. The more precisely this financial engineering is focused on a particular commodity and state, the more likely it is that the state claims prices can be inferred from the prices of the financial assets.

Incomplete Markets

Suppose that the dividends in a security market equilibrium do not span $\mathbb{R}^S$ but instead some subspace of dimension J. We first consider a special case in which the A-D equilibrium allocation is still achieved. We then look at an example in which the SM equilibrium allocation differs.

Suppose that consumer h has an initial portfolio $\overline{\xi}^h$ of the A assets. Asset a has a (real) dividend of d_{sa} in state s. Each consumer has the same homothetic expected utility function

$$U^h(x^h) = \sum_{s=1}^{S} \pi_s u\left(x_s^h\right), \quad h = 1, \ldots, H.$$

Given the homotheticity assumption the complete market equilibrium is the no-trade equilibrium of a single representative consumer. The total wealth is $W = p \cdot \sum_{a=1}^{A} d_a$. Consumer h, with wealth $W^h = p \cdot \sum_{a=1}^{A} d_a \overline{\xi}_a^h \equiv k^h W$ consumes a fraction k^h of the total dividends. That is, final consumption is $x^h = k^h \sum_{a=1}^{A} d_a$. It follows that instead of trading in the A-D markets, each consumer can simply purchase a mutual fund that perfectly tracks the market portfolio. Thus the A-D equilibrium allocation is achieved simply by trading in the asset markets, regardless of the dimension of the subspace spanned by the dividend vectors.

Next we add initial endowments. Intuitively, as long as each consumer's endowment vector is spanned by the dividend vectors, this argument will continue to hold. For then each consumer's total endowment plus initial portfolio can be written as a weighted average of the dividend vectors. We therefore consider an example where this is not the case.

Solving for an Incomplete Security Market Equilibrium

Although we consider only a one-good, two-consumer, S-state example, generalizations are straightforward. There are A securities (no initial holdings). Asset a has dividend vector d_a, $a = 1, \ldots, A$. The aggregate endowment is ω. The two consumers have the same homothetic expected utility function

$$U^h(x^h) = \sum_{s=1}^{3} \pi_s u\left(x_s^h\right), \quad h = 1, 2.$$

Let $\bar{x}^1$ be the SM equilibrium consumption of consumer 1. Then $\bar{x}^2 = \omega - \bar{x}^1$. With incomplete markets the first-order conditions cannot be solved analytically for the most useful special case where consumers exhibit constant relative risk aversion. However, by working in reverse, we can construct equilibria quite easily.

Step 1: Implicit prices and implicit taxes For any expected utility function $U^h(x^h) = \sum_{s=1}^{S} \pi_s u(x_s^h)$ define the gradient vector $m^h = \frac{\partial U^h}{\partial x_s^h}$, that is $m_s^h = \pi_s u'(x_s^h)$. Given this gradient vector, computed at $\bar{x}^h$, consumer h's marginal rate of substitution (MRS) of x_1^h for x_s^h is $r_s^h = m_s^h / m_1^h$.

Because U^h is strictly concave, for any $x^h \neq \bar{x}^h$,

$$U^h(x^h) - U^h(\bar{x}^h) < \frac{\partial U^h}{\partial x} \cdot (x^h - \bar{x}^h) = \frac{1}{m_1^h} r^h \cdot (x^h - \bar{x}^h).$$
$$\leq 0 \text{ if } r^h \cdot (x^h - \bar{x}^h) \leq 0.$$

Thus, once at his optimum, if consumer h were given the opportunity to trade with an implicit price vector equal to r^h he would not wish to do so. We therefore call r^h the SM equilibrium implicit market price vector of consumer h.

Define $\Delta r = r^2 - r^1$. This is the vector of implicit price differentials. In an A-D equilibrium marginal rates of substitution are all equal. Thus these implicit price differentials are a measure of the loss associated with incomplete markets.

Step 2: Equilibrium security prices Consumer h, with endowment ω^h trades in security markets. By hypothesis his final consumption is $\bar{x}^h$. Therefore his equilibrium security holding $\bar{\xi}^h$ satisfies

$$\bar{x}^h = \omega^h + \mathbf{D}\bar{\xi}^h. \tag{8.2-7}$$

Moreover $\bar{\xi}^h$ is his optimal portfolio; that is,

$$\bar{\xi}^h = \arg\max_{\xi}\{\overline{U}(\xi) = U(\omega^h + \mathbf{D}\xi)\,|\,P'\xi \le 0\}.$$

The first-order condition for an optimal portfolio is

$$\frac{\dfrac{\partial \overline{U}^h}{\partial \xi_1^h}}{P_1} = \frac{\dfrac{\partial \overline{U}^h}{\partial \xi_2^h}}{P_2}.$$

This can rewritten as follows:

$$\frac{m^h \cdot d_1}{P_1} = \frac{m^h \cdot d_a}{P_a}, \quad h = 1, 2, a = 2, \ldots, A.$$

Dividing by the marginal utility in state 1,

$$\frac{r^h \cdot d_1}{P_1} = \frac{r^h \cdot d_a}{P_a}, \quad h = 1, 2, a = 2, \ldots, A.$$

Rearranging,

$$\frac{P_a}{P_1} = \frac{r^1 \cdot d_a}{r^1 \cdot d_1} = \frac{r^2 \cdot d_a}{r^2 \cdot d_1}, \quad a = 2, \ldots, A.$$

But $r^2 = r^1 + \Delta r$. Substituting for r^2 in the previous expression and appealing to the Ratio Rule,

$$\frac{P_a}{P_1} = \frac{r^1 \cdot d_a}{r^1 \cdot d_1} = \frac{r^1 \cdot d_a + \Delta r \cdot d_a}{r^1 \cdot d_1 + \Delta r \cdot d_1} = \frac{\Delta r \cdot d_a}{\Delta r \cdot d_1}. \tag{8.2-8}$$

Step 3: Solving for the initial endowments From (8.2-7),

$$\omega^1 = \bar{x}^1 - \mathbf{D}\bar{\xi}^1. \tag{8.2-9}$$

Thus we can choose any positive ω^1 satisfying (8.2-9) where the portfolio also satisfies the portfolio constraint $P'\bar{\xi}^1 = 0$.

Consider the special three-state two-security case, in which $U^h = \sum_{s=1}^{3} \pi_s \ln x_s^h$. To simplify the algebra we assume that the three states are equally likely. The individuals trade two securities with dividend vectors $d_1 = (1, 0, 1)$ and $d_2 = (0, 1, 1)$. Suppose that the aggregate endowment is $\omega = (10, 3, 8)$ and that the SM equilibrium consumption of consumer 1 is $x^1 = (6, 2, 6)$. Then $x^2 = (4, 1, 2)$.

The implicit prices for consumer h are

$$r_s^h = \frac{\dfrac{\partial U^h}{\partial x_s^h}}{\dfrac{\partial U^h}{\partial x_s^i}} = \frac{\pi_s \, x_1^h}{\pi_1 \, x_s^h}. \qquad (8.2\text{-}10)$$

Then

$$r^1 = \left(1, \frac{x_1^1}{x_2^1}, \frac{x_1^1}{x_3^1}\right) = (1, 3, 1) \quad \text{and} \quad r^2 = \left(1, \frac{x_1^2}{x_2^2}, \frac{x_1^2}{x_3^2}\right) = (1, 4, 2).$$

Therefore the implicit price differentials are $\Delta r = (0, 1, 1)$. Appealing to (8.2-8),

$$\frac{P_2}{P_1} = 2.$$

Because $P_1 \bar{\xi}_1^{-1} + P_2 \bar{\xi}_2^{-1} = 0$ it follows that $\bar{\xi}_2^{-1} = -\frac{1}{2}\bar{\xi}_1^{-1}$. Appealing to (8.2-9), $\omega^1 = \bar{x}^1 - \mathbf{D}\bar{\xi}^{-1}$. We may therefore choose any portfolio holding $\bar{\xi}_1^{-1}$ such that $\omega^1 > 0$. For example if $\bar{\xi}_1 = 1$,

$$\omega^1 = \begin{bmatrix} 6 \\ 2 \\ 6 \end{bmatrix} - \begin{bmatrix} 1 & 0 \\ 0 & 1 \\ 1 & 1 \end{bmatrix} \begin{bmatrix} \bar{\xi}_1 \\ -\frac{1}{2}\bar{\xi}_1 \end{bmatrix} = \begin{bmatrix} 5 \\ \frac{1}{2} \\ 5\frac{1}{2} \end{bmatrix}$$

Because the consumers have the same homothetic preferences, the A-D equilibrium is a no-trade equilibrium for the representative consumer. The normalized A-D equilibrium price vector is

$$(1, p_2, p_3) = \left(1, \frac{x_1}{x_2}, \frac{x_1}{x_3}\right) = (1, 3\tfrac{1}{3}, 1\tfrac{1}{4}), \quad \text{since } x = \omega = (10, 3, 8).$$

Note that the A-D equilibrium price lies between the two implicit price vectors $r^1 = (1, 3, 1)$ and $r^2 = (1, 4, 2)$ associated with the incomplete market equilibrium.

Note also that $\frac{p \cdot d_2}{p \cdot d_1} = \frac{65}{27} < 2 = \frac{P_2}{P_1}$. Thus the relative value of security 1 is higher when markets are complete. Therefore, if an individual or firm can predict the effect of adding a new security on the relative price of current securities, there are profitable arbitrage opportunities. This suggests that, in an incomplete market, financial intermediaries have a strong incentive to create new securities.

Exercises

Exercise 8.2-1: Why Incomplete Markets? In this section it was argued that with incomplete markets, there is always an incentive for a new security to be created. Why then are real-world markets incomplete?

Exercise 8.2-2: Asset Prices Consider a single good economy in which there are two dates(0 and 1), and at date 1 there are two states. There are H consumers. Each consumer has the same expected utility function $U(x^h) = \ln x_0^h + \delta \sum_{s=0}^{2} \pi_s \ln x_s^h$. For simplicity suppose that the two states are equally likely. Finally assume that the aggregate endowment is larger in state 2 $(\omega_2 > \omega_1)$.

(a) Let the date 0 commodity be the numeraire so that $p_0 = 1$. Solve for the equilibrium state claims prices.
(b) There are two assets with dividends $d_1 = (1,0)$ and $d_2 = (0,1)$. Both dividends thus are distributed with the same mean and variance. Show that the equilibrium asset prices (valued in terms of the numeraire commodity) must satisfy $P_2 < P_1$. Why is this?

Exercise 8.2-3: SM Equilibrium in an Economy with Identical Homothetic Preferences Suppose that each consumer has a VNM expected utility function

$$U(x^h) = \sum_{s=1}^{3} \pi_s \left(x_s^h\right)^{1/2}.$$

Suppose also that the "endowment" is really two assets. The riskless asset a has a return of 100 in each state. Risky asset b yields nothing in state 1, 400 in state 2, and 800 in state 3.

(a) Solve for the A-D equilibrium state claims prices in terms of the probabilities.
(b) What will be the associated securities (asset) prices?
(c) Suppose each consumer can only trade in securities markets. Show that the A-D equilibrium can be replicated by an SM equilibrium.

Exercise 8.2-4: Asset Prices and Risk Aversion Consider a single good economy with two periods and H consumers. All consumers have the same beliefs and homothetic utility function

$$U(x^h) = u\left(x_0^h\right) + \delta \sum_{s=1}^{S} \pi_s u\left(x_s^h\right) \quad \text{where } u'(x_s) = \left(\frac{1}{x_s}\right)^R.$$

The aggregate endowment in state s is ω_s, $s = 1, \dots, S$.

(a) Confirm that the individuals have constant relative aversion to wealth risk equal to R.

(b) Appeal to the FOC to show that A-D equilibrium prices must satisfy the condition

$$\frac{1}{p_0(\omega_0)^R} = \frac{\delta \pi_s}{p_s(\omega_s)^R}, \quad s = 1, \ldots, S.$$

(c) Let P_1 be the price of a riskless bond paying 1 in every state at date 1. Let P_2 be the price of an asset with a dividend equal to a fraction λ of the aggregate endowment. Use the AD equilibrium prices to obtain an expression for the asset price ratio P_2/P_1. For the two-state case show that the higher the degree of risk aversion, the lower this equilibrium asset price ratio. What is the intuition for this result?

Exercise 8.2-5: Stock Market Equilibrium Consider the following one-good, two-period model. The endowment is $(\omega_0, 0)$. If $(y_0^f, y_1^f) \in \mathcal{Y}^f$ firm f, $f = 1, \ldots, F$ can use $-y_0^f$ units of period 1 input to produce the state-contingent period 1 output $(y_1^f, \ldots, y_S^f) = y_1^f(d_1, \ldots, d_S)$. Thus the aggregate production vector is $(y_0, y_1 d)$. Suppose initially that consumers trade period 0 consumption and units of the period 1 "dividend" vector d. The expected utility of consumer h is therefore

$$U^h\left(x_0^h, x_1^h\right) = u^h\left(x_0^h\right) + \sum_{s=1}^{S} \pi_s u^h\left(x^h d_s\right).$$

Let p_0 be the price of the period 0 good, and let p_1 be the price of a dividend.

(a) Characterize a WE of this economy.
(b) Compare this with the A-D equilibrium for this economy.
(c) By the First welfare theorem, a WE allocation is PE. In what respect is the WE of part (a) a PE allocation?
(d) Next assume that there is no dividend market. Instead consumers trade period 1 endowment and shares in the F firms. Explain why the stock market equilibrium is equivalent to the dividend market equilibrium.
(e) Can you generalize the model to allow for F_j firms to produce a state-contingent dividend d_j, $j = 1, \ldots, m$?

8.3 Capital Asset Pricing Model

Key ideas: portfolio choice, diversification, mutual fund theorem, CAPM

We have seen that if there are as many linearly independent asset returns as states, asset markets are a perfect substitute for markets in state claims. But what if there are fewer asset markets? In general, trading in asset markets will yield a Pareto inferior outcome. Moreover, it is generally not possible to solve analytically for the equilibrium asset prices.

One special case in which it is possible to price assets, regardless of whether there are more assets than states, is when individuals only care about the first and second moments of the distribution of asset returns.

Mean-Variance Preferences

Suppose that consumers care only about the mean and variance of their final wealth so that the expected utility of a portfolio with mean μ and standard deviation σ can be written as $U^h(\sigma, \mu)$. As we shall see, in such a world, even if individuals have very different attitudes toward risk, each will want to hold a portfolio consisting only of the riskless asset and a mutual fund consisting of the entire market portfolio.

Diversification

Suppose that there are A risky assets and one riskless asset (asset 0). Asset a has return $z_a = (z_{a1}, \ldots z_{aS})$. The vector of mean returns is $\mu = (\mu_0, \ldots, .\mu_A)$, and the covariance matrix of returns is $[\sigma_{ij}]$. The vector of asset prices is $P = (P_0, \ldots, P_A)$. We choose units of the riskless asset so that a price per unit is 1. Then the gross riskless return is $\mu_0 = 1 + r$ where r is the riskless interest rate.

Consumer h, with wealth W^h, chooses a portfolio $\xi = (\xi_0, \ldots, \xi_A)$ that maximizes the expected utility given her portfolio constraint

$$P \cdot \xi \leq W^h.$$

Let $\mu(\xi)$ and $\sigma(\xi)$ be the resulting portfolio mean and variance, that is

$$\mu(\xi) = \sum_{a=0}^{A} \xi_a \mu_a \quad \text{and} \quad \sigma^2(\xi) = E\left\{\sum_{a=0}^{A} \xi_a(z_a - \mu_a)\right\}^2 = \xi'[\sigma_{ij}]\xi.$$

Then the individual maximizes her expected utility by solving the following portfolio problem:

$$\text{Max}_q\{U^h(\sigma(\xi), \mu(\xi)) | P \cdot \xi \leq W^h\}.$$

It proves convenient not to focus on the size of an individual's portfolio, but on spending per dollar of wealth, $x = \xi / W^h$. The portfolio constraint can then be rewritten as

$$P \cdot x \leq 1.$$

Note that because $q = W^h x$, it follows that $\mu(\xi) = W^h \mu(x)$ and $\sigma(\xi) = W^h \sigma(x)$. Expected utility can then be expressed as $U^h(W^h \mu(x), W^h \sigma(x))$. Rather than carry the wealth term, we define the derived utility function

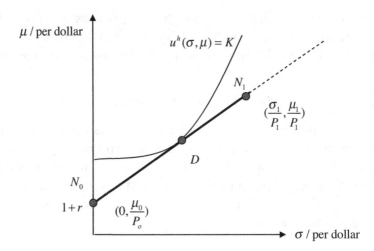

Figure 8.3-1. Choosing an optimal portfolio.

$u^h(\mu(x), \sigma(x)) \equiv U^h(W^h\mu(x), W^h\sigma(x))$. Thus, we may rewrite the optimization problem as follows:

$$\underset{x}{\text{Max}}\{u^h(\sigma(x), \mu(x))|P \cdot x \le 1\}.$$

We have therefore established that we can analyze the portfolio choice of consumer h as if she has a wealth of 1.

Consider first an individual choosing a portfolio consisting of the riskless asset (asset 0) and one risky asset (asset 1). Given a wealth of 1, he can purchase 1 unit of the riskless asset or $1/P_1$ units of the risky asset. If he purchases only the riskless asset (N_0 in Figure 8.3-1) his mean return is $1 + r$. If he purchases only the risky asset 1 (N_1 in Figure 8.3-1) the standard deviation and mean of his portfolio are μ_1/P_1 and σ_1/P_1, respectively.

If he spends a fraction λ of his wealth on the risky asset, the standard deviation of his portfolio return is $\lambda\frac{\sigma_1}{P_1}$, and the mean portfolio return is $(1 - \lambda)$ $\frac{\mu_0}{P_0} + \lambda\frac{\mu_1}{P_0}$. Thus the diversified portfolios are all those on the heavy line. If the consumer borrows funds at the riskless interest rate he can purchase more of the risky asset. Equivalently, he can sell short. That is, he can ask his broker to sell units of the riskless asset that others are holding at the brokerage house, use the funds from the sale to buy more of the risky asset, and then later pay the riskless gross return (from the sale of the risky asset). Through such a short sale the portfolio mean and standard deviation rise even further along the dashed extension of the line depicted in Figure 8.3-1.

Next define R to be the set of feasible means and standard deviations of an individual who invests only in risky assets. These are depicted in Figure 8.3-2.

Pick any point $(\hat{\sigma}, \hat{\mu})$ in this set. This point depicts the standard deviation and mean of a portfolio $(\hat{x}_1, \ldots, \hat{x}_A)$ costing a dollar. Think of this as a dollar

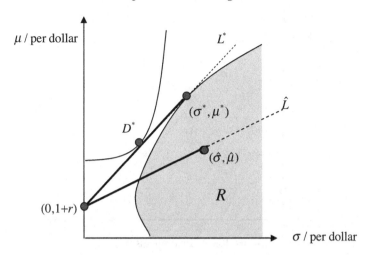

Figure 8.3-2. Choosing an optimal portfolio.

investment in a mutual fund. We have just argued that all portfolios consisting of shares in this mutual fund and the riskless asset must lie on the line $\hat{L}$. Because this argument holds for every point in the set R, the complete set of feasible portfolios is the cone created by drawing all the lines from $(0, 1 + r)$ through a point in R. Thus, the efficient portfolios are those on the line L^* touching the set R at (σ^*, μ^*). Let $(x_1^*, \ldots, x_A^*)$ be the portfolio of risky assets corresponding to this point. Then, if this portfolio is offered by financial intermediaries as a mutual fund, the individual can do no better than to choose a portfolio consisting only of the riskless asset and this mutual fund. Of course, the optimal share of risky assets (the point D^* in the figure) is determined by both the individual's wealth and attitude toward risk.

Mutual Fund Theorem

Note that exactly the same argument holds for every investor. Thus, given the asset price vector P, every individual will wish to purchase the same mutual fund $(x_1^*, \ldots, x_A^*)$.

But the total supply of risky assets is the entire market portfolio. In equilibrium the demand for risky assets (demand for shares in the single mutual fund) must be equal to the total supply of risky asserts (the "market portfolio"). Thus, the equilibrium mutual fund must be the market portfolio. Therefore, risk is fully diversified if all individuals trade only in the riskless asset and the market portfolio.

Proposition 8.3-1: Mutual Fund Theorem
If individuals care only about the first and second moments of the distribution of portfolio asset returns, then, in equilibrium, all hold shares of the market portfolio and invest the rest of their wealth in the riskless asset.

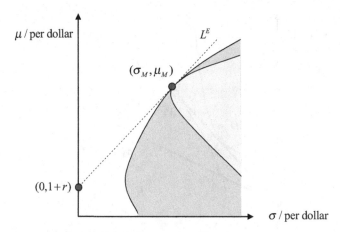

Figure 8.3-3. Pricing asset *a*.

Pricing Individual Assets

Consider a dollar portfolio consisting of the mutual fund M, asset a, and the riskless asset. The portfolio constraint is

$$x_0 + P_M x_M + P_a x_a = 1.$$

From the mutual fund theorem we know that, in equilibrium, the investor will choose only the market portfolio and the riskless asset so that the equilibrium holding of asset a is zero. This is illustrated in Figure 8.3-3. The dark shaded area indicates all (σ, μ) outcomes when the investor invests in all A risky assets. The lightly shaded area indicates the possible outcomes when the investor's portfolio contains only asset a and the market mutual fund. Because this is a more constrained set of opportunities, the lightly shaded area must lie inside the dark shaded area. Then the lightly shaded area must be tangential to the market line. Therefore if the investor is constrained to choose a portfolio consisting only of the riskless asset, the market mutual fund, and asset a, his optimal choice is to purchase only the market mutual fund and the riskless asset. We use this fact to price each individual asset.

If the investor holds only the market portfolio, the mean portfolio return per dollar is μ_M/P_M and the standard deviation is σ_M/P_M. Therefore the slope of the market line (or *Sharpe ratio*) is

$$\frac{\frac{\mu_M}{P_M} - (1+r)}{\frac{\sigma_M}{P_M}} = \frac{\mu_M - (1+r)P_M}{\sigma_M}. \tag{8.3-1}$$

Now consider a portfolio consisting of the riskless asset, the market mutual fund, and asset a. The portfolio return is $c = x_0 z_0 + x_M z_M + x_a z_a$. Substituting for x_0 from the portfolio constraint, the portfolio return can be rewritten as follows:

$$c = 1 + r + x_M(z_M - (1+r)P_M) + x_a(z_a - (1+r)P_a).$$

The mean and variance of this portfolio are therefore as follows:

$$\mu(x) = 1 + r + x_M(\mu_M - (1+r)P_M) + x_a(\mu_a - (1+r)P_a)$$

$$\sigma^2(x) = x_M^2 \sigma_M^2 + 2x_M x_a \sigma_{aM} + x_a^2 \sigma_a^2.$$

Differentiating by x_a,

$$\frac{\partial \mu}{\partial x_a} = \mu_a - (1+r_0)P_a, \quad \text{and} \quad 2\sigma \frac{\partial \sigma}{\partial x_a} = 2x_M \sigma_{aM} + 2x_a \sigma_a^2. \quad (8.3\text{-}2)$$

Finally, we note that, in equilibrium, the best portfolio of risky assets contains only the market portfolio. Thus, in equilibrium, $x_a = 0$ and so $\sigma(x) = x_M \sigma_M$. Substituting into (8.3-2),

$$\frac{d\mu}{d\sigma} = \frac{\dfrac{\partial \mu}{\partial x_a}}{\dfrac{\partial \sigma}{\partial x_a}} = \frac{\mu_a - (1+r)P_a}{\dfrac{\sigma_{aM}}{\sigma_M}}.$$

This must be the slope of the market line given by (8.3-1). Therefore

$$\frac{\mu_a - (1+r)P_a}{\dfrac{\sigma_{aM}}{\sigma_M}} = \frac{\mu_M - (1+r)P_M}{\sigma_M}.$$

Rearranging this expression we have the price of each asset as a function of the underlying means and covariances and the price of the market portfolio. We summarize this in Proposition 8.3-2.

Proposition 8.3-2: Capital Asset Pricing Rule
If individuals care only about the first and second moments of the distribution of portfolio asset returns, then the equilibrium price of asset i satisfies

$$\mu_a - (1+r)P_a = \frac{\sigma_{aM}}{\sigma_M^2}(\mu_M - (1+r)P_M). \quad (8.3\text{-}3)$$

Let $1 + r_a$ be the risky gross yield on asset a. That is,

$$1 + r_a = \frac{z_a}{P_a}, \quad a = 1, \ldots, A$$

Then $\sigma_{aM} = \text{cov}\{z_a, z_M\} = \text{cov}\{P_a r_a, P_M r_M\} = P_a P_M \text{cov}\{r_a, r_M\}$.
Similarly, $\sigma_M^2 = \text{var}\{z_M\} = \text{var}\{P_M r_M\} = P_M^2 \text{var}\{r_M\}$.

Substituting into (8.3-3) and rearranging,

$$\frac{\mu_a}{P_a} - (1+r) = \frac{\text{cov}\{r_a, r_M\}}{\text{var}\{r_M\}} \left(\frac{\mu_M}{P_M} - (1+r) \right).$$

Hence

$$E\{r_a\} - r = \frac{\text{cov}(r_a, r_M)}{\text{var}(r_M)}(E\{r_M\} - r).$$

Investment houses run regressions of each stock's yield on the market yield and report the "beta" of the stock. Suppose two listed firms have the same expected yield, but the return of the first firm has a higher beta (is more highly correlated with the market portfolio). Then the equilibrium expected yield for the first firm must be higher because it offers less of an opportunity to spread risk.

Example of Mean-Variance Preferences

The assumption that individuals only care about the first two moments of the distribution of returns is obviously only a first approximation. However, this is the case if returns are normally distributed. If, in addition, individuals exhibit constant absolute risk aversion, preferences can be expressed as a quadratic function of the portfolio mean and standard deviation.

If the return on each asset is normally distributed, then any portfolio (a linear combination of the assets) is also normally distributed. Let μ and σ^2 be the mean and variance of the portfolio return for individual h. Then $\tilde{c}$ has density function

$$f(c) = \frac{1}{\sigma\sqrt{2\pi}} e^{-\frac{1}{2}\left(\frac{x-\mu}{\sigma}\right)^2}. \tag{8.3-4}$$

We assume that individual h exhibits constant absolute risk aversion so that his utility function (up to a linear transformation) is $v_h(c) = e^{-\alpha c}$ and his expected utility is

$$u = E\{v_h(\tilde{c})\} = \int_{-\infty}^{\infty} e^{-\alpha c} f(c) dc. \tag{8.3-5}$$

We now show that there is a simple representation of these preferences that is linear in the mean and variance of the portfolio return.

Proposition 8.3-3: Quadratic Representation of Preferences

If an individual exhibits constant absolute risk aversion, so that $-\frac{v''(c)}{v'(c)} = \alpha$ and consumption is normally distributed with mean μ and standard deviation σ, then

$$U(\mu, \sigma) = \mu - \tfrac{1}{2}\alpha\sigma^2 \tag{8.3-6}$$

is a representation of the individual's preferences.

Proof: Substituting from (8.3-4) into (8.3-5), expected utility is

$$u = E\{v(\tilde{c})\} = -\frac{1}{\sigma\sqrt{2\pi}} \int_{-\infty}^{\infty} e^{-\frac{1}{2}(2\alpha c + (\frac{c-\mu}{\sigma})^2)} dc$$

$$= -\frac{1}{\sigma\sqrt{2\pi}} e^{-\alpha\mu} \int_{-\infty}^{\infty} e^{-\frac{1}{2}(2\alpha\sigma(\frac{c-\mu}{\sigma}) + (\frac{c-\mu}{\sigma})^2)} dc. \qquad (8.3\text{-}7)$$

Completing the square,

$$u = -\frac{1}{\sigma\sqrt{2\pi}} e^{-\alpha(\mu - \frac{1}{2}A\sigma^2)} \int_{-\infty}^{\infty} e^{-\frac{1}{2}((\alpha\sigma)^2 + \alpha\sigma(\frac{c-\mu}{\sigma}) + (\frac{c-\mu}{\sigma})^2)} dc.$$

Hence

$$u = -e^{-\alpha(\mu - \frac{1}{2}\alpha\sigma^2)} \int_{-\infty}^{\infty} \frac{1}{\sigma\sqrt{2\pi}} e^{-\frac{1}{2}(\frac{c-\mu+\alpha\sigma}{\sigma})^2} dc.$$

But the integral is equal to 1 because it is the integral of a normal density function over its support. Hence $u = -e^{-\alpha(\mu - \frac{1}{2}A\sigma^2)} = -e^{-\alpha U(\mu,\sigma)}$. $\qquad \square$

Exercises

Exercise 8.3-1: Pricing Independent Assets There is one riskless asset with gross yield $1 + r$ and A risky assets. Asset a has mean μ_a and variance σ_a^2. The assets are independently and normally distributed. Individual h, $h = 1, \ldots, H$ has VNM utility function $u(x) = -e^{-\alpha^h x}$ (constant absolute risk aversion).

(a) Initially assume that all individuals have the same risk-aversion parameter α. Solve for the equilibrium price of each asset.
(b) Holding the number of assets constant, what happens as the number of individuals becomes large? Explain.
(c) Holding the number of individuals constant, how does the price of each asset change as the number of assets rises? Is this surprising? Explain.
(d) What if the number of firms and the number of individuals increase at the same rate?
(e) Extend the analysis to the case where each individual has a different risk-aversion parameter.

Exercise 8.3-2: Mutual Fund Theorem

(a) Suppose that all A risky assets are independent. Appeal to the capital asset pricing formula to obtain an expression for the price of asset a in terms of the variances of the A assets and the price of the market portfolio.

(b) If asset 2 has twice the variance of asset 1, compare the expected return of each asset over and above the riskless gross return, that is $\mu_1 - (1+r)P_1$ and $\mu_2 - (1+r)P_2$.

(c) Fixing the A assets, what happens to the price of each asset as the number of consumers grows large?

8.4 Arbitrage Pricing Theory

Key ideas: no arbitrage, implicit state claims prices, Fundamental Theorem of Asset Pricing

Rather than begin with preferences and solve for the implied equilibrium prices, a separate strand of security pricing theory, developed initially by Ross (1976), begins with the dividends of securities in different states and then asks what implications follow under the assumption that security prices do not admit any arbitrage opportunities.

We label the securities $1, \ldots, A$. Security a has price P_a. A portfolio $\xi = (\xi_1, \ldots, \xi_A)$ of A securities then has a market value $\sum_{a=1}^{A} P_a \xi_a \equiv P'\xi$. If markets are complete the market value of the portfolio must also be the value of the dividends in the portfolio. In an A-D equilibrium with state claims price vector p, the market value of the dividends is $\sum_{a=1}^{A} p'd_a \xi_a \equiv P'\mathbf{D}\xi$. Thus

$$P'\xi = p'\mathbf{D}\xi.$$

Next suppose that the asset markets are incomplete so that the dimension of $\mathbf{D}$ is less than S. The central result of arbitrage pricing theory is that if asset prices admit no arbitrage opportunities, there exists an implicit state claims price vector that correctly values these assets; that is, the value of any portfolio of the A assets is equal to the value of the dividends computed using these implicit prices.

Definition: No Arbitrage Given securities with dividend vectors d_a, $a = 1, \ldots, A$, the security price vector $P = (P_1, \ldots, P_A)$ does not admit arbitrage if for any portfolio ξ,

(i) $w = \mathbf{D}\xi = 0 \Rightarrow P'\xi = 0$
(ii) $w = \mathbf{D}\xi > 0 \Rightarrow P'\xi > 0$.

To illustrate, suppose that there are three states and two assets, and the dividend vectors are $d_1 = (1, 0, 1)$ and $d_2 = (0, 1, 1)$. In this case the dividend vectors span a two-dimensional subspace W^2 of the state space $\mathbb{R}^3$, where

$$W^2 = \left\{ w \mid w = \mathbf{D}\xi = \begin{bmatrix} 1 & 0 \\ 0 & 1 \\ 1 & 1 \end{bmatrix} \begin{bmatrix} \xi_1 \\ \xi_2 \end{bmatrix} = \begin{bmatrix} \xi_1 \\ \xi_2 \\ \xi_1 + \xi_2 \end{bmatrix} \right\}.$$

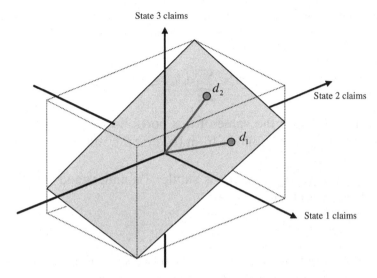

Figure 8.4-1. Dividends spanned by d_1 and d_2.

This is depicted in Figure 8.4-1 for all points inside the box.

For no arbitrage, the value of the dividend vector w must be strictly positive if $w > 0$. But in the example $w = (\xi_1, \xi_2, \xi_1 + \xi_2)$ so the value of w must be greater than zero, if and only if $\xi > 0$. However, the value of the portfolio is $P_1\xi_1 + P_2\xi_2$. Thus, for our example, any price vector $P \gg 0$ is consistent with no arbitrage.[2]

Implicit State Claims Prices without Preferences

We now ask what we can be said about asset prices and returns if we appeal only to no arbitrage.

Proposition 8.4-1: Fundamental Theorem of Asset Pricing (Ross)
For securities $1, \ldots, A$ with dividend vectors $d_1, \ldots, d_A \in \mathbb{R}^S$, and security prices $P = (P_1, \ldots, P_A) \gg 0$ the following are equivalent:

(a) P does not admit arbitrage and
(b) there exists a state price vector $r \in \mathbb{R}^S$, $r \gg 0$ such that any portfolio $\xi = (\xi_1, \ldots, \xi_A)$ has a market value

$$P'\xi = r'\mathbf{D}\xi.$$

---

[2] Suppose that d_2 is replaced $\bar{d}_2 = (1, -1, 0)$. Confirm that no arbitrage implies that any portfolio that is long in asset 1 and short in asset 2 has a positive price if and only if $P_1 > P_2$.

The proof that (b) implies (a) follows almost immediately. If, for some port-folio ξ,

$$w = \sum_{a=1}^{A} d_a \xi_a = 0$$

it follows from (b) that the value of this portfolio is zero. Similarly, if for some portfolio ξ, $w > 0$ it follows from (b) that the value of this portfolio is strictly positive because $r \gg 0$.

The proof that (a) implies (b) is subtle. To understand the method of attack we begin with two examples.

Example 1

Consider an economy with three states and two securities. The first security has a dividend $d_1 = (1, \frac{1}{2}, 1)$ and the second a dividend $d_2 = (0, 1, 1)$. The asset prices are $P = (3, 2)$.

Let W^2 be the two-dimensional subspace of portfolio dividends spanned by the two dividend vectors. Also let $\Xi = \{\xi \mid \mathbf{D}\xi > 0\}$ be the set of portfolios with a dividend $d = \mathbf{D}\xi > 0$.

As can easily be checked $\xi^* = (1, 1) \in \Xi$. Thus Ξ is non-empty. As can also be readily checked Ξ is convex. The set is depicted in Figure 8.4-2.

Note that as long as $P_1 < 2P_2$, the line $P_1\xi_1 + P_2\xi_2 = 0$ is a supporting price line. Hence $\xi \in \Xi$ and $\xi \neq 0$ imply that $P'\xi > 0$. Thus the asset price vector $P = (3, 2)$ does not admit arbitrage.

We now show that we can extend no arbitrage from the subspace W^2 to $\mathbb{R}^3$. Define the portfolio $\xi^* = (1, 1)$. It is readily confirmed that

$$d^{**} = D\xi^* + \begin{bmatrix} 0 \\ 0 \\ 1 \end{bmatrix} = \begin{bmatrix} 1 \\ 1\frac{1}{2} \\ 3 \end{bmatrix} \notin W^2.$$

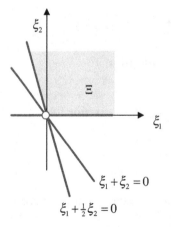

Figure 8.4-2. Portfolios with a positive dividend.

We need to show that there is some price P^{**} for the dividend d^{**} such that (P_1, P_2, P^{**}) admits no arbitrage. Note that

$$\begin{bmatrix} 0 \\ 0 \\ 1 \end{bmatrix} = d^{**} - d^*.$$

The market value of $d^* = \mathbf{D}\xi^*$ is $P'\xi^*$. Thus if there exists such a P^{**}, the market value of a claim to state 3 is

$$r_3 = P^{**} - P'\xi^*. \tag{8.4-1}$$

Step 1: Long positions on the new asset The portfolio (ξ_1, ξ_2, α) has a dividend of $w = \mathbf{D}\xi + \alpha d^{**}$ and a market value of

$$P'\xi + \alpha P^{**}.$$

For no arbitrage, we require that for any $w > 0$, the value of the dividend stream is strictly positive. That is

$$\hat{w} = \mathbf{D}\hat{\xi} + \alpha d^{**} > 0 \Rightarrow P'\hat{\xi} + \alpha P^{**} > 0.$$

Equivalently,

$$\mathbf{D}\hat{\xi} > -\alpha d^{**} \Rightarrow P'\hat{\xi} > -\alpha P^{**}. \tag{8.4.2}$$

This holds if $\alpha = 0$ for then $w \in W^2$.

Suppose that $\alpha > 0$. Then define $\beta = -1/\alpha < 0$ and we can rewrite (8.4-2) as follows:

$$\beta\mathbf{D}\hat{\xi} < d^{**} \Rightarrow \beta P'\hat{\xi} < P^{**}.$$

Define $\xi = \beta\hat{\xi}$. Then we require that

$$\mathbf{D}\xi < d^{**} \Rightarrow P'\xi < P^{**}.$$

Define the set $X = \{\xi \mid \mathbf{D}\xi \leq d^{**}\}$. Then we require that

$$P'\xi \leq P^{**} \quad \text{for all } \xi \in X. \tag{8.4-3}$$

Step 2: Short positions on the new asset Next suppose that $\alpha < 0$. Then define $\beta = -1/\alpha > 0$ and we can rewrite (8.4-2) as follows:

$$\beta\mathbf{D}\hat{\xi} > d^{**} \Rightarrow \beta P'\hat{\xi} > P^{**}.$$

Define $\xi = \beta\hat{\xi}$. Then we require that

$$\mathbf{D}\xi > d^{**} \Rightarrow P'\xi > P^{**}.$$

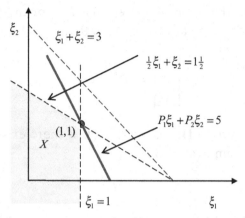

Figure 8.4-3. Lower bound for the price of the third asset.

Define the set $Y = \{\xi | \mathbf{D}\xi \geq d^{**}\}$. Then we require that

$$P'\xi \geq P^{**}, \quad \text{for all} \quad \xi \in Y. \tag{8.4-4}$$

Step 3: Pricing the new asset The set $X = \{\xi | \xi_1 \leq 1, \frac{1}{2}\xi_1 + \xi_2 \leq 1\frac{1}{2}, \xi_1 + \xi_2 \leq 3\}$ is depicted in Figure 8.4-3.

Note that with $P = (3, 2)$,

$$(1, 1) = \arg \operatorname*{Max}_{\xi}\{P'\xi | \xi \in X.$$

Hence (8.4-3) is satisfied as long as $P^{**} > 5$.

The set $Y = \{\xi | \xi_1 \geq 1, \frac{1}{2}\xi_1 + \xi_2 \geq 1\frac{1}{2}, \xi_1 + \xi_2 \geq 3\}$ is depicted in Figure 8.4-4.

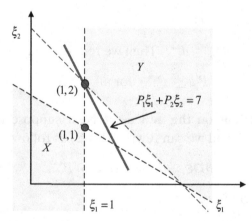

Figure 8.4-4. Upper bound for the price of the third asset.

Note that with $P = (3, 2)$,

$$(1, 2) = \arg \operatorname*{Min}_{\xi}\{P'\xi \mid \xi \in Y.$$

Hence (8.4-4) is satisfied as long as $P^{**} < 7$. Thus as long as $P^{**} \in (5, 7)$ the asset prices admit no arbitrage. Choose $P^{**} = 6$. Appealing to (8.4-1),

$$r_3 = P^{**} - P'\xi^* = 1.$$

Also $P' = r'\mathbf{D}$. Therefore

$$[3, 2, 6] = [r_1, r_2, 1] \begin{bmatrix} 1 & 0 & 1 \\ \frac{1}{2} & 1 & 1\frac{1}{2} \\ 1 & 1 & 3 \end{bmatrix}.$$

Hence $2 = r_2 + r_3$ and $3 = r_1 + \frac{1}{2}r_2 + r_3$. Solving, $r_2 = 1$ and $r_1 = 1\frac{1}{2}$.

Example 2

Consider an economy with three states and two securities. The first security has a dividend $d_1 = (1, 0, -1)$ and the second a dividend $d_2 = (0, 1, -1)$. Thus the portfolio ξ has a dividend of $d = (\xi_1, \xi_2, -\xi_1, -\xi_2)$. It follows that there is no portfolio with a dividend $d > 0$. Hence every asset price vector $P \gg 0$ does not admit arbitrage. Arguing as earlier, choose $\xi^* = (1, 1)$. Then $d^* = \mathbf{D}\xi^* = (1, 1, -2)$. It is readily confirmed that

$$d^{**} = d^* + \begin{bmatrix} 0 \\ 0 \\ 2 \end{bmatrix} = \begin{bmatrix} 1 \\ 1 \\ 0 \end{bmatrix} \notin W^2.$$

Define the set $X = \{\xi \mid \mathbf{D}\xi \leq d^{**}\}$. Then we require that

$$P'\xi \leq P^{**}, \quad \text{for all } \xi \in X. \tag{8.4-5}$$

The set $X = \{\xi \mid \xi_1 \leq 1, \xi_2 \leq 1, -\xi_1 + -\xi_2 \leq 0\}$ is depicted in Figure 8.4-5.

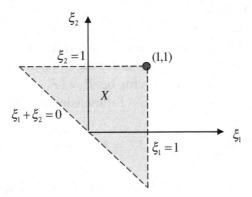

Figure 8.4-5. Bounding the price of the third asset.

Note that for any $P \gg 0$,

$$(1, 1) = \arg \operatorname*{Max}_{\xi} \{P'\xi | \xi \in X.$$

Hence (8.4-5) is satisfied as long as $P^{**} > P_1 + P_2$.
Define the set $Y = \{\xi | \mathbf{D}\xi \geq d^{**}\}$. Then we require that

$$P'\xi \geq P^{**}, \quad \text{for all } \xi \in Y \tag{8.4-6}$$

The set $Y = \{\xi | \xi_1 \geq 1, \xi_2 \geq 1, -\xi_1 - \xi_2 \geq 0\}$ is empty. Thus condition (8.4-6) is satisfied vacuously.

We now follow these same steps to prove the fundamental theorem. Suppose that there are J linearly independent dividend vectors. Label them $1, \ldots, J$. Then we can ignore the other dividend vectors (because they are linear combinations of the J independent vectors) and define $\mathbf{D}$ to be the $S \times J$ dimensional matrix of these J column vectors. We need to show that there exists a state price vector $r \in \mathbb{R}^S$, $r \gg 0$ such that any portfolio $\xi = (\xi_1, \ldots, \xi_J)$ has a market value

$$P'\xi = r' \sum_{a=1}^{J} d_a \xi_a = r'\mathbf{D}\xi.$$

Because it will be important later we note that if $d = \mathbf{D}\xi^1 = \mathbf{D}\xi^2$, then $\mathbf{D}(\xi^1 - \xi^2) = 0$. Because the matrix $\mathbf{D}$ has full rank it follows that $\xi^1 - \xi^2 = 0$. Thus the mapping $\mathbf{D}\xi$ is both continuous and one-to-one. It follows that there exists a continuous inverse one-to-one mapping $\xi(d)$.

Choose any portfolio $\xi^* = (\xi_1^*, \ldots, \xi_J^*) > 0$. We also define $d^* = \mathbf{D}\xi^*$ and $\mathbf{1}_s$ to be the s-th vertex of the unit simplex in $\mathbb{R}^S$. Suppose that $d^{**} = d^* + b\mathbf{1}_s$ is in the set W^J; that is, it is spanned by the J dividend vectors. It follows that $d^{**} - d^* = b\mathbf{1}_s \in W^J$. By hypothesis the span of W^J is less than S so this cannot be true for all s. Then for some t, $d_t^{**} = d_t^* + b\mathbf{1}_t \notin W^J$. Then re-label the components so that $d_S^{**} = d_S^* + b\mathbf{1}_S \notin W^J$.

The key is to show that it is possible to extend no arbitrage from the linear subspace W^J to a linear subspace space W^{J+1} of dimension $J + 1$. Applying this argument $S - J$ times, we can extend no arbitrage to $W^S = \mathbb{R}^S$. We can then use the asset prices in W^S to solve for the implicit state claims prices.

Let the SM equilibrium price vector be $P = (P_1, \ldots, P_J)$. By hypothesis this is strictly positive. Define the $J + 1$ dimensional subspace as

$$W^{J+1} = \left\{ w | w = \sum_{a=1}^{J} d_a \xi_a + \alpha d^{**} = \mathbf{D}\xi + \alpha d^{**}, \text{ for some } (\xi, \alpha). \right\}$$

Let P^{**} be the market value of d^{**}. We must establish that there exists some P^{**} that admits no arbitrage on W^{J+1}.

Any dividend in W^J can be written as $\sum_{a=1}^{J} d_a \xi_a = \mathbf{D}\xi$. For no arbitrage with the $J+1$ securities, the market value of $w = \mathbf{D}\xi + \alpha d^{**}$ must be

$$P'\xi + \alpha P^{**}.$$

Moreover, for no arbitrage, we require that for any $\hat{w} \in W^{J+1}$, if $\hat{w} > 0$, then the value of the dividend stream is strictly positive. That is,

$$\hat{w} = \mathbf{D}\hat{\xi} + \alpha d^{**} > 0 \Rightarrow P'\hat{\xi} + \alpha P^{**} > 0.$$

Step 1 and step 2. These are exactly as in Example 1.

Define the set $X = \{\xi | \mathbf{D}\xi \leq d^{**}\}$. Then we require that

$$P'\xi \leq P^{**}, \quad \text{for all } \xi \in X. \tag{8.4-7}$$

Similarly define the set $Y = \{\xi | \mathbf{D}\xi \geq d^{**}\}$. Then we require that

$$P'\xi \geq P^{**}, \quad \text{for all } \xi \in Y. \tag{8.4-8}$$

Note that for any $\xi^0 \in X$ and $\xi^1 \in Y$, $\mathbf{D}\xi^0 \leq d^{**} \leq \mathbf{D}\xi^1$. If $\mathbf{D}\xi^0 = \mathbf{D}\xi^1$ then $\mathbf{D}\xi^0 = d^{**}$. But this is impossible because $d^{**} \notin W^J$. Then $\mathbf{D}\xi^0 < \mathbf{D}\xi^1$ and so $P'\xi^0 < P'\xi^1$.

Step 3: If Y is empty condition (8.4-8) is satisfied vacuously. Therefore suppose that Y is non-empty.

Let Z be the image of the mapping $\mathbf{D}\xi$ with domain Y. That is $\mathbf{D}z : Y \to Z$. Because Y is closed and the mapping is continuous, Z is closed. Note also that $d \in Z \Rightarrow d \geq d^{**}$ so Z is bounded from below. We have already argued that there is a continuous inverse mapping $\xi(d) : Z \to Y$. Therefore inequality (8.4-8) can be rewritten as follows:

$$P'\xi(d) \geq P^{**}, \quad \text{for all } d \in Z.$$

Because $P'\xi(d)$ is continuous and Z is bounded from below, $P'\xi(d)$ takes on its minimum at some $d^+ \in Z$. Also, because $d^+ \in Z, d^+ \geq d^{**} > d^*$. However $d^* = \mathbf{D}\xi^*$. Then, by no arbitrage

$$\underset{d \in Z}{\text{Min}}\{P'\xi(d)\} > P'\xi^*.$$

Hence we must choose $P^{**} < \underset{d \in Z}{\text{Min}}\{P'\xi(d)\}$.

If X is the empty set we are done. Suppose instead that X is non-empty. Let Z^- be the image of the mapping $\mathbf{D}\xi$ with domain X. Arguing almost exactly as earlier, condition (8.4-7) can be rewritten as

$$P'\xi(d) \leq P^{**}, \quad \text{for all } d \in Z^-.$$

Because $P'\xi(d)$ is continuous and Z^- is bounded from above, $P'\xi(d)$ takes on its maximum at some $d^- \in Z^-$. Appealing to step 2, $P'\xi(d^-) < P'\xi(d^+)$.

Combining these results we have shown that for all $x \in X$, $y \in Y$

$$P'x \leq \operatorname*{Max}_{d \in Z^-}\{P'\xi(d)\} < \operatorname*{Min}_{d \in Z}\{P'\xi(d)\} \leq P'y.$$

Thus conditions (8.4-7) and (8.4-8) hold for any P^{**} satisfying

$$\operatorname*{Max}_{d \in Z^-}\{P'\xi(d)\} < P^{**} < \operatorname*{Min}_{d \in Z}\{P'\xi(d)\}.$$

We have therefore extended no arbitrage from W^J to W^{J+1}. Repeating the argument we can extend no arbitrage to $W^S = \mathbb{R}^S$.

Example 3

Consider an economy with three states and two securities. The first security has a dividend $d_1 = (1, 0, 1)$ and the second a dividend $d_2 = (0, 1, 1)$. The asset prices are $P = (2, 4)$. Consider the portfolio $\xi^* = (1, 1)$. This yields a dividend

$$d^* = \mathbf{D}\xi^* = \begin{bmatrix} 1 & 0 \\ 0 & 1 \\ 1 & 1 \end{bmatrix}\begin{bmatrix} 1 \\ 1 \end{bmatrix} = \begin{bmatrix} 1 \\ 1 \\ 2 \end{bmatrix}. \text{ Then choose } d^{**} = \begin{bmatrix} 1 \\ 1 \\ 2+b \end{bmatrix}.$$

In this case $X = \{\xi \mid \mathbf{D}\xi \leq d^{**}\} = \{\xi \mid \xi_1 \leq 1, \xi_2 \leq 1, \xi_1 + \xi_2 \leq 2 + b\}$ and $Y = \{\xi \mid \mathbf{D}\xi \geq d^{**}\} = \{\xi \mid \xi_1 \geq 1, \xi_2 \geq 1, \xi_1 + \xi_2 \geq 2 + b\}$.

These sets are depicted in Figure 8.4-6. Note that with $P = (2, 4)$, $P'\xi$ takes on its maximum over X at $\xi^* = (1, 1)$, whereas $P'\xi$ takes on its minimum over Y at $(1 + b, 1)$. Thus with $P = (2, 4)$ we can extend no arbitrage to $W^3 = \mathbb{R}^3$ by choosing

$$P^{**} \in (6, 6 + 2b).$$

We write this price as $P^{**} = 6 + 2\beta$ where $\beta \in (0, b)$.

If there exists a vector of implicit state prices r, this must satisfy

$$P' = r'\mathbf{D}.$$

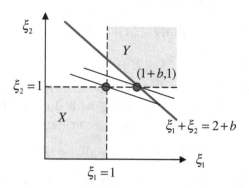

Figure 8.4-6. Bounding the price of the third asset.

That is

$$P' = [2, 4, 6 + 2\beta] = r' \begin{bmatrix} 1 & 0 & 1 \\ 0 & 1 & 1 \\ 1 & 1 & 2+b \end{bmatrix}.$$

Because the columns of **D** are linearly independent, **D** is invertible. Hence

$$r' = [2, 4, 6 + 2\beta] \begin{bmatrix} 1 & 0 & 1 \\ 0 & 1 & 1 \\ 1 & 1 & 2+b \end{bmatrix}^{-1} = [2, 4, 6 + 2\beta] \begin{bmatrix} 1+b & 1 & -1 \\ 1 & 1+b & -1 \\ -1 & -1 & 1 \end{bmatrix} \frac{1}{b}$$

$$= \frac{1}{b}[2(b - \beta), 2b + 2(b - \beta), 2\beta] \quad \beta \in (0, b).$$

Note that by choosing β close to zero we can make the implicit price of state 3 claims arbitrarily small, and by choosing β close to b we can make the implicit price of state 1 claims arbitrarily small. Thus these implicit prices should not be viewed as prices that could be used to guide production decisions. Instead they are accounting prices that can, in principle, be used to test hypotheses about the efficiency of a fixed set of financial instruments.

Exercises

Exercise 8.4-1: Three States and Two Assets Asset 1 has a dividend $d_1 = (-1, 1, 2)$, whereas asset 2 has a dividend $d_2 = (1, 1, 0)$.

(a) Depict the set Ξ of portfolios for which the dividend $d = \mathbf{D}\xi > 0$.
(b) Characterize the set of asset prices that do not admit arbitrage and confirm that the asset price vector $P = (2, 6)$ is a member of this set.
(c) If $P = (2, 6)$ choose $\xi^* = (1, 1)$ and a third asset with dividend $d^{**} = \mathbf{D}\xi^* + 1_3$. Show that $(P_1, P_2, P^{**}) = (2, 6, 11)$ admits no arbitrage.
(d) Solve for a state claims price r with the property that $P_a = r'd_a$ for any asset a, spanned by the two assets.

Exercise 8.4-2: Implicit State Claims Prices Consistent with Asset Prices That Admit No Arbitrage Asset 1 has a dividend $d_1 = (-1, 1, 2)$, whereas asset 2 has a dividend $d_2 = (1, 1, 0)$.

(a) Appeal to your answer to Exercise 8.4-1 to show that $(P_1, P_2, P^{**}) = (2, 6, 8 + b)$ admits no arbitrage if and only if $b \in (0, 4)$. Depict the set Ξ of portfolios for which the dividend $d = \mathbf{D}\xi > 0$.
(b) Choose $\xi^* = (1, 1)$ and a third asset with dividend $d^{**} = \mathbf{D}\xi^* + 1_3$. For each value of b, solve for all the possible state claims prices r with the property that for any asset a, spanned by the two assets $P_a = r'd_a$.

Exercise 8.4-3: An Economy in which All Asset Prices Admit No Arbitrage Asset 1 has a dividend $d_1 = (1, 1, -2)$, whereas asset 2 has a dividend $d_2 = (1, -2, 1)$.

(a) Write down the constraints that must be satisfied so that a portfolio has a dividend $d > 0$ and show that there is no such portfolio.
(b) What asset price admits no arbitrage?
(c) Choose $\xi^* = (1, 1)$ and a third asset with dividend $d^{**} = \mathbf{D}\xi^* + \mathbf{1}_3$ and solve for the asset prices (P_1, P_2, P^{**}) that admit no arbitrage.

References and Selected Historical Reading

Arrow, Kenneth J. (1971). *Essays in the Theory of Risk-Bearing*. Amsterdam: North-Holland.

Arrow, Kenneth J. and Debreu, G. (1954). "Existence of a Competitive Equilibrium for a Competitive Economy." *Econometrica* **22**(3): 265–90.

Chen, Nai-Fu, Roll, Richard, and Ross, Stephen A. (1986). "Economic Forces and the Stock Market." *Journal of Business* **59**(3): 383–403.

Cox, John, Ingersoll, Jonathan, and Ross, Stephen A. (1985). "An Intertemporal General Equilibrium Model of Asset Prices." *Econometrica* **53**: 363–84.

Debreu, Gerard. (1959). *Theory of Value: An Axiomatic Analysis of Economic Equilibrium*. New York: John Wiley and Sons.

Hirshleifer, Jack and Riley, John G. (1994). *The Analytics of Uncertainty and Information*. Cambridge: Cambridge University Press.

Markowitz, H. M. (1959). *Portfolio Selection: Efficient Diversification of Investments*. New York: John Wiley & Sons.

Ross, Stephen. (1976). "The Arbitrage Theory of Capital Asset Pricing." *Journal of Economic Theory* **13**(3): 341–60.

Sharpe, William F. (1964). "Capital Asset Prices: A Theory of Market Equilibrium under Conditions of Risk." *Journal of Finance* **19**(3): 425–42.

9

Strategy

Games in Which Preferences and History Are Common Knowledge

9.1 Strategic Equilibrium

Key ideas: simultaneous move game, normal form, pure and mixed strategies, dominant strategy equilibrium, Nash equilibrium, common knowledge, correlated strategies

In all the previous chapters, the primary focus was on resource allocation via a Walrasian equilibrium (WE). In a WE allocation all players are price takers so there are no strategic issues. However, the price-taking assumption only makes sense if there are a sufficiently large number of competing players. As we have seen, if a production set exhibits increasing returns to scale, one firm can produce at a lower cost than two or more firms so there is a natural monopoly. When a commodity is sold by one firm there is a strategic issue. Instead of being a price taker, the firm is a price setter, choosing a pricing strategy to maximize the firm's payoff. But suppose that production sets in an industry exhibit increasing returns to scale at low outputs and decreasing returns at outputs that are a significant fraction (but less than 50%) of market demand. Then average cost is minimized, with a few firms producing near the average cost-minimizing output. Now strategic issues become much more subtle because a change in the production plan of one firm affects the sales of that firm's competitors. This typically causes a reaction by each competitor. Making a good choice then requires all players to forecast the actions of their competitors. Using the language of social competition (sports, card games, etc.) any such strategic competition is called a game and the participants in the game are called players.

To begin, consider the following simple economic game. There are two players. Player $i, i = 1, 2$ is the manager of firm i. Each player submits the price of the firm's product for the next week to be posted on the web. To keep things simple, each player sets a high price p_H or a low price p_L. Let A_i be the set of possible actions; then $A_i = \{p_H, p_L\}$.

Table 9.1-1a. *Payoff Matrix of Pricing Game*

		Player 2	
		p_H	p_L
Player 1	p_H	4, 4	1, 8
	p_L	8, 1	2, 2

If the information is posted on the web only after both players have submitted a price, then it does not really matter who moves first or whether the players move simultaneously. The games are strategically equivalent. Such games are called *simultaneous move games*. It is this class of games that we consider first.

Simultaneous Move Games

Let $\mathfrak{I}$ be the set of players, so that in the example $\mathfrak{I} = \{1, 2\}$. A list of the actions taken in the game by each player is called an *outcome profile*. Thus, in the example, an outcome profile is an action vector $a = (a_1, a_2)$ where $a_i \in A_i$. We write the set of possible outcome profiles as $A = A_1 \times A_2$. Associated with each outcome profile is a payoff $u_i(a), i \subset \mathfrak{I}$.

In two-player simultaneous move games it is often convenient to represent the game in "matrix" or "normal" form. Each of the possible payoff pairs $u_1(a), u_2(a)$ is listed in a cell in a matrix with the payoff to player 1 listed first (see Table 9.1-1a).[1]

In the example, the payoffs in the game are chosen to reflect a typical situation facing two competing firms. Both would prefer to set a high price resulting in the payoff vector $u(p_H, p_H) = (4, 4)$, rather than set a low price resulting in the payoff vector $u(p_L, p_L) = (2, 2)$. However if one sets a low price and the other sets a high price, the firm with the high price loses almost all of its market share. The payoff vectors are $u(p_L, p_H) = (8, 1)$ and $u(p_H, p_L) = (1, 8)$.

Elimination of Dominated Strategies

For an I player game the set of feasible outcome profiles is $A = A_1 \times \cdots \times A_I \equiv \{(a_1, \ldots, a_I) | a_i \in A_i, i \in \mathfrak{I}\}$.[2]

---

[1] A game of this type is called a prisoner's dilemma game. In such a game both prisoners have the opportunity to keep quiet and get a moderate sentence. However, if one "squeals" he will be set free while the other prisoner will be severely punished. The catch is that if both squeal the sentence will be longer than if both keep quiet.

[2] This is called the Cartesian product set or simply the product set of the action sets of the I players.

Table 9.1-1b. *Deletion of Strictly Dominated Actions*

		Player 2	
		p_H	p_L
Player 1	p_H	4, 4	1, 8
	p_L	8, 1	2, 2

Define $a_{-i} \equiv (a_1, \ldots, a_{i-1}, a_{i+1}, \ldots, a_I)$ to be a feasible action of player i's competitors. Using the product notation, the set of such feasible actions is

$$A_{-i} \equiv A_1 \times \cdots \times A_{i-1} \times A_{i+1} \times \cdots \times A_I = \mathop{\times}_{\substack{j=1 \\ j \neq i}}^{I} A_j.$$

An action $a_i \in A_i$ is said to be strictly dominated if there is some alternative action $\bar{a}_i \in A_i$ that yields a strictly higher payoff regardless of all the other players' actions. The action a_i is said to be weakly dominated if $\bar{a}_i$ yields a payoff that is at least as high regardless of other's actions and yields a strictly higher payoff for at least one action of the opponents.

Definition: Strictly and Weakly Dominated Action Player i's action a_i is strictly dominated by $\bar{a}_i$ if $u_i(\bar{a}_i, a_{-i}) > u_i(a_i, a_{-i})$, $\forall a_{-i} \in A_{-i}$.

Player i's action a_i is weakly dominated by $\bar{a}_i$ if $u_i(\bar{a}_i, a_{-i}) \geq u_i(a_i, a_{-i})$, $\forall a_{-i} \in A_{-i}$ and the inequality is strict for some $a_{-i} \in A_{-i}$.

It is very natural to assume that a player would never knowingly play a strictly dominated action. Suppose that after all dominated actions are eliminated only one action remains. This action then seems a highly plausible outcome of the game. In the simple pricing example it is easy to check that, regardless of the price chosen by player 2, player 1 has a strictly higher payoff when she chooses the low price, so choosing the high price is a strictly dominated action. Given the symmetry of the game the same is true for player 2. Deleting these actions as depicted in Table 9.1-1b, leaves only one possible outcome: Both players choose the low price.

We now modify the game and assume that there are three possible prices, p_H, p_M, and p_L. The payoff matrix is shown in Table 9.1-2a. For each player the one strictly dominated action is choosing the high price. Eliminating this strategy yields the payoff matrix shown in Table 9.1-2b.

Now choosing the low price strictly dominates choosing the medium price, and so p_L is the unique price surviving the successive (or "iterated") elimination of strictly dominated actions.

Table 9.1-2a. *Iterated Strict Dominance*

		Player 2		
		p_H	p_M	p_L
Player 1	p_H	100, 100	30, 150	−40, 90
	p_M	150, 30	50, 50	5, 60
	p_L	90, −40	60, 5	10, 10

Pure and Mixed Strategies

Thus far we have considered strategies that involve choosing a single action. This is called a pure strategy. More generally, players may have an interest in randomizing over their actions. Such a strategy is called a mixed strategy.[3] Given the finite action set $A_i = \{a_{i1}, \ldots, a_{im_i}\}$, a mixed strategy assigns a probability to each of the possible actions. Player i's strategy set S_i is then the set of all probability measures in

$$\Delta(A_i) = \left\{ \pi \,|\, \pi \geq 0, \sum_{j=1}^{m_i} \pi_j = 1 \right\}.$$

As Table 9.1-3 shows, we can sometimes eliminate an action because it is dominated by a mixed strategy. Player 1 chooses from the action set $A_1 = \{Top, Middle, Bottom\}$ and player 2 from action set $A_2 = \{Left, Right\}$.

As you can readily confirm, there is no pure strategy that strictly dominates any action. However, if player 1 mixes between *Middle* and *Bottom* with the probabilities indicated, her payoff is $0 \times (-1) + \frac{2}{3}(-2) + \frac{1}{3}(4) = 0$ if player 2 chooses *Left* and is $0 \times (-1) + \frac{2}{3}(4) + \frac{1}{3}(-8) = 0$ if player 2 chooses *Right*. Thus *Top* is strictly dominated by this mixed strategy. Once *Top* is eliminated, *Left* dominates *Right* for player 2. And if player 2 plays *Left*, player 1's dominant strategy is *Bottom*. Thus the only strategy surviving after the iterated elimination of dominated strategies is (*Bottom, Left*).

We now provide a formal definition of a dominant strategy equilibrium.

Table 9.1-2b. *Payoff Matrix after Deletion of Dominated Actions*

		Player 2	
		p_M	p_L
Player 1	p_M	50, 50	5, 60
	p_L	60, 5	10, 10

---

[3] If a player places strictly positive probability on every action in his action set, the strategy is said to be totally (or completely) mixed.

Table 9.1-3. Top *is a Dominated Action*

			Player 2	
			Left	Right
	0	*Top*	−1, 6	−1, 8
Player 1	2/3	*Middle*	−2, 1	4, 0
	1/3	*Bottom*	4, 2	−8, 1

Definition: Strict (Weak) Dominant Strategy Equilibrium The outcome profile $(\bar{a}_1, \ldots, \bar{a}_I)$ is a strict (weak) dominant strategy equilibrium if for all $i \in \mathfrak{I}$, every other action in player i's action set A_i is strictly (weakly) dominated.

Definition: Iterated Strict (Weak) Dominance Equilibrium The outcome profile $(\bar{a}_1, \ldots, \bar{a}_I)$ is an iterated strict (weak) dominant strategy equilibrium if for all $i \in \mathfrak{I}$, every other action in player i's action set A_i is iteratively strictly (weakly) dominated.

Consider next the game with payoff matrix in Table 9.1-4. We argue that it is not clear that the weak dominance equilibrium is a good predictor of how a game will be played, especially if the players can communicate before playing the game. In Table 9.1-4, note that the row b payoff vector $(5, 2, 3)$ is strictly greater than the row a payoff vector $(4, 1, 0)$ and is greater than the row c payoff vector $(2, 1, 3)$. Given the symmetry of the payoffs, the same is true for the column b payoff vector. Thus for each player strategy, b strictly dominates strategy a and weakly dominates strategy c.

This suggests that players will eliminate strategies a and c so that the payoff for each player is 2. Yet note that each would strictly prefer to pay strategy c if the other player did so. Suppose that the two players discuss this and verbally agree to play c. Would player 1 have an incentive to violate the verbal agreement if he thought that player 2 would keep it? Note that conditional on player 2 choosing c, choosing c is best for player 1. So there is no incentive for player 1 to violate the agreement. An identical argument holds

Table 9.1-4. *Equilibrium in Weakly Dominated Strategies*

		Player 2		
		A	*b*	*c*
	a	4, 4	1, 5	0, 2
Player 1	*b*	5, 1	2, 2	3, 1
	c	2, 0	1, 3	3, 3

for player 2. Thus there is good reason to believe that both players would keep their tentative agreement and choose strategy c.

Mutual Best Response Equilibrium (Nash Equilibrium)

Although there are some important cases of iterated dominant strategy equilibria in economics, they are the exception rather than the rule. Thus we need a weaker strategic equilibrium concept.

Consider the following thought experiment for a game to be played by Alex and Bev. Before the game is played, each is invited to submit a proposed strategy. These proposed strategies are then revealed to the players. Alex can ask himself whether it is a best response for him to do what he said he would do if Bev does what she said she would do. Alex can also ask himself whether it will be Bev's best response to do what she said she would do if he does what he said he would do. If the answer to both of these questions is yes, then the announced strategies are called mutual best responses.

With more than two players, exactly the same thought experiment is possible. A player can ask whether it is a best response for him to do what he said he would do, assuming that all the other players do what they said they would do. The player can also ask this same question about each of the other players. If the answer to every question is yes, then the announced strategies are mutual best responses. Strategies that are mutual best response are called Nash equilibrium (NE) strategies.[4]

To illustrate we examine a simple partnership game. Two players have an equal share in a partnership. Let a_i be the effort level of player i. Total revenue is $R(a) = 12a_1a_2$ and the cost to player i is $C_i(a_i) = a_i^3$. For simplicity we assume that $A_i = \{1, 2, 3\}$. Each player gets a 50 percent share of total revenue. Neither the effort level a_i nor the cost $C_i(a_i)$ is observed by the partner (player $-i$). Thus the two players play a simultaneous move game. The payoff matrix is shown in Table 9.1-5 where the payoff to player i is $u_i(a_i, a_{-i}) = \frac{1}{2}R(a) - C_i(a_{-i})$.

Table 9.1-5. *Partnership Game*

		Player 2		
		$a_2 = 1$	$a_2 = 2$	$a_2 = 3$
Player 1	$a_1 = 1$	5, 5	11, 4	17, −9
	$a_1 = 2$	4, 11	16, 16	28, 9
	$a_1 = 3$	−9, 17	9, 28	27, 27

---

[4] The mutual best response equilibrium concept was first used formally by Augustin Cournot (1842) in his analysis of duopoly. However it was named after John Nash who was the first to apply a fixed-point theorem to establish a general existence theorem for simultaneous move games.

It is readily confirmed that choosing effort level 3 is strictly dominated. However, after elimination of this strategy, neither of the other strategies is dominated. Thus we look instead for strategies that are mutual best responses. Because the partnership game is symmetric, it is natural to begin by looking for a symmetric NE. Consider the strategy profile $(a_1, a_2) = (2, 2)$. With player 2 choosing $a_2 = 2$, player 1's best response is $a_1 = 2$ and vice versa. Therefore the action profile $(a_1, a_2) = (2, 2)$ is an NE. Arguing in exactly the same way it is easy to confirm that the action profile $(a_1, a_2) = (1, 1)$ is also an NE.

In addition to these two pure strategy equilibria there is also a mixed strategy NE. If a player's best response is to randomize between two or more pure strategies, the payoff must be the same when he plays each of the pure strategies. Then for a mixed strategy NE a player will never play a strictly dominated strategy. Therefore if player 2 plays a mixed strategy she must mix over strategies 1 and 2. Let π be the probability that player 2 plays strategy 1. Player 1's expected payoff if he chooses strategy 1 is therefore

$$u_1(a_1, \pi) = \pi 5 + (1 - \pi)11 = 11 - 6\pi.$$

And if he chooses strategy 2 his expected payoff is

$$u_1(a_2, \pi) = \pi 4 + (1 - \pi)16 = 16 - 12\pi.$$

Therefore $u_1(a_1, \pi) - u_1(a_2, \pi) = 6\pi - 5$ and so player 1 is indifferent if $\pi = \frac{5}{6}$. A symmetric argument holds for player 2. Thus a mixed strategy NE is for each player to play strategy 1 with probability $\frac{5}{6}$ and strategy 2 with probability $\frac{1}{6}$.

The continuous version of this game is also easy to analyze. Player i's payoff is

$$u_i(a_i, a_{-i}) = \tfrac{1}{2} R(a) - C_i(a_i) = 6a_i a_{-i} - a_i^3.$$

We look for an equilibrium in pure strategies. For any a_{-i}, player i's set of best responses is

$$BR(a_{-i}) = \arg \operatorname*{Max}_{a_i}\{u_i(a_i, a_{-i})\}.$$

First-Order Conditions

$$\frac{\partial u_i}{\partial a_i} = 6a_{-i} - 3a_i^2 = 0, \quad i = 1, 2.$$

Solving, the unique best response is $a_i = BR_i(a_{-i}) = \sqrt{2a_{-i}}$.

Therefore if $(\bar{a}_1, \bar{a}_2)$ is an NE, $\bar{a}_1 = \sqrt{2\bar{a}_2}$ and $\bar{a}_2 = \sqrt{2\bar{a}_1}$. Solving, $(\bar{a}_1, \bar{a}_2) = (2, 2)$.

Formally, for any strategy profile $s \in S = \Delta_1(A_1) \times \cdots \times \Delta_I(A_I)$ let $BR_i(s_{-i})$ be the set of strategies for player i that maximize player i's payoff. We can then define a *best response mapping* as follows:

$$BR(s) = (BR_1(s_{-1}), \ldots, BR_I(s_{-I})).$$

If for each i $s_i \in BR_i(s_{-i})$ the strategies are mutual best responses; that is, the strategy profile is an NE.

Definition: Nash Equilibrium For a simultaneous move game played by players $1, \ldots, I$, the strategy profile $\bar{s} = (\bar{s}_1, \ldots, \bar{s}_I)$ is a Nash equilibrium if the strategies are mutual best responses. That is, for each $i \in \mathfrak{I}$ and all $a_i \in A_i$, $u_i(\bar{s}_i, \bar{s}_{-i}) \geq u_i(a_i, \bar{s}_{-i})$.

Note that the definition of NE considers only responses that are pure strategies. However, any mixed strategy s_i is a vector of probabilities $\pi(a_i)$ over the action set A_i. Then if $\bar{s}$ is an NE strategy profile, by the linearity of expected utility we have that

$$u_i(s_i, \bar{s}_{-i}) = \sum_{a_i \in A_i} \pi(a_i) u_i(a_i, \bar{s}_{-i})$$

$$\leq \sum_{a_i \in A_i} \pi(a_i) u_i(\bar{s}_i, \bar{s}_{-i}), \text{ because, } \bar{s}_i \text{ is a best response,}$$

$$= u_i(\bar{s}_i, \bar{s}_{-i}) \text{ because } \sum_{a_i \in A_i} \pi(a_i) = 1.$$

Thus if the conditions for an NE hold, there is no deviation by a single player (pure or mixed) that yields a higher expected payoff.

Common Knowledge of the Game

In price theoretic analysis, players make choices consistent with their preferences and opportunities (constraints). These choices require a knowledge of market prices but no knowledge of the preferences of other players. In game theoretic analysis we make much stronger assumptions about the knowledge of the participating players. Typically the outcome of the game depends on the actions taken by all the participants. Thus player i's choice requires him to form beliefs about the possible actions that will be taken by his competitors. To do so, player i must know the other players' actions sets and their preferences over these actions. Thus we assume that the game being played (I, A, u) is known by all the players. Yet even this is not enough. Player i must also know that the other players know the game being played. And he must also know that others know that he knows that others know the game being played and so on. Players who have all these higher orders of knowledge of the game are said to have common knowledge of the game.

To see why these higher levels of common knowledge are crucial, consider the following game. Alex and Bev both have a coin. Each writes down either heads or tails. (These are the players' simultaneous actions.) The coins are then tossed. Each coin will come up heads with probability 1/3. If the players' actions and the two coins all coincide they each receive $1,000. Otherwise they get nothing.

If players have common knowledge that each coin will come up heads with probability 1/3, they have common knowledge that the probability of two heads is (1/3)*(1/3) = 1/9 and common knowledge that the probability of two tails is (2/3)*(2/3) = 4/9. Thus they both write down tails and win $1,000 with probability 4/9.

Suppose that we drop the common knowledge assumption and make the following alternative assumptions. Alex correctly believes that both coins will come up heads with probability 1/3. However, Alex incorrectly believes that Bev believes that Alex's coin will come up heads with probability 1. Similarly Bev correctly believes that both coins will come up heads with probability 1/3. However, Bev incorrectly believes that Alex believes that Bev's coin will come up heads with probability 1.

If Alex believes that Bev's coin will come up heads for sure, he must write down heads to have a positive probability of winning. Given that this is what Bev believes about Alex, Bev will infer that Alex will write down heads. Then she can only win by writing down heads as well. The same argument holds for Alex so he will write down heads as well. The coins are tossed and both come up heads with probability (1/3)*(1/3)=1/9. Thus the players win $1,000 with probability 1/9.

As we see later, we can relax the common knowledge somewhat and assume that players know some parameters of the game but are uncertain about other parameters. But then we need to impose the common knowledge assumption on the beliefs that each player has about the unknown parameters.

Common Knowledge of Rationality

Rational players are those who makes choices consistent with their preferences. Just as with the parameters of the game, there are higher orders of rationality. It is not enough for player i to know that other players choose according to their preferences. She must also know that the other players know that she is rational as well. And she must also know that others know that she knows that they are rational and so on. Players who have all these higher orders of rationality are said to have common knowledge of rationality.

Common Knowledge of the Equilibrium Strategy Profile

It is important to note that appealing to the NE as a solution concept requires an even stronger common knowledge assumption: knowledge that the other players are playing their equilibrium strategies. This is an especially strong assumption if there are multiple equilibria. It is far from clear how beliefs can converge on any particular equilibrium. In some environments this issue can be ameliorated by pre-play communication. Suppose that there are three equilibria, but one has some "nice" property. For example, one equilibrium might be Pareto-preferred over the others or one might be seen as fairer than the others. Discussion of the "nice" property of an equilibrium might well persuade all players that it will be played.

Even if there is a unique NE its predictive power relies on the common knowledge assumption. For without it, a player may believe that some of his opponents are cooperating rather than independently pursuing their self-interests. Given such a belief, the player left out in the cold will typically not want to play his NE strategy.

To illustrate, consider the following simultaneous move three-player matching game. Each player must choose either heads or tails. Player 3's choice determines which of the two matrixes shown in Table 9.1-6 is the payoff matrix.

Note that player 3's strictly dominant strategy is to choose heads so we consider only the left matrix. It is readily checked that the unique NE strategy is for both player 1 and player 2 to choose heads. The NE payoff vector is therefore (2, 2, 2). However, note that when player 1 chooses heads, players 2 and 3 can do better than in the NE if they can agree to both play tails because each then gets a payoff of 3. And if they do both play tails, player 1 is better off switching to tails. Thus choosing heads is a best response for player 1 only given that it is common knowledge that the strategy profile is for everyone to choose heads.

Table 9.1-6. *Three-player penny matching game*

		Player 2				Player 2	
		Heads	Tails			Heads	Tails
Player 1	Heads	2, 2, 2	1, 0, 4	Player 1	Heads	0, 0, 0	−1, 3, 3
	Tails	0, 1, 1	0, 2, 1		Tails	0, 0, 0	0, 0, 0
		Player 3 Chooses Heads				Player 3 Chooses Tails	

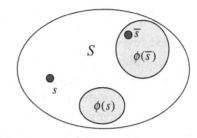

Figure 9.1-1. Fixed point.

Existence of a Nash Equilibrium

For games with finite strategy sets we can appeal directly to Kakutani's fixed point theorem discussed in Chapter 5.

Kakutani's Fixed Point Theorem If $S \subset \mathbb{R}^n$ is compact and convex and if ϕ is an upper hemi-continuous correspondence from S to S such that for all $x \in S$ the set $\phi(x)$ is non-empty and convex, then ϕ has a fixed point.

The mapping $\phi : S \to S$ is depicted in Figure 9.1-1. The correspondence is said to have a fixed point if for some $\bar{s} \in S, s \in \phi(\bar{s})$.

Consider any finite game $(\mathfrak{I}, A, u)$. Note that a strategy for player $i \in \mathfrak{I}$ is a probability measure in $\Delta(A_i)$, the set of all probability measures on player i's feasible actions. Then the strategy set $S = \Delta(A_1) \times \cdots \times \Delta(A_I)$ is compact and convex. For each $i \in \mathfrak{I}$ and any strategy profile $s = (s_1, \ldots, s_I)$, let $BR_i^*(s_{-i})$ be the set of pure strategies that are best responses for player i. Because the game is finite, $BR_i^*(s_{-i})$ is non-empty and finite. Because all the elements of $BR_i^*(s_{-i})$ have the same payoff, all probabilistic mixtures of these actions also have the same payoff and are therefore best responses as well. Let $BR_i(s_{-i})$ be the full set of best responses, pure and mixed. Because the mixed strategies are all the convex combinations of the pure strategies, $BR_i(s_{-i})$ is compact and convex. Then we define the compact and convex response mapping:

$$\phi(s) = (BR_1(s_{-1}), \ldots, BR_I(s_{-I})).$$

Appealing to the Theorem of the Maximum,[5] the best response mapping is upper hemi-continuous. Then the mapping $\phi : S \to S$ satisfies all the requirements of Kakutani's theorem. Therefore we have the following result, first proved by Nash (1950).

Proposition 9.1-1: Existence of Equilibrium
In a game with finite action sets, if players can choose either pure or mixed strategies, there exists an NE.

[5] See Appendix C.

Existence When the Action Sets are Compact and Convex Subsets of $\mathbb{R}^n$

A best response is the solution of a maximization problem. If the feasible set of a player is a closed convex subset of some Euclidean space, we can exploit the tools of calculus to characterize the set of best responses. Thus it is very often preferable to model games in which players make choices over compact, convex subsets of Euclidean space rather than over finite action sets. As we now show, under such an assumption there is very often an NE in pure strategies.

Suppose that player $i \in \mathfrak{I}$ has an action set $A_i \subset \mathbb{R}^n$ that is compact and convex. Suppose also that each player's utility function $u_i(a)$ is continuous. Then for each a_{-i} there is a solution to the maximum problem

$$\underset{a_i \in A_i}{\text{Max}}\, u(a_i, a_{-i}).$$

The set of all such solutions is the best response mapping $BR_i(a_{-i})$ and so this mapping is non-empty. Appealing to the Theorem of the Maximum, the best response mapping $BR_i(a_{-i})$ is also upper hemi-continuous.

Because we are considering only pure strategies, we write the strategy set as $A = A_1 \times \cdots \times A_I$ and define

$$\phi = (BR_1(a_{-1}), \ldots, BR_I(a_{-I})).$$

The best response functions are upper hemi-continuous therefore $\phi : A \to A$ is upper hemi-continuous. This is still not quite enough. Kakutani's fixed point theorem requires that the mapping ϕ be convex valued. Hence we have the following theorem.

Proposition 9.1-2: Existence of an Equilibrium in Pure Strategies
Let $(\mathfrak{I}, A, u)$ be a game in which $A_i \subset \mathbb{R}^n$, $i \in \mathfrak{I}$ is compact and convex and u is continuous. If the best responses sets $BR_i(a_{-i}) \subset A_i$, $i \in \mathfrak{I}$ are convex, there exists an NE in pure strategies.

A special case in which the best responses sets are convex is when the best response mapping is single-valued.[6] More generally, suppose $u_i(a_i, a_{-i})$ is quasi-concave in a_i. Suppose that a_i^0 and $a_i^1 \in BR_i(a_{-i})$. Then $u_i(a_i^0, a_{-i}) = u_i(a_i^1, a_{-i})$. Given the quasi-concavity if $u_i(a_i, a_{-i})$, it follows that for all convex combinations a_i^λ, $u_i(a_i^\lambda, a_{-i}) \geq u_i(a_i^0, a_{-i})$. Hence all convex combinations must be best responses as well. We therefore have the following corollary.

Corollary 9.1-3: Existence of an Equilibrium in Pure Strategies Let $(\mathfrak{I}, A, u)$ be a game in which $A_i \subset \mathbb{R}^n$, $i \in \mathfrak{I}$ is compact and u is continuous. If

---

[6] This is the case, for example, if $u_i(a_i, a_{-i})$, $i \in \mathfrak{I}$ is a strictly quasi-concave function of a_i.

(i) the best response mapping is single-valued or (ii) $u_i(a_i, a_{-i}) \, i \in \mathfrak{I}$ is quasi-concave in a_i, there exists an NE in pure strategies.

Correlated Mixed Strategies

Consider the simple two-player simultaneous move pricing game with payoff matrix in Table 9.1-7.

There are two asymmetric equilibria in which one player has a payoff of 140 and the other 40. There is also a third symmetric equilibrium in which both players choose *High* with probability $p = \frac{1}{5}$ and *Middle* with probability $1 - p = \frac{4}{5}$. The equilibrium expected payoff is 52. Note that the average payoff is higher in the asymmetric equilibria. Both players are therefore better off if they can find some way to each have an equal chance of being the player to take the favored action and receive the high payoff. Putting this another way, suppose that the players find some way of randomizing over which NE strategy to play. Then both can achieve an expected payoff of 90.

Public Randomization Device

The local newspaper provides the players with a simple "correlation device" that achieves this goal. Each day the winning lottery number is announced. The players then agree that if the winning number is odd, it will be player 1 who will choose *Middle* and player 2 who will choose *High*. If the winning number is even the choices will be switched. If each player believes that the other player will follow the agreement, then his best response is to follow the agreement as well. The correlated strategies are therefore NE strategies.

Private Randomization Device

More generally a correlation device instructs the players how to play. The players design a software program to send them messages with predetermined probabilities. Each receives a private message.

Consider the game with a payoff matrix in Table 9.1-7. With probability a player 1 receives a message to choose *High* and player 2 does also. With probability b the correlation device recommends *High* to the row player and

Table 9.1-7. *Correlated Equilibrium*

		Player 2 (Bev)		Probabilities	
		High	Middle	High	Middle
Player 1	*High*	*100, 100*	*40, 140*	a	b
(Alex)	*Middle*	*140, 40*	*30, 30*	c	d

Middle to the column player and so on. Of course, the probabilities must add to 1 so $a + b + c + d = 1$. Thus using the lottery as a correlation device means agreeing to choose $(a, b, c, d) = (0, \frac{1}{2}, \frac{1}{2}, 0)$.

Given the possibility of correlating play in a game, the natural next question is whether the player could do even better using some different correlation device. Because the payoffs are symmetric in this game we consider symmetric equilibria so $b = c$. Also, because neither player wants the outcome in the bottom right corner we will consider correlated equilibria with $d = 0$ so $b = c = \frac{1}{2}(1 - a)$.

Suppose that the row player believes that the column player will follow the recommendation. If the row player receives the recommendation *Middle* she knows that the column player has received a recommendation to play *High* (because $d = 0$) so *Middle* is her best response. If the row player receives the recommendation *High*, she knows that the column player has received the recommendation *High* with probability $a/(a + b)$ (because of Bayes' Rule) and *Middle* with probability $1 - a/(a + b)$. If she plays *High* her expected payoff is

$$100\frac{a}{a + b} + 40\left(1 - \frac{a}{a + b}\right) = 40 + 120\frac{a}{1 + a}, \quad \text{because } a + b = \frac{1 + a}{2}.$$

If she chooses *Middle* her expected payoff is

$$140\frac{a}{a + b} + 30\left(1 - \frac{a}{a + b}\right) = 30 + 220\frac{a}{1 + a}.$$

Thus accepting the recommendation is a best response if

$$40 + 120\frac{a}{1 + a} \geq 30 + 220\frac{a}{1 + a}; \quad \text{that is, } a \leq 1/9.$$

Given the symmetry of the game it follows that the strategies recommended by the correlation device are NE strategies as long as $a \leq 1/9$ From Table 9.1-7, the expected value of the game to each player is $a100 + \frac{1}{2}(1 - a)40 + \frac{1}{2}(1 - a)140 = 90 + 10a$. Thus expected payoffs are maximized by setting $a = 1/9$ and $b = c = \frac{1}{2}(1 - a) = 4/9$.

Note that the set of correlated equilibria includes the three uncorrelated equilibria. For the two pure strategy equilibria, set b or $d = 1$. For the mixed strategy equilibrium, set $a = p^2 = 1/25$, $b = c = p(1 - p) = 4/25$, and $d = (1 - p)^2 = 16/25$.

Exercises

Exercise 9.1-1: Rock, Scissors, Paper Modified to Favor Player 2 Consider Rock, Scissors, Paper modified as indicated in Table 9.1-8. Note that while player 2 gets a double payoff if he plays scissors and player 1 chooses paper,

Table 9.1-8. *Rock, Scissors, Paper with Player 2 Favored*

			Player 2		
			p_2	q_2	$1 - p_2 - q_2$
			Paper	Scissors	Rock
	p_1	*Paper*	0, 0	−24, 24	12, −12
Player 1	q_1	*Scissors*	12, −12	0, 0	−12, 12
	$1 - p_1 - q_1$	*Rock*	−12, 12	12, −12	0, 0

this is not true for player 1. Then player 1 would be unlikely to agree to play unless he were paid something in advance. The question is how much player 2 should be willing to pay to play.

(a) Suppose player 1 plays a mixed strategy as indicated. Write down player 2's payoffs and hence show that there is a unique mixed strategy for player 1 that leaves player 2 indifferent between all three of his strategies.
(b) Show that player 2's expected payoff is $1 if player 1 uses this strategy. What is player 1's expected payoff?
(c) How much should player 2 be willing to pay in advance to play this game?
(d) Solve for the probabilities p_2, q_2, which, if adopted by player 2, will make player 1 indifferent between the three strategies.

Exercise 9.1-2: Vickrey Bidding Game Bidder 1 values an item for sale at 7 (thousand) and bidder 2 at 8 (thousand). Each must submit a sealed bid of 5 thousand or higher in increments of 1 thousand. Because no one values the item higher than 8 we consider only bids up to and including 8. The bidder who bids the most is the winner, but only has to pay the second highest bid. If the bids are the same, the winner is selected by a coin toss and the winner pays the common bid. Bids are submitted in secret.

(a) Explain why the payoff matrix must be as depicted in Table 9.1-9.
(b) Show that (5, 8) and (6, 8) and (7, 8) are all NE.
(c) Are there other equilibria in pure strategies?
(d) Show that one of the NEs is an equilibrium in weakly dominant strategies.

Table 9.1-9. *Vickrey Auction*

		Bidder 2			
		5	6	7	8
Bidder 1	5	1, 1.5	0, 3	0, 3	0, 3
	6	2, 0	0.5, 1	0, 2	0, 2
	7	2, 0	1, 0	0, 0.5	0, 1
	8	2, 0	1, 0	0, 0	−0.5, 0

Exercise 9.1-3: Cournot Duopoly and Iterated Strict Dominance Consider the following Cournot duopoly game. There are two firms. Cost is zero. Each firm chooses its output. Given the strategy profile $q = (q_1, q_2)$, the demand price is $p(q) = 1 - q_1 - q_2$. Because price is negative for $q_i > 1$, we may take the strategy set of each player to be $A_i = [0, 1]$.

(a) Show that the payoffs can be written as follows:

$$u_i(q_i, q_{-i}) = (1 - q_{-i})q_i - q_i^2.$$

(b) Hence explain why $BR_i(q_{-i}) = \frac{1}{2}(1 - q_{-i})$ and show that the NE strategy profile is $q^N = (1/3, 1/3)$.

(c) Show that for any $q_{-i} \in A_{-i}$, $BR_i(q_{-i}) \in [0, 1/2]$. Because $u_i(q_i, q_{-i})$ is a strictly concave function of q_i, show that for each player all the outputs on the interval $(1/2, 1]$ are strictly dominated. Eliminating strictly dominated strategies, it follows that each player will choose an action $q_i \in [0, 1/2]$.

(d) Define $A(\alpha) = [1/3 - \alpha, 1/3 + \alpha]$. From (c) $q_i \in A(1/3)$. If $q_{-i} \in A(\alpha)$, show that $BR_i \in A(\alpha/2) = [1/3 - \alpha/2, 1/3 + \alpha/2]$.

(e) Repeating this argument show that $BR_i \in A(\alpha/2^k) = [1/3 - \alpha/2^k, 1/3 + \alpha/2^k]$.

Hence show that any $q_i \neq 1/3$ is eliminated by iterated strict dominance.

Exercise 9.1-4: Odds and Evens Consider the following simplified version of the widely used "Odds and Evens" game. The players simultaneously call out either "1, 2, 3 Odds!" or "1, 2, 3, Evens!" and raise either one or two fingers. If they make the same call there is no winner. If they make different calls and the number of fingers is odd the player calling "odds" wins. If the number of fingers is even the player calling "even" wins.[7] In this case an action is a number of fingers and a call. Thus each player has four possible actions. The payoff matrix is shown in Table 9.1-10.

(a) Establish that there are no weakly dominated strategies and no NE in pure strategies.

Table 9.1-10. *Odds and Evens game*

			Player 2			
			p_2	q_2	r_2	$1 - p_2 - q_2 - r_2$
			O1	O2	E1	E2
	p_1	O1	0, 0	0, 0	$-1, 1$	$1, -1$
Player 1	q_1	O2	0, 0	0, 0	$1, -1$	$-1, 1$
	r_1	E1	$1, -1$	$-1, 1$	0, 0	0, 0
	$1 - p_1 - q_1 - r_1$	E2	$-1, 1$	$1, -1$	0, 0	0, 0

---

[7] This game was played by the Romans. We have simplified it here by having only one round of the game. Typically the game continues until one or the other player is the winner.

(b) Show that there is a continuum of NE in completely mixed strategies (all strategies played with strictly positive probability).
(c) Show that there are at least six NEs in which each player plays two strategies with positive probability.
(d) Use your result from (b) to draw a conclusion about an NE of the standard "Odds and Evens" game in which play continues until there is a winner.

9.2 Games with a History

Key ideas: finitely repeated game, backward induction, equilibrium threats, extensive form, game tree, sequential move game, sub-game perfect equilibrium, one-stage deviation principle

We now consider games in which not all actions are simultaneous. Thus players moving later can base their strategies on the prior actions of players moving earlier; that is, on the history of the game. Initially we consider finitely repeated games. In the first round or "stage," a simultaneous move game is played. Initially we assume that players observe the prior actions of all their opponents.[8] Let h_i^t be the history of the game as observed by player i before play in stage t. Thus, when the second stage is played, player i's history h_i^2 is the first-stage action profile a^1 and in the t-th stage player i's history is the history of all actions $a^1, \ldots, a^{t-1}$. In each stage the simultaneous stage game is repeated. A stage t strategy is then a function of the history of the game. Thus, in the case of a two-stage repeated game, player i's strategy is a choice $s_i \equiv (s_i^1, s_i^2(h_i^2)) \in S_i \times S_i$.

We write a strategy profile of the T-stage repeated game as $s = (s^1, \ldots, s^T)$ and the set of all strategies profile as $\mathcal{S} = S^1 \times \cdots \times S^T$ where $S^t = \underset{i \in I}{\times} S_i, t = 1, \ldots, T$. The stage t payoff to player $i \in \mathcal{I}$ is $u_i(s^t)$. Future payoffs are discounted at the rate δ. Therefore if the strategy profile is $s \in \mathcal{S}$, the payoff to player i is

$$U_i(s) = \sum_{t=1}^{T} \delta^{t-1} u_i(s^t).$$

Strategic competition among firms typically involves a competition for market share over many periods. In addition to the competition among active firms, there is often the possibility of entry by new firms in later periods. If goods are non-durable each stage of the game may be the same or similar to previous stages. However, as we see, the history of the game can

---

[8] A player who is randomizing could also make his mixed strategy public by allowing a third party to monitor his randomization device. For the cases we consider, the equilibrium strategies are pure strategies so observing past actions is the same as observing past strategies.

affect play in future stages even in this special case. More complex issues arise if goods are durable and new products will become available in future stages. Then a firm introducing a new higher quality product is competing not only with competitors but also with the market for the older versions of its own product.

We will argue that if $\bar{s}^t, t = 1, \ldots, T$ is an NE of the t-th stage game then $\bar{s} = (\bar{s}^1, \ldots, \bar{s}^T)$ is an NE of the repeated game.

Suppose that $\bar{s} \in S$ is an NE strategy profile. Consider a deviation s_i by player i. Then

$$U_i(s_i, \bar{s}_{-i}) - U_i(\bar{s}_i, \bar{s}_{-i}) = \sum_{t=1}^{T} \delta^{t-1} \left[u_i\left(s_i^t, \bar{s}_{-i}^t\right) - u_i\left(\bar{s}_i^t, \bar{s}_{-i}^t\right) \right].$$

By hypothesis $\bar{s}^t$ is an NE of the t-th stage game. Therefore $u_i(s_i^t, \bar{s}_{-i}^t) - u_i(\bar{s}_i^t, \bar{s}_{-i}^t) \leq 0$. Because this is true for all t, it follows that $U_i(s_i, \bar{s}_{-i}) - U_i(\bar{s}_i, \bar{s}_{-i}) \leq 0$.

We have therefore proved part (i) of the following proposition.

Proposition 9.2-1: Nash Equilibria of a Finitely Repeated Game
Suppose that $\bar{s}^t, t = 1, \ldots, T$ is an NE of the stage game. Then (i) the strategy profile $\bar{s} = (\bar{s}^1, \ldots, \bar{s}^T)$ is an NE of the T-stage repeated game and (ii) if $\hat{s}$ is the unique NE of the stage game then $(\hat{s}, \ldots, \hat{s})$ is the unique NE of the repeated game.

To prove (ii) let $\bar{s} \in S$ be an NE of the repeated game. Consider a deviation by player i in stage t. That is, s_i agrees with $\bar{s}_i$ except in stage t. Then

$$U_i(s_i, \bar{s}_{-i}) - U_i(\bar{s}_i, \bar{s}_{-i}) = \delta^{t-1} \left[u_i\left(s_i^t, \bar{s}_{-i}^t\right) - u_i\left(\bar{s}_i^t, \bar{s}_{-i}^t\right) \right].$$

By hypothesis $\hat{s} \in S$ is the unique NE of the stage game. Then there is a unique $\bar{s}^t = \hat{s}$ such that for all $i \in I$ and all $s^t \in S$ $u_i(s_i^t, \bar{s}_{-i}^t) - u_i(\bar{s}_i^t, \bar{s}_{-i}^t) \leq 0$. Because this is true for all t it follows that $\bar{s} = (\hat{s}, \ldots, \hat{s})$.

Example: Two-Stage Partnership Game

We next reconsider the Partnership Game examined in the previous section. The payoffs are shown in Table 9.2-1. There we showed that the two equilibrium pure strategy profiles are $(1, 1)$ and $(2, 2)$.

Arguing as in the discussion of Proposition 9.2-1, any combination of these strategy profiles is an NE of the two-period game. Among these, the best for each player is the repeated strategy profile $(2, 2)$. Given a discount factor $\delta \in [0,1]$, the equilibrium payoff from this game is $16 + \delta 16$.

Table 9.2-1. *Stage Game with Multiple Nash Equilibria*

		Player 2		
		1	*2*	*3*
	1	*5, 5*	*11, 4*	*17, −9*
Player 1	*2*	*4, 11*	*16, 16*	*28, 9*
	3	*−9, 17*	*9, 28*	*27, 27*

Equilibrium Threats

We now argue that, for any sufficiently high discount factor, there is an additional equilibrium in the two-period game that is Pareto preferred. The key idea is that each player can use the threat to play the bad NE in the second period to induce a more favorable action in the first period. Let $s_i^t(h^t)$ be the strategy of player i in period t contingent on the history h^t.

Consider the following strategy:

$$\bar{s}_i^1 = 3, \quad \bar{s}_i^2(h^2) = 2 \text{ if } h^2 = (3,3), \quad \bar{s}_i^2(h^2) = 1 \quad \text{if } h^2 \neq (3,3).$$

Note that in the proposed equilibrium play, each player starts out choosing $s_i = 3$. Then, as long as the opponent actually chooses this strategy in the first stage, player i continues in stage 2 by choosing the good (high payoff) NE strategy of the stage game. However if the opponent "defects" in the first stage and chooses some other strategy, player i continues by choosing the bad (low payoff) NE strategy of the stage game.

Consider the first-period choices of player 1 if player 2 adopts such a strategy. If player 1 chooses the same strategy, both play 3 in the first round and 2 in the second. Thus the payoff to player 1 is $27 + \delta 16$. If player 1 "defects" and switches to 2 he gets 28 in round 1. But then player 2's strategy is to choose action 1 in round 2, and so player 1's best response is to also choose action 1. Thus his second-period payoff is 5. Thus the most that player 1 can gain by defecting is $28 + \delta 5$. Comparing the two payoffs, the net gain to defecting is

$$(28 + \delta 5) - (27 + \delta 16) = 1 - \delta 21 < 0, \quad \text{if } \delta > \tfrac{1}{21}.$$

Thus the proposed strategy is an NE of the two-period game if the discount factor exceeds $\frac{1}{21}$.

With more than two periods, the threat to switch thereafter to action 1 is an even stronger deterrent. For every period remaining, the cost that can be imposed on the defector by playing the bad NE in multiple periods is greater. Suppose for example that the discount factor δ is only slightly less than the critical value $\frac{1}{21}$. The threat to switch is then not credible with one period to go. However, it is credible with more than one period remaining.

Thus with $T > 2$ periods, it is an NE for both players to play $s_i = 3$ in all but the last two rounds and $s_i = 2$ thereafter.

Sequential Move Games

We now consider games in which players move sequentially. As an example, consider the three-player penny matching game of Section 9.1. However, now players move sequentially rather than simultaneously. It is often helpful to represent such a sequential move game graphically in what is called a *game tree*. The possible actions of each player are indicated by branches connecting from nodes as depicted in Figure 9.2-1.

The starting point of the game is called the initial node. At each node one player makes a choice. The branches from a particular node then represent all the player's possible actions. The convention is that the player making the choice at the initial node is called player 1. Other players are labeled according to the order of their first moves.

The end of each branch from the last decision node (called a terminal node) is a possible outcome of the game. Associated with each outcome is a vector of payoffs $u(a)$. Thus, for example, if all the players choose H, the payoff vector is $u(H, H, H) = (2, 2, 2)$. Note that the list of actions leading from the initial node to any terminal node or outcome is an outcome profile. It is important to note that all nodes except the initial node and the terminal nodes are connected to a single prior node and at least two successor nodes. This is what gives the graph its tree structure.

This depiction of the game as a tree is called the extensive form representation of the game or more simply the *extensive form* of the game.

Note that in a sequential move game all players but the first can base their decisions on the history of the game. If, as we assume here, all actions are observable $h^t = (a_1, a_2, \ldots, a_{t-1})$ Thus in the example, the history of the game at player 2's decision node is $h^2 = a_1 \in A_1$ and the history at player

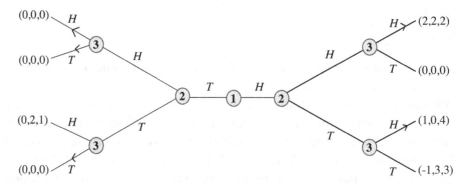

Figure 9.2-1. Sequential move penny matching game.

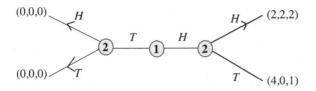

Figure 9.2-2. Backward induction.

3's decision node is $h^3 = (a_1, a_2)$. Player 1 chooses a possibly mixed strategy $s_1 \in \Delta(A_1)$. Player 2 observes the history of the game and then chooses a contingent strategy $s_2(h^2) \in \Delta(A_2)$, and so on.

The key to solving sequential move games is to begin by examining the final stage of the game and then to work backward. For this example consider each decision node for player 3. In Figure 9.2-1 player 3's best response at each node is indicated by an arrow. We can then replace player 3's decision nodes by the best response payoffs. The new decision tree is depicted in Figure 9.2-2.

Player 2's best responses are now shown with arrows. Given these best responses, player 1 chooses H, and so the NE payoff vector is $(2, 2, 2)$ and the NE strategy profile is (H, H, H).

Sub-Games

As we now show, there can be an NE of sequential move games that are highly implausible. We present an example and then show that by introducing a modest "refinement" of the NE, the silly equilibrium is eliminated. In the example, an Incumbent firm faces a potential Entrant. The game tree is depicted in Figure 9.2-3.

Player 1 (the Entrant) moves first, deciding whether or not to choose Enter or Out. If he chooses Enter, player 2 (the incumbent) must choose to

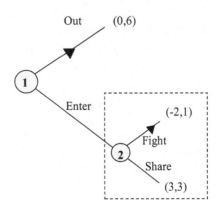

Figure 9.2-3. Entry game with sub-game.

either fight or share the market. Suppose that player 2 chooses *Fight* (indicated by the arrow from her decision node.) Player 1 has a payoff of -2 if he chooses *Enter* and 0 if he chooses *Out*. Thus his best response is *Out*. And given that he chooses Out, *Fight* is a best response by player 2. (Note that player 2 never has to carry out her threat.) A similar argument establishes that (*Enter, Share*) is a second NE.

Which of these equilibria is more plausible? Most would argue that player 1 has failed to look ahead and figure out what is in player 2's interest. If player 1 enters, player 2 is better off choosing *Share*. Thus even if player 2 tells player 1 that her strategy is *Fight*, this is not credible.

We can formalize this as follows. A game tree has a single initial node, branches and nodes for every sequential action, and payoffs at every terminal node. Consider the part of the game inside the dashed rectangle in Figure 9.2-3. This has all the requirements of a game: an initial node and terminal nodes. Any such game is called a sub-game.

Definition: Sub-Game Any branch of a game tree that begins with a single node is a sub-game.

Sub-Game Perfect Equilibrium (SPE)

Consider the sub-game inside the dashed rectangle in Figure 9.2-3. We can strengthen our definition of strategic equilibrium by requiring that the NE strategies must also be equilibrium strategies of each sub-game.

Definition: Sub-Game Perfect Equilibrium An NE strategy profile of a sequential move game is sub-game perfect if the strategy profile is also an NE strategy of each of the sub-games.

For our example, the unique equilibrium of the single sub-game is for player 2 to choose *Share*. We can then lop off this part of the tree and replace it by the NE payoffs of the sub-game as shown in Figure 9.2-4. Player 1's best response is *Enter* so the unique sub-game perfect equilibrium of the Entry game is (*Enter, Share*).

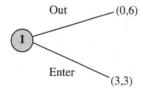

Figure 9.2-4. Entry game with payoffs from sub-game.

The One-Stage Deviation Principle[9]

We now argue that there is an easy way to check whether a strategy profile is sub-game perfect. It is enough to consider one-stage deviations by players at each decision node.

Proposition 9.2-2: One-Stage Deviation Principle
In a T-stage sequential move game, suppose that for the strategy profile $\bar{s} = (\bar{s}^1, \bar{s}^2(h^2), \ldots, \bar{s}^T(h^T))$ there is no one-stage deviation by a player that raises that player's payoff. Then the strategy profile is sub-game perfect.

Proof: The proof follows by backward induction. Let $s = (s^1, s^2(h^2), \ldots, s^T(h^T))$ be some other strategy profile. Define $\bar{s}(\theta)$ to be the strategy profile that agrees with s for $t < \theta$ and with $\bar{s}$ for $t \geq \theta$; that is,

$$\bar{s}(\theta) = (s^1, \ldots, s^{\theta-1}(h^{\theta-1}), \bar{s}^\theta(h^\theta), \ldots, \bar{s}^T(h^T)).$$

Because there is no one-stage deviation from $\bar{s}$ that benefits any player, there is no one-stage deviation from $\bar{s}(\theta)$ for any stage t sub-game where $t \geq \theta$.

We consider deviations by player i. Suppose that stage a is the last stage at which, for some history, player i deviates. Then the strategy profile s agrees with $\bar{s}$ for $t \geq a + 1$ so that $s = \bar{s}(a + 1)$. We now argue that player i must be at least as well off under strategy profile $\bar{s}(a)$ as $\bar{s}(a + 1)$.

Consider the stage a sub-game. By hypothesis, there is no one-stage deviation from $\bar{s}(a)$ that benefits player i. But the only difference between $\bar{s}(a)$ and $\bar{s}(a + 1)$ is the strategy at stage a. Therefore

$$\bar{s}(a) \underset{i}{\succsim} \bar{s}(a + 1) = s. \tag{9.2-1}$$

Let stage b be the second last stage at which player i deviates. Consider the sub-game at stage b. Note that $\bar{s}(b + 1) = \bar{s}(a)$ because there are no deviations between the two stages. Arguing as before $\bar{s}(b + 1)$ is a one-stage deviation from $\bar{s}(b)$. Therefore $\bar{s}(b) \underset{i}{\succsim} \bar{s}(b + 1)$. Therefore $\bar{s}(b) \underset{i}{\succsim} \bar{s}(a)$. Combining this result with (9.2-1) it follows that $\bar{s}(b) \underset{i}{\succsim} s$. Repeating this argument for every stage in which player i deviates it follows that $\bar{s} \underset{i}{\succsim} s$. $\qquad\square$

Although we have considered a sequential move game, the argument is almost identical for a finitely repeated game. We therefore have the following corollary.

Corollary 9.2-3: One-Stage Deviation Principle in Finitely Repeated Games
In a finitely repeated game suppose that for the strategy profile $\bar{s} = (\bar{s}^1, \bar{s}^2(h^2), \ldots, \bar{s}^T(h^T))$ there is no one-stage deviation by a player that raises that player's payoff. Then the strategy profile is sub-game perfect.

---

[9] There is an excellent discussion of this principle for repeated games in Fudenberg and Tirole (1991).

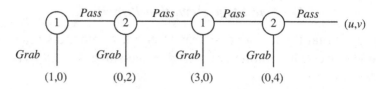

Figure 9.2-5. Centipede game.

Exercises

Exercise 9.2-1: Centipede Game Initially there is a dollar on the table and player 1 can either pick it up or say "Pass." If she picks the money up, the game ends. If she passes, another bill is added and player 2 has the same two options. If there are four passes the game ends and the four bills are removed from the table. Player 1 is paid u and player 2 is paid v. The game tree is depicted in Figure 9.2-5.

(a) Initially suppose that $(u, v) = (5, 5)$. Show that there is a unique SPE.
(b) Characterize the other pure strategy NE.
(c) What are the sub-game perfect equilibria if $(u, v) = (3.5, 3.5)$?
(d) Show that both $(6, 4)$ and $(1, 0)$ are sub-game perfect equilibrium outcomes if $(u, v) - (6, 4)$.
(e) If $(u, v) = (6, 4)$ is there an equilibrium in which every final node is reached with positive probability?

Exercise 9.2-2: Alternating Offer Game An asset of value v is to be shared between two players, but only if they agree on how much each should get. In each round one player makes a demand, and the other either accepts or rejects the offer. Player 1 moves first and makes a demand of x_1 in round 1. Then player 2 has $v - x_1$. If the offer is accepted the game ends. If the offer is rejected player 2 demands x_2 and so on. Between each round the asset value drops by $\frac{1}{4}v$. Thus after four rounds there is nothing left.

(a) Assume that if a player is indifferent he or she will accept the other's demand with probability 1. Consider the sub-game beginning in round 4. Only one-quarter of the asset remains. If player 2 makes any offer $x_4 < \frac{1}{4}v$ it will be accepted by player 1 because this gives player 1 $u_{14} = \frac{1}{4}v - x_4 > 0$. If player 1 rejects the offer then the asset has no value. By hypotheses a player accepts if he or she is indifferent so the best response of player 2 is $x_4 = \frac{1}{4}v$. Apply backward induction to show that the initial offer will be $\frac{1}{2}v$ and that it will be accepted.
(b) Show that if player 1 accepts in the last stage with probability $p_4 < 1$ there is no best response by player 1. Use this argument to establish that the equilibrium of part (a) is the unique SPE.

(c) For any integer T, solve for the sub-game perfect equilibrium payoff if v/T of the asset is lost each round.

(d) What NE is most favorable to player 1? What NE is most favorable to player 2?

Exercise 9.2-3: Rubinstein Bargaining Game An asset of value v is to be divided as in Exercise 9.2-2. However, the asset no longer depreciates. Instead there is a constant discount factor δ between periods. Player 1 moves in the odd periods and player 2 in the even periods. The game has no end date. Define u_{it} to be player i's sub-game perfect equilibrium payoff in round t. Consider round 2 where player 2 makes a demand. Player 1's SPE payoff in period 3 is u_{13}. Discounting back to period 2, player 1's equilibrium payoff if he rejects player 2's demand is δu_{13}.

(a) Explain carefully why player 2's sub-game perfect equilibrium payoff in period 2 is

$$u_{22} = \underset{x_1}{\text{Max}}\{x_1, v - x_1 \geq \delta u_{13}) = v_1 - \delta u_{13}.$$

(b) Make a similar argument to show that player 1's SPE payoff in period 1 is $u_{11} = v - \delta u_{22}$.

(c) Why must it be the case that $u_{11} = u_{13}$?

(d) Hence show that $(u_{11}, u_{21}) = ((\frac{1}{1+\delta})v, (\frac{\delta}{1+\delta})v,)$.

(e) What NE outcome is most favorable to each player?

Exercise 9.2-4: To Take or Not to Take, That is the Question Two participants, A and B have agreed to play a game at a well-known casino. Any winnings will be in the form of a cashier's check, to be mailed the following day. The game is as follows. A prize of \$500 will be offered to A. If he takes it the game will be over. A is also told that if he declines, then after he leaves, a total of \$1,000 + x will be offered to B. She can either take it or decline. If B also declines each will be sent a check for \$1,000.

(a) If $x > 0$ explain why A's unique SPE is for each player to take the money.

(b) Suppose $(i)\, x = \$500$ $(ii)\, x = \$2000$. If you were contestant B what would you do in each case?

(c) If you were contestant A what would you do in each case?

(d) Would your answers change if both contestants remain until the game is over?

(e) What do you think most people would do?

(f) If your answers deviate from the SPE strategies, why do you think this is the case?

9.3 Duopoly Games

Key ideas: continuous strategy space, Bertrand pricing game, best response mapping, alternating move game, second mover advantage, war of attrition

Until now we have primarily considered games in which the strategy set is finite. With two players it is then natural to analyze the game using a table with the strategies of the players and the payoffs all listed. An alternative modeling choice is to assume that the strategic variables are real vectors. We can then use the methods of calculus to characterize an NE.

We now illustrate this by examining two applications. First we consider a variation of the classic Bertrand pricing game. In this game there is a unique pure strategy equilibrium. We characterize the equilibrium and then explore how the equilibrium prices and profits vary as the degree of substitutability between the two products increases. The second example is the war of attrition. Two firms are competing in a market. Both would be better off if one firm were to exit and compete in some other market. However, the firm that stays has a higher payoff than the firm that exits. In this environment the symmetric NE is a mixed strategy over all possible exit times.

Bertrand Pricing Game

Two firms produce products that are imperfect substitutes. The price set by firm i is $P_i, i = 1, 2$. The price set by firm i's competitor is P_{-i}.[10] Product demand is

$$q_i = \alpha - \beta P_i + \theta(P_{-i} - P_i), \quad i = 1, 2.$$

Each firm has a constant unit cost of production c. To simplify the analysis we define the new variable $p_i = P_i - c$. This is the firm's markup over its cost. Then we can rewrite q_i as follows:

$$q_i = \alpha - \beta c - \beta p_i + \theta(p_{-i} - p_i), \quad i = 1, 2.$$

To avoid notational clutter we can carefully choose units for q and p so that $\alpha - \beta c$ and β are both 1; then

$$q_i = 1 - p_i + \theta(p_{-i} - p_i), \quad i = 1, 2.$$

The model is therefore equivalent to one in which firms have no costs of production and $p = (p_1, p_2)$ is the price vector.[11] Note that the greater the

---

[10] We are being a little casual, because market demand cannot be negative. However, as the reader may check, our arguments continue to hold if we take explicit account of the non-negativity constraint.

[11] We continue to refer to p as the price vector in the zero cost model, but it should be remembered that it is really the markup over the firm's cost.

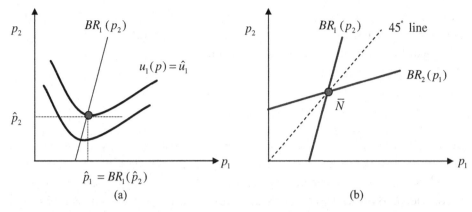

Figure 9.3-1. (a) Best response mapping. (b) Nash equilibrium.

parameter θ, the greater the degree of substitutability across products. We are particularly interested in how the pricing decisions change as this parameter increases.

Given symmetry it is helpful to write the prices as (p_i, p_{-i}). The profit of firm i is then

$$u_i(p_i, p_{-i}) = p_i q_i = p_i(1 - p_i + \theta(p_{-i} - p_i)) \qquad (9.3\text{-}1)$$

Note that $u_i(p_i, p_{-i})$ is an increasing function of p_{-i} and that

$$\frac{\partial u_i}{\partial p_i}(p) = (1 + \theta p_{-i}) - (1 + \theta)p_i \qquad (9.3\text{-}2)$$

Thus for any p_{-i}, firm i's profit increase with p_i until $p_i = \frac{1}{2}(1 + \theta p_{-i})/(1 + \theta)$ and then decreases. Indifference curves for firm 1 are therefore as depicted in Figure 9.3-1a. Because a higher price for the other product is better for firm 1, higher indifference curves yield higher profit.

Note that for any p_{-i}, firm i's profit is maximized at $p_i = \frac{1}{2}(1 + \theta p_{-i})$; that is,

$$BR_i(p_{-i}) = \frac{(1 + \theta p_{-i})}{2(1 + \theta)}.$$

The best response mapping for firm 1 is depicted in Figure 9.3-1a. Given the price $\hat{p}_2$, firm 1 can choose any point on the dotted horizontal line. Then the best response $\hat{p}_1 = BR_1(\hat{p}_2)$ is the point where the indifference curve is horizontal.

At the NE, strategies must be mutual best responses; that is,

$$p_i = BR_i(p_{-i}) = \frac{1 + \theta p_{-i}}{2(1 + \theta)}, \quad i = 1, 2.$$

In Figure 9.3-1b this is the point $\overline{N}$. Although solving the two linear equations is straightforward, an even easier method is to note that the symmetry of the problem yields a symmetric solution, $\overline{p}_1 = \overline{p}_2 = \overline{p}$.

Substituting,

$$\overline{p} = \frac{1 + \theta\overline{p}}{2(1+\theta)}; \quad \text{hence} \quad \overline{p} = \frac{1}{2+\theta} \quad \text{and so} \quad q_1 = q_2 = \frac{1+\theta}{2+\theta}.$$

The results are intuitive. As the degree of substitutability increases, the strategic competition intensifies and so NE prices decline. In the limit, $p_i = P_i - c, i = 1, 2$ approaches zero, and the output of each firm approaches 1. Note that with constant unit cost, the WE price must be equal to unit cost. Thus in the limit, the NE price approaches the WE price.

Thus far we have examined games in which decisions are made simultaneously. We now ask what advantage firm 2 gets if it is able to first observe the price set by firm 1 and then optimally respond.

Duopoly Pricing Game with Alternating Moves

Suppose that firm 1 chooses the price p_1. From our earlier analysis, we know that the best response function for firm 2 is

$$p_2 = BR_2(p_1) = \frac{1 + \theta p_1}{2(1 + \theta)}. \tag{9.3-3}$$

This is depicted in Figure 9.3-2, along with the indifference curve for firm 1 through $\overline{N}$, the NE of the simultaneous move game. As argued earlier, this indifference curve must be horizontal at $\overline{N}$. Because the best response mapping for firm 2 is upward sloping, it follows that the best response of firm 1 is the price p_1^N where the indifference curve is tangential to firm 2's best response line. Thus N is the NE of the alternating move game.

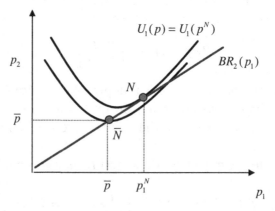

Figure 9.3-2. Nash equilibrium with alternating moves.

Because it is to the northwest of $\overline{N}$, the alternating move equilibrium N prices are higher and both firms are better off than if they move simultaneously.

Arguing more formally, firm 1's profit function is

$$u_1(p_1, BR_2(p_1)) = p_1 q_1 = p_1(1 - p_1 + \theta(BR_2(p_1) - p_1)). \quad (9.3\text{-}4)$$

It is helpful to compare this with firm 1's payoff in the simultaneous play model. From (9.3-1),

$$u_1(p_1, p_2) = p_1(1 - p_1 + \theta(p_2 - p_1)).$$

Note that in the sequential move model there is an extra term that depends on p_1. As we have seen, the best response mapping is strictly increasing; thus the marginal profit from increasing price is higher than in the simultaneous move game.

To solve for the best response function for firm 1, we differentiate (9.3-4):

$$\frac{d}{dp_1} u_1(p_1, BR_2(p_1)) = \frac{\partial u_1}{\partial p_1} + \frac{\partial u_1}{\partial p_2} \frac{d}{dp_1} BR_2(p_1).$$

Substituting from (9.3-2) and (9.3-3),

$$\frac{du_1}{dp_1} = 1 - 2(1 + \theta)p_1 + \theta p_2 + \frac{\theta^2}{2(1 + \theta)} p_1 = 0 \quad \text{at} \quad p_1 = BR_1(p_2).$$

Solving,

$$BR_1(p_2) = \frac{2(1 + \theta)}{4 + 8\theta + 3\theta^2}(1 + \theta p_2). \quad (9.3\text{-}5)$$

For a NE, both (9.3-3) and (9.3-5) must hold. Using (9.3-3) to substitute for θp_2 in (9.3-5) we have at last

$$p_1 = \frac{2 + 3\theta}{2(2 + 4\theta + \theta^2)} \quad \text{and hence} \quad p_2 = \frac{4 + 10\theta + 5\theta^2}{4(1 + \theta)(2 + 4\theta + \theta^2)}. \quad (9.3\text{-}6)$$

From Figure 9.3-3 we know that both firms have higher prices in the alternating move game and that equilibrium payoffs are higher. From (9.3-6), both net prices approach zero as the substitution parameter grows large. Table 9.3-1 provides some numerical results for different values of the substitution parameter. Column 2 is the equilibrium net price $\overline{p} = \overline{P} - c$ in the simultaneous move game. Columns 3 and 4 are the net prices of the two firms in the alternating move game.

Note that the relative advantage of moving second rises with θ. This is intuitive. A higher substitution parameter means that a given price reduction

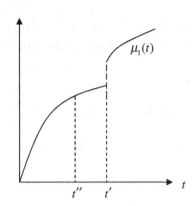

(a) Mass point for firm 1 at t'.

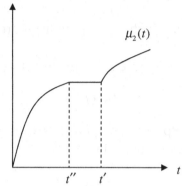

(b) Interval over which firm 2 does not exit

Figure 9.3-3. No mass points for $t > 0$. (a) Mass point for firm 1 at t'. (b) Interval over which firm 2 does not exit.

will result in more customers switching to product 2. Interestingly, even as the substitution parameter grows large, the relative advantage to moving second remains bounded.

Who Goes First?

We have seen that both firms gain if one is willing to go first and announce its price. Suppose there is no natural order of moves so both can announce their prices for the next week at $t = 1$ or choose to wait and announce at $t = 2$. Because both firms have an incentive to wait until the other has announced its price, there is an NE in which both firms wait until $t = 2$ and then play the simultaneous move game. This may suggest that the simultaneous move game is more realistic.

However, the firms can do better if they can correlate their strategies by observing a realization of some random variable. Suppose, for example, that before the first move, each player observes whether the last digit of a winning number in the weekly lottery is odd or even. Now the game has a history

Table 9.3-1. *The Advantage to Moving Second*

θ	$\overline{p}$	p_1	p_2	$p_1/\overline{p}$	$p_2/\overline{p}$	p_1/p_2	q_1	q_2	U_1/U_2
0	0.5	0.5	0.5	1	1	1	0.5	0.5	1
1	0.33	0.36	0.34	1.07	1.02	1.05	0.63	0.68	0.97
5	0.14	0.18	0.16	1.27	1.11	1.14	0.71	0.95	0.85
10	0.08	0.11	0.10	1.35	1.16	1.17	0.73	1.06	0.80
100	0.010	0.015	0.012	1.48	1.24	1.20	0.75	1.23	0.73
1E + 6	1E − 06	1.5E − 06	1.2E − 06	1.50	1.25	1.2	0.75	1.25	0.72

before the first move – $h^1 \in H^1 = \{odd, even\}$. A Pareto superior correlated NE is for firm 1 to move in period 1 if the number is odd and for firm 2 to move in period 1 if the number is even. Although the actual play is asymmetric, each firm has the same expected payoff before the realization of the random variable.

War of Attrition

Just as in the previous example, suppose that two firms are producing products with somewhat similar characteristics. (For example, the firms might produce two different types of cars.) For simplicity, we assume that the differences in the characteristics of the two products are such that the firms are playing a symmetric duopoly pricing game. Let a be the equilibrium duopoly profit of each firm per unit of time. As a result of changing demand or new technology, the two firms simultaneously learn that there is an opportunity for each to make more profit if one of the firms retools and produces a different kind of car.[12] The firm that makes the move can earn a profit per unit of time equal to $m > a$. As a result of the move by one firm, the firm that does not move has increased monopoly power so its profit rises as well to n.

If the profit of the firm that moves is greater than the profit of the firm that stays, each firm will want to move immediately. Yet suppose that it is the firm that stays that has the higher profit stream; that is,

$$n > m > a.$$

Now both firms would rather not move. However, in this case both forego the increased profit. What should the firms do?

To analyze this game we first note that we have not yet described the payoffs if the two firms choose the same moving time. We assume that, in the event of a tie, the mover is selected randomly. (In fact the equilibrium strategies are the same for any tie-breaking rule.)

It is not difficult to see that there are two pure strategy equilibria of this game. If firm 1 chooses the strategy of staying forever, then firm 2's best response is to move immediately. And given that firm 2 is moving immediately, firm 1 earns the maximum profit stream immediately by staying. Thus firm 1's strategy is a best response as well. Of course, there is a second NE in which firm 2 refuses to ever move and firm 1 moves immediately. (In fact these are the only two equilibria in pure strategies.)

Of course, there is a problem here. Each firm likes a different NE. In such cases, economists often look first for a symmetric equilibrium. We now argue

---

[12] For example, consider two auto firms that both initially produce sedans. A taste for SUVs develops so it becomes more profitable for one firm to instead use its plant to produce SUVs. Given that one firm does so, the other firm can raise its prices on sedans.

that there is such an equilibrium involving mixed strategies. Let $\mu(t)$ be the probability that each firm moves by time t. If neither firm has moved at time t the conditional probability that a firm will move in the small interval Δt is given by

$$\frac{\mu(t + \Delta t) - \mu(t)}{1 - \mu(t)} \approx \frac{\mu'(t)\Delta t}{1 - \mu(t)} \equiv p(t)\Delta t. \tag{9.3-7}$$

The key to solving for an equilibrium is the observation that in a mixed strategy equilibrium the firms must be indifferent between all the actions in the support of their probability distribution over moving times. In particular, firm 1 must be indifferent between moving at time t and moving at time $t + \Delta t$. Suppose neither firm has moved before time t. If firm 1 moves at t it earns a profit of $m\Delta t$ over the interval $[t, t + \Delta t]$. If firm 1 waits, it earns the duopoly profit stream of $a\Delta t$. Moreover, with probability $p(t)\Delta t$, firm 2 moves in this time interval, and then firm 1 has a future profit steam of n rather than m. Given an interest rate r, the present value of this future increased profit stream is $\frac{n-m}{r}$. The expected net gain from waiting is therefore

$$\Delta u_1 = a\Delta t + p(t)\Delta t \left(\frac{n - m}{r}\right) - m\Delta t = \left[a - m + p(t)\left(\frac{n - m}{r}\right)\right]\Delta t.$$

But, for an equilibrium, firm 1 must be indifferent between moving at t and moving at $t + \Delta t$. Thus the equilibrium expected net gain from waiting is zero. Rearranging, it follows that the equilibrium probability of moving is

$$p = r\left(\frac{m - a}{n - m}\right).$$

Appealing to (9.3-7), it follows that

$$\frac{-\mu'(t)}{1 - \mu(t)} = -p. \tag{9.3-8}$$

Integrating this expression,

$$\ln(1 - \mu(t)) = \ln k - pt.$$

Hence $\mu(t) = 1 - ke^{-pt}$. If $k < 1$, there is a mass point at zero. It is not too difficult to confirm that there cannot be any mass points in a symmetric equilibrium.[13] Therefore the unique symmetric equilibrium c.d.f. is

$$\mu(t) = 1 - e^{-pt}, \quad \text{where} \quad p = r\left(\frac{m - a}{n - m}\right).$$

---

[13] If both choose t with positive probability then one firm is strictly better off breaking the tie by staying slightly longer than t.

For the reader who remains a bit suspicious of the somewhat informal derivation of the necessary conditions for equilibrium, we now present a more formal analysis.

We begin with the following helpful observation. Given an interest rate r, the present value of a profit stream of 1 over the time interval $[0, t]$ is $B(t) = \int_0^t e^{-rs} ds$. It is readily confirmed that $B(\infty) = \frac{1}{r}$ and $B'(t) = e^{-rt}$.

Let $v_1(t_1, t_2)$ be the payoff to firm 1 if firm 1 decides it will move at t_1 and firm 2 decides it will move at time t_2.

Case (i) $t_1 < t_2$:

Firm 1 earns the duopoly profit stream until time t_1 and the profit stream from moving for all $t > t_1$. Hence $v_1(t_1, t_2) = a B(t_1) + e^{-rt_1} \frac{m}{r}$.

Case (ii) $t_1 > t_2$:

Firm 1 earns the duopoly profit stream until time t_2; then firm 2 moves. So for all higher t firm 1 earns the profit stream from staying. Hence $v_1(t_1, t_2) = a B(t_2) + e^{-rt_2} \frac{n}{r}$.

Case (iii) $t_1 = t_2$:

In this case the actual mover is selected randomly so that each firm has an equal probability of staying and moving. Because $t_1 = t_2$, firm 1's payoff is

$$v_1(t_1, t_1) = a B(t_1) + e^{-rt_1} \frac{\frac{1}{2}(n+m)}{r}.$$

Let $\mu(t)$ be the symmetric equilibrium c.d.f.; that is, $\Pr\{\tilde{t}_i \leq t\} = \mu(t)$. We assume that this distribution is continuous. If firm 2 plays the symmetric equilibrium mixed strategy and firm 1 chooses to move at time t, firm 1's expected payoff is

$$u_1(t, \bar{s}_2) = (1 - \mu(t)) \left[a B(t) + e^{-rt} \frac{m}{r} \right]$$

$$+ \int_0^t \left[a B(s) + e^{-rs} \frac{n}{r} \right] \mu'(s) ds. \tag{9.3-9}$$

In the proposed equilibrium firm 1 also plays a mixed strategy. Thus firm 1 must have the same payoff for all moving times. Hence $\frac{\partial}{\partial t} u_1(t, \bar{s}_2) = 0$. Differentiating (9.3-9) yields the necessary condition (9.3-8).

We have found an NE by conjecturing that the equilibrium probability distributions were identical and continuous. A complete analysis would rule out classes of possible alternative equilibria. We conclude by showing that an NE mixed strategy cannot have a mass point at any moving time $t > 0$. The proof is by contradiction.

Suppose $\mu_1(t)$ is discontinuous at t' as depicted in Figure 9.3-3a. We show that a necessary condition for $\mu_1(t)$ to be a best response is that there is an interval $[t'', t']$ over which firm 2 will never exit. To see this, note that if firm 2 plans to move at $t' + \delta$ rather than $t' - \delta$ its probability of getting the higher payoff as the stayer rises discontinuously. For sufficiently small δ this cannot be offset by the additional flow payoff from moving. It follows that there must be some interval $[t'', t']$ within which firm 2 will never move. This is depicted in Figure 9.3-3b.

Given this interval, firm 1 can move its mass point from t' to t'' and so avoid the duopoly loss over the interval $[t', t'']$. Then moving at t' with positive probability cannot be a best response after all.

Exercises

Exercise 9.3-1: Alternating Move Pricing Game as Substitutability Grows Large

(a) For the pricing game examined in this section, define the new variables $z_i = \theta p_i$ $i = 1, 2$ and write down the two necessary conditions as linear equations in z_1 and z_2.

(b) Show that in the limit as $\theta \to \infty$, $(z_1, z_2) \to (\frac{6}{4}, \frac{5}{4})$.

(c) Hence show that the output of the two firms approaches $(\frac{3}{4}, \frac{5}{4})$.

Exercise 9.3-2: Cournot Production Game

Suppose that the market demand curve is $p = a - q$. There are two firms. The output of firm j is q_j. Each has the same unit cost of production c. The game is played once.

(a) Solve for the NE and compare it with the symmetric collusive outcome.

(b) For n identical firms show that the first-order condition for a best response is

$$\frac{\partial \Pi}{\partial q_i} = a - c - b(s + q_i) = 0, \quad \text{where } s = \sum_{j=1}^{n} q_j.$$

Sum over the n firms and hence show that $n(a - c) - (n + 1)s = 0$.
Hence show that the equilibrium price is $p^n = \frac{1}{n+1}a + \frac{n}{n+1}c$.

(c) Compare the outcome with the WE outcome as n becomes large.

Exercise 9.3-3: Cournot Production Game with a Competitive Fringe

Suppose demand is given by $p = 100 - q$. Firm 1 has a cost function $TC_1(q_1) = c_1 q_1$. Firm 2 has a cost function $TC_2(q_2) = c_2 q_2$.

(a) Obtain the best response functions for each firm. Hence solve for the equilibrium outputs and prices. HINT: Look for conditions under which both firms compete and when only firm 1 enters the market.

(b) Suppose that there are n firms just like firm 2. Solve again for the equilibrium price. (You should assume that in the equilibrium all the identical firms actually choose the same output level.)

(c) Discuss what happens as n gets large.

Exercise 9.3-4: Production Game with Sequential Entry Demand is given by $p = 24 - q$, where $q = q_1 + q_2$. Firm 1 has a cost $C_1 = 4q_1$. Firm 2's cost function is $C_2 = 8q_2$.

(a) Suppose that each firm makes its production decision without observing its competitor's decision. Solve for the best response functions for each firm. Hence solve for the simultaneous move equilibrium.

(b) Suppose firm 1 makes the first move. Utilize the fact that firm 2 will choose a best response to get an expression for firm 1's profit in terms of q_1 alone.

(c) Solve for firm 1's optimal output decision and compare output levels and profits with those in the simultaneous move equilibrium.

Exercise 9.3-5: Production Game with Three Firms and Sequential Entry The market demand price function is $p = a - q_1 - q_2 - q_3$. Each firm has a unit cost of c.

(a) Show that the third mover (firm 3) has a best response $q_3 = BR_3(q_2, q_3) = \frac{1}{2}(a - c - q_1 - q_2)$.

(b) Show that the profit function for firm 2 can be written as follows:

$$U_2(q_1, q_2) = \frac{1}{2}(a - c - q_1 - q_2)q_2.$$

(c) Hence show that firm 2 has a best response of $q_2 = BR_2(q_1) = \frac{1}{2}(a - c - q_1)$.

(d) Write down the profit function for firm 1 and hence show that firm 1's best response is $q_1 = \frac{1}{2}(a - c)$.

(e) Compare the equilibrium outputs of the three firms and solve for the equilibrium price.

Exercise 9.3-6: Existence of Equilibrium Consider two firms producing an identical product. The unit cost for firm i is c_i where $c_1 < c_2$. All consumers purchase from the firm offering the lowest price. If the two firms set the same price firm 1 gets a fraction f_1 of the market and firm 2 a fraction $f_2 = 1 - f_1$. Consumer demand for the two products is as follows:

$$(q_1, q_2) = \begin{cases} (a - p_1, 0), & p_1 < p_2 \\ (f_1(a - p_1), & f_2(a - p_2)), & p_1 = p_2 \\ (0, a - p_2), & p_1 > p_2 \end{cases}.$$

The action set for each firm is the interval $[0, a]$.

(a) Show that there can be no equilibrium in pure strategies with either price strictly greater than c_2.

(b) Suppose that firm 1 adopts a mixed strategy. Let p_1^* be the firm's maximum price. That is, $\mu_1(p_1^*) = 1$ and $\mu_1(p_1) < 1$, for all $p < p_1^*$. Suppose that $p_1^* > c_2$ and obtain a contradiction. HINT: Argue that firm 2's best response is to announce a price $p_2 < p_1^*$ and hence that the price p_1^* cannot be a best response for firm 1.

(c) Show that $(p_1, p_2) = (c_2, c_2)$ is the unique NE if $f_1 = 1$.

(d) Show that there is no NE if $f_1 < 1$.

(e) For finite strategy sets show that there is a unique equilibrium.

(f) Do you think it makes sense to model Bertrand price competition by assuming that $f_1 = 1$?

Exercise 9.3-7: War of Attrition

(a) Appeal to equation (9.3-9) to obtain the necessary condition for the symmetric equilibrium mixed strategy. (This is condition (9.3-8)).

(b) What are the equilibrium expected payoffs?

(c) Show that there are other mixed strategy equilibria in which firm 1 moves immediately with strictly positive probability; that is, $\mu_1(0) > 0$ while $\mu_2(0) = 0$.

(d) Suppose instead that there are three firms. If one moves, then all three are better off but those who stay have bigger profits than the firm that moves. Characterize the NE for this game.

Exercise 9.3-8: Rent-Seeking Contest

Two competing firms spend resources on a politician. The amount spent by firm i is x_i. The firm that spends the most on the politician's re-election wins a favor from the politician. If firm 1 wins the contest, its profit rises by W_1 and the profit of firm 2 falls by L_2. If firm 2 wins, its profit rises by W_2 and the profit of firm 1 falls by L_1. If the two firms spend the same amount, each wins with probability 0.5. The profit gains and losses are common knowledge. Firms choose their spending levels simultaneously.

(a) First consider the special case $(W_i, L_i) = (W, 0)$ $i = 1, 2$. Give an argument as to why there can be no equilibria in pure strategies.

(b) Show that the mixed strategy with probability distribution $\mu_i(x) = \Pr\{x_i \le x\} = x_i / W$ is an NE.

(c) Develop an argument as to why the equilibrium probability distributions $\mu_1(x)$, $\mu_2(x)$ cannot have a mass point at $x > 0$.

(d) Solve for the equilibrium mixed strategy if $(W_i, L_i) = (W, L)$ $i = 1, 2$.

(e) Solve for the equilibrium mixed strategies if $W_1 > W_2 > L_1 = L_2 = 0$.

9.4 Infinitely Repeated Games

Key ideas: stage game, grim strategy, strategies off the equilibrium path, folk theorem, one-stage deviation principle

In an infinitely repeated game a simultaneous move stage game is played repeatedly. Let $S = S_1 \times \cdots S_I$ be the set of feasible strategy profiles of the stage game. For any strategies of player i's opponents, s_{-i}, player i's maximum payoff is

$$\underset{s_i \in S_i}{\text{Max}}\{u_i(s_i, s_{-i})\}.$$

Table 9.4-1. *Stage Game*

| | | Player 2 | | |
		High	Middle	Low
	High	*100, 100*	*40, 170*	*20, 90*
Player 1	Middle	170, 40	50, 50	0, 40
	Low	*90, 20*	*40, 0*	*10, 10*

To analyze the equilibria of the infinitely repeated game we begin by defining the minmax value of the stage game to player i as the highest payoff he can achieve when his opponents' objective is to minimize his payoff. This is the highest payoff that player i can guarantee himself. This minmax value is

$$\underline{u}_i = \underset{s_{-i} \in S_{-i}}{\text{Min}} \ \underset{s_i \in S_i}{\text{Max}} \{u_i(s_i, s_{-i})\}.$$

Define

$$\underline{s}_{-i} \in \arg \underset{s_{-i} \in S_{-i}}{\text{Min}} \ \underset{s_i \in S_i}{\text{Max}} \{u_i(s_i, s_{-i})\}.$$

This is a minmax strategy vector for player i's opponents.

Let $u(s) = (u_1(s), \ldots, u_I(s))$ be the payoff vector for strategy profile s of the stage game. We argue that if players are sufficiently patient (so that their discount factors are sufficiently close to 1), any payoff vector $u(s) \gg \underline{u}$ is a Nash equilibrium payoff of the infinitely repeated game.

To illustrate, consider the simultaneous move pricing stage game in Table 9.4-1. This is a variant of the pricing game examined in Section 9.1. Note that the unique NE payoff vector of this stage game is $(50, 50)$.

If player 2 chooses *High*, player 1's maximum payoff is 170 (when he chooses *Middle*). If player 2 chooses *Middle* player 1's maximum payoff is 50. If player 2 chooses *Low* player 1's maximum payoff is 20. Thus player 1's minmax payoff is 20. Given the symmetry of the game the minmax payoff vector is $\underline{u} = (20, 20)$.

The feasible payoffs in the stage game are depicted in Figure 9.4-1. The union of the lightly and heavily shaded regions is the set of convex combinations of these payoff vectors.

These are all feasible if the players use a public randomization device.[14] For example suppose the randomization device proposes (*High, Middle*) and (*Middle, High*) with equal probability. If the two players follow the proposed strategies each player has a payoff of $\frac{1}{2}(170) + \frac{1}{2}(40) = 105$. The more

---

[14] As long as the discount factor of each player is sufficiently close to 1, it is possible to approximate the expected payoffs with a randomization device by alternating between the strategies at the appropriate rates.

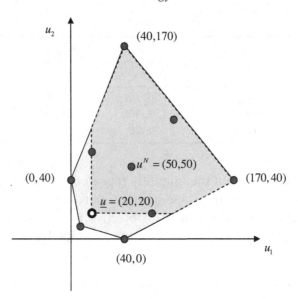

Figure 9.4-1. Pareto-preferred payoffs in the stage game.

heavily shaded area in the figure is the set of payoffs that Pareto dominate the minmax payoffs.

Pick any strategy profile s yielding a strictly Pareto preferred payoff in the stage game; that is, $u(s) \gg \underline{u}$. We consider the "grim strategy" in which players begin by playing according to the strategy profile s and continue to do so until a single player deviates. The deviating player is punished thereafter by all the other players, who gang up on him and play a minmax strategy against him. That is, if the first deviation is in stage t and it is by player i alone, all the other players switch to their minmax strategies $\underline{s}_{-i}$. We have the following proposition.

Proposition 9.4-1: Folk Theorem[15]

For every pure strategy profile s of the stage game with payoff vector $u(s) \gg \underline{u}$, there exists a discount factor $\underline{\delta}$ such that for all $\delta \in (\underline{\delta}, 1)$ the grim strategy is an NE strategy profile of the infinitely repeated game with payoff vector $u(s)$.

Proof: We will seek conditions under which player i has no incentive to deviate in the first stage if all other players play according to the proposed strategy. Let u_i^D be player i's maximum payoff from deviating while all other players choose s_{-i}. For player i to have an incentive to deviate it must be

---

[15] This is called the Folk Theorem because it was a well-known result long before it was formally proved. Perhaps my ancestral Graham clan should take some of the credit. The clan motto is "Never forget a friend, never forgive an enemy."

the case that $u_i^D > u_i(s)$. Given the response to this deviation, player i's discounted payoff is

$$u_i^D + \sum_{t=2}^{\infty} \delta^{t-1} \underline{u}_i = u_i^D + \delta \underline{u}_i \sum_{t=1}^{\infty} \delta^{t-1} = u_i^D + \frac{\delta}{1-\delta} \underline{u}_i.$$

If player i never deviates her payoff is

$$u_i(s) + \sum_{t=2}^{\infty} \delta^{t-1} u_i(s) = u_i(s) + \delta u_i(s) \sum_{t=1}^{\infty} \delta^{t-1} = u_i(s) + \frac{\delta}{1-\delta} u_i(s).$$

Therefore player i is strictly worse off deviating if

$$u_i^D - u_i(s) + \frac{\delta}{1-\delta} (\underline{u}_i - u_i(s)) < 0. \tag{9.4-1}$$

Rearranging this inequality, player i is strictly worse off deviating if

$$\frac{u_i^D - u_i(s)}{u_i^D - \underline{u}_i} < \delta.$$

Making exactly the same argument for each of the other players who have a short-run gain from deviating, it follows that there is some $\delta < 1$ such that no player gains from deviating in stage 1 of the game. Because the game is repeated, exactly the same argument also holds at each stage. □

How plausible is the threat to play the minmax strategy? Consider the payoff matrix in Table 9.4-1. If player 1 defects and player 2 responds by choosing his minmax strategy (*Low*), player 1's best response is *High*. But if player 1 chooses *High*, player 2 can increase his payoff to 170 by choosing *Middle*. Note that at each stage the players are beginning an infinitely repeated sub-game. With player 1 always choosing *High* in this sub-game, it is not a best response for player 2 to choose *Low*. Therefore the NE strategies are not sub-game perfect.

SPE of the Infinitely Repeated Game

Let s^N be an NE strategy profile of the stage game with NE payoff vector u^N. Suppose that the game has reached the t-th stage. Regardless of how many times the stage game is to be repeated (finitely or infinitely), if player i believes that his opponents will choose s_{-i}^N in all future stages, then his best response is s_i^N. Thus the NE of the stage game is a sub-game perfect equilibrium of the repeated game.

Proposition 9.4-2: SPE of the Infinitely Repeated Game
Let $s^N = (s_1^N, \ldots, s_n^N)$ be a NE of the stage game. Then $s^t(h^t) = s^N$ is a sub-game perfect equilibrium (SPE) of the infinitely repeated game.

This observation suggests an alternative grim strategy. Instead of threatening to play the minmax strategies in response to a defection by player i, the opposing players can switch to their stage game NE strategies s_{-i}^N. Given such a response to her defection, player i maximizes her payoff in the continuation of the game by choosing s_i^N. Let $u^N = (u_1^N(s^N), \ldots, u_I(s^N))$ be the stage game NE payoff vector. We can thus replace $\underline{u}$ by u^N in the statement of Proposition 9.4-1. Appealing to Proposition 9.4-2, in the event of a defection, the play in the continuation of the game is sub-game perfect. We have therefore proved the following result.

Proposition 9.4-3: SPE of the Infinitely Repeated Game (Friedman)
Let s^N be an NE of the stage game with payoff vector u^N. For every pure strategy profile s with payoff vector $u(s) \gg u^N$, there exists a discount factor $\underline{\delta} < 1$ such that for all $\delta \in (\underline{\delta}, 1)$ the payoff vector $u(s)$ is an SPE outcome in each stage of the infinitely repeated game.

It should be clear that the grim strategy is not the only response to actions off the equilibrium path that will sustain a Pareto preferred strategy s. All that is required is that the long-run penalty should exceed the short-run payoff. One simple alternative is for each of the other players to respond to a deviation by player i from strategy s_i in the first stage by playing an NE strategy in periods 2 through T and then reverting to the strategy s in period $T + 1$. Then the payoff to player i if he defects is at most

$$u_i^D + \sum_{t=2}^{T} \delta^{t-1} u_i^N + \sum_{t=T+1}^{\infty} \delta^{t-1} u_i(s)$$

$$= u_i^D + \left(\frac{1 - \delta^{T-1}}{1 - \delta} \right) \delta u_i^N + \sum_{t=T+1}^{\infty} \delta^{t-1} u_i(s).$$

If he does not defect, player i's payoff is

$$u_i(s) + \sum_{t=2}^{T} \delta^{t-1} u_i(s) + \sum_{t=T+1}^{\infty} \delta^{t-1} u_i(s)$$

$$= u_i(s) + \left(\frac{1 - \delta^{T-1}}{1 - \delta} \right) \delta u_i(s) + \sum_{t=T+1}^{\infty} \delta^{t-1} u_i(s).$$

Then player i is strictly worse off defecting if

$$u_i^D - u_i(s) - \frac{\delta - \delta^T}{1 - \delta} \left(u_i(s) - u_i^N \right) < 0,$$

that is,

$$\frac{u_i^D - u_i(s)}{u_i(s) - u_i^N} - \frac{\delta - \delta^T}{1 - \delta} < 0.$$

As long as this expression is negative when $T = \infty$, it must be negative for all sufficiently large T.

It may seem immaterial which of these strategies is used, because in equilibrium, neither will ever be played. However, we have assumed here that the strategies chosen in each stage of the game are part of the history of the game. In the next chapter we study an example where this is no longer the case and the length of the punishment then becomes important.

Example: The Repeated Cournot Production Game

Suppose n identical firms simultaneously choose their outputs, $(q_1, \ldots, q_n)$. The demand price is $p = 1 - Q = 1 - \sum_{j=1}^{n} q_j$. For expositional ease we assume that the cost of production is zero. Because we will use the result repeatedly we note that

$$x^* = \arg \max_x (a - x)x = a/2 \quad \text{and} \quad (a - x^*)x^* = (a/2)^2. \quad (9.4\text{-}2)$$

Symmetric Joint Profit-Maximizing Outcome

Total profit is $\Pi(Q) = p(Q)Q = (1 - Q)Q$. Appealing to (9.4-2), this takes on its maximum at $Q = \frac{1}{2}$. Thus the symmetric profit-maximizing output per firm is $q^* = \frac{1}{2n}$, the price is $p^* = \frac{1}{2}$, and so the profit of firm i is $u_i^* = \frac{1}{4n}$.

Symmetric NE

The profit of firm i is

$$u_i = \left(1 - \sum_{\substack{j=1 \\ j \neq i}}^{n} q_j - q_i\right) q_i. \quad (9.4\text{-}3)$$

Appealing to (9.4-2), this takes on its maximum at $q_i = \frac{1}{2}(1 - \sum_{\substack{j=1 \\ j \neq i}}^{n} q_j)$.

Appealing to symmetry, $q_i^N = \frac{1}{n+1}$, then $u_i^N = \frac{1}{(n+1)^2}$.

Deviation

From (9.4-3), if all other firms choose the strategy q^*, firm i's profit is

$$u_i = \left(1 - \frac{n-1}{2n} - q_i\right) q_i = \left(\frac{n+1}{2n} - q_i\right) q_i.$$

Appealing to (9.4-2), this takes on its maximum at $q_i^D = \frac{n+1}{4n}$ and firm i's profit is

$$u_i^D = \left(\frac{n+1}{4n}\right)^2.$$

Substituting these expressions into (9.4-1), all defections are strictly unprofitable if and only if

$$\left(\left(\frac{n+1}{4n}\right)^2 - \frac{1}{4n}\right) - \frac{\delta}{1-\delta}\left(\frac{1}{4n} - \frac{1}{(n+1)^2}\right)$$

$$= \left(\frac{(n+1)^2 - 4n}{16n^2}\right) - \frac{\delta}{1-\delta}\left(\frac{(n+1)^2 - 4n}{4n(n+1)^2}\right)$$

$$= \frac{(n-1)^2}{4n}\left(\frac{1}{4n} - \frac{\delta}{1-\delta}\frac{1}{(n+1)^2}\right) < 0,$$

that is,

$$\frac{(n+1)^2}{4n} < \frac{\delta}{1-\delta}.$$

Note that the left-hand side increases without bound as the number of firms grows large. Thus, regardless of the discount factor, if there are enough firms in the market, the monopoly outcome is not an NE of the repeated game.

The One-Stage Deviation Principle for Infinitely Repeated Games

For finitely repeated games we have seen that to check whether a profile is sub-game perfect, all we need to do is consider the one-stage deviations by each player. We now show that this result applies as well to infinitely repeated games. The idea of the proof is simple. If there is an infinite deviation that yields a strictly higher payoff to the deviating player, then, because the gain to deviating far in the future is discounted, there must also be a gain to some long finite deviation. But by the arguments for finitely repeated games, this is impossible.

Proposition 9.4-4: One-Stage Deviation Principle for Infinitely Repeated Games[16]

In an infinitely repeated game suppose that stage payoffs are bounded from above and that the discount factor is strictly less than 1. If for the strategy profile $\{\bar{s}^t(h^t)\}_{t=1}^{\infty}$ there is no one-stage deviation by a player that raises that player's payoff, then the strategy profile is sub-game perfect.

Proof: Suppose player i deviates so that the strategy profile is $s \equiv \{s^t(h^t)\}_{t=1}^{\infty}$. Define $U_i^t(s)$ to be the payoff to strategy s in the stage t sub-game. If $\bar{s}$

---

[16] This proof follows closely that in Fudenberg and Tirole (1991).

is not sub-game perfect, then there is a stage τ, history h^τ, and associated stage τ sub-game such that player 1's payoff in the sub-game satisfies $U_i^\tau(s) - U_i^\tau(\bar{s}) = \varepsilon > 0$. Consider the strategy profile $\hat{s}$ that agrees with s for $t < \hat{t}$ and with $\bar{s}$ for all higher t. Because payoffs are bounded and the discounted factor $\delta < 1$ it follows that

$$\lim_{\hat{t} \to \infty} U_i^\tau(\hat{s}) - U_i^\tau(s) = 0.$$

Note that

$$U_i^\tau(\hat{s}) - U_i^\tau(\bar{s}) = [U_i^\tau(\hat{s}) - U_i^\tau(s)] + [U_i^\tau(s) - U_i^\tau(\bar{s})].$$

We have argued that the first bracketed expression approaches zero as $\hat{t} \to \infty$ and by hypothesis the second bracketed expression is ε. Hence there exists a stage $\hat{t}$ such that

$$U_i^\tau(\hat{s}) - U_i^\tau(\bar{s}) \geq \tfrac{1}{2}\varepsilon.$$

Note that the strategy profile $\hat{s}$ is a finite stage deviation from $\bar{s}$. But by the arguments for finite stage games, if there is no gain to a one-stage deviation, there can be no gain to any finite stage deviation. Thus we have a contradiction. □

Exercises

Exercise 9.4-1: Repeated Cournot Production Game Suppose $c = 4$, $p = 16 - q_1 - q_2$ and $q_1, q_2 \in \mathbb{R}^+$.

(a) Show that the Pareto efficient strategies of the one-shot game satisfy $q_1 + q_2 = 6$.
(b) Solve for the unique NE.
(c) For what discount factors is the cooperative output vector $(x, x) < (q_1^N, q_2^N)$ a sub-game perfect equilibrium outcome of the infinitely repeated game?

Exercise 9.4-2: NE of the Repeated Game For the data of Exercise 9.4-1, consider the strategy $q^* = (3, 3)$.

(a) Explain why the minmax threat by both players is an NE threat but not an SPE threat.
(b) For what discount factors is $q^* = (3, 3)$ an NE outcome of the infinitely repeated game?

Exercise 9.4-3: Cournot Game With a T Period Threat For the data of Exercise 9.4-1, obtain an inequality of the form $T \leq f(\delta)$ that must be satisfied in order for the T-period threat to support the profit-maximizing output $q^* = (3, 3)$ as a sub-game perfect equilibrium.

References and Selected Historical Reading

Aumann, Robert. (1987). "Correlated Equilibrium as an Extension of Bayesian Rationality." *Econometrica* **55**: 1–18.

Benoit, J. P. and Krishna, V. (1985). "Finitely Repeated Games." *Econometrica* **53**: 890–904.

Bertrand, J. (1883). "Théorie mathématique de la richesse sociale." *Journal des Savants*, 499–508.

Cournot, A. (1838). *Recherches sur les Principes Mathematiques de la Théorie des Richesses*. English edition (ed. N. Bacon): *Researches into the Mathematical Principles of the Theory of Wealth*, New York: Macmillan, 1987.

Dasgupta, P, and Maskin, E. (1986). "The Existence of Equilibrium in Discontinuous Economic Games I: Theory." *Review of Economic Studies* **53**: 1–26.

Debreu, Gerard. (1952). "A Social Equilibrium Existence Theorem." *Proceedings of the National Academy of Sciences* **38**: 886–93.

Fan, K. (1952). "Fixed Point and Minimax Theorems in Locally Convex Topological Linear Spaces." *Proceedings of the National Academy of Sciences* **38**: 121–26.

Friedman J. (1971). "A Noncooperative Equilibrium for Supergames." *Review of Economic Studies* **38**: 1–12.

Fudenberg, D. and Levine, D. (1983). "Sub-Game Perfect Equilibria of Finite and Infinite Horizon Games." *Journal of Economic Theory* **31**: 227–56.

Fudenberg, D., Levine, D., and Maskin, E. (1994). "The Folk Theorem with Imperfect Public Information." *Econometrica* **62**: 997–1039.

Fudenberg, Drew and Maskin, Eric. (1986). "The Folk Theorem in Repeated Games with Discounting or with Incomplete Information." *Econometrica* **54**: 533–54.

Fudenberg, Drew and Tirole, Jean. (1991). *Game Theory*. Cambridge, MA: MIT Press.

Glicksberg I. L. (1952). "A Further Generalization of the Kakutani Fixed Point Theorem with Application to Nash Equilibrium Points." *Proceedings of the National Academy of Sciences* **38**: 170–74.

Nash J. (1950). "Equilibrium Points in N-Person Games." *Proceedings of the National Academy of Sciences* **36**: 48–49.

Rubinstein, A. (1982). "Perfect Equilibrium in a Bargaining Model." *Econometrica* **50**: 97–109.

Selten, R. (1965). "Spieltheoretische Behandlung eines Oligopolmodells mit Nachfrageträgheit." *Zeitschrift für die gesamte Staatswissenschaft* **12**: 301–24.

10

Games with Asymmetric Information

10.1 Games of Incomplete Information

Key ideas: Bayesian games, common knowledge, Nature's move, Bayesian Nash equilibrium in simultaneous and sequential move games, equilibrium in auctions

In the games considered in the previous chapter, the only uncertainty concerns the strategy that each player will employ. Players have full information about their opponents' payoffs. Moreover, in games with more than one round of play, all players have complete information about the history of the strategies played and this is common knowledge. We now relax these assumptions. In this section one or more players must choose an action knowing the preferences of his opponents only probabilistically. Formally, player $i \in \mathfrak{I}$ with utility function $u_i(\cdot, \theta_i)$ is said to be a player of type θ_i where $\theta_i \in \Theta_i = \{\theta_{i1}, \ldots, \theta_{im_i}\}$ is the set of possible types of player i.

Simultaneous Move Game – An Example

To illustrate the issues associated with such games, consider the following variant of the Cournot duopoly game. If firm i is of type θ_i it has a unit cost of $c(\theta_i)$. Firm i knows its own type but not that of its opponent. Firm i, $i = 1, 2$ chooses an output q_i. The products of the two firms are perfect substitutes so the market-clearing price is

$$p(q) = a - q_1 - q_2.$$

Therefore, if the output vector is q, the profit of firm i is

$$u_i(q_i, q_{-i}, \theta_i) = (a - q_i - q_{-i} - c(\theta_i))q_i.$$

If firm i does not know the other firm's type, it maximizes the expectation over all the possible types:

$$U_i(q_i, \theta_i) \equiv \underset{q_{-i}}{E}\{u_i(q_i, q_{-i}, \theta_i)\} = (a - q_i - E\{q_{-i}\} - c(\theta_i))q_i.$$

347

Then

$$q_i(\theta_i) = \arg \underset{q_i}{\mathrm{Max}}\{U_i(q_i, \theta_i)\}.$$

Note that U_i is a strictly concave function of q_i; thus the FOC is both necessary and sufficient.

FOC

$$\frac{\partial U}{\partial q_i} = a - E\{q_{-i}\} - c_i(\theta_i) - 2q_i = 0, \quad i = 1, 2.$$

Therefore

$$q_i^{BR}(\theta_i) = \tfrac{1}{2}(a - E\{q_{-i}\} - c(\theta_i)), \quad i = 1, 2. \tag{10.1-1}$$

Consider the simplest case in which firm 2's cost is known, but firm 1's cost is private information. We now consider how beliefs affect firm 1's decision by examining the implications of a change in beliefs.

First-Order Beliefs

Firm 2 revises upward its beliefs about firm 1's unit cost. Because firm 1 produces less with a higher cost, firm 2 then revises downward its beliefs about q_1. As a result firm 2 will increase its output.

Second-Order Beliefs

Firm 1 believes that firm 2 has revised upward its beliefs about c_1. If this belief is correct, firm 2 will raise its output. Then given these beliefs about firm 2, firm 1 will lower its own output. Thus second-order beliefs also affect best responses.

Third-Order Beliefs

Firm 2 believes that firm 1 believes that firm 2 has revised upward its beliefs about c_1. From the earlier arguments, it follows that firm 2 believes that firm 1 will lower its output. Given such beliefs firm 2 will further raise its own output. Thus third-order beliefs also affect best responses.

This same argument can be extended ad infinitum, so beliefs at every level affect best responses. One way to cut through such complexity is to extend the assumption of common knowledge to beliefs.

Definition: Common Knowledge Beliefs The joint probability distribution, $f(\theta_1, \ldots, \theta_I)$, over the type space $\Theta = \times_{i \in \mathfrak{I}} \Theta_i$, is common knowledge.

We now modify the duopoly example and assume that each firm's type is independently and identically distributed. Therefore $f(\theta_1, \theta_2) = g(\theta_1)g(\theta_2)$. We assume that this is common knowledge.

A pure strategy for firm i is a mapping $q_i(\theta_i)$ of each possible type $\theta_i \in \Theta_i$ into the set of feasible actions $A_i = \mathbb{R}_+$. Given common knowledge about the strategy of the other firm and common knowledge about the distribution of types, it is a straightforward matter for firm i to compute the expected payoff from any output choice q_i

Appealing to (10.1-1),

$$q_i^{BR}(\theta_i) = \tfrac{1}{2}\left(a - \underset{\theta_{-i}}{E}\{q_{-i}(\theta_{-i})\} - c(\theta_i)\right).$$

Taking expectations over firm i's type,

$$\underset{\theta_i}{E}\{q_i(\theta_i)\} = \tfrac{1}{2}\left(a - \underset{\theta_{-i}}{E}\{q_{-i}(\theta_{-i})\} - \underset{\theta_i}{E}\{c(\theta_i)\}\right).$$

Because the cost function $c(\theta_i)$ is the same for each type, and the joint distribution of types is symmetric, it follows that the expected cost, $\bar{c}$, is the same for each type. Setting $i = 1$ and then $i = 2$ and solving,

$$\underset{\theta_i}{E}\{q_i(\theta_i)\} = \tfrac{1}{3}(a - \bar{c}), \quad i = 1, 2.$$

Substituting this into (10.1-1) and rearranging,

$$q_i^{BR}(\theta_i) = \tfrac{1}{3}(a - \bar{c}) - \tfrac{1}{2}(c(\theta_i) - \bar{c}), \quad i = 1, 2$$

Therefore

$$\begin{aligned} p(\theta) &= a - q_1(\theta_1) - q_2(\theta_2) \\ &= \tfrac{1}{3}a + \tfrac{2}{3}\bar{c} + [\tfrac{1}{2}(c(\theta_1) + c(\theta_2)) - \bar{c}]. \end{aligned}$$

Note that the expected price is $\bar{p} = \tfrac{1}{3}a + \tfrac{2}{3}\bar{c}$ and the price exceeds the expected price by the difference between the average of the two unit cost realizations and the mean unit cost.

Simultaneous Move Games

Consider any simultaneous move game in which player $i \in \mathfrak{I}$ has a type $\theta_i \in \Theta_i$ and a set of feasible actions A_i. Let S_i be the set of all probability measures on $\Delta(A_i)$ and define $S = S_1 \times \cdots, \times S_I$. A strategy s_i for player $i \in \mathfrak{I}$ is, for each type $\theta_i \in \Theta_i$, a probability measure $s_i(\theta_i) \in S_i$. The strategy profile $s = (s_1, \ldots, s_I)$ is then a listing of the type of contingent strategies for every player.

Such a game is called a Bayesian game, and an equilibrium of the game is called a Bayesian Nash equilibrium.

Definition: Bayesian Nash Equilibrium of a Simultaneous Move Game Let $u_i(s, \theta_i)s \in S$ be the payoff of player $i \in \mathfrak{I}$ if his type is $\theta_i \in \Theta_i$ and the strategy profile is s. Let $f(\theta_1, \dots, \theta_I)$ be the joint probability distribution over types, where this is common knowledge. The strategy profile is a Bayesian Nash equilibrium if, for each $\theta_i \in \Theta_i$, $i \in \mathfrak{I}$ $s_i(\theta_i)$ is a best response, given the common knowledge beliefs.

Because it emphasizes the role of common knowledge beliefs, we now note that a Bayesian Nash equilibrium is a Nash equilibrium of a sequential move game in which an additional player, "Nature" moves first. In the first move Nature chooses each player's type. Nature's payoff is independent of the actions of the other players, so any mixed strategy is a best response for Nature. In a Nash equilibrium, the strategies of all the players are common knowledge so, after Nature makes her move, the remaining players respond knowing Nature's mixed strategy; that is, the joint probability distribution over types. Therefore a Bayesian Nash equilibrium of the I player game of incomplete information can be viewed as a Nash equilibrium of the $I + 1$ player game with Nature playing first.

Sealed First- and Second-Price Auctions

Bidding games are an important class of simultaneous move Bayesian games. Each player (or bidder) has private information about the value of a prize. The players then bid for the prize by choosing actions. The resulting allocation of the prize is based on the actions chosen.

One such bidding game is an auction. A single item is up for sale. Buyers submit sealed bids and the buyer submitting the highest bid is the winner. In the case of a tie, the winner is chosen randomly from the tying high bidders. In the first-price (or high-bid) auction the winning bidder pays his own high bid (the first price). In the second-price auction the winning bidder pays the second highest bid (the second price).[1]

In the sealed second-price auction it is easy to show that if buyer i's value is θ_i his dominant strategy is bid his value. Let m be the maximum of all the other bids. Suppose that buyer i bids $x < \theta_i$ rather than θ_i. If $m < x$, buyer i remains the winner and continues to pay m (the second highest bid). If $m > \theta_i$, buyer i remains the loser. If $x < m < \theta_i$, buyer i is the loser and so his payoff is zero. If he had bid θ_i he would have been the winner and earned a profit of $\theta_i - m$. Thus bidding θ_i weakly dominates bidding $x < \theta_i$. An almost

---

[1] A simple way to run such an auction as a classroom experiment is to have the players pull a single bill from their wallets and look at (say) the second and third digits of the bank note number. Then valuations lie between 0% and 99% of some cash prize (say ten dollars.) The probability of each number is the same so values are uniformly distributed.

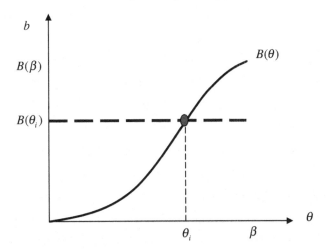

Figure 10.1-1. Equilibrium bid function.

identical argument establishes that bidding θ_i also weakly dominates bidding $x > \theta_i$.

Let $\{\theta_{(1)}, \theta_{(2)}, \ldots, \theta_{(n)}\}$ be the values ordered from highest to lowest.[2] If all buyers bid according to their dominant strategies and buyer i wins, then $\theta_i = \theta_{(1)}$ and his payment is $\theta_{(2)}$. Buyer i's expected payment conditional on being the winner is therefore $E\{\theta_{(2)}|\theta_{(1)} = \theta_i\}$.

We now turn to the sealed first-price auction. Under the assumption of independently and identically distributed (i.i.d.) values it is natural to look for a symmetric equilibrium. A buyer with a higher valuation has more to lose by bidding low so it is also natural to look for an equilibrium bidding strategy $B(\theta_i)$ that is strictly increasing. Finally, given the assumption of a continuously differentiable c.d.f. we assume that $B(\cdot) \in \mathbb{C}^1$. Suppose that all the buyers other than buyer i bid according to the strictly increasing bid function $B(\cdot)$ depicted in Figure 10.1-1. With all other buyers bidding according to the equilibrium bidding strategy, buyer i's win probability if his value is θ_i and he bids $B(\theta_i)$, is the probability that θ_i is the high value; that is, $w(\theta_i) = F^{n-1}(\theta_i)$.

Rather than solve directly for the equilibrium bid function, it is easier to solve for the equilibrium payoff. This is the equilibrium win probability $w(\theta)$ times the net gain $\theta - B(\theta)$; that is,

$$u(\theta) = w(\theta)(\theta - B(\theta)).$$

Because we know the equilibrium win probability we can then use this equation to solve for the equilibrium bid function.

---

[2] The jth highest value is called the jth order statistic.

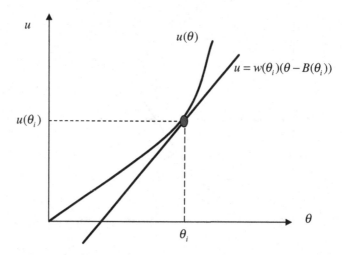

Figure 10.1-2. Equilibrium payoff function.

Suppose that buyer i deviates from the equilibrium strategy and bids $B(\theta_i)$ regardless of his value. His win probability is then $w(\theta_i)$ regardless of his value. If his value is θ, then his expected payoff is

$$u = w(\theta_i)(\theta - B(\theta_i)).$$

Note that the expected payoff rises linearly with buyer i's value as depicted in Figure 10.1-2. Note also that the graph of the function has a slope equal to the win probability $w(\theta_i)$.

Because $u(\theta)$ is the payoff when buyer i responds optimally, it follows that

$$u(\theta) \geq w(\theta_i)(\theta - B(\theta_i)) \quad \text{for all} \quad \theta \in [0, \beta].$$

Also,

$$u(\theta_i) = w(\theta_i)(\theta_i - B(\theta_i)). \tag{10.1-2}$$

Therefore the function $u(\theta)$ must have the same slope as the line at θ_i. Hence

$$\frac{du}{d\theta}(\theta_i) = w(\theta_i).$$

Exactly the same argument holds for each value on $[0, \beta]$. Moreover a buyer with a value of zero bids zero and has a zero payoff. Therefore

$$u(\theta_i) = \int_0^{\theta_i} \frac{du}{d\theta} d\theta = \int_0^{\theta_i} w(\theta) d\theta.$$

Integrating this expression by parts,

$$u(\theta_i) = \theta_i w(v_i) - \int_0^{\theta_i} \theta \, dw(\theta) = w(\theta_i) \left(\theta_i - \frac{\int_0^{\theta_i} \theta \, dw(\theta)}{w(\theta_i)} \right).$$

Comparing this expression with (10.1-2), it follows that the equilibrium bid function is

$$B(\theta_i) = \frac{\int_0^{\theta_i} \theta \, dw(\theta)}{w(\theta_i)}. \tag{10.1-3}$$

Note that

$$\frac{w(\theta)}{w(\theta_i)} = \Pr\{\theta_{(2)} \leq \theta | \theta_{(1)} = \theta_i\}.$$

Therefore the equilibrium bid is the expectation of the second highest value, conditional on buyer i having the highest value.

As we have seen, this is also the equilibrium expected payment of the high-value buyer in the sealed second-price auction. We therefore have the following result.

Proposition 10.1-1: Revenue Equivalence of the Sealed First- and Second-Price Auctions
In an n-bidder auction in which bidders are risk neutral and valuations are independently and identically distributed according to a distribution with c.d.f. $F \in \mathbb{C}^1$ and support $[0, \beta]$, equilibrium expected revenue is the same in the sealed first- and second-price auctions.

To understand this result it is helpful to reconsider the sealed second-price auction.

Let $u(\theta)$ be the equilibrium expected payoff. If buyers bid according to their equilibrium strategies, buyer i, with value θ_i bids $b_i = \theta_i$ and wins with probability $w(\theta_i) = F^{n-1}(\theta_i)$. Let $r(\theta_i)$ be buyer i's equilibrium expected payment. Then buyer i's expected payoff when his value is θ_i is

$$u(\theta_i) = w(\theta_i)\theta_i - r(\theta_i).$$

Now suppose that buyer i deviates from the equilibrium bidding strategy and bids θ_i regardless of his value. His win probability is therefore $w(\theta_i)$ and his expected payment is $r(\theta_i)$. Then his payoff is

$$u = w(\theta_i)\theta - r(\theta_i).$$

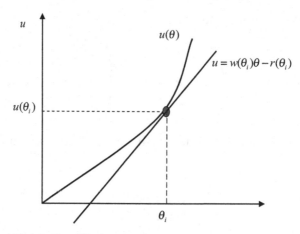

Figure 10.1-3. Equilibrium payoffs in the sealed second-price auction.

Because this strategy is feasible and $u(\theta)$ is the best response payoff it follows that

$$u(\theta) \geq w(\theta_i)\theta - r(\theta_i).$$

Also $u(\theta_i) = w(\theta_i)\theta_i - r(\theta_i)$. Thus the equilibrium payoff function is bounded below by the line $u = w(\theta_i)\theta - r(\theta_i)$ and touches at $\theta = \theta_i$ as depicted in Figure 10.1-3.

It follows that the slope of the payoff function is

$$\frac{du}{dv}(\theta_i) = w(\theta_i).$$

Therefore just as in the sealed first-price auction

$$u(\theta_i) = u(\theta_i) - u(0) = \int\limits_{0}^{\theta_i} \frac{du}{d\theta} d\theta = \int\limits_{0}^{\theta_i} w(\theta) d\theta.$$

We therefore have the following result.

Proposition 10.1-2: Buyer Equivalence of the Sealed First- and Second-Price Auctions

In an n-bidder auction in which bidders are risk neutral and valuations are independently and identically distributed according to a distribution with c.d.f. $F \in \mathbb{C}^1$ and support $[0, \beta]$, the equilibrium payoff for each buyer type is the same in the sealed first- and second-price auctions.

In both of the auctions the total surplus generated is the value of the transfer of the item from the seller to the buyer who values it most. Therefore the total surplus in the two auctions is the same. In equilibrium the buyers are indifferent between the two auctions; therefore the remaining player in the game (the seller) must be as well. Hence we have revenue equivalence.

Strategically Equivalent Open Auctions

As we now show, for each of these auctions there are open auctions in which the equilibrium strategies are identical to those in each of the sealed bid auctions.

Dutch Auction

Traditionally tulips have been sold in Amsterdam using an open descending-price auction. A trolley of tulips is rolled in front of the bidders and a clock starts ticking down. The clock is stopped when a buyer raises her hand and claims the flowers on the trolley. We now argue that this auction is equivalent to a sealed high-bid auction, so that the Bayesian Nash equilibrium strategies are exactly the same. First note that unless a buyer thinks that she can learn how other buyers will bid by watching how they are perspiring or nervously twitching, she learns nothing until the item is sold. Thus she may as well write down her planned bid, $B(\theta_i)$, on a piece of paper. As long as she and all the other bidders do so, the auctioneer can throw away the clock and ask to see all the bits of paper. The buyer who has written down the largest number is the winner and pays the bid. Of course this is how a sealed high-bid auction is conducted so the two auctions are equivalent.

Proposition 10.1-3: Equivalence of the Sealed First-Price and Dutch Auctions
The equilibrium bidding strategies in the sealed first-price and Dutch auctions are identical.

Ascending Bid (English) Auction

Although sealed bidding is standard when firms compete for contracts, the open auction used by auction houses is also commonly used. It is the dominant auction for objets d'art, and its use for other items is increasing.[3] For theoretical purposes it is convenient to model such an "English" auction not with an auctioneer calling successively higher prices but with a clock ticking up.[4] Each buyer has control of a light located on a computer screen

---

[3] In Korea used cars are sold in an electronic open ascending-price auction. By pushing a button a buyer increases the maximum bid by one pre-defined step unless he is already the high bidder. Of course Internet auctions are variants of the open ascending-price auction.

[4] The real-world auctioneer then plays the role of the clock. He can speed the process up when bidding is brisk by jumping the asking price early in the auction.

alongside her bidder number. Initially each buyer's light is on, indicating buyer participation. Once a buyer pushes her button, her light goes out. The clock ticks on until the second to last light flicks off. The remaining buyer is the winner and she pays the price on the clock. If there are m bidders remaining and all the m lights go off simultaneously, the winner is selected randomly from among them.

In such an auction, it is better for each buyer to stay in rather than drop out as long as the asking price (the clock price) is below her value. This is the case regardless of her opponents' bidding strategies. Thus a buyer's dominant strategy is to "bid" her value; that is, stay until the clock price equals her value.

Summarizing, we have the following result.

Proposition 10.1-4: Equivalence of the Sealed Second-Price and English Auctions
The equilibrium bidding strategy in a sealed second-bid and in the open ascending-price auction is for buyers to bid their values.

This last observation and the revenue equivalence of the sealed first- and second-bid auctions explain what would otherwise be a remarkable difference between market institutions in England and Scotland. The canny Scots sell real property primarily in sealed first-price auctions. The English typically sell real property in open ascending-price auctions. The revenue equivalence results thus provide a powerful explanation for the survival of both institutions.

Sequential Move Games

Sequential move games can be similarly generalized to allow for incomplete information.

As in the case of complete information we denote the player who moves in the t-th stage as player i_t. The set of possible pure strategies available to player i_t in stage t is A_t. Let S_t be the set of probability measures on $\Delta(A_t)$. With complete information, the stage t strategy $s_t(h^t)$ is a probability measure for each possible history. With incomplete information, the stage t strategy $s_t(h^t, \theta_t) \in S_t$ is a probability measure for each possible history and type. A payoff $u_i(s, \theta_i)$, $i \in \mathfrak{I}$ is specified for every possible strategy profile s.

Definition: Bayesian Nash Equilibrium of a Sequential Move Game Let $u_i(s, \theta_i)s \in S$ be the payoff of player $i \in \mathfrak{I}$ if his type is $\theta_i \in \Theta_i$. Let $f(\theta_1, \ldots, \theta_I)$ be the joint probability distribution over types, where this is common knowledge. A strategy profile is a Bayesian Nash equilibrium if, for each t and $\theta_{i_t} \in \Theta_{i_t}$ $s_t(h^t, \theta_{i_t})$ is a best response, given the common knowledge beliefs.

When games are sequential, one of the additional complexities is that actions typically reveal information about the type of player taking the action. If types are correlated, all players with decision nodes later in the game update their beliefs based on this information. The common knowledge assumption plays a critical role because it means that all the players can update their beliefs using Bayes' Rule.

Such issues are the subject of Section 10.2. Here we consider a simpler case in which types are independent.

Cournot Duopoly with Sequential Moves

Consider the Cournot output game once more. Firm i, $i = 1, 2$ knows its own unit cost c_i and chooses an output q_i, $i = 1, 2$. The resulting market-clearing demand price is $p = a - q_1 - q_2$. Firm 1 moves first, choosing its output. Firm 2 observes firm 1's output and then chooses its best response $q_2^{BR}(q_1, c_2)$. Firm 1 anticipates this choice. However, in the absence of common knowledge, firm 1 does not know firm 2's unit cost. Instead it forms its own belief about this cost, $E_1\{c_2\}$.

Firm 2's profit is

$$U_2(q, c_2) = (a - q_1 - q_2 - c_2)q_2.$$

Solving,

$$q_2^{BR}(q_1, c_2) = \arg \underset{q_2}{\text{Max}}\{U_2(q, c_2)\} = \tfrac{1}{2}(a - c_2 - q_1).$$

Given firm 1's beliefs, it acts as though firm 2's best response function is

$$q_2^{BR}(\bar{c}_{12}) = \tfrac{1}{2}(a - E_1\{c_2\} - q_1).$$

Then firm 1's expected profit is

$$U_1 = (a - q_1 - q_2^{BR} - c_1)q_1.$$

Substituting for the best response function and solving,

$$q_1^{BR} = \tfrac{1}{2}a - c_1 + \tfrac{1}{2}E_1\{c_2\}.$$

Given this action by firm 1, firm 2's best response is

$$q_2^{BR} = \tfrac{1}{2}(a - c_2 - q_1^{BR}) = \tfrac{1}{4}a + \tfrac{1}{2}(c_2 - c_1) - \tfrac{1}{4}E_1\{c_2\}.$$

Thus total output is a function not only of the marginal cost of each firm but also of firm 1's first-order beliefs about firm 2's marginal cost.

With three firms, industry output depends on second-order beliefs as well. Arguing as earlier, firm 2 (the second mover) chooses its output taking into account its own marginal cost and its expectation of firm 3's marginal cost $E_2\{c_3\}$. Firm 1 must then form an expectation not only of 2's marginal cost $E_1\{c_2\}$ but also of firm 2's expectation of firm 3's marginal cost $E_1\{E_2\{c_3\}\}$.

Extending this argument, adding an nth firm requires adding $n - 1$ additional expected values,

$$E_1\{c_2\}, \; E_1\{E_2\{c_3\}\}, \; \ldots, \; E_1\{\ldots\{E_{n-1}\{c_n\}\ldots\}.$$

Thus total output is a function not only of the n marginal costs but also of

$$1 + 2 + \cdots + (n - 1) = \tfrac{1}{2}(n - 1)n$$

expected values. Under the standard common knowledge assumption the solution is greatly simplified because the $n - 1$ expected marginal costs of later movers are all common knowledge.

Exercises

Exercise 10.1-1: Batman and the Joker Batman has just learned that the Joker plans a big caper for tomorrow, but he does not know if the target of the Joker's attack will be the Museum (M) or the Tower (T). Batman can guard one of these targets but not both. Tomorrow's outcome depends on the actions of Batman and the Joker and on the weather.

- If Batman guards the wrong target (that is, the target that the Joker does not attack) then the Joker will succeed regardless of the weather. Batman values this outcome at −4 and the Joker values it at +4.
- If Batman guards the Museum and the Joker attacks the Museum and the weather is Bad, Batman will foil and catch the Joker. Batman values this outcome at +8 and the Joker values it at −20.
- In every other circumstance the Joker will be foiled but will escape. Batman and the Joker value this outcome at 0.

Batman must make his choice today – before he knows the weather. The Joker can make his choice tomorrow when he sees the weather. Neither player sees the action of the other. It is common knowledge that the probability that the weather will be good is $\tfrac{3}{4}$ and the probability that the weather will be bad is $\tfrac{1}{4}$.

(a) Depict this Bayesian game in extensive (tree) form.
(b) Explain carefully why there can be no equilibrium in pure strategies.
(c) Let y be the probability that Batman chooses the Museum. Show that there is a unique y such that the Joker is indifferent between M and T if the weather is bad and a second y such that the Joker is indifferent if the weather is good.

(d) Let x be the probability that the Joker chooses M. For each y determined in (c) examine the payoff of Batman and show that there is a unique Bayesian Nash equilibrium of this game.

Exercise 10.1-2: Sequential Move Game with Three Firms There are three firms selling an identical product. The market-clearing price is $p(q) = a - q_1 - q_2 - q_3$. Firm i has a unit cost c_i that is private information. Unit costs are independently distributed with support $\Gamma \subset [0, a]$. Each firm's cost is private information. Firm 1 chooses its output and this is observed by firm 2, which then chooses q_2. Firm 3 observes both q_1 and q_2 and then chooses q_3.

(a) Solve for the Nash equilibrium without making the common knowledge assumption.
(b) Compare the choice of firm 1 with its choice when there is common knowledge about the distribution of unit costs.

Exercise 10.1-3: All Pay Auction Suppose that valuations are independent and each buyer's valuation is uniformly distributed on $[0, 1]$. Suppose that the seller changes the rules. The item is to be sold to the high bidder, but all bids will be retained by the seller.

(a) In the two-buyer case, confirm that the new symmetric equilibrium bid function is

$$b(\theta) = \tfrac{1}{2}\theta^2.$$

(b) In the n-buyer case confirm that the perfect Bayesian equilibrium (BPE) bid function is of the form $b(\theta) = k\theta^n$.
(c) Solve for the equilibrium bid function if each buyer's value is i.i.d. on $[0, 1]$ with c.d.f. $F(\cdot) \in^1$.

Exercise 10.1-4: Sealed High-Bid Auction with Two Identical Items for Sale There are three buyers. The support of each buyer's value is $[0, \beta]$ and the p.d.f. of the buyers' values is $f(\theta_1) f(\theta_2) f(\theta_3)$. Each buyer values only one item. Buyers submit sealed bids. The two highest bids are the winning bids, and each winner pays his own bid.

(a) Show that buyer i, with value θ_i, has one of the two highest values with probability $2F(\theta_i) - F(\theta_i)^2$.
(b) Hence argue that, in a symmetric equilibrium, the slope of buyer i's equilibrium payoff function is $\frac{du}{d\theta}(\theta_i) = 2F(\theta_i) - F(\theta_i)^2$.
(c) Hence solve for the equilibrium bid function.
(d) Generalize your answer to the n-buyer case.

10.2 Refinements of Bayesian Nash Equilibrium

Key Ideas: perfect Bayesian equilibrium, trembling-hand perfection, sequential equilibrium, Intuitive Criterion

Even with the heroic assumption of common knowledge, it is typical for there to be many Bayesian Nash equilibria (BNE). Worse still, for the important class of signaling games there is a continuum of BNE. This is highly unsatisfactory, because the plethora of equilibria does not lead to readily testable predictions of the theory. Instead theory explains almost anything. A second problem for the BNE is that some of the multiple equilibria are widely considered to be much less plausible than others. In response, there has been a massive amount of research devoted to "refining" the definition of equilibrium, so that the refined equilibrium concept selects a subset of the BNE and at the same time eliminates equilibria that seem implausible. Here we examine the most widely used of these refinements.

We begin with an example of an implausible NE. Consider the following variant of the entry game examined in Section 9.2. Both player 1 (the potential entrant) and player 2 (the incumbent) must choose a strategy before knowing how strong player 1's financial backing will be.[5] If his backing is weak, the payoff matrix is as shown in Table 10.2-1a. If the entrant's financial backing is strong the payoff matrix is instead as shown in

Table 10.2-1a. *Weak Potential Entrant and Incumbent*

		Player 2: (Incumbent)	
		Fight	Share
Player 1: (Entrant)	Enter	–2, 40	3, 30
	Out	0, 60	0, 60

Table 10.2-1b. *Strong Potential Entrant and Incumbent*

		Player 2: (Incumbent)	
		Fight	Share
Player 1: (Entrant)	Enter	4, 29	3, 30
	Out	0, 60	0, 60

[5] Player 1 (the Entrant) is male and player 2 (the Incumbent) is female.

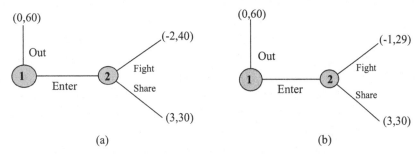

Figure 10.2-1. (a) Game with weak entrant. (b) Game with strong entrant.

Table 10.2-1b. The games are depicted in extensive form in Figures 10.2-1a and 10.2-1b.

First consider these games if there is full information as to whether the entrant is weak or strong. In the game with the weak entrant, if player 1 chooses *Enter*, player 2's best response is *Fight* and so player 1 is strictly better off choosing *Out*. Thus (*Out, Fight*) is the unique Nash equilibrium strategy profile.

In the game with the strong entrant the strategy profiles (*Out, Fight*) and (*Enter, Share*) are both Nash equilibria. Consider the first of these strategy profiles. With player 2 choosing *Fight*, player 1's best response is *Out*. And with player 1 choosing *Out*, any strategy by player 2 is a best response. However, this is an implausible equilibrium because if player 1 were to choose *Enter*, player 2's best response is *Out*.

This equilibrium is eliminated by looking at the sub-game beginning at the second node. The NE strategy of the sub-game with the strong entrant is *Share*. Then we can replace the second node with the payoff at the equilibrium terminal node of the sub-game; that is, (3, 30). Player 1 is then strictly better off choosing *Enter*, and so the NE profile (*Out, Fight*) is not sub-game perfect.

Perfect Bayesian Equilibrium

The least controversial of the refinements extends the notion of sub-game perfection.

To illustrate consider the entry game once more. Remember that we are assuming that both players must choose without knowing whether the entrant will be weak (limited financial backing) or strong (a big war chest.) The game is depicted in extensive form in Figure 10.2-2.

The added dashed line connecting the decision nodes of player 1 indicates that player 1 must choose an action knowing only that he is at one of these

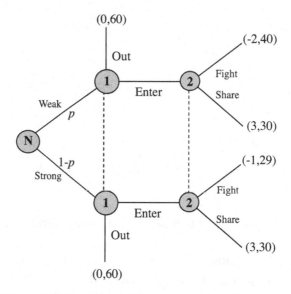

Figure 10.2-2. Game with both players uninformed.

two nodes. Because player 1's information is that he is at one of these nodes, the set of such nodes is called an *information set*. Similarly player 2 must choose her response knowing that she is in an information set. The probability, p, of a weak entrant is common knowledge.

Note that there are no sub-games. Note also that player 2's best response depends on her beliefs about player 1's strength. If she believes player 1 is likely to be weak her best response to *Enter* is *Fight*. If player 1 is almost certainly strong, player 2's best response to *Enter* is *Share*.

To compute his expected payoff from choosing *Enter*, player 1 must look ahead along the branches of the game tree and compute player 2's best response.

Bayesian Nash Equilibrium with Entry

Suppose that player 2 chooses *Share*. The expected payoff to player 1 if he chooses *Enter* is therefore

$$U_1 = pu_{1W}(Enter, Share) + (1-p)u_{1S}(Enter, Share) = 3.$$

Because the payoff to choosing *Out* is zero, player 1's best response is *Enter*.

With player 1 choosing *Enter* the probability that he is Weak is p. Given this probability, we can argue as earlier that player 2's expected payoff to choosing *Share* is $U_2(Share) = 30$ and the expected payoff to choosing *Fight* is $U_2(Fight) = p40 + (1 - p)29 = 29 + 11p$. The net gain to choosing *Fight* is therefore

$$U_2(Fight) - U_2(Share) = 11(p - \tfrac{1}{11}). \qquad (10.2\text{-}1)$$

Thus the proposed strategy *Share* is a best response for player 2 if and only if $p \le \tfrac{1}{11}$. Given that player 2 chooses *Share*, player 1's best response is *Enter*.

Bayesian Nash Equilibrium with No Entry

Suppose that player 2 chooses *Fight*. The expected payoff to player 1 if he chooses *Enter* is therefore

$$\begin{aligned} U_1 &= pu_{1W}(Enter,\ Fight) + (1 - p)u_{1S}(Enter,\ Fight) \\ &= p(-2) + (1 - p)(-1) < 0. \end{aligned}$$

Because the payoff to choosing *Out* is zero, player 1's best response is to choose *Out*.

Note that with player 1 choosing *Out*, player 2's decision node is never reached. Thus (*Out, Fight*) is always a Bayesian Nash equilibrium.

We have shown that if the probability of a weak entrant is sufficiently low ($p < \tfrac{1}{11}$) there are two equilibria. Is one of these equilibria more plausible than the other? Most economists argue that the equilibrium with no entry is implausible. First, if $p = 0$, this equilibrium is ruled out by sub-game perfection. Thus, by continuity, it seems an unlikely outcome if p is extremely small. Moreover, for all $p < \tfrac{1}{11}$ it follows from (10.2-1) that player 2 is strictly better off choosing *Share* rather than *Fight*. And given that player 2 chooses *Share*, player 1 is strictly better off choosing *Enter*. For this reason as well, the equilibrium with entry seems much more plausible.

Beliefs on and off the Equilibrium Path

The conclusion that *Fight* is implausible is based on an argument about what beliefs are sensible in the second stage of the game. In the equilibrium with entry, each of the decision nodes is reached with positive probability. Any such node and the branches leading to these nodes are said to be "on the equilibrium path." All the other nodes and branches are off the equilibrium path. In the equilibrium with no entry, the two nodes in player 2's information set are never reached. Thus the belief that player 2 will choose *Fight* is never tested. Therefore, to eliminate this strategy, we need to find a way to place restrictions on beliefs that are off the equilibrium path.

Definition: Perfect Bayesian Equilibrium A Bayesian Nash equilibrium strategy profile is a perfect Bayesian equilibrium (PBE) if, at all nodes off the equilibrium path, there are strategies and beliefs consistent with Bayes' Rule such that the strategies (on and off the equilibrium path) are best responses.[6]

In the earlier example, (*Enter, Share*) and (*Out, Fight*) are both BNE when $p < \frac{1}{11}$. The first of these is a PBE because all nodes are reached in the BNE so the conditions for a PBE are vacuously satisfied. In the BNE (*Out, Fight*), the two nodes in player 2's information set are off the equilibrium path. For this profile to be a PBE we must consider the best response at this information set. *Fight* is a best response only if player 2 believes that player 1 is weak with probability $p \geq \frac{1}{11}$. But it is common knowledge that the prior probability is $p < \frac{1}{11}$ and there is no additional information that might lead player 2 to update her belief. Therefore player 2's belief that $p \geq \frac{1}{11}$ is not consistent with Bayes' Rule and so (*Out, Fight*) is not a PBE.

Trembling-Hand Perfect Equilibrium

The early literature on perfect Bayesian equilibrium was built on the idea that any node off the equilibrium path would be reached with positive probability if, at each node or information set, a player were to "tremble" and select each of the pure strategies in his strategy set with a small but strictly positive probability. Formally, suppose that the set of feasible actions for the player making the decision at the t-th stage is A_t, where A_t is finite. Let $\overline{\pi}_t, t = 1, \ldots, T$ be the Bayesian Nash equilibrium strategy in stage t so that the strategy profile is $\overline{\pi} = (\overline{\pi}_1 \times \cdots \times \overline{\pi}_T)$. A strategy π_t (assigning probabilities to actions at the t-th stage) is called "totally mixed" if it places positive probability on all actions. Then consider a sequence $\{\pi^k\}_{k=1}^{\infty}$ of totally mixed strategies that approaches $\overline{\pi}$. We can think of these probabilities arising from trembles by each player in the game. Each player tries to play his equilibrium strategy but, with some small probability, trembles and selects the wrong action. The sequence $\{\pi^k\}_{k=1}^{\infty}$ is therefore called a sequence of "trembles." In the limit, the trembling approaches zero, and the strategy profile approaches the BNE strategy profile. Because the totally mixed strategies assign a positive probability to every branch of the tree, players can use Bayes' Rule to assign conditional probabilities to each of the nodes in their information sets and choose best responses.

---

[6] This is a somewhat informal definition. In general, a complete description of a perfect Bayesian equilibrium would spell out the restrictions on posterior beliefs implied by the assumptions made about prior beliefs. Formal definitions of two historically important special cases of a perfect Bayesian equilibrium are presented below.

Definition: Trembling-Hand Perfect Equilibrium A Bayesian Nash equilibrium is a trembling-hand PBE if there exists some sequence of totally mixed strategy profiles, $\{\pi^k\}_{k=1}^\infty$ converging on the equilibrium strategies, such that for all sufficiently large k, the equilibrium strategies are best responses.

Because the trembling-hand perfect equilibrium places restrictions on the beliefs at each of the equilibrium nodes, it further refines the PBE.

Sequential Equilibrium

Introducing trembles induces beliefs about the likelihood of every node. Rather than checking the conditions for trembling-hand perfection, it is often simpler to define the beliefs at each decision node to be the limit of beliefs under trembles, as the probability of trembling approaches zero. This led Kreps to propose the following slight weakening of Selten's equilibrium concept.

Definition: Sequential Equilibrium A Bayesian Nash equilibrium strategy profile of a game is a sequential equilibrium if the strategy at each node of the tree is a best response, when the beliefs at each node are the limits of beliefs associated with trembles, as the probability of trembling approaches zero.

Because the trembling-hand perfect equilibrium considers arbitrarily small trembles, the requirement that strategies be best responses must also hold in the limit. Therefore if an equilibrium is trembling-hand perfect, it is also sequential.[7]

Sequential Move Games with Private Information

Unfortunately, even these refinements do not prove very helpful in sequential move games in which earlier movers have private information.

Example 1: Informed First and Uninformed Second Mover
Consider the following variant of the entry game. Now player 1 knows his type but player 2 remains uninformed about player 1's type. This is indicated in Figure 10.2-3 in the game tree by the dashed line connecting player 2's nodes.

---

[7] Exercise 10.2-2 provides an example where a "crazy" equilibrium is sequential but not trembling-hand perfect. As a practical matter it is often easier to check whether an equilibrium is sequential so this should be the first step.

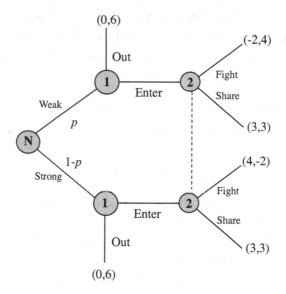

Figure 10.2-3. Game with informed first mover.

Note that if player 1 is strong, his strictly dominant strategy is to choose *Enter*. Suppose player 1 also chooses *Enter* if he is weak. Player 2's expected payoffs are as follows:

$$U_2(\textit{Enter, Fight}) = p(4) + (1 - p)(-2) = 6p - 2.$$

$$U_2(\textit{Enter, Share}) = p(3) + (1 - p)(3) = 3.$$

Suppose first that $p < 5/6$. Then $U_2(\textit{Enter, Fight}) < 3$ and so player 2's best response is *Share*. Given this response, the weak player 1 is also strictly better off choosing *Enter*. Thus the unique perfect Bayesian equilibrium is for player 1 to choose *Enter*, regardless of his type and for player 2 to choose *Share*.

Suppose next that $p > 5/6$. From the earlier argument, if player 1 also chooses *Enter* when he is weak, player 2 will choose *Fight*. But then *Enter* is not a best response by player 1 if he is weak. Thus there can be no equilibrium in pure strategies. We argue that there is a PBE in which player 1 randomizes if he is weak and player 2 also randomizes. The mixed strategies are depicted in the tree diagram in Figure 10.2-4.

Suppose that player 1 chooses *Enter* with probability α when he is the weak type. Applying Bayes' Rule

$$p\{\text{weak}|\textit{Enter}\} = \frac{\text{Pr}\{\text{weak, } \textit{Enter}\}}{\text{Pr}\{\text{weak, } \textit{Enter}\} + \text{Pr}\{\text{strong, } \textit{Enter}\}} = \frac{p\alpha}{p\alpha + 1 - p}$$

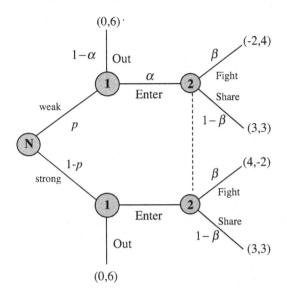

Figure 10.2-4. Equilibrium with mixed strategies.

and

$$p\{strong|Enter\} = \frac{\Pr\{strong, Enter\}}{\Pr\{weak, Enter\} + \Pr\{strong, Enter\}} = \frac{1-p}{p\alpha + 1 - p}.$$

The net expected gain to player 2 if she chooses *Fight* rather than *Enter* is therefore

$$\left(\frac{p\alpha}{1-p+p\alpha}\right)(4) + \left(\frac{1-p}{p\alpha+1-p}\right)(-2) - 3 = \frac{p}{p\alpha+1-p}\left(\alpha - \frac{5(1-p)}{p}\right).$$

Thus player 2 is indifferent and therefore willing to mix if $\alpha = \frac{5(1-p)}{p}$.

The weak player 1 must also be willing to mix. Suppose that player 2 chooses *Fight* with probability β. The weak player 1's net gain to choosing *Enter* rather than *Out* is therefore $\beta(-2) + (1-\beta)3 = 5(\frac{3}{5} - \beta)$. Thus the weak player 1 is indifferent and willing to mix if $\beta = \frac{3}{5}$.

As we now illustrate, such games typically have multiple equilibria.

Example 2

Consider another variant of the entry game. The game tree in Figure 10.2-5 has exactly the same branches as that of Figure 10.2-4 However the payoffs differ. Let $s_1(\theta)$ be player 1's strategy if he is type θ, where $\theta \in \Theta = \{strong, weak\}$ and let $s_2(h^1)$ be player 2's strategy, where $h^1 \in \{Out, Enter\}$ is the information that she has when she makes her choice. We now argue that each of the following strategy profiles is a Bayesian Nash equilibrium:

(i) $s_1(weak) = Out$, $s_1(strong) = Enter$, $s_2(Enter) = Share$
(ii) $s_1(weak) = s_1(strong) = Out$, $s_2(Enter) = Fight$.

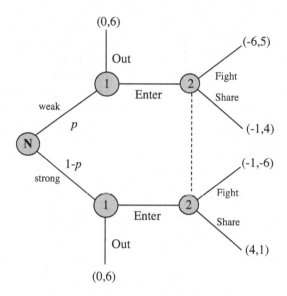

Figure 10.2-5. Game with an informed entrant.

Consider the first strategy profile. Note that, given the choices of the different types of player 1, player 2 can apply Bayes' Rule to determine the probability that the entrant is strong. Because the weak player 1 chooses *Out*, this probability is 1. Then player 2's best response is *Share* yielding a payoff of 1. And if player 2 chooses *Share*, player 1 is better off choosing *Enter* if he is strong and staying *Out* if he is weak. Thus the strategies are mutual best responses.

Consider the second strategy profile. If player 2 chooses *Fight*, regardless of whether player 1 is strong or weak, then player 1 is better off staying out and having a payoff of zero rather than entering and having a negative payoff. And given that player 1 always chooses *Out*, player 2 achieves her maximum possible payoff of 6. Thus again the strategies are mutual best responses.

We now argue that each Bayesian Nash equilibrium is also a PBE. To do so we show that it is a sequential equilibrium. Consider equilibrium (i). Let ε_W be the probability of a tremble by player 1 if he is weak and ε_S be the probability of a tremble if he is strong. Then $\text{Pr}\{\text{Weak}, \textit{Enter}\} = p\varepsilon_W$ and $\text{Pr}\{\text{Strong}, \textit{Enter}\} = (1 - p)\varepsilon_S$. Hence the conditional probability,

$$
\begin{aligned}
\text{Pr}\{W|\textit{Enter}\} &= \frac{\text{Pr}\{\text{Weak}, \textit{Enter}\}}{\text{Pr}\{\text{Weak}, \textit{Enter}\} + \text{Pr}\{\text{Strong}, \textit{Enter}\}} \\
&= \frac{p\varepsilon_W}{p\varepsilon_W + (1 - p)(1 - \varepsilon_S)}.
\end{aligned}
$$

Taking the limit as the probability of trembling approaches zero, the conditional probability $\text{Pr}\{\text{Weak}|\textit{Enter}\} \to 0$. Thus the Bayesian Nash equilibrium beliefs are sequential.

Now consider equilibrium (ii). Because the action *Enter* is not chosen in equilibrium, the Bayesian Nash equilibrium strategies place no restriction on the beliefs of player 2, should a player actually choose *Enter*. We now argue that, in this example, a sequential equilibrium also imposes no restrictions on these beliefs. To compute sequential beliefs we again introduce trembling probabilities ε_W and ε_S for the two types of player 1. Now the conditional probability that the entrant is weak is

$$\Pr\{W|Enter\} = \frac{\Pr\{Weak, Enter\}}{\Pr\{Weak, Enter\} + \Pr\{Strong, Enter\}}$$
$$= \frac{p\varepsilon_W}{p\varepsilon_W + (1-p)\varepsilon_S}.$$

For any ε_W choose $\varepsilon_S = (\frac{p}{1-p})\theta\varepsilon_W$. Then $\Pr\{W|Enter\} = \frac{1}{1+\theta}$. Taking the limit as $\varepsilon_W \to 0$ has no effect on this conditional probability. For large θ, this probability is close to zero and for small θ it is close to 1. Then by choosing a θ sufficiently large, the best response of player 2 is to choose *Share*.[8] Thus both the Bayesian Nash equilibria are trembling-hand perfect.

More complex games with private information typically have many perfect Bayesian equilibria. Indeed, for a widely studied class of signaling games, there is a continuum of PBE. Thus we are left either with a rather fuzzy theory of behavior, or we must seek some further way to refine the equilibrium concept.

Intuitive Criterion

Consider the equilibrium in which both types of player 1 choose *Out*. If player 1 is strong, he might make the following argument to himself or to player 2. "If I were weak and were to choose *Enter*, my possible payoffs would be –1 and –6, while my equilibrium payoff is zero. Thus I would never choose *Enter*. Therefore if I enter, I will be credibly signaling to player 2 that I am strong. Her best response will then be *Share*. As a result, I will end up with a payoff of 1. Because this is better than staying out I should choose to *Enter*."

Any Nash equilibrium in which a particular type can make such an argument is said to fail the Intuitive Criterion. We formalize this as follows.

Consider a game in which player 1 moves first, taking an action $a \in A$. The other players observe player 1's action and then play out the rest of the game. Player 1's type $\theta \in \Theta$ is private so the equilibrium payoffs depend on the beliefs of the other players about his type.

---

[8] We have shown that the conditional probability can lie anywhere on the interval $(0, 1)$. Suppose $(\varepsilon_w, \varepsilon_S) = (\delta, \delta^2)$. Then $\Pr\{\text{Weak}|Enter\} = \frac{p\delta}{p\delta + (1-p)\delta^2} = \frac{p}{p + (1-p)\delta}$.

Note that the limit as $\delta \to 0$ is 1 so the belief that $\Pr\{\text{Weak}|Enter\} = 1$ is also a sequential equilibrium belief.

Weak Intuitive Criterion[9] Consider an action of player 1, $\hat{a}$, that is chosen with zero probability in a PBE. Let $u_1(\hat{a}, \theta, \theta')$ be player 1's payoff if he chooses $\hat{a}$ when his type is θ and is believed to be type $\theta' \in \Theta$. Let $u_1^N(\theta)$ be this type's PBE payoff. The PBE fails the Intuitive Criterion if, for some player *1* of type $\hat{\theta} \in \Theta$, $u_1(\hat{a}, \hat{\theta}, \hat{\theta}) > u_1^N(\hat{\theta})$ and for all other types in Θ, $\text{Max}_{x \in \Theta}\{u_1(\hat{a}, \theta, x)\} < u_1^N(\theta)$.

The implicit message sent by the sender is "I am type $\hat{\theta}$ and you should believe me because if you do I will be better off than in the equilibrium only if I really am type $\hat{\theta}$. Moreover none of the other types will be better off taking this action regardless of which type you believe them to be."

For our example we have seen that the PBE in which both types choose *Out* fails the Weak Intuitive Criterion. The strong type is able to improve on his equilibrium payoff by choosing an out-of-equilibrium strategy. In the other equilibrium, the strong type "signals" that he is strong by choosing *Enter*. There is no out-of-equilibrium strategy that a weak player 1 can use to improve his payoff so this equilibrium satisfies the Intuitive Criterion.

Unfortunately this Weak Intuitive Criterion and Cho and Kreps' original Intuitive Criterion are too weak to be useful where there are more than two types. Cho and Kreps (1987) and Banks and Sobel (1987) suggest stronger refinements to deal with this more general case. Rather than follow either approach exactly, we instead strengthen the Intuitive Criterion as follows.

Strong Intuitive Criterion Consider an action of player 1, $\hat{a}$, that is chosen with zero probability in a PBE. Let $u_1(\hat{a}, \theta, \theta')$ be player 1's payoff if he chooses $\hat{a}$ when his type is θ and is believed to be type $\theta' \in \Theta$. Let $u_1^N(\theta)$ be this type's PBE payoff. The PBE fails the Intuitive Criterion if, for some type $\hat{\theta} \in \Theta$, $u_1(\hat{a}, \hat{\theta}, \hat{\theta}) > u_1^N(\hat{\theta})$ and for all other types in Θ, $u_1(\hat{a}, \theta, \hat{\theta}) < u_i^N(\theta)$.

In the Weak Intuitive Criterion other types are ruled out because there is no response to the action $\hat{a}_i$ that would make them better off, regardless of which type the responders believe then to be. Under the Strong Intuitive Criterion, the implicit message sent by the sender is "I am type $\hat{\theta}$ and you should believe me because, if you do, I will be better off than in the equilibrium only if I really am type $\hat{\theta}$."

For the two-type case the Strong and Weak Intuitive Criteria are equivalent. For more than two types the Strong Intuitive Criterion is a much more

---

[9] This is equivalent to Cho and Kreps' Intuitive Criterion with two types and is weaker with more than two types.

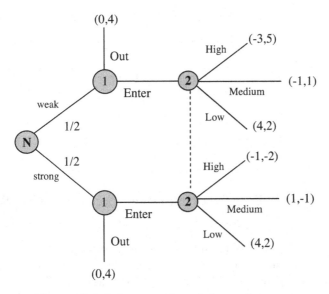

Figure 10.2-6. Game with an informed entrant.

powerful refinement.[10] However, it is weaker than the D1 refinement proposed by Cho and Kreps that modifies the slightly weaker Universal Divinity refinement proposed by Banks and Sobel.

Exercises

Exercise 10.2-1: Multiple Sequential Equilibria Consider the game depicted in extensive form in Figure 10.2-6.

Let $a_1(w)$ be the pure strategy of player 1 if Nature chooses a weak entrant, and let $a_1(S)$ be the pure strategy of player 1 if Nature chooses a strong entrant. Player 2 observes player 1's action and then responds with her action $a_2(a_1)$.

(a) Explain why the strategies in the first 2 rows of Table 10.2-2 are BNE. Are the strategies in row 3 equilibrium strategies?
(b) Explain why the strategies in the first two rows are both sequential equilibria.
(c) Which of these equilibria fails the Intuitive Criterion?

Exercise 10.2-2: Equilibria in Sealed Second-Price Auctions Buyers A and B each have a valuation of the single item for sale that is either 2 or 4. Valuations are independently distributed. A buyer's value is high with probability p. The item is to be sold in a sealed bid auction to the highest bidder at the second highest price. If there is a tie, the winner will be selected randomly

---

[10] It is therefore much more controversial. One common criticism is that the PBE satisfying the Strong Intuitive Criterion is independent of the underlying distribution of types. See Exercise 10.2-3.

Games with Asymmetric Information

Table 10.2-2. *Game with an Informed First Mover*

Player 1 (Entrant)		Player 2 (Incumbent)	
$a_1(w)$	$a_1(s)$	$a_2(O)$	$a_2(E)$
O	O	H	
E	E		L
O	E	H	L

from the high bidders. Each buyer must submit a sealed bid $b \in B = \{2, 3, 4\}$ for the item.

(a) Explain why it is a Bayesian Nash equilibrium for buyer A to bid 4 regardless of his valuation and for buyer B to bid 2 regardless of her valuation.
(b) Explain why the equilibrium is not trembling-hand perfect.

HINT: Consider the game as sequential move game in which buyer A moves first and Buyer B responds without knowing which bid buyer A has made. Draw the game tree. Then consider the tremble by buyer A shown in Table 10.2-3.

(c) Is the BNE sequential?
(d) Show that for a BNE to be trembling-hand perfect, both buyers must bid 4 with probability 1 when their values are high.
(e) Is bidding 2 the unique trembling-hand perfect equilibrium bidding strategy for a buyer with a low value?

Exercise 10.2-3: Signaling Equilibrium with Two Types There are two types of worker. Type θ has a marginal value product of $v_\theta = \theta$ where $\theta \in \Theta = \{1, 2\}$. The cost of signal z for the low type is $C_1(z) = z$ and for the high type is $C_2(z) = (1 - \varepsilon)z$. The worker is type 1 with probability p. There are two firms that play a Bertrand wage bidding game for the services of the worker. Thus the equilibrium wage is the expected marginal value product of the worker.

(a) Show that there is a separating PBE in which type 1 does not signal and type 2 chooses $z \in Z$ where $z \in Z \equiv (1, 1/(1 - \varepsilon))$.

Table 10.2-3. *Trembling by the First Mover*

		Bid		
Buyer A		2	3	4
value	2	ε	ε	$1 - 2\varepsilon$
	4	ε	ε	$1 - 2\varepsilon$

(b) Show that the equilibrium payoff to the worker in the pooling equilibrium with no signaling is $w(p) = 2 - p$.

(c) Show that the unique separating equilibrium satisfying the Weak Intuitive Criterion is the PBE with $z = 1$.

(d) Show that for this equilibrium, as $(p, \varepsilon) \to 0$, the equilibrium payoff of the high productivity type approaches 1. Compare this with the equilibrium payoff of both types in the PBE with no signaling. Also compare the equilibrium with the equilibrium at the limit when $p = \varepsilon = 0$.

Exercise 10.2-4: Cho and Kreps' Intuitive Criterion Consider a PBE and define $u_1(\hat{a}, \theta, \theta')$ to be agent 1's payoff if he takes the action $\hat{a}$ off the equilibrium path, his type is θ and he is believed to be type θ'. Cho and Kreps argue that if $\text{Max}_{\theta' \in \Theta}\{u_1(\hat{a}, \theta, \theta')\} < u_1^N(\theta)$, then type θ will never take such an action. Therefore the respondents should concentrate their beliefs on those types in the subset $\hat{\Theta}$ for whom $\text{Max}_{\theta' \in \Theta}\{u_1(\hat{a}, \theta, \theta')\} \geq u_1^N(\theta)$. The PBE fails the Cho and Kreps Intuitive Criterion if there is some type $\hat{\theta} \in \hat{\Theta}$ who is strictly better off choosing $\hat{a}$ for all beliefs concentrated on $\hat{\Theta}$. Formally, the PBE fails the Cho and Kreps Intuitive Criterion if there exists $\hat{\theta} \in \hat{\Theta}$ such that $\text{Min}_{\theta \in \hat{\Theta}}\{u_1(\hat{a}, \hat{\theta}, \theta)\} > u_1^N(\theta)$.

Again consider the worker model of Exercise 10.2-3, but this time there are three types of workers with productivity levels $v_\theta = \theta$, $\theta \in \Theta = \{1, 2, 3\}$. The signaling cost of type θ is $C_\theta(z) = z/\theta$. The three types are equally likely.

(a) Show that the set of separating PBE that satisfy the Cho and Kreps' Intuitive Criterion are the education wage pairs $\{(z_1, w_1), (z_2, w_2), (z_3, w_3)\} = \{(0, 1), (z_2, 2), (z_2 + 3, 3)\}$ where $z_2 \in Z_2 = [1, 2]$.

(b) Show that the PBE with only type 3 signaling also satisfies the Cho and Kreps' Intuitive Criterion.

(c) Are there other partial pooling equilibria that satisfy the Cho and Kreps' Intuitive Criterion?

10.3 Games with Unobservable Strategies and Public Signals

Key ideas: infinitely repeated production game, trigger strategy, Cournot equilibrium, Pareto preferred Nash equilibrium

Thus far we have assumed that there is complete and common knowledge of the history of the game. In particular, the strategies (pure or mixed) played in all prior rounds are common knowledge. If players learn nothing about the final payoffs until after the game has ended, there is no history. Thus the game is essentially equivalent to a simultaneous move game. But in most economic applications there is a sequence of periods $T = \{1, 2, \ldots, T\}$ and an outcome in each period that is dependent on the period t actions taken.

Thus the outcome reveals information about opponents' actions. More generally, suppose that in period t there is some observable signal p_t that is correlated with the players' actions. In this section we consider infinitely repeated games where actions are not observable, but there is common knowledge of preferences as well as a history of public signals.

Let $p^t = \{p_1, \ldots, p_{t-1}\}$ be the history of public signals and let a_i^t be the corresponding history of player i's actions. Then, for player i, the history of the game $h_i^t = \{a_i^t, p^t\}$. The Nash and sub-game perfect equilibrium of such a game are defined exactly as in Section 9.4. The issue we explore here is what sort of payoffs are feasible if the discount factor is sufficiently close to 1.

We illustrate with an extended example. Once again we consider the Cournot production game. Each firm knows its own sequence of production decisions and observes the market-clearing price. If the demand price function is known, then each firm knows the market-clearing price $p(q^C)$ associated with any cooperative output vector $q^C = (q_1^C, \ldots, q_n^C)$. Thus if firm i defects and produces more, the market-clearing price will be lower, and so all the other firms are able to infer that a defection has taken place and can then switch to a Nash equilibrium of the stage game. The set of equilibria is therefore exactly as in Section 9.4.

Suppose instead that demand is also subject to an i.i.d. shock θ_t. Let $p_t = p(\theta_t, q_t)$ be the resulting market-clearing demand price if the output vector is $q_t = (q_{1t}, \ldots, q_{It})$. If θ_t is unobservable, the market-clearing price is a public signal correlated with the actions of the I players.

To focus on essentials we assume that there are two firms and that the unit cost of production is zero.[11] The demand price function is

$$\tilde{p} = 1 + \tilde{\varepsilon} - q_1 - q_2$$

where the intercept shift parameter $\tilde{\varepsilon}$ is a symmetrically distributed random variable with mean zero, support $[-\alpha, \alpha]$, and c.d.f. $F \in \mathbb{C}^2$. Let $\overline{p}(q)$ be the expected price; that is, $\overline{p}(q) = 1 - q_1 - q_2$. Then $\tilde{p} = \overline{p}(q) + \tilde{\varepsilon}$.

Because realizations of the random variable are independent, then, regardless of history, the one-period expected payoff of firm j is

$$u_j = q_j(1 - q_1 - q_2).$$

From Section 9.4 we know that the symmetric monopoly output is $q_1^* = q_2^* = \frac{1}{4}$ and the Nash equilibrium output is $q_1^N = q_2^N = \frac{1}{3}$. The corresponding expected payoffs are $u_j^* = \frac{1}{8}$ and $u_j^N = \frac{1}{9}$, $j = 1, 2$.

We now seek conditions under which some symmetric cooperative output vector $q^C \equiv (q_1^C, q_2^C)$ is sustainable as a Nash equilibrium. This must be strictly preferred to the NE of the stage game $q^N \equiv (q_1^N, q_2^N)$ so $q_1^C < q_1^N$. We

---

[11] Equivalently, the cost of production is c and p is the markup over this unit cost.

consider the incentive for firm 1 to defect. If firm 1 chooses q_1, its expected payoff in the stage game is

$$u_1\left(q_1, q_2^C\right) = \left(1 - q_2^C - q_1\right) q_1.$$

This takes on its maximum at $\overline{q}_1 = \frac{1}{2}(1 - q_2^C)$. For any $\hat{q}_1 > \overline{q}_1$ there exists $q_1^D < \overline{q}_1$ for which the short-run gain to firm 1 is higher. Moreover, the higher is firm 1's output, the greater is the probability of a low price and thus the greater is the probability of detection. Thus firm 1's profit-maximizing defection is in the interval $D(q_1^C) = [q_1^C, \overline{q}_1]$.

Each firm only knows its own strategy and the history of market-clearing prices.

We consider the following simple trigger strategy for each of the two firms. As long as the equilibrium price is never below the trigger price p, firm j produces q_j^C in each period. However, if there is ever a price strictly below p, firms switch to a punishment phase. For the next t-1 periods, each firm produces its NE output of the stage game. At the end of this punishment phase each firm returns to its cooperative strategy and again continues with it until the trigger is tripped.

Expected Payoff to Cooperation

Even if the firms cooperate they have to face the probability of punishment associated with the price dropping below the trigger price. We define V_j^C to be the present value of player j's payoff stream if both firms cooperate and define V_j^P to be the present value of player j's payoff stream at the moment that punishment begins. Because the punishment lasts for t-1 periods,

$$V_j^P = \sum_{s=1}^{t-1} \delta^{s-1} u_j(q^N) + \delta^{t-1} V_j^C.$$

It turns out to be convenient to use as a reference point the outcome if the NE of the stage game is played forever. Let V_j^N be firm j's payoff if this is the case. By backward induction,

$$V_j^N = \sum_{s=1}^{t-1} \delta^{s-1} u_j(q^N) + \delta^{t-1} V_j^N.$$

Because the payoffs are the same for the first t-1 periods, the difference in present values is simply the difference in discounted payoffs beginning at t. That is,

$$V_j^P - V_j^N = \delta^{t-1}\left(V_j^C - V_j^N\right). \tag{10.3-1}$$

Let $q \equiv (q_1, q_2)$ be the output vector in period 1. Then $\tilde{p} = \overline{p}(q) + \tilde{\varepsilon}$. Define $\lambda(q)$ to be the probability that the trigger is not tripped. That is,

$$\lambda(q) = \Pr\{\tilde{p} \geq p\} = \Pr\{\overline{p}(q) + \tilde{\varepsilon} \geq p\} = \Pr\{\varepsilon \geq p - \overline{p}(q)\}$$
$$= 1 - F(p - \overline{p}(q)). \tag{10.3-2}$$

Let $V_j(q)$ be the expected payoff to firm j if, in all future periods, players choose the cooperative strategy unless they are in a punishment phase. By backward induction, the expected value of cooperating satisfies

$$V_j(q) = u_j(q) + \delta(\lambda(q)V_j(q^C) + (1 - \lambda(q))V_j^P). \tag{10.3-3}$$

Again by backward induction,

$$V_j^N = u_j^N + \delta V_j^N.$$

We can rewrite this as follows:

$$V_j^N = u_j^N + \delta(\lambda(q)V_j^N + (1 - \lambda(q))V_j^N). \tag{10.3-4}$$

Subtracting this expression from (10.3-3),

$$V_j(q) - V_j^N = u_j(q) - u_j^N + \delta\lambda(q)\left(V_j^C - V_j^N\right) + \delta(1 - \lambda(q))\left(V_j^P - V_j^N\right).$$

Substituting for V_j^P, from (10.3-1),

$$V_j(q) - V_j^N = u_j(q) - u_j^N + \delta\lambda(q)\left(V_j^C - V_j^N\right) + \delta^t(1 - \lambda(q))\left(V_j^C - V_j^N\right)$$
$$= u_j(q) - u_j^N + [\delta\lambda(q) + \delta^t(1 - \lambda(q))]\left(V_j^C - V_j^N\right) \tag{10.3-5}$$

Suppose that both firms choose the cooperative strategy in period 1. Setting $q = q^C$ in (10.3-5),

$$V_j^C - V_j^N = u_j(q^C) - u_j^N + [\delta\lambda(q^C) + \delta^t(1 - \lambda(q^C))]\left(V_j^C - V_j^N\right). \tag{10.3-6}$$

Rearranging, we have at last,

$$V_j^C - V_j^N = \frac{u_j(q^C) - u_j^N}{1 - \delta\lambda(q^C) - \delta^t(1 - \lambda(q^C))}. \tag{10.3-7}$$

Note that the denominator increases with the length of the punishment phase. It also increases with the probability that the trigger is not tripped and hence increases as the trigger price is lowered. Thus the expected equilibrium payoff is a decreasing function of the length of the punishment phase and the trigger price. This is very intuitive. A higher trigger price raises the probability of the punishment phase, and a longer punishment phase raises the size of the punishment. Both reduce the equilibrium expected payoff.

Defection by Firm 1

From (10.3-5), if firm 1 defects so that the first period output vector is $q^D = (q_1^D, q_2^C)$, firm 1's expected payoff is

$$V_1(q^D) - V_1^N = u_1(q^D) - u_1^N + [\delta\lambda(q^D) + \delta^t(1 - \lambda(q^D))] \left(V_1^C - V_1^N\right).$$
(10.3-8)

Then, subtracting (10.3-6) from (10.3-8), the net gain to defecting is

$$V_1(q^D) - V_1^C = u_1(q^D) - u_1(q^C) - (\delta - \delta^t)(\lambda(q^C) - \lambda(q^D)) \left(V_1(q^C) - V_1^N\right)$$
(10.3-9)

Also, from (10.3-2), the increase in probability of setting off the trigger, if firm 1 defects is

$$\lambda(q^C) - \lambda(q^D) = F(p - \overline{p}(q^D)) - F(p - \overline{p}(q^C)). \qquad (10.3\text{-}10)$$

The one-period deviation is unprofitable if and only if $V_1(q^D) - V_1(q^C) \leq 0$. Appealing to (10.3-9), this deviation is unprofitable if and only if

$$V_1(q^C) - V_1^N \geq \frac{u_1(q^D) - u_1(q^C)}{(\delta - \delta^t)(\lambda(q^C) - \lambda(q^D))}. \qquad (10.3\text{-}11)$$

Also, from (10.3-7),

$$V_1(q^C) - V_1^N = \frac{u_1(q^C) - u_1^N}{1 - \delta^t - (\delta - \delta^t)\lambda(q^C)}.$$

Combining these last two results, the necessary and sufficient condition for the deviation to be unprofitable is

$$V_1(q^C) - V_1^N = \frac{u_1(q^C) - u_1^N}{1 - \delta^t - (\delta - \delta^t)\lambda(q^C)} \geq \frac{u_1(q^D) - u_1(q^C)}{(\delta - \delta^t)(\lambda(q^C) - \lambda(q^D))}.$$

Small Deviations

For incentive compatibility the incentive constraint must hold for all deviations, in particular for small deviations. Note that as $q_1 \to q_1^C$, both the numerator and denominator on the right-hand side of (10.3-11) approach zero. Appealing to l'Hôpital's Rule,[12] the limit of the ratio at q_1^C is the ratio of the derivatives at q_1^C. Then infinitesimally small defections are unprofitable if and only if

$$V_1^C - V_1^N \geq \frac{\dfrac{\partial u_1}{\partial q_1}(q_1^C, q_2^C)}{(\delta - \delta^t)F'(p - \overline{p}(c^C))}. \qquad (10.3\text{-}12)$$

---

[12] See Appendix C.

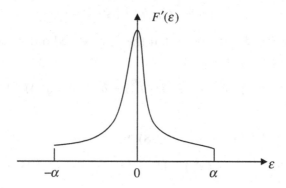

Figure 10.3-1. Density function for demand shift parameter.

Suppose that the density function $F'(\varepsilon)$ is uni-modal as depicted in Figure 10.3-1.

If there is sufficient mass near zero (so that $F'(0)$ is sufficiently large), this inequality must hold if the trigger price is set equal to $\overline{p}(q^C)$, because then $F'(p - \overline{p}(q^C)) = F'(0)$.

In the discussion that follows we assume that this is the case.

A Cooperative Equilibrium with No Price Wars

Suppose first that the unobserved random variable is distributed uniformly. Then

$$F(\varepsilon) = \frac{\alpha + \varepsilon}{2\alpha}, \, \varepsilon \in [-\alpha, \alpha].$$

Small deviations: Appealing to (10.3-12), these are unprofitable if and only if

$$V_1^C - V_1^N \geq \frac{\dfrac{\partial u_1}{\partial q_1}\left(q_1^C, q_2^C\right)}{(\delta - \delta^t)\frac{1}{2\alpha}}. \qquad (10.3\text{-}13)$$

Finite deviations: Because F and $\overline{p}(q)$ are linear, $\lambda(q^C) - \lambda(q^D)$ $= F(p - \overline{p}(q^C)) - F(p - \overline{p}(q^D))$ is a linear function of q_1^D and

$$\lambda(q^C) - \lambda(q^D) = F'(p - \overline{p}(q^C))\left(q_1^C - q_1^D\right).$$

Moreover $u_1(q_1, q_2^C)$ is concave in q_1 so

$$u_1(q^D) - u_1(q^C) \leq \frac{\partial u_1}{\partial q_1}(q^C)\left(q_1^D - q_1^C\right).$$

Hence

$$\frac{u_1(q^D) - u_1(q^C)}{(\delta - \delta^t)\lambda(q^C) - \lambda(q^D)} \leq \frac{\dfrac{\partial u_1}{\partial q_1}(q^C)\left(q_1^D - q_1^C\right)}{(\delta - \delta^t)F'(p - \overline{p}(q^C))\left(q_1^C - q_1^D\right)} = \frac{\dfrac{\partial u_1}{\partial q_1}(q^C)}{(\delta - \delta^t)\frac{1}{2\alpha}}.$$

It follows from (10.3-11) and (10.3-13) that if the incentive constraint for small deviations is satisfied then all the incentive constraints are satisfied.

In the uniform case the right-hand side of (10.3-13) is independent of the trigger price. Moreover, lowering the trigger price lowers the probability that the trigger is tripped and hence raises the payoff to cooperation. It follows that the best equilibrium trigger price strategy is to set the trigger price equal to $\overline{p}(q^C) - \alpha$ so that the market price will drop below the trigger price with positive probability only if a firm deviates. But in equilibrium, no firm has an incentive to deviate. Thus cooperation is sustained forever.

Cooperative Equilibrium with Price Wars

We now argue that this result can only occur if the density is bounded away from zero at the lower support. Consider inequality (10.3-12), the incentive constraint for small defections, once more,

$$V_1^C - V_1^N \geq r(p) \equiv \frac{1}{\delta - \delta^t} \frac{\frac{\partial u_1}{\partial q_1}(q_1^C, q_2^C)}{F'(p - \overline{p}(q^C))}.$$

If the density approaches zero, as $p \to \overline{p}(q^C) - \alpha$, the right-hand side increases without bound. Therefore the constraint cannot be satisfied. Thus the trigger price must be set higher, and so eventually the Nash Equilibrium strategies of the stage game will be played. If the density function is symmetric and uni-modal, the function $r(p)$ must be as depicted in Figure 10.3-2, increasing without bound at the maximum and minimum prices.

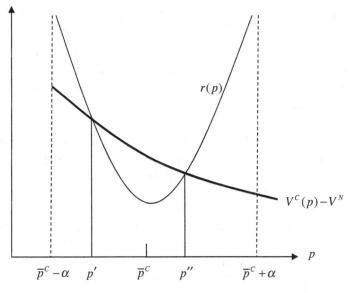

Figure 10.3-2. Incentive-compatible trigger prices.

We have also argued that $V^C(p)$ is a decreasing function. Thus, as depicted in Figure 10.3-2, the set of feasible trigger prices is an interval $[p', p'']$. Moreover the best trigger price is the smallest feasible price p'.

Of course this trigger price depends on the length of the punishment phase. A full analysis of the optimal trigger price would map out the equilibrium payoff for each t and optimal trigger price $p'(t)$. The key points are that the optimal choice of t is finite and the optimal trigger price results in punishment with finite probability. Thus, as Porter first argued, the model explains periods of cooperation interspersed with periods of punishment ("price wars") and then further cooperation.

Exercises

Exercise 10.3-1: One-Stage Deviation Principle with Private Strategies

(a) In a game where past strategies are public information the one-stage deviation principle holds. That is, if no player benefits from a one-stage deviation from a strategy profile $\bar{s}$ then this strategy profile is sub-game perfect. Show that, for games in which players only observe a public signal, if a strategy profile $\bar{s}$ satisfies the one-stage deviation principle, no player can gain from any finite stage deviation.

(b) Can the argument be extended to infinite deviations?

Exercise 10.3-2: Rotemberg and Saloner's "Price War"
Demand is either high or low. If both firms choose the same price p, the profit for each firm is $u_H(p)$ in the high-demand state and $u_L(p)$ in the low-demand state. At the beginning of each period, and before prices are announced, each firm learns the true state. Let p_H and $p_L < p_H$ be the profit-maximizing prices. The cost of production is c so the Nash equilibrium of the price game is $(p_1, p_2) = (c, c)$ with zero profit. The probability of the high-demand state is θ. A firm can deviate from any collusive outcome by lowering its price slightly and capturing all the market. In this case his opponent will play the grim Nash equilibrium strategy.

(a) If the discount factor is δ, obtain expressions for the expected payoff to each player in the two states if they cooperate forever, choosing p_h in the high-demand state and p_l in the low-demand state.

(b) If the initial state is h explain why the necessary and sufficient condition for cooperation in period 1 is $U_h^C \geq 2u_h(p_h)$.

(c) If this condition holds, show that there will also be cooperation in period 1 if the initial state is l.

(d) Hence explain why the condition in (b) is necessary and sufficient for cooperation to be achievable as a sub-game perfect equilibrium.

(e) Show that cooperation is always achievable if $\delta \geq \frac{1}{2}$.

References and Selected Historical Reading

Abreu, D., Pierce, D., and Stachetti, E. (1990). "Towards a Theory of Discounted Repeated Games with Imperfect Monitoring." *Econometrica* **58**: 1041–64.

Banks, J. S. and Sobel, J. (1987). "Equilibrium Selection in Signaling Games." *Econometrica* **55**: 647–62.

Cho, In-Koo and Kreps, D. M. (1987). "Signaling Games and Stable Equilibria," *Quarterly Journal of Economics* **102**.

Fudenberg, Drew and Tirole, Jean (1991). *Game Theory*. Cambridge, MA: MIT Press.

Harsanyi, J. (1967–68). "Games with Incomplete Information Played by Bayesian Players." *Management Science* **14**: 159–82, 320–34, 486–502.

Kohlberg, E. and Mertens, J.-F. (1986). "On the Strategic Stability of Equilibria." *Econometrica* **54**:1003–38.

Kreps, D. M. and Sobel, J. (1994). "Signaling." In *Handbook of Game Theory, Volume II*, (R. Aumann and S. Hart, eds.). New York: Elsevier.

Kreps, D. M. and Wilson, R. (1982). "Sequential Equilibria." *Econometrica* **50**: 889–904.

Porter R. (1983). "Optimal Cartel Trigger Price Strategies." *Journal of Economic Theory* **29**: 313–38.

Selten, R. (1965). "Re-Examination of the Perfectness Concept for Equilibrium Points in Extensive Games." *International Journal of Game Theory* **4**: 25–55.

11

Incentive Compatibility and Mechanism Design

11.1 Incentive Compatibility

Key ideas: incentive constraints, intensity of preferences, single crossing property, local upward and downward constraints

Signaling Games

Consider a sequential move game that begins with Nature choosing the preferences of the first mover. That is, Nature chooses player 1's type. Player 1 learns his type and chooses his action. The other players observe the action that player 1 takes but not his type. The rest of the game is then played out. This is called a signaling game because the choice of the informed player 1 potentially reveals information about his type to the other players and thus influences their responses. An example of such a game is the simple entry game analyzed in Section 10.2. The entrant may be strong or weak. If the equilibrium strategy of the potential entrant is to stay out of the market when weak and enter when strong, the entry signals strength and the incumbent takes this into account when choosing a response.

We consider the signaling game for three reasons. First, it is an important class of economic games. Second, in this class of games the issue of incentives with private information is central. Third, we can apply the insights for the signaling game to the theory of mechanism design.

Let the set of possible types of first movers be Θ. It is simpler to think of Θ as a finite set so that $\Theta = \{\theta_1, \ldots, \theta_T\}$, but continuous types can be similarly analyzed. In the finite types case it is often convenient to define $\mathcal{T} = \{1, \ldots, T\}$ and write the set of types as $\Theta \equiv \{\theta_t\}_{t \in \mathcal{T}}$.

If player 1 is of type θ_t, his preferences are represented by the utility function $u(\theta_t, q, r)$ over $Q \times R$, where Q is the set of possible actions by player 1 and R is the set of possible payoffs to player 1. To simplify the exposition, we often rewrite the utility function of type θ_t as

$$U_t(q, r) \equiv u(\theta_t, q, r).$$

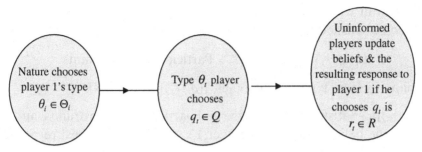

Figure 11.1-1. Sequential move signaling game.

Let $f(\theta_t)$ be the probability measure over types. This probability measure is common knowledge. In the simplest version of the model, a type θ_t player chooses a pure strategy $q_t \in Q$. (The arguments extend naturally to allow for mixed strategies.) A pure strategy for player 1 is then a vector $\{q_t\}_{t \in T}$ in the product space Q^T. If there is a single uninformed player, then that player applies Bayes' Rule to update her beliefs about the type of player 1 she faces and chooses a best response. More generally, with more than one responding player, these players all update their beliefs. Suppose that all the responding players believe that the strategy of player 1 is $\{q_t\}_{t \in T}$. From the particular action that they observe, they apply Bayes' Rule to update their beliefs about player 1's type. Thus each of the actions in player 1's strategy $\{q_t\}_{t \in T}$ induces responses by the other players, which yield player 1 a payoff $r_t \in R$. This game is depicted schematically in Figure 11.1-1.

Player 1 can also compute the best responses given his strategy and thus correctly infer the outcome of the game $\{q_t, r_t\}_{t \in T}$. However, the critical question becomes whether player 1 would choose the strategy $\{q_t\}_{t \in T}$ knowing the other players' responses. Suppose that his type is θ_t and instead of choosing action q_t he chooses q_s. Because the responding players believe they know his strategy is $\{q_t\}_{t \in T}$, the response is r_s and so player 1's payoff is $U_t(q_s, r_s)$ rather than $U_t(q_t, r_t)$. Then player 1 has an incentive to deviate unless $U_t(q_t, r_t) \geq U_t(q_s, r_s)$.

The outcome for type θ_t must satisfy this inequality for each of the other types. Moreover these incentive constraints must hold for every possible type. Thus the following conditions are necessary for $\{q_t, r_t\}_{t \in T}$ to be a BNE outcome of the game:

$U_t(q_t, r_t) \geq U_t(q_s, r_s), \forall t$ and $s \in T$ where $s \neq t$. Incentive constraints

If all the Incentive Constraints are satisfied, the mapping $M \equiv \{q_t, r_t\}_{t \in T}$ is said to be incentive compatible.

In addition, player 1 must be willing to play the game. Let $\{U_{ot}\}_{t \in T}$ be the utility associated with each type's outside option. Then, for an equilibrium in which player 1 always participates, the following constraint must also be satisfied for each type:

$$U_t(q_t, r_t) \geq U_{0t} \ \forall t \in T. \quad \text{Participation constraints}$$

A mapping from types to outcomes, $\{(q_t, r_t)\}_{t \in T}$ is a BNE if

(i) $\{(q_t, r_t)\}_{t \in T}$ satisfies the incentive and participation constraints, and
(ii) given the beliefs induced by player 1's strategy, r_t is a best response by the uninformed responders.

Example: Educational Signaling A consultant's value $\theta_t \in \Theta = \{1, 2\}$ (measured in millions of dollars). His cost of accumulating the educational credential q is $C_t(q) = q/\theta_t$. Note that the marginal cost of a higher education is $1/\theta_t$ so a higher value consultant can obtain a level of education q at a lower cost. Therefore education becomes a potential signal. The consultant's outside opportunities are $(U_{01}, U_{02}) = (\frac{1}{4}, 1\frac{1}{4})$. Firms observe the consultant's education level and then compete in a Bertrand wage game for the consultant's services.

In an equilibrium in which type θ_2 successfully signals, the other players know player 1's value. Thus in such an equilibrium $(r_1, r_2) = (\theta_1, \theta_2) = (1, 2)$.
We argue that $(q_1, r_1) = (0, 1)$ and $(q_2, r_2) = (1 + a, 2)$ is a PBE for all $a \in (0, \frac{1}{2})$.
Note that $U_t(q, r) = r - q/\theta_t$. Therefore

$$U_1(q_1, r_1) = 1 \quad \text{and} \quad U_1(q_2, r_2) = 2 - (1 + a) = 1 - a.$$

Therefore the incentive constraint for type θ_1 is satisfied for $a \geq 0$. Also,

$$U_2(q_1, r_1) = 1 \quad \text{and} \quad U_2(q_2, r_2) = 2 - \tfrac{1}{2}(1 + a) = \tfrac{1}{2}(3 - a).$$

Thus the incentive constraint for type θ_2 is satisfied if

$$U_2(q_2, r_2) - U_2(q_1, r_1) = \tfrac{1}{2}(1 - a) > 0; \quad \text{that is, if} \quad a \in [0, 1].$$

The participation constraints are

$$U_1(q_1, r_1) = 1 \geq \tfrac{1}{4} = U_{01} \quad \text{and} \quad U_2(q_2, r_2) = \tfrac{1}{2}(3 - a) \geq 1\tfrac{1}{4} = U_{02}.$$

The second inequality holds if $a \in [0, \frac{1}{2}]$. Thus all the incentive and participation constraints are satisfied if $a \in [0, \frac{1}{2}]$.
The general signaling game is analyzed in detail in Section 11.2.

Mechanism Design

There is a second class of models with a very similar structure. In its simplest version there are two players. Player 1 moves first and announces the rules of a game G to be played with player 2. The set of possible types of player 2 is Θ. Player 2 knows her type but this information is private. The probability measure over types is common knowledge. If player 2 is of type θ_t, her equilibrium outcome of the game is (q_t, r_t). Then the set of equilibrium outcomes is $\{q_t, r_t\}_{t \in T}$. Any such game is called a mechanism, and the first mover is called the mechanism designer.

As an example,[1] the mechanism designer might be a monopoly seller and player 2 a buyer with demand price function $p(\theta_t, q), \theta_t \in \Theta$. The game G might offer the buyer the choice of buying units of a media service under two different pricing plans. In plan a the price per minute of service is p_a. In plan b the buyer pays a monthly access fee, K_b, and the price per minute is $p_b < p_a$. Given these options, the different types of buyers choose the plans that are best for them and then purchase their optimal quantities and the associated payments $\{q_t, r_t\}_{t \in T}$.

Given a response mapping $M(G) = \{q_t, r_t\}_{\theta_t \in \Theta}$, the expected payoff to the mechanism designer is

$$U^d(G) = \sum_{t \in T} f_t U_t^d(q_t, r_t).$$

As the first mover, the designer chooses the mechanism (i.e., the rules of the game) that maximizes his expected payoff.

Because the mechanism designer does not know player 2's type, player 2 can always choose the best response of any type $\theta_s \in \Theta$ and so obtain an outcome of (q_s, r_s). Let $U_t(q, r) \equiv u(\theta_t, q, r)$ be a type θ_t's utility function. Then for (q_t, r_t) to be a best response outcome for type θ_t, the incentive constraints

$$U_t(q_t, r_t) \geq U_t(q_s, r_s), \; s \in T$$

must be satisfied. That is, just as in the signaling game, the equilibrium outcome of the game $M(G) = \{q_t, r_t\}_{\theta_t \in \Theta}$ must be incentive compatible. Mechanism design is analyzed in Section 11.3.

Necessary and Sufficient Conditions for Incentive Compatibility

Note that if there are T different types of player, there are $T - 1$ incentive constraints that must be satisfied for each type $\theta_t \in \Theta$. For incentive compatibility this must be true for each of the T types of player so that there are $T \times (T - 1)$ incentive constraints. In addition there are T participation constraints.

---

[1] Another example of mechanism design is the choice of auction rules. We consider the design of an optimal auction in Chapter 12.

In general, there is little that one can do with a model that has so many constraints. To proceed, we need to impose additional structure on the nature of the preferences of the different types of players.

Let $U_t(q, r)$ be the payoff function for type θ_t. We make the following very weak assumption about the payoff function.

Assumption 1:

For all $t \in \mathcal{T}$ the payoff function $U_t(q, r)$ is continuously differentiable on the closed set $Q \times R$ and either $\frac{\partial U_t}{\partial r} > 0$ or $\frac{\partial U_t}{\partial r} < 0$.

The key to successful modeling is the assumption that the difference between any pair of types reflects differences in their strength of preference for q.

Definition: Stronger Preference for q Type θ_t has a stronger preference for q than type θ_s if for any $(\hat{q}, \hat{r})$ and $(q, r) \in Q \times R$, where $q > \hat{q}$, $(q, r) \underset{s}{\succsim} (\hat{q}, \hat{r}) \Rightarrow (q, r) \underset{t}{\succ} (\hat{q}, \hat{r})$.

This is depicted in Figure 11.1-2, first with $\frac{\partial U_t}{\partial r} > 0$ and then with $\frac{\partial U_t}{\partial r} < 0$. Consider the set of outcomes to the right of the dashed vertical line through $(\hat{q}, \hat{r})$ in Figure 11.1-2. In each diagram the heavily shaded region is the subset of outcomes that type θ_s player weakly prefers to $(\hat{q}, \hat{r})$. The union of this set and the dotted region is the corresponding subset of outcomes that a type θ_t weakly prefers to $(\hat{q}, \hat{r})$. Note that in each case, as q increases, the indifference curve for type θ_t crosses from the upper contour set for type θ_s to the lower contour set. Because there can be no crossing from the lower contour set to the upper contour set, the assumption that θ_t has a stronger preference for q is called the single crossing property.

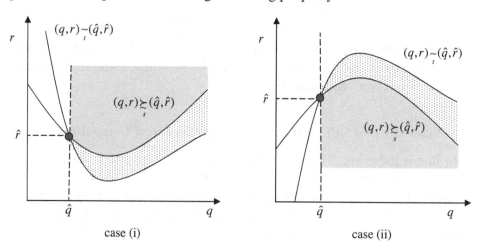

Figure 11.1-2. Type θ_t has a stronger preference for q. case (i) $\partial U_t / \partial r > 0, t \in \mathcal{T}$, case (ii) $\partial U_t / \partial r < 0, t \in \mathcal{T}$.

Assumption 2: Single Crossing Property (SCP)
Higher indexed types have a stronger preference for q.

We then have the following lemma.

Lemma 11.1-1: Preference Rankings under the SCP Suppose that $\hat{q} < q$. If the SCP holds then

(i) $(\hat{q}, \hat{r}) \underset{s}{\precsim} (q, r) \Rightarrow (\hat{q}, \hat{r}) \underset{t}{\prec} (q, r), \forall t > s$

(ii) $(\hat{q}, \hat{r}) \underset{t}{\succsim} (q, r) \Rightarrow (\hat{q}, \hat{r}) \underset{s}{\succ} (q, r), \forall s < t.$

Proof: Condition (i) is simply a restatement of the definition of stronger preferences given the SCP. To confirm condition (ii), suppose that for some $\theta_s < \theta_t$, (ii) is false. That is,

(a) $(\hat{q}, \hat{r}) \underset{t}{\succsim} (q, r)$ and   (b) $(\hat{q}, \hat{r}) \underset{s}{\precsim} (q, r)$,   for some $\theta_s < \theta_t$.

But by the SCP, if (b) holds then $(\hat{q}, \hat{r}) \underset{t}{\prec} (q, r)$ thus contradicting (a). $\square$

Consider the indifference curve in Figure 11.1-2 for type θ_t through $(\hat{q}, \hat{r})$. We define the marginal rate of substitution in the usual way:

$$\text{MRS}_t(\hat{q}, \hat{r}) = \frac{\dfrac{\partial U_t}{\partial q}}{\dfrac{\partial U_t}{\partial r}}.$$

It is tempting to conclude that if the SCP holds, then the marginal rates of substitution (MRS) of the two types must be everywhere different. However, this is not quite true. Instead, we have the following result.[2]

Lemma 11.1-2: Single Crossing Suppose that type θ_t has a stronger preference for q than θ_s on $Q \times R$.
   If $\partial U_\tau / \partial r > 0, \tau \in T$, then for all $(q, r) \in Q \times R$, $\text{MRS}_t(q, r) \geq \text{MRS}_s (q, r)$.
   If $\partial U_t / \partial r < 0, \tau \in T$, then for all $(q, r) \in Q \times R$, $\text{MRS}_t(q, r) \leq \text{MRS}_s (q, r)$.

Proof: The set of points on the indifference curve $U_s(q, r) = U_s(\hat{q}, \hat{r})$ implicitly define the function $r_s(q)$. That is,

$$U_s(q, r_s(q)) - U_s(\hat{q}, r_s(\hat{q})) = 0 \quad \text{for all} \quad q > \hat{q}.$$

---

[2] This is a technical point. As a practical matter, economists usually simply assume strict monotonicity of the MRS with respect to type.

For all $t \in \mathcal{T}$ define $D_t(q) \equiv U_t(q, r_s(q)) - U_t(\hat{q}, r_s(\hat{q}))$. By construction $D_s(q) = 0$. Moreover, if type θ_t has a stronger preference for q then

$$D_t(q) \equiv U_t(q, r_s(q)) - U_t(\hat{q}, r_s(\hat{q})) > 0, \quad \text{for all} \quad q > \hat{q}.$$

Also $D_t(\hat{q}) = 0$. Therefore

$$\frac{d}{dq} D_t(\hat{q}) \geq 0. \tag{11.1-1}$$

Note that because $D_s(q) = 0$, it follows by the Implicit Function Theorem that

$$\frac{dr_s}{dq}(q) = -\frac{\partial U_s}{\partial q} \Big/ \frac{\partial U_s}{\partial r} = -\mathrm{MRS}_s(q, r_s(q)).$$

Then

$$\frac{d}{dq} D_t(q) = \frac{\partial U_t}{\partial q} + \frac{\partial U_t}{\partial r} \frac{dr_s}{dq} = \frac{\partial U_t}{\partial r} \left(\frac{dr_s}{dq} + \frac{\frac{\partial U_t}{\partial q}}{\frac{\partial U_t}{\partial r}} \right)$$

$$= \frac{\partial U_t}{\partial r} [\mathrm{MRS}_t(\hat{q}, \hat{r}) - \mathrm{MRS}_s(\hat{q}, \hat{r})].$$

Appealing to (11.1-1), the right-hand side must be positive. □

To illustrate, consider the following examples.

Example 1: Educational Signaling (Spence)

A consultant of type θ_t has a value $v(\theta_t)$ to potential clients. The consultant knows his type but this is not observed by the clients. The probability that a consultant is of type θ_t is f_t. A type θ_t consultant can obtain an education of observable quality q at a cost of $C_t(q)$. Higher valued types have a lower marginal cost of education; that is, if $\theta_s > \theta_t$ $C_s'(q) < C_t'(q)$. Clients offer different fees, r, for different education levels. An offer can then be written as (q, r). Let $\{(q_t, r_t)\}_{t \in \mathcal{T}}$ be the offers selected by different types. A type θ_t consultant's payoff is $U_t(q_t, r_t) = r_t - C_t(q_t)$ and the profit of the firm (the second mover) that makes the successful offer is $v(\theta_t) - r_t$. Preference directions and the indifference curves for type θ_t and type $\theta_2 > \theta_t$ through $(\hat{q}, \hat{r})$ are depicted in Figure 11.1-3. Because the slope of type t's indifference curve is his marginal cost of q, and because higher types have lower marginal cost, the SCP holds.

Example 2: Insurance (Rothschild-Stiglitz)

An individual "insuree" seeks to purchase coverage in the event of a loss, L, from a risk-neutral insurer. The insuree's probability of not incurring a loss takes on possible values $\theta_t \in \Theta = \{\theta_1, \ldots, \theta_T\}$. The no-loss probability θ_t is

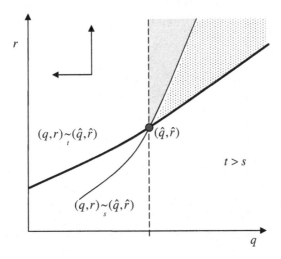

Figure 11.1-3. Educational signaling.

known only to the insuree. An insurance policy is a commitment to cover the loss less some deductible q. The maximum deductible is the total loss L so $Q = [0, L]$. In return for the insurance coverage, the insuree must pay a premium r, regardless of whether there is a loss. The vector (q, r) then completely describes an insurance policy.

Insuree's Expected Utility

In both the loss and no-loss states the insuree pays the premium r. In the loss state the insuree incurs a loss L and the insurer pays out $L - q$. Given a von Neumann Morgenstern utility function u, the expected utility of a type θ_t insuree is

$$U_t(q, r) = \theta_t u(w - r) + (1 - \theta_t)u(w - q - r).$$

Risk-Neutral Insurer

If an insuree who purchases the policy (q, r) is of type θ_t, the joint probability that the insuree is of type θ_t and incurs a loss is $f_t(1 - \theta_t)$. Given the deductible q, the insurer pays out $L - q$. Then if a type θ_t insuree chooses a policy (q_t, r_t), the expected profit of the insurer is

$$U_0 = \sum_{t \in T} f_t(r_t - (1 - \theta_t)(L - q_t).$$

Single Crossing Property

The indifference curves through $(\hat{q}, \hat{r})$, for types θ_s and $\theta_t > \theta_s$, are depicted in Figure 11.1-4. Note that the slope of a type θ_t insuree's indifference curve

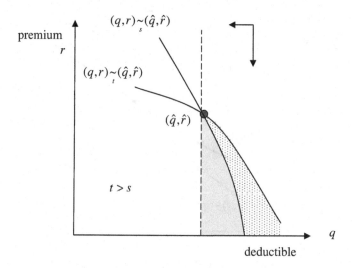

Figure 11.1-4. Signaling by purchasing less coverage.

through $(\hat{q}, \hat{r})$ is

$$\left.\frac{dr}{dq}\right|_{U_t} = -\frac{\partial U_t}{\partial q} \bigg/ \frac{\partial U_t}{\partial r} = -\frac{(1-\theta_t)u'(w - \hat{q} - \hat{r})}{\theta_t u'(w - \hat{r}) + (1-\theta_t)u'(w - \hat{q} - \hat{r})}$$

$$= -\frac{1}{\left(\dfrac{\theta_t}{1-\theta_t}\right)\dfrac{u'(w - \hat{r})}{u'(w - \hat{q} - \hat{r})} + 1}.$$

As θ_t increases the denominator increases and so the slope of the indifference curve becomes less negative. Thus the SCP holds.

Example 3: Bidding

A bidder's value of a single item for sale is $\theta_t \in \Theta$. The bidder is risk neutral. Bidders compete for the item by making bids. Let q be the probability of winning, and let r be the bidder's expected payment. If the bidder has a value θ_t, his expected payoff is

$$U_t(q, r) = q\theta_t - r.$$

The MRS is then

$$\mathrm{MRS}_t(q, r) = \frac{\partial U_t}{\partial q} \bigg/ \frac{\partial U_t}{\partial r} = -\theta_t.$$

Because $\frac{\partial}{\partial r}U_t(q, r) < 0$ and the MRS is more negative for a buyer with a higher value the SCP holds.

We now show that if Assumptions 1 and 2 hold, then the problem of identifying incentive-compatible actions and outcomes $\{(q_t, r_t)\}_{t \in \mathcal{T}}$ is considerably simplified.

Definition: Local Upward and Downward Constraints If type θ_t prefers (q_t, r_t) to (q_{t+1}, r_{t+1}) then the local upward constraint for type θ_t is satisfied.

If type θ_t prefers (q_t, r_t) to (q_{t-1}, r_{t-1}) then the local downward constraint for type θ_t is satisfied.

The following two propositions are the key insights.

Proposition 11.1-3: Monotonicity

If the SCP holds, then the local incentive constraints imply that $q_1 \leq \cdots \leq q_T$.

Proof: Suppose that for some types θ_t and θ_{t+1}, $q_t > q_{t+1}$. The local upward incentive constraint is $(q_{t+1}, r_{t+1}) \underset{t}{\precsim} (q_t, r_t)$. Because $q_t > q_{t+1}$ it follows from Lemma 11.1-1 that $(q_{t+1}, r_{t+1}) \underset{t+1}{\prec} (q_t, r_t)$. But this is impossible because it violates the local downward incentive constraint for type θ_{t+1}. $\square$

Proposition 11.1-4: Local Incentive Compatibility Implies Global Incentive Compatibility

If Assumptions 1 and 2 hold and all the local incentive constraints are satisfied, then the mapping $M \equiv \{(q_t, r_t)\}_{t \in \mathcal{T}}$ satisfies all the incentive constraints.

Proof: It will be assumed that $\frac{\partial U_\tau}{\partial r} > 0, \tau \in \mathcal{T}$. The proof when the partial derivative is always negative is almost identical. By hypothesis the local upward constraint holds for type θ_t and the local downward constraint holds for θ_{t+1}; that is,

(i) $(q_t, r_t) \underset{t}{\succsim} (q_{t+1}, r_{t+1})$ and (ii) $(q_t, r_t) \underset{t+1}{\precsim} (q_{t+1}, r_{t+1})$.

Consider any s and t such that $s < t$ and $\tau \in \{s, s+1, \ldots, t-1\}$. From Proposition 11.1-3 the monotonicity property must be satisfied so $q_\tau \leq q_{\tau+1}$.

Case (a) $q_\tau = q_{\tau+1}$.

It follows from (i) and (ii) that $r_\tau = r_{\tau+1}$. Then $(q_\tau, r_\tau) \underset{\tau}{\sim} (q_{\tau+1}, r_{\tau+1})$.

Case (b) $q_\tau < q_{\tau+1}$.

The local downward constraint holds for type $\theta_{\tau+1}$; that is, $(q_\tau, r_\tau) \underset{t+1}{\precsim} (q_{\tau+1}, r_{\tau+1})$. Because $\tau + 1 \leq t$ it follows from statement (i) of Lemma 11.1-1 that $(q_\tau, r_\tau) \underset{t}{\precsim} (q_{\tau+1}, r_{\tau+1})$. Then we may conclude that for both case (a) and case (b) $(q_\tau, r_\tau) \underset{t}{\precsim} (q_{\tau+1}, r_{\tau+1})$. Because this preference relation holds for each $\tau \in \{s, s+1, \ldots, t-1\}$, it follows that

$$(q_s, r_s) \underset{t}{\precsim} (q_{s+1}, r_{s+1}) \underset{t}{\precsim} \cdots \underset{t}{\precsim} (q_t, r_t).$$

By an almost identical argument, it follows from statement (ii) of Lemma 11.1-1 that

$$(q_s, r_s) \mathrel{\underset{s}{\succsim}} (q_{s+1}, r_{s+1}) \mathrel{\underset{s}{\succsim}} \ldots \mathrel{\underset{s}{\succsim}} (q_t, r_t)$$

We have therefore shown that for all s and $t > s$,[3]

$$(q_s, r_s) \mathrel{\underset{s}{\succsim}} (q_t, r_t) \quad \text{and} \quad (q_s, r_s) \mathrel{\underset{t}{\precsim}} (q_t, r_t).$$

Thus all the incentive constraints hold.   □

As we see in the next two sections, there are important special cases when either the local upward or downward constraint is binding for each type; that is, for $\{q_t, r_t\}_{t \in T}$: either (i) $(q_t, r_t) \mathrel{\underset{t}{\sim}} (q_{t+1}, r_{t+1})$ or (ii) $(q_t, r_t) \mathrel{\underset{t+1}{\sim}} (q_{t+1}, r_{t+1})$.

Because it is a necessary condition for incentive compatibility, we assume monotonicity; that is, $q_t \leq q_{t+1}$. Suppose that (i) holds so that the local upward constraint holds. Appealing to the SCP, it follows that $(q_t, r_t) \mathrel{\underset{t+1}{\precsim}} (q_{t+1}, r_{t+1})$ so the local downward constraint must also hold.

Suppose next that (ii) holds. Then the local downward constraint holds. Suppose that the local upward constraint is violated; that is, $(q_t, r_t) \mathrel{\underset{t}{\prec}} (q_{t+1}, r_{t+1})$. But this cannot be true because by the SCP this implies that $(q_t, r_t) \mathrel{\underset{t+1}{\prec}} (q_{t+1}, r_{t+1})$, contradicting (ii). Then $(q_t, r_t) \mathrel{\underset{t}{\succsim}} (q_{t+1}, r_{t+1})$ so the local upward constraint must also hold. The following result then follows from Proposition 11.1-4.

Corollary 11.1-5: Incentive Constraints with Binding Local Constraints Suppose that $\{q_t, r_t\}_{t \in T}$ is increasing in q, the SCP holds, and for each type either the local upward or downward constraint is binding. Then all the other local constraints must also hold, and so all the incentive constraints are satisfied.

Participation

Thus far we have assumed that the responding player must choose some $q \in Q$. However, for many applications, each type of responding player has an outside alternative in addition to those in Q. We now extend the analysis to take this into account. Let U_{0t} be the payoff to type θ_t if the responding player chooses his outside alternative. Given Assumption 1, there must be some r_{0t} such that $U_t(0, r_{0t}) = U_{0t}$. Thus we can always replace the outside alternative by the outcome $(0, r_{0t})$. If a type θ_t responder prefers some $q \in Q$, he is said to satisfy the participation constraint. In general this significantly complicates matters. For any mapping $M = \{q_t, r_t\}_{t \in T}$ let P be the subset of types that strictly prefer their outside alternative. An outcome is feasible if, for the remaining types $\hat{T} = T \setminus P$, the incentive-compatibility constraints are satisfied.

---

[3] Moreover, if there is some type τ such that $q_s < q_\tau < q_t$ the preference rankings are strict.

As we shall see, there are some applications for which the following assumption is natural.

Assumption 3: Single Outside Alternative
For all types the participation constraint can be expressed as follows:

$$U_t(q, r) \geq U_t(0, r_0).$$

Suppose that Assumption 3 and the SCP hold and $Q \subset \mathbb{R}_+$. Suppose also that the participation constraint holds for the lowest type; that is,

$$U_1(q_1, r_1) \geq U_1(0, r_0).$$

Suppose first that $q_1 = 0$ and that $U_t(q, r)$ is strictly increasing in r. Then $r_1 \geq r_0$, and so for all $t \in \mathcal{T}$, $U_t(q_1, r_1) \geq U_t(0, r_0)$. An identical argument holds if utility is decreasing in r. Suppose next that $q_1 > 0$. Then by the SCP, $U_t(q_1, r_1) \geq U_t(0, r_0)$ for all $t \in \mathcal{T}$. Thus to check the participation constraint, we need only check the constraint for type 1.

Note finally that the participation constraint for type θ_1 is also a local downward constraint. We therefore have the following generalization of Proposition 11.1-4.

Proposition 11.1-6:
If Assumptions 1–3 hold and the local upward and downward incentive constraints are satisfied (including the downward constraint for the lowest type), then $\{q_t, r_t\}_{t \in T}$ satisfies all the incentive and participation constraints.

Continuously Distributed Types

In the continuous version of the model, a type θ player has utility function $u = u(\theta, q, r)$ where $\theta \in \Theta = [\alpha, \beta]$. Assumptions 1 and 2 can then be rewritten as follows.

Assumption 1':
The payoff function $u(\theta, q, r)$ is continuously differentiable and either $\partial u / \partial r > 0$ or $\partial u / \partial r < 0$, for all $(\theta, q, r) \in \Theta \times Q \times R$.

Assumption 2':
SCP
Suppose that $q^1 > q^0$. If $u(\theta, q^1, r^1) \geq u(\theta, q^0, r^0)$, then, for all $\phi > \theta$, $u(\phi, q^1, r^1) > u(\phi, q^0, r^0)$

For the continuous model we consider outcome profiles $\{(q(\theta), r(\theta))\}_{\theta \in \Theta}$ where $q(\theta)$ and $r(\theta)$ are piecewise continuously differentiable. Such a profile is incentive compatible if

$$u(\theta, q(x), r(x)) \leq u(\theta, q(\theta), r(\theta)) \,\forall \theta \quad \text{and} \quad \forall x \in \Theta. \tag{11.1-2}$$

We define

$$U(\theta, x) \equiv u(\theta, q(x), r(x)) \quad \text{and} \quad V(\theta) = U(\theta, \theta).$$

Then we have the following proposition.

Proposition 11.1-7: Incentive Compatibility

If Assumptions 1 and 2 hold and $q(t)$ and $r(t)$ are continuous and piecewise differentiable, then for $\{(q(\theta), r(\theta))\}_{\theta \in \Theta}$ to be incentive compatible: (i) $q(\theta)$ must be non-decreasing and (ii)

$$\frac{dV}{d\theta} = \frac{\partial u}{\partial \theta}(\theta, q(\theta), r(\theta)), \quad \text{where} \quad V(\theta) = u(\theta, q(\theta), r(q)).$$

Together these conditions are sufficient for incentive compatibility.

Proof: If the SCP holds, then arguing exactly as in the finite types case, $q(\cdot)$ is increasing so (i) is true.

For any θ_1 and $\theta_2 > \theta_1$, $U(\theta_1, \theta_2) \le U(\theta_1, \theta_1)$; hence $U(\theta_2, \theta_2) - U(\theta_1, \theta_2) \ge U(\theta_2, \theta_2) - U(\theta_1, \theta_1)$. Also, $U(\theta_2, \theta_1) \le U(\theta_2, \theta_2)$; hence $U(\theta_2, \theta_2) - U(\theta_1, \theta_1) \ge U(\theta_2, \theta_1) - U(\theta_1, \theta_1)$.

Combining these inequalities,

$$\frac{U(\theta_2, \theta_2) - U(\theta_1, \theta_2)}{\theta_2 - \theta_1} \ge \frac{U(\theta_2, \theta_2) - U(\theta_1, \theta_1)}{\theta_2 - \theta_1} \ge \frac{U(\theta_2, \theta_1) - U(\theta_1, \theta_1)}{\theta_2 - \theta_1}.$$

If $\{q(\theta), r(\theta)\}_{\theta \in \Theta}$ is continuous, the upper and lower bounds converge in the limit. Therefore

$$V'(\theta) = \frac{d}{d\theta} U(\theta, \theta) = u_\theta(\theta, q(\theta), r(\theta)).$$

This proves statement (ii) of the proposition. Also

$$\theta = \arg \underset{x \in \Theta}{\text{Max}} \{u(\theta, q(x), r(x))\}.$$

The first-order condition for a maximum is

$$u_q q'(\theta) + u_r r'(\theta) = 0.$$

Thus

$$r'(\theta) = -(u_q/u_r)q'(\theta) = -\text{MRS}(\theta, q(\theta), r(\theta))q'(\theta). \qquad (11.1\text{-}3)$$

Finally note that

$$\frac{\partial U}{\partial x}(\theta, x) = u_q(\theta, q(x), r(x))q'(x) + u_r(\theta, q(x), r(x))r'(x)$$

$$= u_r(\theta, q(x), r(x)) \left[\frac{r'(x)}{q'(x)} + \frac{u_q(\theta, q(x), r(x))}{u_r(\theta, q(x), r(x))} \right] q'(x).$$

Note that (11.1-3) holds for all $\theta \in \Theta$ so it holds for $\theta = x$. Therefore

$$\frac{\partial U}{\partial x}(\theta, x) = u_r[\text{MRS}(x, q(x), r(x)) - \text{MRS}(\theta, q(x), r(x))] q'(x).$$

From Lemma 11.1-2, if the SCP holds then

$$x < \theta \Rightarrow u_r[\text{MRS}(\theta, q(x), r(x) - \text{MRS}(x, q(x), r(x)] \geq 0$$

and

$$x > \theta \Rightarrow u_r[\text{MRS}(\theta, q(x), r(x) - \text{MRS}(x, q(x), r(x)] \leq 0.$$

Also $q(\theta)$ is non-decreasing. Thus $\frac{\partial U}{\partial x}(\theta, x) \geq 0$ for $x < \theta$ and $\frac{\partial U}{\partial x}(\theta, x) \leq 0$ for $x > \theta$. Thus $U(\theta, x)$ takes on its maximum at $x = \theta$, and so the necessary conditions are indeed sufficient. $\qquad\square$

Exercises

Exercise 11.1-1: Sufficient Condition for Single Crossing In the proof of necessity in Proposition 11.1-6 we considered the case in which $u(\theta, q, r)$ is an increasing function of (q, r). For any $q^1 > q^0$ we chose, $(q^1, \hat{r})$ to be on the indifference curve for type θ through (q^0, r^0). We then defined $(q(\lambda), r(\lambda))$ to be the points on the indifference curve through (q^0, r^0) and $(q^1, \hat{r})$ and showed that

$$\frac{d}{d\lambda}u(\phi, q(\lambda), r(\lambda)) = (q^1 - q^0)u_r[\text{MRS}(\phi, q, r)$$
$$- \text{MRS}(\theta, q, r], \quad \text{for all} \quad \lambda \in (0, 1).$$

Use this to prove that if $\text{MRS}(\phi, q, r) > \text{MRS}(\theta, q, r)$, for any $(q, r) \in Q \times R$, then type ϕ has a stronger preference for q.

Exercise 11.1-2: Educational Signaling A type θ_t consultant has a marginal product of $m(\theta_t) = \theta_t$ where $\Theta = \{1, 2, 3\}$. Types are uniformly distributed. The best outside opportunity is $(0, r_0) = (0, \frac{1}{2})$. The cost of accumulating educational credential q is $C(\theta_t, q) = \frac{q}{\theta_t}$ so that the payoff to a type θ consultant, if she receives a payment r for her services, is

$$u(\theta_t, q, r) = r - \frac{q}{\theta_t}.$$

(a) What is the best separating equilibrium of the game?
(b) What is the best pooling equilibrium in which the lower two types are pooled?
(c) What is the best pooling equilibrium with all three types pooled?
(d) Compare the equilibrium payoffs.
(e) Characterize the set of PBE in which the lowest two types are pooled.

Exercise 11.1-3: Educational Signaling with Continuously Distributed Types A type θ consultant has a marginal product of $m(\theta) = k\theta$ where $\Theta = [0, \beta]$.

The cost of accumulating educational credential q is $C(\theta, q) = q/\theta^2$ so that the payoff to a type θ consultant, if she receives a payment r for her services, is

$$u(\theta, q, r) = r - \frac{q}{\theta^2}.$$

(a) Show that a necessary condition for incentive compatibility in a separating equilibrium is

$$q'(\theta) = k\theta^2.$$

(b) Let $V(\theta) = k\theta - q(\theta)/\theta^2$ be the equilibrium payoff. Show that $V'(\theta) = \frac{2q(\theta)}{\theta^3}$.

(c) Hence show that the equilibrium payoff must satisfy the following differential equation:

$$2\theta V(\theta) + \theta^2 V'(\theta) = k\theta^2.$$

(d) Solve this differential equation and hence show that $V(\theta) = \frac{2}{3}k\theta$.

(e) Let $r = R(q)$ be the equilibrium wage offered to a worker who chooses signal level q. Show that

$$R'(q) = \frac{1}{\theta^2}.$$

(f) Hence show that $R(q)^2 R'(q) = k^2$.

(g) Solve for the equilibrium payment function.

11.2 Information Revelation, Adverse Selection, and Signaling

Key ideas: unraveling principle, adverse selection, signaling, signaling equilibrium satisfying the Intuitive Criterion

In this and later sections we appeal to the results on incentive compatibility as we consider different economic environments where private information plays a critical role. As our first topic, we consider games in which a player with favorable private information is eager to communicate this to other players. To illustrate, consider sellers with items of uncertain quality. Let $v(\theta_t)$, $\theta_t \in \Theta = \{\theta_1, \ldots, \theta_T\}$ be the true (i.e., the full information) value of the product or service that a type θ_t player sells (used car, consulting service, etc.) A higher type has a higher valued product for sale. Also define $\mu(\theta_t) = E\{v(\theta_s)|\theta_s \leq \theta_t\}$ to be the average market value of a seller whose type is known to be less than or equal to θ_t. For all $\theta_t > \theta_1$, this average value is strictly less than the value of the highest type in the pool; that is, $\mu(\theta_t) < v(\theta_t)$.

The Unraveling Principle

Suppose that all the different types of sellers are in the pool. The actual value is not directly observable so a buyer's expected value of an item is the population average. Competition among buyers then pushes the equilibrium price to $\mu(\theta_T)$. But this is below the value of the highest type so if this type of seller can credibly reveal his true type he will do so and therefore earn $v(\theta_T)$. Suppose that this is the only type to reveal. Then the market value of the item is the average of the T-1 remaining types; that is, $\mu(\theta_{T-1})$. Because this market value is lower than $v(\theta_{T-1})$, the second highest type of seller is better off revealing. By making this argument repeatedly, it follows that all types of seller except the lowest have an incentive to reveal their private information. But then the market value of a seller who does not reveal is $v(\theta_1)$ so, even by withholding this information, the value of the lowest type of seller is revealed as well.

Crucial to this argument is the assumption that sellers can credibly reveal their private information at no cost. We next consider the outcome when this cost is prohibitive.

Adverse Selection: Exit or Trade

Potential sellers have only two options. They can either trade at a price reflecting the average value of items for sale or withdraw from the market. It proves helpful to switch from the finite types version of the model to the continuous types model. We write the value of a type θ item as $v(\theta)$ where $\theta \in \Theta = [\alpha, \beta]$. The c.d.f. of θ is $F \in \mathbb{C}^1$. Then the average value of types below θ is

$$\mu(\theta) = E\{v(x)|x \le \theta\} = \frac{\int\limits_{\alpha}^{\theta} v(x)F'(x)dx}{F(\theta)}.$$

Note that $\mu(\alpha) = v(\alpha)$ and $\mu(\theta) < v(\theta)$, for $\theta > \alpha$.

Let $v_o(\theta)$ be a type θ seller's best alternative or "outside" opportunity. For example, if the item is a used car, $v_o(\theta)$ is the value to the seller of continuing to drive it. To simplify the analysis we assume that this outside option has a value that is a fraction γ of the true market value of the item $v(\theta)$. The value, the average value of those types below θ, and the outside option value are all depicted in Figure 11.2-1.

Suppose that the outside value for the highest type, $v_0(\beta)$, exceeds the average of all the types $\mu(\beta)$. Then the functions $\mu(\theta)$ and $v_o(\theta)$ must have at least one intersection. For simplicity we assume that there is only one such intersection.

Consider any price $p > \overline{p}$ as depicted in Figure 11.2-1. Note that the type $\theta_o(p)$ is indifferent between selling at this price and choosing his outside alternative. All types above $\theta_0(p)$ are strictly better off withdrawing from the market. All lower types are strictly better off selling. Therefore the

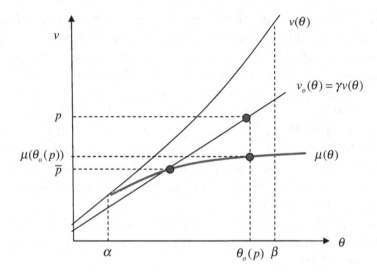

Figure 11.2-1. Adverse selection.

average value of those remaining is $\mu(\theta_o(p))$. But this is less than p so the price is too high. An essentially identical argument establishes that any price $p < \overline{p}$ results in an average value in excess of p so this price is too low. Thus $\overline{p}$ is the unique market-clearing price.

The incomplete information of the buyers therefore has an adverse effect on both the volume of trade and the average quality of the items traded. Note that as γ increases, the value of the outside opportunity, $v_o(\theta)$ shifts up. As a result the equilibrium price, $\overline{p}(\gamma)$, declines. In the limit, as the difference between the outside value and $v(\theta)$ approaches zero, only the very lowest quality items (the "lemons") are traded.[4]

Given the inability of high-value sellers to get a price above their reservation price, such buyers have an incentive to seek some costly way of signaling the quality of their product. As discussed in the previous section, an observable action is a potential signal if it is more costly for low-value sellers. It is to this topic that we now turn.

Signaling Equilibrium

Section 11.1 focused on the first stage of the two-stage signaling game and examined necessary and sufficient conditions for incentive compatibility. To complete the model we need to make some additional assumptions, in particular about the equilibrium outcome of the game for player 1. Let the set of types be $\Theta = \{\theta_1, \theta_2, \ldots, \theta_T\}$, and let the utility of player 1 be $u(\theta_t, q, r)$ if his type is θ_t, where q is the action of the first mover and r is the response

---

[4] The almost total breakdown of the market does not imply that there is a large social loss. If the difference between $v(\theta)$ and $v_o(\theta)$ is small, the social loss from the market failure is also small.

of the other players. As in Section 11.1 we assume that Assumptions 1–3 hold. That is, utility is continuously differentiable, the single crossing property holds, and each player 1 type has the same outside alternative. We also assume that the agent's payoff is an increasing function of r.

We look for an equilibrium in pure strategies; that is, for each type θ_t there is a single action $q(\theta_t)$. Because the SCP holds, incentive compatibility requires that higher types choose higher actions. Then if $q(\theta_\tau)$ is the choice of type θ_τ there must be some subset of types $\hat{\Theta} = \{\theta | \theta_s \leq \theta \leq \theta_t\}$ such that $q(\theta_\tau) = q(\theta_t)$ if and only if $\theta_\tau \in \hat{\Theta}$.

Suppose that the responding players observe the signal q and, based on this signal, believe that the agent's type lies in some set $\hat{\Theta} \subset \Theta$. We assume that for any such beliefs there is a unique equilibrium response by the responding players. In general this payoff depends on the choice of q and the beliefs in the second stage so we write player 1's payoff as $r = R(\hat{\Theta}, q)$. In the special case in which $\hat{\Theta} = \{\theta_t\}$ we write the response as $r = R(\theta_t, q)$ rather than $R(\{\theta_t\}, q)$.

Let Θ' and Θ'' be two different subsets of Θ. If all the types only in Θ' are lower than all the types only in Θ'' we write $\Theta' < \Theta''$.[5] We make the following assumptions about the response function.

Assumption 4: Equilibrium outcome for player 1
Player 1's payoff, $u(\theta_t, q, R(\hat{\Theta}, q))$, if his type is θ_t and believed to be in $\hat{\Theta} \subset \Theta$, is a continuously differentiable strictly quasi-concave function of q with a maximum $q^*(\theta_t, \hat{\Theta}) < q^{\max}$, the maximum feasible action. Higher types generate more favorable responses; that is,

$$\Theta' < \Theta'' \Rightarrow R(\Theta', q) < R(\Theta'', q).$$

Assumption 5:
Participation[6]
(i) For all types the outside option is equivalent to outcome $(0, r_o)$ and (ii) for some q, $(q, R(\theta_1, q)) \underset{\theta_1}{\succ} (0, r_0)$.

Appealing to the SCP, it follows immediately that the preference ranking (ii) holds for all buyer types.[7]

The key implications of Assumptions 4 and 5 are illustrated in Figure 11.2-2. The dashed curves are indifference curves of a type θ_t player. By Assumption 5, there is some action, q, strictly preferred to the outside

---

[5] In set theoretic terms, $\Theta' \backslash \Theta' \cap \Theta'' < \Theta'' \backslash \Theta' \cap \Theta''$,

[6] If condition (ii) is not satisfied, simply define the new set of type $\overline{\Theta} = \{\theta \in \Theta | \theta \geq \theta_s\}$ where θ_s is the smallest type such that for some q, $(q, R(\theta, q)) \underset{\theta_s}{\succ} (0, r_0)$. See the exercises for examples where condition (i) is not satisfied.

[7] We argue later that the lowest possible response in a PBE is $R(\theta_1, q)$. Thus condition (i) implies that, in a PBE, all types are better off participating than choosing their outside alternative.

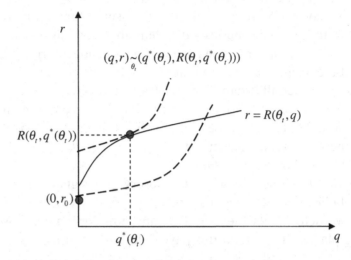

Figure 11.2-2. Preference map of type θ_t and response curves.

alternative $(0, r_0)$. By Assumption 4 $u(\theta_t, q, R(\theta_t, q))$ must take on its maximum at a unique $q^*(\theta_t)$. Moreover $u(\theta_t, q, R(\theta_t, q))$ is increasing in q for $q < q^*(\theta_t)$ and decreasing in q for $q > q^*(\theta_t)$. Graphically, along the response curve $R(\theta_t, q)$ the utility of type θ_t increases until $q = q^*(\theta_t)$ and decreases thereafter. Hence each indifference curve for type θ_t either lies everywhere above the response curve $r = R(\theta_t, q)$ or intersects once to the right of $q^*(\theta_t)$.

Before characterizing a separating equilibrium with private information, suppose first that the responding players all observe player 1's type. Then if the type is θ_t, and the action is q, the equilibrium payoff to player 1 is $R(\theta_t, q)$. Knowing this, type θ_t chooses

$$q^*(\theta_t) = \arg \operatorname*{Max}_{q}\{u(\theta_t, q, R(\theta_t, q)).$$

The outcome of the game is therefore $\{(q^*(\theta_t), R(\theta_t, q^*(\theta_t)))\}_{\theta_t \in \Theta}$. We refer to this full information outcome as the efficient outcome.

Could the full information-efficient outcome be an equilibrium outcome with asymmetric information? As Figure 11.2-3 illustrates, the answer is yes. Let there be two types: θ_1 and $\theta_2 > \theta_1$. Consider the efficient contracts $\{(q^*(\theta_t), R(\theta_t, q^*(\theta_t)))\}_{t \in T}$. Type $\theta_t, t = 1, 2$ maximizes his utility at $q^*(\theta_t)$ where his indifference curve touches the response curve $r = R(\theta_t, q)$. As depicted $(q^*(\theta_2), R^*(\theta_2))$ lies below the indifference curve for type θ_1, so that the upward incentive constraint for type θ_1 is satisfied. Similarly $(q^*(\theta_1), R^*(\theta_1))$ lies below the indifference curve for type θ_2, so that the downward incentive constraint for type θ_2 is also satisfied.

As we now show, this is not possible if neighboring types are sufficiently similar. We therefore ignore this unlikely (and hence uninteresting) case.

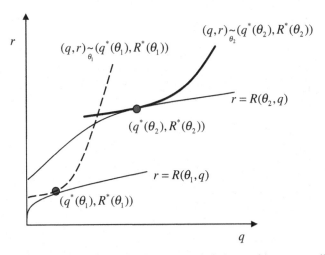

Figure 11.2-3. Full information outcome is incentive compatible.

Lemma 11.2-1: A Separating Equilibrium Cannot Be Efficient if Neighboring Types Are Sufficiently Similar[8] If Assumptions 1–5 hold and the difference between neighboring types is sufficiently small, then the local upward constraints are all violated for the efficient strategy $\{q^*(\theta_t)\}_{\theta_t \in \Theta}$.

Proof: For any θ define the efficient action

$$q^*(\theta) = \arg \underset{q}{\text{Max}}\{u(\theta, q, R(\theta, q)) | q \geq 0\}. \qquad (11.2\text{-}1)$$

Because $u(\theta, q, R(\theta, q))$ is a strictly quasi-concave function of q, then $q^*(\theta)$ is unique. Strict quasi-concavity and the continuity of $u(\theta, q, R(\theta, q))$ imply that $q^*(\theta)$ is continuous.

Appealing to the Envelope Theorem,

$$\frac{d}{d\theta}u(\theta, q^*(\theta), R(\theta, q^*(\theta))) = \frac{\partial u}{\partial \theta} + \frac{\partial u}{\partial r}\frac{\partial R}{\partial \theta}. \qquad (11.2\text{-}2)$$

Also

$$\frac{d}{d\theta}u(\theta, q^*(\theta), R(\theta, q^*(\theta)))\bigg|_{\theta=\theta_t} = \frac{\partial u}{\partial \theta}\bigg|_{\theta=\theta_t} + \frac{d}{d\theta}u(\theta_t, q^*(\theta), R(\theta, q^*(\theta)))\bigg|_{\theta=\theta_t}. \qquad (11.2\text{-}3)$$

The terms on the left-hand side and first terms on the right-hand side of equations (11.2-2) and (11.2-3) are the same at $\theta = \theta_t$. Therefore the second terms on the right-hand side of each equation are also the same. Thus

$$\frac{d}{d\theta}u(\theta_t, q^*(\theta), R(\theta, q^*(\theta)))\bigg|_{\theta=\theta_t} = \frac{\partial u}{\partial r}\frac{\partial R}{\partial \theta}\bigg|_{\theta=\theta_t} > 0.$$

---

[8] The reader may wish to skip this technical proof. Exercise 11.2-2 provides a simple example that illustrates the lemma.

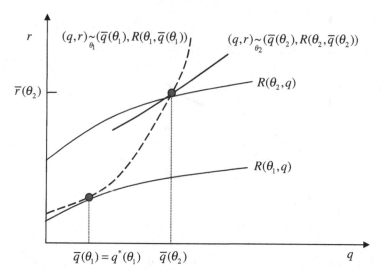

Figure 11.2-4. Choosing the action for types θ_1 and θ_2.

It follows that for any θ_{t+1} sufficiently close to θ_t,

$$u(\theta_t, q^*(\theta_{t+1}), R(\theta_{t+1}, q^*(\theta_{t+1}))) - u(\theta_t, q^*(\theta_t), R(\theta_t, q^*(\theta_t))) > 0. \qquad \square$$

Constructing a Separating PBE

Given our assumptions there is a simple way of constructing a separating PBE strategy $\{\overline{q}(\theta_t)\}_{\theta_t \in \Theta}$.

Choosing $\overline{q}(\theta_1)$: In a separating PBE a type θ_1 player takes a different action from all the other types; thus the responders know he is type θ_1 and so the response function is $R(\theta_1, q)$. Then type θ_1 chooses the full information-efficient action:

$$\overline{q}(\theta_1) = q^*(\theta_1) \equiv \arg \operatorname*{Max}_{q}\{u(\theta_1, q, R(\theta_1, q))\}.$$

Choosing $\overline{q}(\theta_2)$: The dashed curve depicted in Figure 11.2-4 is the graph of the indifference curve for type θ_1 through $q^*(\theta_1)$. By Assumption 4 this intersects the graph of the response function once to the right of $\overline{q}_1(\theta_1)$. Let $(\overline{q}(\theta_2), \overline{r}(\theta_2))$ be this intersection point.

Choosing $\overline{q}(\theta_t)$: Each of the other signaling levels is chosen inductively. Given $\overline{q}(\theta_{t-1})$, choose $(\overline{q}(\theta_t), \overline{r}(\theta_t))$ where the indifference curve for type θ_t through $(\overline{q}(\theta_{t-1}), R(\theta_{t-1}, q(\theta_{t-1})))$ intersects $R(\theta_t, q)$ to the right of $\overline{q}(\theta_{t-1})$.

Because all of the local upward constraints are binding and $\{\overline{q}(\theta_t)\}_{\theta_t \in \Theta}$ is increasing, all the incentive and participation constraints are satisfied. Therefore $\{\overline{q}(\theta_t), \overline{r}(\theta_t)\}_{\theta_t \in \Theta}$ is a BNE.

We next establish the following result.

Proposition 11.2-2:

The BNE separating equilibrium in which local upward constraints are all binding and the lowest type chooses its efficient action is a PBE.

Proof: We show that there are sequential beliefs that support the BNE. Suppose that for all types the distribution of trembles is uniform and let ε_t be the probability that type θ_s trembles. Then the conditional probability that some action q (off the equilibrium path) is chosen by type θ_t is

$$p(\theta_t|q) = \frac{\varepsilon_t}{\sum\limits_{s=1}^{T} \varepsilon_s}.$$

Choose $\varepsilon_t = \delta$ and $\varepsilon_s = \delta^2, s \neq t$. Then

$$p(\theta|q) = \frac{\delta}{\delta + (T-1)\delta^2} = \frac{1}{1 + (T-1)\delta}.$$

Taking the limit as the probability if trembles approaches zero, $p(\theta_t|q) \to 1$. Thus we can use any beliefs that we like as to which type is taking the action q.

Case (i): $q < \overline{q}(\theta_1)$.

Choose type θ_1 to be the player believed to be taking the off the equilibrium path action q. By construction

$$\overline{q}(\theta_1) = \arg \underset{q}{\text{Max}}\{u(\theta_1, q, R(\theta_1, q))\}.$$

Then $(q, R(\theta_1, q)) \underset{\theta_1}{\prec} (\overline{q}(\theta_1), R(\theta_1, \overline{q}(\theta_1)))$.

Appealing to Lemma 11.1-1 it follows that all higher types also strictly prefer $(\overline{q}(\theta_1), R(\theta_1, \overline{q}(\theta_1)))$. And because the BNE is incentive compatible

$$(\overline{q}(\theta_1), R(\theta_1, \overline{q}(\theta_1))) \underset{\theta_t}{\precsim} (\overline{q}(\theta_t), R(\theta_t, \overline{q}(\theta_t))), \forall \theta_t \in \Theta.$$

Thus no type is better off choosing q given these beliefs.

Case (ii): $\overline{q}(\theta_{s-1}) < q < \overline{q}(\theta_s)$.

The argument is similar. This time let the belief be that it is type θ_{s-1} that is choosing action q.

By construction, $u(\theta_{s-1}, q, R(\theta_{s-1}, q))$ is strictly decreasing for $q > \overline{q}(\theta_{s-1})$. Then

$$(q, R(\theta_{s-1}, q)) \underset{\theta_{s-1}}{\prec} (\overline{q}(\theta_{s-1}), R(\theta_{s-1}, \overline{q}(\theta_{s-1}))).$$

Appealing to Lemma 11.1-1 (ii), the preference ranking is the same for all lower types. Also, by construction, the local upward constraint is binding. Therefore

$$(q, R(\theta_{s-1}, q)) \underset{\theta_{s-1}}{\prec} (\overline{q}(\theta_{s-1}), R(\theta_{s-1}, \overline{q}(\theta_{s-1}))) \underset{\theta_{s-1}}{\sim} (\overline{q}(\theta_s), R(\theta_s, \overline{q}(\theta_s))).$$

Appealing to Lemma 11.1-1 (i) it follows that for $\theta_t > \theta_{s-1}$

$$(q, R(\theta_{s-1}, q)) \underset{\theta_t}{\prec} (\overline{q}(\theta_s), R(\theta_s, \overline{q}(\theta_s))).$$

Because the BNE is incentive compatible it follows that

$$(\overline{q}(\theta_s), R(\theta_s, \overline{q}(\theta_s))) \underset{\theta_t}{\precsim} (\overline{q}(\theta_t), R(\theta_t, \overline{q}(\theta_t))).$$

Thus no higher type prefers to choose q either.

The argument for $q > \overline{q}(\theta_T)$ proceeds similarly. Thus at every point off the equilibrium path there are beliefs such that every type is worse off deviating from his BNE strategy. $\qquad\square$

Signaling with Types Continuously Distributed

We now extend the model to the case where types are continuously distributed. Given our results for the finite types case, we seek to characterize a separating equilibrium that is efficient for the lowest type.

A type θ player has utility function $u(\theta, q, r)$. Types are continuously distributed on the interval $[\alpha, \beta]$. If it is believed that the player is type θ and his choice is q, the response in the second stage of the game is $r = R(\theta, q)$. We assume that Assumptions 1–5 hold.

Let $\{(q(\theta)\}_{\theta \in \Theta}$ be the choices of each type in a separating equilibrium. We assume that $q(\theta)$ is continuous. A type t player's equilibrium payoff is $V(\theta) = u(\theta, q(\theta), R(\theta, q))$. Appealing to Section 11.1 this payoff is incentive compatible if it satisfies the differential equation

$$V'(\theta) = u_\theta(\theta, q(\theta), R(\theta, q)). \tag{11.2-1}$$

Let $q^*(\theta)$ be the full information-efficient outcome; that is, $q^*(\theta) = \arg \underset{q}{\text{Max}}\ u(\theta, q, R(\theta, q))$. In the finite types case $q(\theta_t) \geq q^*(\theta_t)$, thus we seek an equilibrium mapping $q(\theta) \geq q^*(\theta)$. Also define $V^*(\theta) = u(\theta, q^*(\theta), R(\theta, q^*(\theta)))$. We know that the lowest type chooses the full information signal. Thus $V(\alpha) = V^*(\alpha)$.

We look for a solution to this differential equation under the assumption that for all types above α, $V^*(\theta) > V(\theta)$; hence $q(\theta) > q^*(\theta)$. Given strict quasi-concavity it follows that for all $q > q^*(\theta)$, $V = u(\theta, q, R(\theta, q))$ is a strictly decreasing function of q. Then we can invert this expression and write $q = h(\theta, V)$. Substituting this into (11.2-4) yields an ordinary differential equation for V,

$$\frac{dV}{d\theta} = u_\theta(\theta, h(\theta, V), R(\theta, h(\theta, V))).$$

In addition, because $V(\theta)$ is the maximum payoff for type θ,

$$V(\theta) = u(\theta, (q(\theta), r(\theta))).$$

We can use these two conditions to solve for the signaling equilibrium.

Example: Educational Signaling
A type θ consultant has a marginal product $m(\theta)$ where $m(\cdot)$ is a strictly increasing continuous function. Types are continuously distributed on $[\alpha, \beta]$ where $\alpha > 0$ and $m(\alpha) = 0$. The cost of accumulating educational credential q is $C(\theta, q) = \frac{q}{\theta}$ so that the payoff to a type θ consultant, if she receives a payment r for her services, is

$$u(\theta, q, r) = r - \frac{q}{\theta}.$$

Let $\{q(\theta), r(\theta)\}_{\theta \in \Theta}$ be a separating equilibrium of the signaling game. Because each type is separated, Bertrand wage competition bids the wage up to the consultant's marginal product. Therefore $r(\theta) = m(\theta)$. Let $V(\theta)$ be the equilibrium payoff of type θ; that is,

$$V(\theta) = u(\theta, q(\theta), r(\theta)) = m(\theta) - \frac{q(\theta)}{\theta}. \tag{11.2-2}$$

By the Envelope Theorem $V'(\theta) = \frac{q(\theta)}{\theta^2}$. Therefore

$$\theta V'(\theta) = \frac{q(\theta)}{\theta}. \tag{11.2-3}$$

Substituting into (11.2-5) and rearranging,

$$V(\theta) + \theta V'(\theta) = m(\theta).$$

Both sides can be integrated. Noting that the lowest type does not signal so $V(0) = 0$, it follows that

$$\theta V(\theta) = \int_\alpha^\theta m(x)dx.$$

Hence the equilibrium payoff is $V(\theta) = \frac{1}{\theta} \int_\alpha^\theta m(x)dx$. Finally, substituting this back into (11.2-5),

$$q(\theta) = \theta(m(\theta) - V(\theta)) = \theta m(\theta) - \int_\alpha^\theta m(x)dx.$$

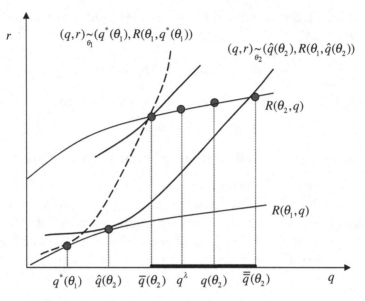

Figure 11.2-5. Pareto-inferior separating PBE.

Continuum of Separating Equilibria with Finite Types

With finite types the best separating equilibrium is not the unique PBE. In fact there is a continuum of such equilibria. To illustrate, consider the two-type case. The best separating PBE strategy, $\{q^*(\theta_1), \overline{q}(\theta_2)\}$, is depicted in Figure 11.2-5.

Define

$$\hat{q}(\theta_2) = \arg \underset{q}{\mathrm{Max}}\{u(\theta_2, q, r)|r \leq R(\theta_1, q)\}.$$

This is also depicted. Also define $\overline{\overline{q}}(\theta_2) > \overline{q}(\theta_2)$ such that

$$(\hat{q}(\theta_2), R(\theta_1, \hat{q}(\theta_2))) \underset{\theta_2}{\sim} (\overline{\overline{q}}(\theta_2), R(\theta_1, \overline{\overline{q}}(\theta_2))).$$

Consider any strategy $\{q^*(\theta_1), q(\theta_2)\}$ where $q(\theta_2) \in [\overline{q}(\theta_2), \overline{\overline{q}}(\theta_2)]$. Note that

$$(q^*(\theta_1), R(\theta_1, q^*(\theta_1))) \underset{\theta_1}{\succ} (q(\theta_2), R(\theta_2, q(\theta_2)))$$

and

$$(q^*(\theta_1), R(\theta_1, q^*(\theta_1))) \underset{\theta_2}{\prec} (q(\theta_2), R(\theta_2, q(\theta_2))).$$

Thus both the incentive constraints are satisfied and so $\{q^*(\theta_1), q(\theta_2)\}$ is a PBE.

We now argue that no such Pareto inferior PBE satisfies the Strong Intuitive Criterion.

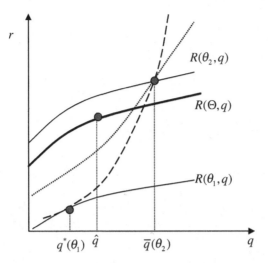

Figure 11.2-6. Pareto-superior pooling PBE.

Suppose that type θ_2 chooses the action off the equilibrium path

$$q^\lambda = (1 - \lambda)\overline{q}(\theta_2) + \lambda q(\theta_2), 0 < \lambda < 1.$$

Because $u(\theta_2, q, R(\theta_2, q))$ is a decreasing function of q for $q > \overline{q}(\theta_2)$, such an action makes this type strictly better off if he is believed to be the high type. Also, by construction, for all $q > \overline{q}(\theta_2)$,

$$u(\theta_1, q, R(\theta_2, q)) < u(\theta_1, \overline{q}(\theta_2), R(\theta_2, \overline{q}(\theta_2))) = u(\theta_1, \overline{q}(\theta_1), R(\theta_1, \overline{q}(\theta_1))).$$

Thus type θ_1 would be worse off mimicking the out-of-equilibrium action, even if he were believed to be the high type.

An almost identical argument applies with more than two types, resulting in the following proposition.

Proposition 11.2-3:
The only separating PBE satisfying the Strong Intuitive Criterion is the best separating equilibrium.

Pooling Equilibria

Although we have focused on separating PBE strategies of the first mover, there exist PBE strategies in which two or more types choose the same action. These are called pooling strategies. Consider the two-type case. Figure 11.2-6 depicts the best separating PBE. Note that the dashed curve is type 1's indifference curve through his separating PBE outcome and the dotted indifference curve is type 2's indifference curve through her separating PBE outcome. Let $R(\Theta, q)$ be the response function if all types choose the same action. As depicted, for all $\hat{q}$ below some threshold, both types prefer the pooling response to their separating equilibrium responses. To see

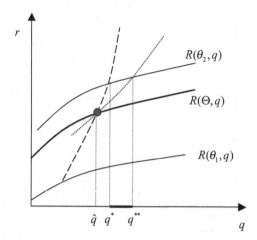

Figure 11.2-7. Intuitive Criterion not satisfied.

that any such $\hat{q}$ is a pooling equilibrium, consider Figure 11.2-7. As we have already argued, we may use any belief for an action off the equilibrium path. So choose the belief to be that it is type θ_1. Both types are strictly better off at $(\hat{q}, R(\Theta, \hat{q}))$ than at any point on $R(\theta_1, q)$ so the pooling BNE is a PBE.

All such pools are eliminated by the Strong Intuitive Criterion. Let q^* and q^{**} be the actions where the indifference curves of each type (through the equilibrium outcome) intersect $R(\theta_2, q)$. A type θ_2 player can argue as follows: "I have chosen $q \in (q^*, q^{**})$ and you should believe I am type θ_2. For if you do, then your response will be $R(\theta_2, q)$ and I will be better off. However this would not be the case if I were type θ_1."

With more than two types, this argument can be easily formalized to show that if the lowest two types are pooled, then the Intuitive Criterion cannot be satisfied. An inductive argument can then be used to establish the following result.

Proposition 11.2-4:
No pooling PBE satisfies the Strong Intuitive Criterion.

Exercises

Exercise 11.2-1: Choice of Signals A type θ worker's marginal product is $m(\theta) = a\theta$ where $\theta \in \{1, 2\}$. Her outside opportunity wage is $w_0 \in (a, 2a)$. She can choose either x, y, or z as a signal, where (i) $C(\theta, x) = x/\theta$, (ii) $C(\theta, y) = y^2/\theta$, and (iii) $C(\theta, z) = z/\theta^2$.

(a) Compare the equilibrium payoffs in the three cases.
(b) Which of the three signals is best for the worker? Provide the intuition behind the ranking.
(c) Extend the analysis to the three-type case where $\theta \in \{1, 2, 3\}$.

Exercise 11.2-2: Can Local Incentive Constraints Hold for Efficient Signals?
The utility of type θ_t is $u(\theta_t, q, r) = r - q^2/2\theta_t$. There are T types and
$\theta_1 < \cdots < \theta_T$. If it is believed that the type sending the signal q is θ, the
second-stage response function is $R(\theta, q) = \theta q$.

(a) Show that the efficient action for type θ_t is $q^*(\theta_t) = \theta_t^2$. Hence solve for the
efficient response $R(\theta_t, q^*(\theta_t))$ and the resulting utility $U^*(\theta_t)$.
(b) Suppose that $\theta_{t+1} = a\theta_t$. Show that the local upward constraint

$$u(\theta_t, q^*(\theta_{t+1}), r^*(\theta_{t+1})) \leq U^*(\theta_t)$$

is satisfied if and only if $2a^3 - a^4 - 1 \leq 0$.

(c) Confirm that this constraint holds for all $a \geq 2$ but is violated if $a \in (1, 1.5]$.

Exercise 11.2-3: Minimum Signals A type θ worker's marginal product
is $m(\theta)$ where $\theta \in \{\theta_1, \ldots, \theta_T\}$. Her outside opportunity wage is $r_0 \in$
$(m(\theta_1), m(\theta_T))$. The signaling cost function is $C(\theta, q)$.

(a) Show that to satisfy the Strong Intuitive Criterion, the lowest type that signals
must satisfy the following conditions: (i) $m(\theta_t) - C(\theta_{t-1}, q_t) = w_0$, (ii) $m(\theta_{t-1}) \leq$
r_0.
(b) Taking the limit as the difference between types approaches zero, show that
$q_t \rightarrow 0$ and $m(\theta_t) \rightarrow r_0$.

Exercise 11.2-4: Choice of Signals with Continuous Types Continue with the
model of the previous exercise, but now types are continuously distributed
on the interval $[1, 2]$. The signalling cost function is $c(\theta, q, \alpha) = q/\theta^\alpha$. The
marginal product of a type θ consultant is $m(\theta) = \theta$. (Appealing to the above
limiting argument, the lowest signal $q(\theta_0)$ is zero.

(a) Solve for θ_0.
(b) Write down the first-order condition for incentive compatibility. Integrate and
hence show that the equilibrium cost of signaling for type θ is $C^e(\theta, \alpha) =$
$\frac{a\theta}{1+\alpha}(1 - \tau^{1+\alpha})$ where $\tau = \theta_0/\theta$,
(c) Confirm that $\frac{C^e(\theta, \beta)}{C^e(\theta, \alpha)} = \frac{1+\alpha}{1+\beta}(\frac{1-\tau^{1+\beta}}{1-\tau^{1+\alpha}})$. Hence show that $C^e(\theta, 2) < C^e(\theta, 1)$ for all
$\theta > \theta_0$.
(d) *Show that $C^e(\theta, \beta) < C^e(\theta, \alpha)$ for all $\theta > \theta_0$ and $\beta > \alpha$.

Exercise 11.2-5: Educational Signaling The utility of a type θ consultant is
$u(\theta, q, r) = r - B(q)/A(\theta)$ where $A'(\theta) > 0$ and $B'(q) > 0$. The set of types
is $\Theta = [\alpha, \beta]$. The marginal product of a type θ consultant is $m(\theta) = \theta$.

(a) Define $V(\theta)$ to be the equilibrium payoff of type $\theta \geq \alpha$. Explain why, in a separating equilibrium,

$$V'(\theta) = u_\theta(t, q(\theta), \theta) = A'(\theta)B(q(\theta))/A^2(\theta) \quad \text{and}$$
$$V(\theta) = \theta - B(q(\theta))/A(\theta).$$

(b) Substituting for $B(q(\theta))$ and rearranging, confirm that

$$A'(\theta)V(\theta) + A(\theta)V'(\theta) = \theta A'(\theta).$$

(c) Integrate and hence show that the equilibrium payoff of type θ satisfies

$$A(\theta)V(\theta) - A(\alpha)\alpha = \int\limits_{\alpha}^{\theta} xA'(x)dx.$$

(d) Hence show that $V(\theta) = \theta - \int_{\alpha}^{\theta} \frac{A(x)}{A(\theta)}dx$.

(e) Suppose there are two possible signaling technologies with signaling costs $C_i(\theta, q) = B_i(q)/A_i(\theta)$ $i = 1, 2$. Suppose also that $A_2(\theta)/A_1(\theta)$ is strictly increasing so that $MC_2(\theta, q)/MC_1(q)$ is a strictly decreasing function of θ. Prove that the payoff to all but the lowest type is higher for the second technology.

HINT: Use the fact that $\frac{A_2(\theta)}{A_1(\theta)} > \frac{A_2(x)}{A_1(x)}$.

Exercise 11.2-6: Productive Signal A worker of type θ has a marginal product of $m(\theta, q) = 2\theta q^{1/2}$ if he achieves education level q. His cost of education is $C(\theta, q) = q/\theta$. Types are continuously distributed on the interval $[0, 4]$. There is no outside opportunity.

(a) With full information show that type t will choose $q^*(\theta) = \theta^4$ and that his wage will be $m(\theta, q^*(\theta)) = \theta^3$.

(b) With asymmetric information, extend this argument to show that the equilibrium wage function $r(q)$ must satisfy the following ordinary differential equation:

$$2r(q)\frac{dr}{dq} = 4q^{1/2}.$$

(c) Solve for the equilibrium level of education $q(\theta)$ and the wage function $r(q)$.

Exercise 11.2-7: Choosing a Signaling Technology Workers can choose one of two signals, y and z. Types are continuously distributed on the interval $[0, 1]$. The value of a type θ worker to competing firms is θ. The cost of signaling at level y is $C_1(\theta, y) = \frac{y}{\theta}$. The cost of signaling at level z is $C_2(\theta, z) = \frac{z}{1+\theta^2}$.

(a) If all choose to signal using y, solve for the equilibrium payoff $V_1(\theta)$.

(b) If all signal using z, show that the equilibrium payoff function is $V_2(\theta) = \frac{2\theta^3}{3(1+\theta^2)}$.

(c) If both signaling technologies were available, what would be the equilibrium outcome for each type?

(d)* Suppose instead that $\Theta = [0, 3]$?

Exercise 11.2-8*: Equilibrium When High-Quality Workers Have Better Outside Opportunities A type θ worker has a value $g(\theta) = \theta$ and a signaling cost $C(\theta, q) = q/\theta$. Types are continuously distributed on $[0, 1]$. The outside payoff to type θ is $w_0(\theta) = \gamma + \beta\theta$, where $\gamma < \alpha$.

(a) Show that with full information, each type $\theta < \theta^* = \gamma/(\alpha - \beta)$ is better off taking his outside opportunity.

(b) Suppose that with asymmetric information, type $\hat{\theta}$ is indifferent between choosing the signal $q(\hat{\theta}) > 0$ and staying out while all higher types signal. For $\theta \geq \hat{\theta}$, define

$$V(\theta) = u(\theta, q(\theta), r(\theta)) = \theta - q(\theta)/\theta.$$

Show that $\frac{dV}{d\theta} = \frac{q(\theta)}{\theta^2}$. Hence show that the equilibrium payoff function $V(\theta)$ must satisfy the differential equation $\theta\frac{dV}{d\theta} + V(\theta) = \theta$. Integrate and so establish that

$$V(\theta, k) = \tfrac{1}{2}\theta + \frac{k}{\theta}.$$

(c) Depict the 45° line and the curve $V(\theta, k)$ for $k > 0$. Show that at the intersection of this curve and the 45° line the slope of the payoff function is zero.

(d) Draw in the outside opportunity line and explain why the Pareto preferred signaling function must be tangential to the outside opportunity line.

(e) Solve for the minimum type that signals $\hat{\theta}$ and the minimum signal $q(\hat{\theta})$.

Exercise 11.2-9: Comparing the Finite Type and Continuous Type Models

(a) In the finite types model, let $V(\theta_t)$ be type θ_t's payoff; that is, $V(\theta_t) \equiv u(\theta_t, q_t, r_t)$. If the local downward constraint holds for type θ_{t+1} explain why $V(\theta_{t+1}) - V(\theta_t) \geq u(\theta_{t+1}, q_t, r_t) - u(\theta_t, q_t, r_t)$.

(b) If the local upward constraint holds for type θ_t explain why $V(\theta_{t+1}) - V(\theta_t) \leq u(\theta_t, q_{t+1}, r_{t+1}) - u(\theta_t, q_{t+1}, r_{t+1})$.

(c) Show that these constraints imply that

$$\frac{u(\theta_{t+1}, q_{t+1}, r_{t+1}) - u(\theta_t, q_{t+1}, r_{t+1})}{\theta_{t+1} - \theta_t}$$

$$\geq \frac{V(\theta_{t+1}) - V(\theta_t)}{\theta_{t+1} - \theta_t} \geq \frac{u(\theta_{t+1}, q_t, r_t) - u(\theta_t, q_t, r_t)}{\theta_{t+1} - \theta_t}.$$

(d) Hence argue that, if quantities converge in the limit, then the local upward and downward constraints become the following ordinary differential equation:

$$\frac{dV}{d\theta} = \frac{\partial u}{\partial \theta}(\theta, q(\theta), r(\theta)).$$

11.3 Mechanism Design

Key ideas: incentive and participation constraints, Revelation Principle, single crossing property, local binding constraints, indirect price discrimination, optimal control, optimal income taxation

Thus far we have considered games in which the rules of play are specified exogenously. We now consider a game in player 1 moves first, announcing the rules of the game G. The other players then play a game with player 1 under the specified rules. For expositional ease we consider a two-player game. Player 2's preferences are defined on $Q \times R$ where $q \in Q$ may be thought of as an allocation of some good and $r \in R$ is player 2's payment.

If player 2's type is $\theta_t \in \Theta$ her preferences are represented by the utility function $u(\theta_t, q, r)$. Let $U_0(\theta_t)$ be player 2's utility if she declines to play. Without loss of generality we may choose r_{0t} so that $U_0(\theta_t) = u(\theta_t, 0, r_{0t})$. To simplify the analysis of participation we assume that r_{0t} is the same for each type. Then declining to participate is equivalent to participating in the game G as long as the set of feasible outcomes includes the outcome $(0, r_0)$. This is the approach that we will take. Player 2 knows her type θ_t. Let $(q_t, r_t) \equiv (q(\theta_t), r(\theta_t))$ be her equilibrium outcome. Then the participation constraint is

$$u(\theta_t, q_t, r_t) \geq u(\theta_t, 0, r_0) \quad t \in \mathcal{T}.$$

Because (q_t, r_t) is an equilibrium best response, type θ_t can be no better off mimicking the equilibrium play of any other type. Therefore

$$u(\theta_t, q_t, r_t) \geq u(\theta_t, q_s, r_s), \forall s \neq t, \quad \text{and} \quad \forall t \in \mathcal{T}.$$

Let $u^D(\theta_t, q, r)$ be the payoff to the designer if player 2's type is θ_t. Player 1 knows only the probability distribution of player 2's type. Let f_t be the probability that player 2's type is θ_t. Then for any particular mechanism G, the mechanism designer can compute the best response mapping $\mathcal{M} = \{q(\theta_t), r(\theta_t)\}_{\theta_t \in \Theta}$ and so compute his expected payoff:

$$U^D(G) = \sum_{\theta_t \in \Theta} f_t u^D(\theta_t, q_t, r_t).$$

Player 1 then chooses the game G (i.e., the mechanism) that maximizes his expected payoff.

Example: Two-Part Pricing

Player 1 is a monopoly that can produce a commodity at a constant unit cost c. Player 2 is a buyer with demand price function $p(\theta_t, q)$. Player 1 does not know player 2's type so offers several alternative payment plans. If player 2 chooses alternative 1 ("plan 1") she can purchase any quantity she wishes at a price P_1. Each of the other plans offers some lower price P_a. However to get the discounted price, player 2 must also pay a monthly access fee K_a. The mechanism is therefore a set of alternative pricing plans $G = \{(P_a, K_a)\}_{a=0}^{A}$. If player 2's type is θ_t she chooses her most preferred plan (P_t, K_t) and then chooses q_t such that her value of the marginal unit is equal to the plan price; that is, $p(\theta_t, q_t) = P_t$. Her total payment is then $r_t = P_t q_t + K_t$.

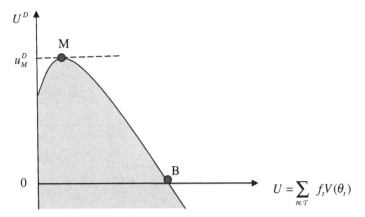

Figure 11.3-1. Set of feasible payoffs.

Player 1 then chooses the set of pricing plans $G = \{(P_a, K_a)\}_{a=0}^{A}$ that maximizes the expected profit of the firm.

We assume that Assumptions 1–2 of Section 11.1 are satisfied. Most importantly, the SCP holds. From the vantage point of the mechanism designer, the expected payoffs of the two players are

$$U^D(G) = \sum_{\theta_t \in \Theta} f_t u^D(\theta_t, q_t, r_t) \quad \text{and}$$

$$U(G) = \sum_{t \in \mathcal{T}} f_t V(\theta_t) \quad \text{where} \quad V(\theta_t) \equiv u(\theta_t, q_t, r_t).$$

The set of feasible expected payoffs are depicted in Figure 11.3-1. If the designer is a monopoly supplying some commodity or service and collecting revenue, then the relevant point on the frontier is the point M where U^D is maximized. Alternatively, if two or more identical mechanism designers play a Bertrand game, competing with the alternatives that they offer, then an equilibrium outcome must yield an expected profit of zero for the successful designer. In this case the relevant point in the feasible set is the point B on the frontier. More generally, however, we will consider other social objectives. Thus the entire frontier is of interest.

There is a second interpretation of the mechanism design problem. Instead of a single informed player 2 we consider a population of players of mass N, where $f(\theta_t)$ is the fraction of type θ_t in the population. The population payoff W is a population-weighted concave function of the utilities of the different types of player 2; that is,

$$W = N \sum_{t \in \mathcal{T}} f_t w(u(\theta_t, q_t, r_t)).$$

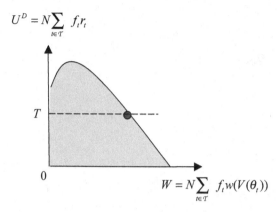

Figure 11.3-2. Optimal taxation.

For example, let r_t be the tax revenue to be raised from a worker of type θ_t so that the total revenue raised by the government is $U^D = N \sum_{t \in T} f_t r_t$. The mechanism design problem becomes the design of a tax scheme to maximize social welfare of the population given the government's tax requirement T (see Figure 11.3-2).

Direct Mechanisms and the Revelation Principle

For any game G selected by the mechanism designer, there is a mapping of best response outcomes, $\mathcal{M} = \{(q(\theta_t), r(\theta_t))\}_{\theta_t \in \Theta}$. Because this is a best response mapping

$$u(\theta_t, q(\theta_t), r(\theta_t)) \geq u(\theta_t, q(\theta_s), r(\theta_s)), \forall t \quad \text{and} \quad s \neq t.$$

Suppose that the designer computes the best responses in the game G. Rather than announce the rules of the game, the designer instead simply announces the best response mapping $\mathcal{M}^D \equiv \{x, (q(x), r(x))\}_{x \in \Theta}$ and then offers the outcome $(q(x), r(x))$ to a player choosing x. A type θ_t player therefore has a payoff of $U(\theta_t, x) \equiv u(\theta_t, q(x), r(x))$. As we have just argued, it is a best response for type θ_t to respond by choosing $x = \theta_t$. Because this equivalent mechanism maps types directly to outcomes it is called a direct mechanism. This very useful insight is called the Revelation Principle.

For the direct mechanism the local upward and downward constraints can be written succinctly as follows:

$$U(\theta_t, \theta_{t-1}) \leq U(\theta_t, \theta_t) \quad \text{and} \quad U(\theta_t, \theta_t) \geq U(\theta_t, \theta_{t+1})$$

Appealing to Proposition 11.1-6, we have the following immediate implication.

Proposition 11.3.1: Incentive Compatible Direct Mechanism
If Assumptions 1-3 of section 11.1 hold and the local upward and downward constraints for a direct mechanism $\mathcal{M}^D \equiv \{x, (q(x), r(x))\}_{x \in \Theta}$ are all satisfied, then $\{q(\theta_t)\}_{\theta_t \in \Theta}$ is increasing and all the incentive and participation constraints are satisfied.

As we shall see, when types are continuously distributed, it is often easier to work with the direct mechanism.

Application 1: Indirect Price Discrimination

As our first application we consider mechanism design by a profit-maximizing monopolist. The total mass of buyers is $N = 1$. A type θ_t buyer's utility gain from purchasing q units of the commodity and paying r is $u(\theta_t, q, r)$. If he stays out of the market he purchases nothing from the monopolist and pays nothing so the outcome is $(q_0, r_0) = (0, 0)$. Because we have defined $u(\theta_t, q, r)$ to be the utility gain, the "outside utility" is zero. We assume that Assumptions 1 and 2 of Section 11.1 hold. Because r is a buyer's payment, $\frac{\partial u}{\partial r}(\theta_t, q, r) < 0$.

An important special case is when utility is quasi-linear so that $u(\theta, q, r) = B(\theta, q) - r$. In this case the benefit $B(\theta, q)$ can be interpreted as the area below the consumer's demand curve $p(\theta, q)$. We can therefore write the utility function as follows:

$$u(\theta, q, r) = B(\theta, q) - r = \int_0^q p(\theta, x)dx - r.$$

The following result drives our analysis.

Proposition 11.3-2: Necessary and Sufficient Conditions with Profit Maximization
If Assumptions 1–3 hold and $\frac{\partial u}{\partial r} < 0$, all the local downward constraints must be binding.

Proof: Consider a mechanism $\mathcal{M} \equiv \{q_t, r_t\}_{t \in T}$ and suppose that type θ_s is the lowest type for which the local downward constraint is not binding; that is,

$$u(\theta_s, q_s, r_s) > u(\theta_s, q_{s-1}, r_{s-1}) \quad \text{and} \quad u(\theta_\tau, q_\tau, r_\tau) = u(\theta_\tau, q_{\tau-1}, r_{\tau-1}), \tau < s.$$

Because utility is strictly decreasing in r we can increase the payment of type θ_s to $\hat{r}_s > r_s$ so that

$$u(\theta_s, q_s, \hat{r}_s) = u(\theta_s, q_{s-1}, r_{s-1}).$$

Because the mechanism is feasible, the local downward constraint must be satisfied for θ_{s+1}. That is,

$$u(\theta_{s+1}, q_{s+1}, r_{s+1}) \geq u(\theta_{s+1}, q_s, r_s).$$

Because the utility of type θ_{s+1} is strictly decreasing in r,

$$u(\theta_{s+1}, q_s, r_s) > u(\theta_{s+1}, q_s, \hat{r}_s).$$

Thus the local downward constraint is no longer binding for type θ_{s+1}. Then we can increase r_{s+1} to $\hat{r}_{s+1}$ where this constraint is satisfied with equality. But this argument can be repeated for all $t > s$ until all the local downward constraints are binding. Appealing to Corollary 11.1-4, if all the local downward constraints are binding then the mechanism is incentive compatible and satisfies the participation constraint. $\qquad\square$

Marginal Payoffs

In a world of complete information and no legal or economic constraints on the exploitation of this information,[9] the seller can extract all consumer surplus by setting the payment at the point where each buyer type is indifferent between purchasing and exiting. With imperfect information a type θ_t buyer has a higher payoff than type θ_{t-1}. We refer to this difference in the payoffs as type θ_t's marginal payoff. (In the literature this difference is often referred to as type θ_t's marginal information rent. However, this is a somewhat different idea than the traditional definition of economic rent.)

Given Proposition 11.3-2, a necessary condition for profit maximization is that the local downward constraint is binding. Therefore

$$V(\theta_t) \equiv u(\theta_t, q_t, r_t) = u(\theta_t, q_{t-1}, r_{t-1}).$$

Then the difference between the payoff of type θ_t and type θ_{t-1} – that is, the marginal payoff of type θ_t – is

$$M_t \equiv V(\theta_t) - V(\theta_{t-1}) = u(\theta_t, q_{t-1}, r_{t-1}) - u(\theta_{t-1}, q_{t-1}, r_{t-1})). \qquad (11.3\text{-}1)$$

In the quasi-linear case

$$u(\theta, q, r) = B(\theta, q) - r = \int_0^q p(\theta, x)dx - r.$$

Appealing to (11.3-1), the marginal payoff of type θ is

$$M_t = B(\theta_t, q_{t-1}) - r_{t-1} - (B(\theta_{t-1}, q_{t-1}) - r_{t-1}) = B(\theta_t, q_{t-1}) - B(\theta_{t-1}, q_{t-1}).$$

---

[9] As an example of an economic restriction, suppose that a buyer can purchase a "q-pack" and repackage it as a number of smaller q^*-packs. This reduces the monopoly power of the mechanism designer.

Total Payoffs to Buyers

Because the participation constraint is binding for a type θ_1 buyer, his payoff is zero. From the difference equation we can then compute the total information rent for each type of buyer. A type θ_t buyer's informational rent (his equilibrium payoff) is

$$V(\theta_t) = \sum_{s=2}^{t} M_s.$$

The total payoff to the buyers is then

$$U = \sum_{\theta_t \in \Theta} f_t V(\theta_t).$$

Note that the marginal payoff of a type θ_t buyer, M_t, appears in the total informational rent of type θ_t and all the higher types. Then, substituting for $V(\theta_t)$ and collecting the marginal payoff terms,

$$U = \sum_{t=2}^{T} (1 - F_{t-1}) M_t, \quad \text{where} \quad F_t \equiv \sum_{s=1}^{t} f_t. \qquad (11.3\text{-}2)$$

To obtain an expression for the designer's total revenue, we note that because the payoff of a type θ buyer is $V(\theta_t) = B(\theta_t, q_t) - r_t$, the total revenue of the designer is

$$TR = \sum_{t=1}^{T} f_t r_t = \sum_{t=1}^{T} f_t B(\theta_t, q_t) - f_t V(\theta_t) = \sum_{t=1}^{T} f_t B(\theta_t, q(\theta_t)) - U.$$

But we have just argued that to maximize profit the local downward constraints must be binding and so the total payoff to the buyers satisfies (11.3-2). Then the maximized total revenue of the mechanism designer is

$$TR^D = \sum_{t=1}^{T} f_t B(\theta_t, q_t) - \sum_{t=2}^{T} (1 - F_{t-1}) M_t$$

$$= \sum_{t=1}^{T} f_t B(\theta_t, q_t) - \sum_{t=1}^{T-1} (1 - F_t) M_{t+1}, \qquad (11.3\text{-}3)$$

where

$$M_{t+1} = B(\theta_{t+1}, q_t) - B(\theta_t, q_t).$$

We assume a constant unit cost of production c. Therefore the total cost is

$$TC^D = \sum_{t=1}^{T} f_t c q_t.$$

The profit of the mechanism designer is therefore

$$U^D = TR^D - TC^D = \sum_{t=1}^{T} f_t B(\theta_t, q_t) - \sum_{t=0}^{T-1} (1 - F_{t+1}) M_{t+1}(q_t).$$

For incentive compatibility the allocation $\{q_t\}_{t=1}^{T}$ must be increasing. The profit-maximizing allocation is therefore the solution to the following standard optimization problem:

$$\underset{q \geq 0}{\text{Max}} \{U^D(q) | q_{t+1} \geq q_t, t = 1, \ldots, T-1\}.$$

To understand the solution it is helpful to consider the marginal contribution of each buyer type to total revenue. Differentiating (11.3-3) by q_t, the marginal revenue generated by type θ_t buyers is

$$\frac{\partial}{\partial q_t} TR^D = f_t p(\theta_t, q_t) - (1 - F_{t+1})(p(\theta_{t+1}, q_t) - p(\theta_{t+1}, q_t))$$

$$= f_t \left[p(\theta_t, q_t) - \left(\frac{1 - F_{t+1}}{f_t} \right) (p(\theta_{t+1}, q_t) - p(\theta_{t+1}, q_t)) \right].$$

Because there are f_t buyers of type θ_t, the marginal revenue of a type θ_t buyer is

$$MR_t(q_t) = p(\theta_t, q_t) - \left(\frac{1 - F_{t+1}}{f_t} \right) (p(\theta_{t+1}, q_t) - p(\theta_{t+1}, q_t)).$$

The analysis is especially straightforward if we impose the following regularity assumption.

Regularity Assumption: Increasing Marginal Revenue

$$MR_t(q_t) = p(\theta_t, q_t) - \left(\frac{1 - F_{t+1}}{f_t} \right) (p(\theta_{t+1}, q_t) - p(\theta_{t+1}, q_t))$$

is higher for higher types.

Given a unit cost of c, the marginal profit per type θ_t buyer is

$$MU_t^D(q_t) = MR_t(q_t) - c.$$

Suppose we ignore the monotonicity constraint and maximize profit for each type. If $MR_1(0) > c$, then the profit-maximizing q_1 is strictly positive. Otherwise it is zero. If the regularity assumption holds, it follows that $MR_2(q) > MR_1(q)$. Therefore if $q_1 > 0$ then the profit-maximizing $q_2 > q_1$.

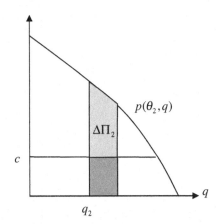

Figure 11.3-3. Marginal profit from increasing q_2.

Otherwise $q_1 = 0$ and so it must be the case that $q_2 \geq q_1$. Exactly the same argument holds for each type so the solution $\{q_t\}_{t \in \mathcal{T}}$ is monotonically increasing. Thus the incentive constraints are all satisfied.

A Two-Type Example

Types θ_1 and θ_2 have demand price functions $p(\theta_1, q)$ and $p(\theta_2, q) > p(\theta_1, q)$. A monopoly has a constant marginal cost of production of c. We present a simple graphical solution.

The local downward constraint for type θ_2 is

$$u(\theta_2, q, r) = B(\theta_2, q) - r \geq u(\theta_2, q_1, r_1).$$

For any q_2, revenue is maximized by choosing $r_2 = B(\theta_2, q_2) - u(\theta_2, q_1, r_1)$. Therefore the extra revenue from increasing q_2 by Δq_2 is $B(\theta_2, q_2 + \Delta q_2) - B(\theta_2, q_2)$. This is depicted in Figure 11.3-3 as the sum of the heavily and lightly shaded areas.

The extra cost is the heavily shaded area. Thus profit is maximized by choosing a plan size so that the demand price $p(\theta_2, q_2)$ is equal to marginal cost.

Now consider increasing the number of units in plan 1. The argument begins as earlier. The extra revenue from raising output by Δq_1 is the additional area under the demand price function and above the marginal cost line. Then the marginal profit from type 1 customers is

$$\Delta \Pi_1 = (p(\theta_1, q_1) - c)\Delta q_1.$$

This is the lightly shaded region in Figure 11.3-4. But there is an additional consideration.

Plan 1 is more attractive to type 2 buyers by the sum of the shaded and cross-hatched areas. However, the increase in plan 1's cost is the sum of the

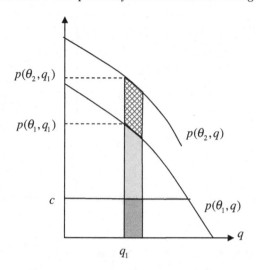

Figure 11.3-4. Marginal profit from increasing q_1.

shaded areas. Because plan 2 is designed so that type 2 buyers are indifferent between plan 1 and plan 2, it follows that the payment for plan 1 must be reduced by the cross-hatched area; that is,

$$\Delta r_2 = -(p(\theta_2, q_1) - p(\theta_1, q_1))\Delta q_1.$$

Multiplying by the number of buyers of each type, the net gain to the designer is

$$\begin{aligned}
\Delta U^D &= f_1 \Delta \Pi_1 - f_2 \Delta r_2 \\
&= f_1(p(\theta_1, q_1) - c)\Delta q_1 - f_2(p(\theta_2, q_1) - p(\theta_1, q_1))\Delta q_1.
\end{aligned}$$

Dividing by Δq_1 and taking the limit,

$$\frac{\partial U^D}{\partial q_1} = f_1(p(\theta_1, q_1) - c) - f_2(p(\theta_2, q_1) - p(\theta_1, q_1)).$$

Let (q_1^*, q_2^*) be solutions to these first-order conditions. If $q_1^* > 0$ then

$$p(\theta_1, q_1^*) - c = \frac{f_2}{f_1}(p(\theta_2, q_1^*) - p(\theta_1, q_1^*)) > 0 = p(\theta_2, q_2^*) - c.$$

Note that the allocation to type θ_2 is efficient because a type θ_2 buyer's demand price (his marginal willingness to pay) is equal to marginal cost. However the designer chooses the allocation to a type θ_1 buyer so that the demand price exceeds marginal cost. Thus, just as in simple monopoly, the monopoly profit is maximized by choosing a total output lower than the socially efficient output.

Suppose that the demand price functions are linear and have the same slope; that is, $p(\theta_t, q) = a_t - bq$. Substituting into the first-order condition for q_1,

$$\frac{\partial U^D}{\partial q_1} = f_1(p(\theta_1, q_1) - c) - f_2(p(\theta_2, q_1) - p(\theta_1, q_1))$$

$$= f_1\left(a_1 - bq_1 - c - \frac{f_2}{f_1}(a_2 - a_1)\right)$$

$$= f_1\left(\left[a_1 - c - \frac{f_2}{f_1}(a_2 - a_1)\right] - bq_1\right).$$

Note that the term in brackets is a decreasing function of the probability ratio and is negative when this ratio is sufficiently large. Thus the greater the ratio of high to low types, the smaller is the allocation to a type 1 buyer. Indeed if the ratio is sufficiently large, $q_1^* = 0$. The low type is squeezed out of the market completely.

Intuitively this must be the case. The monopoly faces a tradeoff. If it decreases the allocation to a type 1 buyer then it can extract less profit from this type. But then the "plan" (q_1, r_1) is less attractive to a type 2 buyer, and so the incentive constraint binds less tightly and the designer can increase r_2. As a result, the higher the fraction of type θ_2 buyers, the bigger the incentive for the monopoly to lower the size of plan 1. In the limit type 1 buyers are squeezed out of the market completely.

Example 2: Three Types and Pooling
There are three types. The demand price function for type θ_t is $p(\theta_t, q) = a_t - q, t = 1, 2, 3$, where $(a_1, a_2, a_3) = (40, 50, 60)$. Marginal cost is 10. The fractions of each type are

$$(f_1, f_2, f_3) = (1/2, 1/8, 3/8).$$

Although this example can also be solved by the graphical approach used for example 1, we follow the general method developed earlier.

$$U^D = \left(\sum_{t=1}^{3} f_t(B(\theta_t, q_t) - cq_t) - \sum_{t=1}^{2}(1 - F_t)(B(\theta_{t+1}, q_t) - B(\theta_t, q_t))\right)$$

$$= \sum_{t=1}^{3} f_t(a_t q_t - \tfrac{1}{2}q_t^2 - 10q_t) - \sum_{t=1}^{2}(1 - F_t)10q_t.$$

Then the marginal profit per unit mass of each type is

$$\frac{\partial U^d}{\partial q_1} = f_1[40 - q_1 - 10] - (f_2 + f_3)10] = \tfrac{1}{2}[20 - q_1]$$

$$\frac{\partial U^d}{\partial q_2} = f_2[50 - q_2 - 10] - f_3 10] = \tfrac{1}{8}[10 - q_2]$$

$$\frac{\partial U^d}{\partial q_3} = f_3[60 - q_3 - 10] = \tfrac{3}{8}[50 - q_3].$$

If we ignore the monotonicity constraints and solve for the profit-maximizing allocation we get the solution $\{q^*(\theta_t)\}_{\theta_t \in \Theta} = \{20, 10, 50\}$. But this is not feasible so we add the constraint that $q_2 \geq q_1$. The Lagrangian for this problem is $\mathcal{L} = U^d + \lambda(q_2 - q_1)$ and this yields the following first-order conditions:

$$\frac{\partial \mathcal{L}}{\partial q_1} = \frac{\partial U^d}{\partial q_1} - \lambda = \tfrac{1}{2}[20 - q_1] - \lambda = 0.$$

$$\frac{\partial \mathcal{L}}{\partial q_2} = \frac{\partial U^d}{\partial q_2} + \lambda = \tfrac{1}{8}[10 - q_2] + \lambda = 0.$$

$$\frac{\partial \mathcal{L}^d}{\partial q_3} = \frac{\partial U^d}{\partial q_3} = \tfrac{3}{8}[50 - q_3] = 0.$$

Because the shadow price is not zero it must be strictly positive. Then $q_1 = q_2 = \hat{q}$. Adding the first two conditions, the marginal profit from type 1 and type 2 is

$$\frac{\partial U^d}{\partial q_1} + \frac{\partial U^d}{\partial q_2} = \tfrac{1}{2}[20 - \hat{q}] + \tfrac{1}{8}[10 - \hat{q}] = 0.$$

Thus $\hat{q} = 18$.

Remark: Quantity or Quality?

We have presented this model as one of price discrimination by a monopolist. However, it can also be interpreted as the choice of a monopolist selling different qualities of a product. Consumers vary in their willingness to pay for a higher quality of some product. Each wishes to purchase either one unit or stay out of the market. Let $B(\theta_t, q)$ be a type θ_t's willingness to pay for quality level q and let $C(q)$ be the cost of producing a unit of quality q. Then the expected cost is

$$C^d = \sum_{\theta_t \in \Theta} f_t C(q_t).$$

The profit-maximizing monopoly chooses among feasible mechanisms to maximize its expected profit.

Continuous Types

The analysis is easily extended to the case of continuous types. Let the family of demand curves be $p(\theta, q)$ where $\theta \in \Theta = [\alpha, \beta]$. The mass of buyer types is $N = 1$. A type θ buyer then has utility

$$u(\theta, q, r) = B(\theta, q) - r.$$

Consider the direct mechanism $\mathcal{M}^D = \{x, (q(x), r(x)\}_{x \in \Theta}$. We define $U(\theta, x)$ to be type θ's payoff if he chooses $(q(x), r(x))$. For incentive compatibility this is maximized at $x = \theta$ and we define $V(\theta) = U(\theta, \theta)$. Appealing to Section 11.1, we have the following necessary condition for incentive compatibility:

$$V'(\theta) = U_\theta(\theta, \theta) = u_\theta(\theta, q(\theta), r(\theta)) = B_\theta(\theta, q(\theta)). \qquad (11.3\text{-}4)$$

As in the finite types case, we sum the marginal payoffs to obtain an expression for the total payoffs of all the buyers.

$$U = \int_\alpha^\beta V(\theta) F'(\theta) d\theta.$$

Integrating by parts and noting that $\frac{d}{d\theta} - (1 - F(\theta)) = F'(\theta)$, we obtain

$$U = V(\alpha) + \int_\alpha^\beta V'(\theta)(1 - F(\theta)) d\theta.$$

For profit maximization, the participation constraint is binding for the lowest type; thus $V(\alpha) = 0$.

Substituting from (11.3-4),

$$U = \int_\alpha^\beta B_\theta(\theta, q(\theta))(1 - F(\theta)) d\theta.$$

The equilibrium payoff of a type θ buyer is $V(\theta) = B(\theta, q(\theta)) - r(\theta)$. Rearranging and summing over types, the expected revenue of the designer is

$$TR = \int_\alpha^\beta B(\theta, q(\theta)) F'(\theta) - U$$

$$= \int_\alpha^\beta TR^D(\theta, q(\theta)) F'(\theta) d\theta,$$

where

$$TR^D(\theta, q) \equiv B(\theta, q) - \left(\frac{1 - F(\theta)}{F'(\theta)} \right) B_\theta(\theta, q).$$

Differentiating by q,

$$MR^D(\theta, q) \equiv p(\theta, q) - \left(\frac{1 - F(\theta)}{F'(\theta)} \right) p_\theta(\theta, q) \qquad (11.3\text{-}5)$$

In the finite types case we introduced the assumption that marginal revenue

$$MR_t^D(q_t) \equiv p(\theta_t, q_t) - \left(\frac{1 - F_{t+1}}{f_t}\right)(p(\theta_{t+1}, q_t) - p(\theta_{t+1}, q_t))$$

$$= p(\theta_t, q_t) - \left(\frac{1 - F_{t+1}}{F_{t+1} - F_t}\right)(p(\theta_{t+1}, q_t) - p(\theta_{t+1}, q_t))$$

is higher for buyers with higher types. Define $\Delta\theta = \theta_{t+1} - \theta_t$. Then marginal revenue can be rewritten as follows:

$$MR_t^D(q_t) = p(\theta_t, q_t) - \left(\frac{1 - F(\theta_t + \Delta t)}{\underbrace{F(\theta_t + \Delta\theta) - F(\theta_t)}_{\Delta\theta}}\right)\left(\frac{p(\theta_t + \Delta\theta, q_t) - p(\theta_t, q_t)}{\Delta\theta}\right).$$

In the limit at $\Delta\theta \to 0$ the right-hand side approaches (11.3-5). Therefore, corresponding to the regularity for the finite types case we make the following assumption.

Regularity Assumption: Increasing Marginal Revenue Marginal revenue

$$MR^D(\theta, q) \equiv p(\theta, q) - (\frac{1 - F(\theta)}{F'(\theta)})p_\theta(\theta, q)$$

is an increasing function of θ.

This is a mild assumption. First note that the demand price is strictly increasing in θ. Second, for many distributions the hazard rate, $h(\theta) = \frac{F'(\theta)}{1 - F(\theta)}$, is increasing. If so, the inverse is decreasing. Then as long as $p_\theta(\theta, q)$ does not increase too quickly as θ increases, the regularity assumption is satisfied.

The solution is easily depicted graphically. Let $\hat{q}(\theta)$ be the solution to $MR^D(\theta, q) = c$. Under the regularity assumption this is an increasing function as depicted in Figure 11.3-5.

Below the graph of $\hat{q}(\theta)$ marginal revenue exceeds marginal cost, and above it marginal revenue is less than marginal cost. Thus ignoring the

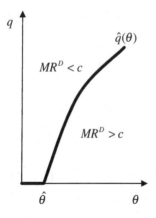

Figure 11.3-5. Solving for the optimal allocation.

monotonicity constraint, profit is maximized by choosing $q(\theta) = 0$ for $\theta < \hat{\theta}$ and $q(\theta) = \hat{q}(\theta)$ for $\theta \geq \hat{\theta}$. Note that $q(\theta)$ so defined is monotonic. Thus the monotonicity constraint is satisfied.

Consider the special linear case where $p = \theta - q$. Substituting into the expression for marginal revenue,

$$MR^D(\theta, q) = J(\theta) - q, \quad \text{where} \quad J(\theta) \equiv \theta - \frac{1 - F(\theta)}{F'(\theta)}.$$

Given a constant unit cost of c, the marginal profit associated with a type θ buyer is

$$MR^D(\theta, q) - c = J(\theta) - c - q.$$

If the regularity assumption holds, $J(\theta)$ is increasing. Then there is some $\hat{\theta} \in [\alpha, \beta)$ such that

$$J(\hat{\theta}) - c = 0. \quad \text{For all} \quad \theta < \hat{\theta}, q(\theta) = 0 \quad \text{and, for all higher} \quad \theta,$$
$$q(\theta) = J(\theta) - c.$$

Example: Implementing the Optimal Direct Mechanism as Non-Linear Pricing

Suppose that types are uniformly distributed on $[0, 1]$ so that

$$J(\theta) = \theta - \frac{1 - F(\theta)}{F'(\theta)} = 2\theta - 1.$$

Then the profit-maximizing allocation is

$$q(\theta) = \begin{cases} 0, & \theta \leq \frac{1}{2}(1 + c) \\ 2\theta - 1 - c, & \theta > \frac{1}{2}(1 + c) \end{cases}. \tag{11.3-6}$$

Because $q(\theta)$ is increasing we can define the increasing function $R(\cdot)$ such that

$$r(\theta) = R(q(\theta)).$$

A type θ buyer who selects the quantity q then must pay $R(q)$. This is depicted in Figure 11.3-6.

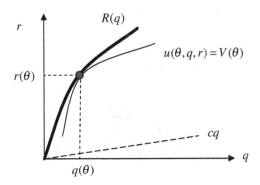

Figure 11.3-6. Non-linear pricing.

To solve for the optimal non-linear payment function we note that

$$\theta = \arg \underset{x}{\text{Max}}\{u(\theta, q(x), R(q(x)))\} = \arg \underset{x}{\text{Max}} \left\{ \int_{0}^{q(x)} p(\theta, x)dx - R(q(x)) \right\}.$$

Then the FOC for incentive compatibility is

$$[p(\theta, q(\theta)) - R'(q)]q'(\theta) = 0 \ \theta \geq \tfrac{1}{2}(1 + c).$$

Therefore $R'(q) = p(\theta, q) = \theta - q$. Also from (11.3-6), $q = 2\theta - 1 - c$. Eliminating θ it follows that

$$R'(q) = \tfrac{1}{2}(1 + c - q).$$

Hence

$$R(q) = \tfrac{1}{2}(1 + c)q - \tfrac{1}{4}q^{2}.$$

We have therefore established that the monopoly can implement the profit-maximizing direct mechanism by offering to sell q units to any customer for a total payment of $R(q)$. Note that the price per unit, $R(q)/q$, declines with the number of units purchased so quantity discounts are optimal. Note also that at $q(1) = 1 - c$, $R'(q(1)) = c$. Thus there is no distortion for the highest type. However, for all other types the marginal payment exceeds marginal cost so the monopolist undersupplies.

Allocation Rule When Marginal Revenue Is Decreasing for a Subset of Types

As in the regular case, define $\hat{q}(\theta)$ to be the solution to $MR^{D}(\theta, q) = c$. If the regularity assumption is not satisfied, $\hat{q}(\theta)$ is not monotonic. However, it is not difficult to characterize the optimal allocation rule. Figure 11.3-7 depicts

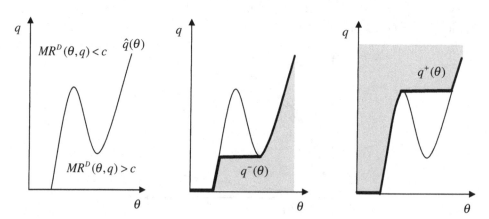

Figure 11.3-7. Characterizing the optimal allocation.

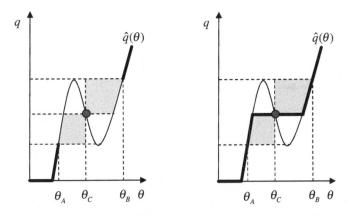

Figure 11.3-8. Pooling.

the case in which there is one interval over which $\hat{q}(\theta)$ is decreasing. Note that $MR^D(\theta, q) > c$ in the interior of the shaded area in the center diagram. Therefore the allocation $q^-(\theta)$ yields a higher revenue than any allocation below it in the shaded area. Similarly, because $MR^D(\theta, q) < c$ in the interior of the shaded area in the right diagram, the allocation $q^+(\theta)$ yields a higher revenue than any allocation above it in the shaded area. It follows that the profit-maximizing allocation $q(\theta)$ satisfies $q^-(\theta) \leq q(\theta) \leq q^+(\theta)$.

Consider the left-hand diagram in Figure 11.3-8. There must be some θ_C in the interval (θ_A, θ_B) such that $q(\theta) = \hat{q}(\theta)$. In the shaded area to the left of θ_C, $MR^D(\theta, q) > c$. Thus over the interval $[\theta_A, \theta_C]$, profit is maximized along the upper boundary of the shaded area. Similarly in the shaded area to the right of θ_C, $MR^D(\theta, q) < c$. Thus over the interval $[\theta_C, \theta_B]$, profit is maximized along the lower boundary of the shaded area. Thus the profit-maximizing allocation rule coincides that $\hat{q}(\theta)$ except over some interval over which $q(\theta)$ is constant.

Application 2: Optimal Income Taxation[10]

Agents' preferences over consumption x and labor supply l are represented by the separable function $U(x, l) = B(x) - C(l) \in \mathbb{C}^2$, where $B(\cdot)$ is a strictly increasing strictly concave function and $C(l)$ is a strictly increasing convex function. A type θ worker has a productivity parameter θ. Types are continuously distributed with support $\Theta = [\alpha, \beta]$ and c.d.f. $F(\cdot) \in \mathbb{C}^1$. A type θ worker has can earn an income of $q = \theta l$ by incurring effort level l. Then if he pays a tax of r, his utility is

$$u(\theta, q, r) = B(q - r) - C\left(\frac{q}{\theta}\right).$$

With full information, for any tax t^* paid by a type θ worker, efficiency requires that the worker's utility be maximized. This is depicted in

---

[10] This more technical application requires a basic understanding of Pontryagin's Maximum Principle.

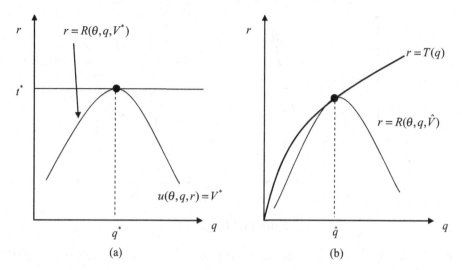

Figure 11.3-9. (a) Efficient lump-sum tax. (b) Inefficient income tax.

Figure 11.3-9a. The worker's maximizing income q^* is the income where the slope of the indifference curve is zero.

Note that the points (q, r) on an indifference curve $u(\theta, q, r) = V$ implicitly define the function $r = R(\theta, q, V)$. Given our assumptions, the upper contour sets of $u(\theta, q, r)$ are strictly convex. Therefore $R(\theta, q, V)$ is a strictly quasi-concave function of q. Thus $R_q > 0$ for all $q < q^*$ and $R_q < 0$ for all $q > q^*$. In the right-hand diagram the income tax function is strictly increasing so that $R_q > 0$ at $\hat{q}$. Thus the worker supplies less than his efficient quantity of labor.

Since it will prove helpful we now further characterize the function $R(\theta, q, V)$. Along an indifference curve

$$u(\theta, q, r) = B(q - R) - C(q/\theta) = V. \qquad (11.3\text{-}7)$$

Differentiating (11.3-7) by V yields $B'(q - r)R_V = 1$:
Therefore

$$R_V = -1/B'(q - r) \qquad (11.3\text{-}8)$$

Also inverting (11.3-7) we obtain $q - R = B^{-1}(V + C(q/\theta))$. Therefore

$$R = q - B^{-1}(V + C(q/\theta)) \qquad (11.3\text{-}9)$$

As a preliminary to solving for an optimal income tax scheme we characterize the set of incentive compatible tax schemes. Note that

$$MRS(\theta, q, r) = \frac{u_q}{u_r} = \frac{B'(q - r) - \frac{1}{\theta}C'(\frac{q}{\theta})}{-B'(q - r)} = -1 + \frac{\frac{q}{\theta}C'(\frac{q}{\theta})}{q B'(q - r)}$$

Since $C(\cdot)$ is an increasing convex function, the right-hand side is strictly decreasing in θ. Therefore the SCP holds.

A mechanism $\{q(\theta), r(\theta)\}_{\theta \in \Theta}$ is incentive compatible if, for all $\theta \in \Theta$

$$\theta = \arg \underset{x \in \Theta}{\text{Max}}\, u(\theta, q(x), r(x))$$

Define $V(\theta) = u(\theta, q(\theta), r(\theta))$. Since the SCP holds the necessary and sufficient conditions for incentive compatibility are the monotonicity condition ($q(\theta)$ is increasing) and the Envelope Theorem condition:

$$V'(\theta) = u_\theta = \frac{q(\theta)}{\theta^2} C' \left(\frac{q(\theta)}{\theta} \right) \tag{11.3-10}$$

We know that $q(\theta)$ is increasing. Consider any s and $\theta > s$ such that $q(\theta) > q(s)$

$$u(\theta, q(\theta), r(\theta)) = B(q(\theta) - r(\theta)) - C(q(\theta)/\theta) < B(q(\theta) - r(\theta)) - C(q(s)/\theta).$$

Then if $q(\theta) - r(\theta) \le q(s) - r(s), u(\theta, q(\theta), r(\theta)) < u(\theta, q(s), r(s))$. But this violates incentive compatibility. Therefore $q(\theta) - r(\theta) > q(s) - r(s)$. That is, after tax income is strictly higher for higher types.

The mechanism designer must raise a total tax of T. Therefore

$$\int_\alpha^\beta r(\theta) f(\theta) d\theta = \int_\alpha^\beta R(\theta, q(\theta), V(\theta)) f(\theta) d\theta \ge T \tag{11.3-11}$$

Since $V(\theta)$ must be increasing, we take as the designer objective, the maximization of a weighted average of the workers' utilities.

$$U^D = \int_\alpha^\beta w(\theta) V(\theta) f(\theta) d\theta \tag{11.3-12}$$

where the weights are (weakly) decreasing. The more rapidly the weights decline, the greater is the degree of egalitarianism.

The mechanism designer maximizes (11.3-12) subject to (11.3-10), (11.3-11) and the monotonicity condition. The Hamiltonian for this problem is

$$H = w(\theta) V(\theta) f(\theta) + \lambda(\theta) \frac{q(\theta)}{\theta^2} C' \left(\frac{q(\theta)}{\theta} \right) + \mu R(\theta, q(\theta), V(\theta)) f(\theta).$$

Let Q be the set of functions that are increasing on Θ. By the Maximum Principle

$$q^*(\theta) = \arg \underset{q \in Q}{\text{Max}} \{ H(\theta, q, V, \lambda) \}.$$

We proceed by ignoring the monotonicity constraint and choosing $q^*(\theta)$ that solves the relaxed problem

$$q^*(\theta) = \arg \max_q \{H(\theta, q, V, \lambda)\}$$

As may be readily checked numerically, it is easy to find examples for which the solution to the relaxed problem is indeed monotonic.

Note that since $q = \theta l$ we can rewrite the Hamiltonian as follows:

$$H = w(\theta)V(\theta)f(\theta) + \frac{\lambda(\theta)}{\theta}lC'(l) + \mu R(\theta, \theta l, V(\theta))f(\theta).$$

Substituting from (11.3-9)

$$H = w(\theta)V(\theta)f(\theta) + \frac{\lambda(\theta)}{\theta}lC'(l) + \mu(\theta l - B^{-1}(V + C(l)))f(\theta)$$

Then

$$q^*(\theta) = \theta l^*(\theta) = \theta \arg \max_l \{H(\theta, \theta l, V, \lambda)\}.$$

Differentiating we obtain

$$\frac{\partial H}{\partial l}(\theta, \theta l, V, \lambda) = \lambda(\theta)\frac{d}{dl}(lC'(l)) + \mu(\theta - \frac{\partial}{\partial V}B^{-1}(V + C(l)))f(\theta) \le 0.$$

The FOC for this maximization problem is then

$$\frac{\partial H}{\partial l} \le 0, \text{ with equality if } l(\theta) > 0.$$

As we shall show below there is some interval $[\hat{\theta}, \beta]$ over which $\lambda(\theta)$ is increasing. Since $C(l)$ is increasing and convex it follows that that $\frac{\partial}{\partial \theta}\frac{\partial H}{\partial l} = \lambda'(\theta)\frac{d}{dl}(lC'(l)) + \mu > 0$ over this interval. Therefore worker effort $l(\theta)$ is increasing for $\theta > \hat{\theta}$.

We next note that the income tax problem imposes no constraints on either the minimum utility $V(\alpha)$ or the maximum utility $V(\beta)$. For such a free end-point problem it follows that $\lambda(\alpha) = \lambda(\beta) = 0$. Therefore

$$\frac{\partial H}{\partial l}(\alpha, \alpha l, V(\alpha), \lambda) = \mu\left(\theta - \frac{\partial}{\partial V}B^{-1}(V + C(l))\right)f(\theta).$$

It follows that if α is sufficiently small, $\frac{\partial H}{\partial l}(\alpha, \alpha l, V(\alpha), \lambda) < 0$. Henceforth we shall assume that this condition holds. Thus the optimal labor supply is zero for a subset of types $[\alpha, \gamma]$. These types are therefore provided a subsidy (or "negative income tax" s.

We now consider types on $[\gamma, \beta]$ who do work. It proves more straightforward to return to the original Hamiltonian

$$H = w(\theta)V(\theta)f(\theta) + \frac{\lambda(\theta)}{\theta}\left(\frac{q}{\theta}C'\left(\frac{q}{\theta}\right) + \mu R(\theta, q, V(\theta))\right)f(\theta)$$

For all who work,

$$\frac{\partial H}{\partial q} = \frac{\lambda(\theta)}{\theta} \frac{d}{dq} \left(\frac{q}{\theta} C' \left(\frac{q}{\theta} \right) + \mu R_q(\theta, q(\theta), V(\theta)) \right) f(\theta) = 0. \quad (11.3\text{-}13)$$

If $\lambda(\theta) = 0$ for all $\theta > \gamma$ it follows that $R_q(\theta, q(\theta), V(\theta)) = 0$. But this is impossible as it would imply that the income tax scheme had no distortions.

The shadow price $\lambda(\theta)$ satisfies

$$\lambda'(\theta) = -\frac{\partial H}{\partial V} = (-w(\theta)V(\theta) + \mu R_V(\theta, q, V(\theta))) f(\theta).$$

Substituting from (11.3-8)

$$\lambda'(\theta) = (-w(\theta)V(\theta) + \frac{\mu}{B'(q-r)}) f(\theta) \quad (11.3\text{-}14)$$

Substituting from (11.3-8), we can rewrite (11.3-14) as follows:

$$\lambda'(\theta) = -\frac{\partial H}{\partial V} = f(\theta)g(\theta) \quad \text{where} \quad g(\theta) \equiv -w(\theta) + \frac{\mu}{B'(q(\theta) - r(\theta))}.$$

We have argued that for incentive compatibility after tax income $q(\theta) - r(\theta)$ must be strictly increasing if $q(\theta)$ is strictly increasing. Also $w'(\theta) \leq 0$. Therefore $g(\theta)$ is a strictly increasing function on $[\gamma, \beta]$.

Suppose that $\lambda'(\beta) < 0$. Then $g(\beta) < 0$. Since $g(\theta)$ is strictly increasing it follows that $g(\theta) < 0$, $\forall \theta < \beta$ and so $\lambda'(\theta) < 0$ on $[\alpha, \beta]$. Then $\lambda(\alpha) > 0$. But this is not true for a free end-point problem. Therefore $\lambda'(\beta) \geq 0$. An almost identical argument establishes that $\lambda'(\alpha) \leq 0$. Then for some $\hat{\theta}$, $\lambda(\hat{\theta}) < 0$ and $\lambda'(\hat{\theta}) = 0$. Again appealing to the fact that $g(\theta)$ is increasing, it follows that $\lambda'(\theta) \leq 0$, $\theta < \hat{\theta}$ and $\lambda'(\theta) \geq 0$, $\theta > \hat{\theta}$. Therefore $\lambda(\theta) \leq 0$ on $[\alpha, \beta]$ and the inequality is strict on (γ, β).

From (11.3-13) it follows that $R_q(\theta, q(\theta), V(\theta)) > 0$ on $[\gamma, \beta]$. Thus the optimal income tax distorts income downward for all but the highest type of worker.

The optimal tax schedule is depicted in Figure 11.3-10. For types below γ, $q(\theta)=0$ so these agents do no work and must receive a fixed subsidy $r(\theta) = s$. All types above γ pay taxes and except for the highest type pay a positive marginal tax. The highest type pays the highest total tax but has a zero marginal tax.

Note that the marginal tax rate must rise over a range of middle income levels and then fall again over high income levels. This is in stark contrast to tax rates that are typically proposed in the political arena.

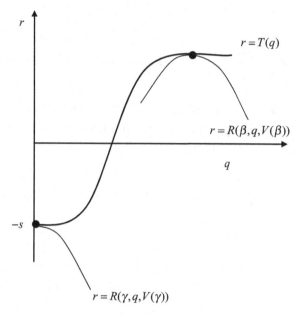

Figure 11.3-10. Optimal income tax schedule.

Exercises

Exercise 11.3-1: Profit-Maximizing Plans with Three Types Suppose that $p(\theta_t, q) = 140 - b(\theta_t)q$ where $(b(\theta_1), b(\theta_2), b(\theta_3)) = (4, 2, 1)$. The unit cost is 20.

(a) If the fraction of each type is the same, solve for the optimal number of units in each plan offered by the monopolist.

(b) Carefully analyze the effect on these plans as the fraction of type 2 falls and the fraction of type 3 rises.

Exercise 11.3-2: Optimal Selling Scheme A store owner has a single unit for sale (e.g., an antique.) A consumer walks into the store. He knows that his valuation of the item is $\theta \in V = [0, \beta]$. However, the store owner knows only the distribution of possible valuations; that is, the p.d.f. $f(\theta)$.

(a) Let $q(\theta)$ be the equilibrium probability that a trade will be made to a type θ buyer. Let $r(\theta)$ be this type's equilibrium expected payment and let $U(\theta)$ be the expected buyer payoff.

Show that the equilibrium marginal informational rent is $U'(\theta) = q(\theta)$. Hence show that the expected revenue of the seller is $\overline{R} = \int_0^\beta q(\theta)J(\theta) f(\theta)d\theta - U(0)$ where $J(\theta) = \theta - (1 - F(\theta))/f(\theta)$.

(b) Is it necessarily the case that $q(\theta)$ is an increasing function?

(c) Suppose that $J(\theta)$ is a strictly increasing function. Explain why there exists some $\theta_0 \in (0, \beta)$ such that $J(\theta) > 0$ if and only if $\theta > \theta_0$.

(d) Hence show that the optimal scheme is to set $q(\theta) = \begin{cases} 0, \theta < \theta_0 \\ 1, \theta \geq \theta_0 \end{cases}$.

(e) What is a simple implementation of this optimal scheme?

(f) *Suppose that $J(\theta)$ changes sign at θ_0, θ_1 and θ_2. Explain why it is that for an optimal scheme $q(\theta) = 0, \theta < \theta_0$ and $q(\theta) = 1, \theta \geq q_2$. Hence

$$\overline{R} = \int_{\theta_0}^{\theta_2} J(\theta)q(\theta)f(\theta)d\theta + \int_{\theta_2}^{\beta} J(\theta)f(\theta)d\theta.$$

Argue that if $q(\theta)$ is strictly increasing on some sub-interval of $[\theta_0, \theta_2]$ it is not revenue maximizing. Thus $q(\theta) = \hat{q}$ in $[\theta_0, \theta_2]$.

(g) Hence show that either $\hat{q} = 0$ or $\hat{q} = 1$ is optimal and again discuss the implementation of the optimal scheme.

Exercise 11.3-3: Monopoly and Product quality Each consumer purchases either one unit from a firm's product line or nothing at all.

Different consumers place different values on product quality. A type θ_t consumer's value of a unit of quality q is

$$B(\theta_t, q) = \theta_t(10q - \tfrac{1}{2}q^2).$$

This is private information. The cost of producing a unit of quality q is $6q$. There are three types, $\theta_t \in \{1, 2, 3\}$, and there are equal numbers of each type.

(a) Solve for the optimal quality levels.
(b) Solve for the profit-maximizing quality levels.
(c) Solve for the price charged for each product in the monopolist's product line.

Exercise 11.3-4: Price Discrimination with a Fixed Supply The demand price functions of type θ are $p(\theta, q) = \theta - q$, where θ is continuously distributed on $[0, 1]$. The fraction of customers whose types are no greater than θ is $F(\theta)$. The aggregate supply of the commodity is Q. It is illegal for the monopoly seller to price discriminate directly. Instead he must offer a schedule of selling plans (q, R); that is, q units for a total cost of R.

(a) Let $V(\theta)$ be the payoff of type θ in the profit-maximizing scheme, and let $q(\theta)$ be the allocation rule under this scheme. Show that $\frac{dV}{d\theta} = q(\theta)$. Hence obtain an expression for the total profit R.
(b) The aggregate supply is fixed so that the monopolist designs an incentive-compatible scheme to solve $\text{Max}_{q(\theta)}\{R| \int_0^q q(\theta)f(\theta)d\theta \leq Q\}$. Explain why the Lagrange multiplier of this constrained optimization problem is the marginal revenue of the monopoly.
(c) Solve for the optimal allocation rule as a function of the shadow price.
(d) Integrate to obtain an expression for that total allocation and hence solve for the shadow price $\lambda(Q) = MR(Q)$ as a function of the aggregate supply.

(e) Hence explain how to solve for the profit-maximizing selling scheme for any cost function $C(Q)$.

Exercise 11.3-5: Indirect Price Discrimination without Quasi-Linear Preferences A type θ buyer has a payoff of $B(\theta, q, r)$ if he purchases q units at a cost r. If he purchases nothing his payoff is $B(\theta, 0, 0)$. Define his net gain $u(\theta, q, r) = B(\theta, q, r) - B(\theta, 0, 0)$ where $u_q > 0$ and $u_r < 0$. The unit cost of production is c. Suppose that $\frac{\partial}{\partial \theta}(u_q/u_r) < 0$ so that the SCP holds.

(a) Explain why the efficient $(q(\theta), r(\theta))$ must be the solution of the following optimization problem:

$$\underset{(q,r)}{\text{Max}}\{r - cq \mid u(\theta, q, r) \geq u(\theta, q(\theta), r(\theta))\}.$$

Hence obtain a necessary condition for efficiency.

(b) Inverting the mapping $V = u(\theta, q, r)$ and writing $r = R(\theta, q, V)$, show that the necessary condition for efficiency can be written as follows:

$$\frac{\partial R}{\partial q}(\theta, q, V(\theta)) = c.$$

(c) Henceforth assume that a buyer's type is private information. Write down the designer's problem if the objective is to maximize profit. Let $V(\theta)$ be the payoff to a type θ buyer. Show that $\frac{dV}{d\theta} = u_\theta(\theta, q(\theta), r(\theta))$.
(d) The mapping $V = u(\theta, q, r)$ implicitly defines the inverse mapping $r = R(\theta, q, V)$. Show that the problem can be reduced to a standard control problem with one fixed endpoint.
(e) Define $g(\theta, q, V) \equiv u_\theta(\theta, q, R(\theta, q, V))$.

Explain why this can be rewritten as

$$g(\theta, q, V) \equiv \frac{\partial}{\partial \theta} u(\theta, q, R(\phi, q, V) \text{ at } \phi = \theta.$$

Then

$$g_q(\theta, q, V) = \frac{\partial}{\partial \theta}\frac{\partial}{\partial q} u(\theta, q, R(\phi, q, V)) \text{ at } \phi = \theta.$$

Hence argue as in the discussion of optimal income taxation that $g_q(\theta, q(\theta), V(\theta)) > 0$.

(f) Show that $\frac{d\lambda}{d\theta} > 0$ if $\lambda(\theta) = 0$. Hence explain why $\lambda(\theta) < 0$, for all $\theta < \beta$.
(g) Use this result to show that the monopoly undersupplies all buyer types except the higher type.

References and Selected Historical Reading

Akerlof, G. (1970). "The Market for Lemons." *Quarterly Journal of Economics* **89**: 488–500.

Maskin, E. S. and Riley, J. G. (1984). "Monopoly with Incomplete Information." *Rand Journal of Economics* **15**: 171–96.

Maskin, E. and Tirole, J. (1990). "The Principal–Agent Relationship with an Informed Principal: The Case of Private Values." *Econometrica* **58**: 379–409.

Mirrlees, J. (1971). "An Exploration in the Theory of Optimum Income Taxation." *Review of Economic Studies* **38**: 175–208.

Mussa, M. and Rosen, S. (1978). "Monopoly and Product Quality." *Journal of Economic Theory* **18**: 301–17.

Myerson, R. (1983). "Mechanism Design by an Informed Principal." *Econometrica* **51**: 1767–97.

Riley, John G. (1979). "Informational Equilibrium." *Econometrica*, **48**: 331–59.

Rothschild, Michael and Stiglitz, J. E. (1976). "Equilibrium in Competitive Insurance Markets: An Essay on the Economics of Imperfect Information." *Quarterly Journal of Economics* **80**: 629–49.

Spence, A. M. (1974). *Market Signaling*. Cambridge, MA: Harvard University Press.

12

Auctions and Public Goods

12.1 Auctions

Key ideas: equilibrium bidding with private and common values

In Chapter 10 we characterized equilibrium bidding for the sealed high-bid and second-price auctions with private values. We begin here with a more complete analysis of bidding with private values. We then consider bidding when the bidders differ in their private information but share the same common value of the auction item.

Auctions with Independent Private Values

In Chapter 11 we showed that the single-crossing property holds for bidding games with independent private values. Therefore we can use the first-order approach to characterize equilibrium bidding. We consider a family of sealed high-bid auctions that includes the sealed first- and second-price auctions as limiting cases.

A single item is to be sold to one of n risk-neutral bidders. Bidder i, $i = 1, \ldots, n$ has a value θ_i (i.e., an independent draw from a distribution with support $[0, \beta]$ and c.d.f. $F(\cdot) \in \mathbb{C}$). All this is common knowledge. The winner pays $\lambda b_{(1)} + (1 - \lambda)b_{(2)}$, a weighted average of the highest and second highest bids. Let $B(\cdot)$ be the equilibrium bid function, and let m be the maximum of all the other buyers' values. If buyer i loses, he pays nothing. If he has the highest value and wins, his equilibrium payment is

$$R(\theta_i, m) = \lambda B(\theta_i) + (1 - \lambda)B(m).$$

It proves helpful to define $w(\theta) = \Pr\{\theta_j \leq \theta, j \neq i\} = F^{n-1}(\theta)$. The values of all the other buyers are below m with probability $w(m)$. Therefore buyer

i's equilibrium expected payment is

$$r(\theta_i) = \int\limits_0^{\theta_i} R(\theta_i, m)w'(m)dm = \int\limits_0^{\theta_i} (\lambda B(\theta_i) + (1-\lambda)B(m))w'(m)dm$$

$$= \lambda B(\theta_i)w(\theta_i) + (1-\lambda)\int\limits_0^{\theta_i} B(m))w'(m)dm.$$

As we see later, it is the derivative of this function that proves most useful. Differentiating by θ_i,

$$r'(\theta_i) = \lambda B'(\theta_i)w(\theta_i) + B(\theta_i)w'(\theta_i). \qquad (12.1\text{-}1)$$

We analyze the auction as a direct revelation mechanism. Let $U(\theta_i, x)$ be the equilibrium payoff to buyer i with value θ_i when he deviates and bids $B(x)$ rather than $B(\theta_i)$. That is,

$$U(\theta_i, x) = \theta_i w(x) - r(x).$$

Because $B(\theta_i)$ is bidder i's best response when his value is θ_i,

$$\theta_i = \arg\underset{x}{\text{Max}}\{U(\theta_i, x)\}.$$

First-order condition

$$\frac{\partial U}{\partial x}(\theta_i, x) = \theta_i w'(x) - r'(x) = 0 \quad \text{at} \quad x = \theta_i.$$

Therefore

$$\theta_i w'(\theta_i) - r'(\theta_i) = 0.$$

Substituting this expression into (12.1-1) and rearranging, we obtain the following ordinary differential equation for the equilibrium bid function:

$$B'(\theta) = \frac{1}{\lambda}\frac{w'(\theta)}{w(\theta)}(\theta - B(\theta)). \qquad (12.1\text{-}2)$$

To solve this differential equation, define $H(\theta) = w(\theta)^{1/\lambda}$; then

$$\frac{H'(\theta)}{H(\theta)} = \frac{1}{\lambda}\frac{w'(\theta)}{w(\theta)}.$$

Thus the differential equation can be rewritten as follows:

$$B'(\theta) = \frac{H'(\theta)}{H(\theta)}(\theta - B(\theta)).$$

Rearranging this equation,

$$H(\theta)B'(\theta) + H'(\theta)B(\theta) = \theta H'(\theta).$$

Integrating both sides then

$$H(\theta_i)B(\theta_i) = \int_0^{\theta_i} \theta H'(\theta)d\theta = \theta_i H(\theta_i) - \int_0^{\theta_i} H(\theta)d\theta.$$

The equilibrium bid function is therefore

$$B(\theta_i) = \theta_i - \int_0^{\theta_i} \frac{H(\theta)}{H(\theta_i)}d\theta = \theta_i - \int_0^{\theta_i} \left(\frac{w(\theta)}{w(\theta_i)}\right)^{1/\lambda} d\theta. \qquad (12.1\text{-}3)$$

The payment by the winner is $\lambda b_{(1)} + (1 - \lambda)b_{(2)}$. If $\lambda = 1$, then this is the sealed first-price auction. As λ declines, the term inside the integral falls and so the equilibrium bid rises. In the limit as $\lambda \to 0$ the integral approaches zero and so the equilibrium bid $B(\theta_i) \to \theta_i$. Of course this is the equilibrium bid in the sealed second-price auction.

Remark: The Minimum Bid Suppose that the support of the values is $[\alpha, \beta]$ where $\alpha > 0$. The earlier arguments can be used to solve for an equilibrium in which $B(\alpha) = \alpha$ so that the equilibrium expected payoff of the lowest type $V(\alpha) = 0$.

Might there be an equilibrium in which the lowest value bidder bids less? We now argue that this cannot be the case.

By hypothesis, the equilibrium bid function is strictly increasing. Thus a bidder with the lowest value α has an equilibrium expected payoff of zero because he wins with zero probability. Thus no other bid can yield a strictly positive payoff. But if $B(\alpha) < \alpha$, a type α bidder wins with a strictly positive probability when he bids $\frac{1}{2}(B(\alpha) + \alpha)$ because by continuity, some positive mass of types bids less than $\frac{1}{2}(B(\alpha) + \alpha)$. Moreover his payoff as the winner is $\alpha - \frac{1}{2}(B(\alpha) + \alpha) = \frac{1}{2}(\alpha - B(\alpha)) > 0$. But this is impossible because we have argued that his equilibrium payoff is zero. Thus $B(\alpha) \geq \alpha$.

If $B(\alpha) > \alpha$, then $B(\theta) > \theta$ for some interval of values $(\alpha, \hat{\theta})$. Any bidder with a value in this interval wins with strictly positive probability and thus has a strictly negative payoff. But this is impossible because such a bidder is better off staying out of the auction.

Comparative Statics of the Sealed First-Price Auction

We now explore how a shift in the distribution of values affects bidding in the sealed first-price auction.

Rightward Shift in the Distribution of Values

Let $B(\cdot)$ be the equilibrium bidding strategy if each buyer's type is distributed with c.d.f. F. Also let $\hat{b}(\cdot)$ be the equilibrium bidding strategy if values are distributed with c.d.f. $\hat{F}$. Suppose that $\hat{F}$ stochastically dominates F. A simple intuitive argument suggests that a shift from F to $\hat{F}$ will lead to higher equilibrium bidding. For if there is less weight in the left tails of the distribution, buyers will be forced to bid more aggressively to compete with their opponents who are more likely to have high values. In fact, we need the somewhat stronger assumption of conditional stochastic dominance. That is, for any y and any $x < y$

$$Pr\{\hat{\theta} \leq x | \hat{\theta} \leq y\} = \frac{\hat{F}(x)}{\hat{F}(y)} \leq \frac{F(x)}{F(y)} = Pr\{\theta \leq x | \theta \leq y\}.$$

The reason is that it is the beliefs about buyers with lower values that determine equilibrium behavior.

Proposition 12.1-1: Conditional Stochastic Dominance (CSD) and Equilibrium Bids

In a sealed first-price auction, if the distribution of values shifts and the new distribution exhibits conditional stochastic dominance over the old distribution, then all bids rise.

Proof: Setting $\lambda = 1$ in (12.1-3),

$$B(\theta_i) = \theta_i - \int_0^{\theta_i} \frac{w(\theta)}{w(\theta_i)} d\theta.$$

We assume that $\hat{F}$ exhibits CSD over F so that

$$\frac{\hat{F}(\theta)}{\hat{F}(\theta_i)} \leq \frac{F(\theta)}{F(\theta_i)}.$$

Because $w(\theta) = F^{n-1}(\theta)$,

$$\frac{\hat{w}(\theta)}{\hat{w}(\theta_i)} \leq \frac{w(\theta)}{w(\theta_i)}.$$

Therefore $\hat{b}(\theta) \geq B(\theta)$. □

Roughly speaking, this proposition reveals that, as the mean of the distribution increases, so do the equilibrium bids.

Mean-Preserving Spreads

We now fix the mean and ask how equilibrium bidding changes as the variance of the distribution increases. From Chapter 7, $\hat{F}$ is a mean-preserving spread of F if

$$\hat{T}(\theta) - T(\theta) \equiv \int_0^\theta (\hat{F}(\theta) - F(\theta))d\theta \geq 0,\ \theta \in [0, \beta] \quad \text{and} \quad \hat{T}(\beta) - T(\beta) = 0.$$

We first examine the effect on the maximum bid. The rate at which the equilibrium payoff rises with type is

$$V'(\theta) = F^{n-1}(\theta). \tag{12.1-4}$$

Therefore the equilibrium payoff of the highest type is $V(\beta) = \int_0^\beta F^{n-1}(\theta)d\theta$.

If $n = 2$ we can integrate by parts to obtain

$$V(\beta) = \beta - \mu, \quad \text{where} \quad \mu = \int_0^\beta \theta f(\theta)d\theta.$$

Thus the maximum bid is the mean value.

If $n > 2$ the change in the payoff of the highest type is

$$\hat{V}(\beta) - V(\beta) = \int_0^\beta (\hat{F}^{n-1} - F^{n-1})d\theta$$

$$= \int_0^\beta (\hat{F}(\theta) - F(\theta))H(\theta)d\theta, \quad \text{where} \quad H(\theta) \equiv \sum_{j=1}^{n-2} \hat{F}^j(\theta)F^{n-1-j}(\theta).$$

Note that $H(\theta)$ is strictly increasing if $n > 2$.

Integrating by parts,

$$\hat{V}(\beta) - V(\beta) = [\hat{T}(\beta) - T(\beta)]H(\beta) - \int_0^\beta (\hat{T}(\theta) - T(\theta))H'(\theta)d\theta.$$

Because $\hat{F}$ is a mean-preserving spread of F, the first term is zero. The second term is negative if $n > 2$. Hence we have proved the following proposition.

Proposition 12.1-2: Change in the Maximum Payoff after a Mean-Preserving Spread

If the distribution of values shifts and the new distribution is a mean-preserving spread of the old distribution, then the bid of a buyer with the highest value is the same when there are two buyers (and equal to the mean value) and is lower if there are more than two buyers.

For the special case of a simple mean-preserving spread there exists some $\hat{\theta}$ such that $\hat{F}(\theta) - F(\theta) \geq 0, \forall \theta < \hat{\theta}$, and $\hat{F}(\theta) - F(\theta) \leq 0, \forall \theta > \hat{\theta}$. It follows immediately from (12.1-4) that

$$\hat{V}'(\theta) - V'(\theta) \geq 0, \quad \forall \theta < \hat{\theta} \quad \text{and} \quad \hat{V}'(\theta) - V'(\theta) \leq 0, \quad \forall \theta > \hat{\theta}.$$

Therefore $\hat{V}(\theta) - V(\theta)$ is first increasing and then decreasing. Also $\hat{V}(0) = V(0) = 0$ and by Proposition 12.1-2 the maximum bid is lower and so $\hat{V}(\beta) \geq V(\beta)$. Hence we have the following corollary.

Corollary 12.1-3: Change in Equilibrium Payoffs after a Mean-Preserving Spread If the distribution of values shifts and the new distribution is a simple mean-preserving spread of the old distribution, then the equilibrium payoffs rise.

To understand this result let $\hat{F}$ be any distribution with mean μ. With two buyers the maximum bid is μ. With more buyers the bid function increases so the maximum bid exceeds μ. Let F be a continuous distribution function that approximates a step function with all the probability mass at the mean. That is,

$$F(\theta) \approx F^*(\theta) = \begin{cases} 0, & \theta < \mu \\ 1, & \theta \geq \mu \end{cases}.$$

Then $\hat{F}$ is a mean-preserving spread of F^* and hence F. With all the mass at the mean there is no informational rent. The symmetric equilibrium bid is the mean μ regardless of the number of bidders.

For the two-buyer case we can analyze the expected revenue of the seller in a similar manner. Given revenue equivalence we focus on the sealed second-price auction. Let $F_{(2)}(\theta)$ be the c.d.f. of the second-order statistic. This is the probability that both of the values are below θ.

Proposition 12.1-4: Revenue Effect of a Mean-Preserving Spread
If there are two buyers and $\hat{F}$ is a mean-preserving spread of F, then expected revenue is lower for $\hat{F}$.

Proof: The c.d.f. for the second highest price is

$$F_{(2)}(\theta) = \Pr\{\theta_{(2)} \leq \theta\} = 1 - \Pr\{\tilde{\theta}_1 \geq \theta \quad \text{and} \quad \tilde{\theta}_2 \geq \theta\}$$
$$= 1 - (1 - F(\theta))^2 = 2F(\theta) - F^2(\theta).$$

In the second-price auction, the expected revenue is the expectation of the second highest value:

$$U^D = \int_0^\beta \theta \, dF_{(2)}(\theta) = \beta - \int_0^\beta F_{(2)}(\theta) d\theta = \beta - \int_0^\beta (2F - F^2) d\theta.$$

Because expected revenue is the same in the sealed first- and second-price auctions, the difference in expected revenue in the sealed first-price auction is

$$\hat{U}^D - U^D = \int_0^\beta (2F - F^2) d\theta - \int_0^\beta (2\hat{F} - \hat{F}^2) d\theta.$$

Because the means are the same this can be rewritten as follows:

$$\hat{U}^D - U^D = \int_0^\beta (\hat{F}^2 - F^2) d\theta = \int_0^\beta (\hat{F}(\theta) - F(\theta)) M(\theta),$$

where $M(\theta) = \hat{F}(\theta) + F(\theta)$ is strictly increasing.

Integrating by parts,

$$\hat{U}^D - U^D = - \int_0^\beta (\hat{T}(\theta) - T(\theta)) M'(\theta) d\theta < 0.$$

The right-hand side is negative because $M(\cdot)$ is increasing.   □

To understand this result, consider again the extreme case in which the variance is zero for F so that both buyers bid μ. Thus the item sells at a price μ. For any continuous distribution $\hat{F}$ with the same mean the maximum bid is μ so the item sells at a lower price with probability 1.

Bidding with Common Values

One key simplifying assumption in the earlier analysis is that buyers' values are private and independent. Although this is a convenient first approximation, there are many situations in which the item up for auction is of equal value to the potential buyers. Asymmetry across buyers arises because the true value of the item is unknown, and each buyer has different private information related to its true value. The private information of buyer i is summarized by his "signal" θ_i.

To simplify the exposition we consider the two-buyer case. If buyer i knew both signals he would use both to compute the estimated value of the item

$\phi(\theta_i, \theta_{-i})$ where the function $\phi(\cdot)$ is strictly increasing and symmetric.[1] The difficulty is that buyer i only learns about the other buyer's signal after he knows whether he has won.

If two signals are related to a common value it is natural to assume that the signals are positively correlated rather than independent. That is, if buyer $-i$ has a higher signal, he also believes that buyer i's signal is more likely to be higher as well. One way of representing this correlation is to assume that all the "left tail" conditional probabilities fall as a buyer's signal increases.

If buyer $-i$'s signal is θ_{-i}, the probability that buyer i's value is less than x, conditional on being less than y, is

$$\Pr\{\theta_i \leq x | \theta_i \leq y, \theta_{-i}\} = \frac{F(x|\theta_{-i})}{F(y|\theta_{-i})}.$$

In the independent signals case this is independent of buyer $-i$'s value. Henceforth we suppose instead that

$$\frac{\partial}{\partial \theta_{-i}} \Pr\{\theta_i \leq x | \theta_i \leq y, \theta_{-i}\} = \frac{\partial}{\partial \theta_{-i}} \frac{F(x|\theta_{-i})}{F(y|\theta_{-i})} \leq 0.$$

Then for any $\theta'_{-i} > \theta_{-i}$

$$\frac{F(x|\theta'_{-i})}{F(y|\theta'_{-i})} \leq \frac{F(x|\theta_{-i})}{F(y|\theta_{-i})}.$$

If this inequality holds we say that the joint distribution satisfies the CSD property.

Definition: Conditional and Strong Conditional Stochastic Dominance Property The symmetric joint density function $f(\theta_1, \theta_2)$ has the CSD property on $\Theta \times \Theta$ where $\Theta = [\alpha, \beta]$ if for all $x, y \in \Theta$:

$$\frac{\partial}{\partial \theta_{-i}} \Pr\{\theta_i \leq x | \theta_i \leq y, \theta_{-i}\} = \frac{\partial}{\partial \theta_{-i}} \frac{F(x|\theta_{-i})}{F(y|\theta_{-i})} \leq 0.$$

If this inequality is strict for all $x, y \in (\alpha, \beta)$ the joint density function has the strong CSD property.

Note that if the CSD property holds, then, for all $\theta' < \theta$ and $x < y$

$$\frac{F(\theta|y) - F(\theta'|y)}{F(\theta|y)} = 1 - \frac{F(\theta'|y)}{F(\theta|y)} \geq 1 - \frac{F(\theta'|x)}{F(\theta|x)} = \frac{F(\theta|x) - F(\theta'|x)}{F(\theta|x)}.$$

---

[1] For example $\phi(\theta) = \frac{1}{2}\theta_1 + \frac{1}{2}\theta_2$.

Dividing both sides by $\theta - \theta'$ and taking the limit as $\theta' \to \theta$, it follows that

$$\frac{f(\theta|y)}{F(\theta|y)} \geq \frac{f(\theta|x)}{F(\theta|x)} \; \forall y \quad \text{and} \quad x < y. \tag{12.1-5}$$

Equilibrium Bidding

Henceforth we shall assume that the CSD property holds and compare the sealed first- and second-price auctions.

In the sealed second-price auction we have the following result.

Proposition 12.1-5: Equilibrium Bidding Strategy in the Sealed Second-Price Auction

If the winning bidder pays the second highest bid, the symmetric equilibrium bidding strategy is $\phi(\theta, \theta)$, $\theta \in \Theta_i = [\alpha, \beta]$, and the equilibrium expected payment conditional on winning is

$$\overline{B}(\theta) = \int_\alpha^\theta \phi(z, z) \frac{f(z|\theta)}{F(\theta|\theta)} dz. \tag{12.1-6}$$

Proof: Suppose that buyer $-i$ follows the equilibrium strategy and buyer i with signal θ bids $\phi(x, x) < \phi(\theta, \theta)$. If buyer $-i$ bids below $\phi(x, x)$ then buyer i wins regardless and pays $\phi(x, x)$. If buyer $-i$ bids above $\phi(\theta, \theta)$ then buyer i loses regardless. Suppose that buyer $-i$ bids; $\phi(\theta_{-i}, \theta_{-i}) \in (\phi(x, x), \phi(\theta, \theta))$; then $\theta_{-i} \in (x, \theta)$. If buyer i bids $\phi(x, x)$ he loses. If he bids $\phi(\theta, \theta)$ he wins and his payoff is $\phi(\theta, \theta_{-i}) - \phi(\theta_{-i}, \theta_{-i}) > 0$ because $\theta_{-i} < \theta$. Thus buyer i's expected payoff is strictly lower if he bids $\phi(x, x)$ rather than $\phi(\theta, \theta)$.

An almost identical argument can be used to show that buyer i is worse off bidding higher than $\phi(\theta, \theta)$. Thus bidding $\phi(\theta, \theta)$ is the unique best response. $\qquad\square$

Now consider bidding in a sealed high-bid auction. If buyer 2 bids according to the symmetric equilibrium bid function $B(\cdot)$ and buyer 1 with value θ bids $B(x)$, buyer 1's expected payoff is

$$U(\theta, x) = \int_\alpha^x (\phi(\theta, z) - B(x)) f(z|\theta) dz.$$

The FOC for a maximum must hold at $x = \theta$.

$$\frac{\partial U}{\partial x} = (\phi(\theta, x) - B(x)) f(x|\theta) - \int_\alpha^x B'(x) f(z|\theta) dz$$

$$= (\phi(\theta, x) - B(x)) f(x|\theta) - B'(x) F(x|\theta).$$

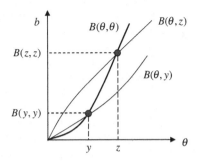

Figure 12.1-1. Equilibrium with naïve beliefs.

Setting this equal to zero at $x = \theta$,

$$(\phi(\theta, \theta) - B(\theta)) f(\theta|\theta) - B'(\theta)F(\theta|\theta) = 0.$$

Rearranging this expression,

$$B'(\theta) = \frac{f(\theta|\theta)}{F(\theta|\theta)}(\phi(\theta, \theta) - B(\theta)). \tag{12.1-7}$$

The challenge is to compare the solution to this differential equation with $\overline{B}(\theta)$ satisfying (12.1-6). The key is to first consider equilibrium bidding if, for each $y \in \Theta$, a buyer with signal y is naïve and believes that values are distributed independently with c.d.f. $F(\theta|y)$. Let the equilibrium bid function associated with such beliefs be $B(\theta, y)$. Suppose each buyer type is naive. Then a buyer with signal y bids as if the equilibrium bid function is $B(\theta, y)$ and therefore bids $B(y, y)$. A buyer with signal $z > y$ bids as if the equilibrium bid function is $B(\theta, z)$ and therefore bids $B(z, z)$. This is depicted In Figure 12.1-1.

The equilibrium bidding strategy when all buyers have such naive beliefs is therefore $B(\theta, \theta)$.

We have already argued that under independence there is revenue equivalence. Therefore the bid by a buyer with signal θ is equal to the equilibrium expected payment in the sealed second-price auction. That is, $B(\theta, \theta) = \overline{B}(\theta)$. Thus to compare revenues in the two auctions we simply need to compare the sealed first-price auctions with correct and naïve beliefs.

The intuition is that the naïve bidder thinks that those with lower values have beliefs that stochastically dominate their true beliefs. So the naïve buyer's belief about how the other buyers will bid is biased upward. As a result his response is to bid higher as well and therefore increase his win probability. Because there is revenue equivalence under naïve bidding, expected revenue is lower in the sealed first-price auction.

As a first step we examine equilibrium bidding under naïve beliefs. If buyer 2 bids according to the naïve symmetric equilibrium bid function

$B(\theta, y)$ and buyer 1 with value θ bids $B(x, y)$, buyer 1's expected payoff is

$$U(\theta, x, y) = \int_\alpha^x (\phi(\theta, z) - B(x, y)) f(z|y) dz.$$

The FOC must hold at $x = \theta$.

$$\frac{\partial U}{\partial x}(\theta, x, y) = (\phi(\theta, x) - B(x, y)) f(x|y) - \frac{\partial B}{\partial x}(x, y) F(x|y).$$

Setting this equal to zero at $x = \theta$,

$$\frac{\partial B}{\partial \theta}(\theta, y) = \frac{f(\theta|y)}{F(\theta|y)}(\phi(\theta, \theta) - B(\theta, y)). \tag{12.1-8}$$

This must hold for all θ. Note that we can rewrite equation (12.1-8) as follows:

$$\frac{\partial}{\partial \theta}(B(\theta, y) F(\theta|y)) = \phi(\theta, \theta) f(\theta|y).$$

Integrating both sides and rearranging,

$$B(\theta, y) = \int_\alpha^\theta \phi(z, z) \frac{f(z|y)}{F(\theta|y)} dz = \phi(\theta, \theta) - \int_\alpha^\theta \frac{d\phi}{dz}(z, z) \frac{F(z|y)}{F(\theta|y)} dz. \tag{12.1-9}$$

We first argue that if the CSD property holds then $B(\theta) \le B(\theta, \theta)$. We suppose that this statement is false and seek a contradiction. If it is not the case that $B(\theta) \le B(\theta, \theta)$, then for some y, $B(y) > B(y, y)$. The graphs of the bid functions $B(\theta)$ and $B(\theta, y)$ are depicted in Figure 12.1-2. Because $B(0) = B(0, y) = 0$, there must be some $x \ge 0$ such that $B(x) = B(x, y)$ and $B(\theta) > B(\theta, y)$ on $(x, y]$.

From (12.1-8),

$$\frac{\partial B}{\partial \theta}(\theta, y) = \frac{f(\theta|y)}{F(\theta|y)}(\phi(\theta, \theta) - B(\theta, y)). \tag{12.1-10}$$

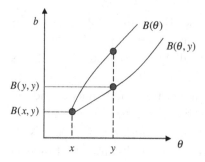

Figure 12.1-2. Equilibrium bid functions.

From (12.1-7),

$$B'(\theta) = \frac{f(\theta|\theta)}{F(\theta|\theta)}(\phi(\theta, \theta) - B(\theta)).$$

Note that $\theta \in (x, y]$. Appealing to the CSD assumption and hence (12.1-5) it follows that

$$B'(\theta) \le \frac{f(\theta|y)}{F(\theta|y)}(\phi(\theta, \theta) - B(\theta))$$

$$< \frac{f(\theta|y)}{F(\theta|y)}(\phi(\theta, \theta) - B(\theta, y)) \text{ on } (x, y], \text{ because } B(\theta) > B(\theta, y)$$

$$= \frac{\partial B}{\partial \theta}(\theta, y), \text{ from (12.1-10).}$$

Then $B(y) < B(y, y)$ in contradiction of our initial hypothesis. Thus for all y

$$B(y) \le B(y, y). \tag{12.1-11}$$

We now argue that if the strict CSD property holds, then the inequality must be strict. Suppose for some $\hat{\theta} > 0$, $B(\hat{\theta}) = B(\hat{\theta}, \hat{\theta})$. Since (12.1-11) holds, it follows that $B'(\hat{\theta}) \ge \frac{d}{d\theta}B(\theta, \theta)$. From (12.1-10) and (12.1-7),

$$\frac{\partial B}{\partial \theta}(\hat{\theta}, y)\bigg|_{y=\hat{\theta}} = \frac{f(\hat{\theta}|\hat{\theta})}{F(\hat{\theta}|\hat{\theta})}(\phi(\hat{\theta}, \hat{\theta}) - B(\hat{\theta}, \hat{\theta}))$$

$$= \frac{f(\hat{\theta}|\hat{\theta})}{F(\hat{\theta}|\hat{\theta})}(\phi(\hat{\theta}, \hat{\theta}) - B(\hat{\theta})) = B'(\hat{\theta}).$$

Also from (12.1-9), because the strong CSD property holds,

$$\frac{\partial B}{\partial y}(\theta, y) = -\int_0^\theta \frac{d}{dz}\phi(z, z)\frac{\partial}{\partial y}\frac{F(z|y)}{F(\theta|y)}dz > 0.$$

Therefore

$$\frac{d}{d\theta}B(\hat{\theta}, \hat{\theta}) = \frac{\partial B}{\partial \theta}(\hat{\theta}, y)\bigg|_{y=\hat{\theta}} + \frac{\partial B}{\partial y}(\hat{\theta}, y)\bigg|_{y=\hat{\theta}} > B'(\hat{\theta}).$$

But this contradicts our earlier conclusion. We have therefore proved the following proposition.

Proposition 12.1-6: Revenue Comparison with Conditional Stochastic Dominance (Milgrom and Weber)
If the (strong) CSD property holds, then in the sealed first-price auction buyers bid (strictly) less than they would if they made the naïve (and incorrect)

assumption that all other buyers share their beliefs. Because the assumption of naïve beliefs implies revenue equivalence, it follows that expected revenue is (strictly) lower in the sealed first-price auction than in the sealed second-price auction.

Exercises

Exercise 12.1-1: Bidding When the Seller Sets a Reserve Price If the seller sets a minimum (or "reserve") price of $\hat{\theta}$, all those with values below $\hat{\theta}$ will not bid.

(a) Explain why all those with values above $\hat{\theta}$ are strictly better off bidding so the equilibrium bidding strategy in a sealed first-price auction is a mapping $B(\theta)$ with domain $[\hat{\theta}, 1]$.

(b) Extend the argument made earlier to show that the equilibrium bid function is

$$B(\theta) = \frac{F(\hat{\theta})^{n-1}\hat{\theta} + \int_{\hat{\theta}}^{\theta} x(n-1)xF(x)^{n-2}dx}{F(\theta)^{n-1}}.$$

(c) Integrate by parts to show that

$$B(\theta) = \theta - \int_{\hat{\theta}}^{\theta} \left(\frac{F(x)}{F(\theta)}\right)^{n-1} dx.$$

(d) If $\overline{F}$ conditionally stochastically dominates F, does it follow that bids will be higher? What will happen if $\overline{F}$ stochastically dominates F?

(e) If the number of bidders rises, show that the equilibrium bid is strictly higher for all $\theta > \hat{\theta}$.

Exercise 12.1-2: All Pay Auction A single item is to be sold to the high bidder in a sealed first-price auction. Each buyer places a cash bid in an envelope and submits his envelope. This is a nonrefundable bid. The envelopes are then opened and the winner is the buyer who has submitted the largest bid.

(a) If the equilibrium bid function is $B(\cdot)$, obtain an expression for the payoff to bidder i if all other bidders employ the equilibrium strategy and bidder i bids $\hat{b} = B(x)$.

(b) Analyze the direct revelation game and solve for the equilibrium bid function. Solve also for the equilibrium payoff for each type.

(c) Compare this with the equilibrium payoff in the standard sealed high-bid auction.

Exercise 12.1-3: Shift in the Distribution of Values Let $B(\theta)$ be the equilibrium bid function when values are continuously distributed on $[\alpha, \beta]$. Suppose that the distribution function shifts to the right so that the new c.d.f.

is $\overline{F}(\theta) = F(\theta - \kappa), \theta \in [\alpha + \kappa, \beta + \kappa]$. Show that the new equilibrium bid function is $\overline{B}(\theta) = \kappa + B(\theta - \kappa)$.

Exercise 12.1-4: Common Value Auction with Two Bidders Bidder i's "type" θ_i is a realization of a random variable with support $[\alpha, \beta]$, c.d.f. $F(\cdot)$ and density $f(\cdot)$. Each bidder's value of the item is the average of the types; that is, $v_i(\theta) = \sum_{j=1}^{n} \frac{1}{n}\theta_j$. Let $B(\cdot)$ be the equilibrium bidding strategy.

(a) With two bidders, show that if her opponent employs the equilibrium bid function and bidder i bids $\hat{b} = B(x)$, then her payoff is

$$u(x, \theta_i) = \int_{\alpha}^{x} \left(\frac{1}{2}\theta_i + \frac{1}{2}y \right) dF(y) - F(x)B(x).$$

(b) Analyze the direct revelation game and hence establish the following necessary condition for equilibrium:

$$xf(x) = \frac{d}{dx} F(x)B(x).$$

(c) Solve for the equilibrium bid function.

Exercise 12.1-5: The Winner's Curse Consider the common value auction with n bidders. Types are uniformly distributed on $[0, 1]$ so $F(\theta) = \theta$. Each buyer's valuation $v_i = \frac{1}{n}\sum_{j=1}^{n} \theta_j$. Thus we can think of a buyer's type as her initial private estimate of the item's value and v_i as the estimate she would have if she knew all the buyers' initial private estimates.

(a) Consider the auction as a direct revelation game and show that

$$u(x, \theta_i) = \frac{1}{n}\theta_i F^{n-1}(x) + \frac{n-1}{n} F^{n-2}(x) \int_{\alpha}^{\theta_i} y\, dF(y) - F^{n-1}(x)B(x)$$

$$= \frac{1}{n}\theta_i x^{n-1} + \frac{n-1}{2n} x^n - x^{n-1} B(x).$$

(b) Write down the first-order condition and hence show that the equilibrium bid function is

$$B(\theta_i) = \left(1 - \frac{1}{n} \right) \left(1 + \frac{2}{n} \right) \frac{\theta_i}{2}.$$

(c) Confirm that for $n \geq 4$, the bid function declines as the number of bidders increases.

Remark: The winner is cursed because she only wins if her initial private estimate of the value is the highest. She will overbid unless she takes this into account in computing her expected value of the item.

Exercise 12.1-6: Bidding with Finite Types There are two bidders. Buyer i has a private value of 2 with probability p_i and 1 with probability $1 - p_i$. The item is to be sold in a sealed high-bid auction with a random tie-breaking rule.

(a) The equilibrium bid of the low-value bidder is $B(1) = 1$. Sketch a proof that this must be the case.
(b) Explain why the bidding strategy of a high-value bidder must be a mixed strategy.
(c) Solve for c.d.f. of the equilibrium mixed strategy if $p_1 = p_2 = p$.
(d) Show that there is no equilibrium if $p_1 \neq p_2$. HINT: Let $[1, \bar{b}_i]$ be the support of buyer i's bid distribution when his value is 2. Explain why $\bar{b}_1 = \bar{b}_2$.

Exercise 12.1-7: More Risk Averse Bidders Bid More in a Sealed First-Price Auction The gain in utility when a buyer with value θ pays b is $U(\theta - b)$. If the buyer is risk neutral $U(\theta - b) = \theta - b$. If the buyer is risk averse, $U(\cdot)$ is strictly concave. There are two buyers. Each buyer's value is i.i.d. on $[0, 1]$ with c.d.f. $F(\cdot) \in C^1$.

(a) If a function $h(\cdot) : \mathbb{R} \to \mathbb{R}$ is increasing, strictly concave, and $h(0) = 0$, show that

$$\frac{h(x)}{h'(x)} > x, \quad x > 0.$$

(b) Let $B_N(\theta)$ be the equilibrium bid function if buyers are risk neutral. Let $B_A(\theta)$ be the equilibrium bid function if buyers are risk averse. Show that the bid functions satisfy the following differential equations:

$$(i) \; B'_N(\theta) = \frac{f(\theta)}{F(\theta)}(\theta - B_N) \quad \text{and} \quad (ii) \; B'_A(\theta) = \frac{f(\theta)}{F(\theta)} \frac{U(\theta - B_A)}{U'(\theta - B_A)}.$$

(c) Appeal to (a) to show that

$$B'_A(\theta) > \frac{f(\theta)}{F(\theta)}(\theta - B_A).$$

(d) Suppose that for some θ^*, $B_A(\theta^*) < B_N(\theta^*)$. Because $B_A(0) = B_N(0) = 0$, there must be some $\theta^{**} \in [0, \theta^*)$ such that $B_A(\theta^{**}) = B_N(\theta^{**})$ and $B_A(\theta^*) < B_N(\theta^*)$, $\theta \in (\theta^{**}, \theta^*]$.
    Then appeal to (c) to show that

$$B_A(\theta^*) - B_A(\theta^{**}) = \int_{\theta^{**}}^{\theta^*} B'_A(\theta)d\theta > B_N(\theta^*) - B_N(\theta^{**}).$$

Hence obtain a contradiction.
(e) It follows that $B_A(\theta) \geq B_N(\theta)$. Appeal to (ii) to show that the inequality is strict for all $\theta > 0$.

12.2 Revenue Equivalence Theorem

Key ideas: equilibrium win probability, equilibrium marginal payoff, optimal reserve price

In Chapter 10 we saw that if n risk-neutral buyers have values that are distributed with a joint density function $f(\theta_1) \times \cdots \times f(\theta_n)$, then the sealed bid and open auctions yield the same expected payoff to each buyer type. Given this buyer equivalence, the expected payment by each buyer type must be the same, and therefore the expected revenue of the seller is the same. We now establish a far more general result.

For any mechanism designed by the seller, the expected gross payoff of buyer i with value θ_i is his probability of winning w times his value. Let r be the expected payment by the buyer (and hence the expected revenue to the seller). Then the expected payoff can be written as follows:

$$u(\theta_i, w, r) = w\theta_i - r.$$

Suppose that the seller designs a symmetric mechanism so that buyers compete on an even playing field. Then it is natural to seek a symmetric equilibrium. Let the equilibrium win probability of a buyer with value $\theta \in \Theta$ be $w(\theta)$ and let the equilibrium expected payment be $r(\theta)$.

As we have argued in Chapter 11, the single crossing property (SCP) holds. Thus a necessary condition for equilibrium is that for any $\hat{\theta}_i > \theta_i$ buyer i's win probability $w(\hat{\theta}_i) \geq w(\theta_i)$. It follows that the equilibrium expected payment $r(\hat{\theta}_i) \geq r(\theta_i)$. Otherwise the buyer with value θ_i would be strictly better off mimicking the buyer with value $\hat{\theta}_i$.

Consider a selling mechanism with the equilibrium property that if the item is awarded to any buyer it is to the buyer who values it the most. (If there are tying high values, the winner is selected randomly from the highest value buyers.) The sealed high bid auction is one such auction. Given the reserve price (and possibly an entry fee as well), those buyers with values below some threshold $\hat{\theta}$ do not bid. All other buyers bid and the high-value buyer wins.

The win probability of a buyer with a value above the threshold is the probability that she has the high value. Thus

$$w(\theta) = \begin{cases} 0, & \theta < \hat{\theta} \\ F^{n-1}(\theta), & \theta \geq \hat{\theta} \end{cases}.$$

Because the equilibrium win probability is a strictly increasing function, the equilibrium expected payment, $r(\theta)$ must be as well.[2] We look for an equilibrium in which the win probability $w(\theta)$ and expected payment $r(\theta)$ are continuously differentiable.

---

[2] Otherwise, a lower value buyer would mimic a higher value buyer and increase his payoff.

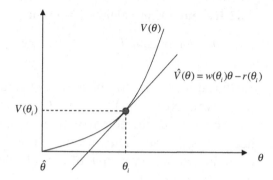

Figure 12.2-1. Equilibrium marginal payoff.

We first present a graphical analysis. Let $V(\cdot)$ be the equilibrium payoff function. Then the equilibrium payoff of buyer i with value θ_i is

$$V(\theta_i) = w(\theta_i)\theta_i - r(\theta_i).$$

Suppose that all other buyers bid according to the equilibrium strategy, but buyer i deviates and regardless of his value, bids as if his value were θ_i. His win probability is therefore $w(\theta_i)$ and his expected payment is $r(\theta_i)$. His payoff is therefore

$$\hat{V}(\theta_i) = w(\theta_i)\theta - r(\theta_i).$$

The two functions $V(\theta)$ and $\hat{V}(\theta)$ are depicted in Figure 12.2-1.

First, note that $V(\theta) \geq \hat{V}(\theta)$, because $V(\theta)$ is the best response payoff. Second, note that $V(\theta_i) = \hat{V}(\theta_i)$, because buyer i bids his best response when his value is θ_i. Finally note that the function $\hat{V}(\theta)$ is linear with slope $w(\theta_i)$. Then, as depicted, the two curves must have the same slope at θ_i and so

$$\frac{dV}{d\theta}(\theta_i) = w(\theta_i).$$

Formally we apply the direct revelation approach. The mechanism designer computes the equilibrium win probability and expected payment functions $\{w(x), r(x)\}_{x\in\Theta}$ and invites each buyer to report some $x \in \Theta$. If buyer i with value θ_i reports x, he has a win probability of $w(x)$ and an expected payment of $r(x)$. Therefore his payoff is

$$U(\theta_i, x) = \theta_i w(x) - r(x).$$

The equilibrium best response yields the outcome $(w(\theta_i), r(\theta_i))$. Let $V(\theta_i)$ be the buyer's equilibrium payoff. Then

$$\theta_i = \arg\underset{x\in\Theta}{\text{Max}}\{U(\theta_i, x)\} \quad \text{and} \quad V(\theta_i) = U(\theta_i, \theta_i).$$

Appealing to the Envelope Theorem,

$$\frac{dV}{d\theta}(\theta_i) = w(\theta_i).$$

Because this argument holds for any θ_i it follows that the equilibrium marginal payoff is the win probability. Because the lowest type that submits a bid has a payoff of zero it follows that

$$V(\theta) = \int_{\hat{\theta}}^{\theta} w(x)dx.$$

Thus the equilibrium payoff is the same for all selling schemes that assign the item to the bidder with the highest value above the entry value $\hat{\theta}$. Also $V(\theta_i) = \theta_i w(\theta_i) - r(\theta_i)$. Thus the equilibrium expected payment is

$$r(\theta_i) = \theta_i w(\theta_i) - \int_{\hat{\theta}}^{\theta_i} w(\theta)d\theta. \tag{12.2-1}$$

This is also the same for all such selling schemes. We therefore have the following striking result.

Proposition 12.2-1: Revenue Equivalence Theorem[3] (Riley and Samuelson)
If buyers' values are jointly distributed with joint density $f(\theta_1) \times \cdots \times f(\theta_n)$ and the item is sold to the buyer with the highest value above some "reserve" value $\hat{\theta}$, then for all θ, the equilibrium payoff to a buyer and hence the expected seller revenue are independent of the selling mechanism.

Example 1: All Pay Auction
Suppose that the item is allocated as in the sealed high-bid auction but that all bidders must pay their bids. Then the equilibrium bid function $B(\theta)$ is the expected payment by a buyer with value θ. That is, $B(\theta) = r(\theta)$ and so the equilibrium bid is given by (12.2-1).

Example 2: War of Attrition
There are two buyers. The auctioneer starts a clock and stops it when told to do so by one of the buyers. Both then pay the "time" on the clock.

---

[3] This result was first proved in the early spring of 1979. Bill Samuelson and I became convinced, by a host of examples, that there must be a general principle underlying them. I well remember the excitement of the moment when everything fell into place on a rainy afternoon in Newton Highlands, Massachusetts. In the following summer, Myerson showed that it was not possible to extract more revenue by assigning the item to anyone other than the high value buyer, except in rather extreme cases.

Let $B(\cdot)$ be the equilibrium bid function. Suppose buyer 1's value is θ and buyer 2's value is θ_2. Then buyer 1 pays $\mathrm{Min}\{B(\theta), B(\theta_2)\}$. His expected payment is therefore

$$r(\theta) = \int_0^\theta B(\theta_2) f(\theta_2) d\theta_2 + \int_\theta^1 B(\theta) f(\theta_2) d\theta_2$$

$$= \int_0^\theta B(\theta_2) f(\theta_2) d\theta_2 + B(\theta)(1 - F(\theta)). \tag{12.2-2}$$

As we see later it is the derivative of the payment function that we will need to solve for the equilibrium bid function. Differentiating (12.2-2),

$$r'(\theta) = B(\theta) f(\theta) + B'(\theta)(1 - F(\theta)) - B(\theta) f(\theta) = B'(\theta)(1 - F(\theta)).$$

The necessary condition for incentive compatibility is easily obtained by applying the direct revelation approach. If bidder i with value θ_i bids $B(x)$ his payoff is

$$U(\theta_i, x) = \theta_i F(x) - r(x).$$

But $B(\theta_i)$ is the bidder's equilibrium best response. Therefore

$$\theta_i = \arg \max_x \{U(\theta_i, x) = \theta_i F(x) - r(x)\}.$$

FOC

$$\theta_i f(x) - r'(x) = 0 \quad \text{at} \quad x = \theta_i$$

Therefore $r'(\theta) = \theta f(\theta)$. Equating the two expressions for $r'(\theta)$,

$$B'(\theta) = \frac{\theta f(\theta)}{1 - F(\theta)}.$$

Hence

$$B(\theta_i) = \int_0^{\theta_i} \frac{\theta f(\theta)}{1 - F(\theta)} d\theta.$$

Optimal Reserve Price

With a reserve price there is some value $\hat{\theta}$ such that the equilibrium payoff $V(\hat{\theta}) = 0$ and $V(\theta) > 0$ if and only if $\theta > \hat{\theta}$. Given the revenue equivalence theorem, we can choose any particular auction to study the revenue implications of varying $\hat{\theta}$. It is simplest to examine the sealed second-price auction.

In this case $\hat{\theta}$ is the reserve price set by the seller. Suppose that the reserve price is raised from $\hat{\theta}$ to $\hat{\theta} + \Delta\theta$.

We consider first order effects. The probability that there is more than one buyer with a value between $\hat{\theta}$ and $\hat{\theta} + \Delta\theta$ is of second order. If there is more than 1 buyer with a value above $\hat{\theta} + \Delta\theta$, the price will be bid up beyond $\hat{\theta} + \Delta\theta$ so changing the reserve price has no effect on revenue. Thus we can ignore these two cases. Suppose then that buyer 1 is the only buyer with a value above $\hat{\theta}$. His value is above $\hat{\theta} + \Delta\theta$ with probability $1 - F(\hat{\theta} + \Delta\theta)$ and between $\hat{\theta}$ and $\hat{\theta} + \Delta\theta$ with probability $F(\hat{\theta} + \Delta\theta) - F(\hat{\theta})$. In the first case the seller's revenue rises by $\Delta\theta$ while in the second there is no sale so the loss is $\hat{\theta}$. Thus the increase in expected seller revenue is

$$F^{n-1}(\hat{\theta})[(1 - F(\hat{\theta} + \Delta\theta))\Delta\theta - \hat{\theta}(F(\hat{\theta} + \Delta\theta)) - F(\hat{\theta})].$$

Because this is the effect of just one buyer, the effect of all n buyers is n times this change. Taking the first order approximation, the increase in expected seller revenue is therefore

$$\Delta r = nF^{n-1}(\hat{\theta})[(1 - F(\hat{\theta}) - \hat{\theta} f(\hat{\theta})]\Delta\theta$$

Dividing by $\Delta\theta$ and taking the limit, the marginal expected revenue of the seller is

$$\frac{dr}{d\hat{\theta}} = nF^{n-1}(\hat{\theta})[(1 - F(\hat{\theta}) - \hat{\theta} f(\hat{\theta})].$$

First, note that if the minimum value α is sufficiently small, this is strictly positive at $\hat{\theta} = \alpha$. Thus the seller maximizes profit by excluding buyers with sufficiently low values. This is the standard monopoly outcome. To maximize profit a monopoly seller compares marginal revenue (MR) and marginal cost (MC) rather than marginal benefit and marginal cost. Thus, unless MR is always higher than MC, the monopoly undersupplies relative to the efficient outcome.

Second, note that we can rewrite the marginal seller revenue as follows:

$$\frac{dr}{d\hat{\theta}} = nF^{n-1}(\hat{\theta})(1 - F(\hat{\theta})[1 - \hat{\theta}h(\hat{\theta})],$$

where $h(\theta) = f(\theta)/(1 - F(\theta))$ is the "hazard rate" of the distribution. For a broad range of distributions this is an increasing function. Then there is a unique reserve price satisfying the first-order condition $dr/d\hat{\theta} = 0$. It follows that the revenue-maximizing reserve price is independent of the number of bidders.

Exercises

Exercise 12.2-1: Optimal Auction with Finite Types There are two buyers. Each has a value in $\Theta = \{1, 2\}$. Values are independently distributed and the probability each buyer has a high value is p.

(a) Confirm that in the sealed first- and second-price auctions the equilibrium payoffs are $(V(1), V(2)) = (0, 1 - p)$.
(b) Show that there exists a $\hat{p}$ such that the seller loses by setting a reserve price if and only if $p < \hat{p}$.
(c) The seller instead announces that the bidders must choose a bid in $B = \{1, b\}$. Solve for the b that maximizes the seller's expected payoff and show that the new payoff to the high-value buyers, $V^*(2)$, is lower than $V(2)$. Therefore revenue is higher.

Exercise 12.2-2: Optimal Reserve Price Buyers are risk neutral. Each buyer's value is an independent draw from a distribution with support $[\alpha, \beta]$, c.d.f. $F(\cdot)$ and p.d.f. $f(\theta)$.

(a) Appeal to the earlier results to show that if the seller sets a reserve value of $\hat{\theta}$, the equilibrium expected payment by buyer i is

$$\bar{r}_i(\hat{\theta}) = \int_{\hat{\theta}}^{\beta} \theta F^{n-1}(\theta) f(\theta) d\theta - \int_{\hat{\theta}}^{\beta} H(\hat{\theta}, \theta) f(\theta) d\theta$$

where $H(\hat{\theta}, \theta) = \int_{\hat{\theta}}^{\theta} F^{n-1}(x) dx$.
(b) Note that $H(\hat{\theta}, \hat{\theta}) = 0$ and $\frac{\partial H}{\partial \theta}(\hat{\theta}, \theta) = F^{n-1}(\theta)$. Hence show that

$$\frac{d\bar{r}_i}{d\hat{\theta}} = -F^{n-1}(\hat{\theta})[\hat{\theta} f(\hat{\theta}) - (1 - F(\hat{\theta}))].$$

(c) Hence characterize the reserve value that maximizes the seller's expected revenue. Suppose that the seller's value of the item θ_0. This is his payoff if the item is not sold. Again characterize the optimal reserve value.
(d) If values are uniformly distributed on $[\alpha, \beta]$, for what values of the parameters is it optimal for the seller to set a reserve price above α?

12.3 Optimal Auctions

Key ideas: Applying the Revelation Principle, expected buyer surplus (informational rent), expected seller surplus, characterizing the revenue-maximizing auction design

In Section 12.2 we considered auctions in which the item is sold to the buyer with the highest value as long as that value exceeds some minimum value $\hat{\theta}$. Most strikingly, we established that, under the baseline assumptions of risk neutrality, symmetry, and independence, changing the rules of the auction has no effect on the expected payoffs of a buyer with value θ. Thus the seller's revenue is independent of the auction rules. We now show that, under one weak additional assumption, it never pays to sell to anyone but the buyer with the highest value. Then a seller can do no better than set an optimal reserve price and sell the item using one of the two common auctions. We also relax the assumption that all buyers are drawing from the same distribution and again characterize the optimal auction.

We assume that all buyers' values are in the interval $[\alpha, \beta]$ and have joint density function $f_1(\theta_1) \times \cdots \times f_n(\theta_n)$ and joint c.d.f. $F_1(\theta_1) \times \cdots \times F_n(\theta_n)$. The seller's reservation value is θ_0. This is his payoff in the event that the item is not sold.

In the analysis of non-linear pricing we introduced the following regularity assumption for a family of demand price functions $p(\theta, q)$.

Regularity Assumption: Increasing Marginal Revenue

$$\text{MR}(\theta, q) = p(\theta, q) - \left(\frac{1 - F(\theta)}{F'(\theta)} \right) p_\theta(\theta, q)$$

is an increasing function of θ.

In an auction, if buyer i with value θ_i wins with probability q, his payoff is $B(\theta_i, q) = \theta_i q$.

Let $p(\theta_i, q)$ be the demand price function. That is,

$$p(\theta_i, q) \equiv \begin{cases} \theta_i, & q \le 1 \\ 0, & q > 1 \end{cases}.$$

Then $B(\theta_i, q) = \int_0^q p(\theta_i, q) = \theta_i q$.

Let $F_i(\cdot)$ be the c.d.f. of buyer i's value. Then for an auction the regularity assumption is satisfied if and only if

$$\text{MR}_i(\theta, q) = J_i(\theta) \equiv \theta - \frac{1 - F_i(\theta)}{F_i'(\theta)}$$

is an increasing function. We will appeal to this assumption in the analysis of optimal auctions.

As argued in the previous section, the payoff of buyer i with value θ_i can be written as $U_i = w\theta_i - r$. Because the SCP holds, buyers with higher values choose higher win probabilities by bidding higher.

We proceed by noting that for any selling mechanism – that is, a set of rules announced by the seller – the equilibrium best responses result in buyer

i winning the item with some equilibrium probability $w_i(\theta_1, \ldots, \theta_n)$ and equilibrium expected payment $r_i(\theta_1, \ldots, \theta_n)$. Taking the expectation over all the other buyers, define

$$\overline{w}_i(\theta_i) = \mathop{E}_{\theta_{-i}}\{w_i(\theta)\} \quad \text{and} \quad \overline{r}_i(\theta_i) = \mathop{E}_{\theta_{-i}}\{r_i(\theta)\}. \tag{12.3-1}$$

Consider the direct revelation game where the seller announces the win probabilities and payoffs and invites each buyer to reveal his type. Suppose that instead of making his best response, buyer i announces that his value is x. Then his expected payoff is

$$U_i(\theta_i, x) = \overline{w}_i(x)\theta_i - \overline{r}_i(x). \tag{12.3-2}$$

Because buyer i's best response is to announce his true value, $U_i(\theta_i, x)$ takes on its maximum at $x = v_i$. That is,

$$\theta_i = \arg\mathop{\text{Max}}_x\{U_i(\theta_i, x\} = \mathop{\text{Max}}_x\{\overline{w}_i(x)\theta_i - \overline{r}_i(x)\}.$$

Also let $V_i(\theta_i)$ be the equilibrium payoff to buyer i with value θ_i; that is,

$$V_i(\theta_i) = \mathop{\text{Max}}_x\{U_i(\theta_i, x\} = \mathop{\text{Max}}_x\{\overline{w}_i(x)\theta_i - \overline{r}_i(x)\}.$$

Appealing to the Envelope Theorem, it follows that

$$\frac{dV_i}{d\theta_i} = \overline{w}_i(\theta_i).$$

Integrating, the equilibrium payoff to buyer i is

$$V_i(\theta_i) = V_i(\alpha) + \int_\alpha^{\theta_i} \overline{w}_i(x)dx.$$

Henceforth we will ignore any selling scheme that gives money away even to the lowest value buyer; therefore $V_i(\alpha) = 0$.

Taking the expectation over all possible values,

$$\mathop{E}_{\theta_i}\{V_i(\theta_i)\} = \int_\alpha^\beta f_i(\theta_i) \int_\alpha^{\theta_i} \overline{w}_i(x)dx d\theta_i.$$

Integrating by parts, the equilibrium *ex ante.* expected payoff of buyer i is

$$\mathop{E}_{\theta_i}\{V_i(\theta_i)\} = \mathop{E}_{\theta_i}\left\{\frac{1 - F_i(\theta_i)}{f_i(\theta_i)}\overline{w}_i(\theta_i)\right\}. \tag{12.3-3}$$

Suppose that the seller's value is θ_0. If the vector of buyer values is θ, the probability that no one is the winner is $1 - \sum_{i=1}^{n} w_i(\theta)$. Then the seller's payoff is

$$u_0(\theta) = \sum_{i=1}^{n} r_i(\theta) + \left(1 - \sum_{i=1}^{n} w_i(\theta)\right)\theta_0.$$

Taking expectations over types, the seller's expected payoff is

$$U_0 = \underset{\theta}{E}\left\{\sum_{i=1}^{n} r_i(\theta) + \left(1 - \sum_{i=1}^{n} w_i(\theta)\right)\theta_0\right\} = \theta_0 + \sum_{i=1}^{n} \underset{\theta}{E}\{r_i(\theta) - w_i(\theta)\}\theta_0$$

$$= \theta_0 + \sum_{i=1}^{n} \underset{\theta_i}{E}\,\underset{\theta_{-i}}{E}\{r_i(\theta) - w_i(\theta)\}\theta_0 = \theta_0 + \sum_{i=1}^{n} \underset{\theta_i}{E}\{\overline{r}_i(\theta) - \overline{w}_i(\theta)\}\theta_0.$$

Also $V(\theta_i) = \theta_i \overline{w}(\theta_i) - \overline{r}(\theta_i)$. Substituting for $\overline{r}_i(\theta_i)$,

$$U_0 = \theta_0 + \sum_{i=1}^{n} \underset{\theta_i}{E}\{(\theta_i - \theta_0)\overline{w}_i(\theta_i) - V_i(\theta_i)\}.$$

Substituting from (12.3-3),

$$U_0 = \theta_0 + \underset{\theta}{E}\left\{\sum_{i=1}^{n}\left[\theta_i - \theta_0 - \frac{1 - F_i(\theta_i)}{f_i(\theta_i)}\right]w_i(\theta)\right\}$$

$$= \theta_0 + \underset{\theta}{E}\left\{\sum_{i=1}^{n}[J_i(\theta_i) - \theta_0]w_i(\theta)\right\}.$$

Note that the equilibrium payoffs to the buyers and mechanism designer depend only on the allocation rule $w(\theta) = (w_1(\theta), \ldots, w_n(\theta))$.

We therefore have the following proposition.

Proposition 12.3-1: Equilibrium Payoffs
The equilibrium payoff to buyer i with value θ_i is $V_i(\theta_i) = \int_\alpha^{\theta_i} \overline{w}_i(x)dx$, and the equilibrium payoff to the seller is $U_0 = \theta_0 + E_\theta\{\sum_{i=1}^{n} w_i(\theta)(J_i(\theta_i) - \theta_0)\}$ where $J_i(\theta_i) = \theta_i - \frac{1 - F_i(\theta_i)}{f_i(\theta_i)}$.

Consider the symmetric case in which each buyer draws from the same distribution $F(\cdot)$. Given the regularity assumption, there is some $\hat{\theta} \in [\alpha, \beta)$ such that $J(\theta_i) \geq \theta_0$, if and only if $\theta_i \geq \hat{\theta}$. We now argue that the selling mechanism is optimal for the mechanism designer if the item is allocated to the buyer with the highest value above $\hat{\theta}$.

Consider the pointwise maximization of $\sum_{i=1}^{n} w_i(\theta)(J(\theta_i) - \theta_0)$. If all values are less than $\hat{\theta}$, the sum is maximized by setting each probability equal to zero. If one or more values exceeds $\hat{\theta}$, the sum is maximized by setting the win probability equal to 1 for the buyer with the highest value. This is precisely the allocation rule if the seller announces a reserve price of $\hat{\theta}$ and sells using either the sealed high-bid or open ascending-bid auctions.

Proposition 12.3-2: Optimal Auction (Myerson)

A single item is available for sale to one of n buyers. The seller's value is θ_0. Buyers' values are identically distributed with c.d.f. $F(\cdot)$, p.d.f. $f(\cdot)$, and $J(\theta) = \theta + (1 - F(\theta))/f(\theta)$ is increasing. If $J(\alpha) \geq \theta_0$, then the optimal selling scheme is a common auction with no reserve price, and if $J(\alpha) < \theta_0$, then the optimal selling scheme is a common auction with reserve price $\hat{\theta}$ satisfying $J(\hat{\theta}) = \theta_0$.

Asymmetric Auctions

Thus far we have focused on symmetric auctions; that is, auctions in which buyers' values are identically distributed. We now consider a two-buyer auction where one bidder is "stronger" (i.e., the distribution of values is more favorable). As we see, the profit-maximizing auction rule offers a subsidy to the weaker bidder. Intuitively, giving him a subsidy makes him bid more aggressively and thus forces the high bidder to bid more aggressively as well.

We consider the special case in which both values are uniformly distributed, but the supports of the distributions are $[0, \beta_1]$ and $[0, \beta_2]$ where $\beta_1 > \beta_2$. Given his more favorable distribution, we refer to buyer 1 as the strong buyer and buyer 2 as the weak buyer. We assume that the seller's value is zero. Given these assumptions,

$$J_i(\theta_i) = 2\theta_i - \beta_i.$$

Appealing to Proposition 12.3-1, it follows that the item should not be sold if both J_1 and J_2 are negative; that is, $\theta_i < \beta_i/2$ $i = 1, 2$. Otherwise it should be sold to the strong buyer, if and only if $J_1(\theta_1) \geq J_2(\theta_2)$; that is, $\theta_1 > \theta_2 + \frac{1}{2}(\beta_1 - \beta_2)$. This outcome can be achieved using an open ascending-bid auction in which the seller sets a reserve price of $\hat{\theta} = \frac{1}{2}\beta_1$ and any bid by the weak bidder is subsidized by an amount $s = \frac{1}{2}(\beta_2 - \beta_1)$. Note that with such a subsidy, bidding the reserve price has a net cost to buyer 2 of

$$\hat{\theta} - s = \frac{1}{2}\beta_1 - \frac{1}{2}(\beta_1 - \beta_2) = \frac{1}{2}\beta_2.$$

Thus buyer 2 will enter as long as $\theta_2 > \frac{1}{2}\beta_2$. Suppose both buyers bid. Given the subsidy, buyer 2's dominant strategy is to remain in the auction until the asking price equals $\theta_2 + s$. If she wins then she pays θ_2. It follows that buyer 1 is a high bidder if $\theta_1 \geq \theta_2 + s$; that is, $\theta_1 \geq \theta_2 + \frac{1}{2}(\beta_1 - \beta_2)$.

Exercises

Exercise 12.3-1: Optimal Reserve Prices

(a) If the seller's value is zero and buyers' values are uniformly distributed on the interval $[0, \beta]$, show that the optimal reserve price $r^* = \beta/2$.
(b) If values are uniformly distributed on the interval $[\alpha, \beta]$ so that $F(\theta) = \frac{\theta - \alpha}{\beta - \alpha}$, establish conditions under which it is profitable to set a reserve price.
(c) Repeat part (b) if the seller has a positive value θ_0.

Exercise 12.3-2: Common Value Auctions
Buyer i's type θ_i is an independent draw from a distribution with support $[\alpha, \beta]$, c.d.f. $F(\cdot)$ and p.d.f. $f(\cdot)$. His value is a symmetric function $v(\theta_1, \ldots, \theta_n)$ of each buyer's type.

(a) Argue as for the private values case that the expected surplus of buyer i is

$$\underset{i}{E}\left\{ \frac{1 - F(\theta_i)}{f(\theta_i)} \frac{\partial v}{\partial \theta_i}(\theta) q_i(\theta) \right\}.$$

(b) Hence show that if the seller's value is zero, the expected profit of the seller is

$$\underset{\theta}{E}\{U_0(\theta)\} = \underset{\theta}{E}\left\{ \sum_{i=1}^{n} q_i(\theta)\left[v(\theta) - \frac{1 - F(\theta_i)}{f(\theta_i)} \frac{\partial v}{\partial \theta_i} \right] \right\}.$$

(c) Hence explain why the sealed high-bid and sealed second-bid auctions are payoff equivalent.
(d) If there are two bidders and each buyer's type is uniformly distributed on $[0,1]$, obtain an expression for expected revenue if the seller only allocates to types above $\hat\theta$. Hence show that revenue is maximized when $\hat\theta = 2/5$.
(e) What is the revenue-maximizing reserve price in this case?

Exercise 12.3-3: Optimal Asymmetric Auctions
Two bidders have values that are continuously distributed on $[0, 1]$. The c.d.f. for bidder i is $F_i(\theta)$. The hazard rate is higher for the second bidder; that is,

$$\frac{f_1(\theta)}{1 - F_1(\theta)} < \frac{f_2(\theta)}{1 - F_2(\theta)}.$$

(a) Show that $F_1(\theta) < F_2(\theta)$, $\theta \in (0, 1)$ so that buyer 1 is the "strong" bidder.
(b) Show that the buyer's payoff from any selling scheme can be expressed simply as a function of the allocation rule $w_i(\theta_1, \theta_2)$, $i = 1, 2$ where these are the probabilities that the item is assigned to bidder j.

(c) Show that expected seller revenue is

$$\int_0^1 \int_0^1 [q_1(\theta)J_1(\theta_1) + q_2(\theta)J_2(\theta_2)] dF(\theta_1) dF_2(\theta_2) \quad \text{where} \quad J_i(v) = v - \frac{1 - F_i(v)}{f_i(v)}.$$

(d) Hence comment on whether the optimal selling scheme is symmetric or whether the playing field should be tilted in favor of the weak player.

Exercise 12.3-4: Finite Types There are two buyers. Values are independent. Each buyer has a value of 1 with probability $1 - p$ and a value of 2 with probability p.

(a) Show that the equilibrium strategy in the sealed first-price auction is for a low-value buyer to bid his value and for a high-value buyer to bid a mixed strategy $\tilde{b}$ with support $[1, 1 + p]$.
(b) Confirm that the payoffs to each buyer type are the same in the sealed first-price and open ascending-price auctions.
(c) For an optimal auction, argue as in the monopoly problem of Section 11.3 that the local downward constraint must be binding. Hence or otherwise characterize an optimal direct revelation scheme.
(d) Show that it is optimal to sell using a sealed second-price auction in which buyers are restricted to making one of two possible bids.

12.4 Designing an Efficient Mechanism

Key ideas: public good, efficient mechanisms, Vickrey-Clarke-Groves mechanism

The discussion of mechanism design has thus far focused primarily on the pursuit of private rather than social goals. A monopolist seeks to maximize profit via indirect price discrimination, or the owner of an objet d'art designs an auction to maximize the expected revenue from its sale. In this section we consider the design of mechanisms to maximize social welfare. We consider a family of problems where the private benefit to agent $i \in \mathfrak{I}$, $B_i(\theta_i, q)$, depends on his type $\theta_i \in \Theta_i = [\alpha_i, \beta_i]$ and an allocation rule $q = (q_1, \ldots, q_n) \in Q$. We assume that for agent i the lowest type is α_i and the highest is β_i and that $B_i(\theta_i, q)$ is an increasing function of θ_i.

Preferences are quasi-linear so if the agent makes a payment of r_i, his payoff is

$$u_i = B_i(\theta_i, q) - r_i.$$

The social surplus is the sum of the private benefits less the cost of the allocation

$$S(\theta, q) = \sum_{i \in \mathfrak{I}} B_i(\theta_i, q) - C(q). \tag{12.4-1}$$

An allocation rule $q^*(\theta)$ is efficient if

$$q^*(\theta) = \arg \underset{q \in Q}{\mathrm{Max}}\{S(\theta, q)\}. \qquad (12.4\text{-}2)$$

We can rewrite social surplus as follows:

$$S(\theta, q) = \sum_{i \in \mathfrak{J}} (B_i(\theta_i, q) - r_i) + \sum_{i \in \mathfrak{J}} r_i - C(q)$$

$$= \sum_{i \in \mathfrak{J}} u_i(\theta_i, q) + \left[\sum_{i \in \mathfrak{J}} r_i - C(q) \right].$$

The expression in brackets is the designer revenue minus the cost of producing the public good. Among the set of efficient mechanisms we seek the one that is least costly (most profitable) for the designer.

One special case that we have already studied is an auction, where a single item is allocated to agent i with probability q_i and the private benefit is $B_i(\theta_i, q) = \theta_i q_i$. The social value of this item is then

$$S(\theta, q) = \sum_{i \in \mathfrak{J}} \theta_i q_i, \quad \text{where} \quad Q = \{q | q \geq 0 \quad \text{and} \quad \sum_{i \in \mathfrak{J}} q_i = 1\}.$$

A second application that we consider in detail later is the efficient production of a public good. A good is "public" if consumption is non-rivalrous. That is, the enjoyment derived from the good by one agent does not reduce the enjoyment of others. For example, suppose that a city authority is considering introducing controls on air pollution that are estimated to cost k. Agent i, $i \in \mathfrak{J}$ places a value θ_i on the cleaner air. For social efficiency the air quality should be improved if and only if the sum of the benefits exceeds the cost. Because consumption is non-rivalrous, the total value of the public good is the sum of individual values $\sum_{i \in \mathfrak{J}} \theta_i$. The cost of the public good is k. Let $q(\theta)$ be the probability that the public good is produced given that agent $i \in \mathfrak{J}$ has a value θ_i. The social surplus is then

$$S(\theta, q(\theta)) = q(\theta) \left(\sum_{i \in \mathfrak{J}} \theta_i - k \right).$$

As we shall see, the key to achieving efficiency is to align private and social incentives. Suppose that $q^*(\theta)$ maximizes social surplus. That is,

$$q^*(\theta) \in \arg \underset{q}{\mathrm{Max}} \left\{ \sum_{j = \mathfrak{J}} B_j(\theta_j, q) - C(q) \right\} \quad \text{for all } \theta \in \Theta.$$

It follows immediately that

$$\theta \in \arg \operatorname*{Max}_{x} \left\{ \sum_{j \in \mathfrak{I}} B_j(\theta_j, q^*(x)) - C(q^*(x)) \right\} \quad \text{for all } x \text{ and } \theta \in \Theta. \quad (12.4\text{-}3)$$

Setting $x_{-i} = \theta_{-i}$

$$\theta_i \in \arg \operatorname*{Max}_{x_i \in \Theta_i} \left\{ \sum_{j \in \mathfrak{I}} B_j(\theta_j, q^*(x_i, \theta_{-i})) - C(q^*(x_i, \theta_{-i})) \right\} \quad \text{for all } \theta \in \Theta$$

It is helpful to focus on agent i and rewrite this as follows:

$$\theta_i \in \arg \operatorname*{Max}_{x_i \in \Theta_i} \{ B_i(\theta_i, q^*(x_i, \theta_{-i})) + t_i(x_i, \theta_{-i}) \quad \text{for all} \quad \theta \in \Theta \quad (12.4\text{-}4)$$

where

$$t_i(x_i, \theta_{-i}) \equiv \sum_{\substack{j \in \mathfrak{I} \\ j \neq i}} B_j(\theta_j, q^*(x_i, \theta_{-i})) - C(q^*(x_i, \theta_{-i})) \} \quad (12.4\text{-}5)$$

Simply changing notation,

$$\theta_i \in \arg \operatorname*{Max}_{x_i \in \Theta_i} \left\{ B_i(\theta_i, q^*(x_i, x_{-i})) + t_i(x_i, x_{-i}) \right\} \quad \text{for all} \quad \theta_i \in \Theta_i, x_{-i} \in \Theta_{-i}$$

where

$$t_i(x_i, x_{-i}) \equiv \sum_{\substack{j \in \mathfrak{I} \\ j \neq i}} B_j(\theta_j, q^*(x_i, x_{-i})) - C(q^*(x_i, x_{-i})) \} . \quad (12.4\text{-}6)$$

With these preliminaries we are ready to consider incentives. Suppose that the designer invites each agent $i \in \mathfrak{I}$ to announce some $x_i \in \Theta_i$. If so the designer will use the allocation rule $q^*(x)$. Once all the agents have made their announcements, agent i, will receive the transfer payment $t_i(x)$. The agent's private benefit is $B_i(\theta_i, q^*(x_i, x_{-i}))$. Therefore his payoff is

$$u_i(\theta_i, x_i, x_{-i}) = B_i(\theta_i, q^*(x_i, x_{-i})) + t_i(x)$$

$$= B_i(\theta_i, q^*(x_i, x_{-i})) + \sum_{\substack{j \in \mathfrak{I} \\ j \neq i}}^{n} B_j(x_j, q^*(x_i, x_{-i})) - C(q^*(x_i, x_{-i})) \} .$$

We have just argued that for all $x_{-i} \in \Theta_{-i}$ the right hand side is maximized at $x_i = \theta_i$. Therefore, regardless of the announcements of the other agents, announcing $x_i = \theta_i$ is optimal for agent i. That is, revealing the truth is a dominant strategy for agent i. Since our argument holds for every agent, it follows that it is a dominant strategy for all agents to announce their private parameters. If all agents play their dominant strategies it follows that allocation is $q^*(\theta)$ so efficiency is achieved.

The equilibrium payoff of agent is therefore

$$U_i(\theta) = u_i(\theta_i, \theta_i, \theta_{-i}) = B_i(\theta_i, q^*(\theta_i, \theta_{-i})) + t_i(\theta_i, \theta_{-i})$$
$$= B_i(\theta_i, q^*(\theta_i, \theta_{-i})) + \sum_{\substack{j \in \mathfrak{J} \\ j \neq i}} B_j(x_j, q^*(\theta_i, \theta_{-i})) - C(q^*(\theta_i, \theta_{-i}))\} = S^*(\theta_i, \theta_{-i})$$

Thus efficiency is achieved by making each agent's equilibrium payoff is equal to the entire social surplus. However there is a cheaper alternative. Maximized social surplus is an increasing function. It follows that the minimum payoff to agent i is $S^*(\alpha_i, \theta_{-i})$. Consider then the alternative transfer $t_i^*(x) = t_i(x) - S_i(\alpha_i, x_{-i})$. Then

$$U_i^*(\theta) = S^*(\theta_i, \theta_{-i}) - S^*(\alpha_i, \theta_{-i}) \qquad (12.4\text{-}7)$$

Note that the participation constraint is now always binding when the agent's i's type is α_i. Thus $t_i^*(x)$ is the smallest transfer that is incentive compatible.

Finally note that the incentive scheme aligns agent i's payoff with his contribution to social surplus over and above the minimum contribution. Following Ostroy we will henceforth refer to this as agent i's marginal contribution to social surplus. Providing a transfer equal to agent i's marginal contribution to social surplus gives agent i the incentive to reveal his type. Our results are summarized in the following proposition.

Proposition 12.4-1: V-C-G Mechanism
The efficient allocation $q^*(\theta)$ can be achieved as a dominant strategy equilibrium if, based on the vector of announced values x, the allocation is $q^*(x)$ and agent i, $i \in \mathfrak{J}$ is given a subsidy (possibly negative)

$$t_i^*(x_i, x_{-i}) = \sum_{\substack{j \in \mathfrak{J} \\ j \neq i}} B(x_j, q^*(x_i, x_{-i})) - S_i^*(\alpha_i, q^*(\alpha_i, x_{-i})).$$

With these payments agent i's equilibrium payoff is his marginal contribution to social surplus $S_i^*(\theta_i, x_{-i}) - S_i^*(\alpha_i, x_{-i})$. Thus the participation constraint is binding for the lowest type.

To complete the analysis we solve for the equilibrium expected payoffs $V_i(\theta_i)$ of each agent. We assume that types are continuously distributed:

$$V_i(\theta_i) = \underset{\theta_{-i}}{E}\left\{S^*(\theta_i, \theta_{-i}) - S^*(\alpha_i, \theta_{-i})\right\}.$$

We have already argued that $V_i(\alpha_i) = 0$. Also,

$$S^*(\theta_i, \theta_{-i}) \equiv S(\theta, q^*(\theta)) = \sum_{j\in\mathfrak{I}} B_j(\theta_j, q^*(\theta)) - C(q^*(\theta)).$$

Appealing to the Envelope Theorem,

$$\frac{\partial}{\partial\theta_i}S(\theta, q^*(\theta)) = \frac{\partial}{\partial\theta_i}B_i(\theta_i, q^*(\theta)).$$

Therefore

$$V_i'(\theta_i) = E\left\{\frac{\partial}{\partial\theta_i}B_i(\theta_i, q^*(\theta))\right\}.$$

We therefore have the following result.

Proposition 12.4-2: Equilibrium Expected Payoff to the Agents Using the V-C-G Mechanism

Suppose types are continuously distributed and the V-C-G mechanism is used to achieve an efficient allocation. Then the minimum equilibrium expected payoff $V_i(\theta_i)$ to agent $i \in I$ satisfies

$$\text{(i) } V_i(\alpha_i) = 0 \quad\text{and}\quad \text{(ii) } V_i'(\theta_i) = \underset{\theta_{-i}}{E}\left\{\frac{\partial B_i}{\partial\theta_i}(\theta_i, q^*(\theta))\right\}.$$

Example: Allocation of a Single Indivisible Good

For the case of a single indivisible item, we already know that the good can be allocated efficiently using a sealed second-price auction. As we now show, the second-price auction is an example of a V-C-G mechanism.

Suppose that there are two agents. The agents' values θ_1, θ_2 are continuously distributed on $\Theta = [0, 1]$. An allocation rule is a probability vector $q^*(\theta)$. For efficiency the good is allocated to the agent with the highest value.[4] Then

$$B_1(\theta_1, q^*(\theta)) = \begin{cases} 0, & \theta_1 < \theta_2 \\ \theta_1, & \theta_1 > \theta_2 \end{cases} \quad\text{and}\quad B_2(\theta_2, q^*(\theta)) = \begin{cases} 0, & \theta_2 < \theta_1 \\ \theta_2, & \theta_2 > \theta_1 \end{cases}.$$

Also, if agent 1 has a value of zero, then maximized surplus is θ_2. Therefore $S_1^*(0, \theta_2) = \theta_2$. Let $r_i(x)$ be the fee charged agent i, that is, $r_i(x) = -t_i^*(x)$.

---

[4] Because values are equal with zero probability we ignore ties in the exposition.

If both agents play their dominant strategies and announce their true types, the fee charged agent 1 is therefore

$$r_1(\theta_1, \theta_2) = S^*(0, \theta_2) - B_2(\theta_2, q^*(\theta)) = \begin{cases} 0, & \theta_1 < \theta_2 \\ \theta_2, & \theta_1 > \theta_2 \end{cases}.$$

Then

$$r_1(x_1, x_2) = \begin{cases} 0, & x_1 < x_2 \\ x_2, & x_1 > x_2 \end{cases}.$$

If the announced values are $x = (x_1, x_2)$, the net payoff to agent 1 is therefore

$$U_1(\theta_1, x) = B_1(\theta_1, q^*(x)) - r_1(x) = \begin{cases} 0, & x_1 < x_2 \\ \theta_1 - x_2, & x_1 > x_2 \end{cases}.$$

Case (i) $x_2 < \theta_1$: Agent 1 always wants to be allocated the item so maximizes his payoff by choosing $x_1 \geq \theta_1$.
Case (ii) $x_2 > \theta_1$: Agent 1 never wants to be allocated the item so maximizes his payoff by choosing $x_1 \leq \theta_1$.

Agent 1 can satisfy both inequalities by choosing $x_1 = \theta_1$. Thus his best response is to announce his true value. Note that the efficient mechanism can be implemented as a second-price auction. If agent 1's announced value is the highest, he wins the item and pays the second announced value.

Efficient Public Good Provision

Agent i, $i \in \mathfrak{I}$, has a private value θ_i for the public good. The cost of the public good is k. Maximized social surplus is then

$$S^*(\theta) = \underset{q}{\text{Max}} \left\{ q \left(\sum_{i \in \mathfrak{I}} \theta_i - k \right) \right\}.$$

If $\sum_{i \in \mathfrak{I}} \alpha_i > k$ it is always optimal to produce the public good. If $\sum_{i \in \mathfrak{I}} \beta_i < k$ it is never optimal to produce the public good. We rule out these uninteresting cases by assuming that

$$\sum_{j \in \mathfrak{I}} \alpha_j < k < \sum_{j \in \mathfrak{I}} \beta_j. \tag{12.4-8}$$

To simplify the exposition it is helpful to define

$$\sigma(\theta_{-i}) \equiv \sum_{\substack{j \in \mathfrak{I} \\ j \neq i}} \theta_j.$$

Then maximized social surplus can be rewritten as follows:

$$S^*(\theta_i, \sigma) = \underset{q}{\text{Max}} \left\{ q \left[\theta_i + \sum_{\substack{j \in \mathfrak{J} \\ j \neq i}} \theta_j - k \right] \right\} = \underset{q}{\text{Max}} \{ q[\theta_i + \sigma - k] \}.$$

The optimal allocation rule is therefore

$$q^*(\theta_i, \sigma) = \arg \underset{q}{\text{Max}} \{ q[\theta_i + \sigma - k] \} = \begin{cases} 0, & \theta_i + \sigma < k \\ 1, & \theta_i + \sigma \geq k \end{cases}.$$

Note that

$$q^* \left(\sum_{\substack{j \in \mathfrak{J} \\ j \neq i}} \theta_j - k \right) = q^*(\theta_i, \sigma)(\sigma - k).$$

Note also that

$$S^*(\alpha_i, \sigma) = q^*(\alpha_i, \sigma)(\alpha_i + \sigma - k).$$

Then the payment by agent i is

$$r_i(\theta_i, \sigma) = -t_i^*(\theta_i, \sigma) = q^*(\alpha_i, \sigma)(\alpha_i + \sigma - k) - q^*(\theta_i, \sigma)(\sigma - k).$$

Case (i): $\theta_i + \sigma < k$ and so $q^*(\theta_i, \sigma) = 0$.

Then $q^*(\alpha_i, \sigma) = 0$ and so $r_i(\theta_i, \sigma) = 0$. Announcing α_i rather than θ_i has no effect on the allocation. Because the benefit is zero (no public good) the participation constraint is binding so no fee can be charged.

Case (ii): $\alpha_i + \sigma \geq k$ and so $q^*(\alpha_i, \theta_{-i}) = 1$.

In this case $q^*(\theta_i, \sigma) = 1$ and so $r_i(\theta) = \alpha_i$. Note that it is efficient to produce the public good even if agent i understates his value. Because the minimum private value is α_i the designer can charge agent i a fee of α_i without violating the participation constraint.

Case (iii): $q^*(\alpha_i, \sigma) = 0$ and $q^*(\theta_i, \sigma) = 1$.

Then $r_i(\theta) = k - \sigma$. Note that $q^*(\alpha_i, \sigma) = 0$ if $\alpha_i + \sigma < k$; that is, if $k - \sigma > \alpha_i$. Thus the fee exceeds α_i. It is efficient to produce the public good if $\theta_i + \sigma \geq k$; that is, $\theta_i \geq k - \sigma$. This outcome is achieved by charging agent i a fee of $k - \sigma$ for the production of the public good.

We have seen that each agent either pays a fee or pays nothing. Unfortunately, as we now show, the sum of these fees is always less than the cost of the public good. Thus the V-C-G mechanism is not feasible unless the designer is willing to accept a loss.

Suppose that it is efficient to produce the public good so that $S_i^*(\theta_i, \theta_{-i}) = S(\theta, q^*(\theta)) > 0$. Then

$$S_i^*(\theta_i, \theta_{-i}) = \text{Max} \left\{ 0, \theta_i + \sum_{\substack{j \in \mathfrak{I} \\ j \neq i}} \theta_j - k \right\} = \theta_i + \sum_{\substack{j \in \mathfrak{I} \\ j \neq i}} \theta_j - k.$$

There are two possibilities. Either (a) $S_i^*(\alpha_i, \theta_{-i}) > 0, i \in \mathfrak{I}$ or (b) $S_i^*(\alpha_i, \theta_{-i}) = 0$ for J of the agents. First consider case (a). Then

$$S_i^*(\alpha_i, \theta_{-i}) = \alpha_i + \sum_{\substack{j \in \mathfrak{I} \\ j \neq i}} \theta_j - k, \quad i \in \mathfrak{I}.$$

Agent i's equilibrium payoff is his marginal contribution to social surplus

$$U_i^e = S_i^*(\theta_i, \theta_{-i}) - S_i^*(\alpha_i, \theta_{-i}).$$

Hence

$$U_i^e = \theta_i - \alpha_i.$$

Summing over agents,

$$\sum_{i \in \mathfrak{I}} U_i^e = \sum_{i \in \mathfrak{I}} \theta_i - \sum_{i \in \mathfrak{I}} \alpha_i.$$

By hypothesis, $\sum_{i \in \mathfrak{I}} \alpha_i < k$. Therefore

$$\sum_{i \in \mathfrak{I}} U_i^e > \sum_{i \in \mathfrak{I}} \theta_i - k = S_i^*(\theta, \theta_{-i}).$$

Thus the total payoff to the agents exceeds the total surplus.

Next consider case (b) in which $S_i^*(\alpha_i, \theta_{-i}) = 0$ for J of the agents. Relabel the agents so that it is the first J for whom this equality holds. Agent i's equilibrium payoff is his marginal contribution to social surplus

$$U_i^e = S^*(\theta_i, \theta_{-i}) - S^*(\alpha_i, \theta_{-i}).$$

Then for the first J agents,

$$U_i^e = S^*(\theta_i, \theta_{-i}), \quad i = 1, \ldots, J.$$

Arguing as earlier, for all the other agents, $U_i^e = \theta_i - \alpha_i$. Summing over agents,

$$\sum_{i \in \mathfrak{I}} U_i^e = J S^*(\theta_i, \theta_{-i}) + \sum_{\substack{i \in \mathfrak{I} \\ i > J}} (\theta_i - \alpha_i) > J S^*(\theta_i, \theta_{-i}). \quad (12.4\text{-}9)$$

Thus in both cases the sum of the payoffs exceeds total surplus. Because the total surplus is divided among the agents and the designer, it follows that the payoff to the designer is negative. We therefore have the following proposition.

Proposition 12.4-3: Designer Payoff with Efficient Public Good Provision Using the V-C-G Mechanism
In the V-C-G mechanism the equilibrium payoff of the designer is strictly less than zero if the public good is produced.

We now illustrate the use of the V-C-G mechanism in a simple case of two agents and two types.

Example: V-C-G Mechanism with Finite Types
There are two agents. Agent i's value of the public good is $\theta_i \in \{0, 1\}$. The cost of the public good is $k < 1$.

Note that it is efficient to produce the public good unless both values are low. Consider agent 1. The maximized social surplus is

$$S^*(\theta_1, \theta_2) = B_1(\theta_1, q^*(\theta)) + [B_1(\theta_1, q^*(\theta)) - C(q^*(\theta))]$$
$$= q^*(\theta)\theta_1 + [q^*(\theta)(\theta_2 - k)].$$

Note that $S^*(0, \theta_2) = \begin{cases} 0, & \theta_2 = 0 \\ 1 - k, & \theta_2 = 1 \end{cases}$.

If both agents reveal their true values, then the fee paid by agent 1 is

$$r_1(\theta) = S^*(0, \theta_2) - q^*(\theta)(\theta_2 - k).$$

These fees are computed in Tables 12.4-1 and 12.4-2 for each cell.

Table 12.4-1. $q^*(\theta)(\theta_2 - k)$

		θ_2	
		0	1
θ_1	0	0	$1 - k$
	1	$-k$	$1 - k$

Table 12.4-2. $r_1(\theta) = S_1^*(0, \theta_2) - q^*(\theta)(\theta_2 - k)$

		θ_2	
		0	1
θ_1	0	0	0
	1	k	0

Table 12.4-3a. $U_1(0, x_1, x_2)$

		x_2	
		Low	High
x_1	*Low*	0	0
	High	–k	0

Table 12.4-3b. $U_1(1, x_1, x_2)$

		x_2	
		Low	High
x_1	*Low*	0	1
	High	1–k	1

The next two tables show agent 1's payoffs when the reports of the two agents are $x = (x_1, x_2)$. In Table 12.4-3a agent 1's value is low and in Table 12.4-3b his value is high.

Note that if agent 1's value is low it is his dominant strategy to announce *low* and if his value is high it is a dominant strategy to announce *high*. Appealing to the symmetry of the model, exactly the same conclusion must hold for agent 2.

Let p be the probability that each agent's value is low. From Table 12.4-2, agent 1 pays k only if his value is high and agent 2's value is low so his expected payment is $p(1 - p)k$. Because the same argument holds for agent 2, the expected revenue of the designer is $2p(1 - p)k$.

The public good is produced unless both have low values. Thus the expected cost of the public good is $(1 - p^2)k$. The expected profit of the designer is therefore

$$E\{U^D\} = 2(1 - p)pk - (1 - p^2)k = -k(1 - p)^2 < 0. \quad (12.4\text{-}10)$$

An important question is how much better might the designer do if he used some mechanism other than the V-C-G mechanism. For this example we will show that the designer can indeed do better. Moreover, for some parameter values the designer's expected profit is positive. Suppose the payment schedule is as shown in Table 12.4-4. Agent 1's payoff for each of his possible values is shown in Tables 12.4-5a and 12.4-5b.

Arguing as earlier, truth-telling is agent 1's strictly dominant strategy as long as $c < 1$. The expected profit of the designer is therefore

$$E\{U^D\} = 2(1 - p)pc - (1 - p^2)k = k(1 - p)\left(\frac{2pc}{k} - 1 - p\right).$$

Table 12.4-4. *Modified Payment Schedule*

		x_2 Low	x_2 High
x_1	*Low*	0	0
	High	c	0

Table 12.4-5a. $U_1(0, x_1, x_2)$

		x_2 Low	x_2 High
x_1	*Low*	0	0
	High	$-c$	0

Table 12.4-5b. $U_1(1, x_1, x_2)$

		x_2 Low	x_2 High
x_1	*Low*	0	1
	High	$1-c$	1

It is easily checked that this is positive for c sufficiently close to 1 as long as $k < \frac{2p}{1+p}$.

This example illustrates a general point. It is possible to raise the designer's payoff above the V-C-G payoff because, in the finite types model, the local downward constraints for types with positive payoffs are not binding. In the limit, as the finite types model approaches a continuous model, the local downward constraints do bind for the V-C-G mechanism. As we see in the next section, the V-C-G mechanism is revenue maximizing.

Exercises

Exercise 12.4-1: Finite Type Example There are two agents. Agent 1's value $\theta_1 \in \{5, 12\}$ and agent 2's value $\theta_2 \in \{0, 10\}$. Values are equally likely. The cost of the public good is 6.

(a) Show that the V-C-G fees are as shown in Table 12.4-6.
(b) Confirm that the V-C-G mechanism incurs a loss if both types are high.
(c) Show that it is possible to lower the net subsidy in some cells and still satisfy incentive compatibility.
(d) Show that the designer can extract an expected profit.

Table 12.4-6. *V-C-G Payments*

$r_1(x_1, x_2)$		x_2		$r_2(x_1, x_2)$		x_2	
		0	10			0	10
x_1	5	0	5	x_1	5	0	1
	12	6	5		12	10	0

Exercise 12.4-2: A V-C-G Mechanism with Continuously Distributed Types
There are two agents each with a value continuously distributed on $[0, 1]$.
The cost of the public good is $k \in (1, 2)$.

(a) Show that in a V-C-G the equilibrium expected payoff of each agent is equal to expected total surplus.
(b) Hence explain why the loss of the mechanism designer is equal to expected total surplus.
(c) Suppose instead that there are three agents and that $k > 2$. Show that again the mechanism designer has a loss. How big is the loss?

Exercise 12.4-3: Implementation of Efficient Public Good Provision by Charging Pivotal Agents Suppose that agent i's value θ_i is a random variable with support $[0, \beta_i]$. Each agent submits a bid x_i. The public good (which costs k to produce) will be produced if $\sum_{i \in \mathfrak{I}} x_i \geq k$. If this condition is not satisfied the agents pay nothing. If $\sum_{i \in \mathfrak{I}} x_i \geq k$ define $\sigma(x_{-i})$ to be the sum of the bids by all the agents other than agent i; that is,

$$\sigma(x_{-i}) = \sum_{\substack{j \in \mathfrak{I} \\ j \neq i}} x_j.$$

If $k - \sigma(x_{-i}) - \beta_i \leq 0 < k - \sigma(x_{-i})$ the public good is produced if and only if agent i's value is sufficiently high. Such an agent is said to be "*pivotal*."
Define

$$p(x_{-i}) = \text{Max}\{0, k - \sigma(x_{-i})\}.$$

If agent i is pivotal and has submitted a bid above this price he pays p_i. Otherwise agent i pays nothing.

(a) Show that if agent i bids his value, his payoff is as depicted in Figure 12.4-1 as a function of σ_i.
(b) Draw the payoff graph (i) with $x_i < \theta_i$ and (ii) with $x_i > \theta_i$.

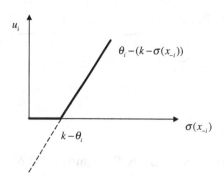

Figure 12.4-1. Implementation of efficient public good provision.

(c) Explain why it is a dominant strategy for agent i to bid his value.

(d) Extend the analysis to the case in which agent i's minimum value is α_i, $i \in \mathfrak{I}$.

Exercise 12.4-4: Total Payments when Pivotal Agents are Charged Suppose that agent i's value θ_i is a random variable with support $[0, \beta_i]$. The implementation scheme is the one described in Exercise 12.4-3.

(a) Show that if all agents are pivotal, the sum of the payments is lower than the cost of the public good.

(b) Show that if all but the first J agents are pivotal, this is again the case.

12.5 Trade-Off between Efficiency and Designer Profit

Key ideas: blocking agent, efficiency and mechanism designer losses, undersupply of the public good to reduce designer loss

In this section we consider general allocation mechanisms when types are independently distributed. Let $B_i(\theta_i, q)$ be the private benefit to agent i, where θ_i $i \in \mathfrak{I}$ is agent i's type. We assume that $\theta_i \in \Theta_i = [\alpha_i, \beta_i]$ and that each agent's value is continuously distributed with $F_i(\cdot)$ and density $f_i(\theta_i)$. For some mechanism m, let $q(\theta)$ be the probability that the public good is produced given the vector of types θ. Social surplus is then

$$S(\theta, q) = \sum_{i \in \mathfrak{I}} B(\theta_i, q) - C(q), \; \theta_i \in \Theta_i.$$

Initially we consider efficient mechanisms. That is, the allocation rule is

$$q^*(\theta) = \underset{q}{\text{Max}}\{S(\theta, q) = \sum_{i \in \mathfrak{I}} B(\theta_i, q) - C(q)\}.$$

Given our assumptions, we will show that the V-C-G mechanism maximizes the expected payoff of the designer. As we have seen the V-C-G mechanism is a loss maker for the designer. Thus efficiency can only be achieved if the mechanism is somehow underwritten. We then examine the trade-off between efficiency and designer profit.

Incentive Compatibility

The analysis of incentive compatibility here is almost identical to the analysis of incentive compatibility in auctions. If all agents announce their true values, the probability that the public good will be produced is $q(\theta)$. From the perspective of agent i, it proves convenient to rewrite this probability as $q_i(\theta_i, \theta_{-i})$. Taking the expectation over the other agents, agents i's payoff is his private value times the probability of the public good provision less the expected cost. That is,

$$u_i(\theta_i, x_i) = \underset{\theta_{-i}}{E}\{B(\theta_i, q_i(x_i, \theta_{-i}))\} - \underset{\theta_{-i}}{E}\{r_i(\theta_i, \theta_{-i})\}$$

$$\equiv \underset{\theta_{-i}}{E}\{B(\theta_i, q_i(x_i, \theta_{-i}))\} - \bar{r}_i(\theta_i).$$

For the mechanism to be incentive compatible, agent i cannot gain by announcing any other value. That is,

$$u_i(\theta_i, x_i) = \underset{\theta_{-i}}{E}\{B(\theta_i, q_i(x_i, \theta_{-i}))\} - \bar{r}_i(x_i), \quad x_i \in \Theta_i$$

$$\leq \underset{\theta_{-i}}{E}\{B(\theta_i, q_i(\theta_i, \theta_{-i}))\}_i - \bar{r}_i(\theta_i), \equiv u_i(\theta_i, \theta_i).$$

Arguing exactly as in the auctions analysis, a necessary and sufficient condition for incentive compatibility is that $E_{\theta_{-i}}\{B_i(\theta_i, q(\theta))\}$ is an increasing function. Let $V_i(\theta_i)$ be the equilibrium payoff. Then

$$V_i(\theta_i) = \underset{\theta_{-i}}{E}\{u_i(\theta_i, x_i)\} = \underset{\theta_{-i}}{E}\{\underset{x_i}{\text{Max}}\{B(\theta_i, q_i(x_i, \theta_{-i})) - \bar{r}_i(x_i)\}\}, \quad x_i \in \Theta_i.$$

Appealing to the Envelope Theorem, the equilibrium marginal payoff is

$$V_i'(\theta_i) = \underset{\theta_{-i}}{E}\left\{\frac{\partial B_i}{\partial \theta_i}(\theta_i, q_i(\theta))\right\}. \tag{12.5-1}$$

For the mechanism to be non-coercive, an agent cannot be worse off if he participates. Thus the participation constraint is $u_i(\alpha_i, \alpha_i) \geq 0, i = 1, \ldots, n$. To maximize revenue the designer minimizes the payoff to the lowest type. Thus $V_i(\alpha_i) = 0, i \in \mathfrak{I}$.

Also, from (12.5-1). $V_i'(\theta_i) = E_{\theta_{-i}}\{\frac{\partial B_i}{\partial \theta_i}(\theta_i, q_i(\theta))\}$. Appealing to Proposition 12.4-2 it follows that agent i's equilibrium payoff in the revenue-maximizing mechanism is exactly the same as in the V-C-G mechanism. We therefore have the following proposition.

Proposition 12.5-1: Revenue-Maximizing Efficient Mechanism If values are independently and continuously distributed, the V-C-G mechanism is a revenue-maximizing efficient mechanism and so the designer has an expected loss.

Recall from the previous section that, in the V-C-G mechanism, agent i's equilibrium payoff is

$$u_i = S^*(\theta_i, \theta_{-i}) - S^*(\alpha_i, \theta_{-i}). \qquad (12.5\text{-}2)$$

Thus agent i's equilibrium payoff is largest (and so designer losses are greatest) when the second term is zero. If it is never efficient to produce the public good when agent i's type is α_i, then agent i can unilaterally block production by announcing that his type is α_i. We call any such agent a blocking agent.

Definition: Blocking Agent Agent i is blocking if it is never efficient to undertake the project when agent i's value is sufficiently low. Formally, for all $\theta_{-i} \in \Theta_{-i}$, $\alpha_i + \sum_{\substack{j \in \mathcal{J} \\ j \neq i}} \theta_j < k$.

It follows from the definition of a blocking agent that $S(\alpha_i, \theta_{-i}) = 0$. Therefore from (12.5-2), the payoff to any blocking agent is equal to the total maximized social surplus. This is summarized in the following proposition.

Proposition 12.5-2: The Cost of an Efficient Mechanism with a Blocking Agent
In the efficient mechanism that maximizes the designer's payoff, any blocking agent has an expected payoff that is equal to the expected social surplus.

Trade-Off between Efficiency and Designer Profit: *The Public Good Case*

We next examine the trade-off between efficiency and designer profit. To simplify the exposition we consider the public goods allocation problem. Then $B_i(\theta_i, q) = \theta_i q$.

In Figure 12.5-1 we depict the trade-off between the profit (or loss) of the mechanism designer and expected social surplus generated by the mechanism. Note that social surplus is maximized at a point below the horizontal axis, reflecting the fact that the expected profit of the designer must be negative.

For any expected social surplus $E_\theta\{S(\theta, q(\theta))\}$ we seek to characterize the mechanism that maximizes designer-expected profit. Let $q(\theta)$ be an incentive-compatible allocation rule. We consider mechanisms with the property that no agent is made strictly worse off by the mechanism. Thus

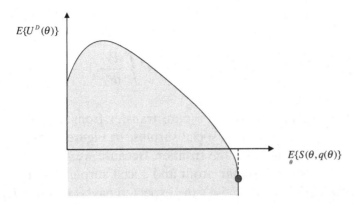

Figure 12.5-1. Trade-off between designer profit and social surplus.

agent i's payment $r_i(\theta)$ is zero if the public good is not produced. The equilibrium payoff to agent i can therefore be written as follows:

$$u_i = (\theta_i - r_i(\theta))q(\theta).$$

As in the analysis of auctions we make the following assumptions.

Assumption 1: Independent Values
Agent $i's$ value is independently distributed with support $[\alpha_i, \beta_i]$, c.d.f. F_i and p.d.f. $f_i(\theta_i)$.

Assumption 2: Regularity Condition

$$J_i(\theta_i) = \theta_i - \frac{1 - F_i(\theta_i)}{f_i(\theta_i)}, \quad i = 1, \ldots, n \text{ is strictly increasing.}$$

Note that it is sufficient that the hazard rate $h_i(\theta_i) = \frac{f_i(\theta_i)}{1-F_i(\theta_i)}$ is increasing. This is the case for a wide range of distributions.

Because it proves helpful later, we define the function

$$J_i(\theta_i, \lambda) \equiv \theta_i - \lambda \left(\frac{1 - F_i(\theta_i)}{f_i(\theta_i)} \right), \quad i = 1, \ldots, n.$$

By Assumption 2 this is strictly increasing in θ_i when $\lambda = 1$. Therefore for all $\lambda \in [0, 1]$ $J_i(\theta_i, \lambda) = (1 - \lambda)\theta_i + \lambda J_i(\theta_i, 1)$ is also increasing. Also, for $\lambda > 0$ $J_i(\theta_i, \lambda) < \theta_i$.

Appealing to (12.5-1),

$$\frac{dV_i}{d\theta_i} = \mathop{E}_{\theta_{-i}}\{q(\theta)\}, \tag{12.5-3}$$

where $E_{\theta_{-i}}\{q(\theta)\}$ must be a non-decreasing function of θ_i.

Integrating by parts, the equilibrium expected payoff of agent i is

$$\underset{\theta_i}{E}\{V_i(\theta_i)\} = \int_{\alpha_i}^{\beta_i} V_i(\theta_i) f_i(\theta_i) d\theta_i = V_i(\alpha_i) + \int_{\alpha_i}^{\beta_i} \frac{dV_i}{d\theta_i}(1 - F_i(\theta_i)) d\theta. \quad (12.5\text{-}4)$$

The payoff to the lowest type is a pure transfer from the designer to the agent so involves no change in social surplus. In Figure 12.5-1 it is a move down the vertical segment of the frontier. Because we seek to characterize the trade-off between designer profit and social surplus we set $V_i(\alpha_i) = 0$. Appealing to (12.5-3) and (12.5-4), the expected payoff of agent i is

$$\underset{\theta}{E}\{u_i(\theta)\} = \int_{\alpha_i}^{\beta_i} \underset{\theta_{-i}}{E}\{q(\theta)(1 - F_i(\theta_i))\} d\theta_i = \underset{\theta}{E}\left\{ q(\theta) \left(\frac{1 - F_i(\theta_i)}{f_i(\theta_i)} \right) \right\}.$$

Also

$$\underset{\theta}{E}\{u_i(\theta)\} = \underset{\theta}{E}\{(\theta_i - r_i(\theta))q(\theta)\}.$$

Combining these results, the expected revenue from agent i is

$$\underset{\theta}{E}\{r_i(\theta)q(\theta)\} = \underset{\theta}{E}\{J_i(\theta_i)q(\theta)\}. \quad (12.5\text{-}5)$$

The expected profit of the designer is the expected revenue from the I. agents less the cost of the public good. Then

$$\underset{\theta}{E}\{U^D\} = \underset{\theta}{E}\left\{ \left(\sum_{i \in \mathfrak{I}} r_i(\theta) - k \right) q(\theta) \right\} = \underset{\theta}{E}\left\{ \left(\sum_{i \in \mathfrak{I}} J_i(\theta_i, 1) - k \right) q(\theta) \right\}.$$

$$(12.5\text{-}6)$$

Expected total surplus is

$$\underset{\theta}{E}\{S(\theta, q(\theta))\} = \underset{\theta}{E}\left\{ \left(\sum_{i \in \mathfrak{I}} \theta_i - k \right) q(\theta) \right\}.$$

To solve for the different points on the social surplus designer profit frontier, we maximize a weighted average[5]

$$W^\lambda = (1 - \lambda) \underset{\theta}{E}\{S(\theta, q(\theta))\} + \lambda \underset{\theta}{E}\{u_0\}$$

---

[5] Because both social surplus and designer profit depend linearly on the allocation rule $q(\theta)$ it is relatively easy to confirm that the feasible set is convex. See Exercise 12.5-3.

Substituting from (12.5-5) and (12.5-6),

$$W = \underset{\theta}{E} \left\{ (1 - \lambda) \left(\sum_{i \in \mathfrak{I}} \theta_i - k \right) + \lambda \left(\sum_{i \in \mathfrak{I}} J_i(\theta_i) \right) - k)) q(\theta) \right\}$$

$$= \underset{\theta}{E} \left\{ \left(\sum_{i \in \mathfrak{I}} J_i(\theta_i, \lambda) \right) - k) q(\theta) \right\}. \qquad (12.5\text{-}7)$$

Pointwise maximization of (12.5-7) yields the solution

$$q(\theta, \lambda) = \begin{cases} 0, & \sum_{i \in \mathfrak{I}} J_i(\theta_i, \lambda) < k \\ 1, & \sum_{i \in \mathfrak{I}} J_i(\theta_i, \lambda) \geq k \end{cases}.$$

Given our assumptions, $q(\theta, \lambda)$ is an increasing function. Thus the requirements of incentive compatibility are satisfied. The solution for the two-agent case is depicted in Figure 12.5-2.

The shaded area indicates those values for which it is efficient to produce the public good. This is the solution when $\lambda = 0$. As the weight on designer profit increases, the boundary curve shifts to the right. This is intuitive. To extract more revenue the designer must charge high-value agents more. But he can only do so by making the alternative of announcing a low value less attractive. In the public goods case the designer can only do this by not supplying the public good.

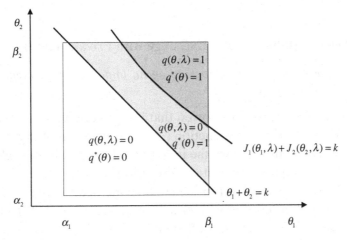

Figure 12.5-2. Undersupply of the public good to reduce designer loss.

Exercises

Exercise 12.5-1: Blocking Agents There are two agents. Agent i's value of the public good is continuously distributed on the interval $\Theta_i = [\alpha_i, \beta_i]$. The cost of the public good is k.

(a) If $\Theta_i = [0, 1]$ and the cost of the public good $k \in (1, 2)$, show that for efficient public good provision the loss to the mechanism designer is at least equal to expected social surplus.
(b) What if $\Theta_1 = [1, 2]$, $\Theta_2 = [2, 3]$, and $k \in (4, 5)$?
(c) What would happen instead if there are three agents, all with values on the interval $[0, 1]$ and $k \in (2, 3)$?

Exercise 12.5-2: Symmetric Uniform Distribution of Values Suppose that each agent's value is uniformly distributed on the interval $[\alpha, \beta]$. For each $\lambda \in [0, 1]$, solve for the allocation rule $\pi(\theta)$ that maximizes

$$W^\lambda = (1 - \lambda) \underset{\theta}{E}\{S(\theta, q(\theta))\} + \lambda \underset{\theta}{E}\{u_0\}.$$

Exercise 12.5-3: Convexity of the Social Choice Set Let m^0 and m^1 be incentive-compatible non-coercive mechanisms that yield a zero payoff to the lowest type. Associated with each are allocation rules $q^0(\theta)$, $q^1(\theta)$.

(a) Show that the mechanism $m^\mu = (1 - \mu)m^0 + \mu m^1$, $0 < \mu < 1$ is incentive compatible and non-coercive and yields agent i an expected payoff of $E_\theta\{u_i^\mu\} = (1 - \mu) E_\theta\{u_i^0\} + \mu E_\theta\{u_i^1\}$, $i = 1, \ldots, n$.
(b) Show also that expected social surplus is

$$\underset{\theta}{E}\{S(\theta, q^\mu(\theta))\} = (1 - \mu) \underset{\theta}{E}\{S(\theta, q^0(\theta))\} + \mu \underset{\theta}{E}\{S(\theta, q^1(\theta))\}.$$

(c) Hence or otherwise show that $E_\theta\{u_0^\mu\} = (1 - \mu) E_\theta\{u_0^0\} + \mu E_\theta\{u_0^1\}$.
(d) Use these results to prove that the set depicted in Figure 12.5-1 is convex.

12.6 Efficient Production and Exchange with Private Values and Costs

Key ideas: value as cost saving, blocking agent, impossibility theorem, profitable mechanisms with two or more buyers

In the analysis of auctions we showed that if there are n buyers and a single seller with a known cost of production (or use value), it is always possible to design a mechanism that assigns the item to the buyer with the highest value (i.e., is efficient) and also generates a profit to the auction designer. Indeed there are many such mechanisms, including the sealed first- and second-price auctions with a reserve price equal to the seller's cost. But there is an important caveat. The auction is efficient because the seller's cost is public information. As we see, we can apply the results of the public goods model to show that there may exist no such self-supporting mechanism when it is necessary to elicit the seller's value as well.

We begin by examining the case in which a commodity is to be produced by a single seller and traded to a single buyer. Agent 1, the buyer, has a value $\theta_1 \in \Theta_1 = [\alpha_1, \beta_1]$. Agent 2, the seller, can produce the commodity at a cost of $c_2 \in C = [\gamma, \kappa]$. We assume that θ_1 and c_2 are independently and continuously distributed. Both value and cost are private information.

The social gain to the exchange is $\theta_1 - c_2$. Because both value and cost are private information, just as in the case of the public good, it is necessary to elicit a linear combination of two private signals. It proves helpful to focus not on the seller's cost but on the difference between the seller's cost and the maximum possible cost $\theta_2 = \kappa - c_2$. We refer to this difference as the cost savings.

Define Θ_2 to be the set of possible cost savings; that is, $\Theta_2 = [\alpha_2, \beta_2] = [0, \kappa - \gamma]$. We can then write maximized social surplus as follows:

$$S^* = \text{Max}\{0, \theta_1 - c_2\} = \text{Max}\{0, \theta_1 - (\kappa - \theta_2)\}$$
$$= \text{Max}\{0, \theta_1 + \theta_2 - \kappa\}, \theta_1 \in \Theta_1, \theta_2 \in \Theta_2.$$

Note that by the change of variables, we have reduced the problem to a two-agent public goods problem.

Recall that a blocking agent is one for whom it is never efficient to produce if an agent's value is sufficiently low. Thus the buyer is blocking if $\alpha_1 + \theta_2 < \kappa$; that is, if

$$\alpha_1 \leq \kappa - \theta_2 = c_2, \forall c_2 \in C.$$

Similarly the seller is blocking if $\theta_1 + \alpha_2 \leq \kappa$. Because $\alpha_2 = 0$, the seller is blocking if

$$\theta_1 \leq \kappa, \forall \theta_1 \in \Theta_1.$$

The following result is then a direct implication of Proposition 12.5-2.

Proposition 12.6-1: Trade between Blocking Agents
If the maximum cost exceeds the maximum value (seller is blocking) and the minimum value is less than the minimum cost (buyer is blocking), then the minimum expected loss of the mechanism designer is equal to the expected gains from trade.

More generally, the following proposition is an immediate implication of Proposition 12.5-1.

Proposition 12.6-2: Myerson-Satterthwaite Impossibility Theorem
Suppose that there is a single buyer and seller. The buyer's value is continuously distributed on the interval $\Theta_1 = [\alpha_1, \beta_1]$, and the seller's cost is continuously distributed on the interval $C = [\gamma, \kappa]$. Suppose also that there are

gains from trade for some but not all realizations ($\alpha_1 < \kappa$). If the cost and value are private and independently distributed, then for efficient exchange between a single buyer and seller the mechanism designer must incur an expected loss.

If there are two or more buyers there is a further generalization of this result. Let the set of buyers be $\mathfrak{I} = \{1, \dots, I\}$ and let agent $I+1$ be the seller. Suppose that the value of each buyer and the cost of the seller all have the same support $[\alpha, \beta]$. Consider the V-C-G mechanism. Maximized total surplus is

$$S^*(\theta, c) = \text{Max}_q \left\{ \sum_{i \in \mathfrak{I}} q_i(\theta_i - c) | 0 \le \sum_{i \in \mathfrak{I}} q_i \le 1 \right\}.$$

Maximized total surplus when the seller has his worst type ($c = \beta$) is

$$S^*(\theta, \beta)) = \text{Max}_q \left\{ \sum_{i \in \mathfrak{I}} q_i(\theta_i - \beta) | 0 \le \sum_{i \in \mathfrak{I}} q_i \le 1 \right\}.$$

By hypothesis $\theta_i \le \beta$ so $S^*(\theta, \beta)) = 0$. The seller is therefore a blocking agent.

In the V-C-G mechanism each agent's equilibrium payoff is the marginal contribution to social surplus. Hence the seller's equilibrium payoff is

$$u_{I+1}(\theta, c) = S^*(\theta, c) - S^*(\theta, \beta) = S^*(\theta, c).$$

Because the seller's payoff is equal to total surplus, the sum of all the payoffs must exceed total surplus so again the V-C-G mechanism generates a loss for the designer.

To complete the proof it must be shown that, for any efficient incentive-compatible mechanism, the expected payoff of each buyer and the seller cannot exceed the equilibrium V-C-G payoffs. The proof for each of the buyers is almost identical to that for the agents in the public goods model. A very similar argument holds for the seller as well. Our result is summarized as follows.

Proposition 12.6-3: Impossibility Theorem with Many Buyers
Suppose that each buyer's value and the seller's cost are all continuously distributed on the interval $\Theta = [\alpha, \beta]$. If the cost and value are private and independently distributed, then for efficient exchange between n buyers and a single seller, seller the mechanism designer must incur an expected loss.

Note that the seller is blocking only because his maximum cost is equal to (or higher than) the maximum value of all the buyers. Henceforth we assume that the maximum cost is lower than the maximum buyer value so that the seller is not blocking.

Proposition 12.6-4: Profitable Efficient Mechanism Design with Unknown Values and Cost

Suppose that each buyer's value is independently and continuously distributed on the interval $\Theta = [\alpha, \beta]$. Also the seller's cost is independently and continuously distributed on $C = [\gamma, \kappa]$ where $\kappa < \beta$. If (i) $\kappa - \gamma$ is sufficiently small or (ii) the number of buyers is sufficiently large, then the V-C-G mechanism is profitable.

To see that (i) is true consider the two-buyer case. The V-C-G payoffs are

$$u_1 = S^*(\theta_1, \theta_2, c) - S^*(\alpha, \theta_2, c), \quad u_2 = S^*(\theta_1, \theta_2, c) - S^*(\theta_1, \alpha, c), \quad \text{and}$$
$$u_3 = S^*(\theta_1, \theta_2, c) - S^*(\theta_1, \theta_2, \kappa).$$

Then the designer payoff is

$$u^D(\theta_1, \theta_2, c) = S^*(\theta_1, \theta_2, c) - \sum_{i=1}^{3} u_i$$
$$= S^*(\alpha, \theta_2, c) + S^*(\theta_1, \alpha, c) + S^*(\theta_1, \theta_2, \kappa) - 2S^*(\theta_1, \theta_2, c).$$
$$(12.6\text{-}1)$$

We solve for the designer's profit when $\theta_1 \geq \theta_2$. To do so we consider each of the six regions in Figure 12.6-1.

In each region, all the terms on the right-hand side of equation (12.6-1) are given in the first four rows of Table 12.6-1. The bottom row shows the designer payoff in each region.

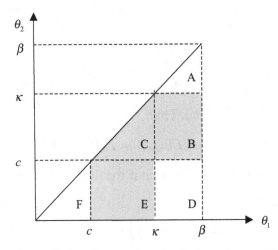

Figure 12.6-1. Computing the designer's payoff.

Table 12.6-1. *Computing the Designer's Payoff*

	A	B	C	D	E	F
$S^*(\alpha, \theta_2, c)$	$\theta_2 - c$	$\theta_2 - c$	$\theta_2 - c$	0	0	0
$S^*(\theta_1, \alpha, c)$	$\theta_1 - c$	$\theta_1 - c$	$\theta_1 - c$	$\theta_1 - c$	$\theta_1 - c$	0
$S^*(\theta_1, \theta_2, \kappa)$	$\theta_1 - \kappa$	$\theta_1 - \kappa$	0	$\theta_1 - \kappa$	0	0
$S^*(\theta_1, \theta_2, c)$	$\theta_1 - c$	$\theta_1 - c$	$\theta_1 - c$	$\theta_1 - c$	$\theta_1 - c$	0
u^D	$\theta_2 - \kappa$	$-(\kappa - \theta_2)$	$-(\theta_1 - \theta_2)$	$-(\kappa - c)$	$-(\theta_1 - c)$	0

Note that as $c \to \kappa$ the three shaded regions vanish. The only remaining regions are regions A, D, and F. In region F the designer's payoff is zero, and in region D the negative payoff approaches zero in the limit. However, in region A the payoff of the designer is strictly positive with probability 1. Thus if $\kappa - c$ is sufficiently small, then the expected payoff of the designer is positive.

There is a simple intuition for this result. As uncertainty about the seller's cost is reduced toward zero, the problem approximates more closely a standard auction problem with known cost.

Next consider the effect of increasing the number of buyers. Let $\theta_{(1)}$ and $\theta_{(2)}$ be the highest and second highest values. If $S^*(\theta, c) = 0$ then all payoffs are zero so the designer's profit is zero. Suppose instead that $S^*(\theta, c) > 0$. Because only the buyer with the highest value has a positive payoff in the V-C-G mechanism, the sum of the buyers' payoffs is

$$\sum_{i=1}^{I} u_i = \text{Min}\{\theta_{(1)} - \theta_{(2)}, \ \theta_{(1)} - c\}.$$

By hypothesis the maximum cost is below the maximum value. Therefore, as the number of buyers increases, the probability that the second highest value, $\theta_{(2)} > c$ approaches 1. Also $E\{\theta_{(1)} - \theta_{(2)}\} \to 0$. Thus

$$E\left\{\sum_{i=1}^{I} u_i\right\} \to 0.$$

Also $u_{I+1} = S^*(\theta, c) - S^*(\theta, k)$. Then

$$E\{S^*(\theta, c)\} - E\{u_{I+1}\} = E\{S^*(\theta, k)\} > 0.$$

Combining these results it follows that if the number of buyers is sufficiently large then

$$E\{S^*(\theta, c)\} - E\left\{\sum_{i=1}^{I+1} u_i\right\} > 0.$$

Designer Profit with Two-Sided Competition

Finally we consider designer profit where there is more than one seller and more than one buyer. Suppose that a government agency owns some land filled with toxic waste. It would like to restore the land for a housing development and then sell the restored land to the housing developer who can add the most value to it. There are m firms in the business of land restoration. Let c_j be firm j's cost and let c_L be the lowest cost. Similarly there are n firms who wish to build houses on the restored land. Let θ_i be the value of the property for housing developer i and let θ_H be the highest value. Then, for efficiency, the land will be restored by the lowest cost detoxification firm and houses will be built by the highest value developer, if and only if $\theta_H - c_L \geq 0$.

As a benchmark we focus on the case in which all values and costs are drawn from the same distribution with support $[\alpha, \beta]$ and c.d.f. $F \in \mathbb{C}^1$. Let $G(\cdot)$ be the c.d.f. of the lowest cost and let $H(\cdot)$ be the c.d.f. of the highest value. Then

$$G = (1 - (1 - F)^m) \quad \text{and} \quad H = F^n.$$

Maximized expected total surplus is therefore

$$E\{S^*(n, m)\} = \int_\alpha^\beta dG \int_0^\theta \text{Max}\{0, \theta_H - c_L)\}dH = \int_\alpha^\beta dG(c_L)I(c_L),$$

where

$$I(x) = \int_x^\beta (\theta - x)dH(\theta).$$

Note that $I(\beta) = 0$ and that $I'(c) = -(1 - H(c))$. Integrating by parts,

$$S^*(n, m) = \int_\alpha^\beta G(c_I)I'(c_L)dc_L = \int_\alpha^\beta G(x)(1 - H(x))dx$$

$$= \int_\alpha^\beta (1 - (1 - F)^m)(1 - F^n)dx. \tag{12.6-2}$$

Buyer i's expected marginal contribution to social surplus is

$$E\{u_i\} = E\{S^*(n, m)\} - E\{S^*(n - 1, m)\}. \tag{12.6-3}$$

Similarly seller j's marginal contribution to social surplus is

$$E\{u_j^S\} = E\{S^*(n, m)\} - E\{S^*(n, m - 1)\}. \tag{12.6-4}$$

The expected profit of the designer is

$$E\{u_0\} = E\{S^*(n, m)\} - \sum_{i=1}^{n} E\{u_i^B\} - \sum_{j=1}^{m} E\{u_j^S\}.$$

Substituting from (12.6-3) and (12.6-4),

$$E\{u_0\} = nE\{S^*(n-1, m)\} + mE\{S^*(n, m-1)\} - (n+m-1)E\{S^*(n, m)\}$$

$$= \int_{\alpha}^{\beta} I(n, m, F(x), 1 - F(x))dx,$$

where

$$I(n, m, F, 1 - F) \equiv n(1 - (1 - F)^m)(1 - F^{n-1})$$
$$+ m(1 - (1 - F)^{m-1}(1 - F^n) - (n + m - 1)(1 - (1 - F)^m)(1 - F^n)$$

Consider the two-buyer, two-seller case. Define $E \equiv 1 - F$.

$$I(2, 2, F, E) \equiv 2(1 - E^2)(1 - F) + 2(1 - E)(1 - F^2) - 3(1 - E^2)(1 - F^2)$$
$$= 2[1 - E^2 - F + E^2 F] + 2[1 - E - F^2 - EF^2] - 3 + 3E^2$$
$$+ 3F^2 - 3E^2 F^2$$
$$= 1 + (E^2 + F^2) - 2(E + F) + 2EF(E + F) - 3E^2 F^2.$$

Since $E + F = 1$, it follows that

$$I(2, 2, F, E) \equiv -3EF^2 = -3(1 - F)^2 F^2 < 0, \forall F \in (0, 1).$$

We therefore have the following result.

Proposition 12.6-5: Designer Loss with Two Buyers and Two Sellers
Suppose that each buyer's value and each seller's cost are independently and continuously distributed on the interval $\Theta = [\alpha, \beta]$ with c.d.f. F. All values and costs are private. If there are two buyers and two sellers, then the efficient exchange mechanism yields an expected loss to the designer.

Next consider the three-buyer, three-seller case. Define $E \equiv 1 - F$. Then

$$I(3, 3, F, E) = 3(1 - E^3)(1 - F^2) + 3(1 - E^2)(1 - F^3) - 5(1 - E^3)(1 - F^3)$$
$$= 3[1 - E^3 - F^2 + E^3 F^2] + 3[1 - E^2 - F^3 + E^2 F^3] - 5$$
$$- 5E^3 - 5F^2 - 5E^3 F^3$$
$$= [1 - 3(E^2 + F^2) + 2(E^3 + F^3)] + 3E^2 F^2(E + F) - 5E^3 F^3$$
$$= [1 - 3(E^2 + F^2) + 2(E + F)(E^2 - EF + F^2)]$$
$$+ 3E^2 F^2(E + F) - 5E^3 F^3$$
$$= 1 - E^2 - 2EF - F^2 + 3E^2 F^2 - 5E^3 F^3, \quad \text{since } E + F = 1$$
$$= 3E^2 F^2 - 5E^3 F^3$$
$$= (1 - F)^2 F^2[3 - 5(1 - F)F].$$

Since $F(1 - F)$ takes on its maximum at $F = \frac{1}{2}$, $I(3, 3, F, 1 - F) > 0$, $\forall F \in (0, 1)$. We have therefore proved the following result.

Proposition 12.6-6: Designer Profit with Three Buyers and Three Sellers
Suppose that each buyer's value and each seller's cost are independently and continuously distributed on the interval $\Theta = [\alpha, \beta]$ with c.d.f. F. All values and costs are private. If there are three buyers and three sellers, then the efficient exchange mechanism yields an expected profit to the designer.

For a larger number of buyers and sellers, the analysis is a bit more messy. However, the function $I(n, m, F, 1 - F)$ expected payoff of the designer is easy to compute numerically. It is left as a computational exercise to show that with at least three buyers and three sellers, the V-C-G mechanism generates a positive expected profit for the designer.

Exercises

Exercise 12.6-1: Blocking Agents with a Single Buyer and Seller Suppose that the buyer's value is distributed on $[3, 5]$ and the seller's cost is distributed on $[4, 6]$.

(a) Convert the problem to a public goods problem and show that both agents are blocking.
(b) If both cost and value are uniformly distributed, what is the minimized expected loss of the designer in an efficient exchange mechanism?

Exercise 12.6-2: Designer Profit in the Uniform Case Suppose that there are two buyers. Each has a value that is independently and uniformly distributed on $[0, 1]$. The seller's cost is independently and uniformly distributed on $[0, \kappa]$, where $\kappa < 1$. Thus the joint density function is $f(\theta_1, \theta_2, c) = 1/k$. Consider the least costly V-C-G mechanism.

(a) Explain why the seller's equilibrium payoff satisfies $u_3 = S(\theta, c) - S(\theta, \kappa)$. Explain also why the social surplus $S(\theta, \kappa)$ is as depicted in Figure 12.6-2a. Take the expectation over buyer values and hence show that

$$\underset{\theta}{E}\{u_3(\theta, c)\} = \underset{\theta}{E}\{S(\theta, c)\} - \frac{1}{3}(2 - 3\kappa + \kappa^3).$$

(b) If the seller's cost is c, explain why the sum of the equilibrium payoffs of the two buyers as depicted in Figure 12.6-2b. Hence show that

$$\underset{\theta}{E}\{u_1(\theta, c) + u_2(\theta, c)\} = \frac{1}{3}(1 - c)^2(1 + 2c).$$

HINT: Consider Figure 12.6-2. Below the 45° line, $u_1(\theta, c) + u_2(\theta, c) = u_1(\theta, c)$ Integrate over the area under the 45° line to solve for $E_\theta\{u_1(\theta, c)\}$. Then appeal to symmetry to obtain $E_\theta\{u_1(\theta, c) + u_2(\theta, c)\}$.

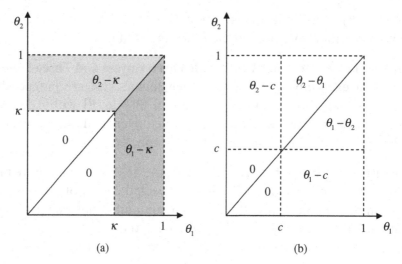

Figure 12.6-2. (a) $u_3(\theta_1, \theta_2, \kappa)$. (b) $u_1(\theta_1, \theta_2, c) + u_2(\theta_1, \theta_2, c)$.

(c) Hence show that the sum of the expected buyer payoffs is

$$E_{\theta,c}\{u_1(\theta, c) + u_2(\theta, c)\} = \frac{1}{3}\left(1 - \kappa^2 + \frac{1}{2}\kappa^3\right).$$

From your answers to parts (a) and (c), show that designer expected profit is positive if $\kappa = \frac{1}{3}$ and solve numerically for the maximum value of κ for which expected profit is positive.

Exercise 12.6-3: Two-Sided Competition

(a) For the uniform case, use a spreadsheet to compute expected designer profit and hence establish numerically that expected designer profit is negative if $m, n \geq 2$ and $n + m \leq 5$.

(b) Establish numerically that expected designer profit is positive if $m, n \geq 2$ and $m + n \geq 6$.

References and Selected Historical Reading

Chattergee, K. and Samuelson, W. "Bargaining under Incomplete Information." *Operations Research* **31**: 835–51.

Clarke, E. (1971). "Multipart Pricing of Public Goods." *Public Choice* **8**: 19–33.

Groves, T. (1973). "Incentives in Teams." *Econometrica* **41**: 617–31.

Klemperer, P. (2002). "What Really Matters in Auction Design." *Journal of Economic Perspectives* **16**: 169–89.

Maskin, E. and Riley, J. (2000). "Asymmetric Auctions." *Review of Economic Studies* **67**: 413–38.

Milgrom, P. and Weber, R. (1982). "A Theory of Auctions and Competitive Bidding." *Econometrica* **50**: 1089–1122.

McAfee, P. and McMillan, J. (1987). "Auctions and Bidding." *Journal of Economic Literature* **25**: 699–738.

Myerson, R. (1981). "Optimal Auction Design." *Mathematics of Operations Research* **6**: 58–73.

Myerson, R. and Satterthwaite, M. (1983). "Efficient Mechanisms for Bilateral Trading." *Journal of Economic Theory* **28**: 265–81.

Riley, J. G. and Samuelson, W. F. (1981). "Optimal Auctions." *American Economic Review* **71**: 381–92.

Vickrey, W. (1961). "Counterspeculation, Auctions and Competitive Sealed Tenders." *Journal of Finance* **16**: 8–37.

Wilson, R.,(1969). "Competitive Bidding with Disparate Information." *Management Science*, **15**: 446–48.

Appendix A

Mathematical Foundations

A.1 Is It Really True?

Key ideas: direct proof, proof by induction, proving the contrapositive, proof by contradiction

The whole point of building a mathematical model is to be able to use the power of mathematical analysis to draw conclusions about economic phenomena. Thus it is essential to have on hand a good toolkit of mathematical propositions. For example, suppose that you wish to analyze the choice of a profit-maximizing firm that sells in a market where the price of the commodity q is p. For any quantity of price pair (q, p), there is some profit $f(q, p)$. To work with this model it is useful to have in the toolkit a clear notion of the rate of change in the function as output changes. Two possible functions are depicted in Figure A.1-1.

Clearly it is easier to characterize the profit-maximizing output in the first case, because the top of the profit hill is the unique point where the slope is zero. In the second case there are lots of outputs where the slope is zero but not all of them yield the profit maximum. Thus, to simplify the model,

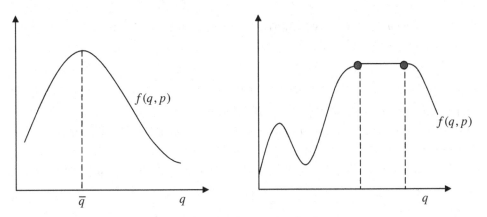

Figure A.1-1. The profit of a firm.

491

it is useful to seek plausible conditions under which the profit curve has a shape that is simple to analyze. This is relatively easy if the firm is choosing a single output. But what if q represents a vector of outputs of different commodities? Taking the example a little further, suppose that $q(p)$ is a solution to the maximization problem for each output price p. To analyze the firm's behavior it is simpler if this output varies smoothly with the output price. But is this a reasonable assumption?

The key to answering such questions might be to put together a toolkit of mathematical methods and results that is large enough to deal with all the basics of economic modeling. However, although this approach works quite well at an introductory level, it is ultimately inadequate for someone wanting a deeper understanding of economic models. Without a clear appreciation of why results hold and how techniques work, it is extremely difficult to decide how to approach a problem. For this reason understanding the derivation of results and how techniques are developed is very important.

How does one go about proving some proposition; that is, demonstrate convincingly that the proposition is true? First there must be some common set of principles or results that are sufficiently familiar that they do not need reiterating or re-proving. Mathematicians then employ several approaches. We discuss each in turn.

Direct Proof

The straightforward approach is built on other accepted propositions. Consider, for example the present value of an investment yielding a constant payment of 1 dollar in each of n periods. With an interest rate r, the present value – discounted to the time of the first payment – is

$$V_n = 1 + \frac{1}{1+r} + \cdots + \left(\frac{1}{1+r}\right)^{n-1}.$$

This is an example of a geometric sum $S_n = 1 + a + a^2 + \cdots + a^{n-1}$. The well-known formula for this sum is

$$S_n = \frac{1 - a^n}{1 - a}, a \neq 1.$$

The direct proof is short. We note that $a S_n = a(1 + a + a^2 + \cdots + a^{n-1})$ and hence, $1 + a S_n = (1 + a + a^2 + \cdots + a^{n-1}) + a^n$. But the term in the parentheses is S_n. Therefore

$S_n(1 - a) = 1 - a^n$. As long as $a \neq 1$, we can divide by $1 - a$ to obtain

$$S_n = \frac{1 - a^n}{1 - a}.$$

Quod erat demonstrandum (Q.E.D.) – Translation: This is what was to be demonstrated.

Note that even this simple proof assumes a common understanding of the rules of algebra.

Proof by Induction

Proof by induction is often helpful if the goal is to establish that some proposition P_n is true for all integers $n = 1, 2, \ldots$. The first step is to establish that the proposition is true for $n = 1$. The second step is to show that if the proposition holds for all integers up to k, it must hold for $n = k + 1$. If both can be proved then we are finished because if P_1 is true, then by the second step P_2 is true. Then, by the second step, because P_1 and P_2 are both true, so is P_3. Because this argument can be repeated over and over again it follows that for all n P_n is true.

Consider the following example. Let S_n be the sum of the first n integers; that is, $S_n = 1 + \cdots + n$. Note that the sequence S_1, S_2, S_3, S_4, S_5 is 1, 3, 6, 10, 15. Someone might note that the formula $S_n = \frac{1}{2}n(n + 1)$ fits for all five elements of this sequence and conjecture (correctly) that the formula must hold for all n. To prove this by induction we begin by supposing that the conjecture holds for all integers up to some integer k and seek to show that it must then hold for the integer $k+1$.

For our example, suppose $S_k = \frac{1}{2}k(k + 1)$. We wish to show that $S_k + (k + 1) = \frac{1}{2}(k + 1)(k + 2)$.

Substituting for S_k,

$$S_k + (k + 1) = \tfrac{1}{2}k(k + 1) + (k + 1) = (\tfrac{1}{2}k + 1)(k + 1) = \tfrac{1}{2}(k + 1)(k + 2).$$

Thus if the proposition is true for $n = k$ it is true for $n = k + 1$. We have already seen that the conjecture is true for $n = 1$; thus it is true for all n.

Proof of the Contrapositive

Suppose we would like to prove that if the statement A is true, then the statement B must also be true. That is, any event in which A is true is also an event in which B is true.[1]

Consider the three Venn diagrams in Figure A.1-2. In each case the box is the set of all possible events. In the left diagram the heavily shaded region is the set of events in which A is true. The set of events in which A is false is the set $\sim A$.

Similarly in the middle diagram, the lightly shaded region is the set of events in which B is true. The two sets are superimposed in the right-hand diagram. As drawn, A is a subset of B. Therefore, if A is true, then B must

---

[1] Equivalently, condition B is a necessary condition for condition A.

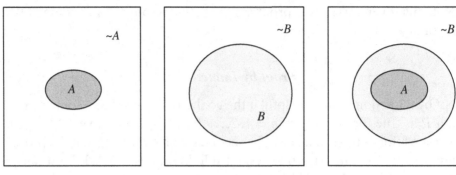

Figure A.1-2. The contrapositive.

be true as well. Thus the goal is to prove that A is a subset of B ($A \subset B$). Note that if this is true, it is also true that any event not in B is also not in A ($\sim B \subset \sim A$). That is, the two statements are equivalent:

$$A \subset B \quad \text{if and only if} \quad \sim B \subset \sim A.$$

Thus instead of attempting a direct proof that A implies B, we can appeal to the contrapositive and attempt to prove that if B is false, then A must also be false.

A good example of this approach can be found in Section A.5 where we show how to construct a proof of the following statement: "If the smooth function f takes on a maximum at $\overline{x}$, then the slope is zero at $\overline{x}$."

The contrapositive of this statement is that if the slope of a function is not zero at $\overline{x}$, then the function does not take on a maximum at $\overline{x}$. The proof then follows from an examination of the formal definition of the "slope" of a function.

Proof by Contradiction

Last but by no means least, we often prove that a statement is true by deriving the implications that follow if the statement is false. Suppose, by a combination of luck and cunning, we find an implication that is impossible. Then we know that the statement cannot be false and so it must be true!

To illustrate, we prove that the sum of two odd numbers must be even. Any even number can be written as $2n$ where n is an integer, and so any odd number can be written as $2n+1$. Suppose that the statement is false so that for some integers, a, b, c

$$(2a + 1) + (2b + 1) = 2c + 1. \tag{A.1-1}$$

Rearranging this equation,

$$2(c - a - b) = 1.$$

The number $2(c - a - b)$ is divisible by 2 so it cannot be equal to 1. Hence equation (A.1-1) leads to a contradiction. Thus there cannot be any such numbers a, b, c and so the statement must be true.

A.2 Mappings of a Single Variable[2]

Key ideas: neighborhood, limit, continuous function, set-valued mappings

A real number is a point in the infinite interval $\mathbb{R} = (-\infty, \infty)$. Throughout this book we consider sets of real numbers. Typically we consider sets of points that are intervals; for example,

$$X = \{x | x \in \mathbb{R}, a \le x \le b\}.$$

Any set such as X that contains its endpoints is known as a closed interval. The mathematical shorthand for such an interval is $[a, b]$. Similarly we define an open interval as $(a, b) = \{x | x \in \mathbb{R}, \ a < x < b\}$.

A function maps each of the points in some set X into a unique point in $(-\infty, \infty)$. We write the output of this mapping as $f(x)$. The set X over which the function is defined is the domain of f, and we write $X = D_f$.

Example 1: Firm's Supply Function

Consider a firm producing a single output. Let $C_1(q)$ be the minimized cost for each level of output q. This is a single-valued mapping from output to cost so it is the firm's *cost function*. Suppose that the cost function is as depicted in Figure A.2-1.

Given the price p, profit is maximized at $q(p)$ where the gap between the cost curve and the revenue line, $R = pq$, is greatest. Thus the profit-maximizing firm supplies $q(p)$ units of output. As long as the slope of the cost curve is everywhere increasing, the profit-maximizing output is unique so the mapping $q(p)$ from price to output is also a function. This is depicted in Figure A.2-2.

Suppose we next modify Example 1 and introduce a fixed cost.

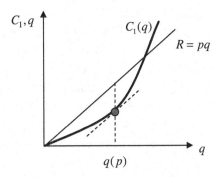

Figure A.2-1. Profit-maximizing output.

---

[2] This chapter is a review of the mathematical foundations. For those readers who find the going tough, it will be helpful to keep open a basic calculus textbook at the same time.

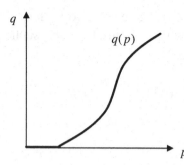

Figure A.2-2. Firm's supply function.

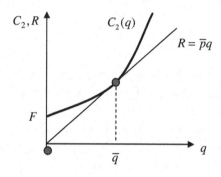

Figure A.2-3. Price yielding a zero profit.

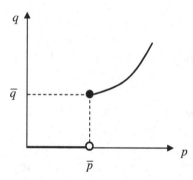

Figure A.2-4. Firm's supply function.

Example 2: Discontinuous Function

The firm's cost is $C_2(q) = F + C_1(q)$. The new cost curve is depicted in Figure A.2-3.

Suppose that the price is $\bar{p}$. That is, the revenue line just touches the cost line at $\bar{q}$. The firm can make a profit of zero by either shutting down or producing $\bar{q}$ units of output. Any other output level yields a strictly negative profit. We assume that in this case it produces $\bar{q}$.[3] At prices higher than $\bar{p}$, the profit-maximizing output $q(p)$ is strictly positive, whereas at prices lower than $\bar{p}$ the firm shuts down. The mapping from price to output is therefore as depicted in Figure A.2-4.

---

[3] The output at price $\bar{p}$ is indicated by the dot in Figure A.1-4. The point indicated by the ring is not on the supply curve. An alternative approach would be to allow either point to be a possible choice by the firm. But then we no longer have a 1–1 mapping from price to output.

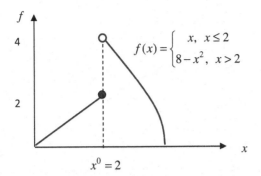

Figure A.2-5. f has no limit at x^0.

There is an important difference between the supply function in example 1 (Figure A.2-2) and the supply function in example 2 (Figure A.2-4). In the former case, output varies smoothly ("continuously") with price. In the latter, there is a jump in output at $\overline{p}$. The supply function is discontinuous at $\overline{p}$.

To provide a precise definition of continuity we appeal to the following preliminary definitions.

Definition: Neighborhood and Deleted Neighborhood The set of points whose distance from x^0 is strictly less than δ is called a neighborhood (or δ – neighborhood) of x^0. When the distance is strictly less than δ but strictly greater than zero (so that x^0 itself is deleted) the set of points is called a deleted neighborhood.

Definition: Limit of a Function The function f has a limit L at x^0 if, for any $\varepsilon > 0$, $|f(x) - L| < \varepsilon$ for all x in some deleted neighborhood of x^0.

Definition: Continuous Function Let f be a function and suppose that $x^0 \in D_f$. Then f is continuous at x^0 if it has a limit point at x^0 equal to $f(x^0)$.

Example 3: Function with No Limit at x^0
Consider some small δ (see Figure A.2-5). For all x in the interval $(2 - \delta, 2)$, $f(x)$ is close to 2. For all x in the interval $(2, 2 + \delta)$, $f(x)$ is close to 4. Thus the function does not approach a limit L as x approaches $x^0 = 2$.

A function f is discontinuous over its domain if it is not continuous at some $x^0 \in D_f$. Consider the following example.

Example 4: A Discontinuous Function with a Limit Point
For all x close to 2, $f(x)$ is close to 2 (see Figure A.2-6). Thus the limit of the function is $L = 2$.

Also $f(x^0) = a$. Therefore the function is discontinuous at x^0 unless $a = 2$.

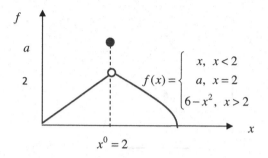

Figure A.2-6. f has a limit point but is not continuous at x^0.

Set-Valued Mappings

In economics, it is sometimes the case that the optimal choice of an economic decision maker is not unique. For example, there can be prices for which a firm may have two or more profit-maximizing outputs. Then the mapping from prices to outputs is not unique. More formally, mappings are sometimes set valued rather than single valued. That is, some or all points in a set X are mapped into sets of points on the real line. Such set-valued mappings are called *correspondences*.

To illustrate, suppose that a firm has two machines. Using machine 1 it can produce up to a units per day at a unit cost of c_1 and using machine 2, it can produce up to b units per day at a unit cost of $c_2 > c_1$. The cost curve is depicted in Figure A.2-7.

If, as depicted, the output price lies in the open interval (c_1, c_2), the vertical distance between the revenue line and the total cost function is greatest at $q = a$. That is, profit is maximized by fully utilizing the first machine. If the output price is below c_1 the profit-maximizing output is zero. If the price is above c_2 it is profitable to fully utilize both machines and produce an output of $a + b$. Finally, if the price is c_1 or c_2, there is an interval of profit-maximizing outputs. The mapping from price to profit-maximizing output is depicted in Figure A.2-8.

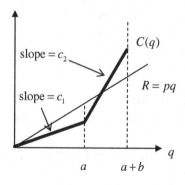

Figure A.2-7. Cost function.

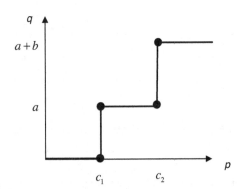

Figure A.2-8. Firm's supply.

In analyzing supply and demand, economists almost always follow Marshall and place the price on the vertical axis. This is depicted in Figure A.2-9. Note that the "inverse mapping" from q to p is also multi-valued. Also shown in the figure are four demand curves. Although a formal mathematical analysis of demand shifts is somewhat more complex with a supply "correspondence" rather than a supply function, the graphical analysis of such shifts is essentially unaffected. If the demand curve shifts from D_0 to D_1, the market-clearing price rises, but output remains at a. If the demand curve rises from D_2 to D_3, output increases, but the market-clearing price remains at c_2.

Exercise A.2-1: Rules for Limits Suppose that the functions f_1 and f_2 have limits L_1 and L_2 at x^0.

(a) Show that the sum of the two functions $g = f_1 + f_2$ has a limit of $L_1 + L_2$.
(b) Show also that $g = f_1 f_2$ has a limit of $L_1 L_2$.

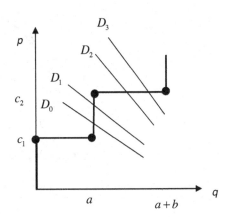

Figure A.2-9. Supply and demand.

A.3 Derivatives and Integrals

Key ideas: rules of derivatives, increasing function, integral as anti-derivative

The Slope of a Function

Consider the function depicted in Figure A.3-1. In graphical terms, the slope of the function at x^0 is the slope of the line just touching the graph of the function at $(x^0, f(x^0))$. This slope is called the derivative of the function art x^0. Analysis of models is further simplified if we assume that each function has an everywhere well-defined derivative and that this derivative varies continuously. Such functions are called *continuously differentiable*. As a shorthand we write $f \in \mathbb{C}^1$.

We now provide a formal definition of the derivative of the function at x^0. Consider the point x^0 and any neighboring point $x^0 + h$, and draw the chord AB connecting the two points on the curve. Then we define the slope of the curve at x^0 to be the limiting value of the slope of the chord as h approaches zero; that is, the slope of the tangent line AC.

Definition: Derivative of a Function[4] The derivative $\frac{df}{dx}(x^0)$ of the function f is the limit point at x^0 of the ratio $g(x) = \frac{f(x) - f(x^0)}{x - x^0}$.

In Figure A.3-1, the line through A with slope $\frac{df}{dx}(x^0)$ is also depicted. The equation of this line is

$$y = f(x^0) + \frac{df}{dx}(x^0)(x - x^0).$$

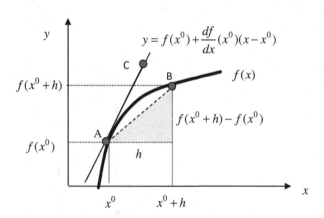

Figure A.3-1. Derivative of a function.

---

[4] It is very common to write the derivative of the function $f(x)$ as $f'(x)$ and in the chapters we often follow this alternative convention. The disadvantage is that it does not naturally generalize to the case of two or more variables.

Because the line and curve take on the same value and have the same derivative at x^0, the line approximates the curve in the neighborhood of x^0. Because the linear approximation has the same first derivative, it is also known as the first-order approximation of f at x^0.

Rules of Differentiation

Appealing to the definition of a derivative as a limit, we have the following basic rules of differentiation.

Chain Rule

Suppose that $y = f(x)$ and $z = g(y) = g(f(x))$. Then

$$\frac{d}{dx} g(f(x)) = \frac{dg}{dy}(y)\frac{dy}{dx}(x).$$

Product Rule

$$\frac{d}{dx}[f(x)g(x)] = \frac{df}{dx}(x)g(x) + f(x)\frac{dg}{dx}(x).$$

Quotient Rule

$$\frac{d}{dx}\frac{f(x)}{g(x)} = \frac{\frac{df}{dx}(x)g(x) - f(x)\frac{dg}{dx}(x)}{g(x)^2}.$$

Each of these properties is said to hold over the domain of a function if it holds at every point in the domain.

Often economic models include functions that everywhere increase (or decrease) with the underlying variable.

Definition: Increasing[5] and Strictly Increasing Function A function f is increasing at x^0 if $\frac{f(x)-f(x^0)}{x-x^0} \geq 0$ for all x in some deleted neighborhood of x^0.

A function f is strictly increasing at x^0 if $\frac{f(x)-f(x^0)}{x-x^0} > 0$, for all x in some deleted neighborhood of x^0.

If a function f is strictly increasing, it is very tempting to conclude that the map of the function must have a strictly positive slope. Indeed if you were to draw some strictly increasing functions you might be able to convince yourself that this was "obvious." But although pictures are often extremely helpful, they are only stepping-stones toward proofs. One way to prove that a statement is false is to find a counterexample.

---

[5] We make no distinction between "increasing" and "non-decreasing." Similarly, if $x_1 \geq 0$ we say either that x_1 is positive or that x_1 is non-negative.

Counterexample: Cubic Function

To see that the slope is not necessarily strictly positive, consider the cubic function $f(x) = x^3$. Then

$$\frac{f(z) - f(x)}{z - x} = \frac{z^3 - x^3}{z - x} = z^2 + xz + x^2 = (z + \tfrac{1}{2}x)^2 + \tfrac{3}{4}x^2. \quad \text{(A.3-1)}$$

This is strictly positive for all x and $z \neq x$. Therefore the cubic is a strictly increasing function over the real line. However,

$$\frac{df}{dx}(x) = \lim_{z \to x} \frac{f(z) - f(x)}{z - x} = \lim_{z \to x}(z^2 + zx + x^2) = 3x^2.$$

Hence $\frac{df}{dx}(0) = 0$. Thus the slope is zero at $x = 0$.

Suppose that the function f is differentiable at x^0. We have just argued that the statement

$A = \{f \text{ is strictly increasing at } x^0\}$ does not imply the statement $B = \{\frac{df}{dx}(x^0) > 0\}$. However, the converse statement is true.[6]

Proposition A.3-1: Sufficient Condition for a Function to be Strictly Increasing/Decreasing at a Point

If $\frac{df}{dx}(x^0) > 0$, then f is strictly increasing at x^0. If $\frac{df}{dx}(x^0) < 0$, then f is strictly decreasing at x^0.

Proof: Suppose that $\frac{df}{dx}(x^0) > 0$. Choose $\varepsilon = \frac{1}{2}\frac{df}{dx}(x^0)$. Because $\varepsilon > 0$, it follows from the definition of a derivative that there exists a $\delta > 0$ such that if $x^0 - \delta < x < x^0 + \delta$ and $x \neq x^0$, then

$$\varepsilon > \frac{f(x) - f(x^0)}{x - x^0} - \frac{df}{dx}(x^0) > -\varepsilon = -\frac{1}{2}\frac{df}{dx}(x^0).$$

Rearranging, it follows that if $x \in (x^0 - \delta, x^0 + \delta)$ and $x \neq x^0$, then

$$\frac{f(x) - f(x^0)}{x - x^0} > \frac{1}{2}\frac{df}{dx}(x^0).$$

Thus if $\frac{df}{dx}(x^0) > 0$, then $\frac{f(x) - f(x^0)}{x - x^0} > 0$ and so f is strictly increasing at x^0. A symmetric argument establishes that if the derivative is negative at x^0, f is strictly decreasing at x^0.   □

Elasticity of a Function

Economists often find it useful to examine proportional changes in a function $y = f(x)$ as the variable x changes. This is the elasticity of a function.

---

[6] In mathematical shorthand, $A \nRightarrow B$; however $B \Rightarrow A$.

For finite changes, the (arc) elasticity is the ratio of the proportional changes in y and x; that is,

$$\frac{\frac{\Delta y}{y}}{\frac{\Delta x}{x}} = \frac{x}{y}\frac{\Delta y}{\Delta x}.$$

Taking the limit as $\Delta x \to 0$, we define the (point) elasticity

$$\mathcal{E}(y, x) = \frac{x}{y}\frac{dy}{dx}.$$

Note that $\frac{d}{dx}\ln y = \frac{1}{y}\frac{dy}{dx}$. Therefore the point elasticity of demand can be written as follows:

$$\mathcal{E}(y, x) = x\frac{d}{dx}\ln y.$$

Example: Elasticity of Demand

Suppose that demand for a product is $y = f(p) = ap^{-v}$. Taking the logarithm, $\ln y = \ln a - v \ln p$. Then $\frac{1}{y}\frac{dy}{dp} = \frac{-v}{p}$ and so $\mathcal{E}(y, p) = -v$.

Rules for Elasticities

Product Rule: $\mathcal{E}(fg, x) = \mathcal{E}(f, x) + \mathcal{E}(g, x)$.
Quotient Rule: $\mathcal{E}(f/g, x) = \mathcal{E}(f, x) - \mathcal{E}(g, x)$.
   To derive the first rule note that $\mathcal{E}(fg, x) = x\frac{d}{dx}\ln fg$.
   Also $\ln fg = \ln f + \ln g$. Then

$$\mathcal{E}(fg, x) = x\frac{d}{dx}(\ln f + \ln g) = x\frac{d}{dx}\ln f + x\frac{d}{dx}\ln g = \mathcal{E}(f, x) + \mathcal{E}(g, x).$$

The derivation of the quotient rule is almost identical.

Integral of a Function

Consider the continuous function f depicted in Figure A.3-2. The integral of a function over some interval $[\alpha, \beta]$ is the area under the curve. One way

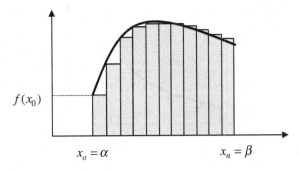

Figure A.3-2. Approximating the area under a curve.

to compute this area is to divide the interval $[\alpha, \beta]$ into n equal segments of length $\delta x = \frac{\beta - \alpha}{n}$. Label the intermediate points $x_1, x_2, \ldots, x_{n-1}$ and then add up the areas of each of the n bars depicted in Figure A.3-2. That is, we compute the following summation:

$$I_n = \sum_{i=0}^{n-1} f(x^i)\delta x.$$

As n increases, the step function approximates the curve better and better. Therefore one way to determine the area under the curve is to take the limit of these approximations.

$$I = \lim_{n \to \infty} \sum_{i=0}^{n-1} f(x^i)\delta x.$$

In mathematical terms, this is the integral of the function f over $[\alpha, \beta]$. Rather than write the expression as a limit, it is convenient to use the following shorthand:

$$I = \int_{\alpha}^{\beta} f(x)dx.$$

In principle, for any particular function, it is possible to find an expression for this limit by following the steps just outlined. However, in many cases, there is a much simpler way to proceed using the rules of differentiation.

Consider the change in the integral as we increase β to $\beta + h$. Because we are varying the right endpoint, we write the integral as $I(\beta)$. Then the change in the area under the curve is $I(\beta + h) - I(\beta)$. For concreteness, suppose that the function f is increasing, as depicted in Figure A.3-3.

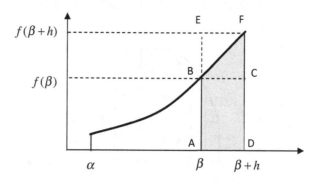

Figure A.3-3. Change in the area under the curve.

Then the change in the area under the curve (the shaded area) is bounded from below by the area of the rectangle ABCD and bounded from above by the rectangle AEFD. That is,

$$f(\beta)h \le I(\beta + h) - I(\beta) \le f(\beta + h)h.$$

Dividing by h,

$$f(\beta) \le \frac{I(\beta + h) - I(\beta)}{h} \le f(\beta + h).$$

Note that in the limit as $h \to 0$, the right-hand expression approaches $f(\beta)$. Also the limiting value of the middle term is the derivative of I. That is,

$$\frac{dI}{d\beta}(\beta) = f(\beta).$$

Because this argument holds for any value β, we may write

$$\frac{dI}{dx}(x) = f(x).$$

Thus the integral of a function is the "anti-derivative" of the function.

Note that the anti-derivative is not unique. We can add any constant to it without affecting its derivative. For this reason, the anti-derivative is called the *indefinite integral*.

The area under the curve over an interval $[\alpha, \beta]$ is called the *definite integral*. For some constant k, the area is

$$\int_{\alpha}^{\beta} f(x)dx = I(\beta) + k.$$

Note that as $\beta \to \alpha$, the area under the curve must approach zero; that is, $I(\alpha) + k = 0$. Then the definite integral

$$\int_{\alpha}^{\beta} f(x)dx = I(\beta) - I(\alpha).$$

Example: Integral as Anti-Derivative
Suppose that $f(x) = x^n$. Because the derivative of x^{n+1} is $(n+1)x^n$, the derivative of $\frac{1}{n+1}x^{n+1}$ is x^n. Then $\frac{1}{n+1}x^{n+1}$ is the anti-derivative of x^n and we may write

$$I(x) = \frac{1}{n+1}x^{n+1}.$$

The definite integral over the interval $[\alpha, \beta]$ is therefore $\frac{1}{n+1}(\beta^{n+1} - \alpha^{n+1})$.

One very useful trick for analyzing the integral of a function f is to see if it can be written in the form $f(x) = u(x)v(x)$ where the function $u(x)$ has a known integral $U(x)$. The integral of f can then be expressed as follows.

Proposition A.3-2: Integration by Parts

Suppose $f(x) = u(x)v(x)$ where $u(x)$ has integral $U(x)$. Then

$$\int_\alpha^\beta f(x)dx = U(\beta)v(\beta) - U(\alpha)v(\alpha) - \int_\alpha^\beta U(x)\frac{dv}{dx}dx.$$

Proof: By the Product Rule,

$$\frac{d}{dx}U(x)v(x) = u(x)v(x) + U(x)\frac{dv}{dx}.$$

Rearranging this expression,

$$u(x)v(x) = \frac{d}{dx}U(x)v(x) - U(x)\frac{dv}{dx}.$$

The proposition then follows by integrating both sides and noting that the integral of the derivative of the function $U(x)v(x)$ is just the function. □

Exercise A.3-1: Rules of Differentiation

(a) Define $y(x) = f(x)g(x)$. Confirm that

$$\frac{y(x+h) - y(x)}{h} = f(x+h)\frac{g(x+h) - g(x)}{h} + g(x)\frac{f(x+h) - f(x)}{h}.$$

(b) Take the limit as $h \to 0$ and so sketch a proof of the Product Rule.

(c) Define $y = f(x)$ and $y + k = f(x+h)$. Confirm that

$$\frac{g(f(x+h)) - g(f(x))}{h} = \frac{g(y+k) - g(y)}{k}\frac{f(x+h) - f(x)}{h}.$$

Hence sketch a proof of the Chain Rule.

Exercise A.3-2:[*] Discontinuously Differentiable Function[7] Consider the following function.

$$f(x) = \begin{cases} x^2 \left(\sin\frac{1}{x} - 1\right), & x \neq 0 \\ 0, & x = 0 \end{cases}.$$

(a) Because $\frac{d}{dx}\sin x = \cos x$, apply the Chain and Product Rules to show that for all $x \neq 0$,

$$\frac{df}{dx}(x) = 2x\left(\sin\frac{1}{x} - 1\right) - \cos\frac{1}{x}.$$

---

[7] An asterisk (*) indicates a somewhat harder question. This exercise is designed for students with strong mathematical backgrounds.

(b) Explain why the slope changes more and more rapidly with x, as x approaches zero.

(c) Explain why $-2x^2 \leq f(x) \leq 0$ and depict the map of the function in a neat figure. Appeal to the definition of the derivative as a limit to show that $\frac{df}{dx}(0) = 0$.

Remark: This is an example of a function that is everywhere differentiable, but is not continuously differentiable at $x = 0$.

Exercise A.3-3 Integrating by Parts

(a) Use the facts that $\ln x = u(x) \ln x$, where $u(x) = 1$ and $\frac{d}{dx} \ln x = \frac{1}{x}$, to show that

$$\int\limits_{\alpha}^{\beta} \ln x \, dx = \beta(\ln \beta - 1) - \alpha(\ln \alpha - 1).$$

(b) Obtain an expression for $\int_{\alpha}^{\beta} x^{\gamma} \ln x \, dx, \ \gamma > 0$.

(c) The exponential function $f(x) = e^x$ has a derivative equal to the value of the function; hence the indefinite integral $\int e^x dx = e^x$. Obtain an expression for $\int_{\alpha}^{\beta} x e^x dx$.

A.4 Optimization

Key ideas: first- and second-order conditions, approximating a function, elasticity

Optimizing behavior underlies almost all economic modeling. In explaining how a model works, it is often extremely helpful to present the implications of optimizing in a relatively informal manner. However, the model itself needs to be built on solid mathematical foundations. Suppose a downward shift in demand has left the profit function of a firm as depicted in Figure A.4-1. Profit $f(q)$ is a decreasing function and is negative for all strictly positive outputs. Thus the firm's profit-maximizing strategy is to close down.

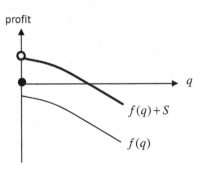

Figure A.4-1. Discontinuous profit function.

To help the domestic industry, the government intervenes and announces that every firm that sells this commodity will receive a subsidy S. As a result, the profit function is

$$\Pi(q) = \begin{cases} 0, & q = 0 \\ f(q) + S, & q > 0 \end{cases}.$$

From Figure A.4-1, the smaller the output of the firm, the greater is the firm's profit. However, if the firm produces nothing, its profit is zero. As a practical matter the firm's output will be "very small." But from a mathematical perspective, there is no solution to the following maximization problem:

$$\text{Max}_{q}\{\Pi(q)|q \geq 0\},$$

so there is no profit-maximizing output.

Intuitively, we can be assured that there is a solution to an optimization problem if we are willing to assume that the function to be optimized is continuous over some interval $[a, b]$. This intuition is confirmed by the following fundamental theorem.

Extreme Value Theorem If the function f is continuous over a closed interval, then f attains its maximizing and minimizing value at some numbers in this interval.

We now seek to characterize the maximizing value of a differentiable (and hence continuous) function. Suppose that $D_f = \mathbb{R}$ and consider any point x^0 where the slope is strictly positive. By Proposition A.3-1, if $\frac{df}{dx}(x^0) > 0$, f is strictly increasing at x^0. Thus there exists $x^1 < x^0$ such that $f(x^1) < f(x^0)$ and $x^2 > x^0$ such that $f(x^2) > f(x^0)$. Thus f does not have maximum or a minimum at x^0. A symmetric argument applies if $\frac{df}{dx}(x^0) < 0$. We have therefore proved the following proposition.

Proposition A.4-1: First-Order Condition (FOC)
Suppose that f takes on its maximum value over $\mathbb{R}$ at x^0. If f is differentiable at x^0 then $\frac{df}{dx}(x^0) = 0$.

In economics it is often natural to restrict the domain of a function. In particular, many variables (ice cream, hours worked, etc.) only have meaning as positive (equivalently, non-negative) numbers. The FOC must be modified to reflect this. Consider the following modified problem:

$$\text{Max}_{x}\{f(x)|x \in \mathbb{R}^+\}.$$

Here we have used the shorthand $\mathbb{R}^+$ to denote the positive real numbers. If the maximum occurs at a point x^0 in the interior of the domain, the FOC is unchanged. If the maximum occurs at the endpoint, $x^0 = 0$, then it continues

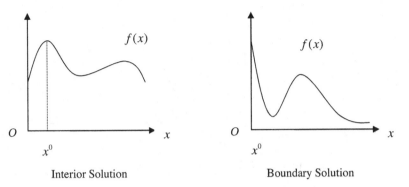

Interior Solution   Boundary Solution

Figure A.4-2. First-order condition.

to be the case that f cannot be strictly increasing at $x = 0$. However, as depicted in Figure A.4-2, f may be strictly decreasing.

The modified FOC then has two parts:

(i) If $x^0 > 0$ then $\frac{df}{dx}(x^0) = 0$.

(ii) If $x^0 = 0$ then $\frac{df}{dx}(x^0) \leq 0$.

This is typically written more compactly as follows:

$$\frac{df}{dx}(x^0) \leq 0, \text{ with equality if } x^0 > 0.$$

Higher-Order Derivatives

If the function f is differentiable over D_f then the derivative is itself a function. Thus, appealing to the definition of a derivative as a limit, we can define the derivative of $\frac{df}{dx}(x)$ at x^0. Because this is the derivative of the derivative of the function f, it is called the second derivative of f. More generally we define $\frac{d^n f}{dx^n}(x^0)$ to be the nth derivative of f at x^0.

Proposition A.4-2: Second-Order Condition

Suppose that f is differentiable on $\mathbb{R}$ and is twice differentiable at x^0. If f takes on its maximum value at x^0 then $\frac{d^2 f}{dx^2}(x^0) \leq 0$.

Proof: Suppose the proposition is false; that is, f takes on its maximum value at x^0 so that $\frac{df}{dx}(x^0) = 0$ and $\frac{d^2 f}{dx^2}(x^0) = \frac{d}{dx}(\frac{df}{dx})(x^0) > 0$. By Proposition A.3-1, if the function g has a strictly positive derivative at x^0, then g is strictly increasing at x^0. Then, because $\frac{d}{dx}(\frac{df}{dx})(x^0) > 0$, $\frac{df}{dx}(x)$ is strictly increasing at x^0. That is, in some deleted $\delta-$ neighborhood of x^0,

$$\frac{\frac{df}{dx}(x) - \frac{df}{dx}(x^0)}{x - x^0} > 0.$$

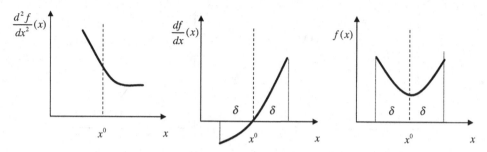

Figure A.4-3. Second-order condition.

Hence $\frac{df}{dx}(x) > 0$ over some interval $(x^0, x^0 + \delta)$. Again appealing to Proposition A.3-1, f is strictly increasing at each point in the interval $(x^0, x^0 + \delta)$ and hence in the interval $(x^0, x^1]$ where $x^1 = x^0 + \frac{1}{2}\delta$.

Because f takes on its maximum at x^0, $f(x^1) \le f(x^0)$. Moreover, because f is strictly increasing at x^1 there exists $\hat{x} \in (x^0, x^1)$ such that $f(\hat{x}) < f(x^1)$. Appealing to the Extreme Value Theorem, f must take on its minimum at some point $c \in (x^0, x^1)$. From the FOC, $\frac{df}{dx}(c) = 0$. But this is impossible because we have already argued that $\frac{df}{dx}(x) > 0$ over some interval $(x^0, x^0 + \delta)$. Then it cannot be the case that $\frac{d^2f}{dx^2}(x^0) > 0$ after all. □

The geometry of the proof is depicted in Figure A.4-3. Suppose that the second derivative is positive at x^0, so that the slope of the function is strictly increasing over some interval $(x^0 - \delta, x^0 + \delta)$. Also, the slope is zero at x^0. Thus the slope is strictly negative for $x \in (x^0 - \delta, x^0)$ and strictly positive for $x \in (x^0, x^0 + \delta)$. This is depicted in the middle diagram. It follows that f must have a local minimum at x^0.

Finally we note that many of the implications of optimization depend only on first and second derivatives of functions. To understand these results it is usually enough to consider a quadratic approximation of the function.

Approximating a Function

Suppose we approximate a function in the neighborhood of x^0 using the following quadratic function:

$$f_a(x) = \alpha_0 + \alpha_1(x - x^0) + \alpha_2(x - x^0)^2.$$

Setting $x = x^0$, $f_a(x^0) = \alpha_0$. Thus the approximating function takes on the same value at x^0 if $\alpha_0 = f(x^0)$. Taking the derivative,

$$\frac{df_a}{dx}(x) = \alpha_1 + 2\alpha_2(x - x^0).$$

Thus the approximating function has the same slope if $\alpha_1 = \frac{df}{dx}(x^0)$.

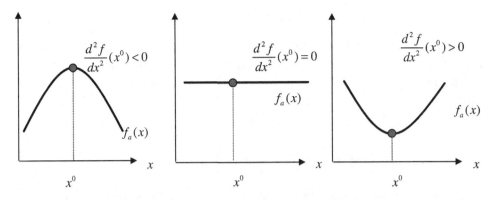

Figure A.4-4. Approximating quadratic functions.

Differentiating again,

$$\frac{d^2 f_a}{dx^2}(x^0) = 2\alpha_2.$$

Thus the approximating function has the same second derivative at x^0 if $\alpha_2 = \frac{1}{2}\frac{d^2 f}{dx^2}(x^0)$.

Collecting these results, we can write the quadratic (or "second-order") approximation of the function f at x^0 as follows:

$$f_a(x) = f(x^0) + \frac{df}{dx}(x^0)(x - x^0) + \frac{1}{2}\frac{d^2 f}{dx^2}(x^0)(x - x^0)^2.$$

Arguing in exactly the same manner we can define higher order approximations as well. However it is the first- and second-order approximations that typically prove most useful.

Consider once more the optimization problem $\text{Max}_x\{f(x)|x \in \mathbb{R}\}$. If f takes on its maximum value at x^0 then we can appeal to the FOC and thus write the second-order approximation as follows:

$$f_a(x) = f(x^0) + \frac{1}{2}\frac{d^2 f}{dx^2}(x^0)(x - x^0)^2.$$

The three possible approximating functions are depicted in Figure A.4-4. In the first two cases, the approximating function takes on its maximum at x^0. In the third case the approximating function takes on its minimum at x^0. As we have shown, if case three holds then the original function f cannot have a maximum at x^0.

Elasticity of a Function

Suppose that the function $x(p)$ represents the solution to some optimization problem given the parameter p. In economics it is often very useful to summarize the sensitivity of the response function in proportional terms. Let the initial price be p^0 and the final price be p^1. Define $x^i = x(p^i)$, $i = 0, 1$. Then the proportional changes as p changes from p^0 to p^1 are

$$\frac{\Delta p}{p^0} = \frac{p^1 - p^0}{p^0} \quad \text{and} \quad \frac{\Delta x}{x^0} = \frac{x^1 - x^0}{x^0}.$$

We define the arc elasticity of x with respect to p to be the ratio of these changes; that is,

$$\frac{\dfrac{\Delta x}{x^0}}{\dfrac{\Delta x}{x^0}} = \frac{p^0}{x^0} \frac{\Delta x}{\Delta p}.$$

Taking the limit, the point elasticity of x at p^0 is

$$\mathcal{E}(x, p^0) = \frac{p^0}{x(p^0)} \frac{dx}{dp}(p^0).$$

Because $\frac{d}{dx} \ln x = \frac{1}{x}$, it is sometimes helpful to write point elasticity as follows:

$$\mathcal{E}(x, p) = p \frac{d}{dp} \ln x. \tag{A.4-1}$$

Point elasticities have very nice properties. For example, the elasticity of a product is the sum of the elasticities

$$\mathcal{E}(xy, p) = \mathcal{E}(x, p) + \mathcal{E}(y, p).$$

This follows from the properties of the logarithmic function. Appealing to (A.4-1),

$$\mathcal{E}(xy, p) = p \frac{d}{dp} \ln xy$$
$$= p \frac{d}{dp} \ln x + p \frac{d}{dp} \ln y$$
$$= \mathcal{E}(x, p) + \mathcal{E}(y, p).$$

Exercise A.4-1: First-Order Conditions Solve the following problem and provide conditions under which $x^* = 0$ and $x^* = b$.

$$\operatorname*{Max}_{x} \{ f(x) = \alpha + \beta x - x^2 | x \in [0, b] \}.$$

Exercise A.4-2: Consumer Choice Suppose that a consumer can purchase units of commodity x at a price of p and commodity y at a price of 1. His utility function is $u(x, y) = B(x) + y$, where B is concave. If he purchases x units and has an income of I, his consumption of the other commodity is $y = I - px$. We can therefore substitute for y in his utility function and write

$$U(x) = B(x) + I - px.$$

The consumer cannot spend more than his income on x so $0 \le x \le \frac{I}{p}$.

(a) Write down the FOC for this example by completing the following statements.

If $x^* \in (0, \frac{I}{p})$ then ... If $x^* = 0$ then.... If $x^* = \frac{I}{p}$ then ...

(b) Solve for the consumer's utility-maximizing choice of x if (i) $B(x) = 10 \ln x$ and if (ii) $B(x) = 10 \ln(5 + x)$.

Exercise A.4-3: Robinson Crusoe Robinson has an endowment of ω units of coconuts. He invests z units in order to produce coconuts next period and consumes $x = \omega - z$ this period. The output of next year's coconuts is $y = a\sqrt{z}$. Robinson's two-period preferences are represented by the utility function $u(x, y) = x + b \ln y$. The parameters a and b are both positive.

(a) Express Robinson's utility as a function of his input choice z.
(b) Under what conditions will Robinson invest less than his endowment (and so enjoy some current consumption)? If this condition is satisfied, how much will he invest?
(c) Under what conditions (if any) will Robinson invest nothing?

Exercise A.4-4: Elasticities

(a) Show that $\mathcal{E}(ax, by) = \mathcal{E}(x, y)$, where a and b are parameters.
(b) Show that the elasticity of the ratio of x and y is the difference in elasticities of x and y.
(c) Show that $\mathcal{E}(x, y)\mathcal{E}(y, z) = \mathcal{E}(x, z)$.
(d) Hence or otherwise show that $\mathcal{E}(y, \frac{1}{x}) = -\mathcal{E}(y, x)$.
(e) Show that $\mathcal{E}(\frac{1}{y}, \frac{1}{x}) = \mathcal{E}(x, y)$.

A.5 Sufficient Conditions for a Maximum

Key ideas: concave and convex functions, quasi-concave function

Characterizing the solution to a maximization problem is especially easy if all we have to do is examine the FOC. This is the case if a function is concave.

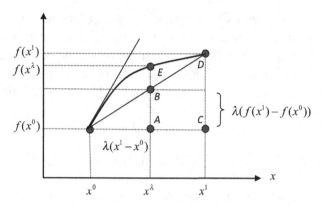

Figure A.5-1. Concave function.

Definition: Concave and Strictly Concave Function A function f is concave on the interval $[a, b]$ if, for any points x^0 and x^1 in this interval, and any convex combination $x^\lambda = (1 - \lambda)x^0 + \lambda x^1$, $0 < \lambda < 1$,

$$f(x^\lambda) \geq (1 - \lambda)f(x^0) + \lambda f(x^1).$$

The function is strictly concave if the inequality is always strict.

In geometric terms, the graph of the function f between any two points x^0 and x^1 lies above the chord connecting the points $(x^0, f(x^0))$ and $(x^1, f(x^1))$.

To see that this is the case, note that

$$x^\lambda - x^0 = \lambda(x^1 - x^0). \tag{A.5-1}$$

That is, the distance between x^0 and the convex combination x^λ is a fraction λ of the distance between x^0 and x^1. Then the vertical distance AB is a fraction λ of the vertical distance CD, so $AB = \lambda(f(x^1) - f(x^0))$. If f is concave, $f(x^\lambda) \geq (1 - \lambda)f(x^0) + \lambda f(x^1)$ so

$$f(x^\lambda) - f(x^0) \geq \lambda(f(x^1) - f(x^0)). \tag{A.5-2}$$

Thus $AE \geq AB$.

If the function is differentiable, the tangent line at any point x^0 must lie above the graph of the function. This is depicted in Figure A.5-1.

Formally we have the following proposition.

Proposition A.5-1:

If f is concave and differentiable at x^0 and x^1, then

$$\tfrac{df}{dx}(x^0)(x_1 - x_0) \geq f(x^1) - f(x^0) \geq \tfrac{df}{dx}(x^1)(x_1 - x_0).$$

Proof: Appealing to equation (A.5-1) $\lambda = \frac{x^\lambda - x^0}{x^1 - x^0}$. Substituting for λ in inequality (A.5-2), $f(x^\lambda) - f(x^0) \geq (\frac{x^\lambda - x^0}{x^1 - x^0})(f(x^1) - f(x^0))$. Rearranging this inequality,

$$\frac{f(x^\lambda) - f(x^0)}{x^\lambda - x^0} x^1 - x^0 \geq f(x^1) - f(x^0).$$

The first inequality then follows by taking the limit as $\lambda \to 0$.

Similarly $x^1 - x^\lambda = (1 - \lambda)(x^1 - x^0)$ and, from the definition of a concave function,

$$f(x^1) - f(x^\lambda) \leq (1 - \lambda)(f(x^1) - f(x^0)).$$

Substituting for $(1 - \lambda)$ from the previous expression,

$$f(x^1) - f(x^0) \geq \frac{f(x^1) - f(x^\lambda)}{x^1 - x^\lambda}(x^1 - x^0).$$

The second inequality then follows by taking the limit as $\lambda \to 1$. □

Note that an immediate implication is that if $x^1 > x^0$, then the slope of the function is lower at x^1. For a strictly concave function we now show that the slope is strictly lower.

Corollary A.5-2: If f is strictly concave on some interval X and is differentiable at $x^0 \in X$, then

$$\frac{df}{dx}(x^0)(x^1 - x^0) > f(x^1) - f(x^0).$$

Moreover, if f is also differentiable at $x^1 > x^0$, then $\frac{df}{dx}(x^0) > \frac{df}{dx}(x^1)$.

Proof: Because Proposition A.5-1 holds for any $x^1 \neq x^0$, the first inequality holds for all convex combinations; that is,

$$\frac{df}{dx}(x^0)(x^\lambda - x^0) \geq f(x^\lambda) - f(x^0).$$

If f is strictly concave, $f(x^\lambda) - f(x^0) > \lambda(f(x^1) - f(x^0))$. Combining these two inequalities,

$$\frac{df}{dx}(x^0)(x^\lambda - x^0) > \lambda(f(x^1) - f(x^0)).$$

Substituting for $x^\lambda - x^0$, by appealing to (A.5-1), it follows that

$$\frac{df}{dx}(x^0)(x^1 - x^0) > f(x^1) - f(x^0).$$

Thus if f is differentiable at x^0 and x^1, we can appeal to the second inequality of Proposition A.5-1 to conclude that

$$\frac{df}{dx}(x^0)(x^1 - x^0) > \frac{df}{dx}(x^1)(x^1 - x^0).$$ □

A further implication of Proposition A.5-1 is that if a concave function is everywhere differentiable, all the tangent lines lie above the graph of the function. We now show that the converse is also true.

Proposition A.5-3:
A differentiable function f is concave on the interval X if and only if for any x^0 and $x^1 \in X$,

$$f(x^1) \leq f(x^0) + \frac{df}{dx}(x^0)(x^1 - x^0). \tag{A.5-3}$$

Proof: We have already established necessity. To demonstrate sufficiency, consider any x^0, x^1 and convex combination $x^\lambda = (1 - \lambda)x^0 + \lambda x^1$. Appealing to (A.5-3),

$$f(x^0) \leq f(x^\lambda) + \frac{df}{dx}(x^\lambda)(x^0 - x^\lambda)$$

and

$$f(x^1) \leq f(x^\lambda) + \frac{df}{dx}(x^\lambda)(x^1 - x^\lambda).$$

Multiplying the first inequality by $(1 - \lambda)$, the second by λ, and then adding the two inequalities, it follows that

$$(1 - \lambda)f(x^0) + \lambda f(x^1) \leq f(x^\lambda).$$ □

We have also seen that if a function is concave and differentiable, the slope of the function declines as x increases. Thus if a concave function is twice differentiable, the second derivative must be negative. The converse of this statement is also true.

Proposition A.5-4:
A twice differentiable function f is concave on the interval X if and only if, for all $x \in X$, $\frac{d^2 f}{dx^2}(x) \leq 0$.

Proof: To demonstrate sufficiency, define
$g(\lambda) = f(x^\lambda) = f(x^0 + \lambda(x^1 - x^0))$; then

$$\frac{dg}{d\lambda}(\lambda) = (x^1 - x^0)\frac{df}{dx}(x^\lambda) \quad \text{and so} \quad \frac{d^2 g}{d\lambda^2}(\lambda) = (x^1 - x^0)^2\frac{d^2 f}{dx^2}(x^\lambda).$$

Because the second derivative of f is negative, it follows that $\frac{dg}{d\lambda}(\lambda)$ is decreasing over the interval $(0, 1)$.

Then $f(x^1) - f(x^0) = g(1) - g(0) = \int_0^1 \frac{dg}{d\lambda}(\lambda)d\lambda \leq \int_0^1 \frac{dg}{d\lambda}(0)d\lambda$, because the derivative is everywhere decreasing.

Taking $\frac{dg}{d\lambda}(0)$ outside the integral and noting that $\frac{dg}{d\lambda}(0) = (x^1 - x^0)\frac{df}{dx}(x^0)$, it follows that

$$f(x^1) - f(x^0) \le \frac{df}{dx}(x^0)(x^1 - x^0). \qquad\qquad \square$$

Maximization

Suppose that the function f is differentiable on $\mathbb{R}$ and there is a point x^0 satisfying the FOC $\frac{df}{dx}(x^0) = 0$. Although this might be a maximum there are three possibilities, all depicted in Figure A.5-2.

However, if f is concave, then it is maximized at x^0. This follows from Proposition A.5-4. Because $\frac{df}{dx}(x^0) = 0$, for any $x^1 \ne x^0$,

$$f(x^1) \le f(x^0) + \frac{df}{dx}(x^0)(x^1 - x^0) = f(x^0).$$

We have therefore proved the following result.

Proposition A.5-5: Sufficient Conditions for a Maximum
Suppose f is concave on $[a, b]$ and for some $x^0 \in (a, b)$, $\frac{df}{dx}(x^0) = 0$. Then

$$f(x) \le f(x^0), \quad \text{for all } x \in [a, b].$$

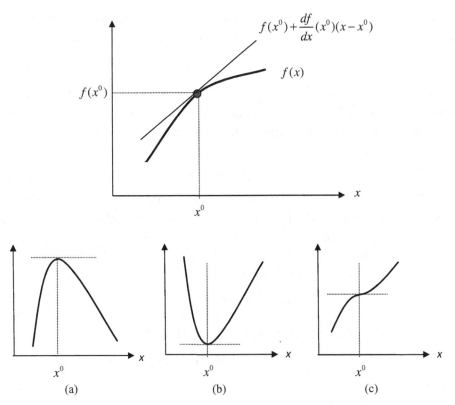

Fig. A.5-2. Tangent line. (a) Maximum, (b) minimum, and (c) point of inflection.

Although concavity assures that the FOC is both necessary and sufficient for a maximum, this is an undesirably strong assumption for many economic applications.

Definition: Local Property of a Function A function f satisfies the property P locally at x^0 if the property P holds in some neighborhood of x^0.

It follows from Corollary A.5-2 that if the FOC holds at x^0 and the function is locally strictly concave, then $f(x) < f(x^0)$ for all $x \neq x^0$ in some neighborhood of x^0. In this case f is said to have a local maximum at x^0.

A local maximum must be the "global" maximum if the function only has one turning point. This is the case if the function is *quasi-concave*.

Definition: Quasi-Concave Function The function f is quasi-concave over the interval $[a, b]$ if, for any x^0 and x^1 in this interval such that $f(x^1) \geq f(x^0)$, $f(x^\lambda) \geq f(x^0)$ where $x^\lambda = (1 - \lambda)x^0 + \lambda x^1$ and $\lambda \in (0, 1)$.

Proposition A.5-6: Quasi-Concavity and Sufficient Conditions for a Maximum

If $\frac{df}{dx}(x^0) = 0$ and f is locally strictly concave at $x^0 \in [a, b]$, then f has a local maximum at x^0. In addition, if f is quasi-concave on this interval, then $f(x) < f(x^0)$ for all $x \in [a, b]$.

Proof: We have just argued that the first statement follows from Corollary A.5-2. That is, there is some neighborhood $N(x^0, \delta)$ within which

$$f(x) < f(x^0), \quad \text{for all} \quad x \neq x^0. \tag{A.5-4}$$

Suppose that there is some point x^1 such that $f(x^1) > f(x^0)$. If f is quasi-concave, then for all convex combinations, $f(x^\lambda) \geq f(x^0)$. In particular, this must be true in $N(x, \delta)$. But this contradicts (A.5-4). □

Minimization

We can appeal to the sufficient conditions for a maximum to obtain similar sufficient conditions for the FOC to yield the minimum. We simply note that if f takes on its minimum at x^0, so that $f(x) \geq f(x^0)$, then $-f(x) \leq -f(x^0)$. Thus one sufficient condition is that $-f$ must be concave. That is, for any x^0 and $x^1 \neq x^0$, and any convex combination x^λ,

$$-f(x^\lambda) \geq (1 - \lambda)(-f(x^0)) + \lambda(-f(x^1)).$$

Multiplying the inequality by –1 changes the sign so

$$f(x^\lambda) \leq (1 - \lambda)f(x^0) + \lambda f(x^1).$$

This is depicted in Figure A.5-3. The map of the function lies everywhere below the chord. Such functions are called convex functions.

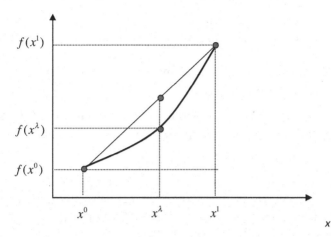

Figure A.5-3. Convex function.

Definition: Convex and Strictly Convex Function A function f is convex on the interval $[a, b]$ if for any points x^0, x^1 in this interval and any convex combination $x^\lambda = (1 - \lambda)x^0 + \lambda x^1$, $0 < \lambda < 1$,

$$f(x^\lambda) \leq (1 - \lambda)f(x^0) + \lambda f(x^1).$$

The function is strictly convex if the inequality is always strict.

Proposition A.5-7: Sufficient Conditions for a Minimum
Suppose $D_f = \mathbb{R}$ and f is convex. If the FOC holds at x^0 then $f(x) \geq f(x^0)$ for all $x \in \mathbb{R}$.

Although this condition is stated for completeness, it is certainly not important to remember it. For, as we have just argued, we can always convert any minimization problem into a maximization problem. This is the approach that we usually adopt.

Exercise A.5-1: Profit-Maximizing Firm A firm hiring x units of labor can produce an output $q(x) = 10x^{\frac{1}{2}}$. The price of output is p and the wage rate is w

(a) Show that the profit function of the firm $f(x) = pq(x) - wx$ is concave.
(b) Solve for the profit-maximizing labor demand and supply of the firm as a function of the wage and price.

Exercise A.5-2: Cost-Minimizing Inputs A firm has a production function $q = 4K + \sqrt{L}$. The wage rate is w and the cost of renting capital equipment is r

(a) Write down an expression for the capital equipment requirements if L units of labor are hired and the objective is to produce q units of output. Hence obtain an expression for total cost $C(L)$ as a function of L and the three parameters, w, r, and q. Explain why $L \in [0, q^2]$.

(b) Show that $-C(L)$ is a concave function of L.

(c) Use the first-order condition for a maximum to solve for the optimal demand for labor.

(d) For what parameter values is the demand for both labor and capital strictly positive?

Exercise A.5-3: Properties of Concave and Quasi-Concave Functions Use the primary definition of concave and quasi-concave functions to establish the following:

(a) The sum of n concave functions is concave. (Start with $n = 2$.)

(b) An increasing function of a quasi-concave function is quasi-concave.

(c) An increasing concave function of a concave function is concave.

(d) If f is concave, show that it is quasi-concave.

Exercise A.5-4: Family of Concave Functions A widely used family of utility functions satisfies the following condition:

$$\frac{d}{dx} \ln \frac{dU}{dx} = \frac{\dfrac{d^2U}{dx^2}}{\dfrac{dU}{dx}} = -\frac{1}{a + bx}, \quad \text{where } a \geq 0, b \geq 0.$$

In each of the following cases, integrate to obtain the implied utility function (i) $a > 0 = b$, (ii) $b = 1$, and (iii) $b > 0$, $b \neq 1$.

Exercise A.5-5: Quasi-Concavity

(a) Depict some quasi-concave functions.

(b) Draw the following function in a neat figure.

$$f(x) = \begin{cases} 8 - (x-2)^2, & x < 2 \\ 8, & 2 \leq x \leq 3. \\ 8 + (x-3)^3, & x > 3 \end{cases}$$

Confirm that f is concave on $[2, 3]$ and is quasi-concave on $\mathbb{R}^+$.

(c) For what values of x are the first- and second-order necessary conditions satisfied? Show that the sufficient conditions for a local maximum fail at each of these points.

Appendix B

Mappings of Vectors

B.1 Vectors and Sets

Key ideas: orthogonal vector, hyperplanes, convex sets, open and closed sets

We now extend our analysis to ordered n-tuples or "vectors." Each component of the vector $x = (x_1, \ldots, x_n)$ is a real number. Where it is important to make clear the dimension of the vector, we write $x \in \mathbb{R}^n$. If each component is positive, then x is positive and we write $x \in \mathbb{R}^n_+$.

We describe the vector y as being larger than the vector x if every component of y is at least as large as x and write $y \geq x$. If at least one component of y is strictly larger we say that y is strictly larger than x and write $y > x$. (We occasionally use the notation $x \gg y$ to indicate that all components are strictly larger.)

A neighborhood of a vector is the set of points near it. Thus to define a neighborhood we need some measure of distance $d(y, z)$ between any two vectors $y = (y_1, \ldots, y_n)$ and $z = (z_1, \ldots, z_n)$. If $n = 1$, a natural measure is the absolute value of the difference so that $d(y, z) = |y - z|$. Similarly with $n = 2$, a natural measure is the Euclidean distance $\|y - z\|$ between the two vectors. This is depicted in Figure B.1-1. Appealing to Pythagoras Theorem,

$$\|y - z\|^2 = (y_1 - z_1)^2 + (y_2 - z_2)^2.$$

Extending this to n-dimensions, the square of Euclidean distance between ordered n-tuples is defined as follows:

$$\|y - z\|^2 = \sum_{j=1}^{n} (y_j - z_j)^2.$$

It is sometimes more convenient to express distance as a vector product.

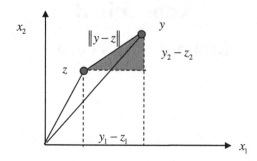

Figure B.1-1. Distance between two vectors.

Vector Product The product ("inner product" or "sumproduct") of two n-dimensional vectors y and z is

$$y \cdot z = \sum_{i=1}^{n} y_i z_i.$$

From this definition, it follows that the distributive law for multiplying vectors is the same as for numbers.

Distributive Law for Vector Multiplication

$$a \cdot (b + c) = a \cdot b + a \cdot c.$$

Orthogonal Vectors

Two vectors, x and p, are depicted in Figure B.1-2 in three-dimensional space.

The length of each vector is its distance to the origin. If x and p are perpendicular it follows from Pythagoras' Theorem that the square of the hypotenuse equals the sum of the squares of the other two sides; that is,

$$\|p - x\|^2 = \|p\|^2 + \|x\|^2. \tag{B.1-1}$$

From the definition of a vector product, the square of Euclidean distance between two vectors can then be written as follows:[1]

$$\|p - x\|^2 = \sum_{i=1}^{n} (p_i - x_i)(p_i - x_i) = (p - x) \cdot (p - x).$$

---

[1] The alternative distance measure $d(y, z) = (\sum_{j=1}^{n} (y_j - z_j)^{2i})^{\frac{1}{2i}}, i = 2, 3 \ldots$ places more weight on larger differences. In the limit this is equivalent to placing all the weight on the maximum difference; that is, $d(y, z) = \underset{j=1,\ldots,n}{Max} |y_j - z_j|$.

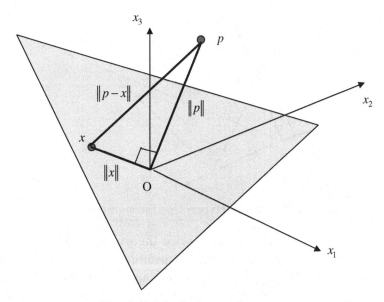

Figure B.1-2. Orthogonal vectors.

Substituting into (B.1-1),

$$(p - x) \cdot (p - x) = p \cdot p + x \cdot x.$$

Applying the rules of vector multiplication,

$$p \cdot p + 2p \cdot x + x \cdot x = p \cdot p + x \cdot x.$$

Hence

$$p \cdot x = 0.$$

We generalize perpendicularity to higher dimensions as follows.

Definition: Orthogonal Vectors The vectors x and p are orthogonal if their product $p \cdot x = \sum_{i=1}^{n} p_i x_i = 0$.

Consider Figure B.1-2 again. Let H be the set of vectors perpendicular to p. In mathematical terms, $H = \{x | p \cdot x = 0\}$. This is the plane created by extending the shaded region. If p is two-dimensional, the set H is a line. If p is of a dimension greater than three, the set H is called a hyperplane.

If we add the vector x^0 to each point in the hyperplane, we shift the plane as depicted in Figure B.1-3. Note that the vector x is in the hyperplane through x^0, orthogonal to p if the vectors p and $x - x^0$ are orthogonal. Thus the hyperplane through x^0 is the set of vectors

$$H^0 = \{x | p \cdot (x - x^0) = 0\}.$$

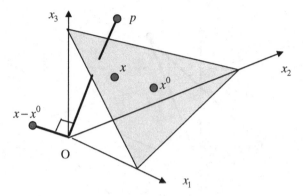

Figure B.1-3. Hyperplane through x^0.

Hyperplanes have a central role in price theory. Take, for example, the expenditure of a consumer purchasing a consumption bundle x given a price vector p. The set of consumption bundles costing the same as the bundle x^0 is the set $H = \{x | p \cdot x = p \cdot x^0\}$; that is, the hyperplane through x^0, orthogonal to p.

Linear and Convex Combinations of Vectors

Let $x^0, \ldots, x^{m-1}$ be m vectors in $\mathbb{R}^n$. Then $y \in \mathbb{R}^n$ is a linear combination of these m vectors if for some $(\alpha_0, \ldots, \alpha_{m-1})$,

$$y = \sum_{i=0}^{m-1} \alpha_i x^i.$$

If $m < n$, the set of all possible linear combinations of m vectors in $\mathbb{R}^n$ is a space of lower dimension. To illustrate, consider the two vectors depicted in Figure B.1-4 in $\mathbb{R}^3$. Taking all the linear combinations of these vectors, a two-dimensional plane is mapped out.

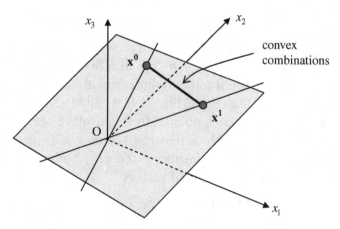

Figure B.1-4. Linear and convex combinations.

A convex combination of two vectors is a weighted average of the vectors where the weights are both positive and sum to 1.

Convex Combination of Two Vectors The vector y is a convex combination of x^0 and $x^1 \in \mathbb{R}^n$ if

$$y = (1 - \lambda)x^0 + \lambda x^1, 0 \le \lambda \le 1.$$

It is often useful to rewrite a convex combination as follows:

$$y = x^0 + \lambda(x^1 - x^0), \quad \lambda \in [0, 1].$$

Thus the vector y is the vector x^0 plus some fraction of the vector $x^1 - x^0$. The weight λ thus indicates the distance along the line joining x^0 and x^1.

To further emphasize this connection, we often write the convex combination of x^0 and x^1 as x^λ. As λ approaches zero, x^λ approaches x^0, and as λ approaches 1, x^λ approaches x^1.

Convex Sets of Vectors

A set S in $\mathbb{R}^n$ is any collection of vectors. In one dimension we have seen that two especially useful sets are the closed and open intervals. Both of these sets have the property that if points x^0 and x^1 are in the set then so is any convex combination,

$$x^\lambda = (1 - \lambda)x^0 + \lambda x^1, \quad 0 \le \lambda \le 1.$$

This suggests the following generalization of an interval.

Convex Set $X \subset \mathbb{R}^n$ is convex if, for any $x^0, x^1 \in X$, every convex combination $x^\lambda \in X$.

Graphically, if two points are in the set X, then every point on the line joining these two points also lies in X. In two dimensions, the boundary of the set must have the "bowed out" or convex shape as depicted in Figure B.1-5.

A set is strictly convex if it is convex and, for every pair of vectors x^0 and $x^1 \in X$, no convex combination lies on the boundary of the set.

To formalize this we need to make precise the idea of a boundary point. First we extend our definition of a neighborhood. A "$\delta-$ neighborhood" of a vector y is the set of points whose distance from y is no greater than δ; that is,

$$N(y, \delta) = \{x \in \mathbb{R}^n, \|x - y\| \le \delta\}.$$

Boundary Point of a Set The vector y is a boundary point of the set X, if every $\delta-$ neighborhood of y contains points in X and points not in X.

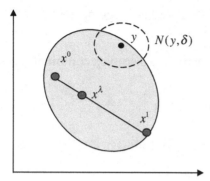

Figure B.1-5. Neighborhood and boundary point.

Any point in a set that is not a boundary point is called an interior point. That is, y is an interior point of X if it has a $\delta-$ neighborhood that lies in X.

Open and Closed Sets A subset of $\mathbb{R}^n$ is closed if it includes all its boundary points. A subset is open if it does not include any of its boundary points.

Compact Set A set is compact if it is both closed and bounded.
     We have the following generalization of the Extreme Value Theorem.

Extreme Value Theorem ($\mathbb{R}^n$) If f is continuous in some compact subset S of $\mathbb{R}^n$, then there are points x^0 and x^1 in S, where f takes on its maximum and minimum values.

     For example, the set $B = \{x \in \mathbb{R}_+^n \mid p \cdot x \leq I, I > 0\}$ is closed. If $p \gg 0$, we can interpret this set as a budget set. Note that x_j is bounded from below by 0 and from above by I/p_j. Thus B is also bounded. Let f be a utility function defined on B. Then by the Extreme Value Theorem, f takes on its maximum at some point x^0 in the budget set.

Exercise B.1-1: Convex Sets Suppose the sets X_1, $X_2 \subset \mathbb{R}^n$ are both convex.

(a) Show that the intersection of the two sets is convex.
(b) Show by counterexample that the union of the two sets need not be convex.
(c) Show that $Y = X_1 + X_2$ and $Z = X_1 - X_2$ are both convex.

B.2 Functions of Vectors

Key ideas: partial and total derivatives, functions of vectors, contour sets, concave and quasi-concave functions

A function f maps each vector $x = (x_1, \ldots, x_n)$ to a point on the real line. Typically we assume that the domain of the function, D_f is convex. For example, a production function $q = f(z)$ maps an input vector z into output q, and a utility function $u = U(x)$ maps a consumption vector into consumer utility. In each case a natural domain of the function is the convex set of non-negative vectors $\mathbb{R}_+^n$.

Partial and Total Derivatives

For a function of n variables, we can fix all but one variable and consider the derivative with respect to this one variable. This is known as a *partial derivative*:

$$\frac{\partial f}{\partial x_j} = \lim_{h \to 0} \frac{f(x_1, \ldots, x_{j-1}, x_j + h, x_{j+1}, \ldots, x_n) - f(x)}{h}.$$

Higher-order partial derivatives are similarly defined.[2]

Definition: Gradient Vector A function f with domain $D_f \subset \mathbb{R}^n$ is differentiable at x if it is partially differentiable with respect to $x_i, i = 1, \ldots, n$. The vector of partial derivatives

$$\frac{\partial f}{\partial x}(x) \equiv \left(\frac{\partial f}{\partial x_1}(x), \ldots, \frac{\partial f}{\partial x_n}(x) \right)$$

is the gradient of f at x.

Next suppose all the components of x vary with some other variable α; that is, $x = x(\alpha)$. This is depicted in Figure B.2-1 for the two-variable case.

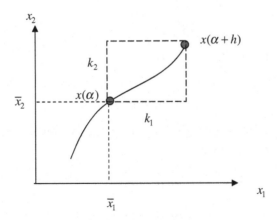

Figure B.2-1. The vector x changes with α.

---

[2] Although we usually write the partial derivatives of $f(x, y)$ as $\frac{\partial f}{\partial x}$ and $\frac{\partial f}{\partial y}$, we sometimes find it more helpful to write them as $f_x(x, y)$ and $f_y(x, y)$.

Following the definition of a derivative we seek to evaluate the limit of the following ratio:

$$\frac{\Delta f}{\Delta \alpha} = \frac{f(x(\alpha + h)) - f(x(\alpha))}{h}.$$

Define $\bar{x} = x(\alpha)$, $k_1 = x_1(\alpha + h) - x_1(\alpha)$ and $k_2 = x_2(\alpha + h) - x_2(\alpha)$.
Then we can rewrite the above ratio as follows:

$$\frac{\Delta f}{\Delta \alpha} = \frac{f(\bar{x}_1 + k_1, \bar{x}_2 + k_2) - f(\bar{x}_1, \bar{x}_2)}{h}$$

$$= \frac{f(\bar{x}_1 + k_1, \bar{x}_2) - f(\bar{x}_1, \bar{x}_2) + f(\bar{x}_1 + k_1, \bar{x}_2 + k_2) - f(\bar{x}_1 + k_1, \bar{x}_2)}{h}$$

$$= \left[\frac{f(\bar{x}_1 + k_1, \bar{x}_2) - f(\bar{x}_1, \bar{x}_2)}{k_1}\right]\left[\frac{x_1(\alpha + h) - x_1(\alpha)}{h}\right]$$

$$+ \left[\frac{f(\bar{x}_1 + k_1, \bar{x}_2 + k_2) - f(\bar{x}_1 + k_1, \bar{x}_2)}{k_2}\right]\left[\frac{x_2(\alpha + h) - x_2(\alpha)}{h}\right].$$

Each of the four ratios becomes a partial derivative as $h \to 0$. Taking the limit,

$$\frac{df}{d\alpha} = \frac{\partial f}{\partial x_1}\frac{\partial x_1}{\partial \alpha} + \frac{\partial f}{\partial x_2}\frac{\partial x_2}{\partial \alpha}.$$

The argument generalizes immediately when there are more than two variables. Expressing the result in vector notation, the total derivative is

$$\frac{df}{d\alpha} = \frac{\partial f}{\partial x} \cdot \frac{\partial x}{\partial \alpha}.$$

Rather than make explicit the underlying variable leading to the change in x, this is often left implicit as follows:

$$df = \frac{\partial f}{\partial x} \cdot dx.$$

This is called the total differential of f.

Special Functions

The following two special mappings from $\mathbb{R}^n$ onto $\mathbb{R}$ have a very central role in the theory of optimization.

Linear Function[3]

$$f(x) = a_0 + \sum_{i=1}^{n} a_j x_j = a_0 + a \cdot x$$

---

[3] Mathematicians typically reserve the term "linear function" for functions where each term is linear in one of the variables. However, economists typically include the constant.

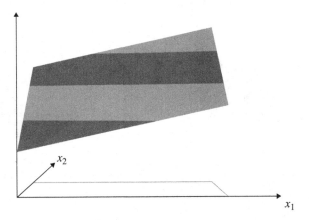

Figure B.2-2. Linear function.

For the two-variable case, the graph of the function $y = a_0 + a_1 x_1 + a_2 x_2$ is a plane in three-dimensional space. An example is depicted in Figure B.2-2.

Quadratic Function

$$f(x) = a_0 + \sum_{i=1}^{n} a_i x_i + \sum_{i=1}^{n} \sum_{j=1}^{n} a_{ij} x_i x_j.$$

Note that a quadratic function f is the sum of a linear function and the function

$$q(x) = \sum_{i=1}^{n} \sum_{j=1}^{n} a_{ij} x_i x_j.$$

This function is called a quadratic form. For every pair x_i and x_j, where $j \neq i$, the quadratic form includes the two terms $a_{ij} x_i x_j + a_{ji} x_j x_i = (a_{ij} + a_{ji}) x_i x_j$. Thus there is no loss of generality in assuming that $a_{ij} = a_{ji}$.

For the two-variable case, we can therefore write the quadratic form as follows:

$$q(x) = \sum_{i=1}^{2} \sum_{j=1}^{2} a_{ij} x_i x_j = a_{11} x_1^2 + 2 a_{12} x_1 x_2 + a_{22} x_2^2.$$

Figure B.2-3 depicts some of the possible graphs of a quadratic form. Both the graphs in the top row depict functions that have a minimum at $x = 0$. On the bottom left we have a maximum and on the bottom right a saddle point.

Example: Quadratic Form with a Saddle Point
Consider the quadratic form $q(x_1, x_2) = -x_1^2 + 4 x_1 x_2 - x_2^2$. Then $q(x_1, 0) = -x_1^2$ and $q(0, x_2) = -x_2^2$. Thus, taking one variable at a time, it appears that the quadratic form has a maximum at $x = 0$. However, setting $x_1 = x_2 = z$

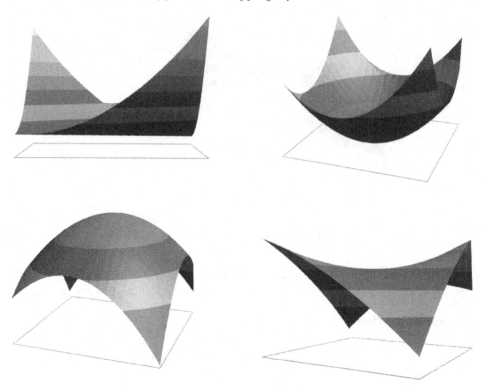

Figure B.2-3. Quadratic forms.

we have $q(z, z) = 2z^2$. Therefore the quadratic form has the saddle shape depicted in the bottom right of Figure B.2-3.

The properties of the quadratic form lie at the heart of the theory of optimization. The reason is that the graph of a function can be approximated by a quadratic function that takes on the same value and has the same first- and second-partial derivatives at x^0. For the two-variable case we have the following quadratic approximation:

$$h(x) = f(x^0) + \sum_{i=1}^{2} \frac{\partial f}{\partial x_i}(x^0)\left(x_i - x_i^0\right) + \frac{1}{2} \sum_{i=1}^{2} \sum_{j=1}^{2} \frac{\partial^2 f}{\partial x_i \partial x_j}(x^0)\left(x_i - x_i^0\right)\left(x_j - x_j^0\right).$$

Note first that $h(x^0) = f(x^0)$. Differentiating by x_1,

$$\frac{\partial h}{\partial x_1}(x) = \frac{\partial f}{\partial x_1}(x^0) + \frac{\partial^2 f}{\partial x_1^2}(x^0)\left(x_1 - x_1^0\right) + \frac{\partial^2 f}{\partial x_1 \partial x_2}(x^0)\left(x_2 - x_2^0\right).$$

Setting $x = x^0$, $\frac{\partial h}{\partial x_1}(x^0) = \frac{\partial f}{\partial x_1}(x^0)$. Note that $\frac{\partial h}{\partial x_1}$ is a linear function with partial derivatives of $\frac{\partial^2 f}{\partial x_1^2}(x^0)$ and $\frac{\partial^2 f}{\partial x_1 \partial x_2}(x^0)$. Thus the second-partial derivatives of h and f are also the same.

As a preliminary step we consider the two-variable case and seek conditions that ensure that a quadratic form is negative. If the quadratic form is negative for all x, (that is, $q(x) \leq 0$), it is said to be negative semi-definite. If $q(x)$ is strictly negative for all $x \neq 0$ it is said to be negative definite.

Proposition B.2-1:

Necessary and sufficient conditions for $q(x_1, x_2) \equiv \sum_{i=1}^{2} \sum_{j=1}^{2} a_{ij} x_i x_j$ to be negative definite:[4]

If (i) $a_{11} < 0$ and (ii) $a_{11} a_{22} - a_{12} a_{21} > 0$, then $q(x_1, x_2) < 0$ for all $x \neq 0$.

Proposition B.2-2:

Necessary and sufficient conditions for $q(x_1, x_2) \equiv \sum_{i=1}^{2} \sum_{j=1}^{2} a_{ij} x_i x_j$ to be negative semi-definite:

$q(x_1, x_2) \leq 0$ if and only if (i) $a_{11}, a_{22} \leq 0$ and (ii) $a_{11} a_{22} - a_{12} a_{21} \geq 0$.

We now derive Proposition B.2-2.[5] Setting $x_2 = 0$ in

$$q(x_1, x_2) \equiv \sum_{i=1}^{2} \sum_{j=1}^{2} a_{ij} x_i x_j, \tag{B.2-1}$$

then

$$q(x_1, x_2) = a_{11} x_1^2. \tag{B.2-2}$$

Thus for $q(x_1, x_2)$ to be negative, a necessary condition is that $a_{11} \leq 0$. A symmetric argument establishes that it is also necessary that $a_{22} \leq 0$.

Suppose first that $a_{11} = 0$. Then, for any $x_1 \neq 0$,

$$q(x_1, x_2) = 2a_{12} x_1 x_2 + a_{22} x_2^2 = \left(2a_{12} + a_{22} \left(\frac{x_2}{x_1} \right) \right) x_1 x_2.$$

If $a_{12} > 0$ we can choose x_2/x_1 sufficiently close to zero that the term in parentheses is strictly positive. If $x_1 x_2 > 0$ then $q(x_1, x_2) > 0$ so $q(x)$ is not negative semi-definite. An identical argument establishes that it cannot be the case that $a_{12} < 0$ either. Then a necessary condition for $q(x)$ to be negative semi-definite is $a_{12} = 0$. (Note that with $a_{11} = 0$ the condition $a_{11} a_{22} - a_{12} a_{21} \geq 0$ is equivalent to the condition $a_{12} = 0$.)

Next suppose that $a_{11} < 0$. Completing the square, (B.2-1) can be rewritten as

$$q(x_1, x_2) = a_{11} \left(x_1 + \frac{a_{12}}{a_{11}} x_2 \right)^2 + \frac{1}{a_{11}} (a_{11} a_{22} - a_{12} a_{12}) x_2^2.$$

---

[4] Note that if (i) and (ii) both hold, then $a_{22} < 0$ as well.
[5] The proof of Proposition B.2-1 is very similar.

Actually, because $a_{12} = a_{21}$ we can write this more conveniently as

$$q(x_1, x_2) = a_{11}\left(x_1 + \frac{a_{12}}{a_{11}}\right)^2 + \frac{1}{a_{11}}(a_{11}a_{22} - a_{12}a_{21})x_2^2. \qquad \text{(B.2-3)}$$

Suppose we choose x_1 so that the first term on the right-hand side of (B.2-3) is zero. Because $a_{11} < 0$, a necessary condition for the right-hand side to be negative is

$$a_{11}a_{22} - a_{12}a_{21} \geq 0. \qquad \text{(B.2-4)}$$

We have therefore established the necessity of conditions (i) and (ii). Sufficiency follows almost immediately. If $a_{11} = 0$ it follows from (B.2-4) that $a_{12} = 0$ and hence that $q(x_1, x_2) = a_{22}x_2^2$. Appealing to (i) in the statement of the proposition, it follows that $q(x) \leq 0$. If $a_{11} < 0$ if follows directly from (B.2-3) that $q(x_1, x_2) \leq 0$.

Concave Functions

In Chapter 1 a function was defined to be concave if, for any two points on the graph of f, the line joining these two points lies below the graph of the function. This definition generalizes naturally.

Definition: Concave Function The function f is concave on the convex set $X \subset \mathbb{R}^n$ if for any vectors x^0 and x^1 in X, and any convex combination $x^\lambda = (1 - \lambda)x^0 + \lambda x^1, 0 < \lambda < 1,$

$$f(x^\lambda) \geq (1 - \lambda)f(x^0) + \lambda f(x^1).$$

If the inequality is always strict, the function is strictly concave.

The two-variable case is depicted in Figure B.2-4. Starting from x^0, pick any other point x^1; then the curve must bend forward in the direction of x^1. In the second figure, the linear approximation of the function at x^0 has been added.

Because the tangent line is a line tangential to a curve, it is called the tangent plane. In higher dimensions it is called the *tangent hyperplane.*

Tangent Hyperplane The set $H = \left\{x \mid \frac{\partial f}{\partial x}(x^0) \cdot (x - x^0) = 0\right\}$ is the tangent hyperplane of the function f at x^0

As is intuitively clear, a differentiable function is concave if and only if the graph of all the tangent hyperplanes lies above the graph of the function.

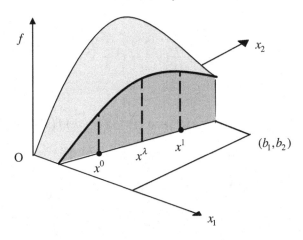

Figure B.2-4. Concave function.

Proposition B.2-3:
A differentiable function f is concave on the convex set $X \subset \mathbb{R}^n$ if and only if for any x^0 and $x^1 \in X$,

$$f(x^1) \le f(x^0) + \frac{\partial f}{\partial x}(x^0) \cdot (x^1 - x^0). \qquad (\text{B.2-5})$$

Proof: The proof of sufficiency proceeds exactly as in the proof for the one-dimensional case (see Proposition A.5-3).

To prove necessity, define

$$g(\lambda) = f(x^\lambda) = f(x^0 + \lambda(x^1 - x^0)).$$

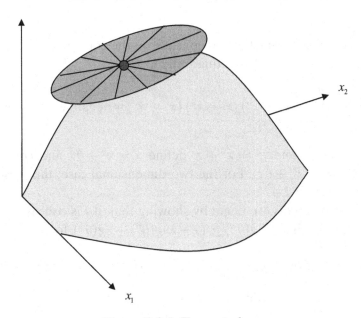

Figure B.2-5. Tangent plane.

Note that

$$g'(\lambda) = \frac{\partial f}{\partial x}(x^\lambda) \cdot (x^1 - x^0). \qquad (\text{B.2-6})$$

Because f is concave,

$$g(\lambda) = f(x^\lambda) = f(x^0 + \lambda(x^1 - x^0)) \geq (1 - \lambda)f(x^0) + \lambda f(x^1).$$

Because $g(0) = f(x^0)$, it follows that for all $\lambda \in (0, 1)$,

$$g(\lambda) - g(0) \geq \lambda(f(x^1) - f(x^0)).$$

Rearranging,

$$\frac{g(\lambda) - g(0)}{\lambda - 0} \geq f(x^1) - f(x^0).$$

Taking the limit as $\lambda \to 0$,

$$g'(0) \geq f(x^1) - f(x^0).$$

Finally, appealing to (B.2-6) and setting $\lambda = 0$,

$$\frac{\partial f}{\partial x}(x^0) \cdot (x^1 - x^0) \geq f(x^1) - f(x^0). \qquad \square$$

The second equivalence theorem for the one-variable case (Proposition A.5-4) also has its generalization.

Proposition B.2-4:
A twice differentiable function f is concave on the convex set $X \subset \mathbb{R}^n$ if and only if, for all x^0 and $x \in X$, the quadratic form

$$q(x) = \sum_{i=1}^{n} \sum_{j=1}^{n} \frac{\partial^2 f}{\partial x_i \partial x_j}(x^0)\left(x_i - x_i^0\right)\left(x_j - x_j^0\right) \text{ is negative semi-definite.}$$

Proof: For any x^0 and $x^1 = x^0 + z$, define $x = x^0 + \theta z$ and consider the function $g(\theta) = f(x^0 + \theta z)$. For the two-dimensional case, this is the curve depicted in Figure B.2-4.

To establish necessity we begin by showing that, if f is concave then $g(\theta)$ must be concave; that is, $g(\theta^\lambda) \geq (1 - \lambda)g(\theta^0) + \lambda g(\theta^1)$ for any θ^0, θ^1 and convex combination θ^λ.

From the definition of g,

$$\begin{aligned} g(\theta^\lambda) &= f(x^0 + (1 - \lambda)\theta^0 z + \lambda \theta^1 z) \\ &= f((1 - \lambda)(x^0 + \theta^0 z) + \lambda(x^0 + \theta^1 z)). \end{aligned}$$

Appealing to the concavity of f it follows that

$$g(\theta^{\lambda}) \geq (1 - \lambda) f(x^0 + \theta^0 z) + \lambda f(x^0 + \theta^1 z)$$
$$= (1 - \lambda) g(\theta^0) + \lambda g(\theta^1).$$

Thus g is concave and so $g''(0) \leq 0$.

From the definition of g,

$$g'(\theta) = \frac{\partial f}{\partial x}(x^0 + \theta z) \cdot z \quad \text{and} \quad g''(\theta) = \sum_{i=1}^{n} \sum_{j}^{n} \frac{\partial^2 f}{\partial x_i \partial x_j}(x^0 + \theta z) z_i z_j.$$

Hence $\sum_{i=1}^{n} \sum_{j}^{n} \frac{\partial^2 f}{\partial x_i \partial x_j}(x^0) z_i z_j = \sum_{i=1}^{n} \sum_{j}^{n} \frac{\partial^2 f}{\partial x_i \partial x_j}(x^0) \left(x_i - x_i^0\right) \left(x_j - x_j^0\right) \leq 0.$

To prove sufficiency, note that if the quadratic form is negative, then $g''(\theta) \leq 0$; that is, $g'(\theta)$ is decreasing on the interval $[0, 1]$. Thus $g'(\theta) \leq g'(0)$ for all $\theta \in [0, 1]$.

From the definition of g,

$$f(x^1) - f(x^0) = g(1) - g(0) = \int_0^1 g'(\theta) d\theta \leq \int_0^1 g'(0) d\theta = g'(0)$$

$$= \frac{\partial f}{\partial x}(x^0) \cdot z = \frac{\partial f}{\partial x}(x^0) \cdot (x^1 - x^0).$$

$\square$

Appealing to Propositions B.2-2 and B.2-4, it follows that a twice differentiable function of two variables $f(x_1, x_2)$, is concave if and only if

$$\text{(i)} \ \frac{\partial^2 f}{\partial x_j^2} \leq 0, \quad j = 1, 2 \quad \text{and} \quad \text{(ii)} \ \frac{\partial^2 f}{\partial x_1^2} \frac{\partial^2 f}{\partial x_2^2} - \left(\frac{\partial^2 f}{\partial x_1 \partial x_2}\right)^2 \geq 0.$$

Example: Cobb-Douglas Function

Because of its simplicity, economists make much use of the following Cobb-Douglas function:

$$f(x) = x_1^{\alpha} x_2^{\beta}, \alpha, \beta \geq 0, x \geq 0.$$

First note that $\frac{\partial^2 f}{\partial x_1^2} = \alpha(\alpha - 1) x_1^{\alpha-2} x_2^{\beta}$ and $\frac{\partial^2 f}{\partial x_2^2} = \beta(\beta - 1) x_1^{\alpha} x_2^{\beta-2}$. Appealing to (i), it follows that for f to be concave, both α and β must lie on the interval $[0, 1]$. Moreover $\frac{\partial^2 f}{\partial x_1 \partial x_2} = \alpha \beta x_1^{\alpha-1} x_2^{\beta-1}$. Appealing to (ii)

$$\frac{\partial^2 f}{\partial x_1^2} \frac{\partial^2 f}{\partial x_2^2} - \left(\frac{\partial^2 f}{\partial x_1 \partial x_2}\right)^2 = [(\alpha - 1)(\beta - 1)\alpha\beta - \alpha^2 \beta^2] x_1^{2(\alpha-1)} x_1^{2(\beta-1)}$$

$$= \alpha\beta(1 - \alpha - \beta) x_1^{2(\alpha-1)} x_1^{2(\beta-1)}.$$

Thus for concavity $\alpha + \beta \leq 1$.

The following propositions are often helpful in determining whether a function is concave.

Proposition B.2-5: Sum of Concave Functions
If f and g are concave then $f + g$ is concave.

Proposition B.2-6: Concave Function of a Function
The function $h(x) = g(f(x))$ is concave if g is concave and either
(a) g is increasing and f is concave or (b) f is linear.

The proofs are left as exercises.

Example 1:
$f(x) = \sum_{j=1}^{n} \ln x_j, x \in \mathbb{R}_+^n$ This is concave because each term in the summation is a concave function.

Example 2:
$f(x) = (x_1^\alpha + x_2^\beta)^\gamma, \alpha, \beta, \gamma \in (0, 1]$ and $x \gg 0$ Note that $f(x) = y(x)^\gamma$, where $y(x) = x_1^\alpha + x_2^\beta$. Because $\alpha \in (0, 1)x^\alpha$ has a negative second derivative, x_1^α is concave. By a symmetrical argument x_2^β is concave. Then $y(x)$ is concave because it is the sum of two concave functions. Also y^γ is an increasing concave function on $\mathbb{R}_+^2$ because it has a negative second derivative. Then f is concave because it is an increasing concave function of a concave function.

Quasi-Concave and Quasi-Convex Functions

In Appendix A we also considered quasi-concave functions. Again the definition generalizes naturally.

Definition: Quasi-Concave and Quasi-Convex Functions The function f is quasi-concave on the convex set X if for any vectors x^0 and x^1 in X and any convex combination $x^\lambda, 0 < \lambda < 1, f(x^\lambda) \geq \text{Min}\{f(x^0), f(x^1)\}$.

The function is quasi-convex if, for any convex combination, $f(x^\lambda) \leq \text{Max}\{f(x^0), f(x^1)\}$.

Note that we can always re-label the vectors x^0 and x^1 so that $f(x^1) \geq f(x^0)$. The following definition of a quasi-concave function is therefore equivalent.

Definition: Quasi-Concave Function The function f is quasi-concave on the convex set X if, for any vectors x^0 and x^1, $f(x^1) \geq f(x^0) \Rightarrow f(x^\lambda) \geq f(x^0)$ for all convex combinations x^λ.

The following propositions are especially helpful in checking for quasi-concavity.[6]

---

[6] The proofs are left as exercises.

Proposition B.2-7:
A concave function is quasi-concave.

Proposition B.2-8:
An increasing function of a concave function is quasi-concave.
 If f is concave and g is increasing then $h(x) = g(f(x))$ is quasi-concave.

Example: Cobb-Douglas Function
$f(x) = x_1^{\alpha_1} x_2^{\alpha_2} \dots x_n^{\alpha_n}, x \gg 0$ Note that $g(x) = \ln f(x) = \sum_{j=1}^{n} \alpha_j \ln x_j$.
Because each term in the summation is a concave function, $g(x)$ is concave.
Inverting, $f(x) = \ln^{-1} g(x) = e^{g(x)}$. Because the exponential function is
increasing, it follows from Proposition B.2-8 that f is quasi-concave.

 The next proposition is especially helpful in production theory where it is
often assumed that production functions are homogeneous of degree 1; that
is, for all $x \in \mathbb{R}_+^n$ and $\mu > 0$, $f(\mu x) = \mu f(x)$.

Proposition B.2-9:
A quasi-concave function that is homogeneous of degree 1 is concave.

Proof: Because f is homogeneous of degree 1 it follows that for any x^0, x^1
and $\lambda \in (0, 1)$

$$(1 - \lambda) f(x^0) + \lambda f(x^1) = f((1 - \lambda)x^0) + f(\lambda x^1),$$

Also, for some $\theta > 0$

$$f((1 - \lambda)x^0) = \theta f(\lambda x^1). \tag{B.2-7}$$

Then

$$(1 - \lambda) f(x^0) + \lambda f(x^1) = (1 + \theta) f(\lambda x^1). \tag{B.2-8}$$

Because f is homogeneous of degree 1 it follows from (B.2-7) that
$f((1 - \lambda)x^0) = f(\theta \lambda x^1)$. Note that

$$\frac{\theta}{1 + \theta}((1 - \lambda)x^0 + \lambda x^0) = \frac{\theta}{1 + \theta}(1 - \lambda)x^0 + \frac{1}{1 + \theta}\theta \lambda x^0$$

is a convex combination of $(1 - \lambda)x^0$ and $\theta \lambda x^1$. Therefore, by the quasi-
concavity of f

$$f\left(\frac{\theta}{1 + \theta}((1 - \lambda)x^0 + \lambda x^0)\right) \geq f(\theta \lambda x^0). \tag{B.2-9}$$

Because f is homogeneous of degree 1 it follows that

$$\frac{\theta}{1 + \theta} f((1 - \lambda)x^0 + \lambda x^0) \geq \theta f(\lambda x^0)$$

and hence that

$$f((1 - \lambda)x^0 + \lambda x^0) \geq (1 + \theta) f(\lambda x^0).$$

Appealing to (B.2-8),

$$f((1 - \lambda)x^0 + \lambda x^0) \geq (1 - \lambda)f(x^0) + \lambda f(x^1). \qquad \square$$

Suppose that x^0 and x^1 are linearly independent so that $(1 - \lambda)x^0 \neq \theta \lambda x^1$. Then if f is strictly quasi-concave the inequality in (B.2-9) is strict. We therefore have the following corollary.

Corollary B.2-10: A strictly quasi-concave function that is homogeneous of degree 1 is concave; moreover, if x^0 and x^1 are linearly dependent (i.e. $x^1 \neq \mu x^0$), then

$$f((1 - \lambda)x^0 + \lambda x^0) > (1 - \lambda)f(x^0) + \lambda f(x^1), \quad 0 < \lambda < 1.$$

Example: Cobb-Douglas Function
$f(x) = x_1^{\alpha_1} x_2^{\alpha_2} \dots x_n^{\alpha_n}, \alpha, x \gg 0$ We have already seen that for any α, f is quasi-concave. If $\sum_{i=1}^{n} \alpha_i = 1$,

$$f(\lambda x) = (\lambda x_1)^{\alpha_1}(\lambda x_2)^{\alpha_2} \dots (\lambda x_n)^{\alpha_n} = \lambda x_1^{\alpha_1} x_2^{\alpha_2} \dots x_n^{\alpha_n} = \lambda f(x).$$

Therefore f is homogeneous of degree 1. By Corollary B.2-10 it follows that f is concave.

Suppose next that $\sum_{i=1}^{n} \alpha_i = \theta < 1$. Then define $\beta_i = \alpha_i/\theta$. Because $\sum_{i=1}^{n} \beta_i = 1$, the function $g(x) = x_1^{\beta_1} x_2^{\beta_2} \dots x_n^{\beta_n}$ is concave. Also

$$f(x) = x_1^{\alpha_1} x_2^{\alpha_2} \dots x_n^{\alpha_n} = x_1^{\theta\beta_1} x_2^{\theta\beta_2} \dots x_n^{\theta\beta_n} = (x_1^{\beta_1} x_2^{\beta_2} \dots x_n^{\beta_n})^{\theta} = g(x)^{\theta}.$$

Thus f is an increasing concave function of g. By proposition B.2-6, f is concave.

Contour Sets

The function $y = f(x_1, x_2)$, depicted in Figure B.2-6, can be represented on the horizontal plane by mapping all the points for which the function takes on a particular value.

This is called a *contour set* (or "level curve"). In mathematical shorthand,

$$C(x^0) = \{x | f(x) = f(x^0)\}.$$

The set of vectors for which the function is above some value, that is,

$$C_U(x^0) = \{x | f(x) \geq f(x^0)\}$$

is called an upper contour set. In the figure this is the set of points inside the circle.

The lower contour sets $C_L(x^0)$, are similarly defined.

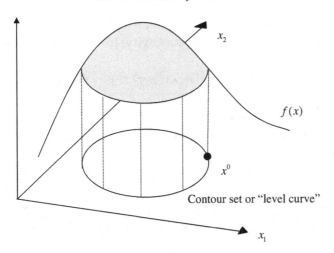

Figure B.2-6. Contour set.

Example: Consumer Choice

Suppose that x^* solves $\underset{x}{\text{Max}}\{U(x)|p \cdot x \leq I\}$. With $n = 2$ we can depict the solution in a standard indifference curve budget-line diagram (Figure B.2-7).

The set of consumption vectors to the right of the indifference curve is an upper contour set of the utility function U. The set of consumption vectors below the budget line is a lower contour set of the expenditure function $e(x) = p \cdot x$. Often in economic analysis it is helpful (and natural) to assume that the upper contour sets of certain functions are convex. As we now see, this is equivalent to assuming that the function is quasi-concave.

Proposition B.2-11:

A function is quasi-concave if and only if the upper contour sets of the function are convex.

Proof: Suppose f is quasi-concave and for any $\hat{x}$, consider vectors x^0 and x^1 that lie in the upper contour set $C_U(\hat{x})$ of this function. That is, $f(x^0) \geq f(\hat{x})$

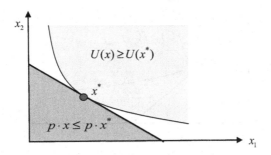

Figure B.2-7. Upper and lower contour sets.

and $f(x^1) \geq f(\hat{x})$. Without loss of generality we may assume that $f(x^1) \geq f(x^0)$. From the definition of quasi-concavity, for any convex combination,

$$x^\lambda = (1 - \lambda)x^0 + \lambda x^1, \quad f(x^\lambda) \geq f(x^0).$$

Because $f(x^0) \geq f(\hat{x})$, it follows that for all convex combinations $f(x^\lambda) \geq f(\hat{x})$. Hence all convex combinations lie in the upper contour set. Thus $C_U(\hat{x})$ is convex.

Conversely, if the upper contour sets are convex, then f is quasi-concave. To demonstrate this, suppose $f(x^1) \geq f(x^0)$. Then x^0 and x^1 are both in $C_U(x^0)$. Therefore, by the convexity of $C_U(x^0)$, all convex combination lie in this set. That is, $f(x^\lambda) \geq f(x^0)$ for all λ, $0 < \lambda < 1$. □

If f is differentiable, then it has the following linear approximation at x^0:

$$f^L(x) = f(x^0) + \frac{\partial f}{\partial x}(x^0) \cdot (x - x^0).$$

The contour set for $f^L(x)$ through x^0 is the set of points satisfying

$$f^L(x) = f^L(x^0), \quad \text{that is,} \quad \frac{\partial f}{\partial x}(x^0) \cdot (x - x^0) = 0.$$

This contour set is depicted in Figure B.2-8 along with the upper contour set $X_U = \{x \mid f(x) \geq f(x^0)\}$. In the two-dimensional case the contour set for the linear approximation is the tangent line. With $n > 2$ this becomes the tangent hyperplane.

From Figure B.2-8 it is clear that if f is quasi-concave, so that the boundary of the upper contour set is bowed out, then the upper contour set for f must be everywhere above the tangent hyperplane. We now show that this is true for the n-dimensional case and that the converse is also true.

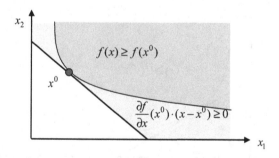

Figure B.2-8. Tangent line.

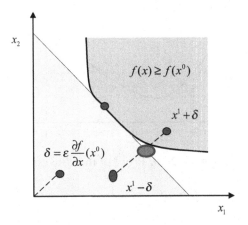

Figure B.2-9. Quasi-concave function.

Proposition B.2-12: Quasi-Concavity of a Differentiable Function

The function $f \in \mathbb{C}^1$ is quasi-concave if and only if

$$f(x) \geq f(x^0) \Rightarrow \frac{\partial f}{\partial x}(x^0) \cdot (x - x^0) \geq 0. \tag{B.2-10}$$

Proof: We first show that quasi-concavity implies (B.2-10). The upper contour set $\{x \mid f(x) \geq f(x^0)\}$ and supporting hyperplane through x^0 are depicted in Figure B.2-9. Consider any point x in the upper contour set. Given that f is quasi-concave, if $f(x) \geq f(x^0)$, then for any convex combination $x^\lambda = (1 - \lambda)x^0 + \lambda x = x^0 + \lambda(x - x^0)$, $f(x^\lambda) \geq f(x^0)$.

Define $g(\lambda) \equiv f(x^\lambda) = f(x^0 + \lambda(x - x^0))$. Differentiating by λ,

$$\frac{dg}{d\lambda}(\lambda) = \frac{\partial f}{\partial x}(x^\lambda) \cdot (x - x^0).$$

But we have just argued that for all $\lambda \in (0, 1)$, $g(\lambda) = f(x^\lambda) \geq f(x^0) = g(0)$. Hence $\frac{dg}{d\lambda}(0) \geq 0$; that is, $\frac{\partial f}{\partial x}(x^0) \cdot (x - x^0) \geq 0$.

To prove the converse, we suppose that the hypothesis is false and seek a contradiction. That is we assume that condition (B.2-10) holds and there exists some x^0, x^1 and convex combination $x^\beta = (1 - \beta)x^0 + \beta x^1$ such that

$$f(x^1) \geq f(x^0) > f(x^\beta).$$

Once again we define the function $g(\lambda) = f((1 - \lambda)x^0 + \lambda x^1) = f(x^0 + \lambda(x^1 - x^0))$. Then

$$g(1) \geq g(0) > g(\beta).$$

It follows from the continuity of f that $g(\lambda)$ is continuous. Thus there exists some $\alpha \in [0, \beta)$ such that

$$g(\alpha) = g(0) \quad \text{and} \quad g(\lambda) < g(0) \quad \text{for all} \quad \lambda \in (\alpha, \beta]. \tag{B.2-11}$$

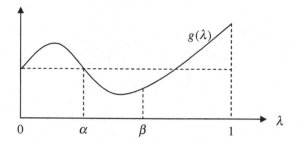

Figure B.2-10. Proof of the converse.

This is depicted in Figure B.2-10.

Then for all $\lambda \in [\alpha, \beta]$

$$f(x^\lambda) = g(\lambda) \le g(1) = f(x^1).$$

Appealing to (B.2-10), it follows that for all $\lambda \in [\alpha, \beta]$,

$$\frac{\partial f}{\partial x}(x^\lambda) \cdot (x^1 - x^\lambda) \ge 0.$$

Also $x^1 - x^\lambda = (1 - \lambda)(x^1 - x^0)$. Therefore

$$\frac{\partial f}{\partial x}(x^\lambda) \cdot (x^1 - x^0) \ge 0 \quad \text{for all} \quad \lambda \in [\alpha, \beta]. \tag{B.2-12}$$

Next note that

$$g'(\lambda) = \frac{d}{d\lambda} f(x^0 + \lambda(x^1 - x^0)) = \frac{\partial f}{\partial x}(x^\lambda) \cdot (x^1 - x^0).$$

Appealing to (B.2-12), it follows that $g'(\lambda) \ge 0$ for all $\lambda \in [\alpha, \beta]$. Then $g(\beta) \ge g(\alpha)$. But this is impossible because it contradicts (B.2-11). $\qquad\square$

We also have the following corollary.

Corollary B.2-13: Upper Contour Sets and Tangent Hyperplanes of a Quasi-Concave Function For any quasi-concave and differentiable function f such that $\frac{\partial f}{\partial x}(x^0) \ne 0$,

$$f(x) > f(x^0) \Rightarrow \frac{\partial f}{\partial x}(x^0) \cdot (x - x^0) > 0.$$

Proof: From Proposition B.2-12 we know that

$$f(x) > f(x^0) \Rightarrow \frac{\partial f}{\partial x}(x^0) \cdot (x - x^0) \ge 0. \tag{B.2-13}$$

Either the corollary holds, or there is some $x^1 \ne x^0$ such that $\frac{\partial f}{\partial x}(x^0) \cdot (x^1 - x^0) = 0$. If so x^1 is on the supporting hyperplane and $f(x^1) > f(x^0)$. Consider x^1 in Figure B.2-9. Also shown is the gradient vector scaled down by the factor ε; that is, $\delta = \varepsilon \frac{\partial f}{\partial x}(x^0)$. Consider $x^2 = x^1 - \delta$. Because $f(x^1) > f(x^0)$ it follows that if we choose ε positive and sufficiently small ε, we can make δ positive and sufficiently small so that $f(x^2) = f(x^1 - \delta) > f(x^0)$.

Also

$$\frac{\partial f}{\partial x}(x^0) \cdot (x^2 - x^0) = \frac{\partial f}{\partial x}(x^0) \cdot (x^2 - x^1) + \frac{\partial f}{\partial x}(x^0) \cdot (x^1 - x^0).$$

But the second term on the right-hand side is zero and $x^2 - x^1 = -\varepsilon \frac{\partial f}{\partial x}(x^0)$. We have therefore established that

$$f(x^2) > f(x^0) \quad \text{and} \quad \frac{\partial f}{\partial x}(x^0) \cdot (x^2 - x^0) = -\varepsilon \frac{\partial f}{\partial x}(x^0) \cdot \frac{\partial f}{\partial x}(x^0) < 0.$$

But this result contradicts (B.2-13) so there can be no such x^2. □

Exercises

Exercise B.2-1: Positive Semi-Definite Quadratic Form What are the necessary and sufficient conditions for $q(x) = \sum_{i=1}^{2} \sum_{j=1}^{2} a_{ij} x_i x_j$ to be everywhere non-negative? HINT: If $q(x)$ is non-negative, $-q(x)$ must be non-positive.

Exercise B.2-2: Positive Definite Quadratic Form What are the necessary and sufficient conditions for $q(x) = \sum_{i=1}^{2} \sum_{j=1}^{2} a_{ij} x_i x_j$ to be strictly positive for all $x \neq 0$?

Exercise B.2-3: Concave and Quasi-Concave Functions Sketch proofs of Propositions B.2-5 and B.2-6.

Exercise B.2-4: Convex Lower Contour Sets

(a) Show that the lower contour sets of a function are convex if and only if the function is quasi-convex.
(b) The output of commodity j has labor input requirements $f_j(q_j)$, $j = 1, \ldots, n$ where $f_j(\cdot)$ is convex. Show that the total labor requirements function $L(q) = \sum_{j=1}^{n} f_j(q_j)$ is quasi-convex.
(c) Hence show that if the supply of labor is fixed, the set of feasible outputs is convex.

Exercise B.2-5: Contour Sets In each case depict the contour sets $f(x) = 0$, $f(x) = k$, $f(x) = -k$, where $k > 0$.

(a) $f(x) = p_1 x_1 + p_2 x_2$, where $p > 0$
(b) $f(x) = x_1 x_2$
(c) $f(x) = x_2^2 - 4x_1^2 = (x_2 - 2x_1)(x_2 + 2x_1)$
(d) * $f(x) = -x_1^2 + 6x_1 x_2 + 7x_2^2$

B.3 Transformations of Vectors

Key ideas: linear transformations, matrix, quadratic form, inverse

A function transforms an n-dimensional vector into a real number (a one-dimensional vector). More generally "transformations" map n-dimensional vectors into m-dimensional vectors. Here we consider the family of linear transformations. Consider the following $m \times n$ "matrix," an array of m rows and n columns:

$$\mathbf{A} = \begin{bmatrix} a_{11} & \cdot & \cdot & \cdot & a_{1n} \\ \cdot & & \cdot & \cdot & \cdot \\ \cdot & & \cdot & \cdot & \cdot \\ a_{m1} & \cdot & \cdot & \cdot & a_{mn} \end{bmatrix}.$$

Each of the rows is an n-dimensional vector. Denote the ith row as $a_i = (a_{i1}, \dots, a_{in})$. Then we transform the n-dimensional vector x into an m-dimensional vector y by taking the product of each row and x:

$$y_1 = a_1 \cdot x$$
$$\cdot$$
$$\cdot$$
$$\cdot$$
$$y_m = a_m \cdot x$$

It proves useful to write the vectors x and y as special matrices with one column ("column vectors"). Then we write

$$y = \mathbf{A}x \quad \text{where} \quad y_i = (i\text{th row of } \mathbf{A}) \cdot x.$$

Next suppose we make two such linear transformations, $y = \mathbf{A}x$ and $z = \mathbf{B}y$. These are depicted in Figure B.3-1. Combining the two transformations we may write

$$z = \mathbf{B}(\mathbf{A}x).$$

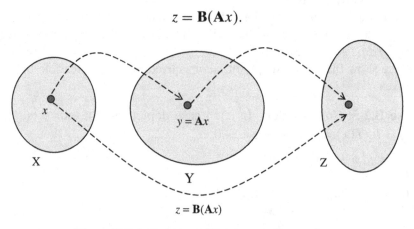

Figure B.3-1. Product of linear transformations.

An important property of linear transformations is that the product of two such transformations is itself a linear transformation; that is,

$$z = \mathbf{B}(\mathbf{A}x) = \mathbf{C}x.$$

Moreover there is a simple rule for computing the elements of the new matrix $\mathbf{C}$:

$c_{ij} = (i\text{th row of } \mathbf{B}) \cdot (j \text{ th column of } \mathbf{A})$.

We demonstrate this for the 2×2 case. Consider two linear transformations of two-dimensional vectors:

$$\begin{bmatrix} y_1 \\ y_2 \end{bmatrix} = \begin{bmatrix} a_{11} & a_{12} \\ a_{21} & a_{22} \end{bmatrix} \begin{bmatrix} x_1 \\ x_2 \end{bmatrix} \quad \text{and} \quad \begin{bmatrix} z_1 \\ z_2 \end{bmatrix} = \begin{bmatrix} b_{11} & b_{12} \\ b_{21} & b_{22} \end{bmatrix} \begin{bmatrix} y_1 \\ y_2 \end{bmatrix}.$$

Multiplying each row of the matrix $\mathbf{A}$ by the column vector x,

$$\begin{bmatrix} y_1 \\ y_2 \end{bmatrix} = \begin{bmatrix} a_{11}x_1 + a_{12}x_2 \\ a_{21}x_1 + a_{22}x_2 \end{bmatrix}$$

and hence

$$\begin{bmatrix} z_1 \\ z_2 \end{bmatrix} = \begin{bmatrix} b_{11} & b_{12} \\ b_{21} & b_{22} \end{bmatrix} \begin{bmatrix} y_1 \\ y_2 \end{bmatrix} = \begin{bmatrix} b_{11} & b_{12} \\ b_{21} & b_{22} \end{bmatrix} \begin{bmatrix} a_{11}x_1 + a_{12}x_2 \\ a_{21}x_1 + a_{22}x_2 \end{bmatrix}$$

$$= \begin{bmatrix} (b_{11}a_{11} + b_{12}a_{12})x_1 + (b_{11}a_{12} + b_{12}a_{22})x_2 \\ (b_{21}a_{11} + b_{22}a_{21})x_1 + (b_{21}a_{12} + b_{22}a_{22})x_2 \end{bmatrix}$$

$$= \begin{bmatrix} b_{11}a_{11} + b_{12}a_{21} & b_{11}a_{12} + b_{12}a_{22} \\ b_{21}a_{11} + b_{22}a_{21} & b_{21}a_{12} + b_{22}a_{22} \end{bmatrix} \begin{bmatrix} x_1 \\ x_2 \end{bmatrix}$$

$$= \begin{bmatrix} c_{11} & c_{12} \\ c_{21} & c_{22} \end{bmatrix}, \quad \text{where} \quad c_{ij} = (i\text{th row of } \mathbf{B}) \cdot (j\text{th column of } \mathbf{A}).$$

Transpose of a Matrix

A matrix is "transposed" by rotating it around its leading diagonal. Let $\mathbf{A}'$ be the transpose of $\mathbf{A}$; that is, $a'_{ij} = a_{ji}$. Then the ith row and jth column of $\mathbf{A}$ become, respectively, the ith column and jth row of $\mathbf{A}'$. From the rules of matrix multiplication,

$$(\mathbf{AB})' = \mathbf{B}'\mathbf{A}'.$$

To confirm this, let $\mathbf{C} = \mathbf{AB}$. We need to establish that $\mathbf{C}' = \mathbf{B}'\mathbf{A}'$; that is, the ijth element of $\mathbf{C}'$ is the product of the ith row of $\mathbf{B}'$ and the jth column of $\mathbf{A}'$:

$$c'_{ij} = c_{ji} = (j\text{th row of } \mathbf{A}) \cdot (i\text{th column of } \mathbf{B})$$
$$= (i\text{th column of } \mathbf{B}) \cdot (j\text{th row of } \mathbf{A})$$
$$= (i\text{th row of } \mathbf{B}') \cdot (j\text{th column of } \mathbf{A}').$$

Note that the transpose of a $n \times 1$ column vector x is a $1 \times n$ row vector x'. Thus the square of the distance between two vectors x and y can be written either as an inner product or a matrix product:

$$\|x - y\|^2 = (x - y) \cdot (x - y) = (x - y)'(x - y).$$

Quadratic Form

Consider the matrix product $x'\mathbf{A}x$. In the two-dimensional case,

$$x'\mathbf{A}x = \begin{bmatrix} x_1 & x_2 \end{bmatrix} \begin{bmatrix} a_{11} & a_{12} \\ a_{21} & a_{22} \end{bmatrix} \begin{bmatrix} x_1 \\ x_2 \end{bmatrix} = \begin{bmatrix} x_1 & x_2 \end{bmatrix} \begin{bmatrix} a_{11}x_1 + a_{21}x_2 \\ a_{21}x_1 + a_{22}x_2 \end{bmatrix}$$
$$= a_{11}x_1^2 + (a_{12} + a_{21})x_1x_2 + a_{22}x_2^2.$$

This is the general quadratic function of a vector $x \in \mathbb{R}^2$. Generally, with an n vector x and $n \times n$ matrix $\mathbf{A}$, the general quadratic function (or "quadratic form" of the matrix $\mathbf{A}$) can be expressed as follows:

$$q(x) = x'\mathbf{A}x = \sum_{i=1}^{n} \sum_{j=1}^{n} a_{ij}x_ix_j.$$

The x_ix_j term is $a_{ij} + a_{ji}$. Thus there is no loss in generality in assuming that the matrix $\mathbf{A}$ is symmetric; that is, $a_{ij} = a_{ji}$.

Consider the partial derivatives of the quadratic form $q(x)$. Collecting all the terms in x_1,

$$q(x) = a_{11}x_1^2 + a_{12}x_1x_2 + \cdots + a_{1n}x_1x_n$$
$$+ a_{21}x_2x_1 + \cdots + a_{n1}x_nx_1 + \text{other terms independent of } x_1.$$

Given the symmetry of $\mathbf{A}$,

$$q(x) = a_{11}x_1^2 + 2(a_{12}x_1x_2 + \cdots + a_{1n}x_1x_n) + \text{terms independent of } x_1.$$

Then

$$\frac{\partial q}{\partial x_1} = 2(a_{11}, \ldots, a_{1n}) \cdot (x_1, \ldots, x_n) = 2(\text{first row of } \mathbf{A}) \cdot x.$$

Similarly,

$$\frac{\partial q}{\partial x_i} = 2(i\text{th row of } \mathbf{A}) \cdot x. \tag{B.3-1}$$

Thus the vector of partial derivatives,

$$\frac{\partial q}{\partial x} = 2\mathbf{A}x.$$

Also, from (B.3-1),

$$\frac{\partial^2 q}{\partial x_j \partial x_i} = 2a_{ij}.$$

Thus the matrix of second-partial derivatives,

$$\left[\frac{\partial^2 q}{\partial x_i \partial x_j} \right] = 2\mathbf{A}.$$

We have therefore proved the following proposition.

Proposition B.3-1: Derivatives of a Quadratic Form
If $q(x) = x'\mathbf{A}x$ then $\frac{\partial q}{\partial x} = 2\mathbf{A}x$ and $\left[\frac{\partial^2 q}{\partial x_i \partial x_j} \right] = 2\mathbf{A}$.

Square Matrices

One important class of linear transformations maps n-dimensional vectors into other n-dimensional vectors (that is, $y = \mathbf{A}x$) where both x and y are n-dimensional vectors. To multiply $\mathbf{A}$ and x the matrix must have n columns. For y to have n elements, there must be n rows of $\mathbf{A}$ so the matrix $\mathbf{A}$ is an n-dimensional square matrix. Consider the simplest case $n = 2$.

$$\begin{bmatrix} y_1 \\ y_2 \end{bmatrix} = \begin{bmatrix} a_{11} & a_{12} \\ a_{21} & a_{22} \end{bmatrix} \begin{bmatrix} x_1 \\ x_2 \end{bmatrix} = \begin{bmatrix} a_{11}x_1 + a_{12}x_2 \\ a_{21}x_1 + a_{22}x_2 \end{bmatrix}$$

$$= \begin{bmatrix} a_{11} \\ a_{21} \end{bmatrix} x_1 + \begin{bmatrix} a_{21} \\ a_{22} \end{bmatrix} x_2 \equiv x_1 a_{(1)} + x_2 a_{(2)}.$$

Thus the vector y is a linear combination of the two column vectors $a_{(1)}$ and $a_{(2)}$. In the n-dimensional case the vector y is the linear combination of the n columns of $\mathbf{A}$ Geometrically, we can draw this linear combination by first drawing each column vector and then scaling each vector and summing the scaled vectors.

With $n = 2$, two possibilities are depicted in Figure B.3-2. In the first case the two column vectors do not differ simply by scale so the mapping is onto the entire two-dimensional space. In this case the columns of $\mathbf{A}$ are said to be linearly independent. In the second case $a_{(2)} = \theta a_{(1)}$ and the mapping is from the two-dimensional space of vectors $x = (x_1, x_2)$ onto a one-dimensional line. In this case the column vectors are said to be linearly dependent.

Similarly, with three dimensions,

$$y = Ax = \begin{bmatrix} a_{11} \\ a_{21} \\ a_{31} \end{bmatrix} x_1 + \begin{bmatrix} a_{12} \\ a_{22} \\ a_{32} \end{bmatrix} x_2 + \begin{bmatrix} a_{31} \\ a_{32} \\ a_{33} \end{bmatrix} x_3 \equiv x_1 a_{(1)} + x_2 a_{(2)} + x_3 a_{(3)}.$$

In Figure B.3-3, the linear combinations of the first two vectors map out a plane in three-dimensional space. If the third vector is in this plane it must

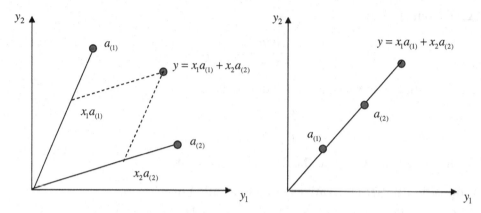

Figure B.3-2. Linearly dependent and independent vectors.

be a linear combination of the other two vectors. Then all the linear combinations of the three vectors also lie in the plane.

Generally, the columns of a square n-matrix are independent if no column can be expressed as a linear combination of the other n-1 columns. In this case the mapping is onto the entire n-dimensional space. For any n-dimensional matrix **A** we can determine whether the columns are independent by computing the determinant of **A** denoted $|\mathbf{A}|$.

Definition: Determinant of a Square Matrix $n = 2$

$$|\mathbf{A}| = \begin{vmatrix} a_{11} & a_{12} \\ a_{21} & a_{22} \end{vmatrix} = a_{11}a_{22} - a_{21}a_{12}$$

$n > 2.$

The determinant is defined recursively as follows:

$|\mathbf{A}| = \sum_{j=1}^{n} (-1)^{i+j} a_{ij} |\mathbf{A}_{(ij)}|$ where $\mathbf{A}_{(ij)}$ is the matrix obtained after deleting the ith row and jth column of **A**.

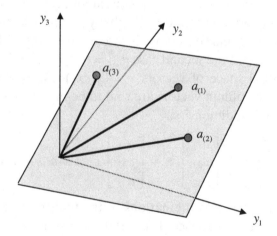

Figure B.3-3. Linear dependence.

Example 1: Linearly Independent Columns

Expanding along the first row,

$$|\mathbf{A}| = \begin{vmatrix} 2 & 3 & 0 \\ 4 & 1 & 3 \\ 1 & 1 & 2 \end{vmatrix} = (-1)^2(2)\begin{vmatrix} 1 & 3 \\ 1 & 2 \end{vmatrix} + (-1)^3(3)\begin{vmatrix} 4 & 3 \\ 1 & 2 \end{vmatrix} + (-1)^4(0)\begin{vmatrix} 4 & 1 \\ 1 & 1 \end{vmatrix}$$

$$= (-1)^2(2)(-1) + (-1)^3(3)(5) = -17.$$

Example 2: Linearly Dependent Columns

Expanding along the third row,

$$|\mathbf{A}| = \begin{vmatrix} 2 & 0 & 4 \\ 1 & 1 & 4 \\ 0 & 2 & 4 \end{vmatrix} = (-1)^4(0)\begin{vmatrix} 0 & 4 \\ 1 & 4 \end{vmatrix} + (-1)^5(2)\begin{vmatrix} 2 & 4 \\ 1 & 4 \end{vmatrix} + (-1)^6(4)\begin{vmatrix} 2 & 0 \\ 1 & 1 \end{vmatrix} = 0.$$

Note that in the second example, the third column vector is twice the sum of the first two columns. Therefore the vectors are not independent.

Identity Matrix

The identity matrix $\mathbf{I}$ has all off-diagonal elements of zero and all on-diagonal elements of 1. Following the rules of matrix multiplication, the identity matrix maps every vector onto itself; that is, $\mathbf{I}x = x$.

Inverse Matrix

Let $\mathbf{A}$ be a square matrix with non-zero determinant. Let $\mathbf{B}$ be a second matrix that maps the vector y back to x (see Figure B.3-4). Then

$$x = \mathbf{B}y = \mathbf{B}(\mathbf{A}x) = (\mathbf{B}\mathbf{A})x = \mathbf{I}x.$$

Thus the "inverse" mapping $\mathbf{B}$ times the matrix $\mathbf{A}$ must equal the identity matrix. Also, starting from a vector y and mapping to x and back again,

$$y = \mathbf{A}x = \mathbf{A}(\mathbf{B}y) = (\mathbf{A}\mathbf{B})y = \mathbf{I}y.$$

Thus regardless of the order of multiplication, the product of the matrix $\mathbf{A}$ and its inverse is the identity matrix. We write the inverse as $\mathbf{A}^{-1}$. Then

$$\mathbf{A}\mathbf{A}^{-1} = \mathbf{A}^{-1}\mathbf{A} = \mathbf{I}.$$

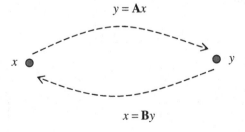

Figure B.3-4. Transformation and its inverse.

To compute the inverse we first define the "minor determinants" of a matrix **A** For each element a_{ij} of **A**, the minor matrix $\mathbf{M}_{ij}$ is obtained by eliminating the ith row and jth column of **A**. The minor determinant $\left|\mathbf{M}_{ij}\right|$ is the determinant of this minor matrix.

Computation of the Inverse

If $|\mathbf{A}| \neq 0$ the square matrix A has an inverse $\mathbf{A}^{-1} = [a_{ij}^{-1}]$, where

$$a_{ij}^{-1} = \frac{(-1)^{i+j}\left|\mathbf{M}_{ji}\right|}{|\mathbf{A}|}.$$

Example:

$$\mathbf{A} = \begin{bmatrix} a_{11} & a_{12} \\ a_{21} & a_{22} \end{bmatrix}$$

$$|\mathbf{M}_{11}| = a_{22}, \ |\mathbf{M}_{12}| = a_{21}, \ |\mathbf{M}_{21}| = a_{12}, \ |\mathbf{M}_{22}| = a_{11}.$$

Then

$$\mathbf{A}^{-1} = \begin{bmatrix} \dfrac{a_{22}}{|\mathbf{A}|} & -\dfrac{a_{12}}{|\mathbf{A}|} \\ -\dfrac{a_{21}}{|\mathbf{A}|} & \dfrac{a_{11}}{|\mathbf{A}|} \end{bmatrix} = \frac{1}{|\mathbf{A}|}\begin{bmatrix} a_{22} & -a_{12} \\ -a_{21} & a_{11} \end{bmatrix}.$$

If the columns of **A** are independent, we have argued that the mapping is onto the entire n-dimensional space. Thus for any vector b there must be some vector x such that

$$\mathbf{A}x = b.$$

Mathematically, because the inverse exists,

$$\mathbf{A}^{-1}(\mathbf{A}x) = (\mathbf{A}^{-1}\mathbf{A})x = \mathbf{I}x = x = \mathbf{A}^{-1}b.$$

Cramer's Rule

Having computed an inverse, it is simply a mechanical exercise to solve a system of linear equations. Cramer's Rule provides a convenient way of summarizing this computation. Define $\mathbf{A}_{j,b}$ to be the matrix A with the jth column replaced by b. Then

$$x_j = \frac{\left|\mathbf{A}_{j,b}\right|}{|\mathbf{A}|}.$$

Example:

$$\begin{array}{l} 3x_1 + 4x_2 = 11 \\ 2x_1 + 3x_2 = 8 \end{array}, \quad \text{that is,} \quad \begin{bmatrix} 3 & 4 \\ 2 & 3 \end{bmatrix}\begin{bmatrix} x_1 \\ x_2 \end{bmatrix} = \begin{bmatrix} 11 \\ 8 \end{bmatrix}.$$

Appealing to Cramer's Rule,

$$x_1 = \frac{\begin{vmatrix} 11 & 4 \\ 8 & 3 \end{vmatrix}}{\begin{vmatrix} 3 & 4 \\ 2 & 3 \end{vmatrix}} = 1, \quad x_2 = \frac{\begin{vmatrix} 3 & 11 \\ 2 & 8 \end{vmatrix}}{\begin{vmatrix} 3 & 4 \\ 2 & 3 \end{vmatrix}} = 2.$$

You can plug back into the equations to confirm that this is the solution.

Negative Semi-Definite Matrix

In the last section we examined the two-variable case and derived necessary conditions under which a quadratic form is negative semi-definite. We now state an important generalization of this result.

Definition: Principal Minor Determinant The ith principal minor of the square matrix $\mathbf{A}$ is the matrix obtained by deleting all but the first i rows and i columns of $\mathbf{A}$ The principal minor determinant is the determinant of this matrix.

Proposition B.3-2: Necessary and Sufficient Conditions for a Quadratic Form to be Negative Semi-Definite
The quadratic form $x'\mathbf{A}x$ is negative semi-definite if and only if the ith principal minor determinant of $\mathbf{A}$ is of sign $(-1)^i, i = 1, \ldots, n$.

Consider the two-variable case. The principal minors of $\mathbf{A}$ are $|a_{11}|$ and $\begin{vmatrix} a_{11} & a_{12} \\ a_{21} & a_{22} \end{vmatrix}$. Thus the necessary and sufficient conditions are $a_{11} \le 0$ and $a_{11}a_{22} - a_{12}a_{21} \ge 0$.

Finally consider the quadratic form $x'\mathbf{A}x$ where the n variables satisfy the linear constraint $b'x = 0$ where $b \neq 0$. Suppose that $b_i \neq 0$. Then

$$x_i = \frac{1}{b_i} \sum_{\substack{j=1 \\ j \neq i}}^{n} b_j x_j.$$

We can therefore substitute for x_i in the quadratic form and obtain a new quadratic form with $n - 1$ variables. Tedious algebra then yields the following proposition.

Proposition B.3-3:
The quadratic form $x'\mathbf{A}x$ is negative for all x satisfying the linear constraint $b'x = 0$ if and only if the ith principal minor of the matrix

$$\begin{bmatrix} 0 & b' \\ b & \mathbf{A} \end{bmatrix}$$

is of sign $(-1)^{1+i}, i = 1, \ldots, n+1$.

Application: Necessary Condition for Quasi-Concavity

An appeal to this last result makes it relatively easy to determine the restrictions that quasi-concavity places on a twice continuously differentiable function. From the previous section we know that for a quasi-concave function

$$f(x) > f(x^0) \Rightarrow \frac{\partial f}{\partial x}(x^0) \cdot (x - x^0) > 0.$$

It follows that if $\frac{\partial f}{\partial x}(x^0) \cdot (x - x^0) \leq 0$ then $f(x) \leq f(x^0)$.

Consider any x^1 on the tangent hyperplane at x^0. That is, $\frac{\partial f}{\partial x}(x^0) \cdot (x^1 - x^0) = 0$. Then all convex combinations $x^\lambda = x^0 + \lambda(x^1 - x^0)$ lie on this tangent hyperplane; that is

$$\frac{\partial f}{\partial x}(x^0) \cdot (x^1 - x^0) = 0. \tag{B.3-2}$$

Thus for any x^λ, $f(x^\lambda) \leq f(x^0)$.

Define $g(\lambda) = f(x^\lambda) = f(x^0 + \lambda\Delta)$, where $\Delta = x^1 - x^0$. Given the earlier arguments $g(\lambda) \leq g(0)$. But

$$g'(\lambda) = \frac{d}{d\lambda} f(x^0 + \lambda\Delta) = \frac{\partial f}{\partial x}(x^\lambda) \cdot \Delta = \frac{\partial f}{\partial x}(x^\lambda) \cdot (x^1 - x^0).$$

Appealing to (B.3-2), it follows that $g'(0) = 0$.

We wish to show that $g''(0) \leq 0$. To do so we suppose instead that $g''(0) > 0$ and seek a contradiction. If $g''(0) > 0$, then in some neighborhood of 0, $g'(\lambda)$ is strictly increasing, and because $g'(0) = 0$, it follows that $g'(\lambda) > 0$ over this neighborhood and so for some $\lambda > 0, g(\lambda) > 0$. But we have already argued that $g(\lambda) \leq g(0)$. Thus we have a contradiction. It follows that $g''(0) \leq 0$. But

$$g''(\lambda) = \frac{d^2}{d\lambda^2} f(x^0 + \lambda\Delta) = \frac{d}{d\lambda}\frac{\partial f}{\partial x}(x^0 + \lambda\Delta) \cdot \Delta.$$

Then $g''(0) = \sum_j \sum_i f_{x_i x_j}(x^0)\Delta_i \Delta_j$ where we use subscripts to indicate partial derivatives.

Thus if f is quasi-concave,

$$\sum_i f_{x_i}(x^0)\Delta_i = 0 \Rightarrow \sum_j \sum_i f_{x_i x_j}(x^0)\Delta_i \Delta_j \leq 0.$$

Appealing to Proposition B.3-3 we have the following result.

Proposition B.3-4: Necessary Conditions for Quasi-Concavity

If U is quasi-concave, then the ith principal minor of

$$\begin{bmatrix} 0 & U_{x_1} & \cdot & \cdot & U_{x_n} \\ U_{x_1} & U_{x_1x_1} & \cdot & \cdot & U_{x_1x_n} \\ \cdot & \cdot & & & \cdot \\ \cdot & \cdot & & & \cdot \\ U_{x_n} & U_{x_nx_1} & \cdot & \cdot & U_{x_nx_n} \end{bmatrix}$$

has sign $(-1)^{1+i}$.

Exercise B.3-1: Linear Economy Production of x_j units of commodity j ($j = 1, 2$) uses up a_{j1} units of commodity 1 and a_{j2} units of commodity 2. Each unit of gross output of commodity j also requires a_{0j} units of labor. The supply of labor is L.

(a) If the gross output vector is x, confirm that the net output vector is $y = (I - A)x$.

(b) Suppose that

$$a_0 = \begin{bmatrix} 1 \\ 1 \end{bmatrix} \mathbf{A} = \begin{bmatrix} \frac{1}{2} & \frac{1}{4} \\ \frac{3}{4} & \frac{1}{4} \end{bmatrix} L = 80.$$

Show that if only commodity 1 is produced, the net output vector is $y^0 = (40, -60)$ and solve for the net output vector y^1 if only commodity 2 is produced.

(c) Depict these vectors in a neat figure and depict also the net output if half the labor is used to produce commodity 1 and half to produce commodity 2. Which of the three net output vectors is feasible?

(d) Show that net output must satisfy the following constraint

$$b \cdot y = a_0'(I - A)^{-1}y \le L,$$

and solve for the vector b given the data of the problem.

(e) What is the maximum feasible net output of commodity 1?

Exercise B.3-2: Simple Regression A data analyst wishes to estimate the relationship between X and Y. She has n observations of each variable. Define the vectors $X^0 = (1, \ldots, 1)$, $X^1 = (X_1, \ldots, X_n)$, and $Y = (Y_1, \ldots, Y_n)$. The estimated relationship is to be a linear combination of X^0 and X^1. That is, $\hat{Y} = aX^0 + bX^1$. This is depicted in Figure B.3-5 for the case of three observations.

(a) Explain why the square of the distance between Y and $\hat{Y}$ is

$$\|Y - \hat{Y}\|^2 = \sum_{j=1}^n (Y_j - a - bX_j)^2.$$

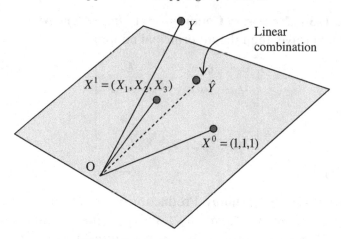

Figure B.3-5. Simple regression.

(b) Show that the distance-minimizing parameter is $a = \overline{Y} - b\overline{X}$ where $\overline{X}$ and $\overline{Y}$ are the sample means.

(c) Define $x = X - \overline{X}$ and $y = Y - \overline{Y}$ and appeal to (b) to show that

$$\| Y - \hat{Y} \|^2 = \sum_{j=1}^{n} (y_j - bx_j)^2.$$

(d) Solve for the distance-minimizing value of b.

Exercise B.3-3: Least-Squared Error The $t \times n$ matrix $\mathbf{X}$ is a matrix composed of n column vectors each of dimension t.

(a) If a is a n-dimensional column vector, explain why $\mathbf{X}a$ is a linearly weighted combination of the column vectors $x_{(1)}, \dots, x_{(n)}$ of $\mathbf{X}$.

(b) Let y be another t-dimensional column vector. Show that the distance between this vector and the linear combination can be written as follows:

$$e'e = y'y - 2a'\mathbf{X}'y + a'\mathbf{X}'\mathbf{X}a.$$

(c) Show that the gradient of this difference is

$$\frac{\partial}{\partial a} e'e = -2\mathbf{X}'y + 2\mathbf{X}'\mathbf{X}a.$$

(d) Choosing a to minimize $e'e$ is the same as choosing a to maximize $-e'e$. Show that $-e'e$ is a concave function of a. Thus the FOC are both necessary and sufficient for a maximum.

HINT: Appeal to Proposition B.3-1 to obtain an expression for the matrix of second-partial derivatives and then show that this matrix is negative definite.

(e) Hence confirm that to minimize this difference, the weights chosen must satisfy

$$a = (\mathbf{X}'\mathbf{X})^{-1}\mathbf{X}'y.$$

B.4 Systems of Linear Difference Equations

Key ideas: phase diagram, eigenvalues, eigenvectors, Walrasian price dynamics

Economists often study the evolution of a vector of economic variables over time. Consider the following difference equation system.

$$x(t+1) = \mathbf{A}x(t), \tag{B.4-1}$$

where $x(t)$ is an n-dimensional vector and $\mathbf{A}$ is an $n \times n$ matrix. We refer to $x(t)$ as the "state" variable at t.

We focus on the special two-dimensional case. The general principles apply also for higher n

$$\begin{bmatrix} x_1(t+1) \\ x_2(t+1) \end{bmatrix} = \begin{bmatrix} a_{11} & a_{12} \\ a_{21} & a_{22} \end{bmatrix} \begin{bmatrix} x_1(t) \\ x_2(t) \end{bmatrix}.$$

Note that $x(t+1) - x(t) = \mathbf{A}x(t) - \mathbf{I}x(t) = (\mathbf{A} - \mathbf{I})x(t)$. Thus if there is a stationary point $\bar{x}$, $(\mathbf{A} - \mathbf{I})\bar{x} = \mathbf{0}$. Therefore as long as the determinant of $\mathbf{A} - \mathbf{I}$ is non-zero, the unique stationary point is $\bar{x} = \mathbf{0}$. We make this assumption throughout.

An Example

We can readily characterize the dynamics. Suppose that

$$\mathbf{A} = \begin{bmatrix} 5 & -1 \\ 3 & 1 \end{bmatrix}.$$

Then

$$\begin{bmatrix} \Delta x_1(t) \\ \Delta x_2(t) \end{bmatrix} \equiv x(t+1) - x(t) = (\mathbf{A} - \mathbf{I})x(t) = \begin{bmatrix} 4x_1(t) - x_2(t) \\ 3x_1(t) \end{bmatrix}. \tag{B.4-2}$$

Thus $\Delta x_2(t) = 3x_1(t)$, so that $x_2(t)$ is increasing if and only if $x_1(t) \geq 0$. Also, from (B.4-2),

$$\Delta x_1(t) = x_1(t+1) - x_1(t) = 4x_1(t) - x_2(t).$$

Thus $x_1(t)$ is increasing if and only if $x_2(t) \leq 4x_1(t)$.

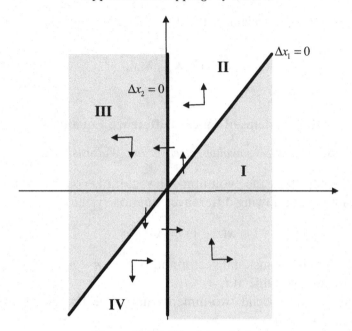

Figure B.4-1. The four phases.

Consider Figure B.4-1. The two lines $\Delta x_1 = 0$ and $\Delta x_2 = 0$ separate the plane into four regions. In each region the state moves in a particular direction (NE, SE, NW, or SW). Thus the dynamic paths are said to be in a particular "phase." For example in phase I, shaded in the figure, $x_1 \geq 0$ and $x_2 \leq 4x_1$ so that state variables are increasing.

We can learn a lot more about the dynamics by seeking a subspace of the state space in which the two variables grow at the same rate. From (B.4-2)

$$\frac{\Delta x_2}{\Delta x_1} = \frac{a_{21}x_1 + (a_{22} - 1)x_2}{(a_{11} - 1)x_1 + a_{12}x_2} = \frac{3x_1}{4x_1 - x_2}.$$

Suppose that $x(t)$ grows proportionally; that is, $x(t + 1) = \lambda x(t)$. If this is the case then

$$\frac{\Delta x_2}{\Delta x_1} = \frac{x_2(t + 1) - x_2(t)}{x_1(t + 1) - x_1(t)} = \frac{(\lambda - 1)x_2(t)}{(\lambda - 1)x_1(t)} = \frac{x_2(t)}{x_1(t)}.$$

(Given our assumption that $|\mathbf{A} - \mathbf{I}| \neq 0$, $\lambda \neq 1$.)

Then, for the example,

$$\frac{\Delta x_2}{\Delta x_1} = \frac{3x_1}{4x_1 - x_2} = \frac{x_2}{x_1}.$$

Hence $3x_1^2 - 4x_1x_2 + x_2^2 = (3x_1 - x_2)(x_1 - x_2) = 0$.

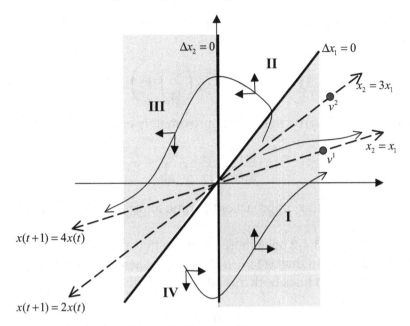

Figure B.4-2. Phase diagram.

Solving this quadratic equation, either $x_2 = x_1$ or $x_2 = 3x_1$. In the first case, by substituting back into the difference equation we obtain

$$\begin{bmatrix} x_1(t+1) \\ x_2(t+1) \end{bmatrix} = \begin{bmatrix} 5 & -1 \\ 3 & 1 \end{bmatrix} \begin{bmatrix} x_1(t) \\ x_1(t) \end{bmatrix} = 4 \begin{bmatrix} x_1(t) \\ x_1(t) \end{bmatrix}.$$

Thus the growth factor $\lambda_1 = 4$. Similarly it can be shown that the growth factor in the second case is $\lambda_2 = 2$. The constant growth lines are also shown as the dashed lines in the "phase diagram" (see Figure B.4-2). Along the dashed line $x_2 = 3x_1$, $x(t)$ doubles from period to period. Along the dashed line $x_2 = x_1$, $x(t)$ quadruples from period to period.

Pick the vector $v^1 \gg 0$ on the line $x_2 = x_1$ and vector $v^2 \gg 0$ on the line $x_2 = 3x_1$. Any initial vector $x(1)$ can be expressed as a linear combination of the vectors v^1 and v^2 because they are linearly independent; that is,

$$x(1) = \alpha_1 v^1 + \alpha_2 v^2.$$

Then

$$\begin{aligned} x(2) = \mathbf{A}x(1) &= \mathbf{A}(\alpha_1 v^1 + \alpha_2 v^2) \\ &= \alpha_1 \mathbf{A}v^1 + \alpha_2 \mathbf{A}v^2 \\ &= \alpha_1 \lambda_1 v^1 + \alpha_2 \lambda_2 v^2. \end{aligned}$$

Repeating this argument, $x(t+1) = \alpha_1\lambda_1^t v^1 + \alpha_2\lambda_2^t v^2$. Because $|\lambda_1| > |\lambda_2|$, it follows that for large t

$$x(t+1) = \lambda_1^t \left(\alpha_1 v^1 + \alpha_2 \left(\frac{\lambda_2}{\lambda_1}\right)^t v^2\right) \approx \lambda_1^t \alpha_1 v^1. \qquad \text{(B.4-3)}$$

Thus for large t, the growth rate is approximately equal to λ_1. Moreover

$$\frac{x_2(t+1)}{x_1(t+1)} \rightarrow \frac{v_2^1}{v_2^1}.$$

Thus the ratio of x_2 to x_1 approaches the ratio along the high constant growth line.

Consider Figure B.4-2 once more. Suppose that $x(1) > 0$. The parameters (α_1, α_2) are chosen so that $x(1) = \alpha_1 v^1 + \alpha_2 v^2$. Then if $x(1)$ lies between the two constant growth lines both α_1 and α_2 are positive. Then for all t,

$$x(t+1) = \alpha_1\lambda_1^t v^1 + \alpha_2\lambda_2^t v^2.$$

Therefore $x(t+1)$ is a weighted average of v^1 and v^2 where both weights are positive. Thus the path lies between $x_2 = x_1$ and $x_2 = 3x_1$, for all t. Moreover, as t grows large, $x_2(t+1)/x_1(t+1) \rightarrow 1$ and the growth rate approaches $\lambda^1 = 4$.

Suppose next that $x(1)$ lies below the high constant growth line $x_2 = x_1$. Then $\alpha_2 < 0 < \alpha_1$ and so $x(t+1)$ lies below the high constant growth line. In the limit $x_2(t+1)/x_1(t+1) \rightarrow 1$ and again the growth factor approaches $\lambda_1 = 4$.

The third possibility is that $x(1)$ lies above the low constant growth rate line $x_2 = 3x_1$. Then $\alpha_1 < 0 < \alpha_2$ and it follows that for sufficiently large t, $x(t+1)$ is negative. As depicted, $x(1)$ is in phase I. The path moves through phase II and ends in phase III.

The General Two-Variable Model

In the example, the long-run outcome is for both state variables to grow at approximately the same rate. We now show that for a big class of linear difference equation systems this will be the case. We begin by seeking initial state $x(1)$ such that

$$x(t+1) = \mathbf{A}x(t) = \lambda x(t) = \lambda \mathbf{I}x(t).$$

Rearranging,

$$x(t+1) - \lambda x(t) = \mathbf{A}x(t) - \lambda \mathbf{I}x(t) = (\mathbf{A} - \lambda\,\mathbf{I})x(t) = 0.$$

For a stationary state this must hold with $\lambda = 1$; that is, $(\mathbf{A} - \mathbf{I})x(t) = 0$. We assume that $|\mathbf{A} - \mathbf{I}| \neq 0$, so that the matrix $\mathbf{A} - \mathbf{I}$ is invertible. Then the unique solution to the equation system $(\mathbf{A} - \mathbf{I})x(t) = 0$ is $x(t) = 0$.

Next consider $\lambda \neq 1$. For a constant growth path the equation system $(\mathbf{A} - \lambda \mathbf{I})x(t) = 0$ must have a non-zero solution. Arguing as earlier, this is not possible if $\mathbf{A} - \lambda \mathbf{I}$ is invertible. Hence for constant growth,

$$|\mathbf{A} - \lambda\mathbf{I}| = \begin{vmatrix} a_{11} - \lambda & a_{12} \\ a_{21} & a_{22} - \lambda \end{vmatrix} = \lambda^2 - (a_{11} + a_{22})\lambda + |\mathbf{A}| = 0. \quad \text{(B.4-4)}$$

This equation is known as the characteristic equation of the matrix $\mathbf{A}$. The two roots λ_1, λ_2 of the quadratic equation are known as the characteristic roots or eigenvalues. Associated with each eigenvalue is a value of the state vector v^i on the unit circle. These are known as eigenvectors. Suppose that the two eigenvalues differ. To show that the eigenvectors must be independent, suppose instead that $v^1 = \theta v^2 = v$. Because both eigenvectors lie on the unit circle, $(\mathbf{A} - \lambda_1\mathbf{I})v = 0 = (\mathbf{A} - \lambda_2\mathbf{I})v$ and therefore $(\lambda_2 - \lambda_1)\mathbf{I}v = (\lambda_2 - \lambda_1)v = 0$. But this is impossible because $v \neq 0$. Therefore the two eigenvectors are indeed independent.

Real Eigenvectors

We can also write the characteristic equation

$$\lambda^2 - (a_{11} + a_{22})\lambda + |\mathbf{A}| = 0$$

as follows, where λ_1 and λ_2 are the characteristic roots:

$$(\lambda - \lambda_1)(\lambda - \lambda_2) = \lambda^2 - (\lambda_1 + \lambda_2)\lambda - \lambda_1\lambda_2 = 0. \quad \text{(B.4-5)}$$

Note that the sum of the roots is the sum of the terms in the leading diagonal of $\mathbf{A}$ and the product of the roots is the determinant of $\mathbf{A}$.

Solving the quadratic characteristic equation yields the two roots

$$\lambda_1 = \frac{1}{2}(a_{11} + a_{22}) + \sqrt{\frac{1}{4}(a_{11} + a_{22})^2 - |A|} \quad \text{(B.4-6)}$$

$$\lambda_2 = \frac{1}{2}(a_{11} + a_{22}) - \sqrt{\frac{1}{4}(a_{11} + a_{22})^2 - |A|}.$$

Thus there are two distinct real roots if and only if

$$(a_{11} + a_{22})^2 - 4|A| = (a_{11} - a_{22})^2 + 4a_{21}a_{12} > 0.$$

Thus a sufficient condition for two distinct real roots is that $a_{12}a_{21} > 0$.

Suppose this condition holds. Arguing exactly as in the example, any initial state vector $x(1)$ can be expressed as a linear combination of v^1 and v^2; that is,

$$x(1) = \alpha_1 v^1 + \alpha_2 v^2.$$

Because $Av^i = \lambda_i v^i, i = 1, 2$, it follows that $A^t v^i = \lambda_i^t v^i, i = 1, 2$. Then

$$x(t+1) = \alpha_1 \lambda_1^t v^1 + \alpha_2 \lambda_2^t v^2.$$

Thus the long-run dynamics are determined by the eigenvalue with the larger absolute value.

Example: Walrasian Price Dynamics

Suppose that the Walrasian auctioneer adjusts prices in proportion to excess demand. Let $\bar{p}$ be the equilibrium price and define $x(t) = p(t) - \bar{p}$. Then the excess demand vector can be written as follows:

$$\hat{e}(x(t)) = e(\bar{p} + x(t)).$$

Note that $\hat{e}(0) = \mathbf{0}$. Consider the linear approximation of $\hat{e}(x)$ in the neighborhood of the equilibrium

$$\hat{e}(x) = \mathbf{E}x = \begin{bmatrix} e_{11} & e_{12} \\ e_{21} & e_{22} \end{bmatrix} \begin{bmatrix} x_1 \\ x_2 \end{bmatrix}.$$

Then the dynamic adjustment process can be written as follows:

$$x(t+1) = \mathbf{A}x(t), \quad \text{where} \quad \mathbf{A} = k\mathbf{E} \quad \text{and} \quad k > 0.$$

Assumptions:

(a) Own price effects are strictly negative $e_{11}, e_{22} < 0$.
(b) Cross price effects are strictly positive $e_{12}, e_{21} > 0$.
(c) Own price effects dominate cross price effects $|\mathbf{E}| = e_{11}e_{22} - e_{21}e_{12} > 0$.
(d) The rate of adjustment is slow $k(e_{11} + e_{22}) > -1$.

By assumption (b) the cross effects are of the same sign and it follows that $a_{12}a_{21} = k^2 e_{12}e_{21} > 0$ so that there are two distinct real roots. By assumption (c) the product of the roots is positive so both have the same sign. By assumption (a) the sum of the roots, $\lambda_1 + \lambda_2 = a_{11} + a_{22}$ is negative. Because λ_1 and λ_2 have the same sign it follows that both must be negative. Finally, by assumption (d), $a_{11} + a_{22} = k(e_{11} + e_{22}) > -1$.

Because $|\mathbf{A}| > 0$, $\sqrt{\frac{1}{4}(a_{11} + a_{22})^2 - |\mathbf{A}|} < \frac{1}{2}|a_{11} + a_{22}|$. Then, from (B.4-6)

$\lambda_2 = \frac{1}{2}(a_{11} + a_{22}) - \sqrt{\frac{1}{4}(a_{11} + a_{22})^2 - |\mathbf{A}|} > a_{11} + a_{22} > -1$. Because both

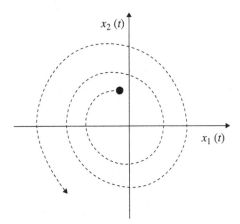

Figure B.4-3. Solution with complex eigenvalues.

eigenvalues are negative both therefore lie in the interval (0, 1). Then the dynamic system is stable and oscillates toward the equilibrium point.[7]

Complex Eigenvalues

Consider the solution to the characteristic equation. Suppose that the expression under the square root in (B.4-6) is negative. Then define $\alpha = \frac{1}{2}(a_{11} + a_{22})$ and $\beta^2 = |A| - \frac{1}{4}(a_{11} + a_{22})^2$. Then (B.4-6) can be rewritten as follows:

$$\lambda_1 = \alpha + \sqrt{-\beta^2}$$
$$\lambda_2 = \alpha - \sqrt{-\beta^2}.$$

Thus there is no solution in terms of real numbers, and so there can be no constant growth paths. We employ a remarkable mathematical sleight of hand and introduce complex numbers. We define $i = \sqrt{-1}$. Then

$$\lambda_1 = \alpha + i\beta \quad \text{and} \quad \lambda_2 = \alpha - i\beta.$$

Example:

Suppose that $\mathbf{A} = \begin{bmatrix} 1 & -\frac{1}{2} \\ \frac{1}{2} & 1 \end{bmatrix}$.

An example of an explosive cycle is depicted in Figure B.4-3. The initial values $x(1) = (x_1(1), x_2(1))$ are indicated by the dot.

The characteristic equation is

$$|\mathbf{A} - \lambda\mathbf{I}| = \begin{vmatrix} 1 - \lambda & -1/2 \\ 1/2 & 1 - \lambda \end{vmatrix} = (1 - \lambda)^2 + \tfrac{1}{4} = 0.$$

Although there is no real root we note that $i^2 = -1$ and so $(1 - \lambda)^2 = \frac{1}{4}i^2$.

---

[7] If the rate of adjustment parameter k is large enough, $\lambda_2 < \frac{1}{2}(a_{11} + a_{22}) = \frac{1}{2}k(e_{11} + e_{22}) < -1$, thus making the adjustment system unstable.

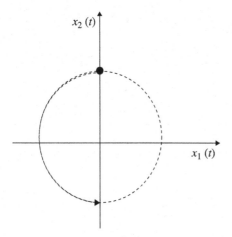

Figure B.4-4. Cycle is neither damped nor explosive.

Taking the square root,

$$\lambda = 1 \pm \tfrac{1}{2}i.$$

As we shall see, the example illustrates a general result. Both $x_1(t)$ and $x_2(t)$ must cycle indefinitely. As depicted the state moves farther and farther from the stationary point so the system is unstable. However, for other parameter values, the state vector oscillates toward the stationary point. The third possibility is that the system has a cycle that is neither damped not explosive. This is the case, for example, if

$$\mathbf{A} = \begin{bmatrix} \cos \pi/n & -\sin \pi/n \\ \sin \pi/n & \cos \pi/n \end{bmatrix}.$$

The solution is depicted in Figure B.4-4.

As the first step in solving for the general solution, note that the eigenvalue λ_1 and associated eigenvector v must satisfy the constant growth condition:

$$(\mathbf{A} - \lambda_1 \mathbf{I})v = 0.$$

That is, $(a_{11} - \lambda_1)v_1 + a_{12}v_2 = 0$. Without loss of generality we may choose $v_1 = 1$ then $v_2 = -(a_{11} - \lambda_1)/a_{12}$. Because λ_1 is a complex number, so is v_2. We write this more succinctly as $v_2 = k_1 + ik_2$.

It proves extremely useful to express the vector of parameters (α, β) in polar coordinates. See Figure B.4-5. Note that $r = \sqrt{\alpha^2 + \beta^2}$ and $\tan \theta = \beta/\alpha$.

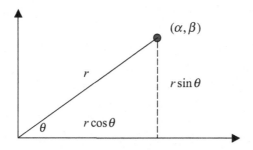

Figure B.4-5. Polar coordinates.

Then we can rewrite the eigenvalue as $\lambda_1 = r(\cos \theta + i \sin \theta)$. Next we note[8] that for any z,

$$\cos z + i \sin z = e^{iz}.$$

Then

$$(\cos \theta + i \sin \theta)^t = e^{i\theta t} = \cos \theta t + i \sin \theta t.$$

And so if $x(1) = v$,

$$x(t+1) = Ax(t) = A^t v = \lambda_1^t v$$

$$= r^t e^{i\theta t} \begin{bmatrix} v^1 \\ v^2 \end{bmatrix} = r^t e^{i\theta t} \begin{bmatrix} 1 \\ k_1 + ik_2 \end{bmatrix}$$

$$= r^t (\cos \theta t + i \sin \theta t) \begin{bmatrix} 1 \\ k_1 + ik_2 \end{bmatrix}.$$

Collecting real and complex terms,

$$x(t+1) = r^t \begin{bmatrix} \cos \theta t \\ k_1 \cos \theta t - k_2 \sin \theta t \end{bmatrix} + ir^t \begin{bmatrix} \sin \theta t \\ k_1 \sin \theta t + k_2 \cos \theta t \end{bmatrix}. \qquad \text{(B.4-7)}$$

Define

$$v^1(t+1) = r^t \begin{bmatrix} \cos \theta t \\ k_1 \cos \theta t - k_2 \sin \theta t \end{bmatrix} \quad \text{and}$$

$$v^2(t+1) = r^t \begin{bmatrix} \sin \theta t \\ k_1 \sin \theta t + k_2 \cos \theta t \end{bmatrix}.$$

We now argue that both $v^1(t)$ and $v^2(t)$ are solutions to the difference equation system. Because $v^1(t) + iv^2(t)$ is a solution,

$$x(t+1) = v^1(t+1) + iv^2(t+1) = \mathbf{A}x(t) = \mathbf{A}v^1(t) + i\mathbf{A}v^2(t).$$

---

[8] In Exercise B.4-1 you are asked to confirm this by appealing to Taylor's Expansion.

Collecting real and complex terms,

$$v^1(t+1) = \mathbf{A}v^1(t) \quad \text{and} \quad v^2(t+1) = \mathbf{A}v^2(t).$$

Choose α_1 and α_2 so that $\alpha_1 v^1(1) + \alpha_2 v^2(1) = x(1)$. Because $v^1(t)$ and $v^2(t)$ are solutions, so is any linear combination. Then

$$x(t) = \alpha_1 v^1(t) + \alpha_2 v^2(t)$$

is the general solution, given the initial state $x(1)$.

Stable and Unstable Systems

From (B.4-6),

$$\lambda_1 = \alpha + i\beta = \tfrac{1}{2}(a_{11} + a_{22}) + \sqrt{\tfrac{1}{4}(a_{11} + a_{22})^2 - |A|}$$

$$\lambda_2 = \alpha - i\beta = \tfrac{1}{2}(a_{11} + a_{22}) - \sqrt{\tfrac{1}{4}(a_{11} + a_{22})^2 - |A|}.$$

From Figure B.4-5, we can rewrite these eigenvalues in polar coordinates as follows:

$$\lambda_1 = r(\cos\theta + i\sin\theta), \quad \lambda_2 = r(\cos\theta - i\sin\theta),$$

where $r = \sqrt{\alpha^2 + \beta^2}$ and $(\alpha, \beta) = (\tfrac{1}{2}(a_{11} + a_{22}), \sqrt{|A| - \tfrac{1}{4}(a_{11} + a_{22})^2})$.

Substituting for α and β, $r = \sqrt{|A|}$.

From (B.4-7), the amplitude of the oscillation is r^t at time t. Thus the amplitude of the oscillations is increasing if $r > 1$ and decreasing if $r < 1$. Therefore the cycles of an oscillating system with complex eigenvalues are damped if and only if $|A| < 1$.

Example (continued)

If $\mathbf{A} = \begin{bmatrix} 1 & -\tfrac{1}{2} \\ \tfrac{1}{2} & 1 \end{bmatrix}$, we have seen that the eigenvalues are $\lambda_1 = 1 + \tfrac{1}{2}i$ and $\lambda_2 = 1 - \tfrac{1}{2}i$.

Transforming the eigenvalues into polar coordinates,

$\lambda_1 = \tfrac{\sqrt{5}}{2}(\cos\bar{\theta}t + i\sin\bar{\theta}t)$ and $\lambda_2 = \tfrac{\sqrt{5}}{2}(\cos\bar{\theta}t - i\sin\bar{\theta}t)$, where $\tan\bar{\theta} = \tfrac{1}{2}$.

Note that because $r = |A| > 1$, the amplitude of the oscillations is increasing. Thus the dynamic system is unstable.

Exercise B.4-1: Polar Representation of a Complex Number

(a) Appeal to Taylor's Expansion around $z = 0$ to show that

$$\cos z = 1 - \frac{z^2}{2!} + \frac{z^4}{4!} \quad \text{and} \quad \sin z = z - \frac{z^3}{3!} + \frac{z^5}{5!}.$$

Therefore $\cos z + i \sin z = 1 + iz - \frac{z^2}{2!} + i\frac{z^3}{3!} + \frac{z^4}{4!}+$.

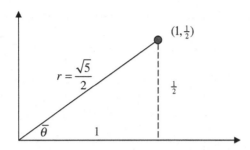

Figure B.4-6. Polar coordinates.

(b) Confirm that this summation can be rewritten as follows:

$$\cos z + i \sin z = 1 + iz + \frac{i^2 z^2}{2!} + \frac{i^3 z^3}{3!} + \frac{i^4 z^4}{4!} + \cdots.$$

(c) Appeal to Taylor's Expansion around $z = 0$ to show that

$$e^{iz} = 1 + \frac{iz}{1!} + \frac{i^2 z^2}{2!} + \frac{i^3 z^3}{3!} + \frac{i^4 z^4}{4!} + \cdots.$$

Hence $e^{iz} = \cos z + i \sin z$.

Exercise B.4-2: Saddle Point Dynamics Suppose that $x(t+1) = \mathbf{A}x(t)$, where $\mathbf{A} = \begin{bmatrix} 2 & \frac{3}{2} \\ \frac{1}{2} & 1 \end{bmatrix}$.

(a) Show that the eigenvalues are $\lambda_1 = \frac{5}{2}$ and $\lambda_2 = \frac{1}{2}$ and solve for the corresponding eigenvectors.
(b) Draw the phase portrait.
(c) For what values of $x(1)$ does the solution converge to zero?

Exercise B.4-3: Oscillations Suppose that $x(t+1) = \mathbf{A}x(t)$, where $\mathbf{A} = \begin{bmatrix} -1 & 1 \\ -5 & 1 \end{bmatrix}$.

(a) Solve for the eigenvalues.
(b) Obtain expressions for the two eigenvalues in polar coordinates.
(c) Hence show that $x(t)$ oscillates explosively with cycles of four periods.

Exercise B.4-4: Walrasian Dynamics The difference between the period t Walrasian price vector and the equilibrium price vector is $x(t)$. The price adjustment is proportional to excess demand; that is,

$$x(t+1) = k\mathbf{E}x(t) \quad \text{where} \quad \mathbf{E} = \begin{bmatrix} -\frac{1}{4} & \frac{1}{4} \\ \frac{1}{8} & -\frac{3}{4} \end{bmatrix}.$$

(a) If $k = 1$ show that both of the eigenvectors $\hat{\lambda}_1$ and $\hat{\lambda}_2$ lie on the interval $(-1, 0)$ so the dynamic adjustment process is stable.

(b) If $k \neq 1$ show that the new eigenvectors $(\lambda_1, \lambda_2) = k(\hat{\lambda}_1, \hat{\lambda}_2)$.

(c) For what values of k is the system stable?

Appendix C

Optimization

C.1 Maximization with Two Variables

Key ideas: Necessary and sufficient conditions

Rather than leap directly to the analysis of multi-variable optimization problems we begin by examining the two-variable case. Suppose that the function f is differentiable at $x^0 = (x_1^0, x_2^0)$. If f takes on its maximum over $\mathbb{R}^2$ at x^0, then taking one variable at a time, we know that each of the first-partial derivatives must be zero.

Proposition C.1-1: First-Order Conditions (FOC) for a Maximum
If $f(x_1, x_2)$ takes on its maximum over $\mathbb{R}^2$ at x^0, then $\frac{\partial f}{\partial x_i}(x^0) = 0, i = 1, 2$.

We also know that each of the second-partial derivatives must be negative. To obtain a further necessary condition we consider the change in f as x changes from x^0 in the direction of some other vector x^1. We do this by considering the weighted average x^λ of x^0 and x^1; that is,

$$x^\lambda = (1 - \lambda)x^0 + \lambda x^1 = x^0 + \lambda(x^1 - x^0),$$

and define $g(\lambda) = f(x^0 + \lambda(x^1 - x^0))$. This function is depicted in Figure C.1-1.

The mapping, $g(\lambda)$, depicted in the cross-section, is a function from $\mathbb{R}$ into $\mathbb{R}$. Then we can appeal to the necessary conditions for one-variable maximization. In particular, for a maximum at x^0, the second derivative of $g(\lambda)$ must be negative at $\lambda = 0$. Define $z \equiv x^1 - x^0$. Then

$$g(\lambda) = f(x^0 + \lambda z) = f\left(x_1^0 + \lambda z_1, x_2^0 + \lambda z_2\right).$$

The first derivative of g is therefore

$$\frac{dg}{d\lambda}(\lambda) = \frac{\partial f}{\partial x_1}(x^\lambda)z_1 + \frac{\partial f}{\partial x_2}(x^\lambda)z_2.$$

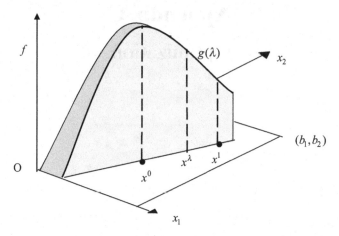

Figure C.1-1. Cross-section of f.

For a maximum this must be zero for all z; hence the partial derivatives at $\lambda = 0$ must both be zero.

Differentiating again and setting $\lambda = 0$

$$\frac{d^2 g}{d\lambda^2}(0) = z_1^2 \frac{\partial^2 f}{\partial x_1^2}(x^0) + 2z_1 z_2 \frac{\partial^2 f}{\partial x_1 \partial x_2}(x^0) + z_2^2 \frac{\partial^2 f}{\partial x_2^2}(x^0)$$

$$= \begin{bmatrix} z_1 & z_2 \end{bmatrix} \begin{bmatrix} \dfrac{\partial^2 f}{\partial x_1^2} & \dfrac{\partial^2 f}{\partial x_1 \partial x_2} \\[2ex] \dfrac{\partial^2 f}{\partial x_1 \partial x_2} & \dfrac{\partial^2 f}{\partial x_1^2} \end{bmatrix} \begin{bmatrix} z_1 \\[1ex] z_2 \end{bmatrix}.$$

In matrix notation,

$$\frac{d^2 g}{d\lambda^2}(0) = (x^1 - x^0)' \left[\frac{\partial^2 f}{\partial x_i \partial x_j}(x^0) \right] (x^1 - x^0) \quad \text{because} \quad z = x^1 - x^0.$$

Note that the right-hand side of the last equation is a quadratic form. Appealing to Proposition B.2-2 we have the following result.

Proposition C.1-2: Second-Order Conditions (SOCs) for a Maximum
If $f(x_1, x_2)$ takes on its maximum over $\mathbb{R}^2$ at x^0, then

$$(i)\ \frac{\partial^2 f}{\partial x_i^2}(x^0) \leq 0, i = 1, 2 \quad \text{and} \quad (ii)\ \frac{\partial^2 f}{\partial x_1^2}(x^0) \frac{\partial^2 f}{\partial x_2^2}(x^0) - \left(\frac{\partial^2 f}{\partial x_1 \partial x_2}(x^0) \right)^2 \geq 0.$$

Exercise C.1-1: Consumer Choice Bev faces prices p_1 and p_2 and her income is I. Her utility function $U(x_1, x_2)$ satisfies $\frac{\partial U}{\partial x_j}(x) > 0, j = 1, 2$, $x \in \mathbb{R}_+^2$.

(a) Argue that the budget constraint must be binding and hence reduce Bev's optimization problem to a one-variable problem. Hence obtain first-order necessary conditions for a corner solution.

(b) Suppose that $\lim_{x_j \downarrow 0} \frac{\partial U}{\partial x_j}(x) = \infty$, $j = 1, 2$. That is, the marginal utility of each commodity increases without bound as consumption of the commodity declines to zero.

Show that the necessary conditions for a maximum cannot be satisfied at a corner.

(a) If $U(x) = \sum_{j=1}^{2} \alpha_j \ln x_j$, where $\alpha_j > 0$, $j = 1, \ldots, n$, show that the solution cannot be at a corner.

(b) Hence solve for Bev's optimal choice.

(c) What if instead $U(x) = x_1^{\alpha_1} x_2^{\alpha_2}$?

Exercise C.1-2: Firm with Interdependent Demands A firm sells two products. Demand prices for these products are as follows:

$$p_1 = 180 - q_1 - \tfrac{1}{2}q_2, \quad p_2 = 180 - \tfrac{1}{2}q_1 - q_2.$$

The cost of production is $C(q) = q_1^2 + \alpha q_1 q_2 + q_2^2$.

(a) If $\alpha = 1$, show that the profit function is concave and solve for the outputs that satisfy the first-order conditions.

(b) Show that the FOC for profit maximization are satisfied at $q = (20, 20)$ if $\alpha = 4$.

(c) Are the second-order (necessary) conditions satisfied at $q = (20, 20)$?

(d) Show that there are two corner solutions to the FOC. Explain why profit must be maximized at these outputs.

(e) Show that profit is a concave function of q_1 and hence solve for $q_1^*(q_2)$, the profit-maximizing output of commodity 1 for all possible values of q_2.

(f) Totally differentiate $\Pi(q_1^*(q_2), q_2)$ and explain why

$$\frac{d\Pi}{dq_2}(q_1^*(q_2), q_2) = \frac{\partial \Pi}{\partial q_2}(q_1^*(q_2), q_2).$$

Hence show that

$$\frac{d\Pi}{dq_2} = \frac{\partial \Pi}{\partial q_2}(q_1^*, q_2) = 180 - 45(1 + \alpha) - (4 - \tfrac{1}{4}(1 + \alpha)^2)q_2.$$

(g) Hence characterize the function $\Pi(q_1^*(q_2), q_2)$ for different values of α.

C.2 Unconstrained Optimization

Key ideas: necessary and sufficient conditions, quasi-concavity

Consider the following problem where the function f is twice continuously differentiable:

$$\text{Max}_{x}\{f(x)|x \in \mathbb{R}^n\}.$$

In the previous section, we examined both the necessary and sufficient conditions for f to take on its maximum at x^0 for the special case when $n = 2$. With n variables the analysis is similar. First we consider the optimization problem one variable at a time. Appealing to the necessary conditions for the one-variable model it follows that the following first- and second-order necessary conditions must hold; that is,

$$\frac{\partial f}{\partial x_j}(x^0) = 0 \quad \text{and} \quad \frac{\partial^2 f}{\partial x_j^2}(x^0) \le 0, \quad j = 1, \ldots, n.$$

The intuition behind these and the further necessary conditions comes from a consideration of the quadratic approximation of the function at the point x^0. Consider the following quadratic function:

$$h(x) = f(x^0) + \frac{\partial f}{\partial x}(x^0) \cdot (x - x^0) + \tfrac{1}{2}(x - x^0)' \left[\frac{\partial^2 f}{\partial x_i \partial x_i}\right](x - x^0).$$

As is readily confirmed, h and f take on the same value and have the same first- and second-partial derivatives at x^0. For x sufficiently close to x^0 the linear terms dominate; thus, if any of the first-partial derivates is non-zero, the function cannot take on its maximum at x^0. Suppose then that the gradient vector, $\frac{\partial f}{\partial x}(x)$ is zero at x^0. Again, for x sufficiently close to x^0 the quadratic terms dominate all higher order terms. Therefore, if f takes on its maximum at x^0, it is necessarily the case that the quadratic form is negative semi-definite at x^0.

Proposition C.2-1: Necessary Conditions for a Maximum

Suppose f takes on its maximum over $\mathbb{R}^n$ at x^0. If f is differentiable at x^0, then $\frac{\partial f}{\partial x}(x^0) = 0$. If f is twice differentiable at x^0, then the quadratic form of the matrix of second-partial derivatives $\mathbf{H}(x^0) = [\frac{\partial^2 f}{\partial x_i \partial x_j}]$ must be negative semi-definite.

Proof: Define $g(\lambda) = f(x^\lambda) = f(x^0 + \lambda z)$, where $z \equiv x^1 - x^0$. We now argue that

$$g''(\lambda) = z'\mathbf{H}(x^\lambda)z \quad \text{where} \quad \mathbf{H}(x) = \left[\frac{\partial^2 f}{\partial x_i \partial x_j}\right].$$

First note that for any function $\phi(x^0 + \lambda z)$,

$$\frac{d}{d\lambda}\phi(x^0 + \lambda z) = \frac{\partial\phi}{\partial x}(x^0 + \lambda z) \cdot z = z'\frac{\partial\phi}{\partial x}(x^0 + \lambda z).$$

In particular, setting $\phi = f$,

$$g'(\lambda) = \frac{d}{d\lambda}f(x^0 + \lambda z) = z'\frac{\partial f}{\partial x}(x^0 + \lambda z).$$

And so

$$g''(\lambda) = z'\frac{d}{d\lambda}\frac{\partial f}{\partial x}(x^0 + \lambda z). \tag{C.2-1}$$

Also, setting $\phi = \frac{\partial f}{\partial x_i}$,

$$\frac{d}{d\lambda}\frac{\partial f}{\partial x_i} = \left(\frac{\partial}{\partial x_1}\frac{\partial f}{\partial x_i}, \cdots, \frac{\partial}{\partial x_n}\frac{\partial f}{\partial x_i}\right)' z = \left(\frac{\partial}{\partial x_i}\frac{\partial f}{\partial x_1}, \cdots, \frac{\partial}{\partial x_i}\frac{\partial f}{\partial x_n}\right)' z.$$

Then

$$\frac{d}{d\lambda}\frac{\partial f}{\partial x} = \begin{bmatrix} \dfrac{d}{d\lambda}\dfrac{\partial f}{\partial x_1} \\ \vdots \\ \dfrac{d}{d\lambda}\dfrac{\partial f}{\partial x_n} \end{bmatrix} z = \left[\frac{\partial^2 f}{\partial x_i \partial x_j}\right] z.$$

Substituting this column vector into (C.2-1),

$$g''(\lambda) = \frac{d^2}{d\lambda^2}f(x^\lambda) = z'\left[\frac{\partial^2 f}{\partial x_i \partial x_j}\right] z.$$

Appealing to the results for a single variable, it follows that a further necessary condition for a maximum is that, for all x^1, the second derivative of $g(\lambda)$ must be negative at $\lambda = 0$. $\square$

In Appendix A we also established sufficient conditions for a maximum. The proofs of Propositions A.5-5 and A.5-6 generalize directly.

Proposition C.2-2: Sufficient Conditions for a Maximum
Suppose $D_f = \mathbb{R}^n$ and f is concave. If the FOC hold at x^0 then

$$f(x) \le f(x^0), \quad \text{for all} \quad x \in D_f.$$

Proposition C.2-3: Quasi-Concavity and Sufficient Conditions for a Maximum
If $\frac{\partial f}{\partial x}(x^0) = 0$ and f is strictly concave in a neighborhood of x^0, then f has a local maximum at x^0. If, in addition, f is quasi-concave on D_f, then $f(x) < f(x^0)$, for all $x \in D_f$.

Exercises

Exercise C.2-1: Profit Maximization A firm has monopoly power in all of its n markets. The demand price for commodity j is

$$p_j = \alpha_j - \beta q_j - \gamma s, \quad \text{where} \quad s \equiv \sum_{j=1}^{n} q_j.$$

Total cost is $C(q) = \sum_{j=1}^{n} c_j q_j$.

(a) Write down the total profit of the firm and show that it can be written as follows:

$$\Pi(q) = \sum_{j=1}^{n} (\alpha_j - c_j) q_j - \sum_{j=1}^{n} \beta q_j^2 - \gamma s^2.$$

Hence (or otherwise) show that profit is a concave function of the output vector q.

(b) Assuming that the profit-maximizing output vector $q^* = (q_1^*, \ldots, q_n^*)$ is strictly positive, show that

$$\alpha_j - c_j - 2\beta q_j^* - 2\gamma s = 0, \quad j = 1, \ldots, n.$$

(c) Sum over the commodities and hence solve for the output sum s.
(d) Appeal to (b) to solve for the output of commodity j.
(e) Hence show that the profit-maximizing outputs are all strictly positive if and only if

$$\frac{\alpha_j - c_j}{\displaystyle\sum_{j=1}^{n} (\alpha_j - c_j)} > \frac{1}{n + \dfrac{\beta}{\gamma}}.$$

(f) Use this inequality to show that if the demand interdependency is sufficiently small or the demand price functions and costs are sufficiently alike, output of all commodities will be strictly positive.

Exercise C.2-2: Quality and Quantity Choice A firm that produces q units of quality z commands a demand price $p(q, z) = 8z - 2q$. The cost of production is $C(q, z) = z^\alpha q$, where $0 \leq z \leq 12$.

(a) If $\alpha = 2$, write down the FOC for a profit maximum and confirm that they all hold at $(q^*, z^*) = (4, 4)$.
(b) Confirm that the profit function is concave in a neighborhood of $(4, 4)$. Explain why it follows that $\Pi(q, z)$ has a local maximum at $(4, 4)$.
(c) To establish that the local maximum is in fact the global maximum, show that regardless of the output decision of the firm, it is optimal to choose a quality level of 4. Hence or otherwise explain why the local maximum must also be the (global) maximum.
(d) Re-examine the problem if $\alpha = 1$.

C.3 Implicit Function Theorem

Key ideas: comparative statics, continuous mapping from parameters to choice variables

To take theory to data, a model must have some predictive power. Consider, for example, a profit-maximizing firm. Suppose that the firm has a profit $f(x, \alpha)$ where $x = (x_1, \ldots, x_n)$ is the output vector and $\alpha = (\alpha_1, \ldots, \alpha_m)$ is a vector of parameters (prices and cost characteristics). The predictive power of the model then depends on the ability of the modeler to derive implications about the way the firm responds to changes in the environment; that is, changes in the parameter vector α. Such an analysis is greatly simplified if it is reasonable to assume that the profit-maximizing response $x = g(\alpha)$ is a differentiable function. But when is this true?

To illustrate the issues, consider first the simplest case in which there is a single output and a single cost parameter. We assume that the profit $f(x, \alpha)$ is a twice continuously differentiable function. The necessary condition for a profit maximum is

$$\frac{\partial f}{\partial x}(x^*, \alpha) \leq 0, \quad \text{with equality if} \quad x^* = 0.$$

We define the function $h(x, \alpha)$ to be the gradient of f; that is, $h(x, \alpha) = \partial f / \partial x(x, \alpha)$. Suppose that h is a decreasing function of x so that the contour set $\{x | h(x, \alpha) = 0\}$ is as depicted in Figure C.3-1.

For each α, there is a unique $x = g(\alpha)$ satisfying the FOC. That is, the FOC implicitly defines the profit-maximizing output $x = g(\alpha)$ as a function

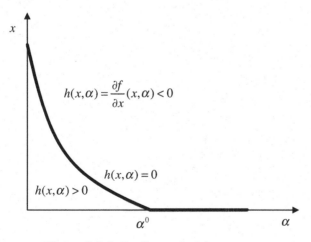

Figure C.3-1. Profit-maximizing output.

of the cost parameter. In the figure this is the heavy curve. The profit-maximizing output is strictly positive, for all $\alpha < \alpha^0$ and is zero for all higher α.

Example:
A firm can sell at a price $p = 10$ and has a cost function $C(x, \alpha) = \alpha x + \frac{1}{2}(1 + \alpha)x^2$. The profit is therefore $f(x, \alpha) = 10x - (\alpha x + \frac{1}{2}(1 + \alpha)x^2)$. Differentiating by x, we obtain

$$h(x, \alpha) = \frac{\partial f}{\partial x}(x, \alpha) = 10 - \alpha - (1 + \alpha)x.$$

Note that this function can be rewritten as $h(x, \alpha) = (1 + \alpha)(\frac{11}{1+\alpha} - 1 - x)$. The FOC for a maximum at x^* is $\frac{\partial f}{\partial x} = h(x^*, \alpha) \leq 0$, with equality if $x^* > 0$. Thus the profit-maximizing output is

$$x = g(\alpha) = \begin{cases} \dfrac{11}{1 + \alpha} - 1, & \alpha \leq 10 \\ 0, & \alpha > 10 \end{cases}.$$

Thus for the example we can solve explicitly for $g(\alpha)$.

In general we cannot solve explicitly so that all we have is an "implicit function" $g(\alpha)$ that satisfies the equation $h(x, \alpha) = 0$. As long as the function h is continuously differentiable, it is tempting to believe that this implicit function must be differentiable as well. Then, as depicted in Figure C.3-1, the profit-maximizing output is continuously differentiable, except at the kink $(g(\alpha^0), \alpha^0)$ where the profit-maximizing output drops to zero. However, our assumptions are not quite strong enough.

To understand why, suppose that $h(x, \alpha) = 2 - \alpha - (2 - x)^3$. The set of points $x = g(\alpha)$ satisfying $h(x, \alpha) = 0$ is depicted in Figure C.3-2. Note that the curve is vertical at $\alpha = 2$ so the derivative of $g(\alpha)$ is not well defined at $\alpha = 2$.

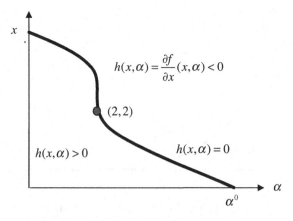

Figure C.3-2. Profit-maximizing output.

Another way of seeing this is to begin by assuming that the function $g(\alpha)$ is differentiable and test whether this leads to a contradiction. Substituting for x, we have $h(g(\alpha), \alpha) = 0$. If both functions are differentiable then

$$\frac{\partial h}{\partial x} g'(\alpha) + \frac{\partial h}{\partial \alpha} = 0 \quad \text{and so} \quad g'(\alpha) = -\frac{\partial h}{\partial \alpha} \Big/ \frac{\partial h}{\partial x}.$$

Note that the right-hand side is only well defined if $\frac{\partial h}{\partial x}(g(\alpha), \alpha)) \neq 0$. The problem then arises because $\frac{\partial h}{\partial x}(2, 2) = 0$.

More generally, suppose that $x = (x_1, \ldots, x_n)$ must satisfy the n equations $h_i(x, \alpha) = 0, i = 1, \ldots, n$, where $\alpha = (\alpha_1, \ldots, \alpha_m)$ is a vector of parameters. Suppose also that $(\overline{x}, \overline{\alpha})$ satisfies these n equations. We would like to know whether these equations implicitly define a continuously differentiable function $x = g(\alpha)$. Although we do not provide a complete proof here, the basic insight comes from taking the linear approximations of the functions and asking the same question for the linearized system. The linearized system is

$$\frac{\partial h_i}{\partial x}(\overline{x}, \overline{\alpha}) \cdot (x - \overline{x}) + \frac{\partial h_i}{\partial \alpha}(\overline{x}, \overline{\alpha}) \cdot (\alpha - \overline{\alpha}) = 0, \quad i = 1 \ldots, n.$$

Rewriting these n equations in matrix form,

$$\left[\frac{\partial h_i}{\partial x_j}(\overline{x}, \overline{\alpha}) \right] (x - \overline{x}) = -\left[\frac{\partial h_i}{\partial \alpha_k}(\overline{x}, \overline{\alpha}) \right] (\alpha - \overline{\alpha}).$$

The matrix of all gradient vectors of $h = (h_1, \ldots, h_n)$, evaluated at $(\overline{x}, \overline{\alpha})$, is known as the Jacobean matrix of the equation system $h(\overline{x}, \overline{\alpha}) = 0$. If this matrix is invertible,

$$x - \overline{x} = -\left[\frac{\partial h_i}{\partial x_j}(\overline{x}, \overline{\alpha}) \right]^{-1} \left[\frac{\partial h_i}{\partial \alpha_k}(\overline{x}, \overline{\alpha}) \right] (\alpha - \overline{\alpha}).$$

Thus, for the linearized system, there is a mapping $x = g(\alpha)$ as long as the Jacobean matrix is invertible.

Proposition C.3-1: Implicit Function Theorem
Let $h_i(x, \alpha), i = 1, \ldots, n$ be a continuously differentiable function of $(x, \alpha) = (x_1, \ldots, x_n, \alpha_1, \ldots, \alpha_m)$ and suppose that $(\overline{x}, \overline{a})$ satisfies the system of equations

$$h_i(x, \alpha) = 0, \quad i = 1, \ldots, n.$$

If the Jacobean matrix of partial derivatives $[\partial h_i / \partial x_j(\overline{x}, \overline{\alpha})]$ is invertible, then there exists an open neighborhood of $\overline{\alpha}$, $N_1(\overline{\alpha}, \delta_1)$ and an open neighborhood of $\overline{x}$, $N_2(\overline{x}, \delta_2)$ and a unique continuously differentiable function $g : N_1 \to N_2$ such that for any $\alpha \in N_1, h_i(g(\alpha), \alpha) = 0, i = 1, \ldots, n$.

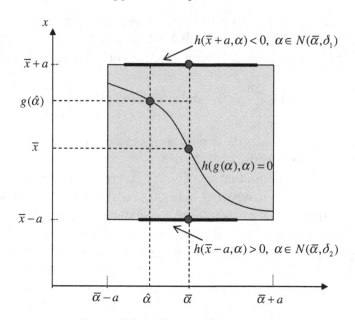

Figure C.3-3. The implicit function.

We now return to the simple example of the profit-maximizing firm and sketch a proof of the existence of a unique continuous implicit function $g(\alpha)$ satisfying

$$h(g(\alpha), \alpha) = \frac{\partial f}{\partial x}(g(\alpha), \alpha) = 0.$$

By hypothesis $h(\overline{x}, \overline{\alpha}) = 0$. In addition we assume that h is continuously differentiable in some neighborhood of $(\overline{x}, \overline{\alpha})$ and that $\frac{\partial h}{\partial x}(\overline{x}, \overline{\alpha}) \neq 0$. A necessary condition for a maximum is that $\frac{\partial h}{\partial x}(\overline{x}, \overline{\alpha}) = \frac{\partial}{\partial x}\frac{\partial f}{\partial x}(\overline{x}, \overline{\alpha}) \leq 0$. Then if $\frac{\partial h}{\partial x}(\overline{x}, \overline{\alpha}) \neq 0$ it must be strictly less than zero. Because h is continuously differentiable if follows that there is some $a > 0$ and a square with side of length $2a$, centered on $\overline{\alpha}$ and $\overline{x}$, within which $\frac{\partial h}{\partial x}(x, \alpha) < 0$. This is the shaded region in Figure C.3-3.

Because $h(\overline{x}, \overline{\alpha}) = 0$, it follows that

$$h(\overline{x} + a, \overline{\alpha}) < 0 \quad \text{and} \quad h(\overline{x} - a, \alpha) > 0. \tag{C.3-1}$$

Appealing to the continuity of h it is an implication of the first inequality in (3-1) that there is some $\delta_1 > 0$ such that

$$h(\overline{x} + a, \alpha) < 0, \quad \text{for all} \quad \alpha \in N(\overline{\alpha}, \delta_1). \tag{C.3-2}$$

By the same argument, it is an implication of the second inequality in (C.3-1) that there is some number $\delta_2 > 0$ such that

$$h(\overline{x} - a, \alpha) > 0, \quad \text{for all} \quad \alpha \in N(\overline{\alpha}, \delta_2). \tag{C.3-3}$$

The two neighborhoods are depicted as heavy line segments in Figure C.3-3.

Define $\delta = \text{Min}\{\delta_1, \delta_2\}$. Then (C.3-2) and (C.3-3) both hold for all $\alpha \in N(\overline{\alpha}, \delta)$.

Consider any $\hat{\alpha} \in N(\overline{\alpha}, \delta)$. Because $h(\overline{x} - a, \hat{\alpha}) > 0 > h(\overline{x} + a, \hat{\alpha})$ and h is a strictly decreasing function of x, it follows that there exists a unique $x = g(\alpha)$ such that $h(g(\alpha), \alpha) = 0$. Because h is continuous, the implicit function g must also be continuous.

Application: Input Demand

Consider a price-taking firm with a concave production function $f(z_1, z_2) \in \mathbb{C}^2$. Let p be the output price and let r be the input price vector. The firm's profit is therefore

$$\Pi = pf(z) - r \cdot z.$$

Suppose that the profit-maximizing input vector $z(p, r)$ is strictly positive. Then the FOC are as follows:

$$\frac{\partial \Pi}{\partial z_1} = p\frac{\partial f}{\partial z_1}(z) - r_1 = 0 \quad \text{and} \quad \frac{\partial \Pi}{\partial z_2} = p\frac{\partial f}{\partial z_2}(z) - r_2 = 0.$$

We now ask how input demand, $z(p, r)$ varies as the price of input 1 changes. The FOC must hold at $z^*(r)$ for all r. Differentiating the FOC by r_1 we obtain the following equations:

$$p\frac{\partial^2 f}{\partial z_1^2}\frac{\partial z_1}{\partial r_1} + \frac{\partial^2 f}{\partial z_2 \partial z_1}\frac{\partial z_2}{\partial r_1} = 1 \quad \text{and} \quad p\frac{\partial^2 f}{\partial z_1 \partial z_2}\frac{\partial z_1}{\partial r_1} + \frac{\partial^2 f}{\partial z_2^2}\frac{\partial z_2}{\partial r_1} = 0.$$

It is helpful to write these equations in matrix form as follows:

$$p\begin{bmatrix} \dfrac{\partial^2 f}{\partial z_{11}} & \dfrac{\partial^2 f}{\partial z_{12}} \\ \dfrac{\partial^2 f}{\partial z_{21}} & \dfrac{\partial^2 f}{\partial z_{22}} \end{bmatrix}\begin{bmatrix} \dfrac{dz_1}{dr_1} \\ \dfrac{dz_2}{dr_1} \end{bmatrix} = \begin{bmatrix} 1 \\ 0 \end{bmatrix}.$$

By the Implicit Function Theorem $z(p, r)$ is a continuously differentiable function of r_1 as long as the determinant of the matrix is non-zero. By hypothesis the production function is concave; thus

$$\begin{vmatrix} \dfrac{\partial^2 f}{\partial z_{11}} & \dfrac{\partial^2 f}{\partial z_{12}} \\ \dfrac{\partial^2 f}{\partial z_{21}} & \dfrac{\partial^2 f}{\partial z_{22}} \end{vmatrix} \geq 0.$$

Thus strengthening this necessary condition for concavity so that the inequality is strict is sufficient to ensure that $z(r)$ is continuously differentiable.[1]

Exercise C.3-1: Guns and Roses A country produces guns and roses. The set of possible outputs $y = (y_1, y_2)$ is $Y = \{(y_1, y_2) | y \geq 0, h(y) \geq 0\}$ where h is a strictly decreasing function and $h(0) > 0$. Under what assumptions can the frontier of this set be expressed as the implicit continuously differentiable function (i) $y_2 = f(y_1)$ and (ii) $y_1 = g(y_2)$?

Exercise C.3-2: Profit-Maximizing Firm A firm sells two products. The marginal revenue functions $MR_1(q_1)$ and $MR_2(q_2)$ are strictly decreasing. The cost of production is $C(q) = g(\alpha_1 q_1 + \alpha_2 q_2), \alpha > 0$, where g is a strictly increasing and strictly convex function. Under what conditions is the profit-maximizing output vector a continuously differentiable function of the cost parameters $\alpha = (\alpha_1, \alpha_2)$?

C.4 Constrained Maximization

Key ideas: convergent sub-sequence, parametric changes in preferences and constraints, hemi-continuity, Theorem of the Maximum, Envelope Theorem

In economics we are typically interested in learning how the decisions of economic agents are affected by changes in their preferences and in the constraints that they face. Suppose first that the preferences of an agent change, but the set of feasible actions is fixed. We model this by introducing the parameter α and writing the preference function or maximand as $f(x, \alpha)$. In general there is no reason why the decision of the agent should vary continuously with the preference parameter α. This is depicted in Figure C.4-1.

Suppose that the preference map gets flatter as α increases. For preference parameter α^0 the contour set through x^A touches the feasible set twice so there are two optimal choices. For smaller α (and so steeper contour sets) the choice is to the southeast of x^A, and for larger α the solution is to the northwest of x^B. Thus the solution to the optimization problem

$$\underset{x}{\text{Max}} \left\{ f(x, \alpha) | x \in X \subset \mathbb{R}^2_+ \right\}$$

has a discontinuity at α^0. We show later that this cannot be the case if there is a unique solution. To do so we appeal to the following simple but important theorem.

---

[1] For example given a Cobb-Douglas production function $f(z) = z_1^\alpha z_2^\beta$, the inequality is strict as long as $\alpha + \beta < 1$.

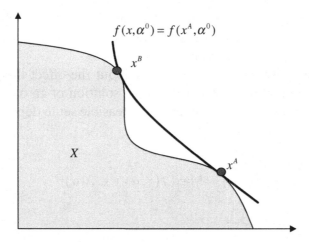

Figure C.4-1. Discontinuous solution.

Bolzano-Weierstrass Theorem: Any bounded sequence of vectors $\{p^t\}_{t=1}^{\infty}$ has a convergent subsequence.

Here we describe the construction of such a sub-sequence for the two-dimensional case. The method of proof is essentially identical for higher dimensions. Because the sequence is bounded, there must be some a and $\delta > 0$ such that $(a, a) \le (p_1^t, p_2^t) < (a + \delta, a + \delta)$. That is, the sequence lies in a square with side of length δ. Partition the square into four equal squares each with a side of length $\delta/2$. This is depicted in Figure C.4-2. Because the sequence is infinite, at least one of the smaller squares must contain an infinite sub-sequence. Select one such square and again split it into four equal smaller squares, each with a side of length $\delta/4$. Repeating this partition n times yields an infinite sub-sequence located in a square with side of length $\delta/2^n$.

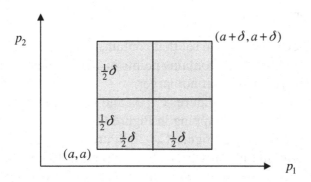

Figure C.4-2. Constructing a convergent subsequence.

At the nth stage, one of the squares with a side of length $\delta/2^n$ must contain an infinite sub-sequence. In the limit the square becomes a point; thus this process yields a convergent infinite sub-sequence.

We use this theorem to derive results about the effect that a change in some environmental parameter has on the solution of an optimizing problem. We allow both the maximand and the feasible set to depend on a vector of environmental parameters α.

Define

$$F(\alpha) = \underset{x}{\text{Max}}\{ f(x, \alpha) | x \in X(\alpha)\}$$

and

$$X^*(\alpha) = \arg \underset{x}{\text{Max}}\{ f(x, \alpha) | x \in X(\alpha)\}.$$

We seek to characterize the properties of the set of maximizers $X^*(\alpha)$ if the maximand is continuous and the feasible set $X(\alpha)$ varies continuously with α. In the language of mathematics, $X(\alpha)$ is a correspondence. To define continuity it turns out to be convenient to proceed in two steps.

Definition: Upper Hemi-Continuous Correspondence The set-valued mapping $X(\alpha)$ is upper hemi-continuous at α^0 if for any open neighborhood V of $X(\alpha^0)$ there exists a δ-neighborhood of α^0, $N(\alpha^0, \delta)$, such that $X(\alpha) \subset V$, for all $\alpha \in N(\alpha^0, \delta)$

Informally, let V be an open set containing the set $X(\alpha^0)$. Then for all α sufficiently close to α^0, the set $X(\alpha)$ is contained in V. Thus the mapping $X(\alpha)$ can be discontinuously larger at α^0 but not discontinuously smaller.

Definition: Lower Hemi-Continuous Correspondence The set-valued mapping $X(\alpha)$ is lower hemi-continuous at α^0 if for any open set V that intersects $X(\alpha^0)$, there exists a δ-neighborhood of α^0, $N(\alpha^0, \delta)$, such that $X(\alpha)$ intersects V for all $\alpha \in N(\alpha^0, \delta)$.

Informally, let V be an open set that contains points in $X(\alpha^0)$. Then for all α sufficiently close to α^0, V contains points in $X(\alpha)$. Thus the mapping can be discontinuously smaller but not larger.

Consider the examples in Figures C.4-3a and C.4-3b. In both cases $X(\alpha)$ is an interval. Note that the mapping in Figure C.4-3a is continuous from the right α^0 and the mapping in Figure C.4-3b figure is continuous from the left but neither is continuous. However, the mapping in Figure C.4-3a is upper but not lower hemi-continuous, whereas the opposite is true for the mapping in Figure C.4-3b.

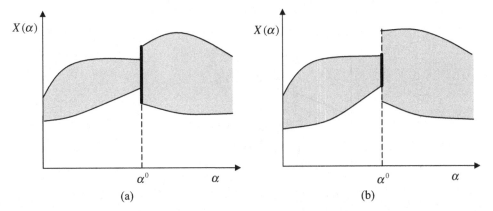

Figure C.4-3. (a) Upper hemi-continuity. (b) Lower hemi-continuity.

A mapping is continuous if it is both upper and lower hemi-continuous. We first consider the case when there is a unique maximizer $x^*(\alpha)$.

Proposition C.4-1: Theorem of the Maximum I

Define $F(\alpha) = \text{Max}_x\{f(x, \alpha)|x \geq 0, x \in X(\alpha) \subset \mathbb{R}^n, \alpha \in A \subset^m\}$ where f is continuous.

If

(i) for each α there is a unique

$$x^*(\alpha) = \arg\underset{x}{\text{Max}}\{f(x, \alpha)|x \geq 0, \quad x \in X(\alpha), \alpha \in A\}$$

and

(ii) $X(\alpha)$ is a compact-valued correspondence that is continuous at α^0, then $x^*(\alpha)$ is continuous at α^0.

Proof: Because $X(\alpha)$ is compact, $x^*(\alpha)$ exists. If $x^*(\alpha)$ is discontinuous at α^0, there exists some $\varepsilon > 0$ and a sequence $\{\alpha^t\} \to \alpha^0$, such that $\|x^*(\alpha^t) - x^*(\alpha^0)\| > \varepsilon$. Because $X(\alpha)$ is bounded, the sequence $\{x^*(\alpha^t)\}$ has a convergent sub-sequence. That is, for some sub-sequence $\{x^*(\alpha^s)\}$,

$$\{x^*(\alpha^s)\} \to x^0 \neq x^*(\alpha^0).$$

The correspondence $X(\alpha)$ is depicted in Figure C.4-4. The heavy line segment is $X(\alpha^0)$. The upper dotted curve is the convergent subsequence $\{(\alpha_s, x^*(\alpha^s))\}_{s=1}^{\infty}$ with limit point (α^0, x^0).

Because $x^*(\alpha^0)$ is maximal, and this is the unique maximizing value of x it follows that

$$f(x^*(\alpha^0), \alpha^0) > f(x^0, \alpha^0).$$

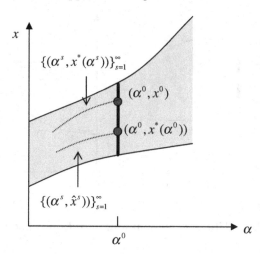

Figure C.4-4. Theorem of the Maximum.

Because $X(\alpha)$ is continuous, there exists a sequence $\{\hat{x}^s\}$ where $\hat{x}^s \in X(\alpha^s)$ such that $\hat{x}^s \to x^*(\alpha^0)$. This is also depicted in Figure C.4-4. By the continuity of f, for all s sufficiently large,

$$f(\hat{x}^s, \alpha^s) > f(x^*(\alpha^s), \alpha^s).$$

But this is impossible because $x^*(\alpha^s)$ is the maximizer at $\alpha = \alpha^s$. Thus we have established that the hypothesis that $x^*(\alpha)$ has a discontinuity at α^0 leads to a contradiction.   □

Remark: Suppose that the feasible set is the intersection of upper contour sets of $g_m(x)$; that is, $X = \{x|x \geq 0, g_i(x) \geq b_i, i = 1, \ldots, m\}$. If $g_i, i = 1, \ldots, m$ is quasi-concave then X is convex. If, in addition, the maximand is a strictly quasi-concave continuous function, then the solution is unique and so $x^*(\alpha)$, the maximizer for

$$\underset{x}{\text{Max}}\{f(x, \alpha)|x \in X \subset \mathbb{R}^n, \alpha \in [a, b]\}$$

is continuous.

We now generalize this result to cases where the set of maximizing values is not unique.

Proposition C.4-2: Theorem of the Maximum II
Define $F(\alpha) = \text{Max}_x\{f(x, \alpha)|x \geq 0, x \in X(\alpha) \subset \mathbb{R}^n, \alpha \in A \subset \mathbb{R}^m\}$ where f is continuous.

Also define $X^*(\alpha) = \arg\text{Max}_x\{f(x, \alpha)|x \geq 0, x \in X(\alpha), \alpha \in A\}$. If $X(\alpha)$ is a compact-valued correspondence that is continuous (i.e., both upper and lower hemi-continuous) at α^0, then $F(\alpha)$ is continuous at α^0 and $X^*(\alpha)$ is compact valued and upper hemi-continuous at α^0.

Proof: Because $X(\alpha)$ is compact, it follows from the Extreme Value Theorem that

$$X^*(\alpha) = \arg \underset{x}{\text{Max}}\{ f(x)|x \in X(\alpha)\}$$

is a non-empty set. Let $\{\alpha^t\}$ be a sequence converging to α^0. Consider any sequence $\{x(\alpha^t)\}$ where $x(\alpha^t) \in X^*(\alpha^t)$. Because the sequence is bounded, there exists a sequence $\{\alpha^s\}$ and a sub-sequence of $\{\alpha^t\}$, such that $\{x(\alpha^s)\}$ converges to some x^0. Because $X(\alpha)$ is upper hemi-continuous, $x^0 \in X(\alpha^0)$. If $x^0 \in X^*(\alpha^0)$ we will have established both the continuity of $F(\alpha)$ and the upper hemi-continuity of $x = X^*(\alpha)$.

Suppose instead that $x^0 \notin X^*(\alpha^0)$. Then for sufficiently small ε there exists some $\hat{x} \in X(\alpha^0)$ such that $f(\hat{x}, \alpha^0) > f(x^0, \alpha^0) + \varepsilon$. By the lower hemi-continuity of $X(\alpha)$, there exists some sequence $\{\alpha^k\}$, a sub-sequence of $\{\alpha^s\}$ such that $\hat{x}^k \in X(\alpha^k)$ converges to $\hat{x}$. Then for all k sufficiently large

$$f(\hat{x}^k, \alpha^k) > f(x(\alpha^k), \alpha^k).$$

But by construction $x(\alpha^k) \in X^*(\alpha^k)$ is a maximizer at $\alpha = \alpha^k$ so this is impossible.

Therefore $x^0 \in X(\alpha^0)$ after all.

A similar argument establishes that $X^*(\alpha^0)$ is compact valued at α^0. □

In many economic models the set of maximizers,

$$X^*(\alpha) = \arg \underset{x}{\text{Max}}\{ f(x, \alpha)|x \geq 0, \quad x \in X(\alpha), \alpha \in A\}$$

is monotonic. Without loss of generality, we may define the parameters so that $X^*(\alpha)$ is monotonically increasing. Then both $\underline{x}(\alpha) = Sup\{X^*(\alpha')|\alpha' < \alpha\}$ and $\overline{x}(\alpha) = Inf\{X^*(\alpha')|\alpha' > \alpha\}$ are well defined. Then we have the following further result.

Proposition C.4-3: Envelope Theorem with Set-Valued Maximizers
Define $F(\alpha)= \underset{x}{\text{Max}}\{ f(x, \alpha)|x \geq 0, x \in X \subset \mathbb{R}^n, \alpha \in A \subset \mathbb{R}^m\}$ where $f \in \mathbb{C}^1$.

Also define $X^*(\alpha) = \arg \underset{x}{\text{Max}}\{ f(x, \alpha)|x \geq 0, x \in X, \alpha \in A\}$. If X is compact and $X^*(\alpha)$ is monotonically increasing at α^0, then $F(\alpha)$ is continuous and semi-differentiable at α^0, where the left and right derivatives are

$$\frac{dF}{d\alpha_-}(\alpha^0) = \frac{\partial f}{\partial \alpha}(\underline{x}(\alpha^0), \alpha^0) \quad \text{and} \quad \frac{dF}{d\alpha_+}(\alpha^0) = \frac{\partial f}{\partial \alpha}(\overline{x}(\alpha^0), \alpha^0).$$

Proof: Consider the decreasing sequence $\{\alpha^t\} \downarrow \alpha^0$. By the Theorem of the Maximum, $X^*(\alpha)$ is upper hemi-continuous and compact valued. Thus $\bar{x}(\alpha^0) = Inf\{X^*(\alpha') | \alpha' > \alpha^0\} \in X(\alpha^0)$, and there is some decreasing sequence $x(\alpha^t) \in X^*(\alpha^t)$ such that $\{x(\alpha^t)\} \downarrow \bar{x}(\alpha^0)$.

Because $\bar{x}(\alpha^0) \in X^*(\alpha^0)$ and $x(\alpha^t) \in X^*(\alpha^t)$,

$$f(\bar{x}(\alpha^0), \alpha^t) - f(\bar{x}(\alpha^0), \alpha^0) \le F(\alpha^t) - F(\alpha^0) \le f(\bar{x}(\alpha^t), \alpha^t) - f(\bar{x}(\alpha^t), \alpha^0).$$

Diving by $\alpha^t - \alpha^0$ and taking the limit,

$$\frac{\partial f}{\partial \alpha}(\bar{x}(\alpha^0), \alpha^0) \le \frac{dF}{d\alpha_+}(\alpha^0) \le \frac{\partial f}{\partial \alpha}(\bar{x}(\alpha^0), \alpha^0).$$

Hence $\frac{dF}{d\alpha_+}(\alpha^0) = \frac{\partial f}{\partial \alpha}(\bar{x}(\alpha^0), \alpha^0)$.

An almost identical argument establishes that $\frac{dF}{d\alpha_-}(\alpha^0) = \frac{\partial f}{\partial \alpha}(\underline{x}(\alpha^0), \alpha^0)$. $\square$

C.5 Supporting Hyperplanes

Key ideas: bounding hyperplane for a convex set, supporting hyperplane

Central to economic theory is the idea that prices are an effective guide to decision making. As a simple illustration, suppose that a firm has a fixed quantity of land and can produce the output vectors in the convex set $\mathcal{Y}$ depicted in Figure C.5-1. Consider any point $\bar{y}$ on the boundary of $\mathcal{Y}$. If the set is convex, it is intuitively clear that there must be some non-zero vector p such that $p \cdot y \le p \cdot \bar{y}$ for all $y \in \mathcal{Y}$. Thus the value of the vector $\bar{y}$ exceeds the value of any other feasible vector.

To prove this takes several steps. We begin by considering vectors that are outside the set.

Proposition C.5-1: Bounding Hyperplane
Let $\mathcal{Y} \subset \mathbb{R}^n$ be a non-empty, convex set. Let $\bar{y}$ be a vector not in $\mathcal{Y}$. Then there exists $p \ne 0$ such that for all y in $\mathcal{Y}$, $p \cdot y < p \cdot \bar{y}$.

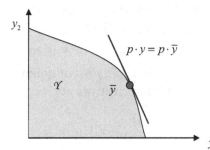

Figure C.5-1. Supporting hyperplane.

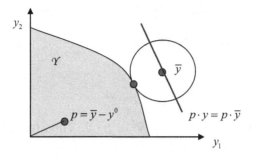

Figure C.5-2. Bounding hyperplane.

The method of proof is illustrated in Figure C.5-2. The ball around the vector $\bar{y}$ just touches the set $\mathcal{Y}$. Thus y^0 is closer to $\bar{y}$ than any other point in $\mathcal{Y}$. Then define $p = \bar{y} - y^0$. The proof is completed by showing that the hyperplane orthogonal to p through $\bar{y}$ lies strictly outside the set $\mathcal{Y}$.

Because $\bar{y} \notin S$, the vector $p \equiv \bar{y} - y^0 \neq 0$.

Thus

$$\|\bar{y} - y^0\|^2 = (\bar{y} - y^0) \cdot (\bar{y} - y^0) = p \cdot (\bar{y} - y^0) > 0.$$

Hence

$$p \cdot y^0 < p \cdot \bar{y}.$$

For any $y \in \mathcal{Y}$, consider the convex combination

$$y^\lambda = (1 - \lambda)y^0 + \lambda y = y^0 + \lambda(y - y^0), \quad 0 < \lambda < 1.$$

Because y^0 and $y \in \mathcal{Y}$ and $\mathcal{Y}$ are convex, the convex combination is $y^\lambda \in \mathcal{Y}$. Then

$$\|\bar{y} - y^\lambda\| \geq \|\bar{y} - y^0\|.$$

Equivalently,

$$(\bar{y} - y^\lambda) \cdot (\bar{y} - y^\lambda) \geq (\bar{y} - y^0) \cdot (\bar{y} - y^0),$$

that is,

$$(\bar{y} - y^0 - \lambda(y - y^0)) \cdot (\bar{y} - y^0 - \lambda(y - y^0)) \geq (\bar{y} - y^0) \cdot (\bar{y} - y^0).$$

Multiplying out and rearranging, it follows that

$$-2\lambda(\bar{y} - y^0) \cdot (y - y^0) + \lambda^2(y - y^0) \cdot (y - y^0) \geq 0.$$

But $p = \bar{y} - y^0$. Then substituting and dividing by λ,

$$-2p \cdot (y - y^0) + \lambda(y - y^0) \cdot (y - y^0) \geq 0.$$

Letting $\lambda \to 0$, we have at last

$$-2p \cdot (y - y^0) \geq 0.$$

Hence

$$p \cdot y \leq p \cdot y^0.$$

But we have already shown that $p \cdot y^0 < p \cdot \bar{y}$. Thus for all $y \in \mathcal{Y}$, $p \cdot y < p \cdot \bar{y}$.

We now show how this result can be extended to cases in which the vector y^0 is a boundary point of $\mathcal{Y}$.

Proposition C.5-2: Supporting Hyperplane Theorem
Suppose $\mathcal{Y} \subset \mathbb{R}^n$ is convex and $\bar{y}$ does not belong to the interior of $\mathcal{Y}$. Then there exists $p \neq 0$ such that for all $y \in \mathcal{Y}$, $p \cdot y \leq p \cdot \bar{y}$.

Proof: Consider any sequence of points $\{\bar{y}^t | \bar{y}^t \notin \mathcal{Y}\}$ that approaches $\bar{y}$. By the Bounding Hyperplane Theorem, there exists a sequence of vectors p^t such that for all t, and all $y \in \mathcal{Y}$

$$p^t \cdot \bar{y}^t - p^t \cdot y > 0.$$

Define $\bar{p}^t = \frac{p^t}{\|p^t\|}$. Then $\bar{p}^t \cdot y < \bar{p}^t \cdot \bar{y}^t$ and, for all t, each element of $\bar{p}^t$ lies in the interval $[-1, 1]$. From the previous section we know that any bounded sequence of vectors in $\mathbb{R}^n$ has a convergent sub-sequence. Thus $\{\bar{p}^t\}_{t=1...}$ has a convergent sub-sequence, $\{\bar{p}^s\}_{s=1...}$. Let $\bar{p}$ be the limit point of this sub-sequence. For all points in the convergent sub-sequence $p^t \cdot \bar{y}^t - p^t \cdot y > 0$.

Then, taking the limit, $\bar{p} \cdot \bar{y} - \bar{p} \cdot y \geq 0$.   □

C.6 Taylor Expansion

Key Ideas: Mean Value Theorem, first-order Taylor expansion, nth-order Taylor Expansion

It is often helpful to consider polynomial approximations of functions. The Taylor Expansion provides a way of representing the error made in using such an approximation.

We begin with the one-variable case using the following result as our basic building block (see Figure C.6-1).

Proposition C.6-1: Mean Value Theorem
Suppose that f is differentiable on the interval $[a, b]$. Then there is some c in this interval such that

$$\frac{df}{dx}(c) = \frac{f(b) - f(a)}{b - a}.$$

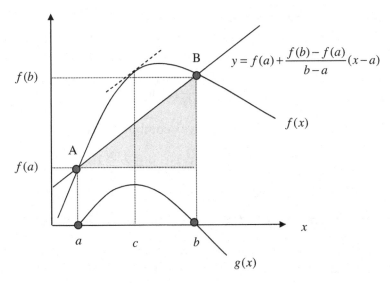

Figure C.6-1. Mean Value Theorem.

Proof: Consider Figure C.6-1. In graphical terms, there must be some c on the interval $[a, b]$ where the slope of the curve is equal to the slope of the chord through A and B.

Note first that the slope of the line through A and B is $\frac{f(b)-f(a)}{b-a}$. Then the equation of the line AB is

$$y = f(a) + \frac{f(b) - f(a)}{b - a}(x - a).$$

Define a new function g to be the difference between f and this line. That is,

$$g(x) = f(x) - f(a) - \frac{f(b) - f(a)}{b - a}(x - a).$$

This is also depicted in the figure. Because $g(a) = g(b) = 0$, either $g(x) = 0$ for all points in the interval, or there is some $\hat{x} \in (a, b)$ such that $g(\hat{x}) \neq 0$. If $g(\hat{x}) > 0$ then there must be some point $c \in (a, b)$ where g takes on its maximum. If $g(\hat{x}) < 0$ then there must be some point $c \in (a, b)$ where g takes on its minimum.[2]

Because f is differentiable, then so is g. From the FOC, there must be some c such that $\frac{dg}{dx}(c) = \frac{df}{dx}(c) - \frac{f(b)-f(a)}{b-a} = 0$. $\qquad\square$

---

[2] In an advanced calculus text a preliminary step would be to prove that if a function is continuous over a closed interval $[a, b]$ then the function must have a maximum and minimum value at some point in this interval.

Proposition C.6-2: First-Order Taylor Expansion
Let f be differentiable on an interval containing x^0 and x^1. Then there is some convex combination $x^\mu = (1 - \mu)x^0 + \mu x^1$ such that

$$f(x^1) = f(x^0) + \frac{df}{dx}(x^\mu)(x^1 - x^0).$$

Proof: For any x^0, x^1 consider the convex combinations

$$x^\lambda = x^0 + \lambda(x^1 - x^0), \quad 0 \le \lambda \le 1.$$

Define the function

$$F(\lambda) \equiv f(x^\lambda) = f(x^0 + \lambda(x^1 - x^0)), \quad 0 \le \lambda \le 1. \qquad \text{(C.6-1)}$$

If f is differentiable over some interval containing x^0 and x^1, then $F(\lambda)$ is differentiable for all convex combinations of x^0 and x^1; that is, for all λ between 0 and 1. Differentiating by λ,

$$\frac{dF}{d\lambda}(\lambda) = (x^1 - x^0)\frac{df}{dx}(x^\lambda).$$

By the Mean Value Theorem, there is some $\mu \in [0, 1]$ such that

$$F'(\mu) = \frac{F(1) - F(0)}{1 - 0}. \qquad \text{(C.6-2)}$$

Note that $F(0) = f(x^0)$ and $F(1) = f(x^1)$. Substituting for each term in equation (C.6-2) yields the following result:

$$f(x^1) = f(x^0) + \frac{df}{dx}(x^\mu)(x^1 - x^0). \qquad \square$$

Corollary C.6-3: First-Order Expansion with n Variables
$$f(x^1) - f(x^0) = (x^1 - x^0) \cdot \frac{\partial f}{\partial x}(x^\mu).$$

Proof: We can apply exactly the same argument if $x \in \mathbb{R}^n$. Now the derivative of the function $F(\lambda) \equiv f(x^\lambda) = f(x^0 + \lambda(x^1 - x^0)), 0 \le \lambda \le 1$ is

$$F'(\lambda) = \frac{d}{d\lambda}f(x^0 + \lambda(x^1 - x^0)) = (x^1 - x^0) \cdot \frac{\partial f}{\partial x}(x^\lambda).$$

Appealing to the Mean Value Theorem, for some $\mu \in [0, 1]$

$$\frac{F(1) - F(0)}{1} = f(x^1) - f(x^0) = (x^1 - x^0) \cdot \frac{\partial f}{\partial x}(x^\mu). \qquad \square$$

This result can be generalized quite easily to higher orders. In each case it is simply a matter of writing down the appropriate higher order polynomial approximation and then adding the last "remainder" term.

Proposition C.6-4: An *m*th Order Taylor Expansion
If f is differentiable n times on the interval $[x^0, x]$ there is some convex combination $x^\lambda = (1 - \lambda)x^0 + \lambda x$ such that

$$f(x) = f(x^0) + \frac{df}{dx}(x^0)(x - x^0) + \cdots + \frac{1}{m-1!}\frac{d^{m-1}f}{dx^{m-1}}(x^0)(x - x^0)^{m-1}$$

$$+ \frac{1}{m!}\frac{d^m f}{dx^m}(x^\lambda)(x - x^0)^m.$$

Taylor's Second-Order Expansion is especially useful. Setting $m = 2$, there is some convex combination x^λ such that

$$f(x) = f(x^0) + \frac{df}{dx}(x^0)(x - x^0) + \frac{1}{2}\frac{d^2 f}{dx^2}(x^\lambda)(x - x^0)^2. \quad \text{(C.6-3)}$$

Proof: ($m = 2$). Consider any x^0, x^1 and convex combination $x^\lambda = x^0 + \lambda(x^1 - x^0)$ and define

$$G(\lambda) = f(x^0 + \lambda(x^1 - x^0)) - f(x^0) - \frac{df}{dx}(x^0)(x^\lambda - x^0) - a\lambda^2$$

$$= f(x^0 + \lambda(x^1 - x^0)) - f(x^0) - \lambda\frac{df}{dx}(x^0)(x^1 - x^0) - a\lambda^2.$$

Setting $\lambda = 0$ it follows immediately that $G(0) = 0$. If we choose a so that $G(1) = 0$ and set $\lambda = 1$ in the above expression then

$$0 = f(x^1) - f(x^0) - \frac{df}{dx}(x^0)(x^1 - x^0) - a. \quad \text{(C.6-4)}$$

Differentiating $G(\lambda)$,

$$\frac{dG}{d\lambda}(\lambda) = (x^1 - x^0)\left[\frac{df}{dx}(x^0 + \lambda(x^1 - x^0)) - \frac{df}{dx}(x^0)\right] - 2a\lambda.$$

Setting $\lambda = 0$, $\frac{dG}{d\lambda}(0) = 0$. Also, differentiating again,

$$\frac{d^2 G}{d\lambda^2}(\lambda) = (x^1 - x^0)^2\frac{d^2 f}{dx^2}(x^\lambda) - 2a. \quad \text{(C.6-5}$$

Because $G(0) = G(1) = 0$ it follows from the Mean Value Theorem that for some $\nu \in [0, 1]$, $\frac{dG}{d\lambda}(\nu) = 0$. We have also seen that $\frac{dG}{d\lambda}(0) = 0$. Appealing to the Mean Value Theorem again, there must be some $\mu \in [0, \nu]$ such that $\frac{d^2 G}{d\lambda^2}(\mu) = 0$.

Appealing to (C.6-5), $\frac{d^2 G}{d\lambda^2}(\mu) = (x^1 - x^0)^2\frac{d^2 f}{dx^2}(x^\mu) - 2a = 0$. It follows that $a = \frac{1}{2}\frac{d^2 f}{dx^2}(x^\mu)(x^1 - x^0)^2$. Appealing to (C.6-4), and evaluating at $\lambda = 1$ (so that $G(1) = 0$)

$$f(x^1) = f(x^0) + \frac{df}{dx}(x^0)(x^1 - x^0) + \frac{1}{2}\frac{d^2 f}{dx^2}(x^\mu)(x^1 - x^0)^2. \qquad \square$$

Corollary C.6-5: Second-Order Taylor Expansion with *n* variables

$$f(x^1) = f(x^0) + (x^1 - x^0) \cdot \frac{\partial f}{\partial x}(x^0) + \tfrac{1}{2}(x^1 - x^0)'\mathbf{H}(x^\mu)(x^1 - x^0), \ \mu \in [0, 1],$$

where $\mathbf{H}(x) = [\frac{\partial^2 f}{\partial x^2}(x)]$ is the Hessian of f.

The following result is a direct application of Taylor's (first-order) expansion.

Proposition C.6-6: l'Hôpital's Rule
Suppose f and $g \in C^1$. If $f(x^0) = g(x^0) = 0$ and $g'(x^0) \neq 0$, then

$$\lim_{x \to x^0} \frac{f(x)}{g(x)} = \frac{f'(x^0)}{g'(x^0)}.$$

Exercise C.6-1: Second-Order Expansion Prove Corollary C.6-5.

Exercise C.6-2: Implicit Function Theorem In Section C.3 we showed that, under the hypotheses of Proposition C.3-2, if $h(x^0, \alpha^0) = 0$, then over some neighborhood of α^0 there is a unique continuous function $g(\alpha)$ satisfying $h(g(\alpha), \alpha) = 0$. Appealing to Taylor's Expansion, you can now prove that this function is differentiable. Choose α^1 and $x^1 = g(\alpha^1)$.

(a) Explain why, as long as α^1 is sufficiently close to α^0

$$F(\lambda) = h(x^0 + \lambda(x^1 - x^0), \alpha^1 + \lambda(\alpha^1 - \alpha^0))$$

is differentiable for all $\lambda \in [0, 1]$.

(b) Appeal to Taylor's Expansion to show that for some $\lambda \in [0, 1]$,

$$F'(\lambda) = \frac{\partial h}{\partial x}(x^\lambda, \alpha^\lambda)(x^1 - x^0) + \frac{\partial h}{\partial \alpha}(x^\lambda, \alpha^\lambda)(\alpha^1 - \alpha^0) = 0.$$

(c) Define $\Delta x = x^1 - x^0$ and $\Delta \alpha = \alpha^1 - \alpha^0$. Show that

$$\frac{\Delta x}{\Delta \alpha} = -\frac{\frac{\partial h}{\partial \alpha}(x^\lambda, \alpha^\lambda)}{\frac{\partial h}{\partial x}(x^\lambda, \alpha^\lambda)}.$$

(d) Given the hypothesis that h is continuously differentiable, make a limiting argument to establish that

$$g'(\alpha^0) = \frac{dx}{d\alpha} = -\frac{\frac{\partial h}{\partial \alpha}(x^0, \alpha^0)}{\frac{\partial h}{\partial x}(x^0, \alpha^0)}.$$

Exercise C.6-3: l'Hôpital's Rule

(a) Appeal to the Mean Value Theorem to establish that for any x^0 and x there exist convex combinations x^λ and x^μ such that

$$\frac{f(x)}{g(x)} = \frac{f(x^0) + f'(x^\lambda)(x - x^0)}{g(x^0) + g'(x^\mu)(x - x^0)}.$$

(b) Hence prove l'Hôpital's Rule by taking the limit.

Answers to Odd-Numbered Exercises

1 Prices and Optimization

1.1 Supporting Prices

Exercise 1.1-1: Supporting Hyperplane

(a) Each term in the summation has a negative second derivative and is therefore concave. Thus U is concave because the sum of concave functions is concave. It is therefore quasi-concave.

(b) The gradient vector $\frac{\partial U}{\partial x}(\overline{x}) = (\frac{\alpha_1}{\overline{x}_1}, \ldots, \frac{\alpha_n}{\overline{x}_n})$. Thus the supporting hyperplane is

$$\sum_{i=1}^{n} \frac{\alpha_i}{\overline{x}_i}(x_i - \overline{x}_i) = 0.$$

(c) We can interpret the contour set $U(x) = U(\overline{x})$ as an indifference curve touching the "budget line" at the point $\overline{x}$. This is depicted in Figure 1.6-1.

Exercise 1.1-3: Supporting Prices

(a) The production set is

$$\mathcal{Y} = \left\{ (z_1, z_2, q) | h(z, q) = q - z_1^{\alpha_1} z_2^{\alpha_2} \le 0 \right\}.$$

The function h is convex because it is the sum of two convex functions. The lower contour sets of a convex function are convex. Thus the production set is convex.

(b) By substitution / lies on the boundary of the production set. Then the gradient of h is supporting at this point.

(c) The gradient vector is $(-r, p) = (\frac{\partial h}{\partial z_1}, \frac{\partial h}{\partial z_2}, \frac{\partial h}{\partial q}) = (-\frac{1}{3}, -\frac{2}{3}, 1)$. This is the supporting hyperplane; that is,

$$(-r, p) \cdot (z_1 - z_1^0, z_2 - z_2^0, q - q^0) \le 0.$$

We can rewrite this as follows:

$$pq - r \cdot z \le pq^0 - r \cdot z^0.$$

593

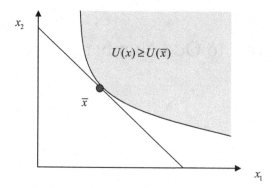

Figure 1.6-1. Supporting line.

(d) As is easily checked, this is the same production set as in part (a). Thus $p = (\frac{1}{3}, \frac{2}{3}, 1)$ is a supporting price vector.

Exercise 1.1-5: Robinson Crusoe Economy with Three Commodities

(a) If Robinson chooses input vector z, his consumption of commodity 1 is $x_1 = \omega_1 - z_1 = 32 - z_1$ and consumption of commodity 2 is $x_2 = \omega_2 - z_2 = 160 - z_2$. Output of commodity 3 is $y_3 = z_1^{1/3} z_2^{2/3}$. Because his endowment of commodity 3 is zero, his consumption of commodity 2 is $x_3 = y_3$. His utility is therefore

$$U = \sum_{j=1}^{3} \ln x_j = \ln(32 - z_1) + \ln(160 - z_2) + \ln z_1^{1/3} z_2^{2/3}$$

$$= \ln(32 - z_1) + \ln(160 - z_2) + \tfrac{1}{3}\ln z_1 + \tfrac{2}{3}\ln z_2.$$

The FOC are very similar to the FOC is the previous exercise. Solving, $z_1^* = 8$ and $z_2^* = 64$. Therefore $y_3 = 32$ and $x^* = (24, 96, 32)$.

(b) Prices are supporting if they are profit maximizing.

$$\Pi = p \cdot y = p_3 y_3 - p_1 z_1 - p_2 z_2 = p_3 z_1^{1/3} z_2^{2/3} - p_1 z_1 - p_2 z_2.$$

FOC:

$$\frac{\partial \Pi}{\partial z_1} = p_3 \tfrac{1}{3} z_1^{-2/3} z_2^{2/3} - p_1 = 0 \quad \text{and} \quad \frac{\partial \Pi}{\partial z_2} = p_3 \tfrac{2}{3} z_1^{1/3} z_2^{-1/3} - p_2 = 0.$$

Substituting for $z^* = (8, 64)$,

$$\frac{\partial \Pi}{\partial z_1} = p_3 \tfrac{1}{3} 4 - p_1 = 0 \quad \text{and} \quad \frac{\partial \Pi}{\partial z_2} = p_3 \tfrac{2}{3} \tfrac{1}{2} - p_2 = 0.$$

(c) It is readily confirmed that $p = (4, 1, 3)$ satisfies these two necessary conditions. Thus this is the supporting price vector. Maximized profit is zero so Crusoe's budget constraint is $p \cdot x = p \cdot \omega$.

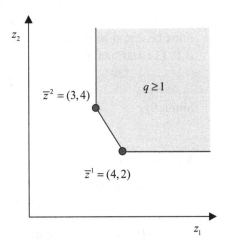

Figure 1.6-2. Isoquant.

Crusoe then solves the following optimization problem:

$$\underset{x}{\text{Max}}\{U(x)|4x_1 + x_2 + 3x_3 \le p \cdot \omega = 288\}.$$

As may be confirmed, x^* is the solution to this optimization problem. Then markets clear at the supporting prices.

Exercise 1.1-7: Linear Technology The production set is

$$\mathcal{Y} = \{(z, q)|x \ge 0, \mathbf{A}x \le z, q \le a_0'x\},$$

where

$$\mathbf{A} = \begin{bmatrix} 4 & 3 \\ 2 & 4 \end{bmatrix} \quad \text{and} \quad a_0 = \begin{bmatrix} 1 \\ 1 \end{bmatrix}.$$

Operating plant 1 at a level of 1 yields an output of 1 and requires an input vector of $\bar{z}^1 = (4, 2)$. Operating plant 2 at a level of 1 yields an output of 1 and requires n input vector of $\bar{z}^2 = (3, 4)$. Any convex combination of thee inputs yields the same output. Thus the unit isoquant is as depicted in Figure 1.6-2.

(b) For any input vector z^0, (z^0, q^0) is on the boundary if q^0 is maximal. Thus

$$q^0 = \text{Max}\{a_0'x|, x \ge 0, \mathbf{A}x \le z^0\}.$$

(c) This problem can be solved graphically. Draw the feasible set and show that the slope of the iso-output lines is between the slope of the two constraints. It is readily confirmed that $x^0 = (2, 2)$.[1]

---

[1] Alternatively solve by trial and error. Pick an x and then compute the implied shadow prices. If marginal value is less than MC and equal to MC for all plants that are utilized, this must be the solution.

(d) Because both plants are in operation, the marginal gain to increasing output must be equal to the marginal cost. The marginal value of increasing x_1 by 1 is 1. The marginal cost is $\lambda_1 4 + \lambda_2 2$. Therefore

$$\lambda_1 4 + \lambda_2 2 = 1.$$

Similarly,

$$\lambda_1 3 + \lambda_2 4 = 1.$$

Solving, $\lambda = (\frac{1}{5}, \frac{1}{10})$.

1.2 Shadow Prices

Exercise 1.2-1: How Many Goods Should She Consume?

(i) Writing the problem in standard form, we seek to solve

$$\text{Max}_x \{U(x) | h(x) = 20 - 4x_1 - x_2 \geq 0, x \geq 0\}.$$

Because the maximand is strictly concave, there is a unique solution: $\bar{x}$ concave. Because the constraint is linear hence concave, and $\frac{\partial h}{\partial x}(x) = (-4, -1) \neq 0$, the necessary conditions are also sufficient. Then all we need to do is find a solution to the first-order conditions.
Form the Lagrangian:

$$\mathcal{L}(x, \lambda) = \ln(a + x_1) + \ln x_2 + \lambda(20 - 4x_1 - x_2).$$

FOC

$$\frac{\partial \mathcal{L}}{\partial x_1} = \frac{1}{a + x_1} - 4\lambda \leq 0, \quad \text{with equality if} \quad \bar{x}_1 > 0.$$

$$\frac{\partial \mathcal{L}}{\partial x_2} = \frac{1}{x_2} - \lambda \leq 0, \quad \text{with equality if} \quad \bar{x}_2 > 0.$$

$$\frac{\partial \mathcal{L}}{\partial \lambda} = (20 - 4x_1 - x_2) \geq 0, \quad \text{with equality if} \quad \lambda > 0.$$

Note that the second condition cannot hold if $x_2 = 0$; thus $\bar{x}_2 > 0$ and hence $\lambda > 0$ and so the constraint is satisfied with equality. Suppose $x_1^* > 0$. Then all three conditions are equalities. In this case,

$$\frac{1}{4(a + x_1)} = \lambda = \frac{1}{x_2} \quad \text{and so} \quad x_2 = 4(a + x_1).$$

Substituting back into the budget constraint,

$$4x_1 + 4(a + x_1) = 20 \quad \text{and so} \quad x_1 = \tfrac{1}{2}(5 - a) \quad \text{and} \quad x_2 = 10 + 2a.$$

Note that our assumption that $\bar{x}_1 > 0$ is satisfied if $a < 5$. Next suppose that $a \geq 5$. It is easy to check that $\bar{x} = (0, 20)$ satisfies the first-order conditions.

(ii) Arguing as in (a), because the utility function is strictly concave, there is a unique solution $\bar{x}$ to Bev's maximization problem:

$$\underset{x \geq 0}{\text{Max}}\{\ln(a + x_1) + x_2 | I - p \cdot x \geq 0\}.$$

The FOC are

$$\frac{\partial \mathcal{L}}{\partial x_1} = \frac{1}{a + x_1} - p_1 \lambda \leq 0, \quad \text{with equality if} \quad \bar{x}_1 > 0.$$

$$\frac{\partial \mathcal{L}}{\partial x_2} = \frac{1}{x_2} - p_2 \lambda \leq 0, \quad \text{with equality if} \quad \bar{x}_2 > 0.$$

$$\frac{\partial \mathcal{L}}{\partial \lambda} = I - p_1 x_1 - p_2 x_2 \geq 0, \quad \text{with equality if} \quad \lambda > 0.$$

Because the problem is concave these conditions are both necessary and sufficient.

To satisfy the second of these conditions, the shadow price must be positive so the budget constraint is satisfied with equality. We first seek conditions under which the solution $\bar{x} \gg 0$. Rewriting the FOC and appealing to the ratio rule yields the following results:

$$\lambda = \frac{1}{p_1(a_1 + x_1)} = \frac{1}{p_2 x_2} = \frac{2}{p_1 a_1 + p \cdot x} = \frac{2}{p_1 a_1 + I}.$$

Therefore $\bar{x}_2 = \dfrac{I + a_1 p_1}{2 p_2}$ and $\bar{x}_1 = \dfrac{I - a_1 p_1}{2 p_2}.$

Note that $\bar{x}_1 > 0$ if and only if $a_1 p_1 < I$. It remains to solve for $\bar{x}$ is this inequality is violated. The natural guess is that $\bar{x}_1 = 0$. Then $\bar{x}_2 = I/p_2$ and so the FOC are as follows:

$$\frac{\partial \mathcal{L}}{\partial x_1} = \frac{1}{a + x_1} - p_1 \lambda = \frac{1}{a} - p_1 \lambda \leq 0,$$

$$\frac{\partial \mathcal{L}}{\partial x_2} = \frac{1}{x_2} - p_2 \lambda = \frac{p_2}{I} - p_2 \lambda = 0.$$

Then $\lambda = 1/I$ and so $\frac{\partial \mathcal{L}}{\partial x_1} = \frac{1}{a} - \frac{p_1}{I} \leq 0$. Therefore $\bar{x} = (0, I/p_2)$ is indeed the solution if $p_1 < I/a$.

Exercise 1.2-3: Multi-Plant Firm The firm must produce q units. Thus the amount produced at each plant must satisfy the constraint $\sum_{j=1}^{n} q_j \geq q$. Total cost $TC(q) = \sum_{j=1}^{n} \frac{q_j^2}{2\alpha_j}$. The firm's optimization problem is therefore as follows:

$$\underset{q}{\text{Min}} \left\{ TC(q) | \sum_{j=1}^{n} q_j \geq q, q \geq 0 \right\}.$$

To be consistent with our economic approach we convert this to the standard form. Note that instead of minimizing TC we maximize $-TC$.

$$\text{Max}_{q}\left\{-TC(q)|h(q) = \sum_{j=1}^{n} q_j - q \geq 0, q \geq 0\right\}.$$

Because $\frac{\partial h}{\partial q} \neq 0$ the Constraint Qualifications are satisfied:

$$\mathcal{L}(q,\lambda) = -\sum_{j=1}^{n}\frac{q_j^2}{2\alpha_j} + \lambda\left(\sum_{j=1}^{n} q_j - q\right).$$

(a) First-order conditions:

$$\frac{\partial\mathcal{L}}{\partial q_j} = -\frac{q_j}{\alpha_j} + \lambda \leq 0 \quad \text{with equality if } q_j^* > 0, \; j = 1,\ldots,n.$$

At least one plant must produce output. Suppose it is the first. Then

$$\frac{\partial\mathcal{L}}{\partial q_1} = -\frac{q_1}{\alpha_1} + \lambda = 0.$$

It follows that $\lambda^* > 0$. Hence, for the first-order conditions $q_j^* > 0$ for every plant and so $q_j^* = \alpha_j\lambda^*$.

(b) Substituting into the constraint,

$$\sum_{j=1}^{n} q_j^* = \sum_{j=1}^{n}\alpha_j\lambda^* = q. \text{ Hence } \lambda^* = \frac{q}{\sum_{1}^{n}\alpha_j} = \frac{q}{n\bar{\alpha}}.$$

(c) $q_j = \alpha_j\lambda = \frac{\alpha_j}{n}\frac{q}{\bar{\alpha}}$. Hence $C_j(q_j) = \frac{\alpha_j}{2n^2}\frac{q^2}{\bar{\alpha}^2}$. Summing over the n plants,

$$TC = \sum_{j=1}^{n}\frac{\alpha_j}{2n^2}\frac{q^2}{\bar{\alpha}^2} = \frac{1}{2n}\frac{q^2}{\bar{\alpha}}.$$

(d) Differentiating yields $MC(q) = \frac{q}{n\bar{\alpha}}$.

(e) The shadow price is the marginal value of relaxing the constraint. In this case it is the effect on total cost of increasing output by 1; that is, marginal cost. Thus it was not necessary to go through all the mathematics to solve for marginal cost. From (b), $MC(q) = \lambda = \frac{q}{n\bar{\alpha}}$. Integrating this expression, $TC(q) = \frac{1}{2n}\frac{q^2}{\bar{\alpha}}$.

1.3 The Envelope Theorem

Exercise 1.3-1: Price Elasticity of Profit

(a) $\Pi(p) = \text{Max}_{q}\{p \cdot q - C(q)\}$

With output constant $\frac{\partial\Pi}{\partial p_i} = q_i(p)$.

From the data $\Pi(10) = 1000 - 600 = 400$; $\frac{\partial \Pi}{\partial p_1} = q_1(p) = 100$.

$$\mathcal{E}(\Pi, p_1) = \frac{p_1}{\Pi} \frac{\partial \Pi}{\partial p_1} = \frac{10}{400} 100 = 2.5.$$

(b) By the Envelope Theorem, $\frac{\partial \Pi}{\partial p_i} = q_i(p)$ so the answer is the same.

(c) From the data, profit is now $10 \times 80 + 20 \times 50 - 1000 = 800$.

By the Envelope Theorem, $\frac{\partial \Pi}{\partial p_1} = q_1(p) = 80$. Therefore

$$\mathcal{E}(\Pi, p_1) = \frac{p_1}{\Pi} \frac{\partial \Pi}{\partial p_1} = \frac{10}{800} 80 = 1.$$

Exercise 1.3-3: Cross Price Effects

(a) The profit of the firm is $\pi = p \cdot q - r \cdot z$. Thus the firm solves the following maximization problem.

$$\underset{z,q}{\text{Max}} \{ p \cdot q - r \cdot z | q, z \geq 0, h(q, z) \geq 0 \}.$$

Let $q(r, p)$ be the profit-maximizing output vector and let $\Pi(r, p)$ be maximized profit. We assume that $\Pi(r, p) \in C^2$ so that $\frac{\partial}{\partial p_i} \frac{\partial \Pi}{\partial p_j} = \frac{\partial}{\partial p_j} \frac{\partial \Pi}{\partial p_i}$.
The Lagrangian for this problem is

$$\mathcal{L}(z, q, \lambda) = p \cdot q - r \cdot z + \lambda h(z, q).$$

By the Envelope Theorem,

$$\frac{\partial \Pi}{\partial p_j} = \frac{\partial \mathcal{L}}{\partial p_j} = q_j(r.p).$$

(b) Differentiating this by p_i,

$$\frac{\partial}{\partial p_i} \frac{\partial \Pi}{\partial p_j} = \frac{\partial q_j}{\partial p_i}(r, p).$$

Reversing the order of differentiation,

$$\frac{\partial}{\partial p_j} \frac{\partial \Pi}{\partial p_i} = \frac{\partial q_i}{\partial p_j}(r, p).$$

Because the order of partial differentiation does not matter, it follows that

$$\frac{\partial q_j}{\partial p_i}(r, p) = \frac{\partial q_i}{\partial p_j}(r, p).$$

(c) Exactly the same argument can be used for two input price changes and for one input and one output price change.

1.4 Foundations of Constrained Optimization

Exercise 1.4-1: Sufficient Conditions for a Unique Maximum If each constraint function is quasi-concave, the feasible set X is convex. Suppose $\bar{x}^0$
and $\bar{x}^1$ both solve $\underset{x}{\text{Max}}\{f(x)|x \in X\}$. Then

$$f(\bar{x}^0) = f(\bar{x}^1) \geq f(x), x \in X.$$

If X is convex it follows that every convex combination, $x^\mu \in X$. If f is strictly quasi-concave, $f(x^\mu) > \text{Min}\{f(\bar{x}^0), f(\bar{x}^1)\}$. But this contradicts the earlier inequality.

Exercise 1.4-3: Dual Linear Programming Problem

(a) Let $\bar{x}$ be a solution to the standard linear programming problem; that is,

$$\bar{x} = \arg\underset{x}{\text{Max}}\{a_0'x|x \geq 0, \mathbf{A}x \leq \bar{z}\}.$$

Appealing to the Fundamental Theorem on Linear Programming, there exists a shadow price vector $\bar{\lambda} \geq 0$ such that the complementary slackness conditions hold. That is,

$$\text{(i) } (a_0' - \bar{\lambda}'\mathbf{A})\bar{x} = 0 \quad \text{and} \quad \text{(ii) } \bar{\lambda}'(\bar{z} - \mathbf{A}\bar{x}) = 0.$$

Together these two conditions imply that

$$a_0'\bar{x} = \bar{\lambda}'\mathbf{A}\bar{x} = \bar{\lambda}'\bar{z}. \tag{1.6-1}$$

The dual problem is $\underset{\lambda}{\text{Min}}\{\lambda'\bar{z}|\lambda'\mathbf{A} \geq a_0', \lambda \geq 0\}$. Consider any $\lambda \geq 0$ satisfying the dual constraints.

(b) Because $\bar{x} \geq 0$ it follows that

$$\lambda'\mathbf{A}\bar{x} \geq a_0'\bar{x}. \tag{1.6-2}$$

(c) Because $\bar{x}$ is feasible, $\mathbf{A}\bar{x} \leq \bar{z}$. Hence

$$\lambda'\mathbf{A}\bar{x} \leq \lambda'\bar{z}. \tag{1.6-3}$$

Combining (1.6-2) and (1.6-3), $\lambda'\bar{z} \geq a_0'\bar{x}$. From (1.6-1) it follows that for all λ satisfying the dual constraints, $\lambda'\bar{z} \geq \bar{\lambda}'\bar{z}$. Therefore

$$\bar{\lambda} = \arg\underset{\lambda}{\text{Min}}\{\lambda'\bar{z}|\lambda'\mathbf{A} \geq a_0', \lambda \geq 0\}.$$

1.5 Application – Monopoly with Joint Costs

Exercise 1.5-1: Multi-Product Firm and Joint Costs The firm is depicted schematically in Figure 1.6-3.

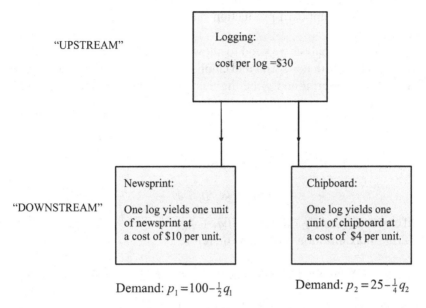

"UPSTREAM"

Logging:

cost per log =$30

"DOWNSTREAM"

Newsprint:

One log yields one unit of newsprint at a cost of $10 per unit.

Chipboard:

One log yields one unit of chipboard at a cost of $4 per unit.

Demand: $p_1 = 100 - \frac{1}{2}q_1$

Demand: $p_2 = 25 - \frac{1}{4}q_2$

Figure 1.6-3. Vertically integrated firm.

(a) If all the logs cut are marketed, total revenue is

$$R = p_1(q_1)q_1 + p_2(q_2)q_2.$$

Substituting for q_1 and q_2,

$$R = 125q - \tfrac{3}{4}q^2.$$

The cost of the logs and of converting them into final products is

$$C = 30q_0 + 10q_1 + 4q_2.$$

Then, because $q_1 = q_2 = q_0$ total cost is $44q_0$ and so the firm's profit is

$$\Pi = 125q_0 - \tfrac{3}{4}q_0^2 - 44q_0.$$

The marginal profit of the firm is therefore

$$\frac{d\Pi}{dq_0} = 81 - \frac{3}{2}q_0.$$

It is readily checked that profit is maximized at $q_0 = 54$. From the demand price functions, it follows that the firm sells newsprint at a price of $73 and chipboard at a price of $11.50.

(b) Next suppose that the firm were to decrease its output of chipboard trays by 1 unit. The unit cost is $4 so division 2 reduces cost by $4. What happens to revenue? Because $p_2 = 25 - \frac{1}{4}q_2$, marginal revenue is $MR_2 = 25 - \frac{1}{2}q_2 = -2$.

Thus reducing chipboard production raises revenue and reduces cost. Hence profit goes up.

(c) For a complete analysis we need to allow for the possibility that not all logs are converted into both newsprint and chipboard. Let q_1 be the number of logs converted into newsprint and q_2 be the number of logs converted into chipboard. The revenue from selling the two products can then be written as

$$R_1 = (100 - \tfrac{1}{2}q_1)q_1 \quad \text{and} \quad R_2 = (25 - \tfrac{1}{4}q_2)q_2.$$

If q_0 logs are cut, the firm faces the constraints:

$$q_1 \leq q_0, q_2 \leq q_0.$$

Total cost is $C(q_0, q_1, q_2) = 30q_0 + 10q_1 + 4q_2$.
The firm's maximization problem is therefore

$$\underset{x,q}{\text{Max}}\{R(q_1) + R(q_2) - C(q_0, q_1, q_2)|q_0 \geq q_1, q_0 \geq q_2\}.$$

Mathematically, this is exactly the same as the electricity pricing problem. Because the Lagrangian is a concave function of (q_0, q_1, q_2). The necessary conditions are also sufficient for a maximum.

Forming the Lagrangian, we obtain

$$\mathcal{L}(q_0, q, \lambda) = R_1(q_1) + R_2(q_2) - 30q_0 - 10q_1 - 4q_2$$
$$+ \lambda_1(q_0 - q_1) + \lambda_2(q_0 - q_2).$$

Differentiating this equation yields the following first-order conditions:

$$MR_1 - 10 - \lambda_1 = 90 - q_1 - \lambda_1 = 0, \quad \text{if} \quad q_1^* > 0,$$
$$MR_2 - 4 - \lambda_2 = 21 - \tfrac{1}{2}q_2 - \lambda_2 = 0 \quad \text{if} \quad q_2^* > 0,$$
$$\lambda_1 + \lambda_2 - 30 = 0, \quad \text{if} \quad q_0^* > 0.$$

Moreover if $q_t < q_0$ then $\lambda_t = 0$.

Given our earlier discussion, we know that profit must be maximized with only one of the constraints binding. Suppose that the chipboard constraint is not binding. Then the shadow price, λ_2^* is zero and so $\lambda_1^* = 30$. It follows from the other first-order conditions that $q_1^* = 60$ and $q_2^* = 42$.

(d) The social surplus is the area under the demand price functions less total cost; that is,

$$\int_0^{q_1} p_1(x)dx + \int_0^{q_2} p_2(x)dx - 30q_0 - 10q_1 - 4q_2.$$

The Lagrangian for maximizing social surplus is therefore

$$\mathcal{L}(q_0, q, \lambda) = \int\limits_0^{q_1} p_1(x)dx + \int\limits_0^{q_2} p_2(x)dx - 30q_0 - 10q_1 - 4q_2$$
$$+ \lambda_1(q_0 - q_1) + \lambda_2(q_0 - q_2).$$

FOC:

$$p_1(q_1) - 10 - \lambda_1 = 90 - \tfrac{1}{2}q_1 - \lambda_1 = 0, \quad \text{if} \quad q_1^* > 0,$$
$$p_2(q_2) - 4 - \lambda_2 = 21 - \tfrac{1}{4}q_2 - \lambda_2 = 0, \quad \text{if} \quad q_2^* > 0,$$
$$\lambda_1 + \lambda_2 - 30 = 0, \quad \text{if} \quad q_0^* > 0.$$

Again if $q_t < q_0$ then $\lambda_t = 0$ and social surplus must be maximized with only one of the constraints binding. Suppose that the chipboard constraint is not binding. Then the shadow price λ_2^* is zero and so $\lambda_1^* = 30$. It follows from the other FOC that $q_1^* = 120$ and $q_2^* = 84$.

(e) Consider the profit-maximization problem in (a) when the demand price for product 2 rises to $p_2 = 35 - \frac{q_2}{4}$. If $q_2^* < q_1^* = q_0^*$, the shadow price, λ_2^*, is zero and so $\lambda_1^* = 30$. Checking the FOC, $q_1^* = 60$ and $q_2^* = 62$. But this contradicts our hypothesis that $q_2^* < q_1^*$. The same considerations can be applied to show that q_1^* cannot be less than q_2^*. The only possibility then is that $q_1^* = q_2^* = q_0$. Solving the three equations with three unknowns ($q_0; \lambda_1$ and λ_2) we can obtain the optimum with the new demand for commodity 2 as $q_1^* = q_2^* = q_0 = 60\tfrac{2}{3}$.

Exercise 1.5-3: Electricity Supply

(a) From the production function $q_t^2 = K_t L_t$. Thus, given that K_t units of capital have been rented, labor demand is $L_t = q_t^2 / K_t$. Hence total cost is

$$\frac{2q_1^2}{K_1} + \frac{2q_2^2}{K_2} + 2K_1 + 2K_2 + 6K_0$$

and the Lagrangian is

$$\mathcal{L} = - \left(\frac{2q_1^2}{K_1} + \frac{2q_2^2}{K_2} + 2K_1 + 2K_2 + 6K_0 \right) + \lambda_1(K_0 - K_1) + \lambda_2(K_0 - K_2).$$

(b) The FOC are therefore

$$\frac{\partial \mathcal{L}}{\partial K_0} = -6 + \lambda_1 + \lambda_2 = 0.$$
$$\frac{\partial \mathcal{L}}{\partial K_t} = \frac{2q_t^2}{K_t^2} - 2 - \lambda_t = 0, t = 1, 2.$$

If outputs are similar the shadow prices must be similar; hence both must be positive. Then $K_t = K_0, t = 1, 2$ and so

$$\frac{2q_1^2}{K_0^2} + \frac{2q_2^2}{K_0^2} = 10.$$

Thus $K_t = \frac{1}{\sqrt{5}}(q_1^2 + q_2^2)^{\frac{1}{2}}$ and so

$$C(q) = 4\sqrt{5}\left(q_1^2 + q_2^2\right)^{\frac{1}{2}}.$$

(c) Substituting for K_t in the FOC for period t,

$$\lambda_t = \frac{10q_t^2}{q_1^2 + q_2^2} - 2.$$

Thus the shadow price of product 1 is lower because $q_1 < q_2$. We can rewrite the shadow price for product 1 as follows:

$$\lambda_1 = \frac{10}{1 + (\frac{q_2}{q_1})^2} - 2.$$

Note that this is positive if and only if $q_1 > q_2/2$. Outside this range not all the capital is used to produce product 1.

(d) In this case the shadow price for product 1 is zero. Hence

$$\frac{\partial \mathcal{L}}{\partial K_1} = \frac{2q_1^2}{K_1^2} - 2 = 0, \quad \frac{\partial \mathcal{L}}{\partial K_2} = \frac{2q_2^2}{K_2^2} - 2 - \lambda_2 = 0.$$

It follows that $K_1 = q_1$. Because $\lambda_2 = 6$ it follows that $K_2 = \frac{1}{2}q_2$. Total cost is therefore

$$C(q) = 4q_1 + 8q_2, q_1 < \tfrac{1}{2}q_2.$$

(e) Arguing symmetrically,

$$C(q) = 8q_1 + 4q_2, q_1 > 2q_2.$$

Fixing q_2, the marginal cost curve for the firm is sketched in Figure 1.6-4.

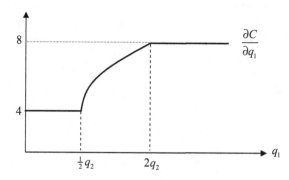

Figure 1.6-4. Marginal cost curve.

2 Consumers

2.1 Theory of Choice

Exercise 2.1-1: Transitivity

(a) Because $x \succsim_i y$ and $y \succsim_i z$ it follows from transitivity that $x \succsim_i z$. Either $x \succ_i z$ or $x \sim_i z$. We suppose the latter and seek a contradiction. Then $z \succsim_i x$. Because $x \succsim_i y$ it follows by transitivity that $z \succsim_i y$. Yet this contradicts the initial hypothesis that the consumer strictly prefers y to z.

(b) Yes it is true. The proof is similar.

Exercise 2.1-3: Sufficient Condition for Convex Preferences

(a) We wish to show that for any $x^0, x^1 \succsim y$ all convex combinations are also preferred to y.

That is, if $U(x^0) \geq U(y)$ and $U(x^1) \geq U(y)$ then $U(x^\lambda) \geq U(y)$. Because $u(x) = f(U(x))$ is concave,

$$u(x^\lambda) \geq (1 - \lambda)u(x^0) + \lambda u(x^1).$$

That is,

$$f(U(x^\lambda)) \geq (1 - \lambda)f(U(x^0)) + \lambda f(U(x^1)).$$

Because f is increasing, $f(U(x^0)) \geq f(U(y))$ and $f(U(x^1)) \geq f(U(y))$. It follows that

$$f(U(x^\lambda)) \geq (1 - \lambda)f(U(y)) + \lambda f(U(y)) = f(U(y)).$$

Again, because f is increasing, $U(x^\lambda) \geq U(y)$.

(b) The proof is almost identical.

(c) No. Suppose $U(x) = a_1 x_1 + a_2 x_2$. Then $u(x) = f(a \cdot x)$. Indifference curves are lines.

Exercise 2.1-5: Strictly Convex Preferences

(a) The logarithm of $U(x)$ is well defined over $\mathbb{R}_+^2$. Define $u(x) = \ln U(x) = \ln(1 + x_1) + \ln(1 + x_2)$. Because each term on the right-hand side is concave it follows from the previous exercise that preferences are convex. Indeed because $\ln(1 + x_j)$ is a strictly concave function, $u(x)$ is strictly concave and so preferences are strictly convex.

(b) For all $x > 0$ the logarithm of $U(x)$ is well defined and strictly concave. Then preferences are strictly convex. It follows that for all strictly positive x^0, x^1 and convex combination x^λ $(0 < \lambda < 1)$, such that $U(x^1) \geq U(x^0)$, $U(x^\lambda) > U(x^0)$. Because $U(x)$ is continuous it follows that, for all non-negative x,

$$U(x^\lambda) \geq U(x^0).$$

Thus preferences are quasi-concave.

Note that if $x^0 = (0, a)$ and $x^1 = (0, b)$, $U(x^0) = U(x^\lambda) = U(x^1) = 0$ so that preferences are not strictly convex.

Exercise 2.1-7: Quasi-Linear Preferences

(a) Because a linear function is concave it follows that if $V(z)$ is concave, the sum $U(x) = y + V(z)$ is concave and hence quasi-concave.

(b) For any vectors z^0, z^1, choose y^0, y^1 so that

$$U(y^0, z^0) = y^0 + V(z^0) = y^1 + V(z^1) = U(y^1, z^1).$$

If U is quasi-concave, then $U(y^\lambda, z^\lambda) \geq U(y^0, z^0)$ and $U(y^\lambda, z^\lambda) \geq U(y^1, z^1)$. Multiply the first inequality by $(1 - \lambda)$ and the second by λ.

$$U(x^\lambda) = y^\lambda + V(z^\lambda) \geq (1 - \lambda)(y^0 + V(z^0)) + \lambda(y^1 + V(z^1))$$
$$= y^\lambda + (1 - \lambda)V(z^0) + \lambda V(z^1).$$

Subtracting y^λ from both sides it follows that V is concave.

2.2 Budget-Constrained Choice with Two Commodities

Exercise 2.2-1: Consumer Choice

(iii) If $U(x) = \ln(1 + x_1) + \ln(1 + x_2)$ the marginal rate of substitution

$$\text{MRS}(x_1, x_2) = \frac{\frac{\partial U}{\partial x_1}}{\frac{\partial U}{\partial x_2}} = \frac{1 + x_2}{1 + x_1}.$$

If $x_1^* = 0$, then $x_2^* = \frac{I}{p_2}$ and $\text{MRS}(x^*) = 1 + \frac{I}{p_2} \leq \frac{p_1}{p_2}$.

Rearranging this expression, $p_2 \leq p_1 - I$. Given the symmetry of the utility function, if the consumer only consumes commodity 1 then $p_1 \leq p_2 - I$; that is, $p_2 \geq p_1 + I$. Thus case (a) corresponds to the third diagram.

Exercise 2.2-3: Elasticity Rules

(a) $\mathcal{E}(y, z) = \frac{z}{y}\frac{dy}{dz} = \frac{z}{y}\frac{dy}{dx} / \frac{dz}{dx} = \frac{1}{y}\frac{dy}{dx} / \frac{1}{z}\frac{dz}{dx} = \frac{d\ln y}{dx} / \frac{d\ln z}{dx}$.

(b) Therefore

$$\mathcal{E}\left(\frac{1}{y}, \frac{1}{x}\right) = \frac{d\ln y^{-1}}{dx} / \frac{d\ln x^{-1}}{dx} = \frac{d\ln y}{dx} / \frac{d\ln x}{dx} = \frac{x}{y}\frac{dy}{dx} = \mathcal{E}(y, x).$$

Also

$$\mathcal{E}\left(\frac{y_2}{y_1}, x\right) = \frac{d}{dx} \ln \frac{y_2}{y_1} \bigg/ \frac{d \ln x}{dx} = x \frac{d}{dx} \ln \frac{y_2}{y_1} = x \frac{d}{dx} \ln y_2 - x \frac{d}{dx} \ln y_1$$

$$= \mathcal{E}(y_2, x) - \mathcal{E}(y_1, x).$$

(c) Appealing to (a)

$$\mathcal{E}(y, \alpha x) = \frac{d \ln y}{dx} \bigg/ \frac{d \ln \alpha x}{dx} = \frac{d \ln y}{dx} \bigg/ \frac{d \ln x}{dx} = \mathcal{E}(y, x).$$

Therefore

$$\mathcal{E}\left(\frac{x_2^c}{x_1^c}, \frac{p_1}{p_2}\right) = \mathcal{E}\left(\frac{x_2^c}{x_1^c}, p_1\right) = p_1 \frac{d}{dp_1} \ln \frac{x_2^c}{x_1^c}$$

$$= p_1 \frac{d}{dp_1} \ln x_2^c - p_1 \frac{d}{dp_1} \ln x_1^c = \mathcal{E}(x_2^c, p_1) - \mathcal{E}(x_1^c, p_1).$$

Exercise 2.2-5: CES Preferences ($\sigma > 1$) $U^{1-\frac{1}{\sigma}} = x_1^{1-\frac{1}{\sigma}} + x_2^{1-\frac{1}{\sigma}}$.

Define $\bar{u} = \bar{U}^{1-\frac{1}{\sigma}}$. Then around an indifference curve $\bar{u} = x_1^{1-\frac{1}{\sigma}} + x_2^{1-\frac{1}{\sigma}}$. Hence on the indifference curve through (a, a),

$$x_1^{1-\frac{1}{\sigma}} + x_2^{1-\frac{1}{\sigma}} = 2a^{1-\frac{1}{\sigma}}.$$

(a) If $\sigma = 2$ this becomes $x_1^{1/2} + x_2^{1/2} = 2a^{1/2}$.

Note that as $x_i \to 0$, $x_{-i} \to 4a$.

(b) $\text{MRS}(x_1, x_2) = \frac{\partial U}{\partial x_1} \bigg/ \frac{\partial U}{\partial x_2} = \left(\frac{x_2}{x_1}\right)^{1/\sigma}$.

Thus $\text{MRS}(x_1, x_2) \to 0$ along the indifference curve as $x_1 \to 4a$ and $\text{MRS}(x_1, x_2) \to \infty$ along the indifference curve as $x_1 \to 0$.

(c) Around the indifference curve through (a, a),

$$x_1^{1-\frac{1}{\sigma}} + x_2^{1-\frac{1}{\sigma}} = 2a^{1-\frac{1}{\sigma}}.$$

Therefore at $x_2 = 0$, $x_{-i} = 2^{\frac{\sigma-1}{\sigma}} a$.

Note that $\ln x_{-i} = (1 - \frac{1}{\sigma}) \ln 2 + \ln a$. Because the right-hand side increases with σ, the intercept x_{-i} is an increasing function of σ.

(d) In the limit $x_{-i}(\sigma) \to 2a$. Thus the indifference curve passes through the points $(2a, 0)$, (a, a), and $(0, 2a)$. Because preferences are convex, this must be a line of slope -1.

2.3 Consumer Choice with *n* Commodities

Exercise 2.3-1: The Expenditure Function with Cobb-Douglas Preferences Suppose a consumer has a Cobb-Douglas utility function

$$U(x) = \mathop{\times}_{j=1}^{n} x_j^{\alpha_j} \equiv x_1^{\alpha_1} \ldots x_n^{\alpha_n}, \quad \sum_{i=1}^{n} \alpha_i = 1.$$

Given a price vector p and a budget I, the consumer chooses inputs to solve

$$V(p, I) = \mathop{\mathrm{Max}}_{x}\{U(x) \mid x \geq 0, \, p \cdot x \leq I\}.$$

Because it will be useful in what follows, we note that $\ln U = \sum_{i=1}^{n} \alpha_i \ln x_i$. Therefore

$$\frac{\partial}{\partial x_i} \ln U = \frac{1}{U} \frac{\partial U}{\partial x_i} = \frac{\alpha_i}{x_i} \quad \text{and so} \quad \frac{\partial U}{\partial x_i} = \frac{\alpha_i U}{x_i}.$$

Because the marginal utility of each commodity increases without bound as consumption declines toward zero, we know that the optimal consumption of each commodity is strictly positive. The Lagrangian is

$$\mathcal{L}(x, \lambda) = U(x) + \lambda(I - p \cdot x).$$

Thus the FOC for the optimal choice of inputs are:

$$\frac{\partial U}{\partial x_i} - \lambda p_i = \frac{\alpha_i U(x)}{x_i} - \lambda p_i = 0.$$

Rearranging, we obtain

$$\frac{\alpha_1}{p_1 x_1} = \cdots = \frac{\alpha_n}{p_n x_n} = \frac{\lambda}{U(x)}.$$

Appealing to the Ratio Rule it then follows immediately that

$$\frac{\alpha_1}{p_1 x_1} = \cdots = \frac{\alpha_n}{p_n x_n} = \frac{\sum_{i=1}^{n} \alpha_i}{p \cdot x} = \frac{1}{I}.$$

Therefore,

$$x_i = \frac{\alpha_i I}{p_i}, \, i = 1, \ldots, n.$$

Finally, substituting back into the utility function, maximized utility is

$$V(p, I) = \mathop{\times}_{i=1}^{n} x_j^{\alpha_i} = I \mathop{\times}_{i=1}^{n} \left(\frac{\alpha_i}{p_i}\right)^{\alpha_i}.$$

Because $U^* = V(p, I)$ is the maximum utility that can be achieved given a budget I, it therefore follows that I is the smallest budget that will yield a utility of U^*. That is, I is the solution to the following "dual" problem:

$$M(q, U^*) \equiv \underset{z}{\text{Min}}\{p \cdot x | x \geq 0, U(x) \geq U^*\}.$$

Inverting, we obtain the expenditure function

$$M(p, U^*) = U^* \overset{n}{\underset{j=1}{\times}} \left(\frac{p_j}{\alpha_j}\right)^{\alpha_j}.$$

Exercise 2.3-3: Consuming Pairs of Commodities Suppose that the consumer decides to spend y on the first pair of commodities and z on the second pair of commodities. The choice of how much to spend on commodity 1 and commodity 2 is a standard Cobb-Douglas utility maximization problem. Therefore

$$p_1 x_1 = p_2 x_2 = \tfrac{1}{2}y.$$

Similarly $p_3 x_3 = p_4 x_4 = \tfrac{1}{2}z$. Substituting back into the utility function yields the following derived utility function:

$$u(y, z, p) = (p_1 p_2)^{-1/2}y + (p_3 p_4)^{-1/2}z.$$

Note that the marginal utility of y and of z are as follows:

$$\frac{\partial u}{\partial y} = (p_1 p_2)^{-1/2} \quad \text{and} \quad \frac{\partial u}{\partial z} = (p_3 p_4)^{-1/2}.$$

If these are equal, the consumer is indifferent as to the fraction of his income he spends on the first two commodities. However, if they differ, he maximizes utility by spending only on the pair of commodities with the higher marginal utility.

Exercise 2.3-5: Compensated Price Elasticities The expenditure function is $M(p, \overline{U}) = \underset{x \geq 0}{\text{Min}}\{p \cdot x | U(x) \geq \overline{U}\}$.

Converting this to a maximization problem,

$$-M(p, \overline{U}) = \underset{x \geq 0}{\text{Max}}\{-p \cdot x | U(x) \geq \overline{U}\}.$$

The Lagrangian of this maximization problem is

$$\mathcal{L}(x, \lambda) = -p \cdot x + \lambda(U(x) - \overline{U}).$$

Appealing to the Envelope Theorem,

$$-\frac{\partial M}{\partial p_i} = \frac{\partial \mathcal{L}}{\partial p_i} = -x_i^c.$$

Hence

$$\frac{\partial^2 M}{\partial p_i \partial p_j} = \frac{\partial}{\partial p_j}\frac{\partial M}{\partial p_i} = \frac{\partial x_i^c}{\partial p_j}.$$

The expenditure function is a concave function of p. Thus, any pair of prices, the Hessian matrix

$$\left[\frac{\partial^2 M}{\partial p_i \partial p_j} \right]$$

must be negative semi-definite. Therefore

$$\frac{\partial^2 M}{\partial p_i \partial p_i} \frac{\partial^2 M}{\partial p_j \partial p_j} - \frac{\partial^2 M}{\partial p_i \partial p_j} \frac{\partial^2 M}{\partial p_j \partial p_j} \geq 0.$$

Appealing to our earlier result, it follows that

$$\frac{\partial x_i^c}{\partial p_i} \frac{\partial x_j^c}{\partial p_j} - \frac{\partial x_i^c}{\partial p_j} \frac{\partial x_j^c}{\partial p_i} \geq 0.$$

Converting this into elasticities yields the desired result.

2.4 Consumer Surplus and Willingness to Pay

Exercise 2.4-1: Consumer Surplus, Compensating Variation, and Equivalent Variation

(a) Consider Figure 2.6-1a,b.
(b) Let $(\overline{x}_j, \overline{y})$ be the choice when the price is p_j. The budget line is

$$p_j x_j + y_j = p_j \overline{x}_j + \overline{y}_j \equiv y_A.$$

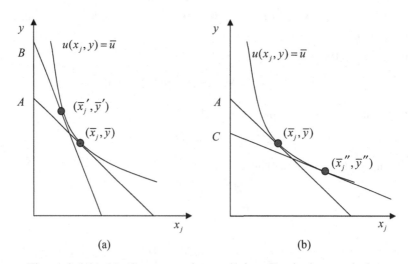

Figure 2.6-1(a,b). Compensating variation. Equivalent variation.

Note that y_A is OA in Figure 2.6-1a. At the new higher price, the compensated budget line is

$$p'_j x_j + y_j = p'_j \bar{x}_j + \bar{y}_j \equiv y_B.$$

Then the extra income needed to compensate the consumer is $y_B - y_A = AB$.

(c) An almost identical argument can be used to show that AC is the equivalent variation when the price is lowered to p''_j.

2.5 Choice over Time

Exercise 2.5-1: Choice over Time with Many Commodities

(a) Let $\{x^i_t\}^T_{t=1}, i = 0, 1$ be optimal with expenditure sequence $\{c^i_t\}^T_{t=1}$. That is, $U^*(c^i) = U(x^i)$. Because $p_t \cdot x^i_t \le c^i_t$, $p \cdot x^\lambda = (1 - \lambda)p \cdot x^0 + \lambda p \cdot x^1 \le (1 - \lambda)c^0 + \lambda c^1 = c^\lambda$. Thus x^λ is feasible given the expenditure sequence $\{c^\lambda_t\}^T_{t=1}$. Suppose $U^*(c^1) \ge U^*(c^0)$. Then $U(x^1) \ge U(x^0)$ and by quasi-concavity, $U(x^\lambda) \ge U(x^0)$. Because x^λ is feasible, $U^*(c^\lambda) \ge U(x^\lambda) \ge U(x^0)$.

(b) We can always convert the optimization problem into a two-stage optimization problem. In the first stage the consumer chooses her optimal consumption each period for any given expenditure vector $(c_1, \dots, c_T)$. In the second stage she allocates her expenditure actress periods subject to his lifetime wealth constraint.

(c) Because the utility function is additively separable, the choice of how to allocate expenditure in period t is independent of consumption in other periods. Thus, in period t the consumer solves the following problem:

$$\underset{x_t}{\text{Max}} \left\{ \sum_{j=1}^{n} \alpha_j \ln x_j \,|\, p_t \cdot x_t = c_t \right\}.$$

This is a standard Cobb-Douglas problem. Solving, $x^*_{tj} = \frac{\alpha_j c_t}{p_{jt}}$. Substituting back into the period t utility function, $u^*(c_t) = \sum_{j=1}^{n} \alpha_j \ln \frac{\alpha_j c_t}{p_{tj}} = \ln c_t +$ terms independent of c_t.

Hence $U^*(c) = \sum_{t=1}^{T} \delta^{t-1} u^*(c_t) = \sum_{t=1}^{T} \delta^{t-1} \ln c_t +$ terms independent of c_t.

(d) Let W_1 be the present value of her endowment. Her lifetime expenditure constraint is $c_1 + \frac{c_2}{1+r} + \cdots + \frac{c_T}{(1+r)^{T-1}} \le W_1$. We form the Lagrangian:

$$\mathcal{L} = \sum_{t=1}^{T} \delta^{t-1} \ln c_t + \lambda \left(W_1 - \sum_{t=1}^{T} \frac{c_t}{(1+r)^{t-1}} \right).$$

FOC:

$$\frac{\partial \mathcal{L}}{\partial c_1} = \frac{1}{c_1} - \lambda = 0, \quad \frac{\partial \mathcal{L}}{\partial c_{t+1}} = \frac{\delta^t}{c_{t+1}} - \lambda(1+r)^t = 0.$$

Eliminating λ, $c_{t+1} = (1+r)^t \delta^t c_1$.

(e) Substituting back into the lifetime budget constraint,

$$c_1(1 + \delta + \cdots + \delta^{T-1}) = W_1.$$

Using the formula for a geometric sum,

$$c_1 = \left(\frac{1-\delta}{1-\delta^T}\right) W_1.$$

Exercise 2.1-3: Saving and Borrowing with a Continuum of Types Each consumer has a wealth of

$$\omega_1 + \frac{\omega_2}{1+r} = \omega(1 + \frac{1}{1+r}) = \frac{2+r}{1+r}\omega.$$

Given his logarithmic preferences, a type α consumer has first-period consumption

$$x_1(\alpha) = \frac{2+r}{1+r}\alpha\omega.$$

Hence his saving $s(\alpha) = \omega - x_1(\alpha) = \omega(1 - \frac{2+r}{1+r}\alpha)$.

(a) Solving for the type with zero saving it follows that type α is a saver if

$$\alpha < \hat{\alpha} \equiv \frac{1+r}{2+r}.$$

(b) The total saving by those who save is

$$S(r) = \int_0^{\hat{\alpha}} s(\alpha)d\alpha = \omega\left.\left(\alpha - \frac{1}{2}\frac{2+r}{1+r}\alpha^2\right)\right|_0^{\hat{\alpha}} = \frac{\omega}{2}\frac{1+r}{2+r}.$$

(c) For all the other consumers, $s(\alpha) < 0$. Thus total borrowing is

$$B(r) = -\int_{\hat{\alpha}}^1 s(\alpha)d\alpha = -\omega\int_{\hat{\alpha}}^1 \left(1 - \frac{2+r}{1+r}\alpha\right)d\alpha$$

$$= -\omega\left.\left(\alpha - \frac{1}{2}\frac{2+r}{1+r}\alpha^2\right)\right|_{\hat{\alpha}}^1, = \frac{\omega}{2}\left(\frac{1+r}{2+r}\right) - \left(\frac{r}{1+r}\right) = \frac{\omega}{2}\frac{1}{(1+r)(2+r)}.$$

Both $S(r)$ and $B(r)$ are depicted in Figure 2.6-2.

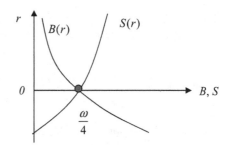

Figure 2.6-2. Saving and borrowing.

3 Equilibrium and Efficiency in an Exchange Economy

3.1 The 2×2 Exchange Economy

Exercise 3.1-1: Prices with Quasi-Linear Preferences Because preferences are convex, an allocation is a Walrasian equilibrium if and only if it is Pareto efficient. We begin by characterizing the Pareto efficient allocations and then solve for the no-trade equilibrium prices given that an endowment is Pareto efficient. Agent h has a $\mathrm{MRS}(x_1^h, x_2^h) = 2(x_2^h)^{1/2}$.

For an efficient allocation in the interior of the Edgeworth Box, the two agents must have the same MRS; hence $x_2^1 = x_2^2 = 100$. Along the line AB in Figure 3.3-1, the MRS is 20. Thus the equilibrium price ratio $p_1/p_2 = 20$.

(a) Along the line segment BO_2,

$$\mathrm{MRS}(x_1^1, x_2^1) = 2(100 + \alpha)^{1/2} > 2(100 - \alpha)^{1/2} = \mathrm{MRS}(x_1^2, x_2^2).$$

Thus agent 1's indifference curve is steeper than that of agent 2 and so all the allocations on BO_2 are Pareto efficient. Along the line segment $O_1 A$ agent 2's indifference curve is steeper so these allocations are also Pareto efficient.

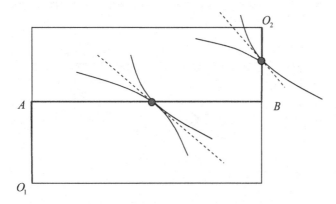

Figure 3.3-1. Efficient allocations.

Consider the line segment BO_2. Because these points are in the interior of agent 1's consumption set, the equilibrium price line must be tangential. That is,

$$p_1/p_2 = \text{MRS}(x_1^1, x_2^1) = 2(100 + \alpha)^{1/2}.$$

Thus the price ratio rises along BO_2 from 20 to $20\sqrt{2}$.

Arguing symmetrically, the price ratio again rises from 20 to $20\sqrt{2}$ along AO_1.

Exercise 3.1-3: Walrasian Equilibrium

(a) Each Bigg has symmetric Cobb-Douglas preferences with endowment $(24, 8)$. Thus a Bigg spends half his income $p_1 24 + p_2 8$ on each commodity. His demand for commodity 2 is therefore $x_2^B = 12r + 4$, where $r = p_1/p_2$.

Define $\hat{x}^L = x^L + a$, where $a = (4, 6)$ and $\hat{\omega} = \omega + a = (24, 16)$. Then each Little's optimization problem can be rewritten as follows:

$$\underset{\hat{x}}{\text{Max}}\{\ln \hat{x}_1 + \ln \hat{x}_2 | p \cdot \hat{x} = p \cdot (x + a) \le p \cdot \hat{\omega}\}.$$

This is again the symmetric Cobb-Douglas case so $p_2 \hat{x}_2^L = \frac{1}{2} p \cdot \hat{\omega}$. Hence $\hat{x}_2^L = 12r + 8$ and so $x_2^L = 12r + 2$. Summing, the market demand for commodity 2 by each Bigg–Little pair is $x_2 = 24r + 6$. Supply is 18. Equating supply and demand, the equilibrium price is $\frac{1}{2}$.

(b) At an interior PE allocation the marginal rates of substitution must be equal. Thus

$$\text{MRS}^L = \frac{6 + x_2^L}{4 + x_1^L} = \frac{x_2^B}{x_1^B} = \text{MRS}^B.$$

Applying the Ratio Rule, $\text{MRS} = \frac{6 + x_2^L}{4 + x_1^L} = \frac{x_2^B}{x_1^B} = \frac{6 + x_2}{4 + x_1} = \frac{6 + \omega_2}{4 + \omega_1} = \frac{24}{48} = \frac{p_1}{p_2}$.

(c) Note that the MRS is constant for all interior PE allocations so that a change in the distribution of the total endowment has no effect on the equilibrium price unless the new equilibrium is no longer in the interior of the Edgeworth box.

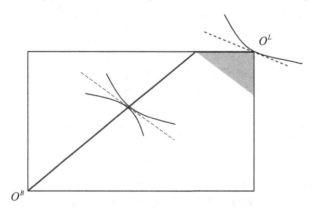

Figure 3.3-2. Equilibrium Price Ratios.

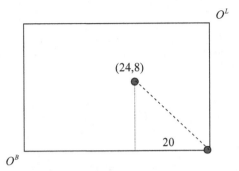

Figure 3.3-3. Unique equilibrium allocation.

(d) This is the endowment point C. Because it is Pareto efficient there is no trade and the equilibrium price ratio is $\frac{1}{2}$.
(e) For any endowment in the unshaded region in Figure 3.3-2 the Walrasian equilibrium price is $\frac{1}{2}$.

For any endowment in the shaded region in Figure 3.3-2 the equilibrium allocation is on the boundary of the Edgeworth box. Because $(42, 18)$ is a Pareto efficient allocation in the interior of the Biggs' consumption set,

$$\text{MRS}^B(x_1, x_2) = \frac{x_2^B}{x_1^B} = \frac{18}{42} = \frac{3}{7} = \frac{p_1}{p_2}.$$

Thus the new Walrasian equilibrium price is $\frac{3}{7}$.

Exercise 3.1-5: More on the Biggs and Littles Because the Littles get no satisfaction from commodity 1 an efficient allocation gives all of this commodity to the Biggs. Similarly, all of commodity 2 must be allocated to the Littles. Thus the only PE allocation is the point in the southeast corner of the Edgeworth box depicted in Figure 3.3-3.

The slope of the line segment connecting the endowment point and the PE allocation is $\frac{8}{20} = \frac{2}{5}$. Thus the Walrasian equilibrium price is $\frac{2}{5}$. Biggs sells his 8 units of commodity 2 and purchases 20 units of commodity 1.

3.2 The Fundamental Welfare Theorems

Exercise 3.2-1: Walrasian Equilibrium with Identical Homothetic Preferences Consider the economy with a single representative agent with utility function $U(\cdot)$ and endowment $\omega = \sum_{h=1}^{H} \omega^h$. Because U is quasi-concave, by Lemma 1.1-2, $U(x) \geq U(\omega) \Rightarrow \frac{\partial U}{\partial x}(\omega) \cdot (x - \omega) \geq 0$. Choose $p = \frac{\partial U}{\partial x}(\omega)$. Then

$$U(x) \geq U(\omega) \Rightarrow p \cdot (x - \omega) \geq 0.$$

If $U(x) > U(\omega)$ then $p \cdot x \geq p \cdot \omega$. We argue that the inequality must be strict. If not, then for some $\hat{x}$, $U(\hat{x}) > U(\omega)$ and $p \cdot \hat{x} = p \cdot \omega$. Then if U is strictly increasing, for $\delta > 0$ and sufficiently small, $U(\hat{x} - \delta) > U(\omega)$ and $p \cdot (\hat{x} - \delta) < p \cdot \omega$. But this contradicts our earlier result.

Therefore

$$U(x) > U(\omega) \Rightarrow p \cdot x > p \cdot \omega.$$

Hence

$$\omega \in \arg \mathrm{Max}\{U(x) | p \cdot x \leq p \cdot \omega\}.$$

Chose θ^h so that $p \cdot \omega^h = p \cdot \theta^h \omega$. Note that $\sum_{h=1}^{H} \theta^h = 1$.

By homotheticity

$$\hat{x}^h \equiv \theta^h \omega \in \arg \mathrm{Max}\{U(x) | p \cdot x \leq p \cdot \omega^h = p \cdot \theta^h \omega\}.$$

Then aggregate excess demand is $\sum_{h=1}^{H} \overline{x} - \omega = \sum_{h=1}^{H} \theta^h \omega - \omega = 0$.

4 Firms

4.2 Decision Making by Price-Taking Firms

Exercise 4.2-1: Cost Minimization Let $\mathcal{Y}$ be the set of feasible input-output vectors (z, q). Let z^0 and z^1 be cost-minimizing input vectors when the input price vectors are, respectively, r^0 and r^1. Finally let z^λ be the cost-minimizing input vector when the input price vector is the convex combination $r^\lambda = (1 - \lambda)r^0 + \lambda r^1$.

The cost function is

$$C(r, q) = \underset{z}{\mathrm{Min}}\{r \cdot z | (z, q) \in \mathcal{Y}\}.$$

(a) Because z^0, z^1 and z^λ are cost minimizing at r^0, r^1 and r^λ, respectively, it follows that

$$C(r^0, q) = r^0 \cdot z^0 \leq r^0 \cdot z^\lambda \text{ and } C(r^1, q) = r^1 \cdot z^1 \leq r^1 \cdot z^\lambda.$$

Multiplying the first inequality by λ and the second by $1 - \lambda$ and adding the inequalities it follows that

$$\lambda C(r^0, q) + (1 - \lambda)C(r^1, q) \leq \lambda r^0 \cdot z^\lambda + (1 - \lambda)r^1 \cdot z^\lambda = r^\lambda \cdot z^\lambda = C(r^\lambda, q).$$

(b) Appealing to the Envelope Theorem, $\frac{\partial C}{\partial r_i} = z_i^*$. Alternatively, arguing as earlier,

$$C(r^1, q) = r^1 \cdot z^1 \leq r^1 \cdot z^0,$$

hence

$$C(r^1, q) - C(r^0, q) \leq r^1 \cdot z^0 - r^0 \cdot z^0 = (r^1 - r^0) \cdot z^0.$$

Also

$$C(r^0, q) = r^0 \cdot z^0 \le r^0 \cdot z^1.$$

Hence

$$C(r^0, q) - C(r^1, q) \le r^0 \cdot z^1 - r^1 \cdot z^1 = (r^0 - r^1) \cdot z^1.$$

Combining these inequalities,

$$(r^1 - r^0) \cdot z^1 \le C(r^1) - C(r^0) \le (r^1 - r^0) \cdot z^0.$$

If only the jth price changes, we can divide through by the price change. Then

$$z_j(r^1) \le \frac{C(r^1) - C(r^0)}{r_j^1 - r_j^0} \le z_j(r^0).$$

By hypothesis $z(r)$ is continuous. Taking the limit it follows that $\frac{\partial C}{\partial r_j} = z_j(r)$. Differentiating by r_i, $\frac{\partial}{\partial r_i}\frac{\partial C}{\partial r_j} = \frac{\partial z_j}{\partial r_i}(r)$.

Applying exactly the same argument to a change in the ith price it follows that $\frac{\partial C}{\partial r_i} = z_i(r)$ and hence that $\frac{\partial}{\partial r_j}\frac{\partial C}{\partial r_i} = \frac{\partial z_i}{\partial r_j}(r)$. By Young's Theorem the order of differentiation is immaterial; hence $\frac{\partial z_i}{\partial r_j}(r) = \frac{\partial^2 C}{\partial r_i \partial r_j} = \frac{\partial^2 C}{\partial r_j \partial r_i} = \frac{\partial z_j}{\partial r_i}(r)$.

(c) Let z^0 be the cost-minimizing input vector when the output vector is q^0 and let z^1 be cost minimizing when the output vector is q^1. Because the production set is convex, the production plan (z^λ, q^λ) is feasible. Thus the cost of producing q^λ is bounded above by $r \cdot z^\lambda = (1 - \lambda)r \cdot z^0 + \lambda r \cdot z^1 = (1 - \lambda)C(q^0, r) + \lambda C(q^1, r)$. That is,

$$C(q^\lambda, r) \le (1 - \lambda)C(q^0, r) + \lambda C(q^1, r), \lambda \in [0, 1].$$

Exercise 4.2-3: CES Production Function

(a) Consider the dual problem of maximizing output subject to a total cost constraint. This has as its Lagrangian,

$$\mathcal{L} = \sum_{j=1}^{2} z_j^{\frac{1}{2}} + \lambda(C - r \cdot z).$$

The first-order conditions are therefore

$$\frac{\partial \mathcal{L}}{\partial z_j} = \frac{1}{2}z_j^{-\frac{1}{2}} - \lambda r_j = 0. \text{ Hence } z_j = \frac{1}{4\lambda^2 r_j^2}.$$

Substituting this back into the production function,

$$q = \sum_{j=1}^{2} z_j^{\frac{1}{2}} = \frac{1}{2\lambda} \sum_{j=1}^{2} \frac{1}{r_j}.$$

Also from the FOC, $r_j z_j = \frac{1}{4\lambda^2} \frac{1}{r_j}$. Summing over j,

$$C = \sum_{j=1}^{2} r_j z_j = \frac{1}{4\lambda^2} \sum_{j=1}^{2} \frac{1}{r_j}.$$

Using these two equations to eliminate the shadow price,

$$C = \frac{q^2}{\sum_{j=1}^{2} \frac{1}{r_j}}.$$

(b) The production set is $\{(z, q) | q^{\frac{1}{2}} \leq z_1^{\frac{1}{2}} + z_2^{\frac{1}{2}}\}$. This is identical to the production set in part (a) if we replace q by $q^{\frac{1}{2}}$. The cost function is therefore

$$C = \frac{q}{\sum_{j=1}^{2} \frac{1}{r_j}}.$$

Exercise 4.2-5: Marginal Cost Independent of an Input Price

(a) Define $v = h(z_1) + z_2$. Consider the dual-output maximization problem,

$$\text{Max}_{z}\{F(h(z_1) + z_2) | r \cdot z \leq C\}.$$

Suppose the optimal level of input 2 is zero. Then $z_1 > 0$ and the FOC are as follows:

$$\frac{\partial \mathcal{L}}{\partial z_1} = F'(v) h'(z_1) - \lambda r_1 = 0.$$

$$\frac{\partial \mathcal{L}}{\partial z_2} = F'(v) - \lambda r_2 \leq 0.$$

Eliminating the shadow price, it follows that $h'(z_1) \geq r_1/r_2$. Since we have assumed that $z_2 = 0$, z_1 must grow large with q, Because $h(\cdot)$ is concave and $h'(\infty) = 0$ it follows that for all sufficiently large output and hence z_1, $h'(z_1) < r_1/r_2$. But this contradicts our earlier conclusion. Thus for sufficiently large output the FOC cannot hold with $z_2 = 0$.

(b) Henceforth we assume that q is sufficiently large that both inputs are strictly positive. From the production function $F^{-1}(q) = h(z_1) + z_2$. Therefore $z_2 = F^{-1}(q) - h(z_1)$ and so total cost is

$$C = r_1 z_1 + r_2(F^{-1}(q) - h(z_1)).$$

The FOC for minimizing total cost is $C'(z_1) = r_1 - r_2 h'(z_1) = 0$. Thus the cost-minimizing level of input 1 is a function only of the input price ratio and not of output. Appealing to the Envelope Theorem, $\frac{\partial C}{\partial q} = r_2 \frac{d}{dq} F^{-1}(q)$. Note that this is independent of r_1.

Exercise 4.2-7: Short Run versus Long Run The proof of the Le Chatelier Principle makes use only of the assumption that the firm is a price taker in a specific market. Thus the principle continues to hold.

4.3 Returns to Scale

Increasing Returns to Scale

For any $\mu \in (0, 1)$ we can write $z = \frac{1}{\mu}(\mu z)$. Because $\frac{1}{\mu} > 1$ and $F(\cdot)$ exhibits IRS it follows that $F(\frac{1}{\mu}\mu z) > \frac{1}{\mu}F(\mu z)$. Rearranging this inequality, $F(\mu z) < \mu F(z)$.

Exercise 4.3-3 Local and Global Increasing Returns to Scale

(a) The function exhibits local IRS at k if the elasticity $\mathcal{E}(F(\lambda k), \lambda)\big|_{\lambda=1} = \frac{k \cdot \frac{\partial F}{\partial k}(k)}{F(k)} > 1$. By hypothesis, the function exhibits local IRS at μk. Therefore

$$\mathcal{E}(F(\lambda \mu k), \lambda)\big|_{\lambda=1} = \frac{\mu k \cdot \frac{\partial F}{\partial k}(\mu k)}{F(\mu k)} > 1.$$

Finally note that $\mathcal{E}(F(\mu k), \mu) = \frac{\mu k \cdot \frac{\partial F}{\partial k}(\mu k)}{F(\mu k)}$.

(b) $\frac{\partial}{\partial \mu} \ln F(\mu k) = \frac{k \cdot \frac{\partial F}{\partial k}(\mu k)}{F(\mu k)}$. From (a) the right-hand side exceeds $\frac{1}{\mu}$.

(c) For any $\lambda > 1$, we may write

$$\ln \frac{F(\lambda k)}{F(k)} = \ln F(\lambda k) - \ln F(k) = \int_1^\lambda \frac{\partial}{\partial \mu} \ln F(\mu k) d\mu.$$

Appealing to (b) the right-hand side exceeds $\int_1^\lambda \frac{1}{\mu} d\mu = \ln \lambda$. Hence $\frac{F(\lambda k)}{F(k)} > \lambda$.

4.4 Firm and Industry Analysis

Exercise 4.4-1: The Social Optimum

(a) Social surplus is $S(q) = B(q) - \sum_{j=1}^n C_j(q_j)$.

The necessary conditions for social surplus maximization are as follows:

$$\frac{\partial S}{\partial q_j} = \frac{\partial B}{\partial q_j} - C_j'(q_j) \le 0, \text{ with equality if } q_j > 0.$$

The demand price function, $p(q)$, satisfies

$$\frac{\partial B}{\partial q}(q) = p(q).$$

(b) Hence, for social surplus maximization,

$$p_j(q) - C'_j(q_j) \leq 0, \quad \text{with equality if} \quad q_j > 0.$$

Exercise 4.4-3: Scale of Competitive Firms

(a) $C = r \cdot z$. Differentiating by q,

$$MC = \frac{\partial C}{\partial q} = \sum_{j=1}^{n} r_j \frac{\partial z_j}{\partial q} = \sum_{j=1}^{n} \frac{r_j z_j}{q} \frac{q}{z_j} \frac{\partial z_j}{\partial q} = \sum_{j=1}^{n} \frac{r_j z_j}{q} \mathcal{E}(z_j, q).$$

Rewriting the last expression,

$$MC = \sum_{j=1}^{n} \frac{r_j z_j}{q} \mathcal{E}(z_j, q) = \sum_{j=1}^{n} \frac{r_j z_j}{C} \frac{C}{q} \frac{q}{z_j} \frac{\partial z_j}{\partial q} = AC \sum_{j=1}^{n} k_j \mathcal{E}(z_j, q).$$

At min AC, $MC = AC$. Therefore

$$1 = \sum_{j=1}^{n} k_j \mathcal{E}(z_j, q).$$

(b) We can rewrite this as follows:

$$\sum_{j=1}^{n} k_j (\mathcal{E}(z_j, q) - 1) = 0.$$

Thus with $n = 2$, either both elasticities are equal to 1 or one is greater and the other is less than 1.

(c) Because $r_2 z_2 = \frac{\beta}{\alpha}(r_1 z_1 - \alpha r_1)$ is follows that

$$r_2 z_2 < \frac{\beta}{\alpha} r_1 z_1 \quad \text{and} \quad r_2 \frac{\partial z_2}{\partial q} = \frac{\beta}{\alpha} r_1 \frac{\partial z_1}{\partial q}.$$

Hence

$$\frac{\beta}{\alpha} \frac{r_1 z_1}{r_2 z_2} > 1 \quad \text{and} \quad r_2 z_2 \frac{q}{z_2} \frac{\partial z_2}{\partial q} = \frac{\beta}{\alpha} r_1 z_1 \frac{q}{z_1} \frac{\partial z_1}{\partial q}.$$

The last expression can be rewritten as follows:

$$\mathcal{E}(z_2, q) = \left(\frac{\beta}{\alpha} \frac{r_1 z_1}{r_2 z_2} \right) \mathcal{E}(z_1, q).$$

Hence $\mathcal{E}(z_2, q) > \mathcal{E}(z_1, q)$ because $\left(\frac{\beta}{\alpha} \frac{r_1 z_1}{r_2 z_2} \right) > 1$.

(c) Appealing to Proposition 4.4-2, MC rises faster than AC and r_2 rise. Thus at the initial cost-minimizing output, $MC > AC$. Therefore as r_2 rises the average cost-minimizing output rises.

4.5 Monopoly Pricing

Exercise 4.5-1: Price Discrimination by Group

(a) The total profit of the monopolist is

$$\Pi(p_1, p_2) = p_1 q_1(p_1) + p_2 q_2(p_2) - c(q_1 + q_2).$$

Where $q_j(p) = a_j - p$. The FOC for an interior maximum are

$$\frac{\partial \Pi}{\partial p_j} = a_j - 2p_j - c = 0, \ j = 1, 2.$$

Hence $p_j^* = \frac{1}{2}(a_j - c)$ and $q_{j*} = \frac{1}{2}(a_j + c)$.

(b) If buyers can purchases from either outlet at no extra cost, the two prices must be the same. Then

$$\Pi(p) = p q_1(p) + p q_2(p) - c(q_1(p) + q_2(p)).$$

As long as $p \leq a_1$, $q_j(p) = a_j - p$, $j = 1, 2$, For $a_1 \leq p \leq a_2$, $q_1(p) = 0$ and $q_2(p) = a_2 - p$. Therefore

$$\Pi = \begin{cases} (p - c)(a_1 - p + a_2 - p), & p \leq a_1 \\ (p - c)(a_2 - p), & a_1 \leq p \leq a_2 \end{cases}.$$

Hence

$$\frac{\partial \Pi}{\partial p} = \begin{cases} a_1 + a_2 - 4p - 2c, & p < a_1 \\ a_2 - 2p - c, & a_1 \leq p \leq a_2 \end{cases}. \tag{4.6-1}$$

Consider first the solution to $\text{Max}\{\Pi(p) | p \leq a_1\}$. From (4.6-1),

$$\frac{\partial \Pi}{\partial p} = 4 \left(\frac{1}{4}(a_1 + a_2) - \frac{1}{2}c - p \right), \ p \leq a_1.$$

The maximization has an interior solution if

$$\frac{\partial \Pi}{\partial p}(a_1) = 4 \left(\frac{1}{4}(a_1 + a_2) - \frac{1}{2}c - p \right) < 0.$$

That is, if $a_2 < 2c + 3a_1$. If this inequality fails the solution lies in the interval $[a_1, a_2]$. Assuming an interior solution, the FOC is

$$\frac{\partial \Pi}{\partial p} = a_2 - 2p - c = 0.$$

Then $p = \frac{1}{2}(c + a_2)$. Note that, because $a_2 \geq 2c + 3a_1$, $p \geq \frac{3}{2}(c + a_1) > a_1$. Thus the profit-maximizing price jumps discontinuously as a_2 rises above $2c + 3a_1$.

5 General Equilibrium

5.1 The Robinson Crusoe Economy

Exercise 5.1-1: Equilibrium

(a) $x = (y + \omega) = (y_1 + 147, y_2)$. Then $-y_1 = 147 - x_1$. Substituting for y in the production function, $x_2 = y_2 = 2(147 - x_1)^{1/2}$. Robinson's utility is therefore $U = x_1 x_2 = 2x_1(147 - x_1)^{1/2}$ Taking the logarithm and differentiating, $\frac{\partial}{\partial L} \ln U = -\frac{1}{147-x_1} + \frac{1}{2x_1}$. Setting this equal to zero, $x_1^* = 98$. Hence $y_1^* = x_1^* - \omega_1 = -49$ and so $x_2^* = 14$.

(b) Let the price vector be p. The production set is $\mathcal{Y} = \{(y_1, y_2)|y_1 + \frac{1}{4}y_2^2 \le 0\}$. Robinson then seeks the solution of the following problem:

$$\Pi = \underset{y}{\text{Max}} \left\{ p \cdot y | y_1 + \tfrac{1}{4}y_2^2 \le 0 \right\}.$$

The constraint is binding at the maximum; therefore we can substitute for y_1 and write the profit as follows:

$$\pi(y_2) = -\tfrac{1}{4}p_1 y_2^2 + p_2 y_2.$$

FOC for profit maximization:

$$\frac{\partial \pi}{\partial y_2} = -\frac{1}{2}p_1 y_2 + p_2 = 0.$$

Hence coconut supply is $y_2 = \frac{2p_2}{p_1}$. Substituting back into the production function, labor demand is $L_D = (\frac{2p_2}{p_1})^2$. For labor demand to be optimal we therefore require that $p_1/p_2 = 2/7$.

Exercise 5.1-3: Existence with a Non-Convexity

(a) The boundary of the production set, $y_1 + \gamma + \frac{1}{8}y_2^2 = 0$ can be rewritten as follows:

$$y_2 = \sqrt{8(-y_1 - \gamma)}.$$

The graph of this function is depicted in Figure 5.7-1.

Adding the endowment $\omega = (2\gamma, 0)$ shifts the boundary horizontally by 2γ.

(b) Crusoe's consumption vector is $x = y + \omega$ where $y_1 = -\gamma - \frac{1}{8}y_2^2$ and so $x_1 = \gamma - \frac{1}{8}y_2^2$. Then Crusoe's utility is

$$U(x) = U(y + \omega) = y_1 + 2\gamma + \ln y_2 = \gamma - \tfrac{1}{8}y_2^2 + \ln y_2.$$

FOC

$$-\frac{1}{4}y_2 + \frac{1}{y_2} = 0.$$

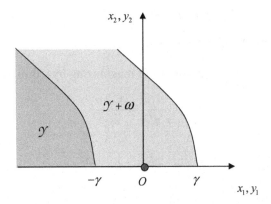

Figure 5.7-1. Feasible allocations.

(c) Hence $y_2^* = 2$ and so $y_1^* = -\gamma - \frac{1}{2}$.

$$y(p) = \arg \underset{y}{\text{Max}}\{p \cdot y | y \in \mathcal{Y}\}.$$

(d) First ignore the option of producing nothing. Then Robinson solves the following maximization problem:

$$\underset{y_2}{\text{Max}}\{p_1(-\gamma - \tfrac{1}{8}y_2^2) + p_2 y_2\}.$$

Solving, $y_2 = 4p_2/p_1$. The resulting profit is

$$\Pi(p) = 2p_2^2/p_1 - p_1\gamma = p_1(2(p_2/p_1)^2 - \gamma).$$

This is positive if and only if $2(p_2/p_1)^2 - \gamma \geq 0$. Therefore the supply curve if the firm is

$$y_2(p) = \begin{cases} 0 & , \quad 2(p_2/p_1)^2 \leq \gamma \\ 4p_2/p_1, & 2(p_2/p_1)^2 \geq \gamma \end{cases}.$$

Note that this is a supply correspondence because it is multi-valued at the critical point where $2(p_2/p_1)^2 = \gamma$.

(e) If there is a Walrasian equilibrium it must be efficient. Because the efficient output of coconuts is 2, it follows that $4p_2/p_1 = 2$.

Thus if a WE exits, the WE price ratio is $p_2/p_1 = \frac{1}{2}$.

(f) The implied equilibrium profit is

$$\Pi(p) = p_1(2(p_2/p_1)^2 - \gamma) = p_1(\tfrac{1}{2} - \gamma).$$

(g) Thus a WE exists if and only if $\gamma \leq \frac{1}{2}$.

5.2 Equilibrium and Efficiency

Exercise 5.2-1: Cobb-Douglas Economy

(a) The FOC for cost-minimization profit maximizing by a firm in industry j are

$$\frac{\alpha_j}{r_1 z_{1j}^f} = \frac{1 - \alpha_j}{r_2 z_{2j}^f}.$$

Rewriting this equation, $\frac{z_{2j}^f}{z_{1j}^f} = \frac{1 - \alpha_j}{\alpha_j} \frac{r_1}{r_2}$, $f = 1, \ldots, F$.

Therefore $\frac{z_{2j}^f}{z_{1j}^f} = \frac{z_{2j}}{z_{1j}}$ and so $z^f = \theta^f z$ for some $\theta^f > 0$, where $\sum_{f=1}^{F} \theta_f = 1$. Hence

$$q_j = \sum_{f=1}^{F} q_j^f = \sum_{f=1}^{F} (\theta^f z_{1j})^{\alpha_j} (\theta^f z_{2j})^{1-\alpha_j}$$

$$= (z_{1j})^{\alpha_j} (z_{2j})^{1-\alpha_j} \sum_{f=1}^{F} \theta^f = (z_{1j})^{\alpha_j} (z_{2j})^{1-\alpha_j}$$

(b) $U = a_1 \ln q_1 + a_2 \ln q_2$
$$= a_1(\alpha_1 \ln z_{11} + (1 - \alpha_1) \ln z_{21}) + a_2(\alpha_2 \ln z_{12} + (1 - \alpha_2) \ln z_{22})$$

Utility is maximized subject to the constraint $z_{11} + z_{12} = \omega_1$, $z_{21} + z_{22} = \omega_2$.
Note that the optimization problem separates into two simpler optimization problems. The first is

$$\max_{z_{11}, z_{12}} \{a_1 \alpha_1 \ln z_{11} + a_2 \alpha_2 \ln z_{12} | z_{11} + z_{12} \le \omega_1\}.$$

This is easily solved.

$$(z_{11}^*, z_{12}^*) = \left(\frac{a_1 \alpha_1 \omega_1}{a_1 \alpha_1 + a_2 \alpha_2}, \frac{a_2 \alpha_2 \omega_1}{a_1 \alpha_1 + a_2 \alpha_2} \right).$$

Similarly,

$$(z_{21}^*, z_{22}^*) = \left(\frac{a_1(1 - \alpha_1)\omega_1}{a_1(1 - \alpha_1) + a_2(1 - \alpha_2)}, \frac{a_2(1 - \alpha_2)\omega_1}{a_1(1 - \alpha_1) + a_2(1 - \alpha_2)} \right).$$

(c) From (a), $\frac{r_1}{z_{11}^*} = \frac{r_2}{z_{21}^*}$. Hence $r = (\frac{\alpha_1}{z_{11}^*}, \frac{1-\alpha_1}{z_{21}^*})$ is a WE.

The cost function for industry j is $C(q_j, r) = (\frac{r_1}{\alpha_j})^{\alpha_j} (\frac{r_2}{1-\alpha_j})^{1-\alpha_j} q_j$.

$$MC_j = AC_j = p_j = \left(\frac{r_1}{\alpha_j} \right)^{\alpha_j} \left(\frac{r_2}{1 - \alpha_j} \right)^{1-\alpha_j}.$$

Exercise 5.2-3: Robinson and Friday

(a) Because both consumers have the same preferences consider this as a representative agent problem. Because $x_1 = \omega_1 - z_1$ and $x_2 = z_1^{1/4}$, the utility of the representative agent is

$$U = \ln(\omega_1 - z_1) + 4a \ln(z_1)^{1/4} = \ln(\omega_1 - z_1) + a \ln z_1.$$

It is readily confirmed that $z_1^* = \frac{a\omega_1}{1+a}$ and hence $x^* = (\frac{\omega_1}{1+a}, (\frac{a\omega_1}{1+a})^{1/4})$.

(b) The representative consumer has the following budget constraint:

$$p_1 x_1 + p_2 x_2 \leq p_1 \omega_1 + \Pi(p).$$

He therefore solves

$$\underset{x}{\text{Max}}\{\ln x_1 + 4a \ln x_2 | p_1 x_1 + p_2 x_2 \leq p_1 \omega_1 + \Pi(p)\}.$$

FOC:

$$\frac{1}{p_1 x_1} = \frac{4a}{p_2 x_2} = \lambda.$$

Rearranging,

$$\frac{p_1}{\left(\frac{1}{x_1}\right)} = \frac{p_2}{\left(\frac{4a}{x_2}\right)}.$$

The WE must be efficient. Hence $x = x^*$ and so $p = (\frac{1}{x_1^*}, \frac{4a}{x_2^*})$ is a WE price vector.

(c) Friday has no profit. His endowment of time is half the total endowment. His optimal consumption bundle is therefore

$$x^F = \arg \underset{x}{\text{Max}}\{\ln x_1 + 4a \ln x_2 | p_1 x_1 + p_2 x_2 \leq p_1(\tfrac{1}{2}\omega_1)\}.$$

FOC

$$\frac{1}{p_1 x_1^F} = \frac{4a}{p_2 x_2^F} = \frac{1+4a}{p_1 x_1^F + p_2 x_2^F} = \frac{1+4a}{\frac{1}{2}p_1 \omega_1}.$$

Therefore

$$x_1^F = \frac{\omega_1}{2(1+4a)}.$$

Hence Robinson's demand for leisure is $x_1^R = x_1^* - x_1^F = (\frac{1}{1+a} - \frac{1}{2(1+4a)})\omega_1$. Note that this approaches $\frac{1}{2}\omega_1$ as $a \to 0$. Moreover it is readily checked that x_1^R is an increasing function of a for a greater than zero and sufficiently small. But Robinson's endowment of time is only $\frac{1}{2}\omega_1$. Thus the representative agent approach must be modified.

The only other possibility is that Robinson consumes all this time in the form of leisure. Then Friday is the only consumer supplying labor. We have already solved for his labor supply. The WE price ratio must be chosen so that the firm's demand for labor is

$$z_1^D = \arg \underset{z_1}{\mathrm{Max}}\{p_2 z_1^{1/4} - p_1 z_1\} = z_1^F = \tfrac{1}{2}\omega_1 - x_1^F.$$

5.3 Existence of Equilibrium

Exercise 5.3-1: Continuity of the Supply Function We first show that the profit-maximizing production vector is unique. Because $\mathcal{Y}$ is compact and $p \cdot y$ is continuous, there is a solution to the maximization problem $\mathrm{Max}_y\{p \cdot y|y \in \mathcal{Y}\}$. To prove that there is a unique solution, we suppose instead that there are at least two solutions y^0 and y^1. Then for every convex combination y^λ is also a solution, because $p \cdot y^\lambda = (1 - \lambda)p \cdot y^0 + \lambda p \cdot y^0 = p \cdot y^0$. Because $\mathcal{Y}$ is strictly convex, every convex combination $y^\lambda \in \mathrm{int}\mathcal{Y}$. Then for sufficiently small $\delta \gg 0$, $y = y^\lambda + \delta \in \mathcal{Y}$. Then $p \cdot y = p \cdot y^\lambda + p \cdot \delta > p \cdot y^0$. But then$y^0$ is not a solution to the optimization problem after all. Thus the profit-maximizing response is a supply function $y(p)$. By the Theorem of the Maximum (I), this function is continuous.

Exercise 5.3-3: Existence and Non-Existence with a Minimum Consumption Threshold

(a) This is a standard case of two consumers with different homothetic preferences. From Section 5.2, the PE allocations are as depicted in Figure 5.7-2, and the WE price ratio p_1/p_2 rises along the PE allocations as the utility of consumer A increases. The highest price ratio is where Alex has the entire endowment (ω, ω). Because his marginal rate of substitution is α^A/β^A along the 45° line, this is the maximum price ratio. Making an identical argument for Bev, the minimum price ratio is α^B/β^B.

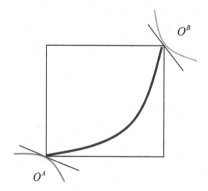

Figure 5.7-2. Edgeworth Box diagram.

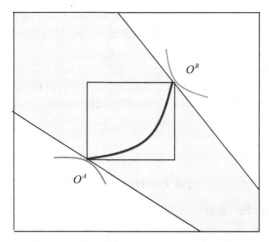

Figure 5.7-3. Edgeworth Box diagram.

(b) The only part of the Edgeworth Box on which neither consumer has a consumption below γ is the inner square depicted in Figure 5.7-3. Redefining units, $U^h = \hat{x}_1^{\alpha^h} \hat{x}_2^{\beta^h}$. The budget constraint $p \cdot x^h \leq p \cdot \omega^h$ becomes

$$p \cdot \hat{x}^h = p_1(x_1^h - \gamma) + p_2(x_2^h - \gamma) \leq p_1(\omega_1^h - \gamma) + p_2(\omega_2^h - \gamma) = p \cdot \hat{\omega}^h.$$

We can therefore appeal to the answer to part (a) for all the points in the inner square of the Edgeworth Box depicted in Figure 5.7-3.

By the First welfare theorem, if there is a WE allocation, it must be PE. Thus there are no WE for endowments outside the shaded region.

Exercise 5.3-5: Continuum of Equilibria with No Consumption Threshold The Edgeworth Box diagram is shown in Figure 5.7-4. For PE allocations outside the

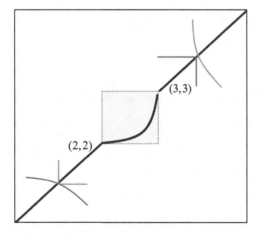

Figure 5.7-4. Edgeworth Box diagram.

shaded region the price is determined by the slope of the high wealth consumer. Along the 45° line the slope of Alex's indifference curve is 2, whereas the slope of Bev's indifference curve is $\frac{1}{2}$.

For the PE allocations inside the shaded region we can redefine units so that $z_i = x_i - 2$. Preferences are homothetic in z; thus we can appeal to our earlier results and conclude that along the PE allocations the WE price ratio rises from $\frac{1}{2}$ to 2.

Arguing as in the previous exercise, there is a continuum of equilibria for one endowment point.

5.4 Public Goods

Exercise 5.4-1: A Public "Bad"

(a) The problem is to solve $\text{Max}_{(y,b)}\{U(y,b)|G(y,b) \leq 0\}$. The Lagrangian is

$$\mathcal{L} = U(y,b) - \lambda G(y,b).$$

The FOC are therefore

$$\frac{\partial \mathcal{L}}{\partial y_j} = \frac{\partial U}{\partial y_j}(y,b) - \lambda \frac{\partial G}{\partial y_j}(y,b) = 0, \quad j = 1, 2.$$

and

$$\frac{\partial \mathcal{L}}{\partial b} = \frac{\partial U}{\partial b}(y,b) - \lambda \frac{\partial G}{\partial b}(y,b) = 0.$$

(b) Introduce prices p_1 and p_2 for the two commodities and the pollution tax t. The firm's optimization problem is $\text{Max}_{(y,b)}\{p \cdot y - tb | G(y,b) \leq 0\}$. Form the Lagrangian $\mathcal{L} = p \cdot y - tb - \mu G(y,b)$. The FOC are therefore

$$\frac{\partial \mathcal{L}}{\partial y_j} = p_j - \mu \frac{\partial G}{\partial y_j}(y,b) = 0, \quad j = 1, 2$$

and

$$\frac{\partial \mathcal{L}}{\partial b} = -t - \mu \frac{\partial G}{\partial b}(y,b) = 0.$$

The consumer equates his marginal utility per dollar.

$$\frac{\frac{\partial U}{\partial y_1}}{p_1} = \frac{\frac{\partial U}{\partial y_2}}{p_2}.$$

(c) It is easy to confirm that these conditions are the FOC for the optimum if $\frac{\partial U}{\partial y_j} = v p_j$ and $\mu = v/\lambda$

(d) The analysis generalizes directly. The new optimization problem is

$$\underset{(y,b)}{\text{Max}}\{U(y,b)| \sum_{f=1}^{2} b^f \leq b, \quad G^f(y,b) \leq 0, \quad f = 1,2\}$$

(e) The government intervention creates a new commodity, "pollution rights," and sets the endowment of this commodity at the optimal level. To price-taking firms, a pollution right is in effect a third input. Markets clear when demand for this right equals the fixed supply so the additional market replaces the need for a direct tax.

5.5 Futures Prices

Exercise 5.5-1: Robinson Crusoe Economy

(a) Define $u = 2 \ln U = \ln x_1 + \ln x_2$. Because utility is strictly increasing $x_2 = y_2$. Hence

$$u = \ln(108 - z_1) + \ln 12 + \tfrac{1}{2} \ln z_1.$$

FOC:

$$\frac{1}{108 - z_1} = \frac{\frac{1}{2}}{z_1} = \frac{\frac{3}{2}}{108}.$$

Hence $z_1^* = 36$ and so $x^* = (72, 72)$.

(b) The profit of the firm is

$$\Pi(p) = \underset{z_1}{\text{Max}} \left\{ -p_1 z_1 + p_2 12 z_1^{1/2} \right\} = p_1 \underset{z_1}{\text{Max}} \left\{ -z_1 + \frac{p_2}{p_1} 12 z_1^{1/2} \right\}.$$

FOC:

$$-1 + 6 \frac{p_2}{p_1} z_1^{-1/2} = 0.$$

Hence $z_1(p) = 36(\frac{p_2}{p_1})^2$.

(c) The WE is a PE allocation. Let $\bar{p}$ be the equilibrium price vector. Then $z_1(\bar{p}) = z_1^* = 36$ and so $\bar{p} = (1, 1)$ is the WE price vector. Equilibrium profit is $\Pi(\bar{p}) = 36$.

The budget constraint of the representative consumer is

$$p \cdot x \leq p_1 108 + \Pi(p).$$

Setting $p = \bar{p}$ this can be rewritten as follows:

$$x_1 + x_2 \leq 144.$$

(d) Alternatively, let r be the real interest rate. That is, by forgoing 1 unit of the commodity in period 1, a consumer earns $1 + r$ units in period 2. In the first period the firm borrows z_1 and in the second earns $12z_1^{1/2}$. The maximized present value of the firm is therefore

$$\Pi(r) = \text{Max}\left\{-z_1 + \frac{12z_1^{1/2}}{1+r}\right\}.$$

Note that this is exactly the same as in the WE with spot and futures markets if $1 + r = \frac{p_1}{p_2}$. Thus the equilibrium "real" interest rate is zero.

Exercise 5.5-3: Rational Expectations Equilibrium

(a) Let $x_t = (x_{t1}, x_{t2})$ be period t consumption. Then

$$x_{11} = \omega_{11} - z_{11}, \quad x_{12} = \omega_{12} - z_{12}, \quad x_{21} = 2z_{11} + \omega_{12} \quad \text{and} \quad x_{22} = 4z_{12} + \omega_{22}.$$

Substituting into the utility function

$$U = 2\ln(120 - z_{11}) + \ln(120 - z_{12}) + \ln(2z_{11} + 120) + \tfrac{1}{2}\ln(4z_{12} + 120).$$

FOC:

$$\frac{\partial U}{\partial z_{11}} = -\frac{2}{120 - z_{11}} + \frac{1}{2z_{11} + 120} \leq 0, \quad \text{with equality if } z_{11} > 0.$$

$$\frac{\partial U}{\partial z_{21}} = -\frac{1}{120 - z_{21}} + \frac{4}{4z_{21} + 120} = 0, \quad \text{with equality if } z_{21} > 0.$$

It is readily checked that $\frac{\partial U}{\partial z_{11}} < 0$ for all $z_{11} \geq 0$ and that the second condition is satisfied if $z_{12} = 45$. Thus the optimal consumption vector is $(x_1^*, x_2^*) = (120, 120, 75, 300)$.

(b) First consider an economy with spot and futures prices. The FOC for utility maximization is

$$\frac{\partial U}{\partial x} = \left(\frac{2}{x_{11}^*}, \frac{1}{x_{21}^*}, \frac{1}{x_{12}^*}, \frac{\frac{1}{2}}{x_{22}^*}\right) = \left(\frac{1}{60}, \frac{1}{120}, \frac{1}{75}, \frac{\frac{1}{2}}{300}\right) = \lambda p.$$

If $p_{11} = 1$, then $\lambda = \frac{1}{60}$. Hence $p = (1, \frac{1}{2}, \frac{4}{5}, \frac{1}{8})$.

(c) If the interest rate is zero, the spot price vector is $p_1 = (1, \frac{1}{2})$ and the future spot price vector is $p_2^{fs} = (1 + r)p_2 = p_2 = (\frac{4}{5}, \frac{1}{8})$. Note that the spot prices are no guide to future spot prices. Thus the representative consumer has no easy way of predicting the future spot prices in this economy.

Exercise 5.5-5: WE in a Two-Period Model

(a) $U(x) = \ln x_{11} + 2 \ln x_{21} + \delta \ln x_{12} + 2\delta \ln x_{22}$.

If there is no storage, the gradient vector must be proportional to the WE price vector at the endowment. Therefore

$$\frac{\partial U}{\partial x}(\omega) = \left(\frac{1}{\omega_{11}}, \frac{2}{\omega_{21}}, \frac{\delta}{\omega_{21}}, \frac{2\delta}{\omega_{22}} \right) = \left(\frac{1}{2}, 1, \delta, 2\delta \right) = \lambda p.$$

Therefore $p = (\frac{1}{2}, 1, \delta, 2\delta)$ is a WE price vector.

(b) The spot price vector is $p_1 = (\frac{1}{2}, 1)$ and the futures price vector is $p_2 = (\delta, 2\delta)$. The future spot price vector is $p_2^{fs} = (1 + r)p_2 = (1 + r)(\delta, 2\delta) = (1 + r)2\delta(\frac{1}{2}, 1)$. Thus the spot prices and future spot prices are identical if $(1 + r)2\delta = 1$; that is $1 + r = 1/2\delta$.

(c) Storing z_{11} units of commodity 1 and z_{21} units of commodity 2 yields a profit of

$$(p_{12} - p_{11})z_{11} + (p_{22} - p_{21})z_{21}.$$

The optimum is a WE. Thus if the optimum involves storage, profit must be maximized at $z \gg 0$. Then $p_{12} = p_{11}$ and $p_{22} = p_{21}$.

(d) If there is no storage the WE prices are $p = (\frac{1}{2}, 1, \delta, 2\delta)$. Storing z_{11} units of commodity 1 and z_{21} units of commodity 2 yields a profit of

$$(p_{12} - p_{11})z_{11} + (p_{22} - p_{21})z_{21} = (\delta - \tfrac{1}{2})z_{11} + (2\delta - 1)z_{21}.$$

Thus it is profit maximizing to do no storage if and only if $\delta \le \frac{1}{2}$.

5.6 Equilibrium with Constant Returns to Scale

Exercise 5.6-1: Market Adjustment Let input 1 be labor so that commodity A is more labor intensive. Let r be the Walrasian equilibrium input price vector. If the supply of input 1 increases there is excess supply, resulting in a downward shift in r_1. This lowers the average and marginal cost of production in both industries so both industries have an incentive to expand. The additional labor input raises the marginal product of input 2 in both industries so there is excess demand for input 2. The price of input 2 must therefore rise until it is profitable for one of the industries to contract. Because industry 1 is more input 1 intensive, its unit cost is lowered more; thus it is industry 2 that contracts. The contraction of industry 2 and expansion of industry 1 continue. This places upward pressure on the price of input 1 and downward pressure on the price of input 2. By Proposition 5.6-3, if both goods are produced, then, in the long run, both input prices must return to their original levels.

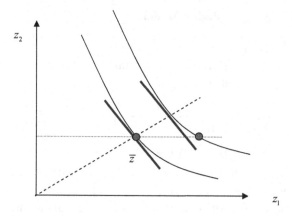

Figure 5.7-5. Input price change with specialization.

If the increase in supply of labor is large, industry B contracts completely so the economy is specialized in the production of commodity A. As depicted in Figure 5.7-5, the equilibrium cost line is tangent to the isoquant at $\bar{z}$. With constant returns to scale the slope is constant along a ray; thus, as labor increases, the wage rental rate must fall.

Exercise 5.6-3: Corollary of the Rybczynski Theorem From the derivation of the Rybczynski Theorem $q_A v_{A1} + q_B v_{B1} = \bar{z}_1$. Hence

$$dq_A v_{A1} + dq_B v_{B1} = d\bar{z}_1.$$

From the Rybczynski Theorem $dq_B < 0$. Therefore $dq_A v_{A1} > d\bar{z}_1$. It follows that

$$\frac{\bar{z}_1}{q_A} \frac{dq_A}{d\bar{z}_1} > \frac{\bar{z}_1}{q_A v_{A1}} = \frac{q_A v_{A1} + q_B v_{B1}}{q_A v_{A1}} > 1.$$

Exercise 5.6-5: Which Input Prices?

(a) Because $F_A(v_A) = F_A(8, 8) = 1$ this is the unit isoquant. Note that $r \cdot v_A = 1 = p_A$ so this is the dollar isoquant. For commodity B, it is a standard result that for a symmetric Cobb-Douglas production function, the cost shares are equal. Because the total cost of each input are $\frac{1}{2}$ when the input vector is $v_B = (5, 20)$ this is indeed efficient. Because output is 1 and the price of commodity B is 1, this is the dollar isoquant for commodity B. The dollar isoquants for both commodities are depicted in Figure 5.7-6 along with the dollar cost line.

(b) The second equilibrium cost line is depicted in Figure 5.7-7. Because the isoquants are symmetric the equilibrium input price vector must be $r' = (\frac{1}{40}, \frac{1}{10})$.

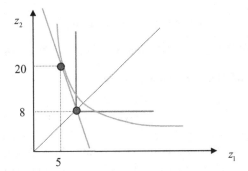

Figure 5.7-6. Dollar isoquants and iso-cost line.

(c) Given the unit input requirements of part (a), total demand for inputs is

$$\begin{bmatrix} 8 & 5 \\ 8 & 20 \end{bmatrix} \begin{bmatrix} q_A \\ q_B \end{bmatrix} = q_A \begin{pmatrix} 8 \\ 8 \end{pmatrix} + q_B \begin{pmatrix} 5 \\ 20 \end{pmatrix}.$$

Thus the input demands are a positively weighted average of vectors with slopes of 1 and 4. With the unit input requirements of part (c) total demand for inputs is

$$\begin{bmatrix} 8 & 20 \\ 8 & 5 \end{bmatrix} \begin{bmatrix} q_A \\ q_B \end{bmatrix} = q_A \begin{pmatrix} 8 \\ 8 \end{pmatrix} + q_B \begin{pmatrix} 20 \\ 5 \end{pmatrix}.$$

Thus the input demands are a positively weighted average of vectors with slopes of 1 and $\frac{1}{4}$. Because the supply ratio is $\frac{1}{2}$, only the second case is consistent with equilibrium.

(d) Now the supply ratio is 2 so only the first case is consistent with equilibrium. Thus $r = (\frac{1}{10}, \frac{1}{40})$.

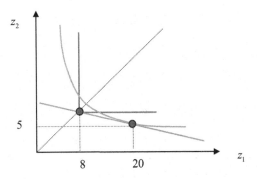

Figure 5.7-7. Second equilibrium iso-cost line.

6 Dynamic Optimization

6.1 Life-Cycle Consumption and Wealth

Exercise 6.1-1: Optimal Wealth Accumulation

(a) The phase diagram 6.1-2 is shown in Figure 6.6-1. Consider the sequence $\{x_t, W_t\}$ satisfying the growth equation and first-order condition $u'(x_t) = u'(x_{t+1})(1+r)\delta$ beginning at B.

    For this path and all those on the dotted line above B, (in phase II) wealth is decreasing. For all those paths starting below B, wealth is initially increasing.

(b) In the final period $x_T = W_T$ thus the optimal path must end on the dashed line. Note that, if first period consumption is higher, consumption is higher in all periods. Thus wealth declines faster. Thus the paths beginning above B reach the terminal line more quickly and are therefore the short horizon paths. It follows that there is a unique first period consumption such that $x_T = W_T$. The optimal path is depicted in Figure 6.6-2 as the curve AC. Note also that since the problem is concave, the FOC are both necessary and sufficient.

    As argued in the answer to part (a), long horizon paths begin to the South-East of B so wealth is initially increasing if T is sufficiently large.

(c) Let $\{x_t, W_t\}$ be optimal with $R = T$ and let $\{\hat{x}_t, \hat{W}_t\}$ be optimal with $R < T$. With retirement, initial total wealth is lower, that is, $\hat{W}_1 < W_1$ as depicted in Figure 6.6-2. From the FOC, either $\{\hat{x}_t\} \geq \{x_t\}$ or $\{\hat{x}_t\} < \{x_t\}$. Since the present value of consumption must be equal to first period wealth, it follows that $\{\hat{x}_t\} < \{x_t\}$. Then $\hat{x}_T < x_T$. Note finally that final period consumption and wealth are equal. Therefore $\hat{W}_T < W_T$.

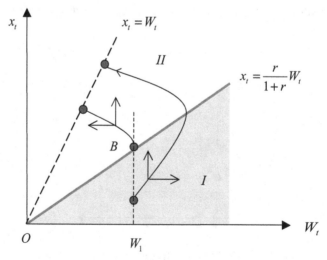

Figure 6.6-1. Consumption-wealth phase diagram with $(1+r)\delta > 1$.

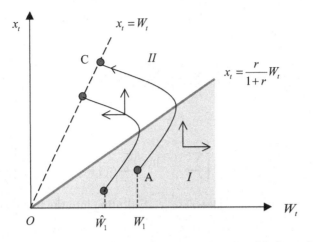

Figure 6.6-2. Consumption-capital phase diagram with $(1+r)\delta > 1$.

Exercise 6.1-3: Optimal Saving with More Than One Commodity and Logarithmic Preferences

(a) The total wealth growth equation is

$$W_{t+1} = (1+r)(W_t - p \cdot x_t) = (1+r)(W_t - c_t).$$

The optimal sequence of expenditures is therefore

$$\{\bar{c}_t\}_{t=1}^{T} = \arg \operatorname*{Max}_{\{c_t\}} \left\{ \sum_{t=1}^{T} \delta^{t-1} v(p_t, c_t) | W_{t+1} = (1+r)(W_t - c_t) \right\}.$$

The period t indirect utility function is

$$v(p_t, c_t) = \operatorname*{Max}_{x_t} \left\{ \sum_{j=1}^{n} \alpha_j \ln x_{jt} | p_t \cdot x_t \le c_t \right\}.$$

For this Cobb-Douglas optimization problem the solution satisfies $p_{jt} \bar{x}_{jt} = \alpha_j c_t$. Therefore

$$v(p_t, c_t) = \sum_{j=1}^{n} \alpha_j \ln \left(\frac{a_j}{p_{jt}} c_t \right) = \ln c_t + \sum_{j=1}^{n} \alpha_j \ln \left(\frac{\alpha_j}{p_{jt}} \right).$$

The second term on the right-hand side is constant. Thus the optimization problem can be rewritten as follows:

$$\operatorname*{Max}_{\{c_t\}} \left\{ \sum_{t=1}^{T} \delta^{t-1} \ln c_t | W_{t+1} = (1+r)(W_t - c_t) \right\}.$$

(b) Because $\overline{W}_{T+1} = 0$, the constraints can be combined into the single lifetime budget constraint

$$\sum_{t=1}^{T} \frac{c_t}{(1+r)^{t-1}} = W_1.$$

Therefore

$$\{\bar{c}_t\}_{t=1}^{T} = \arg \underset{\{c_t\}}{\text{Max}} \left\{ \sum_{t=1}^{T} \delta^{t-1} \ln c_t \, \middle| \, \sum_{t=1}^{T} \frac{c_t}{(1+r)^{t-1}} = W_1 \right\}.$$

The FOC reduces to $c_{t+1} = (1+r)\delta c_t$. Substituting into the budget constraint,

$$\sum_{t=1}^{T} c_1 \delta^{t-1} = c_1 \frac{1 - \delta^T}{1 - \delta} = W_1.$$

Hence $\bar{c}_1 = (\frac{1-\delta}{1-\delta^T})W_1$ and so $\bar{c}_t = ((1+r)\delta)^{t-1}(\frac{1-\delta}{1-\delta^T})W_1$.
Because $p_{jt}\bar{x}_{jt} = \alpha_j \bar{c}_t$ we can immediately solve for the optimal consumption bundle in period t.

(c) First-period consumption $\bar{c}_1 = (\frac{1-\delta}{1-\delta^T})W_1 > (1-\delta)W_1$. Because consumption grows at the rate $(1+r)\delta$, total expenditure in period t is

$$\bar{c}_t = ((1+r)\delta)^{t-1}\bar{c}_1 > ((1+r)\delta)^{t-1}(1-\delta)W_1.$$

Given constant spot prices, consumption of every commodity increases without bound as t increases.

6.2 Family of Dynamic Optimization Problems

Exercise 6.2-1: Linear Utility

(a) The finite horizon problem is

$$\underset{c}{\text{Max}} \left\{ \sum_{t=1}^{T} \delta^t c_t \, \middle| \, W_{t+1} = (1+r)(W_t - c_t) \right\}.$$

We can combine all the wealth accumulation constraints into a single lifetime constraint:

$$\sum_{t=1}^{T} \frac{c_t}{(1+r)^{t-1}} \leq W_1.$$

The Lagrangian for this optimization problem is

$$\mathcal{L} = \delta^{t-1}c_t + \lambda \left(W_1 - \sum_{t=1}^{T} \frac{c_t}{(1+r)^{t-1}} \right)$$

$$= \sum_{t=1}^{T} \frac{1}{(1+r)^{t-1}}[((1+r)\delta)^{t-1} - \lambda)] + \lambda W_1.$$

Because this is concave, the necessary conditions are also sufficient.

$$\frac{\partial \mathcal{L}}{\partial c_t} = \frac{1}{(1+r)^{t-1}}[((1+r)\delta)^{t-1} - \lambda)] \leq 0 \quad \text{with equality if} \quad c_t > 0.$$

This must hold for all t; hence $((1+r)\delta)^{T-1} - \lambda \leq 0$. Then for all $t < T$, the inequality is strict and so $\bar{c}_t = 0, t < T$. Thus the consumer saves all his wealth until the last period and then splurges.

(b) This cannot be the solution to the infinite horizon problem because it implies that the consumer would wait forever. This is strictly clearly worse than consuming the entire wealth in period 1. Thus there is no solution to the infinite horizon optimization problem.

6.3 The Ramsay Problem

Exercise 6.3-1: Optimal Rate of Investment

(a) Let $z^i, i = 0, 1$ be optimal with capital stock K^i. Define the convex combinations z^λ and K^λ. Then

$$N(K^\lambda) = \text{Max}_z\{R(K^\lambda, z) - r \cdot z\} \geq R(K^\lambda, z^\lambda) - r \cdot z^\lambda.$$

Because $R(K, z)$ is strictly concave and $-r \cdot z$ is concave, $R(K, z) - r \cdot z$ is strictly concave. Therefore

$$R(K^\lambda, z^\lambda) - r \cdot z^\lambda > (1 - \lambda)(R(K^0, z^0) - r \cdot z^0) + \lambda(R(K^1, z^1) - r \cdot z^1)$$
$$= (1 - \lambda)N(K^0) + \lambda N(K^1).$$

Combining the two inequalities it follows that $N(K)$ is strictly concave.

(b) The firm seeks to solve the following maximization problem:

$$\text{Max}_{\{x_\tau, K_\tau\}} \sum_{\tau=1}^{\infty} \left(\frac{1}{1+r} \right)^{\tau-1} (N(K_t) - C(x_t)) | K_{t+1} = (1 - \theta)K_t + x_t, \tau = 1, \ldots, T\}$$

(c) Subtracting K_t from both sides of the growth equation,

$$K_{t+1} - K_t = x_t - \theta K_t.$$

Thus capital increases if and only if $x_t - \theta K_t > 0$.

(d) If K_{T+1}^* is optimal, then the solution must also be the solution to the following T period optimization problem:

$$\max_{\{x_t, K_t\}} \sum_{t=1}^{T} \left(\frac{1}{1+r}\right)^{t-1} (N(K_t) - C(x_t)) | K_{t+1}$$

$$= (1-\theta)K_t + x_t, \tau = 1, \ldots, T, K_{T+1} \geq K_{T+1}^*\}.$$

Forming the Lagrangian,

$$\mathcal{L} = \sum_{t=1}^{T} \left(\frac{1}{1+r}\right)^{t-1} (N(K_t) - C(x_t)) + \sum_{t=1}^{T} \lambda_t ((1-\theta)K_t + x_t - K_{t+1}).$$

Given our assumptions, investment will be strictly positive. The FOC are therefore

$$\frac{\partial \mathcal{L}}{\partial x_t} = - \left(\frac{1}{1+r}\right)^{t-1} C'(x_t) + \lambda_t = 0, \tag{6.6-1}$$

and

$$\frac{\partial \mathcal{L}}{\partial K_t} = \left(\frac{1}{1+r}\right)^{t-1} N'(K_t) - \lambda_{t-1} + \lambda_t (1-\theta) = 0. \tag{6.6-2}$$

It is then a straightforward exercise to obtain the necessary condition,

$$N'(K_t) = (1+r)C'(x_{t-1}) - (1-\theta)C'(x_t). \tag{6.6-3}$$

Subtracting $(r + \theta)C'(x_t)$ from both sides of this expression,

$$N'(K_t) - (r + \theta)C'(x_{t-1}) = (1-\theta)(C'(x_{t-1}) - C'(x_t)).$$

Because the cost function is strictly convex,

$$x_t > x_{t-1} \Leftrightarrow N'(K_t) < (r + \theta)C'(x_{t-1}).$$

(e) The phase diagram is depicted in Figure 6.6-3.
(f) From the phase diagram, there is a unique path that approaches the stationary point S. From (6.6-1) the shadow prices decline toward zero along this path. Thus the Transversality Condition holds. It follows that the path DS depicts the solution to the infinite horizon problem.

The intuition should be clear. Because rapid investment is more costly, it pays to spread the period of capital accumulation over many periods. But the gain to investing is greatest initially when the marginal revenue product of capital is highest. So investment is highest at the beginning.

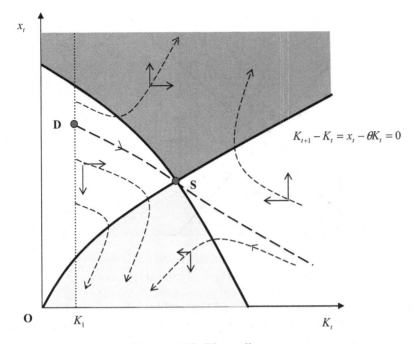

Figure 6.6-3. Phase diagram.

Stationary State Analysis

There is another simple way to see that, with an infinite horizon, the path must approach the saddle point S. Suppose that we simply compare stationary paths. That is, the firm chooses a stationary path, $(\overline{K}, \overline{x})$, one in which new investment just offsets depreciation. Output is then the same in each period, as is the price. A question that we can readily answer is what steady-state capital stock $K_t = \overline{K}, t = 1, 2 \ldots$, yields the highest steady (or stationary) profit. To do so we look at the marginal benefit and cost of increasing the capital stock by one. To maintain a new steady state, this will mean increasing gross investment each period by $\theta C'(\overline{x})$ to offset the greater depreciation associated with the higher capital stock. The simplest way to think about the cost is to suppose that the firm borrows the funds for the new investment. Then each period it pays an interest cost of $rC'(\overline{x})$ as well as for the extra depreciation. On the benefit side, the extra capital brings in a marginal net revenue of $N'(\overline{K})$. Thus the profit-maximizing steady state $(\overline{K}, \overline{x})$ satisfies

$$N'(\overline{K}) = (\theta + r)C'(\overline{x}), \quad \text{where} \quad \overline{x} = \theta \overline{K}.$$

This is the saddle point S.

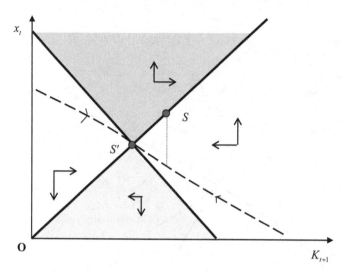

Figure 6.6-4. Increased cost of capital replacement.

Exercise 6.3-3: Comparative Dynamics of Optimal Investing In each case we begin by determining the effect of the parameter change on the phase boundary curves. The consumption growth phase boundary is

$$N'(K_{t+1}) = (r + \theta)C'(x_t), \tag{6.6-4}$$

whereas the capital growth phase boundary is $x_t = \theta K_{t+1}$

(a) The increase in the cost of investment raises the right-hand side of (6.6-4). Thus, holding K_{t+1} constant, x_t must fall. Therefore the consumption-growth phase boundary shifts down. The new steady state S' therefore lies to the southeast of S as shown in Figure 6.6-4. Thus the long-run capital stock and investment are both lower. The new optimal path is downward sloping and therefore lies below S. Thus the initial response to the unanticipated parameter change is for investment to decline even more in the short run. Investment then increases steadily.

  The intuition should be clear. With a higher cost of capital replacement, the long-run capital stock must decline until the marginal product of capital has increased enough to offset the higher marginal cost. Investment declines less in the long run because the marginal product of capital rises as the capital stock declines.

(b) An interest rate increase also increases the right-hand side of the consumption-growth equation. Thus the analysis is almost exactly as in part (a).

(c) If the depreciation rate falls, the capital growth phase boundary shifts downward and the consumption growth phase boundary shifts upward. Thus the new steady-state capital is higher. Investment then rises most rapidly initially. As the capital stock increases, the marginal product of capital falls and thus the incentive to further increase capital falls. Thus the rate of investment declines steadily over time.

6.4 Dynamic Programming Reformulation

Exercise 6.4-1: Solving for the Value Function

(a) $V(K_1) = \underset{c_1, K_2}{\text{Max}} \{\ln c_t + \beta \delta \ln K_2 | c_1 + K_2 = K_1^\alpha\}$

Substituting for K_2, $V(K_1) = \underset{c_1}{\text{Max}} \{\ln c_t + \beta \delta \ln(K_1^\alpha - c_1)\}$.

FOC:

$$\frac{1}{c_1} = \frac{\alpha \beta \delta}{K_2} = \frac{\alpha \beta \delta}{K_1^\alpha - c_1} = \frac{1 + \alpha \beta \delta}{K_1^\alpha}.$$

Hence $c_1 = \frac{1}{1+\alpha\beta\delta} K_1^\alpha$ and $K_1^\alpha - c_1 = \frac{\alpha\beta\delta}{1+\alpha\beta\delta} K_1^\alpha$.

(b) Substituting back into the maximand,

$$V(K_1) = \ln K_1^\alpha + \beta\delta \ln K_1^\alpha + \text{const} = \alpha(1 + \beta\delta)\ln K_1 + \text{const}.$$

Thus the guess is correct if $\alpha(1 + \beta\delta) = \beta$, that is $\beta = \frac{\alpha}{1-\alpha\delta}$.

(c) From the FOC $c_1 = \frac{1}{1+\alpha\beta\delta} K_1^\alpha$. Substituting for β,

$$c_t = \frac{1 - \alpha\delta}{1 - \alpha\delta(1 - \alpha)} K_t^\alpha.$$

Exercise 6.4-3: Solving the A-K Model

(a) From the growth equation,

$$x_t = AK_t - K_{t+1}.$$

$$x_{t+1} = AK_{t+1} - K_{t+2} \Rightarrow \frac{x_{t+1}}{A} = K_{t+1} - \frac{K_{t+2}}{A}$$

$$x_{t+2} = AK_{t+2} - K_{t+3} \Rightarrow \frac{x_{t+2}}{A^2} = K_{t+2} - \frac{K_{t+3}}{A^2}$$

Summing over t,

$$x_t + \frac{x_{t+1}}{A} + \cdots + \frac{x_T}{A^{T-t-1}} = AK_t.$$

(b) The Lagrangian for the finite horizon model is therefore

$$\mathcal{L} = \sum_{t=1}^{T} (u_t(x_t)) + \mu \left(AK_1 - x_1 - \frac{x_2}{1+r} - \cdots - \frac{x_T}{(1+r)^{T-1}} \right),$$

where $u_t(x_t) = \frac{\sigma}{\sigma-1} \delta^{t-1} x_t^{1-1/\sigma}, \sigma \neq 1$.

FOC:

$$\frac{\partial \mathcal{L}}{\partial c_t} = \delta^{t-1} x_t^{\frac{1}{\sigma}} - \frac{\mu}{A^{t-1}} = 0.$$

Hence $\left(\frac{x_{t+1}}{x_t}\right)^{\frac{1}{\sigma}} = A\delta$ and so $\frac{x_{t+1}}{x_t} = (A\delta)^{\sigma} \equiv 1 + \gamma$.

(c) At time t the constraint facing the consumer is as follows:

$$x_t + \frac{x_{t+1}}{A} + \cdots + \frac{x_T}{A^{T-t-1}} = AK_t.$$

Hence

$$x_t 1 + \frac{1+\gamma}{A} + \cdots + \left(\frac{1+\gamma}{A}\right)^{T-t-1} = AK_t.$$

Appealing to the formula for a geometric sum,

$$x_t = \frac{1 - \frac{1+\gamma}{A}}{1 - \left(\frac{1+\gamma}{A}\right)^{T-t}} AK_t.$$

(d) The denominator approaches 1 in the limit if $\frac{1+\gamma}{A} = \frac{(A\delta)^{\sigma}}{A} < 1$. By hypothesis $\delta < 1$ and $A\delta > 1$. Therefore if $\sigma \le 1$ $\frac{(A\delta)^{\sigma}}{A} < \frac{A\delta}{A} = \delta < 1$. Hence for $T - t$ sufficiently large

$$x_t \approx \left(1 - \frac{1+\gamma}{A}\right) AK_t = (A - 1 - \gamma)K_t.$$

However, if σ is sufficiently large,

$$\frac{1+\gamma}{A} = \frac{(A\delta)^{\sigma}}{A} > 1$$

and so

$$x_t = \frac{\frac{1+\gamma}{A} - 1}{\left(\frac{1+\gamma}{A}\right)^{T-t} - 1} AK_t.$$

Thus x_t approaches zero as T grows large.

(e) We argue that solution is the limit of the solution with a finite horizon; that is,

$$x_t = \left(1 - \frac{1+\gamma}{A}\right) AK_t = (A - 1 - \gamma)K_t.$$

Note that if this is the case,

$$K_{t+1} = AK_t - x_t = (1 + \gamma)K_t \text{ where } 1 + \gamma = (A\delta)^{\sigma}.$$

Also from the FOC $c_{t+1} = (1 + \gamma)c_t$. It remains to confirm that $V(K_1) = \sum_{t=1}^{\infty} u_t$ exists.

We wish to show that $u_{t+1} = \frac{1+\gamma}{A}u_t$. We can rewrite u_t and u_{t+1} as follows:

$$u_t = \delta^{t-1}x_t^{1-\frac{1}{\sigma}} = \frac{\delta^{t-1}x_t}{x_t^{\frac{1}{\sigma}}} \quad \text{and} \quad u_{t+1} = \frac{\delta^t x_{t+1}}{x_{t+1}^{\frac{1}{\sigma}}}.$$

Note that $x_{t+1} = (1+\gamma)x_t$ and so $x_{t+1}^{\frac{1}{\sigma}} = (1+\gamma)^{\frac{1}{\sigma}}x_t^{\frac{1}{\sigma}} = A\delta x_t^{\frac{1}{\sigma}}$.
Therefore

$$u_{t+1} = \frac{\delta^t x_{t+1}}{x_{t+1}^{\frac{1}{\sigma}}} = \frac{\delta^t(1+\gamma)x_t}{A\delta x_t^{\frac{1}{\sigma}}} = \frac{1+\gamma}{A}u_t.$$

It follows that

$$\sum_{t=1}^{\infty} u_t = \sum_{t=1}^{\infty} u_1 \left(1 + \frac{1+\gamma}{A} + \left(\frac{1+\gamma}{A}\right)^2 + \cdots \right) = \left(\frac{A}{A-1-\gamma}\right)x_1^{1-\frac{1}{\sigma}}.$$

But $x_1 = (A - 1 - \gamma)K_1$. Therefore

$$V(K_1) = \sum_{t=1}^{\infty} u_t = \left(\frac{A}{A-1-\gamma}\right)(A-1-\gamma)^{1-\frac{1}{\sigma}}K_1^{1-\frac{1}{\sigma}} = \frac{A}{(A-1-\gamma)^{\frac{1}{\sigma}}}K_1^{1-\frac{1}{\sigma}}.$$

6.5 Optimal Control

Exercise 6.5-1: Maximum Indebtedness

(a) The growth equation is

$$\frac{dk}{dt} = rk(t) + w - x(t).$$

We write down the Hamiltonian

$$H = e^{-\delta t}u(x) + \lambda(rk + w - x).$$

Then $\frac{d\lambda}{dt} = -\frac{\partial H}{\partial k} = -r\lambda$ and $\frac{\partial H}{\partial x} = e^{-\delta t}u'(x) - \lambda = 0$.
Integrating the differential equation for λ, $\lambda(t) = \lambda(0)e^{-rt}$. Then

$$u'(x) = \lambda(t)e^{\delta t} = \lambda(0)e^{(\delta-r)t}.$$

It follows that marginal utility grows at the rate $\delta - r > 0$. Hence $x(t)$ is decreasing.
   From the growth equation,

$$\frac{dk}{dt} = rk + w - x \geq 0 \quad \text{if and only if} \quad x \leq w + rk.$$

The phase diagram is therefore as depicted in Figure 6.6-5. Given an initial capital $k(0)$, the optimal path $(\bar{c}(t), \bar{k}(t))$ cannot begin in phase I because the terminal condition $k(T) = 0$ would be violated. Then the starting consumption

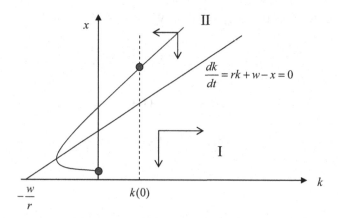

Figure 6.6-5. Phase diagram.

$c(0)$ is in phase II. Because $u'(x) = u'(x(0))e^{(\delta - r)t}$, a higher initial consumption implies higher consumption for all t and hence a lower capital stock. It follows that $k(t)$ is a decreasing function of initial consumption.

Suppose that the path depicted is optimal for some T. Then for all lower $c(1)$, the capital at T is positive and so the terminal condition cannot be satisfied. Thus the longer the time horizon, the higher is initial consumption. Because the optimal path must end at $k(T) = 0$, the path must move from phase II to phase I as depicted. Let $k(t^*)$ be the capital at the time that there is a phase switch. Then $k(t^*) > -w/r$. The present value of the wage stream is w/r. Therefore the consumer's debt is bounded from below by w/r.

Clearly this must be the case because if a consumer were to borrow more, he could never repay the debt.

(b) Initially $\frac{dk}{dt} = rk(t) + w - x(t) < -\varepsilon$. This can only remain true until some t_1 to satisfy the constraint on total indebtedness. Suppose that at t_2, $\frac{dk}{dt} = rk(t) + w - x(t) > \varepsilon$. Phase I is absorbing; therefore this inequality must hold for all higher t. Because $k(T) = 0$ it follows that $T - t_2$ is bounded. Then as $t_2 - t_1 \to \infty$ as $T \to \infty$.

This is depicted in Figure 6.6-6. The consumer goes deeply into debt, borrowing almost up to the bound on indebtedness. He remains there for a long time and near the end of his life pays off his debt.

Exercise 6.5-3: Bequest Motive

(a) The growth equation is

$$\frac{dk}{dt} = rk(t) + w - x(t).$$

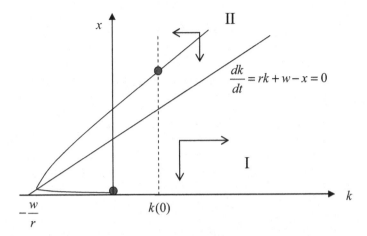

Figure 6.6-6. Phase diagram.

We write down the Hamiltonian

$$H = e^{-\delta t} u(x) + \lambda(rk + w - x).$$

Then $\frac{d\lambda}{dt} = -\frac{\partial H}{\partial k} = -r\lambda$, $\frac{\partial H}{\partial x} = e^{-\delta t} u'(x) - \lambda = 0$ and $\lambda(T) = e^{-\delta T} V'(K(T))$. Integrating the differential equation for λ, $\lambda(t) = \lambda(0)e^{-rt}$. Then

$$u'(x(t)) = \lambda(t)e^{\delta t} = \lambda(0)e^{-(r-\delta)t} = u'(x(0))e^{-(r-\delta)t}.$$

It follows that marginal utility decreases at the rate $r - \delta > 0$. Hence $x(t)$ is increasing. Consider any $(x(t), k(t))$ satisfying the initial condition and the necessary conditions for all $t \in [0, T]$. The higher is the initial consumption $x(0)$, the higher is $x(t), t > 0$ and therefore the lower is the capital stock $k(t)$. Then the mapping $x(0) \to (x(T), k(T))$ implicitly defines the decreasing function $x(T) = g(k(T))$.

The terminal condition is $\lambda(T) = e^{-\delta T} V'(k(T))$. Also $u'(x(T)) = e^{\delta T} \lambda(T)$. Hence the terminal condition can be rewritten as $u'(x(T)) = V'(k(T))$.

Since both $u(\cdot)$ and $V(\cdot)$ are concave, this condition implicitly defines the increasing function $x(T) = m(k(T))$. Since $g(\cdot)$ is decreasing and $m(\cdot)$ is increasing, there is a unique $(x(T), k(T))$ satisfying both the necessary conditions and the terminal condition.

(b) Since the discount factor exceeds the interest rate, $x(t)$ is a decreasing rather than an increasing function. However the analysis proceeds essentially as in the answer to (a).

7 Uncertainty

7.1 Risky Choices

Exercise 7.1-1: Equivalence of the Independence Axioms Suppose $\pi^m \succsim \hat{\pi}^m, m = 1, \ldots, M$

(a) For $M = 2$, it is easy to show that IA implies IA'. From IA, for any probability vector (p_1, p_2),

$$\pi^1 \succsim \hat{\pi}^1 \Rightarrow (p_1, p_2 : \pi^1, \pi^2) \succsim (p_1, p_2 : \hat{\pi}^1, \pi^2)$$

and

$$\pi^2 \succsim \hat{\pi}^2 \Rightarrow (p_1, p_2 : \hat{\pi}^1, \pi^2) \succsim (p_1, p_2 : \hat{\pi}^1, \hat{\pi}^2).$$

Therefore $\pi^1 \succsim \hat{\pi}^1$ and $\pi^2 \succsim \hat{\pi}^2 \Rightarrow (p_1, p_2 : \pi^1, \pi^2) \succsim (p_1, p_2 : \hat{\pi}^1, \hat{\pi}^2)$

(b) Define $\pi^* = (\frac{p_1}{1-p_k}, \ldots, \frac{p_{k-1}}{1-p_k} : \pi^1, \ldots, \pi^{k-1})$ and $\hat{\pi}^* = (\frac{p_1}{1-p_k}, \ldots, \frac{p_{k-1}}{1-p_k} : \hat{\pi}^1, \ldots, \hat{\pi}^{k-1})$.

By hypothesis the equivalence holds for $M = k - 1$. Thus $\pi^* \succsim \hat{\pi}^*$. Next note that

$$(p_1, \ldots p_k : \pi^1, \ldots, \pi^k) = (1 - p_k, p_k : \pi^*, \pi^k)$$

and

$$(p_1, \ldots p_k : \hat{\pi}^1, \ldots, \hat{\pi}^k) = (1 - p_k, p_k : \hat{\pi}^*, \hat{\pi}^k).$$

Because IA' holds for $M = 2$, it follows that

$$(1 - p_k, p_k : \pi^*, \pi^k) \succsim (1 - p_k, p_k : \hat{\pi}^*, \hat{\pi}^k).$$

Exercise 7.1-3: Linear and Monotonic Transformations

(a) Consider any pair of lotteries (c, π) and $(\hat{c}, \hat{\pi})$. If the first is (weakly) preferred then $\sum_{s=1}^S \pi_s v(c_s) \geq \sum_{s=1}^S \hat{\pi}_s v(\hat{c}_s)$. Hence $A + B \sum_{s=1}^S \pi_s v(c_s) \geq A + B \sum_{s=1}^S \hat{\pi}_s v(\hat{c}_s)$. Because the probabilities sum to 1, we can rewrite this as follows:

$$\sum_{s=1}^S \pi_s (A + Bv(c_s)) \geq \sum_{s=1}^S \hat{\pi}_s (A + Bv(\hat{c}_s)).$$

(b) Any increasing monotonic transformation of a utility function is an equivalent representation of preferences. Consider the logarithmic transformation of U, $\ln U = \sum_{s=1}^S \pi_s(c_s) \ln c_s$. Because this is an expected utility function, the consumer's preferences are consistent with the expected utility axioms.

7.2 Attitudes toward Risk

Exercise 7.2-1: Risk Aversion and Trading in State Claims Markets Define

$$\bar{x} = \arg \underset{x}{\text{Max}}\{\pi_1 v(x_1) + \pi_2 v(x_2) | p \cdot x \le I\}.$$

FOC:

$$\frac{\pi_1 v'(\bar{c}_1)}{\pi_2 v'(\bar{c}_2)} = \frac{p_1}{p_2}.$$

Suppose that $\frac{p_1}{p_2} > \frac{\pi_1}{\pi_2}$ so that $v'(\bar{c}_1) > v'(\bar{c}_2)$ and hence that $\bar{c}_2 > \bar{c}_1$.
Consider the logarithm of the MRS. This can be expressed as follows:

$$\ln \text{MRS}(c_1, c_2) - \ln \text{MRS}(c_1, c_1) = \int_{c_1}^{c_2} \frac{d}{dc} \ln \text{MRS}(c_1, c) dc = \int_{c_1}^{c_2} \frac{d}{dc} \ln \frac{v'(c_1)}{v'(c)} dc$$

$$= \int_{c_1}^{c_2} -\frac{v''(c)}{v'(c)} dc = \int_{c_1}^{c_2} A(c) dc.$$

Thus the higher the degree of absolute risk aversion, the greater the change in the MRS. Also on the certainty line the MRS is equal to the ratio of probabilities and is therefore independent of the degree of risk aversion. We have therefore shown that at all points above the certainty line the MRS is higher for an individual with higher absolute aversion to risk. It follows that the more risk-averse individual will choose a final consumption bundle (c_1, c_2) closer to the certainty line.

Exercise 7.2-3: Risky Choices with Two Commodities

(a) Within each state the consumer has a Cobb-Douglas utility function. From Chapter 2, the indirect utility function is

$$V(p, I) = \left[\frac{I}{\alpha + \beta}\right]^{\alpha + \beta} \left(\frac{\alpha}{p_x}\right)^\alpha \left(\frac{\beta}{p_y}\right)^\beta.$$

This is concave in income if and only if the second derivative with respect to income is non-positive; that is, $\alpha + \beta \le 1$.

(b) It is easily checked that the second derivative with respect to p_x is positive. Thus, holding income constant, it follows from Jensen's Inequality that such individuals strictly prefers an uncertain price to its expectation.

(c) In a market economy, price uncertainty is generated by some underlying (technological) shock. This shock affects both the income in each state and the price. Thus it makes little sense to simply study the effect of price uncertainty.

Exercise 7.2-5: Wealth Effects on Asset Shares

(a) If an individual invests a fraction z of his wealth in the risky asset, the consumption in each state s would be $c_s = (W - Wz)(1 + r_1) + Wz(1 + \tilde{r}_{2s})$. Then the expected utility can be written as $U(z) = E\{V(W(1+r_1) + Wz\theta_s)\}$, where $\theta_s = r_{2s} - r_1$.

The marginal utility of increasing his share of asset 2 is

$$U'(z) = \sum_{s=1}^{S} \pi_s \theta_s W v' \left(W(1+r_1) + Wz\theta_s\right).$$

We then ask what is the effect of an increase in wealth on the marginal utility of investing in the risky asset.

$$\frac{d}{dW}U'(z) = \sum_{s=1}^{S} \pi_s \theta_s v'(c_s) + \sum_{s=1}^{S} \pi_s \theta_s W(1+r_1+z\theta_s)v''(c_s), \qquad (7.5\text{-}1)$$

where $c_s = W(1+r_1) + \theta_s Wz$.

That is,

$$\frac{d}{dW}U'(z) = \sum_{s=1}^{S} \pi_s \theta_s v'(c_s) + \sum_{s=1}^{S} \pi_s \theta_s c_s v''(c_s)$$

$$= \sum_{s-1}^{S} \pi_s \theta_s v'(c_s) - \sum_{s=1}^{S} \pi_s \theta_s R(c_s)v'(c_s). \qquad (7.5\text{-}2)$$

Let z^* be the optimal fractional holding of the risky asset. If $\frac{d}{dW}U'(z^*) > 0$, increasing wealth raises the marginal utility of investing in the risky asset. Then, at the higher wealth level, the individual invests more in the risky asset. Appealing to (7.5-1), the first term in (7.5-2) is zero if $z = z^*$. Moreover, if relative risk aversion is constant the second term is also zero. Therefore $\frac{d}{dW}U'(z^*) = 0$. It follows that a change in wealth has no effect on the optimal investment.

(b) The trick to analyzing is to make use of our assumption that relative risk aversion is increasing (IRRA). Index states so that θ_s is decreasing. Then for some state t, $\theta_1 > \cdots > \theta_t \geq 0 > \theta_{t+1} > \cdots > \theta_S$. Because $R(c)$ is increasing

$$\sum_{s=1}^{t-1} \pi_s \theta_s R(c_s)v'(c_s) \geq \sum_{s=1}^{t-1} \pi_s \theta_s R(W(1+r_1))v'(c_s) \qquad (7.5\text{-}3)$$

and

$$\sum_{s=t}^{S} \pi_s(-\theta_s) R(c_s)v'(c_s) \leq \sum_{s=t}^{S} \pi_s(-\theta_s) R(W(1+r_1))v'(c_s).$$

Multiplying the second inequality by -1 and adding the two inequalities (7.5-3),

$$\sum_{s=1}^{S} \pi_s \theta_s R(c_s)v'(c_s) \geq \sum_{s=1}^{S} \pi_s \theta_s R(W(1+r_1))v'(c_s)$$

Hence, arguing as in the answer to (a), it follows from (7.5-2), that $\frac{d}{dW}U'(z^*) \leq 0$.

7.3 Comparing Risky Alternatives

Exercise 7.3-1: Portfolio Choice

(a) Final consumption is $c = (w - x) + x(1 + \tilde{\theta}) = w + x\tilde{\theta}$ and so expected utility is

$$U(x) = E\{u(w + x\tilde{\theta})\}.$$

(b) Differentiating by x,

$$U'(x^*) = E\{\tilde{\theta}u'(w + x\tilde{\theta})\} = 0.$$

$$\frac{\partial u}{\partial x} = \theta v'(w + x\theta).$$

(c) Hence

$$\frac{\partial^2 u}{\partial x \partial \theta} = v'(w + x\theta) + \theta x v''(w + x\theta) = v'(w + x\theta)\left(1 + \theta x \frac{v''(w + x\theta)}{v'(w + x\theta)}\right)$$

$$= v'(c)\left(1 + c\frac{v''(c)}{v'(c)} - w\frac{v''(c)}{v'(c)}\right) = v'(c)(1 - R(c) + A(c)).$$

(d) We can appeal to Proposition 7.3-6 if we can show that $\frac{\partial u}{\partial x}(x, \theta)$ is a concave function of θ. Appealing to (c)

$$\frac{\partial}{\partial \theta}\frac{\partial}{\partial \theta}\frac{\partial u}{\partial x} = v''(c)(1 - R(c) + A(c)) + v'(c)(-xR' + xA').$$

The right-hand side is negative if $R \leq 1$, $R'(c) \geq 0$, and $A'(c) > 0$.

Exercise 7.3-3: Mean Utility-Preserving Increase in Risk

(a) $\theta = h(u)$ is the inverse function; that is, $u = v(w + xh(u))$. Differentiating by u,

$$1 = xh'(u)v'(w + xh(u)).$$

(b) $G(u) = \Pr\{\tilde{u} \leq u\} = \Pr\{v(w + x\tilde{\theta}) \leq v(w + x\theta)\} = \Pr\{\tilde{\theta} \leq \theta\} = F(\theta)$

(c) $\frac{\partial}{\partial x}v(w + xh(u)) = h(u)v'(w + xh(u))$.

Therefore

$$\frac{\partial}{\partial u}\frac{\partial}{\partial x}v(w + xh(u)) = h'(u)v'(w + xh(u)) + h(u)xh'(u)v''(w + xh(u)).$$

Appealing to (a) it follows that

$$\frac{\partial}{\partial u}\frac{\partial}{\partial x}v\left(w + xh(u)\right) = \frac{1}{x}\left(1 + xh\frac{v''(w + xh)}{v'(w + xh)}\right)$$

$$= \frac{1}{x}\left(1 + (w + xh)\frac{v''(w + xh)}{v'(w + xh)} - w\frac{v''(w + xh)}{v'(w + xh)}\right)$$

$$= \frac{1}{x}(1 + (w - R(w + xh) - wA(w + xh)).$$

(d) It follows that $\frac{\partial}{\partial x} v(w + xh(u))$ is a concave function of u if relative risk aversion is increasing and absolute risk aversion is decreasing.

(e) $U(x) = E\{v(w + xh(u))\}$ is a strictly concave function of x. By Proposition 7.3-6, if A represents a mean utility-preserving in risk over B then $U'_B(x) > U'_A(x)$ and so $x^*_A < x^*_B$.

Exercise 7.3-5: Simple Mean-Preserving Spread

(a) $\ln \frac{F(\theta_2)}{F(\theta_1)} = \ln F(\theta_2) - \ln F(\theta_1) = \int_{\theta_1}^{\theta_2} \frac{d}{dx} \ln F(x) dx = \int_{\theta_1}^{\theta_2} \frac{F'(x)}{F(x)} dx.$

(b) For all $x > \theta^*$, $\frac{F'_A(x)}{F_A(x)} > \frac{F'_B(x)}{F_B(x)}$.
Appealing to (a),

$$\ln \frac{F_A(\beta)}{F_A(\theta)} \geq \ln \frac{F_B(\beta)}{F_B(\theta)}, \forall \theta \in [\theta^*, \beta].$$

Hence $F_B(\theta) > F_A(\theta), \forall \theta \in [\theta^*, \beta)$.

(c) Because the distributions have the same mean, there must be some $\underline{\theta}$ and $\hat{\theta}$ where $< \underline{\theta} < \theta^*$ such that $F_A(\underline{\theta}) - F_B(\underline{\theta}) = F_A(\hat{\theta}) - F_B(\hat{\theta}) = 0$ and $F_A(\theta) - F_B(\theta) > 0$ on $(\underline{\theta}, \hat{\theta})$. We first suppose that $\alpha < \underline{\theta}$ and seek a contradiction. Because $\hat{\theta} < \theta^*$,

$$\ln \frac{F_A(\hat{\theta})}{F_A(\underline{\theta})} = \int_{\underline{\theta}}^{\hat{\theta}} \frac{F'_A(x)}{F_A(x)} dx < \int_{\underline{\theta}}^{\hat{\theta}} \frac{F'_B(x)}{F_B(x)} dx = \ln \frac{F_B(\hat{\theta})}{F_B(\underline{\theta})}.$$

Then $\frac{F_A(\hat{\theta})}{F_A(\underline{\theta})} < \frac{F_B(\hat{\theta})}{F_B(\underline{\theta})}$ and so $\frac{F_A(\hat{\theta})}{F_B(\hat{\theta})} < \frac{F_A(\underline{\theta})}{F_B(\underline{\theta})}$. But this is impossible because the two c.d.f.'s have the same value at $\underline{\theta}$ and $\hat{\theta}$.

(d) The only remaining possibility is $\underline{\theta} = \alpha$. Therefore (ii) holds.

7.4 Principal-Agent Problem

Exercise 7.4-1: Increasing Likelihood Ratio and Stochastic Dominance

(a) $\frac{\pi_1(x')}{\pi_1(x)} \leq \cdots \leq \frac{\pi_t(x')}{\pi_t(x)}$ hence $\pi_s(x') < (\frac{\pi_t(x')}{\pi_t(x)})\pi_s(x), s = 1, \cdots, t - 1$.
Summing these inequalities,

$$\sum_{s=1}^{t} \pi_s(x') \leq \left(\frac{\pi_t(x')}{\pi_t(x)}\right) \sum_{s=1}^{t} \pi_s(x).$$

Hence

$$\frac{\sum_{s=1}^{t} \pi_s(x')}{\sum_{s=1}^{t} \pi_s(x)} \leq \frac{\pi_t(x')}{\pi_t(x)}.$$

(b) Define $\Pi_t(x) = \sum_{s=1}^{t} \pi_s(x)$ and $\Pi_t(x') = \sum_{s=1}^{t} \pi_s(x')$. From (a),

$$\frac{\Pi_t(x')}{\Pi_t(x)} \leq \frac{\pi_t(x')}{\pi_t(x)} \quad \text{hence} \quad \frac{\pi_t(x)}{\Pi_t(x)} \leq \frac{\pi_t(x')}{\Pi_t(x')}.$$

Appealing to Proposition 7.3-5, the output distribution under x' exhibits conditional stochastic dominance over that for action x.

Exercise 7.4-3: Principal's Virtual Cost Function

(a) The agent receives his reservation utility. Therefore

$$\overline{U}_A = v(w) - C(x).$$

Differentiating by x, the extra wage needed to induce a higher x satisfies

$$v'(w(x))\frac{dw}{dx} = C'(x).$$

Therefore

$$\frac{dw}{dx} = \frac{C'(x)}{v'(w(x))}.$$

The extra cost of inducing the higher action is therefore

$$w(x_2) - w(x_1) = \int_{x_1}^{x_2} \frac{dw}{dx}dx = \int_{x_1}^{x_2} \frac{C'(x)}{v'(w(x))}dx.$$

(b) Note that $v(w(x)) = \overline{U}_A + C(x)$. Therefore the higher the reservation utility, the higher is the wage $w(x, \overline{U}_A)$ needed to induce action x. Then the marginal utility, $v'(w(x, \overline{U}_A))$, is lower. Appealing to (a), $w(x_2) - w(x_1)$ is higher.

8 Equilibrium in Financial Markets

8.1 Complete Market Equilibrium

Exercise 8.1-1: Uncertainty in an Economy with CES Preferences

(a) $u(kc) = k^{1-\frac{1}{\sigma}}u(c)$ so preferences are homothetic. WE prices are therefore prices at which the representative individual will not wish to trade.

Equating the price ratio and marginal rate of substitution,

$$\frac{p_1}{p_2} = \frac{\pi_1}{\pi_2}\left(\frac{w_2}{w_1}\right)^{\frac{1}{\sigma}}.$$

(b) $R(c) = \frac{cv''(c)}{v'(c)} = \frac{1}{\sigma}$.

(c) The greater the degree of risk aversion, the higher the relative price of the less abundant state claim.

(d) When $\sigma \to 0$, (so, when $RRA \to \infty$), the contour sets of u approach Leontief (L-shaped) contour sets. In the limit the price of the abundant state claim approaches zero.

Exercise 8.1-3: Time, Uncertainty, and Production

(a) From the FOC, the equilibrium spot and contingent future prices for each state are

$$\frac{p_{21}}{p_1} = \delta\pi_1 \frac{w_1}{w_{21}} \quad \text{and} \quad \frac{p_{22}}{p_1} = \delta\pi_2 \frac{w_1}{w_{22}}.$$

(b) Appealing to the hint, the representative consumer chooses z to maximize $U(z) = \ln(100 - z) + \pi_1 \ln(2z) + \pi_2 \ln(\frac{1}{2}z)\}$.

The FOC for the maximization problem is

$$\frac{1}{100 - z^*} = \frac{1}{z^*} \Rightarrow z^* = 50.$$

Hence $x^* = (50, \ 100, \ 25)$. Using the equations for the equilibrium prices from the answer to (a) the price vector is

$$(p_1 \ p_{21} \ p_{22}) = (1, \tfrac{1}{2}\pi_1, 2\pi_2).$$

8.2 Security Market Equilibrium

Exercise 8.2-1: Why Incomplete Markets? If individuals are to trade a state claim, a third party must be able to verify that the state has indeed occurred. The more exotic the state claims that are marketed, the greater the verification costs. Eventually such transaction costs offset the gains to trading. Further difficulties arise if the states are relevant to only a few individuals. Then the number of individuals directly benefiting from the trade is small and so the price-taking assumption underlying an A-D equilibrium is no longer plausible.

Exercise 8.2-3: SM Equilibrium in an Economy with Identical Homothetic Preferences

(a) The utility function is homothetic so we can consider a single representative agent. In equilibrium this agent cannot trade; therefore

$$\omega = \arg \underset{x}{\text{Max}}\{U(x)|p \cdot x \le W\}.$$

FOC:

$$\frac{\tfrac{1}{2}\pi_1}{p_1\omega_1^{1/2}} = \frac{\tfrac{1}{2}\pi_2}{p_2\omega_2^{1/2}} = \frac{\tfrac{1}{2}\pi_2}{p_3\omega_3^{1/2}}.$$

The aggregate endowment is $\omega = (100, 400, 900)$. Substituting into the FOC, $p = (\pi_1, \tfrac{1}{2}\pi_2, \tfrac{1}{3}\pi_3)$ is an A-D equilibrium price vector.

(b) The value of the riskless asset is $P_1 = 100(\pi_1 + \frac{1}{2}\pi_2 + \frac{1}{3}\pi_3)$, and the value of the risky asset is $P_2 = 400p_1 + 900p_2 = 100(2\pi_2 + 3\pi_3)$. The representative agent holds the market portfolio. Because consumers have the same homothetic utility function, all wish to hold a fraction of the market portfolio. They can trade in securities markets to do so. The cost of the market portfolio is $P_1 + P_2$. Individual h can trade his initial holding of the two-asset $\bar{\xi}^h$ for ζ_M^h units of the market portfolio, where

$$(P_1 + P_2)\xi_M^h = P \cdot \bar{\xi}^h.$$

Exercise 8.2-5: Stock Market Equilibrium

(a) Firms purchase inputs and sell units of the "dividend" vector d. The maximized profit or "value" of the firm is

$$\hat{\Pi}^f = \underset{y^f}{\text{Max}}\{p_0 y_0^f + p_1 y_1^f \mid y^f \in \mathcal{Y}^f\}.$$

Consumers also trade in the date 0 commodity and dividends. Consumer h chooses

$$\hat{x}^h = \arg\underset{x^h}{\text{Max}}\{U^h(x^h) \mid p \cdot x^h \leq p_0\omega_0^h + \bar{\xi}^{hf}\hat{\Pi}^f\},$$

where $\bar{\xi}^{hf}$ is his initial portfolio.
(b) In the A-D equilibrium consumers trade claims to all $S + 1$ commodities.
(c) The A-D equilibrium allocation is PE among all feasible allocation is the S+1 dimensional commodity space. The dividend trading equilibrium spans only a two-dimensional subspace. By the First welfare theorem, the WE is a Pareto efficient allocation in this two-dimensional subspace of the commodity space.
(d) Let $\hat{y}^f$ be profit maximizing in the dividend trading equilibrium. That is,

$$p \cdot y^f \leq p \cdot \hat{y}^f = \hat{\Pi}^f, \ y^f \in \mathcal{Y}^f.$$

Note that even if there is no explicit price of a dividend, it remains the implicit price. Therefore no deviation from $\hat{y}^f$ can raise the stock market value of the firm.
A consumer purchasing a portfolio ξ^h has a period 2 consumption of $x_1^h = \sum_{f=1}^{F} \xi^{hf}\hat{y}_1^f d$.
Summing over consumers,

$$\sum_{h=1}^{H} x_1^h = \sum_{h=1}^{H} \xi^{hf} \sum_{f=1}^{F} \hat{y}_1^f d.$$

If there is equilibrium in the stock market, $\sum_{h=1}^{H} \xi^{hf} = 1$. Then

$$\sum_{h=1}^{H} x_1^h = \sum_{f=1}^{F} \hat{y}_1^f d.$$

Thus all period 2 markets clear. Trade in the stock market therefore replicates trade in the dividend market.

(e) Suppose F_1 firms produce a dividend vector d_1 and F_2 firms produce a dividend vector d_2. The arguments above are unchanged. In the dividend market equilibrium there is a price for each of the dividends. The WE allocation is PE in a three-dimensional subspace of $\mathbb{R}^{S+1}$. In the stock market equilibrium the profit (market value) of each firm reflects the implicit price of each of the dividends.

8.3 Capital Asset Pricing Model

Exercise 8.3-1: Pricing Independent Assets

(a) From Proposition 8.3-3, the expected utility of consumer h can be written as

$$U^h(\mu, \sigma) = \mu - \tfrac{1}{2}\alpha^h \sigma^2.$$

The portfolio ξ yields a mean return of $\mu(\xi) = \xi_0(1+r) + \sum_1^A \xi_a \mu_a$ and variance $\sigma^2(\xi) = \sum_1^A \xi_a^2 \sigma_a^2$. The portfolio constraint is $\xi_0 + \sum_{a=1}^A P_a \xi_a \leq W^h$. Substituting for ξ_0, the mean return is $\mu(\xi) = W(1+r) + \sum_1^A \xi_a(\mu_a - (1+r)P_a)$. Then the individual chooses

$$\hat{\xi} = \text{arg } \underset{\xi}{\text{Max}} \left\{ \sum_1^A \xi_a(\mu_a - (1+r)P_a) - \tfrac{1}{2}\alpha^h \left(\sum_1^A \xi_a^2 \sigma_a^2 \right) \right\}.$$

FOC

$$\frac{\partial U}{\partial \xi_a} = \mu_a - (1+r)P_a - \alpha^h \xi_a^h \sigma_a^2 = 0.$$

Hence

$$\xi_a^h = \frac{\mu_a - (1+r)P_a}{\alpha^h \sigma_a^2}.$$

Summing over consumers (with $\alpha^h = \alpha$),

$$1 = \frac{H}{\sigma_a^2}(\mu_a - (1+r)P_a).$$

Hence

$$\mu_a - (1+r)P_a = \alpha \frac{\sigma_a^2}{H}.$$

(b) Note that as $H \to \infty$ the right-hand side approaches zero. Thus the mean return is approximately equal to the return on investing the funds in the riskless asset. The reason is that each individual is purchasing a smaller and smaller share of the market portfolio. In the limit the riskiness of the individual's shareholding approaches zero. Then the individual's wealth in all but the most extreme states is approximately the same, and so the marginal utility in each state is proportional to the probability of each state. Thus, in the limit, the individual values the risky asset as if he were risk neutral.

(c) Note also that the price of the asset is independent of the number of assets or their variance. The explanation is that with constant absolute aversion to risk and independence, the trade-off between holding the riskless asset and risky asset a is independent of the holding of other assets.

(d) Regardless of the number of assets, each individuals holding of a particular asset approaches zero as it grows large. Thus the conclusion in (b) continues to hold.

(e) Suppose that there are two risky assets. Expected utility is

$$U(\xi) = - \underset{z}{E}\{\exp(-\alpha(\xi \cdot z))$$

$$= - \underset{z_0, z_1}{E} \{\exp(-\alpha(\xi_0(1+r) + \xi_1 z_1)\} \underset{z_2}{E}\{\exp(-\alpha(\xi_2 z_2).$$

Note that $\mathrm{MRS}_{01}(\xi)$ is independent of ξ_2. At the consumer's optimum, $\mathrm{MRS}_{01}(\xi) = P_1$.

From (a)

$$\xi_a^h = \frac{\mu_a - (1+r)P_a}{\alpha^h \sigma_a^2}.$$

Summing over consumers,

$$1 = \overline{\alpha}(\frac{\mu_a - (1+r_0)P_a}{\sigma_a^2}),$$

where $\overline{\alpha} = \sum_{h=1}^{H} \frac{H}{\alpha^h}$.

Hence

$$\mu_a - (1+r)P_a = \overline{\alpha}\frac{\sigma_a^2}{H}.$$

8.4 Arbitrage Pricing Theory

Exercise 8.4-1: Three States and Two Assets

(a) The portfolio ξ has dividend $d = \mathbf{D}\xi = \begin{bmatrix} -1 & 1 \\ 1 & 1 \\ 2 & 0 \end{bmatrix} \begin{bmatrix} \xi_1 \\ \xi_2 \end{bmatrix} = \begin{bmatrix} -\xi_1 + \xi_2 \\ \xi_1 + \xi_2 \\ 2\xi_1 \end{bmatrix}.$

Therefore the set of portfolios with $d > 0$ is $\Xi = \{\xi | -\xi_1 + \xi_2 > 0, \xi_1 + \xi_2 > 0, 2\xi_1 > 0\}$. This is the shaded region depicted in Figure 8.5-1.

(b) For no arbitrage, the price line $P'\xi = 0$ must be supporting. The asset price vector P is perpendicular to the price line. Therefore it must lie in the shaded region. Hence $P_1 < P_2$ and so $P = (2, 6)$ admits no arbitrage.

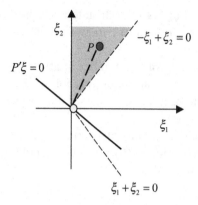

Figure 8.5-1. No arbitrage.

Choose $\xi^* = (1, 1)$. Then

$$d^* = \mathbf{D}\xi^* = \begin{bmatrix} 1 & -1 \\ 1 & 1 \\ 2 & 0 \end{bmatrix} \begin{bmatrix} 1 \\ 1 \end{bmatrix} = \begin{bmatrix} 0 \\ 2 \\ 2 \end{bmatrix}.$$

The first two rows are linearly independent; thus the portfolios span a subspace W^2. Define

$$d^{**} = d^* + \mathbf{1}_3.$$

Stage 1

$$X = \{\xi \mid \mathbf{D}\xi < d^{**}\} = \left\{ \xi \mid \begin{bmatrix} -1 & 1 \\ 1 & 1 \\ 2 & 0 \end{bmatrix} \begin{bmatrix} \xi_1 \\ \xi_2 \end{bmatrix} = \begin{bmatrix} -\xi_1 + \xi_2 \\ \xi_1 + \xi_2 \\ 2\xi_1 \end{bmatrix} < \begin{bmatrix} 0 \\ 2 \\ 3 \end{bmatrix} \right\}.$$

This is depicted in Figure 8.5-2.

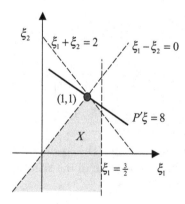

Figure 8.5-2. No arbitrage.

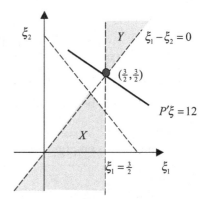

Figure 8.5-3. No arbitrage.

Stage 2

$$Y = \{\xi \mid \mathbf{D}\xi > d^{**}\} = \left\{ \xi \mid \begin{bmatrix} -1 & +1 \\ 1 & 1 \\ 2 & 0 \end{bmatrix} \begin{bmatrix} \xi_1 \\ \xi_2 \end{bmatrix} = \begin{bmatrix} -\xi_1 + \xi_2 \\ \xi_1 + \xi_2 \\ 2\xi_1 \end{bmatrix} > \begin{bmatrix} 0 \\ 2 \\ 3 \end{bmatrix} \right\}.$$

This is depicted in Figure 8.5-3.

(c) It follows that $(P_1, P_2, P^{**}) = (2, 6, P^{**})$ admits no arbitrage if $8 < P^{**} < 12$.
     Hence $(P_1, P_2, P^{**}) = (2, 6, 11)$ admits no arbitrage.
(d) Because $\mathbf{1}_3 = d^{**} - d^* = d^{**} - \mathbf{D}\xi^*$ it follows that $r_3 = P^{**} - P'\xi^* = 3$.
     Also $P' = r'\mathbf{D}$. Therefore

$$[2, 6, 11] = [r_1, r_2, 3] \begin{bmatrix} -1 & 1 & 0 \\ 1 & 1 & 2 \\ 2 & 0 & 3 \end{bmatrix}.$$

Hence $2r_2 + 9 = 11$ and so $r_2 = 1$. Also $r_1 + r_2 = 6$ and so $r_1 = 5$.

Exercise 8.4-3: An Economy in Which All Asset Prices Admit No Arbitrage

(a) The portfolio ξ has dividend

$$d = \mathbf{D}\xi = \begin{bmatrix} 1 & 1 \\ 1 & -2 \\ -2 & 1 \end{bmatrix} \begin{bmatrix} \xi_1 \\ \xi_2 \end{bmatrix} = \begin{bmatrix} \xi_1 + \xi_2 \\ \xi_1 + \xi_2 \\ -2\xi_1 + \xi_2 \end{bmatrix}.$$

Therefore the set of portfolios with $d > 0$ is $\Xi = \{\xi \mid \xi_1 + \xi_2 > 0, \xi_1 - 2\xi_2 > 0, -2\xi_1 + \xi_2 > 0\}$. The second and third inequalities cannot both be satisfied.
(b) Therefore the no arbitrage condition is satisfied vacuously.
(c) With $\xi^* = (1, 1)$ and $d^{**} = d^* + \mathbf{1}_3$.

Stage 1

$$X = \{\xi \,|\, \mathbf{D}\xi < d^{**}\} = \left\{ \xi \,\Bigg|\, \begin{bmatrix} 1 & 1 \\ 1 & -2 \\ -2 & 1 \end{bmatrix} \begin{bmatrix} \xi_1 \\ \xi_2 \end{bmatrix} = \begin{bmatrix} \xi_1 + \xi_2 \\ \xi_1 - 2\xi_2 \\ -2\xi_1 + \xi_2 \end{bmatrix} < \begin{bmatrix} 2 \\ -1 \\ 0 \end{bmatrix} \right\}.$$

As may ready be checked, the vertices of X are the points $(1, 1)$, $(\frac{2}{3}, \frac{4}{3})$, $(\frac{1}{3}, \frac{2}{3})$.

Stage 2
The set Y is empty.

Stage 3
Define $\hat{\xi} = \arg \text{Max}\{P'\xi \,|\, \xi \in X\}$. For $P_1 > P_2$, $\hat{\xi} = (1, 1)$. Therefore
$\text{Max}\{P'\xi \,|\, \xi \in X\} = P_1 + P_2$
It follows that the price of the third asset must satisfy $P^{**} > P_1 + P_2$. For
$P_1 < P_2$, $\hat{\xi} = (\frac{2}{3}, \frac{4}{3})$. Therefore
$\text{Max}\{P'\xi \,|\, \xi \in X\} = \frac{2}{3}P_1 + \frac{4}{3}P_2$
It follows that the price of the third asset must satisfy $P^{**} > \frac{2}{3}P_1 + \frac{4}{3}P_2$.

9 Strategy

9.1 Strategic Equilibrium

Exercise 9.1-1: Rock, Scissors, Paper Modified to Favor Player 1

(a) If player 1 adopts the totally mixed strategy $(p_1, q_1, 1 - p_1 - q_1)$, player 2's expected payoffs from each of his pure strategies are as follows.

$$\begin{bmatrix} u_2(P) \\ u_2(S) \\ u_2(R) \end{bmatrix} = \begin{bmatrix} p_1 & q_1 & 1 - p_1 - q_1 \end{bmatrix} \begin{bmatrix} 0 & 24 & -12 \\ -12 & 0 & 12 \\ 12 & 12 & 0 \end{bmatrix}. \qquad (9.5\text{-}1)$$

If player 2 also plays a totally mixed strategy he must have the same expected payoff from each of his pure strategies. Setting $u_2(P) = u_2(R)$, it follows that $q_1 = 4/12$. Setting $u_2(P) = u_2(S)$ it follows that $p_1 = 3/12$. Then player 1 chooses Rock with probability $5/12$.

(b) Substituting the equilibrium probabilities into (9.5-1), player 2's expected payoff is 1. Because this is a constant sum game, player 1's expected payoff is -1.

(c) Player 2 should be willing to pay up to 1 to play and player 1 should play only if offered at least 1.

(d) Arguing as above

$$\begin{bmatrix} u_1(P) \\ u_1(S) \\ u_1(R) \end{bmatrix} = \begin{bmatrix} 0 & -24 & 12 \\ 12 & 0 & -12 \\ -12 & 12 & 0 \end{bmatrix} \begin{bmatrix} p_2 \\ q_2 \\ 1 - p_2 - q_2 \end{bmatrix}.$$

Equating player 1's expected payoffs it follows that $p_2 = 4/12$ and $q_2 = 3/12$.

Exercise 9.1-3: Cournot Duopoly and Iterated Strict Dominance

(a) Player i's payoff is

$$u_i(q_i, q_{-i}) = p(q_i, q_{-i})q_i = (1 - q_i - q_{-i})q_i = (1 - q_{-i})q_i - q_i^2.$$

This a strictly concave function of q_i with a maximum at $q_i = \frac{1}{2}(1 - q_{-i})$. Hence

$$BR_i(q_{-i}) = \frac{1}{2}(1 - q_{-i}), q_{-i} \in A_{-i} = [0, 1].$$

(b) Therefore in a Nash equilibrium, $q_1 = \frac{1}{2}(1 - q_2)$ and $q_2 = \frac{1}{2}(1 - q_1)$. Solving, $q^N = (\frac{1}{3}, \frac{1}{3})$.

(c) We have shown that $BR_i(q_{-i}) = \frac{1}{2}(1 - q_{-i}), q_{-i} \in A_{-i} = [0, 1]$. Hence

$$BR_1(q_2) \le \underset{q_{-i} \in A_{-i}}{\text{Max}} \{\frac{1}{2}(1 - q_{-i})\} = \frac{1}{2}.$$

Moreover, by strict concavity $u_i(q_i, q_{-i})$ is strictly decreasing for all $q_i > \frac{1}{2}(1 - q_{-i})$. But $q_{-i} \in A_{-i} = [0, 1]$. Therefore

$$u_i(\tfrac{1}{2}, q_{-i}) > u_i(q_i, q_{-i}), q_i > \tfrac{1}{2}, \quad \text{for all} \quad Aq_{-i} \in A_{-i}.$$

Thus $q_i > \frac{1}{2}$ is dominated by $q_i = \frac{1}{2}$.

Eliminating the dominated strategies, we have shown that player i will choose $q_i \in [0, \frac{1}{2}]$.

(d) Define $A(\alpha) = [\frac{1}{3} - \alpha, \frac{1}{3} + \alpha]$. From (c), if $\alpha = \frac{1}{3}$ all strategies not in $A(\alpha)$ are strictly dominated. Arguing as in (c), $u_i(q_i, q_{-i})$ is strictly increasing for all $q_i < \frac{1}{2}(1 - q_{-i})$ and decreasing for all $q_i > \frac{1}{2}(1 - q_{-i})$. Suppose $A_{-i} \subset A(\alpha) = [\frac{1}{3} - \alpha, \frac{1}{3} + \alpha]$. It follows that $u_i(q_i, q_{-i})$ is strictly increasing for all

$$q_i < \underset{q_{-i} \in A(\alpha)}{\text{Min}} \{\tfrac{1}{2}(1 - q_{-i})\} = \tfrac{1}{3} - \tfrac{1}{2}\alpha.$$

And it is strictly decreasing, for all

$$q_i > \underset{q_{-i} \in A(\alpha)}{\text{Max}} \{\tfrac{1}{2}(1 - q_{-i})\} = \tfrac{1}{3} + \tfrac{1}{2}\alpha.$$

Thus $q_i \notin A(\frac{1}{2}\alpha) = [\frac{1}{3} - \frac{1}{2}\alpha, \frac{1}{3} + \frac{1}{2}\alpha]$ is a dominated strategy.

Eliminating these strategies, player i must choose a strategy in the interval $A(\frac{1}{2}\alpha) = [\frac{1}{3} - \frac{1}{2}\alpha, \frac{1}{3} + \frac{1}{2}\alpha]$.

(e) Repeating this argument k times, player i must choose a strategy in

$$A(\tfrac{1}{2^k}\alpha) = [\tfrac{1}{3} - \tfrac{1}{2^k}\alpha, \tfrac{1}{3} + \tfrac{1}{2^k}\alpha].$$

By choosing k large enough any $q_i \ne \frac{1}{3}$ can be eliminated in this way. Thus the only output satisfying iterated strict dominance is $q_i = \frac{1}{3}$.

9.2 Games with a History

Exercise 9.2-1: Centipede Game

(a) There are three sub-games. Consider the sub-game beginning with player 2's second move. He is better of choosing *Across* so the sub-game perfect equilibrium payoff vector is $(5, 5)$. Next consider the sub-game beginning with player 1's second move. If she chooses *Across* she gets the equilibrium payoff described above. Thus her best response is also *Across*. Repeating this argument, the unique sub-game perfect strategies are all *Across* so the equilibrium payoffs are $(5, 5)$.

(b) If in any round but the first, a player chooses *Down* then the best response of all players in prior rounds is to choose *Down*. And if player 1 chooses *Down* in the first round, the payoffs in the future rounds are irrelevant so playing *Down* in a future round is a best response. Thus the other Nash equilibrium outcome is $(1, 0)$.

(c) Player 2 prefers down at his second move. Then, arguing as in (b) all prior players will choose *Down* and so $(1, 0)$ is the sub-game perfect equilibrium outcome.

(d) In his second turn, Player 2 is indifferent. If he chooses *Across* with a sufficiently high probability all prior round players are strictly better off choosing *Across* and so the equilibrium outcome is $(6, 4)$. If in his second turn player 2 choose *Down* with sufficiently high probability, all prior players choose *Down* as well. Thus $(1, 0)$ is also a sub-game perfect equilibrium outcome.

(e) Consider the sub-game beginning at the final decision node. With $v = 4$, player 2 is indifferent between the two actions. Thus any mixed strategy is a best response. If player 2 chooses *Pass* with a probability of $p = 1/2$, player 1's expected payoff is $up = 3$. Therefore player 1 is indifferent between the two actions at the second last decision node. This argument can be repeated for each decision node. Thus there is a unique totally mixed strategy SPE of this game.

Exercise 9.2-3: Rubinstein Bargaining Game

(a) Suppose player 2 asks for x_2 in period 2. If player 1 rejects the present discounted value of his SPE payoff is δu_{13}. Thus it is a best response for player 1 to accept if and only if $v - x_2 \geq \delta u_{13}$. Then player 2's best response is to choose

$$\bar{x}_2 = \arg \text{Max}\{x_2 | v - x_2 \geq \delta u_{13}\} = v - \delta u_{13}.$$

It follows that player 2's SPE payoff in period 2 is $u_{22} = \bar{x}_2 = v - \delta u_{13}$.

(b) We can repeat this argument for player 1 in period 1 to show that

$$\bar{x}_1 = \arg \text{Max}\{x_1 | v - x_1 \geq \delta u_{22}\} = v - \delta u_{22}.$$

Therefore

$$u_{11} = \bar{x}_1 = v - \delta u_{22}.$$

(c) The sub-game at $t = 3$ is identical to the infinitely repeated game.

(d) Setting $u_{13} = u_{11}$ yields two linear equation in two unknowns. Eliminating u_{22}, it follows that $u_{11} = \frac{1}{1+\delta}v$. Hence

$$u_{12} = v - u_{11} = \frac{\delta}{1+\delta}v.$$

(e) If player 1 demands the entire value of the project in every odd numbered period, a best response by player 2 is to accept every such demand. Given that player 2 acquiesces, player 1's best response is to demand the full value pie in every odd numbered period. If instead player 2 demands the entire value in every even numbered period it is best response for player 1 to end the game in period 1. Since the present value of player 2's period 2 demand is δv player 1 asks for $\bar{x}_1 = v - \delta v$.

9.3 Duopoly Games

Exercise 9.3-1: Alternating Move Pricing Game as Substitutability Grows Large

(a) From (9.3-3), $\theta p_2 = \frac{\theta}{2(1+\theta)}(1 + \theta p_1)$. Hence $z_2 = \frac{\theta}{2(1+\theta)}(1 + z_1)$.

From (9.3-5), $\theta p_1 = \frac{2\theta + 2\theta^2}{4 + 8\theta + \theta^2}(1 + \theta p_2)$. Hence $z_1 = \frac{2\theta + 2\theta^2}{4 + 8\theta + 3\theta^2}(1 + z_2)$.

(b) Taking the limit as $\theta \to \infty$,

$$z_2 = \tfrac{1}{2}(1 + z_1) \quad \text{and} \quad z_1 = \tfrac{2}{3}(1 + z_2).$$

Solving, $(z_1, z_2) = (\tfrac{6}{4}, \tfrac{5}{4})$.

(c) Because $q_i = 1 - p_i + \theta(p_j - p_i) = 1 - \frac{z_i}{\theta} + (z_j - z_i)$. In the limit as $\theta \to \infty$ it follows that $(q_1, q_2) \to (\tfrac{3}{4}, \tfrac{5}{4})$.

Exercise 9.3-3: Cournot Production Game with a Competitive Fringe

(a) Arguing as in the previous exercise,

$$U_j(q) = (a - c_j - q_1 - q_2)q_j.$$

For an equilibrium $q^N = (q_1^N, q_2^N)$ with only firm 1 producing (so that $q_2^N = 0$), it is necessarily the case that $\frac{\partial}{\partial q_1} U(q^N) = 0$ and $\frac{\partial}{\partial q_2} U(q^N) \leq 0$. That is,

$$a - c_1 - 2q_1^N = 0 \quad \text{and} \quad a - c_2 - q_1^N \leq 0.$$

From the first condition $q_1^N = \tfrac{1}{2}(a - q_1)$. This is the monopoly output. Then the equilibrium price is the monopoly price, $p = \tfrac{1}{2}(a + c_1)$. Substituting for q_1^N in the second condition yields the following inequality:

$$c_2 \geq \tfrac{1}{2}(a + c_1).$$

Thus firm 2 will enter if and only if its unit cost is below the monopoly price. If this condition holds the first-order condition for firm 2 is $\frac{\partial}{\partial q_2} U(q^N) = 0$. The Nash equilibrium output vector must therefore satisfy the following FOC:

$$a - c_1 - q_2 - 2q_1 = 0 \quad \text{and} \quad a - c_2 - q_1 - 2q_2 = 0.$$

Solving, $q_1^N = \frac{2}{3}(a - c_1) + \frac{1}{3}(a - c_2)$ and $q_2^N = \frac{2}{3}(a - c_2) + \frac{1}{3}(a - c_1)$.

(b) $\frac{\partial U_j}{\partial q_j} = (a - c_2 - \sum_{i=1}^{n} q_i) - q_j = p - c_2 - q_j$.

Thus if the price is above c_2, the unit cost for each fringe firm, all $n-1$ of these firms produce a strictly positive quantity. Moreover, if the price is below c_2 none of the fringe firms will produce. Thus the necessary and sufficient condition for entry is exactly the same as in the case of two firms. Given that this is the case, the FOC for firm 1 is

$$\frac{\partial U_1}{\partial q_1} = (a - c_1 - s) - q_1 = 0, \quad \text{where} \quad s = \sum_{i=1}^{n} q_i.$$

The FOC for each of the other firms is

$$\frac{\partial U_1}{\partial q_j} = (a - c_2 - s) - q_j = 0.$$

Summing over the n firms,

$$(a - c_1 - s) + (n - 1)(a - c_2 - s) = s.$$

Then $s = \frac{1}{n+1}(a - c_1) + \frac{n-1}{n+1}(a - c_2)$. Hence

$$p - c_2 = a - c_2 - s = \frac{2}{n+1}\left[(a - c_2) - \frac{1}{2}(a - c_1)\right].$$

(c) Note that as the number of fringe firms increases, the Nash equilibrium price declines toward the unit cost of the fringe firms.

Exercise 9.3-5: Production Game with Three Firms and Sequential Entry

(a) Firm j's profit is $U_j(q) = (p(q) - c)q_j$.

Firm 3 observes the preceding moves and chooses q_3 to maximize $U_3(q) = (p(q) - c)q_3$. The FOC is

$$\frac{\partial}{\partial q_3} U_3(q) = (p(q) - c) + \frac{\partial p}{\partial q_3} q_3 = a - c - q_1 - q_2 - 2q_3 = 0.$$

Hence $q_3^{BR} = \frac{1}{2}(a - c - q_1 - q_2)$.

(b) Firm 2 anticipates firm 3's best response so its profit is

$$U_2(q_1, q_2) = (p - c)q_2 = (a - c - q_1 - q_2 - q_3^{BR})q_2$$
$$= \frac{1}{2}(a - c - q_1 - q_2)q_2.$$

(c) Setting $\frac{\partial U_2}{\partial q_2} = 0$ it follows that $q_2^{BR} = \frac{1}{2}(a - c - q_1)$.

(d) Appealing to part (a), $q_3^{BR} = \frac{1}{2}(a - c - q_1 - q_2) = \frac{1}{4}(a - c - q_1)$. Then

$$U_1 = (a - c - q_1 - q_2^{BR} - q_3^{BR})q_1 = \frac{1}{4}(a - c - q_1)q_1.$$

It follows that $U_1(q_1)$ takes on its maximum at $q_1^N = \frac{1}{2}(a - c)$.

(e) From (c) $q_2^N = \frac{1}{4}(a - c)$. From (a) $q_3^N = \frac{1}{8}(a - c)$. Total output is therefore $s = (\frac{1}{2} + \frac{1}{4} + \frac{1}{8})(a - c)$, and so the difference between the equilibrium price and unit cost is

$$p - c = a - c - s = (1 - (\tfrac{1}{2} + \tfrac{1}{4} + \tfrac{1}{8}))(a - c) = \tfrac{1}{8}(a - c).$$

Remark: Note that each firm produces half of the output of the firm that moves immediately before it. Extending this argument it can be shown that with four firms the fourth firm produces $\frac{1}{16}(a - c)$ and so on. Then, in the limit,

$$p - c = a - c - s = \left(1 - \left(\sum_1^\infty \frac{1}{2^n}\right)\right)(a - c) = 0.$$

Exercise 9.3-7: War of Attrition

(a) Appealing to (9.3-9),

$$u_1(t, \bar{s}_2) = (1 - \mu(t))[a B(t) + e^{-rt}\frac{m}{r}] + \int_0^t [a B(s) + e^{-rs}\frac{n}{r}]\mu'(s)ds.$$

Then

$$\frac{\partial}{\partial t}u_1(t, \bar{s}_2) = (1 - \mu(t))[a B'(t) + -re^{-rt}\frac{m}{r}]$$
$$- \mu'(t)[a B(t)e^{-rt}\frac{m}{r}] + [a B(t) + e^{-rt}\frac{n}{r}]\mu'(t).$$

Substituting for $B'(t) = e^{-rt}$,

$$\frac{\partial}{\partial t}u_1(t, \bar{s}_2) = e^{-rt}[(1 - \mu(t))(a - m) - \mu'(t)\frac{n - m}{r}].$$

Setting this expression equal to zero yields condition (9.3-8).

(b) Because $\mu(0) = 0$, $u_1(0, \bar{s}_2) = \frac{m}{r}$. Thus the symmetric equilibrium expected profit is the payoff to the mover. The war of attrition wipes out the additional gain to not moving.

(c) From the analysis in the chapter we know that in equilibrium

$$\frac{\mu_1'(t)}{1 - \mu_1(t)} = p = \frac{\mu_2'(t)}{1 - \mu_2(t)}$$

and therefore that $\mu_i(t) = 1 - k_i e^{-pt}, i = 1, 2$.

We also know that there can be no mass points at $t > 0$. An almost identical argument establishes that both cannot choose zero with positive probability.

However, all the necessary and sufficient conditions for equilibrium are satisfied if

$$\text{Min}\{k_1, k_2\} < 1 = \text{Max}\{k_1, k_2\}.$$

(d) Let $\mu(t)$ be the symmetric equilibrium mixed strategy. Let $v(t)$ be the probability that at least one of any two firms moves before time t. Then

$$1 - v(t) = (1 - \mu(t))^2.$$

Arguing as earlier, firm i will be indifferent between moving and staying at every moment if the probability it faces is given by the following equation:

$$1 - v(t) = e^{-pt}.$$

Then $1 - \mu(t) = (1 - v(t))^{1/2} = e^{-pt/2}$.

9.4 Infinitely Repeated Games

Exercise 9.4-1: Repeated Cournot Production Game

(a) Given output vector q, the payoff to firm j is

$$u_j(q) = (p - c - q_1 - q_2)q_j = (12 - q_1 - q_2)q_j, \quad j = 1, 2. \qquad (9.5\text{-}2)$$

Hence $u_1(q) + u_2(q) = (12 - q_1 - q_2)(q_1 + q_2)$. This takes on its maximum at $q_1 + q_2 = 6$.

(b) If firm 2 chooses q_2, firm 1's best response solves

$$\text{Max}_{q_1}\{u_1(q_1, x) = (12 - q_1 - q_2)q_1 = (12 - q_2)q_1 - q_1^2\}.$$

Solving,

$$q_1^* = \tfrac{1}{2}(12 - q_2). \qquad (9.5\text{-}3)$$

Arguing symmetrically, firm 2 has a best response $q_2^* = \tfrac{1}{2}(12 - q_1)$. In a Nash equilibrium both outputs are best responses. Solving, $q^N = (4, 4)$; hence $u_j(q^N) = 16$.

(c) Consider the symmetric cooperative output vector $q = (x, x)$. From (9.5-2),

$$u_1^C = u_1(x, x) = (12 - 2x)x.$$

If firm 1 chooses to defect, it maximizes its short-run gain by choosing its best response $q_1^D = \tfrac{1}{2}(12 - x)$. Then the short-run payoff to defecting is

$$u_1^D = u_1(q_1^D, x) = \tfrac{1}{4}(12 - x)^2.$$

From (9.4-1), the defection is unprofitable if

$$\delta \le \frac{N(x)}{D(x)}.$$

where

$$\frac{N(x)}{D(x)} = \frac{u_1^C - u_1^N}{u_1^D - u_1^C} = \frac{(12 - 2x)x - 16}{\frac{1}{4}(12 - x)^2 - (12 - 2x)x}. \qquad (9.5\text{-}4)$$

The symmetric efficient outcome $q^C = (3, 3)$ is therefore an equilibrium of the repeated game if the inequality holds for $x = 3$. Substituting, $\delta > \frac{9}{17}$.

(d) Define $\frac{N(x)}{D(x)} = \frac{\frac{1}{4}(12-x)^2 - (12-2x)x}{\frac{1}{4}(12-2x)^2 - 16}$.

Both the numerator and denominator approach zero as $x \to 4$. Appealing to l'Hopital's Rule

$$\lim_{x \to 4} \frac{N(x)}{D(x)} = \lim_{x \to 4} \frac{N'(x)}{D'(x)} = \lim_{x \to 4} \frac{7x - 12}{12 - x} = 2.$$

Thus for all cooperative output vectors $q^C = (x, x)$, sufficiently close to $q^N = (4, 4)$, $\frac{N(x)}{D(x)} > 1$ so that cooperation is sustainable for all discount factors.

Exercise 9.4-3: Cournot Game with a *T*-Period Threat From Section 9.3, all defections are unprofitable if and only if

$$u_j^D - u_j^C - \frac{\delta - \delta^T}{1 - \delta}(u_j^C - u_j^N) \le 0.$$

From (D-15),

$$\frac{u_1^C - u_1^N}{u_1^D - u_1^C} = \frac{(12 - 2x)x - 16}{\frac{1}{4}(12 - x)^2 - (12 - 2x)x} = \frac{8}{9} \quad \text{with} \quad x = 3.$$

Thus defections are unprofitable if and only if

$$\frac{1 - \delta}{\delta - \delta^T} \le \frac{8}{9}.$$

10 Games with Asymmetric Information

10.1 Games of Incomplete Information

Exercise 10.1-1: Batman and the Joker

(a) The extensive form of the game is depicted in Figure 10.4-1.
(b) Suppose that Batman chooses the Tower. The Joker's best response is to go to the Museum. And given that the Joker chooses the Museum, Batman is better off doing so as well. Thus it is not an equilibrium strategy for Batman to

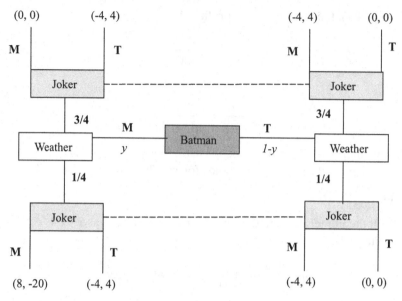

Figure 10.4-1. Game tree.

choose the Tower. An almost identical argument establishes that it is not an equilibrium strategy for Batman to choose the Museum.

(c) Let y be the probability Batman chooses M.

Suppose that the weather is bad and consider the Joker's payoffs.

$$U_J^{Bad}(M) = y(-20) + (1 - y)4 = 4 - 24y, \quad U_J^{Bad}(T) = 4y.$$

Then mix if $4 - 24y = 4y$ (that is, if $y = \frac{1}{7}$), and choose T if $y > \frac{1}{7}$. Suppose that the weather is good

$$U_J^G(M) = 4(1 - y), \quad U_J^G(T) = 4y$$

so mix if $y = \frac{1}{2}$ and choose T if $y > \frac{1}{2}$.

Thus for an equilibrium in mixed strategies there are two possible values of y.

(d) We consider here $y = \frac{1}{2}$. Then if the weather is good the Joker chooses the Tower. Suppose that the Batman chooses the Museum. The Joker plays a mixed strategy when the weather is bad so his expected payoff is

$$U_B(M) = (3/4)(-4) + (1/4)(x8 + (1 - x)(-4)) = 3x - 4.$$

If he chooses the Tower his payoff is $U_B(T) = \frac{1}{4}x(-4) = -x$. For equilibrium Batman must be indifferent so $3x - 4 = -x$. Then $x = 1$.

Exercise 10.1-3: All Pay Auction

(a) Let $B(\theta)$ be the symmetric equilibrium bid function. Then, if all other bidders bid according to the equilibrium strategy, buyer i, with value θ_i, wins if he has the highest value. Thus his win probability is $w(\theta_i) = F^{n-1}(\theta_i)$. If he bids when his value is θ his payoff is

$$u = w(\theta_i)\theta - B(\theta_i).$$

This is a lower bound for his equilibrium payoff $u(\theta) = w(\theta)\theta - B(\theta)$. Arguing exactly as earlier, it follows that

$$\frac{du}{d\theta}(\theta_i) = w(\theta_i) = F^{n-1}(\theta_i).$$

In the uniform case with two bidders, it follows that

$$\frac{du}{d\theta} = F(\theta) = \theta.$$

Integrating,

$$u(\theta) = \tfrac{1}{2}\theta^2.$$

Also $u(\theta) = w(\theta)\theta - B(\theta) = \theta^2 - B(\theta)$. Therefore $B(\theta) = \tfrac{1}{2}\theta^2$.

(b) With n bidders $\frac{du}{d\theta} = w(\theta) = \theta^{n-1}$. Integrating,

$$u(\theta) = \tfrac{1}{n}\theta^n.$$

Also $u(\theta) = w(\theta)\theta - B(\theta) = \theta^n - B(\theta)$. Therefore $B(\theta) = \frac{n-1}{n}\theta^n$.

(c) In the general case,

$$\frac{du}{d\theta} = w(\theta) = F^{n-1}(\theta).$$

Therefore $u(\theta) = \int_0^\theta F^{n-1}(x)dx = w(\theta)\theta - B(\theta) = F^{n-1}(\theta)\theta - B(\theta)$.
Then $B(\theta) = F^{n-1}(\theta)\theta - \int_0^\theta F^{n-1}(x)dx$.

10.2 Refinements of Nash Equilibrium

Exercise 10.2-1: Multiple Sequential Equilibria

(a) In a BNE beliefs are common knowledge. Thus player 2 responds knowing that the two types are equally likely. If both types choose *Out*, the game is over so it is a best response for player 2 to choose *High*. And if this is the case, both Type 1 players are worse off choosing *Enter* than choosing *Fight*. Thus the strategies in the first row are BNE strategies.

If both types enter, player 2's expected payoff if she chooses *High* is $(\tfrac{1}{2})(5) + (\tfrac{1}{2})(-2) = 1\tfrac{1}{2}$. If player 2 chooses *Medium* her expected payoff is $(\tfrac{1}{2})(-1) + (\tfrac{1}{2})(1) = 0$. If she chooses *Low* her payoff is 2. Thus *Low* is a best response. Given that she chooses *Low*, both entrants are better off choosing *E*.

On the proposed equilibrium path it is only the strong player 1 that enters. Given common knowledge beliefs, player 2 knows this so her best response is

Low. But if player 2 chooses *Low* player 1's best response is to *Enter* when weak. Therefore *Out* is not a best response.

(b) In a perfect Bayesian equilibrium there must be a strategy at every node in the tree. There must also be beliefs that are consistent with Bayes' Law so that the strategy at every node is a best response. Consider the first equilibrium and suppose that the weak player trembles with probability ε while the strong player trembles with probability ε^2. Then if player 1 enters, the conditional probability that he is weak is

$$\Pr\{w|E\} = \frac{p\varepsilon}{p\varepsilon + (1-p)\varepsilon^2} = \frac{p}{p + (1-p)\varepsilon}.$$

As $\varepsilon \to 0$ the probability approaches 1. Thus it is a best response for player 2 to choose *High* when ε is sufficiently small. Then the equilibrium is trembling-hand perfect and so is sequential.

In the second equilibrium all decision nodes are reached so it is sequential as well.

(c) Consider the equilibrium in which neither enters. Suppose instead that the strong entrant chooses E and claims to be the strong type. He argues that player 2 should respond with *Medium* rather than *High*. Note that if player 2 does so, player 2's payoff is -1 rather than -2, and player 1's payoff is 1 rather than -1. Moreover, if it were anticipated that player 2 would make such a response, player 1 is worse off entering if he is the weak type. Thus the equilibrium fails the Intuitive Criterion.

Exercise 10.2-3: Signaling Equilibrium with Two Types

(a) In a PBE the minimum expected productivity is 1; thus the wage of the low type in a separating equilibrium is 1. If the equilibrium is separating, the firms bid up the wage of that worker who chooses $z > 0$ to $w(z) = 2$. Type 1 workers must prefer not to signal. Thus

$$u_1(z, w(z)) = w(z) - z = 2 - z \le 1.$$

Therefore $z \ge 1$. Type 2 workers must prefer the separating outcome to not signaling. Therefore

$$u_2(z, w(z)) = 2 - z(1 - \varepsilon) \ge 1.$$

Hence $z \le 1/(1 - \varepsilon)$.

(b) If no one signals, the expected productivity is $1p + 2(1 - p) = 2 - p$. Thus the equilibrium wage is $2 - p$.

(c) Consider the PBE depicted in Figure 10.4-2 and the off-the-equilibrium action $\hat{z}$. Type 1 workers are worse off choosing $\hat{z}$ regardless of which type they are believed to be. A type 2 worker is better off choosing $\hat{z}$ if it is believed that she

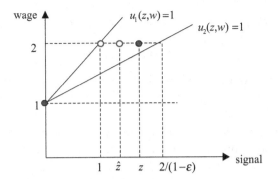

Figure 10.4-2. Separating PBE.

cannot be a type 1 worker (and must therefore be a type 2 worker.) Thus the PBE fails the Intuitive Criterion. Because thus argument holds for any $z > 1$, all such PBE fail the Intuitive Criterion. Finally, if $z = 1$, for any $\hat{z} < 1$ a type 1 worker is better off choosing $\hat{z}$ if beliefs are sufficiently favorable.

(d) With signal $z = 1$ the PBE payoffs are $u_1(1, 1) = 1$ and $u_2(2, z) = 1 + \varepsilon$. Thus in the limit the payoffs both approach 1. In the pooling PBE the equilibrium wage is $w(p) = 2 - p$. Thus the pooling PBE wage approaches 2. With full information the wages are 1 and 2. Note that as $(p, \varepsilon) \to 0$ the worker is almost certainly a high-productivity worker. Thus there is an extreme discontinuity between the separating PBE and the other equilibria at the limit.

10.3 Games with Unobservable Strategies and Public Signals

Exercise 10.3-1: One-Stage Deviation Principle with Private Strategies

(a) The history of the game for player i is his history of strategies played and the history of public signals. A strategy at stage t is $s^t(h^t) = (s_1^t(h_1^t), \ldots, s_I^t(h_I^t))$. Suppose that $\bar{s} = \{\bar{s}^t(h^t)\}_{t=1}^{\infty}$ satisfies the one-stage deviation principle. Let $s = \{s^t(h^t)\}_{t=1}^{\infty}$ be some other strategy profile. Define $\bar{s}(\theta)$ to be the strategy profile that agrees with s for $t < \theta$ and with $\bar{s}$ for $t \geq \theta$; that is,

$$\bar{s}(\theta) = (s^1, \ldots, s^{\theta-1}(h^{\theta-1}), \bar{s}^{\theta}(h^{\theta}), \ldots).$$

Because there is no one-stage deviation from $\bar{s}$ that benefits any player, there is no one-stage deviation from $\bar{s}(\theta)$ for any stage t sub-game where $t \geq \theta$.

We consider finite deviations by player i. Suppose that stage a is the last stage at which, for some history, this player deviates. Then the strategy profile s agrees with $\bar{s}$ for $t \geq a + 1$ so that $s = \bar{s}(a + 1)$. The rest of the argument follows exactly that in the proof of Proposition 9.2-2.

(b) The proof is exactly the same as the proof of Proposition 9.4-4.

11 Incentive Compatibility and Mechanism Design

11.1 Incentive Compatibility

Exercise 11.1-1: Sufficient Condition for Single Crossing Consider any (q^0, r^0) and (q^1, r^1) where $q^1 > q^0$ such that $u(\theta, q^1, r^1) - u(\theta, q^0, r^0) \geq 0$. As in the proof of necessity choose $\hat{r}$ so that $u(\theta, q^1, \hat{r}) - u(\theta, q^0, r^0) = 0$ and consider points $(q(\lambda), r(\lambda))$ on the indifference curve through (q^0, r^0) where $q(\lambda) = q_0 + \lambda(q^1 - q^0)$. Arguing as in the proof of necessity, for any $\phi > \theta$

$$\frac{d}{d\lambda} u(\phi, q(\lambda), r(\lambda)) = (q^1 - q^0) u_r [\text{MRS}(\phi, q, r) - \text{MRS}(\theta, q, r)].$$

By hypothesis $\text{MRS}(\phi, q, r) > \text{MRS}(\theta, q, r)$ for $\phi > \theta$. Thus, for all $\lambda \in [0, 1]$

$$\frac{d}{d\lambda} u(\phi, q(\lambda), r(\lambda)) > 0.$$

Therefore $u(\phi, q^1, \hat{r}) = u(\phi, q(1), r(1)) > u(\phi, q^0, r^0)$. By hypothesis $u(\cdot)$ is an increasing function and $\hat{r} \leq r^1$. Thus $u(\phi, q^1, r^1) > u(\phi, q^0, r^0)$.

Exercise 11.1-3: Educational Signaling with Continuously Distributed Types Assume $\{q(\theta), r(\theta)\}_{\theta \in \Theta}$ is (piecewise) differentiable. In a separating equilibrium the consultant's wage is bid up to his value so $r(\theta) = k\theta$. To satisfy incentive compatibility (IC)

$$u(\theta, q(x), r(x)) \leq u(\theta, q(\theta), r(\theta)).$$

Then $u(\theta, q(x), kx) = kx - \frac{q(x)}{\theta^2}$ takes on its maximum at $x = \theta$.

(a) FOC: $k - \frac{q'(\theta)}{\theta^2} = 0$.

(b) Define $V(\theta) = u(\theta, q(\theta), r(\theta)) = k\theta - \frac{q(\theta)}{\theta^2}$.

Then

$$V'(\theta) = \frac{d}{d\theta}\left(k\theta - \frac{q(\theta)}{\theta^2}\right) = \left(k - \frac{q'(\theta)}{\theta^2}\right) + \frac{2q(\theta)}{\theta^3}.$$

Appealing to the FOC, the expression in parentheses is zero. Therefore

$$V'(\theta) = \frac{2q(\theta)}{\theta^3}.$$

(c) Hence $\frac{1}{2}\theta V'(\theta) = \frac{q(\theta)}{\theta^2}$. Substituting into the expression for $V(\theta)$,

$$V(\theta) = k\theta - \frac{1}{2}\theta V'(\theta).$$

Hence

$$2\theta V(\theta) + \theta^2 V'(\theta) = k\theta^2.$$

(d) Integrating,

$$\theta^2 V(\theta) = \tfrac{2}{3}\theta^3 + k.$$

Because $V(0) = 0$ it follows that $k = 0$ and so $V(\theta) = \tfrac{2}{3}k\theta$.

(e) $u(\theta, q(x), r(x)) = u(\theta, q(x), R(q(x))) = R(q(x)) - \frac{q(x)}{\theta^2}$.

Then the FOC is

$$\left(R'(q(\theta))\right) - \frac{1}{\theta^2}q'(\theta) = 0.$$

so that

$$R'(q(\theta)) = \frac{1}{\theta^2}.$$

(f) Also, in equilibrium $R(q(\theta)) = k\theta$. Then $R(q)^2 R'(q) = k^2$.
(g) Integrating, $\tfrac{1}{3}R(q)^3 = k^2 q$. Then $R(q) = (3k^2 q)^{1/3}$.

11.2 Information Revelation, Adverse Selection, and Signaling

Exercise 11.2-1: Choice of Signals

(a) There are two types. Type 1 has a value of a so is better off not signaling and earning his outside wage of $r_0 > a$. We look for a separating equilibrium satisfying the Intuitive Criterion. Then the local upward constraint must be binding.
  (i) The equilibrium payoffs are $\{(0, r_0), (x, 2a)\}$. With signal x, the payoff to signaling is $u_1(\theta, r_2, x) = u_1(\theta, 2, x) = 2a - C(\theta, x) = 2a - x/\theta$.

The local upward constraint must be binding. Therefore

$$u_1(1, 2, x) = 2a - x = r_0.$$

Thus $x = 2a - r_0$ and so type 2's equilibrium payoff is

$$u_1(2, 2, x) = 2a - \tfrac{1}{2}x = a + \tfrac{1}{2}r_0.$$

  (ii) With signal y the payoff to signaling is $u_2(\theta, r_2, y) = 2a - C(\theta, y) = 2a - y^2/\theta$. Type 1 must be indifferent between signaling and accepting the outside alternative. Therefore

$$u_2(1, 2, y) = 2a - y^2 = r_0.$$

Thus $y^2 = 2a - r_0$ and so type 2's equilibrium payoff is

$$u_2(2, 2, y) = 2a - \tfrac{1}{2}y^2 = a + \tfrac{1}{2}r_0.$$

Note that the outcome is exactly the same as with signal x. There is an easy explanation. We could have begun by defining the new variable $x = y^2$ and then (ii) is identical to (i).

(iii) With signal z the payoff to signaling is $u_3(\theta, \theta_2, z) = 2a - C(\theta, z) = 2a - z/\theta^2$. Type 1 must be indifferent between signaling and accepting the outside alternative. Therefore

$$u_3(1, 2, z) = 2a - z = r_0.$$

Thus $z = 2a - r_0$ and so type 2's equilibrium payoff is

$$u_3(2, 2, z) = 2a - z/\theta_2^2 = 2a - z/4 = \tfrac{3}{2}a + \tfrac{1}{4}w_0.$$

(b) $u_3(2, 2, z) - u_1(2, 2, x) = (\tfrac{3}{2}a + \tfrac{1}{4}w_0) - (a + \tfrac{1}{2}w_0) = \tfrac{1}{4}(2a - w_0) > 0.$

Thus the high type is strictly better off using signal z rather than signal x (or y.) The reason is that the high type's cost of signaling is one-quarter that of the low type with signal z and one-half with signal x. Thus it is relatively more costly for the low type to mimic under signal x.

Exercise 11.2-3: Minimum Signals

(a) In a PBE the lowest type To satisfy the Intuitive Criterion the local upward constraint must be binding. Thus if θ_t is the lowest type that signals, type θ_{t-1} must be indifferent between signaling and staying out. Therefore $r_0 = u(\theta_{t-1}, r_t, q_t) = m(\theta_t) - C(\theta_{t-1}, q_t)$.

(b) If $m(\theta_{t-1}) > r_0$ there is some $\bar{q} \in (0, q_t)$ such that $r_0 = u(\theta_{t-1}, m(\theta_{t-1}), \bar{q}) = m(\theta_{t-1}) - C(\theta_{t-1}, \bar{q})$. Since higher types have lower signaling costs it follows that $u(\theta_{t-2}, \bar{q}, m(\theta_{t-1})) < r_0$. Also, from (a) $u(\theta_t, \bar{q}, m(\theta_{t-1})) < u(\theta_t, q_t, m(\theta_t))$. Then for $\delta > 0$ and sufficiently small, $r_0 < u(\theta_{t-1}, m(\theta_{t-1}), \bar{q} - \delta)$, $u(\theta_t, \bar{q} - \delta, m(\theta_{t-1})) < u(\theta_t, q_t, m(\theta_t))$ and $u(\theta_{t-2}, \bar{q} - \delta, m(\theta_{t-1})) < r_0$. Therefore if type θ_{t-1} takes the off-the-equilibrium-path action $\bar{q}$ and is believed to be type θ_{t-1}, this type is strictly better off while any other mimicking type would be strictly worse off. Thus the PBE fails the strong Intuitive Criterion. Therefore $m(\theta_{t-1}) \leq r_0$

(c) Combining the results, $C(\theta_t, q_t) = m(\theta_t) - r_0 \leq m(\theta_t) - m(\theta_{t-1})$. Taking the limit as $\theta_t - \theta_{t-1} \to 0$ it follows that $C(\theta_t, q_t) \to 0$ and hence $q_t \to 0$ and $m(\theta_t) \to r_0$.

Exercise 11.2–5: Educational Signaling

(a) $u(\theta, q, r) = r - B(q)/A(\theta).$

For incentive compatibility, $u(\theta, q(x), r(x))$ takes on its maximum at $x = \theta$. Therefore,

$$V(\theta) = \theta - B(q(\theta))/A(\theta)$$

(b) By the Envelope Theorem, the derivative of the maximized value $V(\theta) = \text{Max}_x\{u(\theta, q(x), r(x))\}$ is the partial derivative of the maximand; that is,

$$V'(\theta) = u_\theta(\theta, q(\theta), r(\theta)) = A'(\theta)B(q(\theta))/A^2(\theta).$$

Multiplying the expression for $V(\theta)$ by $A'(\theta)$ and the last expression by $A(\theta)$ and adding,

$$A(\theta)V'(\theta) + A'(\theta)V(\theta) = \theta A'(\theta).$$

(c) Integrating both sides,

$$A(\theta)V(\theta) - A(\alpha)V(\alpha) = \int_\alpha^\theta x A'(x)dx.$$

(d) Integrating the right-hand side by parts and rearranging,

$$V(\theta) = \theta - \int_\alpha^\theta \frac{A(x)}{A(\theta)}dx.$$

(e) Because $A_2(\theta)/A_1(\theta)$ is strictly increasing, $\frac{A_2(\theta)}{A_1(\theta)} > \frac{A_2(x)}{A_1(x)} \forall x < \theta$. Rearranging this inequality, $\frac{A_1(x)}{A_1(\theta)} > \frac{A_2(x)}{A_2(\theta)}, x < \theta$. Appealing to (d), $V_1(\theta) < V_2(\theta), \theta > \alpha$.

Exercise 11.2-7: Choosing a Signaling Technology

(a) This is the case discussed in Section 11.1. The equilibrium payoff is $V_1(\theta) = \frac{1}{2}\theta$.
(b) The utility of a type θ worker who chooses the outcome $(z(x), r(x)) = (z(x), x)$ is

$$u(\theta, z(x), r(x)) = x - \frac{z(x)}{1 + \theta^2}.$$

Then $V_2(\theta) = \theta - \frac{z(\theta)}{1+\theta^2}$. Appealing to the Envelope Theorem, $V_2'(\theta) = \frac{2\theta z(\theta)}{(1+\theta^2)^2}$. Eliminating $z(\theta)$,

$$(1 + \theta^2)V_2'(\theta) + 2\theta V_2(\theta) = 2\theta^2.$$

Integrating,

$$V_2(\theta) = \frac{2\theta^3}{3(1 + \theta^2)}.$$

(c) It is easily checked that $\frac{V_2(\theta)}{\theta} < \frac{V_1(\theta)}{\theta}$ on $[0, 1]$ so the first technology is superior.
(d) Technology 2 is now better for high types. The tricky issue is determining the set of types $[0, \hat{\theta}]$ that choose the first technology.

Exercise 11.2-9: Comparing the Finite Type and Continuous Type Models

(a) Since the local downward constraint holds, $V(\theta_{t+1}) = u(\theta_{t+1}, q_{t+1}, r_{t+1}) \geq u(\theta_{t+1}, q_t, r_t)$. Also $V(\theta_t) = u(\theta_t, q_t, r_t)$. Therefore $V(\theta_{t+1}) - V(\theta_t) \geq u(\theta_{t+1}, q_t, r_t) - u(\theta_t, q_t, r_t)$.

(b) Argue essentially as in the answer to (a).

(c) Divide each of the inequalities by $\theta_{t+1} - \theta_t$.

(d) Take the limit under the assumption of continuity.

11.3 Mechanism Design

Exercise 11.3-1: Profit-Maximizing Plans with Three Types

(a) First note that $B_t(q) = 140q - \frac{1}{2}b_t q^2$. Hence the informational rent for type 2 is

$$B_2(q_1) - B_1(q_1) = \frac{1}{2}(b_1 - b_2)q_1^2 = q_1^2.$$

Also the informational rent for type 3 is

$$[B_2(q_1) - B_1(q_1)] + [B_3(q_2) - B_3(q_2)]$$
$$= \frac{1}{2}(b_1 - b_2)q_1^2 + (b_2 - b_3)q_2^2 = q_1^2 + \frac{1}{2}q_2^2.$$

Appealing to (11.2-6)–(11.2-8), the revenue for the three types is as follows:

$$R_1 = 140q_1 - 2q_1^2.$$

$$R_2 = 140q_2 - q_2^2 - q_1^2.$$

$$R_3 = 140q_3 - \frac{1}{2}q_3^2 - (q_1^2 + \frac{1}{2}q_2^2).$$

Subtracting the costs, total profit is

$$U_0 = \sum_{t=1}^{3} f_t(R_t - C_t) = f_1\left(120q_1 - 2q_1^2\right) + f_2\left(120q_2 - q_2^2 - q_1^2\right)$$

$$+ f_3\left(120q_3 - \frac{1}{2}q_3^2 - (q_1^2 + \frac{1}{2}q_2^2)\right).$$

Then

$$\frac{\partial U_0}{\partial q_1} = f_1(120 - 4q_1) - 2f_2q_1 - 2f_3q_1 = f_1(120 - 4q_1) - 2(1 - f_1)q_1.$$

$$\frac{\partial U_0}{\partial q_2} = f_2(120 - 2q_2) - 2f_3q_2.$$

$$\frac{\partial U_0}{\partial q_3} = f_3(120 - q_2).$$

Then U_0 takes on its maximum at

$$\bar{q} = \left(\frac{60 f_1}{1 + f_1}, \frac{60 f_2}{f_2 + f_3}, 120 \right) = \left(\frac{60 f_1}{1 + f_1}, \frac{60 f_2}{1 - f_1}, 120 \right).$$

Note that the denominator of $\bar{q}_2$ is smaller than the denominator of $\bar{q}_1$. Thus $\bar{q}_2 \geq \bar{q}_1$. Also $1 - f_1 = f_2 + f_3 \geq f_2$; thus $\bar{q}_2 \leq 60 < \bar{q}_3$. Thus the monotonicity constraint is satisfied and so $\bar{q}$ is the vector of optimal quantities.

(b) Note that fixing f_1 and increasing f_2 only affects the quantity of plan 2. Clearly $\bar{q}_3$ is unaffected because type 3 receives the socially optimal quantity. Also the revenue from all other types is affected equally by the informational rent of type 2. Thus the marginal profit from increasing q_1 is

$$\frac{\partial U_0}{\partial q_1} = f_1 \frac{d}{dq_1} (B_1(q_1) - C_1(q_1) - (1 - f_1)[B_2'(q_1) - B_1'(q_1)].$$

Then q_1^* is independent of f_2 and f_3.
Remark: This is a general property. Regardless of the number of types, the optimal quantity for type t depends on $(f_1, \ldots, f_t)$ but not on the way higher types are distributed.

Exercise 11.3-3: Monopoly and Product Quality

(a) Without loss of generality we suppose that there is one buyer of each type. Then the total surplus is

$$\sum_{t=1}^{3} (B_t(q_t) - 6q_t).$$

It is readily checked that the surplus-maximizing quality vector is $q^* = (4, 7, 8)$.

(b) The lowest type has no informational rent so pays $R_1 = B_1(q_1) = 10q_1 - \frac{1}{2}q_1^2$. The intermediate type has a rent equal to the difference between his value of the low-quality item and the low type's value; that is, $U_2 = B_2(q_1) - B_1(q_1) = 10q_1 - \frac{1}{2}q_1^2 = B_1(q_1)$. Then

$$R_2 = B_2(q_2) - U_2 = B_2(q_2) - B_1(q_1).$$

Type 3 has an additional rent of $B_3(q_2) - B_2(q_2) = 10q_2 - \frac{1}{2}q_2^2 = \frac{1}{2}B_2(q_2)$. Then

$$R_3 = B_3(q_3) - U_3 = B_3(q_3) - B_1(q_1) - \frac{1}{2}B_2(q_2).$$

Without loss of generality we suppose that there is one buyer of each type. Then the monopolist's profit is $U_0 = \sum_{t=1}^{3} (R_t - 6q_t)$.
Substituting for the revenue of each type and rearranging,

$$U_0 = [-B_1(q_1) - 6q_1] + [\tfrac{1}{2}B_2(q_2) - 6q_2] + [B_3(q_3) - 6q_3].$$

We solve by ignoring the monotonicity constraints. For a type 1 buyer to make a purchase, $B_1(q_1) \geq 0$. Thus the first bracket is maximized by setting $q_1 = 0$. For type 2 the gain is $\frac{1}{2} B_2(q_2) - 6q_2 = (10q_2 - \frac{1}{2}q_2^2) - 6q_2$. This is maximized at $q_2^M = 4$. For type 3 the gain is $B_3(q_3) - 6q_3 = 24q_3 - \frac{3}{2}q_3^2$. This is maximized at $q_3^M = 8$.

(c) Substitute back into the equations for R_2 and R_3.

Exercise 11.3-5: Indirect Price Discrimination without Quasi-Linear Preferences

(a) For the allocation $(q(\theta), r(\theta))$ to be efficient, no alternative allocation yielding at least as high a payoff to a type θ buyer can be more profitable. The Lagrangian for this optimization problem is

$$\mathcal{L} = r - cq + \lambda(u(\theta, q, r) - u(\theta, q(\theta), r(\theta))).$$

From the FOC

$$-\frac{u_q}{u_r} = c.$$

(b) Because $r = R(\theta, q, V)$ is the inverse of $V = u(\theta, q, r)$, $V = u(\theta, q, R(\theta, q, V))$. Differentiating by q,

$$u_q + u_r R_q = 0.$$

Then the necessary condition for efficiency can be rewritten as

$$R_q(\theta, q(\theta), r(\theta)) - c = 0.$$

The left-hand side is the consumer's marginal willingness to pay. Thus a type θ buyer is undersupplied if $R_q(\theta, q(\theta), r(\theta)) - c > 0$.

(c) Let $(q(\theta), r(\theta))_{\theta \in \Theta}$ be the incentive-compatible allocation rule and let $V(\theta) = u(\theta, q(\theta), r(\theta))$ be the payoff function. Applying standard arguments,

$$\frac{dV}{d\theta} = u_\theta(\theta, q(\theta), r(\theta)) = u_\theta(\theta, q(\theta), R(\theta, q(\theta), V(\theta))).$$

The profit of the monopolist is $R(\theta, q(\theta), V(\theta)) - cq(\theta)$. The monopoly than seeks an IC mechanism that maximizes total profit

$$\int_\alpha^\beta R(\theta, q(\theta), V(\theta)) f(\theta) d\theta \text{ where } \frac{dV}{d\theta} = u_\theta(\theta, q(\theta), R(\theta, q(\theta), V(\theta))).$$

(d) Given our assumptions an allocation rule $q(\theta)$ is incentive compatible if and only if it is non-decreasing. This is a standard control problem. The Hamiltonian is

$$H = R(\theta, q, V) - cq + \lambda g(\theta, q, V).$$

(e) Define $g(\theta, q, V) = u_\theta(\theta, q, R(\theta, q, V))$. The right-hand side is the partial derivative of $u(\theta, q, R(\phi, q, V))$ evaluated at $\phi = \theta$. Then

$$g_q(\theta, q, V) = \frac{\partial}{\partial q} \frac{\partial}{\partial \theta} u(\theta, q, R(\phi, q, V)) \text{ at } \phi = \theta$$

$$= \frac{\partial}{\partial \theta} \frac{\partial}{\partial q} u(\theta, q, R(\phi, q, V)) \text{ at } \phi = \theta.$$

The rest of the steps are exactly as in the discussion of optimal income taxation. It follows that

$$g_q(\theta, q, V) = u_r \frac{\partial}{\partial \theta} \left(\frac{u_q}{u_r} \right) > 0.$$

(f) The shadow price satisfies

$$\frac{d\lambda}{d\theta} = -\frac{\partial H}{\partial V} = -R_V - \lambda g_V.$$

Because $R_V < 0$ it follows that $\frac{d\lambda}{d\theta} > 0$ if $\lambda(\theta) = 0$. Then if $\lambda(\theta) \geq 0$, the shadow price is strictly positive for all higher types. But this is impossible because this is a free endpoint problem so $\lambda(\beta) = 0$. Therefore $\lambda(\theta) < 0$ for all $\theta < \beta$.

(g) At any point where the monotonicity constraint is not binding, the FOC is

$$R_q - c + \lambda(\theta)g_q = 0.$$

We have already argued that $g_q > 0$ and $\lambda(\theta) \leq 0$. Moreover the second inequality is strict unless $\theta = \beta$. Therefore $R_q(\theta, q(\theta), V(\theta)) - c \geq 0$ and the inequality is strict unless $\theta = \beta$.

Thus all but the highest type are undersupplied. Suppose finally that there is some interval $[\theta_1, \theta_2]$ over which the monotonicity constraint is binding and so $q(\theta)$ is constant overt this interval. By this argument, the types at the endpoints of this interval are undersupplied. Thus all those in between must be as well.

12 Auctions and Public Goods

12.1 Auctions

Exercise 12.1-1: Bidding When the Seller Sets a Reserve Price

(a) Suppose that the equilibrium bid function is $B(\cdot)$. All those with valuations above the reserve price will wish to bid somewhere between r and their valuation, because they win if they are the only bidder. Thus $b(r) = r$.

(b) Let $V(\theta) = u(\theta, w(\theta), B(\theta))$ be the equilibrium payoff for a buyer with value θ. If all other buyers bid according to their equilibrium strategies and, regardless of his value, buyer i bids $b(\theta_i)$, his win probability is the probability that θ_i is the highest value. Then $w(\theta_i) = F^{n-1}(\theta_i)$ and so his payoff is $u = F^{n-1}(\theta_i)(\theta - B(\theta_i))$. Note that the graph of this function is a line of slope $F^{n-1}(\theta_i)$. Because $B(\theta)$ is buyer i's best response when his value is θ, it follows that

$$V(\theta) \geq F^{n-1}(\theta_i)(\theta - B(\theta_i)).$$

Also $V(\theta_i) \geq F^{n-1}(\theta_i)(\theta_i - b(\theta_i))$. Then the equilibrium payoff function and the line have the same slope and so

$$\frac{dV}{d\theta}(\theta_i) = F^{n-1}(\theta_i).$$

(c) We have argued that $V(\theta) > 0$ if and only if $\theta > r$. Therefore

$$V(\theta_i) = V(\theta_i) - V(r) = \int_r^{\theta_i} F^{n-1}(\theta)d\theta.$$

Also $V(\theta_i) = F^{n-1}(\theta_i)(\theta_i - B(\theta_i))$. Then

$$B(\theta_i) = \theta_i - \int_r^{\theta_i} \frac{F(\theta)}{F(\theta_i)} d\theta.$$

(d) Under CSD $\frac{\overline{F}(x)}{\overline{F}(v)} \leq \frac{F(x)}{F(v)}$, $x < v$ Thus $\overline{B}(\theta) \geq B(\theta)$.

(e) The maximum bid is

$$B(1) = 1 - \int_r^1 F(x)^{n-1}dx.$$

It follows that if $\overline{F}(v) \leq F(v)$, then the maximum bid is higher.

Exercise 12.1-3: Shift in the Distribution of Values

(a) By standard arguments,

$$B(\theta_i) = \theta_i - \int_\alpha^{\theta_i} \frac{F^{n-1}(\theta)}{F^{n-1}(\theta_i)} d\theta.$$

and

$$\overline{B}(\theta_i) = \theta_i - \int_{\alpha+\kappa}^{\theta_i} \frac{\overline{F}^{n-1}(\theta)}{\overline{F}^{n-1}(\theta_i)} d\theta = \theta_i - \int_{\alpha+\kappa}^{\theta_i} \frac{F^{n-1}(\theta - \kappa)}{F^{n-1}(\theta_i - \kappa)} d\theta, \theta_i \in [\alpha + \kappa, \beta + \kappa].$$

Define $v = \theta - \kappa$. Then

$$\overline{B}(\theta_i) = \theta_i - \int_\alpha^{\theta_i-\kappa} \frac{F^{n-1}(v)}{F^{n-1}(v_i)} dv, \theta_i \in [\alpha + \kappa, \beta + \kappa].$$

Exercise 12.1-5: The Winner's Curse

(a) If buyer 1 bids $B(y)$ and all other buyers make their equilibrium bids $B(t_j)$, $j = 2, \ldots, n$, the expected benefit for buyer 1 is $\frac{1}{n} E\{t_1 + t_2 + \cdots + t_n | t_2, \ldots, t_n \leq y\}$ and the expected payment is $F(y)^{n-1} B(y)$.

Because types are independent, $\frac{1}{n} E\{t_1 | t_2, \ldots, t_n \leq y\} = t_1 F(y)^{n-1}$ and

$$E\{t_2 | t_2, \ldots, t_n \leq y\} = \int_{t_2=\alpha}^{y} \cdots \int_{t_n=\alpha}^{y} t_2 f(t_2) \ldots f(t_n) dt_2 \ldots dt_n$$

$$= \int_{t_2=\alpha}^{y} t_2 f(t_2) dt_2 F(y)^{n-2}.$$

Given symmetry it follows that

$$\frac{1}{n} E\{t_1 + t_2 + \cdots + t_n | t_2, \ldots, t_n \leq y\} = \frac{1}{n} t_1 F(y)^{n-1}$$

$$+ \frac{n-1}{n} F(y)^{n-2} \int_{t_2=\alpha}^{y} t_2 f(t_2) dt_2.$$

Thus the expected payoff for buyer 1 is

$$u_1(t_1, y) = \frac{1}{n} t_1 F(y)^{n-1} + \frac{n-1}{n} F(y)^{n-2} \int_{t_2=\alpha}^{y} t_2 f(t_2) dt_2 - F(y)^{n-1} B(y).$$

For the uniform case this can be rewritten as follows:

$$u_1(t_1, y) = \frac{1}{n} t_1 y^{n-1} + \frac{n-1}{2n} y^n - y^{n-1} B(y).$$

(b) Differentiating by y,

$$\frac{\partial}{\partial y} u_1(t_1, y) = \frac{n-1}{n} t_1 y^{n-2} + \frac{n-1}{2} y^{n-1} - \frac{d}{dy}(y^{n-1} B(y)).$$

For incentive compatibility, this must be zero at $y = t_1$.
Hence

$$0 = \frac{n-1}{n} y^{n-1} + \frac{n-1}{2} y^{n-1} - \frac{d}{dy}(y^{n-1} B(y)).$$

Rearranging yields

$$\frac{d}{dy}(y^{n-1} B(y)) = \frac{n-1}{2n}(n+2) y^{n-1}.$$

Integrating by y and noting that $B(0) = 0$ yields the equilibrium bid function.

(c) Define $a(x) = (1 - x)(1 + 2x)$, $x > 0$ and show that this is an increasing function if and only if $x \leq 1/4$.

Exercise 12.1-7: More Risk-Averse Buyers Bid More in a Sealed First-Price Auction

(a) If $h(x)$ is concave,

$$h(y) \leq h(x) + h'(x)(y - x).$$

Setting $y = 0$ yields the desired result.

We take the direct revelation approach. With risk-averse buyers, if all other buyers bid according to $B_A(\theta)$ and buyer i bids $B(x)$, his win probability is $w(x) = F^{n-1}(x)$ and so his expected utility is

$$u = F^{n-1}(x)U(\theta_i - B(x)).$$

Because $B(\theta_i)$ is his equilibrium best response,

$$\theta_i = \arg \underset{x}{\text{Max}} \{ F^{n-1}(x)U(\theta - B(x)) \}.$$

FOC

$$f(x)U(\theta - B_A(x)) - F(x)U'(\theta - B_A(x))B_A'(x) = 0 \quad \text{at} \quad x = \theta_1.$$

Therefore

$$B_A'(\theta) = \frac{f(\theta)}{F(\theta)} \frac{U(\theta - B_A(\theta))}{U'(\theta - B_A(\theta))}.$$

In the special risk-neutral case this reduces to

$$B_N'(\theta) = \frac{f(\theta)}{F(\theta)}(\theta - B_N(\theta)).$$

(c) Appealing to (a), $B_A'(\theta) > \frac{f(\theta)}{F(\theta)}(\theta - B_A(\theta))$, $\theta > 0$.

Suppose that $B_N(\theta^*) > B_A(\theta^*)$. Because $B_N(0) = B_A(0) = 0$, one possibility is that $B_N(\theta) > B_A(\theta)$ on the interval $(0, \theta^*]$. Alternatively there is some $\theta^{**} \in (0, \theta^*)$ such that

$$B_N(\theta^{**}) = B_A(\theta^{**}) \quad \text{and} \quad B_N(\theta) > B_A(\theta) \quad \text{on} \quad (\theta^{**}, \theta^*). \qquad (*)$$

Then

$$B_A(\theta^*) - B_A(\theta^{**}) = \int_{\theta^{**}}^{\theta*} B_A'(\theta)d\theta.$$

Appealing to (c),

$$\int_{\theta^{**}}^{\theta*} B_A'(\theta)d\theta > \int_{\theta^{**}}^{\theta^*} \frac{f(x)}{F(x)}(x - B_A(\theta)d\theta > \int_{\theta^{**}}^{\theta*} \frac{f(x)}{F(x)}(x - B_N(\theta)d\theta$$

$$= B_N(\theta^*) - B_N(\theta^{**}).$$

Then

$$B_A(\theta^*) - B_A(\theta^{**}) > B_N(\theta^*) - B_N(\theta^{**}).$$

(d) But this contradicts (*). Therefore there can be no such θ^*. We have therefore proved that $B_N(\theta) \le B_A(\theta)$. The final step is to show that the inequality must be strict for all $\theta > 0$. Suppose that for $\theta^* > 0$, $B_N(\theta^*) = B_A(\theta^*)$. Then compare the slopes of the bid functions at θ^* and show that $B_A'(\theta^*) > B_N'(\theta^*)$ and hence obtain a further contradiction.

12.2 Revenue Equivalence Theorem

Exercise 12.2-1: Optimal Auction with Finite Types

(a) In the sealed second-price auction a buyer's dominant strategy is to bid her value. Then the minimum bid is 1 and so $V(1) = 0$. A high-value buyer wins that item at a price of 1 with probability p or must pay 2. Therefore $V(2) = 1 - p$.

In the sealed first-price auction a low-value buyer bids 1 while the high-value buyer bids a mixed strategy with support $[1, \overline{b}]$ and c.d.f. $G(b) \in \mathbb{C}^1$. For all $b > 1$ his expected payoff is

$$V(2) = (1 - p + pG(b))(2 - b).$$

Because $G(1) = 0$ and $G(\overline{b}) = 1$ we can solve and show that $V(2) = 1 - p$.

(b) If the seller sets a reserve price he will set the price equal to 2. He sells at this price unless both buyers have a low value. Thus his expected payoff is

$$U_0(2) = 2(1 - (1 - p)^2) = 2p(2 - p).$$

In the sealed second-price auction with no reserve price the winning bid is 2 if both have a high value. Otherwise it is 1. Therefore the seller's expected payoff is

$$U_0(1) = 2p^2 + 1(1 - p^2) = 1 + p^2.$$

Then $U_0(1) - U_0(2) = 1 - 4p + p^2$. This is negative if and only if $p < \hat{p} = 2 - (3)^{1/2}$.

(c) We seek an equilibrium in which the high-value buyers bid b and the low-value buyers bid 1. The seller then chooses b so that a high-value buyer is indifferent between bidding 1 and bidding b. If his opponent bids according to the equilibrium strategy and buyer I bids 1 he ties with probability $1 - p$. Given the tie-breaking rule his win probability is $\frac{1}{2}(1 - p)$, and so his expected payoff is $\frac{1}{2}(1 - p)(2 - 1) = \frac{1}{2}(1 - p)$. If buyer I bids b he wins if his opponent's value is low and half the time if his opponent's value is high. Thus his win probability is $w(b) = 1 - p + \frac{1}{2}p = 1 - \frac{1}{2}p$. His expected payoff is therefore $(1 - \frac{1}{2}p)(2 - b)$. Thus

$$V^*(2) = \tfrac{1}{2}(1 - p) = (1 - \tfrac{1}{2}p)(2 - b).$$

12.3 Optimal Auctions

Exercise 12.3-1: Optimal Reserve Prices

(a) From Proposition 12.3-1,

$$\underset{\theta}{E}\{U_0(\theta)\} = \theta_0 + \underset{\theta}{E}\left\{\sum_{i=1}^{n} q_i(\theta)J_i(\theta_i)\right\} \quad \text{where } J_i(\theta_i) = \theta_i - \theta_0 - \frac{1 - F_i(\theta_i)}{f_i(\theta_i)}.$$

If the seller's value is zero and valuations are uniformly distributed on $[0, \beta]$ this reduces to

$$\underset{\theta}{E}\{U_0(\theta)\} = \underset{\theta}{E}\left\{\sum_{i=1}^{n} q_i(\theta)(2\theta_i - 1)\right\}.$$

If all values are below $\frac{1}{2}$ this is maximized by setting $q_i = 0$, $i = 1, \ldots, n$. If at least one value exceeds $\frac{1}{2}$, this is maximized by allocating the item to the buyer with the highest value. The principal can implement this allocation rule by setting a reserve price of $\frac{1}{2}$ and using either of the common auctions.

(b) With the shift in the distribution the principal's expected payoff becomes

$$\underset{\theta}{E}\{U_0(\theta)\} = \underset{\theta}{E}\left\{\sum_{i=1}^{n} q_i(\theta)(2\theta_i - \beta)\right\}.$$

If $\beta < 2\alpha$ then $2\theta_i - \beta < 0$ and so getting a reserve price lowers expected revenue. if $\beta > 2\alpha$ then the optimal reserve price is $\beta/2$.

(c) If the principal's value is θ_0, the principal's expected payoff becomes

$$\underset{\theta}{E}\{U_0(\theta)\} = \theta_0 + \underset{\theta}{E}\left\{\sum_{i=1}^{n} q_i(\theta)(2\theta_i - \beta - \theta_0)\right\}.$$

Thus the expected revenue-maximizing reserve price is $\frac{1}{2}(\theta_0 + \beta)$.

Exercise 12.3-3: Optimal Asymmetric Auctions

(a) $\frac{d}{d\theta}\ln(1 - F_1(\theta)) = \frac{-f_1(\theta)}{1-F_1(\theta)} > \frac{-f_2(\theta)}{1-F_2(\theta)} = \frac{d}{dv}\ln(1 - F_2(\theta))$.

Integrating and noting that $F_1(0) = F_2(0) = 0$ it follows that for all $\theta \in (0, 1)$ $\ln(1 - F_1(\theta)) > \ln(1 - F_2(\theta))$ and hence $F_1(\theta) < F_2(\theta)$.

(b) The argument proceeds exactly as earlier. The expected surplus for bidder 1 is

$$\bar{u}_1 = \int_0^1 \int_0^1 [q_1(\theta)(1 - F_1(\theta_1))\, f_2(\theta_2)d\theta_1 d\theta_2.$$

(c) The expected social surplus generated by bidder 1 is

$$\int_0^1 \int_0^1 [q_1(\theta)\theta_1\, f_1(\theta_1)\, f_2(\theta_2)d\theta_1 d\theta_2.$$

Thus the expected revenue generated by bidder 1 is

$$\int_0^1 \int_0^1 q_1(\theta)J_1(\theta_1)dF(\theta_1)dF_2(\theta_2) \quad \text{where} \quad J_1(\theta) = \theta - \frac{1 - F_1(\theta)}{f_1(\theta)}.$$

Add the expected revenue generated by bidder 2 to obtain total revenue.

The item should be sold to the weak bidder if $J_2(\theta_2) > J_1(\theta_1)$. Because the hazard rate is higher for bidder 2, $J_2(\theta) > J_1(\theta)$; thus even if buyer 2 has a somewhat lower valuation, she should be assigned the item. That is, the playing field should be tilted in favor of the weaker bidder.

12.4 Designing an Efficient Mechanism

Exercise 12.4-1: Finite Type Example

(a) Maximized social surplus is shown in Table 12.7-1.

Table 12.7-1. *Social Surplus*

$S(\theta_1, \theta_2)$		θ_2	
		0	10
θ_1	5	0	9
	12	6	16

Table 12.7-2. *Marginal Contributions to Social Surplus*

Agent 1		θ_2		Agent 2		θ_2	
		0	10			0	10
θ_1	5	0	0	θ_1	5	0	9
	12	6	7		12	0	10

Subtracting each type's payoff when value is lowest yields each agent's marginal contribution to social surplus (see Table 12.7-2).

In the V-C-G mechanism each agent receives an equilibrium payoff equal to his marginal contribution to social surplus. Thus the sum of equilibrium payoffs is as shown in Table 12.7-3.

Note that in each cell the sum of marginal contributions is never less then social surplus and is greater (by 1) in the bottom right cell. Thus the mechanism loses money for the designer.

The private payoffs with efficient public goods provision are as shown in Table 12.7-4.

Finally subtract the private payoffs from the marginal contributions to social surplus, as in Table 12.7-5.

We then compute the payoffs to the two agents for all possible values and announcements (see Tables 12.7-6 and 12.7-7).

It is readily checked that each agent's dominant strategy is to announce his true value.

(b) It follows from our earlier examination of the sum of payoffs that the V-C-G mechanism is unprofitable.

(c) However, suppose that both agents announce that their values are high. The payment by agent 1 is increased by α. The new payoff matrix for agent 1 when his value is high is shown in Table 12.7-8.

As long as $\alpha < 6$, agent 1 has a higher expected payoff when announcing that his value is high if agent 2 always tells the truth (because values are equally likely.) For any $\alpha > 1$ the sum of payoffs in the bottom right cell is reduced by more than 1 so the mechanism is profitable for the designer.

Exercise 12.4-3: Implementation of Efficient Public Good Provision by Auction

(a) If agent i bids his value, θ_i and $\theta_i + \sigma(x_{-i})_i < k$ – that is, $\sigma(x_{-i})_i < k - \theta_i$ – then the item is not produced and $p = 0$. Therefore the agent's payoff is zero. If $\sigma(x_{-i})_i \geq k - \theta_i$ the good is produced and the agent pays $p(x_{-i}) = \text{Max}\{0, k - \sigma(x_{-i})\}$. Agent i's payoff is therefore as depicted in Figure 12.7-1.

Table 12.7-3. *Sum of Marginal Contributions*

$u_1 + u_2$		θ_2	
		0	10
θ_1	5	0	9
	12	6	17

Table 12.7-4. *Private Payoffs*

Agent 1		θ_2		Agent 2		x_2	
		0	10			0	10
θ_1	5	0	5	x_1	5	0	10
	12	12	12		12	0	10

Table 12.7-5. *Net Payments to Each Agent*

$N_1(x_1, x_2)$		x_2		$N_2(x_1, x_2)$		x_2	
		0	10			0	10
x_1	5	0	-5	x_1	5	0	-1
	12	-6	-5		12	0	0

Table 12.7-6. *Payoffs to Each Agent If Values Are Low*

$u_1(5, x_1, x_2)$		x_2		$u_2(0, x_1, x_2)$		x_2	
		5	10			0	10
x_1	5	0	0	x_1	5	0	-1
	12	-1	0		12	0	0

Table 12.7-7. *Payoffs to Each Agent If Values Are High*

$u_1(12, x_1, x_2)$		x_2		$u_2(10, x_1, x_2)$		x_2	
		0	10			0	10
x_1	5	0	7	x_1	5	0	9
	12	6	7		12	0	10

Table 12.7-8. *New Payoff Matrix*

$u_1(12, x_1, x_2)$		x_2	
		0	10
x_1	5	0	7
	12	6	$7-\alpha$

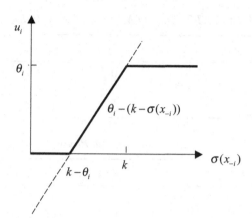

Figure 12.7-1. Maximized social surplus.

(b) If agent i announces $x_i > \theta_i$ the public good is produced if $x_i + \sigma(x_{-i}) \geq k$; that is, $\sigma(x_{-i}) \geq k - x_i$. Also $k - x_i < \theta_i - x_i$. Thus the new payoff function is as shown in Figure 12.7-2.

Note that agent i's payoff is negative if $\sigma \in [k - x_i, k - \theta_i)$ and is otherwise unaffected. Thus agent i's expected payoff is strictly lower if he announces $x_i > \theta_i$. An almost identical argument shows that his expected payment is also strictly lower if he announces $x_i < \theta_i$.

(c) This argument holds independent of the announcement of the other agents. Thus truth-telling is a dominant strategy.

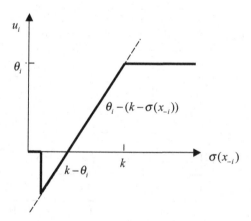

Figure 12.7-2. Agent's payoff if he chooses $x_i = \theta_i$.

12.5 Trade-Off between Efficiency and Designer Profit

Exercise 12.5-1: Blocking Agents

(a) In this case each agent can announce a value of zero. Then regardless of the value announced by the other agent, the total announced value is less ten the cost and so each agent is a blocking agent. Because a blocking agent must be paid the total surplus, it follows that any efficient mechanism must generate a loss of at least the total surplus.

(b) Both agents can block with probability 1, so again the loss must be at least equal to the expected social surplus.

(c) Again each agent is blocking with probability 1. Then the expected payment to each agent must be at least equal to the social surplus. Thus total payments to the three agents must be three times the social surplus.

Exercise 12.5-3: Convexity of the Social Choice Set

(a) $E\{u_i(\theta)\} = \int_{\alpha_i}^{\beta_i} E_{\theta_{-i}}\{q(\theta)(1 - F_i(\theta_i))\}d\theta_i.$

This is linear in the allocation rule. Thus the payoff under the allocation rule

$$q^\mu(\theta) = (1 - \mu)q^0(\theta) + \mu q^1(\theta).$$

is a convex combination of the payoffs under $q^0(\theta)$ and $q^0(\theta)$.

(b) The designer's payoff is also linear in the allocation rule so the same conclusion holds.

(c) From Proposition 12.5-1, for mechanism m^0, $\frac{dU_i^0}{d\theta_i} = E_{\theta_{-i}}\{q^0(\theta_i, \theta_{-i})\}$ and, for mechanism m^1, $\frac{dU_i^1}{d\theta_i} = E_{\theta_{-i}}\{q^1(\theta_i, \theta_{-i})\}$. For incentive compatibility both $E_{\theta_{-i}}\{q^0(\theta_i, \theta_{-i})\}$ and $E_{\theta_{-i}}\{q^1(\theta_i, \theta_{-i})\}$ are increasing functions. Then for any $\mu \in (0, 1)$,

$$\frac{dU_i^\mu}{d\theta_i} = E_{\theta_{-i}}\{(1 - \mu)q^0(\theta_i, \theta_{-i}) + \mu q^1(\theta_i, \theta_{-i})\}.$$

is an increasing function. Thus the rule

$$q^\mu(\theta_i, \theta_{-i}) = (1 - \mu)q^0(\theta_i, \theta_{-i}) + \mu q^1(\theta_i, \theta_{-i})$$

is incentive compatible. Because payoffs are linear in the allocation rule, it follows that all convex combinations of the allocations under m^0 and m^1 are feasible.

12.6 Efficient Production and Exchange with Private Values and Costs

Exercise 12.6-1: Blocking Agents with a Single Buyer and Seller

(a) Define $\theta_2 = 6 - c$. Then maximized social surplus is

$$S^*(\theta_1, \theta_2) = \text{Max}\{0, \theta_1 - c\} = \text{Max}\{0, \theta_1 - (6 - \theta_2)\}$$
$$= \text{Max}\{0, \theta_1 + \theta_2 - 6\}, \quad \text{where} \quad \theta_1 \in [3, 5] \quad \text{and} \quad \theta_2 \in [0, 2].$$

Note that $S^*(3, \theta_2) = \underset{\theta_2 \in \Theta_2}{\text{Max}}\{0, 3 + \theta_2 - 6\} = 0$ and $S^*(\theta_1, 0) = \underset{\theta_1 \in \Theta_1}{\text{Max}}\{0, \theta_1 - 6\} = 0$.
Therefore each agent can block the exchange by announcing the minimum type.

(b) In the V-C-G mechanism

$$u_1(\theta) = S^*(\theta_1, \theta_2) - S^*(3, \theta_2) = S^*(\theta_1, \theta_2).$$

Also

$$u_2(\theta) = S^*(\theta_1, \theta_2) - S^*(\theta_1, 0) = S^*(\theta_1, \theta_2).$$

Thus $S^*(\theta) - u_1(\theta) - u_2(\theta) = -S^*(\theta)$.
The set of parameter values where maximized surplus is positive are depicted in Figure 12.7-3.
In the uniform case

$$S^* = \int_0^2 \frac{1}{2} d\theta_2 \int_3^5 \frac{1}{2} \text{Max}\{\theta_1 + \theta_2 - 6\} d\theta_1$$

$$= \frac{1}{4} \int_1^2 d\theta_2 \int_{6-\theta_2}^5 (\theta_1 + \theta_2 - 6) d\theta_1 = \frac{1}{8} \int_1^2 (\theta_2 - 1)^2 d\theta_2 = \frac{1}{24}.$$

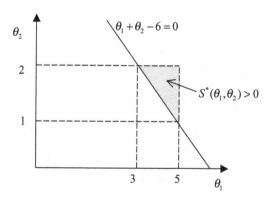

Figure 12.7-3. Agent's payoff if he chooses $x_i > \theta_i$.

Table 12.7-9. *Expected Payoff to Designer*

				M			
$E\{u_0\}/E\{SS\}$		1	2	3	4	5	6
	1	-1	-0.67	-0.15	-0.4	-0.33	-0.28
	2	-0.67	-0.27	-0.08	0.04	0.12	0.17
	3	-0.15	-0.08	0.12	0.25	0.32	0.38
n	4	-0.4	0.04	0.25	0.36	0.44	0.49
	5	-0.33	0.12	0.32	0.44	0.51	0.56
	6	-0.28	0.17	0.38	0.49	0.56	0.6

Exercise 12.6-3: Two-Sided Competition

(a) Without loss of generality we may assume that $[\alpha, \beta] = [0, 1]$. For the uniform case $F(x) = x$. Approximate the continuous c.d.f by the finite uniform distribution with values $\{0, x_1, \ldots, x_{100}\} = \{0, \frac{1}{100}, \ldots, \frac{99}{100}, 1\}$. For each value compute $I(m, n, x_i, 1 - x_i)$. Designer revenue is $\sum_{i=0}^{100} I(m, n, x_i, 1 - x_i) \frac{1}{100}$. This is negative if $m + n = 5$.

(b) If $m + n > 3$ then $I(m, n, x_i, 1 - x_i) > 0$ for all $i = 1, \ldots, 99$.

Index

acceptable gambles, 230
activity vector, 9
Adam Smith, 85
Adam Smith Theorem, 147
Adam Smith's invisible hand, 142
adverse selection, 397
aggregate production function, 173
aggregate risk, 261
all pay auction, 359
Allais paradox, 222
approximating a function, 510
arbitrage pricing theory, 292
Arrow-Debreu equilibrium, 259, 270
ascending bid auction, 355
asset holdings, 270
attitudes toward risk, 229
auctions, 436
aversion to risk, 232

Bayesian games, 347
Bayesian Nash equilibrium, 349, 356
beliefs on and off the equilibrium path, 363
Bellman equation, 202
Bertrand pricing game, 328
best response mapping, 310
bidding games, 350
binary relation, 43
blocking agent, 476
boundary point, 525
bounding hyperplane, 584
Brouwer's fixed point theorem, 154

capital accumulation, 191
capital asset pricing model, 284
capital asset pricing rule, 289
CES preferences, 12, 55
CES production function, 107
characteristic equation, 559
characteristic root, 559
closed set, 526
Cobb-Douglas preferences, 54

Cobb-Douglas production function, 107
common knowledge, 310
common knowledge beliefs, 348
common values, 442
compact set, 526
compensated demand, 58
compensated own price elasticity, 60
compensating variation, 74
complementary slackness, 9
complex eigenvalue, 561
compound prospects, 220
concave function, 6, 514, 532
conditional stochastic dominance, 243, 439, 443
constant returns to scale, 118, 173
constant returns to scale production function,
   119
constrained maximization, 578
constrained optimization, 14
constraint qualification, 20
consumer surplus, 73
continuous function, 497
continuous order, 45
continuum of separating equilibria, 406
contour sets, 538
control variables, 206
convergent subsequence, 28, 579, 581, 586
convex combination, 5, 525
convex function, 519
convex set, 4, 525
correlated mixed strategies, 315
cost function, 109
Cramer's Rule, 550

decomposition of own price effects, 61
decomposition of own price elasticity, 63
decreasing returns to scale, 118
decreasing returns to scale production function,
   119
degree of absolute risk aversion, 233
deleted neighborhood, 497
derivative of a function, 500

designer profit with two-sided competition,
   485
determinant of a square matrix, 548
difference equation system, 555
direct mechanism, 414
direct proof, 492
discontinuous function, 497
discontinuous preference order, 44
diversification, 285
dominated strategies, 304
dual linear programming problem, 37
dual optimization problem, 56
Dutch auction, 355

Edgeworth box, 174
Edgeworth box diagram, 87
educational signaling, 388
efficient production and exchange, 480
efficient public good provision, 463
eigenvalue, 559
elasticity of a function, 502, 512
elasticity of substitution, 59
Ellsberg paradox, 223
English auction, 355
envelope theorem, 23
equilibrium futures prices, 167
equilibrium threats, 321
equilibrium win probability, 351
equivalent variation, 76
Euclidean distance, 521
excess demand correspondence, 158
exchange economy, v, vii, 85
excludable public goods, 166
existence of equilibrium, 153
existence of equilibrium with unbounded excess
   demand, 159
existence of Nash equilibrium, 313
Existence with bounded production, 157
expected utility, 221
expected utility rule, 221
expenditure function, 57
expenditure minimization, 56
expenditure shares, 53
extensive form, 322
Extreme Value Theorem, 508, 526

feasible allocation, 146
financial assets, 270
firm, 106
first-order beliefs, 348
first-order conditions, 15
first-order stochastic dominance, 240
First welfare theorem, 85, 92, 147
first-order conditions, 508, 567
First-Order Taylor Expansion, 588
folk theorem, 340
free disposal, 6
functions of vectors, 526

Fundamental theorem of asset pricing, 293
Fundamental Theorem of Linear Programming,
   31
future commodity, 168
future spot markets, 273
future spot prices, 81
futures price vector, 168
futures prices, 81

game, 303
game show paradox, 225
game tree, 322
games of incomplete information, 347
global incentive compatibility, 391
gradient vector, 20, 527

Hamiltonian, 208
hidden actions, 250
higher order beliefs, 348
homogeneous function, 69, 537
homothetic preferences, 68, 97
hyperplane, 523

identity matrix, 549
implicit function theorem, 28
Implicit Function Theorem, 573
implicit prices, 280
implicit state claims prices, 293
incentive compatibility, 382, 394
incentive constraints, 383
income expansion path, 52
incomplete markets, 279
increasing function, 501
increasing returns to scale, 118
increasing returns to scale production function,
   118
independence axiom, 220
independent private values, 436
indifference order, 44
indirect price discrimination, 133, 415
indirect utility function, 57, 67
industry supply with free entry, 126
inferior good, 53
inferior input, 111
infinitely repeated game, 338
information set, 362
initial node, 322
inner product, 522
input price equalization, 177
insurance, 388
integral, 503
intuitive criterion, 369
inverse matrix, 549
iso-profit line, 3

Jacobean matrix, 575
Jensen's Inequality, 235
Jeremy Bentham, 86

John Rawls, 86
joint costs, 37
joint products, 163

Kakutani's fixed point theorem, 158, 313
Kuhn-Tucker conditions, 20

l'Hôpital's Rule, 590
Lagrange multiplier, 15
Lagrangian, 15
Le Chatelier Principle, 115
life-cycle consumption, 182
limit of a function, 497
Lindahl equilibrium, 165
linear combination, 524
linear function, 528
linear model, 7
linear transformation, 544
local downward constraint, 391
local incentive compatibility, 391
local non-satiation, 46
local property of a function, 518
local returns to scale, 121
local upward constraint, 391
lower hemi-continuity, 580

mapping, 495
market clearing prices, 90
matrix, 544
maximum principle, 212
mean preserving spread, 246, 440
Mean Value Theorem, 586
mean-variance preferences, 285
measures of risk aversion, 232
mechanism design, 384, 411
minmax value, 339
minor determinant, 550
minor matrix, 550
monopoly pricing, 37, 130
monotone likelihood property, 244
moral hazard, 250
multi-stage games, 319
mutual fund theorem, 287
Myerson-Satterthwaite Impossibility Theorem, 481

Nash equilibrium, 308
necessary conditions, 14, 570
negative definite quadratic form, 531
negative semi-definite matrix, 551
negative semi-definite quadratic form, 531
neighborhood, 497
no arbitrage, 292
node, 322
nodes, 322
normal form, 304
normal goods, 53
normal input, 111

one-stage deviation principle, 325, 344
open auction, 355
open set, 526
optimal auction, 460
optimal auctions, 456
optimal control, 206
optimal income taxation, 427
optimal reserve price, 454
optimization, 507
orthogonal vectors, 522
outcome profile, 322
output-efficient, 107

pairwise elasticity of substitution, 72
Pareto efficiency, 86
Pareto efficient allocation, 87, 102, 146
partial derivative, 527
participation constraints, 384
Perfect Bayesian equilibrium, 361
perfect foresight, 279
personalized commodity, 165
personalized price, 165
phase diagram, 187, 557
players, 303
Pontryagin's Maximum Principle, 209
pooling equilibria, 407
portfolio, 270
preferences over prospects, 219
price discrimination by buyer type, 133
price discrimination by group, 132
price-taking, 146
price-taking firms, 108
principal agent problem, 250
private non-rivalrous goods, 163
private randomization device, 315
production efficient, 2
production efficient allocation, 174
production function, 107
production possibility set, 175
production set, 3, 107
proof by contradiction, 494
proof by induction, 493
proof of the contrapositive, 493
prospect, 45, 219
public goods, 163
public randomization device, 315

quadratic form, 546
quadratic function, 529
quasi-concave function, 518, 536
quasi-concave utility function, 49
quasi-convex function, 536
quasi-linear preferences, 54

Rabin paradox, 226
Ramsey problem, 196
Ratio Rule, 89
rational expectations, 169

Refinements of Bayesian Nash equilibrium, 360
regularity assumption, 424, 457
regularity condition, 477
relative risk aversion, 234
representative preferences, 70
returns to scale, 118
revelation principle, 414
Revenue Equivalence Theorem, 453
Revenue-maximizing public goods provision, 475
risky alternatives, 240
risky assets, 265
risky choices, 218
Robinson Crusoe economy, 139
Roy's Identity, 67
Rybczynski Theorem, 178

scale elasticity of output, 120
scale of competitive firms, 129
sealed first price auction, 350
sealed second price auction, 350
second-order stochastic dominance, 242
second-order condition, 509
second-order conditions, 568
Second-Order Taylor Expansion, 590
Second welfare theorem, 85, 103
security market equilibrium, 270
security markets, 274
Separating Hyperplane Theorem, 150
separating perfect Bayesian equilibrium, 402
sequential equilibrium, 365
sequential move game, 322
sequential move games with private information, 365
set-valued mapping, 498
shadow prices, 14
signaling equilibrium, 398
signaling game, 382
simple mean preserving spread, 441
simultaneous move games, 304
single crossing property, 387
Slutsky equation, 62
social choice ranking, 87
social optimum, 124
social surplus, 125
square matrices, 547
stage game, 319
state contingent commodities, 270
state contingent consumption, 262
state dependent dividend, 270
state variable, 206
stochastic dominance, 240
stock market equilibrium, 278
Stolper-Samuelson Theorem, 178
strategic competition, 319
strategic equilibrium, 303
strength of preference, 386
strict preference order, 44

strictly concave function, 514
strictly convex function, 519
strictly dominated action, 305
strictly increasing function, 501
strictly monotonic preferences, 46
strong conditional stochastic dominance, 443
Strong Intuitive Criterion, 370
sub-game, 324
sub-game perfect, 324
substitution effect, 59
successor node, 322
sufficient condition for a maximum, 35
sufficient conditions, 22, 513, 571
sufficient conditions for a maximum, 517
sumproduct, 522
supporting hyperplane, 586
Supporting Hyperplane Theorem, 4
supporting prices, 1

tangent hyperplane, 532
Taylor expansion, 586
terminal node, 322
terminal value problem, 209
theorem of the maximum, 51
theory of choice, 43
total derivative, 528
trading instate claims markets, 235
transfer price, 3
transitive order, 44
transpose of a matrix, 545
trembling-hand perfect equilibrium, 364
two-part pricing, 133, 412

unit hyperplane, 159
unit simplex, 153, 159
unobservable strategies and public signals, 373
unraveling principle, 396
upper contour set, 4, 43
upper hemi-continuity, 580
Upper hemi-continuous correspondence, 158
utility function representation of preferences, 47
utility possibility set, 86

value function, 26
vector product, 521
vectors, 521
Vickrey-Clark-Groves Mechanism, 465

Walras' Law, 90
Walrasian equilibrium, 90, 147
war of attrition, 333
Weak Intuitive Criterion, 370
weakly dominated action, 305
welfare theorems, 102
willingness to pay, 73

Printed in the United States
By Bookmasters